NEW TESTAMENT

THE LIBERATING KING AND HIS CHURCH

A SCRIPTURE PROJECT TO REDISCOVER THE STORY OF THE BIBLE

THOMAS NELSON
Since 1798

NASHVILLE   DALLAS   MEXICO CITY   RIO DE JANEIRO   BEIJING

Published in Nashville, Tennessee, by Thomas Nelson.
Thomas Nelson is a trademark of Thomas Nelson, Inc.

Published in association with Eames Literary Services, Nashville, Tennessee

Typesetting by Rainbow Graphics
Cover design by Scott Lee Designs

Printed in the United States of America

08 09 10 11 12 13 14 15—8 7 6 5 4 3 2 1

the Voice™

NEW TESTAMENT

THE LIBERATING KING AND HIS CHURCH

New Testament Contributors

BIBLICAL SCHOLARS

Joseph Blair, ThD
Darrell L. Bock, PhD
David B. Capes, PhD
Alan Culpepper, PhD
Peter H. Davids, PhD
Joseph Dodson, PhD
Peter Rhea Jones, Sr., PhD
Troy Miller, PhD
Felisi Sorgwe, PhD
Kenneth Waters, Sr., PhD
Jack Wisdom, JD

CONTRIBUTING WRITERS

David B. Capes
Greg Garrett
Kelly Hall
Justin Hyde
Phuc Luu
Brian McLaren
Chris Seay
Alison Thomas
Matthew Paul Turner
Lauren Winner

EDITORIAL REVIEW BY:

Maleah Bell
James F. Couch, Jr.
Marilyn Duncan
Amanda Haley
Kelly Hall
Merrie Noland
Holly Perry

Other Contributors

OLD TESTAMENT BIBLICAL SCHOLARS

David B. Capes, PhD
Peter H. Davids, PhD
J. Andrew Dearman, PhD
Brett Dutton, PhD
Dave Garber, PhD
Mark Gignilliat, PhD
Sheri Klouda, PhD
Tremper Longman, PhD
Creig Marlowe, PhD
Frank Patrick, PhD
Chuck Pitts, PhD
Brian Russell, PhD
Felisi Sorgwe, PhD
Kristin Swenson, PhD
Nancy de Claissé Walford, PhD

OLD TESTAMENT CONTRIBUTING WRITERS

Ginny Allen
Lee Allen
Isaac Anderson
Eric Bryant
Cathy Capes
Daniel Capes
David B. Capes
Don Chaffer
Lori Chaffer
Tara Leigh Cobble
Greg Garrett
Christena Graves
Sara Groves
Amanda Haley
Charlie Hall
Kelly Hall
Greg Holder
Justin Hyde
E. Chad Karger
Tim Keel

Greg LaFollette
Katie Lerch
Paul Littleton
Todd Littleton
Christian McCabe
Donald Miller
Mike Morrell
Damien O'Farrell
Sean Palmer
Jonathan Hal Reynolds
Matthew Ronan
Chris Seay
Robbie Seay
Allison Smythe
Leonard Sweet
Kristin Swenson
Phyllis Tickle
Matthew Paul Turner
Seth Woods
Dieter Zander

Associate Contributors

SONGS FROM THE VOICE MUSIC PROJECT

Kipton Blue
Tyler Burkum
Steven Delopoulos
Jill Paquette DeZwaan
Brandon Graves
Andy Gullahorn
Steve Hindalong
Will Hunt
Kelly Jackson
Matthew P. Jones
Phil Keaggy
Russ Long
Maeve
Steve Mason

Sandra McCracken
Andrew Osenga
Kendall Payne
UJ Pesonen
Andrew Peterson
Jay Pfeifer
Jill Phillips
Robbie Seay Band
Jami Smith
Luke Sullivant
Amy Wallenbeck
Derek Webb
Matt Wertz

CONTRIBUTORS TO BOOKS

R. Robert Creech
Andrew Jones
Evan Lauer
Rob Pepper
Kerry Shook
Chuck Smith, Jr.

WEB SITE

Tyndall Wakeham
Travis Weerts

Table of Contents

The Books of the New Testament

Preface

 ———————————————

the voice.
A Scripture project to rediscover the story of the Bible

Any literary project reflects the age in which it is written. **The Voice** is created for and by a church in great transition. Throughout the body of Christ, extensive discussions are ongoing about a variety of issues including style of worship, how we separate culture from our theology, what it means to live the gospel, and how we faithfully communicate the essential truth of historic Christianity. At the center of this discussion is the role of Scripture. Instead of furthering the division over culture and theology, it is time to bring the body of Christ together again around the Bible. Thomas Nelson Publishers and Ecclesia Bible Society together are developing Scripture products that foster spiritual growth and theological exploration out of a heart for worship and mission. We have dedicated ourselves to hearing and proclaiming God's voice through this project.

Previously most Bibles and biblical reference works were produced by professional scholars writing in academic settings. **The Voice** uniquely represents collaboration among scholars, pastors, writers, musicians, poets, and other artists. The goal is to create the finest Bible products to help believers experience the joy and wonder of God's revelation. Four key words describe the vision of this project:

- holistic   considers heart, soul, and mind
- beautiful   achieves literary and artistic excellence
- sensitive   respects cultural shifts and the need for accuracy
- balanced   includes theologically diverse writers and scholars

Uniqueness of *The Voice*

About 40 different human authors are believed to have been inspired by God to write the Scriptures. **The Voice** retains the unique literary perspective of the human writers. Most English translations attempt to even out the styles of the different authors in sentence structure and vocabulary. Instead, **The Voice** distinguishes the uniqueness of each author. The heart of the project is retelling the story of the Bible in a form as fluid as modern literary works yet remaining painstakingly true to the original manuscripts. Accomplished writers and biblical scholars are teamed up to create an English rendering that, while of great artistic value, is carefully aligned with the original texts. Attention is paid to the use of idioms, artistic elements, confusion of pronouns, repetition of conjunctions, modern sentence structure, and the public reading of the passage. In the process, the writer or scholar may adjust the arrangement of words or expand the phrasing to create an English equivalent.

To help the reader understand how the new rendering of a passage compares to the original manuscripts, several indicators are embedded within the text.

- **Italic type** indicates words not directly tied to a dynamic translation of the original language. These words or sentences in italics may contain information that would have been obvious to those originally addressed in the Gospel or letter (for example, Matthew is speaking directly to Jews, and Paul may be speaking to believers in a specific city) and are meant to help the reader better understand the text without having to stop and read footnotes or a study guide.
- **Outlined boxes** delineate material that expands on the theme. This portion is not taken directly from the original language.
- **Screenplay format** is used to avoid the endless repetition of simple conjunctions and to identify dialog. The speaker is indicated, the dialog is indented, and quotation marks are not used. This helps greatly in the public reading of Scripture. Sometimes the original text includes interruptions in the dialog to indicate attitude of the speaker or who is being spoken to. This is shown either as a stage direction immediately following the speaker's name or as part of the narrative section that immediately precedes the speaker's name. The screenplay format clearly shows who is speaking.

Throughout *The Voice,* other language devices improve readability. We follow the standard conventions used in most translations regarding textual evidence. *The Voice* is based on the earliest and best manuscripts from the original languages (Greek, Hebrew, and Aramaic). When significant variations influence a reading, we follow the publishing standard by bracketing the passage and placing a note at the bottom of the page while maintaining the traditional chapter and verse divisions. The footnotes reference quoted material and help the reader understand the translation for a particular word. Words that are borrowed from another language or words that are not common outside of the theological community (such as "baptism," "repentance," and "salvation") are translated into more common terminology. For clarity, some pronouns are replaced with their antecedents. Word order and parts of speech are sometimes altered to help the reader understand the original passage.

Our purpose in using these literary devices is to enhance the beauty of the Scriptures and to assist the reader in clearly and quickly understanding the meaning of the text. We are constrained to be faithful to these ancient texts while giving the present reader a respectful and moving experience with the Word of God.

—Ecclesia Bible Society

About The Voice Project

*As retold, edited, and illustrated by a gifted team
of writers, scholars, poets, and storytellers*

A New Way to Process Ideas

Chris Seay's (president of Ecclesia Bible Society) vision for **The Voice** goes back 20 years to his early attempts to teach the whole biblical narrative as the story of God's redemptive work in the Liberating King. As Western culture has moved into what is now referred to as postmodernism, Chris observed that the way a new generation processes ideas and information raises obstacles to traditional methods of teaching biblical content. His desire has grown to present the Bible in ways that overcome these obstacles to people coming to faith. Instead of propositional-based thought patterns, people today are more likely to interact with events and individuals through complex observations involving emotions, cognitive processes, tactile experiences, and spiritual awareness. Much as in the parables of Jesus and in the metaphors of the prophets, narrative communication touches the whole person.

Hence, out of that early vision comes the need in a postmodern culture to present Scripture in a narrative form. The result is a retelling of the Scriptures: **The Voice**, not of words, but of meaning and experience.

The Timeless Narrative

The Voice is a fresh expression of the timeless narrative known as the Bible. Stories of God's goodness that were told to each generation by their grandparents and tribal leaders were recorded and assembled to form the Christian Scriptures. Too often, the passion, grit, humor, and beauty have been lost in the translation process. **The Voice** seeks to recapture what was lost.

From these early explorations by Chris and others has come **The Voice**: a Scripture project to rediscover the story of the Bible. Thomas Nelson Publishers and Ecclesia Bible Society have joined together to stimulate unique creative experiences and to develop Scripture products and resources to foster spiritual growth and theological exploration out of a heart for the mission of the church and worship of God.

Traditional Translations

Putting the Bible into the language of modern readers has too often been a painstaking process of correlating the biblical languages to the English vernacular. The Bible is filled with passages intended to inspire, captivate, and depict beauty. The old school of translation most often fails at attempts to communicate beauty, poetry, and story. *The Voice* is a collage of compelling narratives, poetry, song, truth, and wisdom. *The Voice* will call you to enter into the whole story of God with your heart, soul, and mind.

A New Retelling

The Voice is essentially a retelling of the story of God's love and redemption of creation. The "retelling" involves translation and elaboration, but mostly entering into the story of the Scriptures and recreating the event for our culture and time. It doesn't ignore the role of scholars, but it also values the role of writers, poets, songwriters, and artists. Instead, a team of scholars partner with the writers to blend the mood and voice of the original author with an accurate rendering of the words of the text in English.

The Voice is unique in that it represents collaboration among scholars, writers, musicians, and other artists. Its goal is to create the finest Bible products to help believers experience the joy and wonder of God's revelation. In this time of great transition within the church, we are seeking to give gifted individuals opportunities to craft a variety of products and experiences: a translation of the Scriptures, worship music, worship film festivals, biblical art, worship conferences, gatherings of creative thinkers, a Web site for individuals and churches to share biblical resources, and books derived from exploration during the Bible translation work.

The heart of each product within *The Voice* project is the retelling of the Bible story. To accomplish the objectives of the project and to facilitate the various products envisioned within the project, the Bible text is being translated. We trust that this retelling will be a helpful contribution to a fresh engagement with Scripture. The Bible is the greatest story ever told, but it often doesn't read like it. *The Voice* brings the biblical narratives to life and reads more like a great novel than the traditional versions of the Bible that are seldom opened in contemporary culture.

Readable and Enjoyable

A careful process is being followed to assure that the spiritual, emotional, and artistic goals of the project are met. First, the retelling of the Bible has been designed to be readable and enjoyable by emphasizing the narrative nature of Scripture. Beyond simply providing a set of accurately translated individual words, phrases, and sentences, our teams were charged to render the biblical texts with sensitivity to the flow of the unfolding story. We asked them to see themselves not only as guardians of the sacred text, but also as storytellers, because we believe that the Bible has always been intended to be heard as the sacred story of the people of God. We assigned each literary unit (for example, the writings of John or Paul) to a team that included skilled writers and biblical and theological scholars, seeking to achieve a mixture of scholarly expertise and literary skill.

Personal and Diverse

Second, as a consequence of this team approach, **The Voice** is both personal and diverse. God used about 40 human instruments to communicate His message, and each one has a unique voice or literary style. Standard translations tend to flatten these individual styles so that each book reads more or less like the others—with a kind of impersonal textbook-style prose. Some versions have paid more attention to literary style—but again, the literary style of one writer, no matter how gifted, can unintentionally obscure the diversity of the original voices. To address these problems, we asked our teams to try to feel and convey the diverse literary styles of the original authors.

Faithful

Third, we have taken care that **The Voice** is faithful and that it avoids prejudice. Anyone who has worked with translation knows that there is no such thing as a completely un-biased or objective translation. So, while we do not pretend to be purely objective, we asked our teams to seek to be as faithful as possible to the biblical message as they un-derstood it together. In addition, as we partnered biblical scholars and theologians with our writers, we intentionally built teams that did not share any single theological tradi-tion. Their diversity has helped each of them not to be trapped within his or her own in-dividual preconceptions, resulting in a faithful and fresh rendering of the Bible.

Stimulating and Creative

Fourth, we have worked hard to make **The Voice** both stimulating and creative. As we en-gaged the biblical text, we realized again and again that certain terms have conventional associations for modern readers that would not have been present for the original read-ers—and that the original readers would have been struck by certain things that remain invisible or opaque to modern readers. Even more, we realized that modern readers from different religious or cultural traditions would hear the same words differently. For ex-ample, when Roman Catholic or Eastern Orthodox readers encounter the word "bap-tism," a very different set of meanings and associations comes to mind than would arise in the minds of Baptist or Pentecostal readers. And a secular person encountering the text would have still different associations. The situation is made even more complex when we realize that *none* of these associations may resemble the ones that would have come to mind when John invited Jewish peasants and Pharisees into the water of the Jordan River in the months before Jesus began His public ministry. It is far harder than most people realize to help today's readers recapture the original impact of a single word like "baptism." In light of this challenge, we decided, whenever possible, to select words that would stimulate fresh thinking rather than reinforce unexamined assump-tions. We want the next generation of Bible readers—whatever their background—to have the best opportunity possible to hear God's message the way the first generation of Bible readers heard it.

Transformative

Finally, we desire that this translation will be useful and transformative. It is all too common in many of our Protestant churches to have only a few verses of biblical text read in a service, and then that selection too often becomes a jumping-off point for a sermon that is at best peripherally related to, much less rooted in, the Bible itself. The goal of **The Voice** is to promote the public reading of longer sections of Scripture—followed by thoughtful engagement with the biblical narrative in its richness and fullness and dramatic flow. We believe the Bible itself, in all its diversity and energy and dynamism, is the message.

The various creations of the project bring creative application of commentary and interpretive tools. These are clearly indicated and separated from the Bible text that is drawn directly from traditional sources. Along with the creative resources and fresh expressions of God's Word, the reader has the benefit of centuries of biblical research applied dynamically to our rapidly changing culture.

The products underway in **The Voice** include dynamic and interactive presentations of the critical passages in the life of Jesus and the early church, recorded musical presentations of Scripture originally used in worship or uniquely structured for worship, artwork commissioned from young artists, dramatized audio presentations from the Gospels and the Old Testament historical books, film commentary on our society using the words of Scripture, and exploration of the voice of each human author of the Bible.

The first product for **The Voice**, entitled *The Last Eyewitness: The Final Week*, released Spring 2006, follows Jesus through His final week of life on earth through the firsthand account of John the apostle. This book combines the drama of the text with the artwork of Rob Pepper into a captivating retelling of Jesus' final days. The second product, *The Dust Off Their Feet: Lessons from the First Church*, released September 2006, includes the entire Book of Acts retold by Brian McLaren with commentary and articles written by nine scholars and pastors. *The Voice of Matthew* was released January 2007 with the Gospel of Matthew retold by Lauren Winner including Lauren's devotional commentary, along with cultural and historical notes. *The Voice of Luke: Not Even Sandals,* released June 2007, contains the Gospel of Luke retold by Brian McLaren and includes his devotional notes.

The Voice from on High, published in the fall of 2007, contains over 700 verses from 19 Old Testament and New Testament books. The story of the Liberating King is shown to run through the Bible from Genesis to Revelation. Over a dozen writers have contributed to the retelling of the Scriptures with reflections by Jonathan Hal Reynolds. *The Voice Revealed,* also published in the fall of 2007, is the full Gospel of John retold by Chris Seay in a compact edition to introduce others to the faith.

The Voice of Hebrews: The Mystery of Melchizedek, released February 2008, combines the Book of Hebrews retold by Greg Garrett with commentary by David B. Capes. This retelling helps readers understand how Jesus completes the law and prophets and compares the character from Genesis, Melchizedek, and the Liberator, Jesus.

The Voice of Mark: Let Them Listen, released March 2008, completes the gospel story for **The Voice** and pairs the retelling of Mark's Gospel by Greg Garrett with commentary by Matthew Paul Turner.

The latest product from the project is *The Voice of Romans: The Gospel According to Paul.* This book gives great hope to those struggling with the moral collapse of our society. The text of Romans, retold by Chris Seay with David B. Capes and Kelly Hall, breathes new life into an emerging generation.

The Team

The team writing **The Voice** brings unprecedented gifts to this unique project. An award-winning fiction writer, an acclaimed poet, a pastor renowned for using art and narrative in his preaching and teaching, Greek and Hebrew authorities, and biblical scholars are all coming together to capture the beauty and diversity of God's Word.

A Word from Ecclesia

I speak for every artist, musician, editor, writer, and scholar involved in this project when I tell you that we are all honored to have a small part in the sacred work of translating the Scriptures. It has been an honor to have labored, studied, fasted, and prayed over the work that we believe God has placed before us. We have not taken the task lightly, and through the process we have been changed. We are thrilled to see the ways that God uses His Word to speak to His people and reveal Himself to those who had never heard His voice clearly.

As you engage in this story, you may experience a strange feeling that may be best described as a vague sense that you are being followed or pursued. If so, your instincts are correct. This pursuit is what distinguishes Christianity from other faiths. This is the story of God's relentless pursuit of us, and in the story we will begin to hear His footsteps following unfailingly behind us. All other faiths invite seekers to study a new language before they can read their sacred text and are asked to chase after a god that dwells in the heavens. But those of us who walk in the path of Jesus, the Liberating King, are able to read the truth about God in our native tongue, and we experience the beauty of the true God who has drawn near to us in the person of Jesus; He continues to speak to us through His Spirit and the Scriptures as He has to other men and women, boys and girls, since the beginning of time.

We believe that as you read you will be able to experience God taking the broken pieces of your life and making you whole; your anger and resentment will be replaced with hope and grace; you will imagine a new way to live as a participant in God's redemptive work in this world.

I invite you to listen to **The Voice** with an open heart. You will hear God as He whispers of His love to you.

Chris Seay
President, Ecclesia Bible Society

Introduction

God's Covenants with His People

Covenants are all around us

Our lives are filled with many different kinds of commitments or promises that may then be formalized into contracts. When couples exchange vows in a wedding, for example, they are entering into the covenant of marriage. Each person brings something to the relationship and can expect certain things in return. When someone buys or sells in the market, they are making a covenant for goods or services. When a person goes to work for a company, covenants and contracts—some formal, others informal—are necessarily involved. When students receive a syllabus from an instructor, they are taking part in a covenant with their university. In every covenant, the agreeing parties bring something to the table. As we know from experience, different kinds of covenants have different kinds of expectations.

If we think about it, we realize that covenants are woven into the fabric of our everyday lives. Since so much of our lives are lived in covenant-making and covenant-keeping actions, the "covenant" became the perfect vehicle to carry God's plan to restore the broken world.

But what is a "testament"? Simply put, a testament is a covenant, a contract, an agreement between two or more people or parties. So "testament" is a relational term; it implies that a relationship exists between at least two people. Often it is the act that establishes the relationship in the first place and makes the future possible.

The story of God's promises

The heart of the Christian Scriptures, both Old and New Testaments, is a narrative of God's covenants with and promises to His people and the world. Concerned with the proliferation of evil, sin, and its dire consequences on His creation, God decides that the best route to reclaim His broken creation is to reveal Himself to one person, and to another, and then to another, on the way to redeeming the entire world.

Part two

The New Testament is part two of the Christian Scriptures. It consists of 27 books that were written originally in Greek within a generation or two of Jesus' death and resurrection. So while it may seem that you have in hand one book, it is not one book at all. The New Testament is a collection of books, the Book of books—Gospels, letters, a history, and an apocalypse—that tell us about the life of Jesus and the beginnings of the movement He founded. For most believers throughout history it has spoken as the norm for what they believe and how they live. So in that sense, it is the church's book. Here we find the beginnings of our own story.

The foundation: four covenants

The other part of the Bible is the Old Testament, and it essentially tells the story of four covenants that lay the foundation for the new covenant inaugurated in Jesus, our Liberating King. The first covenant involves God's promise to Noah, his family, and the world that He will never again destroy the earth with a flood. God places a rainbow in the sky as a sign of that promise. When God sees the rainbow, He remembers His covenant. After the floodwaters recede and the ark is resting on dry land, He instructs Noah and his family to populate the earth. This is the same command He gave the first man and woman in the garden. Creation starts over with Noah, Mrs. Noah, and their children. Still, it isn't long before sin's presence is once again felt in the world.

God makes a second covenant with a man named Abraham many generations after Noah's descendants have divided into nations and wandered far from their Creator. He brings to the table a number of promises for the wandering nomad and his family. He promises to give him a land, to make him a great nation, to give him a great name, and perhaps, most significantly, to bless all the nations of the world through his descendants (Genesis 12:1-3). Abraham responds to God's call with faith and obedience. His journey ahead is difficult; nevertheless, he continues in faith and becomes the father of a great nation. Abraham doesn't live long enough to see all of God's promise fulfilled. After Abraham's death, God renews this covenant with each successive heir. Jacob wrestles with God and struggles to remain faithful. Eventually, Abraham's descendants sojourn south to Egypt and become slaves in that land under Pharaoh's heel. The promise that Abraham would become a great nation seemed all but impossible to generations of Hebrew slaves.

The third covenant in the Old Testament is between God and Israel, the descendants of Abraham. This covenant begins with a powerful act of deliverance when God rescues the Hebrew slaves from bondage in Egypt. The Eternal One answers the prayers of Abraham's hurting people, raising up Moses to demand from Pharaoh that the Hebrew people be set free. After a convincing display of power over the gods of Egypt and the waters of the sea, God instructs Moses to lead the former slaves to Mount Sinai. With the people camped at its base, Moses ascends the mountain to receive God's law, His blueprint for their lives and society. God promises to be with His people, to protect and deliver them, and to lead them into the promised land, a land flowing with milk and honey. In this covenant, the people of Israel pledge to obey and worship God alone, or else they will face harsh consequences. While obedience to God is guaranteed to bring blessing and prosperity in the land, disobedience brings adversity and the curse. Ultimately that will mean exile from the land of promise.

Centuries later, God comes to King David through the prophet Nathan to establish a fourth covenant. He promises David three things: David's son (Solomon) will build God a temple, his dynasty will continue forever, and God will relate to David's son (heir) as His own son (2 Samuel 7:12-16). God's covenant with David becomes the basis for what is known as the messianic promise. That is the expectation that one day David's son (descendant) would be the Liberating King. According to the prophets, the Liberating King would be God's agent to realize all of God's promises, to renew the world, and to bring salvation to the ends of the earth.

The Liberating King fulfills the covenants

These covenant promises and relationships comprise the central story of the Old Testament, bearing witness to God's dealings with the world, His people, and finally all the nations. As God's plan and will unfold, each covenant brings the world nearer to God's kingdom, His ultimate rule over creation. These covenants become the basis for all the promises and hopes that are fulfilled in Jesus, the Liberating King. That's why this collection of books known as the Old Testament is so important to early Christians. The followers of Jesus found His coming anticipated on almost every page. As you will see, the Old Testament stands in relationship to the New Testament as promise does to fulfillment, as foundation to temple, as classic to contemporary. You cannot have one without the other. The earlier covenants pave the way and make the last covenant, the new covenant, possible.

The new covenant

The phrase "New Testament" goes back to the prophet Jeremiah. About 600 years before Jesus performed His first miracle, the prophet received a message from the Eternal One. In that oracle, he said that a day will come when God establishes a new covenant with His people. Unlike His earlier covenant, this time God will write His words upon the hearts of His people. The new covenant makes it possible for everyone to know the Eternal One and for forgiveness of sins to be extended to all (Jeremiah 31:31-34). Other prophets had seen and prophesied about how God would go about restoring His people and rescuing the world, but Jeremiah is known uniquely as the prophet of the new covenant.

Jesus knew these prophecies. So on the night before He died, He ate with His disciples for the last time. He took the bread and wine that commemorated God's deliverance of the Hebrew slaves and offered them to His followers.

> [19]Then He took bread, gave thanks, broke it, and shared it with them.
>
> Jesus: This is My body, My body given for you. Do this to remember Me.

[20]And similarly, after the meal had been eaten, He took the cup.

Jesus: This cup, which is poured out for you, is the new covenant, made in My blood.

Luke 22:19-20

Reshaping the world

According to Jesus, the new covenant promised by Jeremiah—a covenant that would shake and radically shape the world—was being fulfilled through His death on the cross. God's plan to deal with sin and redeem creation reached its climax in the covenant established by Jesus, the Liberating King.

As you read through the New Testament, we invite you to enter into this story of beauty and grace. Unlike other stories you may hear, ancient and modern, this story is completely true.

David B. Capes, PhD

NEW TESTAMENT

THE LIBERATING KING AND HIS CHURCH

Matthew

Royal lineage of Jesus of Nazareth
By Matthew, the apostle

All the Gospels are anonymous. But when early Christians began collecting them in the second century, they needed a way to distinguish each one from the others. So they gave them titles. The title "According to Matthew" is affixed to this Gospel because church tradition had credited it to Matthew, one of the twelve. It is fitting that Matthew's Gospel is the first book in the New Testament because it was the favorite Gospel of the early Christians. You see, the first disciples were all Jews; and Matthew sought to prove beyond any reasonable doubt that Jesus was the Messiah, the Liberating King, the Son of David, sent by God to rule His kingdom. So Matthew, more than the other Gospel writers, found Jesus' messiahship in strange and wonderful places where Jews would know to look: in genealogies, titles, numerology, and fulfilled prophecies.

Matthew wants his mainly Jewish audience, as God's chosen people, to consider how Jesus is the true son of Abraham, the ideal for Israel, even the perfect candidate to be their Liberating King. So he shows how Jesus identified with Israel—even with their spending time in exile in Egypt—and yet, unlike Israel, He did not fall into disobedience. As Matthew tells the story, Jesus has come to fill the Scripture full by His teachings and His example. In this way, Jesus is a new Moses, a new Lawgiver. But again, He is greater than Moses because He gives the law and writes it directly on the hearts of His disciples and of any who care to overhear the message of the kingdom of heaven. According to Matthew, five sermons of Jesus complete the picture of Jesus as Lawgiver. They don't replace the five books of Torah, but His words refine and complement God's instruction to the people of the new covenant.

For Matthew, Jesus is more than the Messiah, the fulfiller of prophecies, the true son of Abraham, and the new Moses who brings a new law: He is "God with us" who promises to be with us forever. That means that Jesus is no mere mortal: He is God in the flesh who saves us from our sins. The coming of Jesus into the world fulfills God's earlier promises to bring about redemption and a new creation. These images of Jesus that Matthew paints so beautifully fired the imaginations of Christians for centuries so that today, when we open our New Testaments, we find Matthew first in line.

*T*his is the story of Jesus the Son of David, our Liberating King, as told by Matthew, a disciple of our Lord. Now this account has been recorded for all those children of Abraham who have become followers of the true heir of the line of David so that they may know in whom they have believed. Because of our common Jewish heritage we can understand Jesus of Nazareth—His miraculous healings, countless teachings filled with parables, righteous life, and lineage traced back to our father Abraham—as the One the prophets have spoken of since the early days.

This same Jesus is the Liberating King whom we have been waiting for all these years. From the time when John the Teacher was ritually cleansing people in the Jordan, as a sign of rethinking their life of sin, to the wonderfully inspired teaching on the mountain in Galilee, throughout His parables, in His horrible death, and after His marvelous resurrection just days later, He is the King of the kingdom of heaven that He taught us about. There is no one like Jesus. The prophets of old looked for Him, David sang of Him, and our leaders feared Him. He is the Liberator, the Teacher of wisdom, and the Prophet that Moses said was coming into the world.

We will begin our story with the lineage that establishes Jesus as the true Son of David. Next we will examine His life, beginning with His birth and finishing with His resurrection. We will find that in His great teachings and in His exemplary life of holiness and service, Jesus is the great King we have anticipated.

1 This is the family history, the genealogy, of Jesus the Liberator, *the coming King. You will see in this history that* Jesus is descended from King David, and that He is also descended from Abraham.

2 Abraham, *whom God called into a special, chosen, covenanted relationship, and who was the founding father of the nation of Israel,* was the father of Isaac; Isaac was the father of Jacob; Jacob was the father of Judah and of Judah's 11 brothers; 3 Judah was the father of Perez and Zerah (and Perez and Zerah's mother was Tamar, *who was Judah's widowed daughter-in-law; she dressed up like a prostitute and seduced her father-in-law, all so she could keep this very family line alive*); Perez was the father of Hezron; Hezron was the father of Ram; 4 Ram was the father of Amminadab; Amminadab was the father of Nahshon; Nahshon was the father of Salmon; 5 Salmon was the father of Boaz (and Boaz's mother was Rahab, *a Canaanite prostitute who heroically hid Israelite spies from hostile authorities who wanted to kill them*); Boaz was the father of Obed (his mother was Ruth, *a Moabite woman who converted to the Hebrew faith*); Obed was the father of Jesse; 6 and Jesse was the father of David, who was the king *of the nation of Israel*. David was the father of Solomon (his mother *was Bathsheba, and she* was married to a man named Uriah);

*S*olomon's mother was Bathsheba, the wife of Uriah, a soldier in David's army. She was bathing in her courtyard one evening when David spied her and became interested in her. Later Bathsheba got pregnant during an adulterous liaison with David, so David had Uriah killed in battle and then married his widow. David and Bathsheba's first baby died, but later Bathsheba got pregnant again and gave birth to Solomon.

7 Solomon was the father of Rehoboam; Rehoboam was the father of Abijah; Abijah was the father of Asa; 8 Asa was the father of Jehoshaphat; Jehoshaphat was the father of Joram; Joram was the father of Uzziah; 9 Uzziah was the father of Jotham; Jotham was the father of Ahaz; Ahaz was

the father of Hezekiah; [10]Hezekiah was the father of Manasseh; Manasseh was the father of Amon; Amon was the father of Josiah; [11]Josiah was the father of Jeconiah and his brothers, and Josiah's family lived at the time *when God's chosen* people *of Israel* were deported *from the promised land* to Babylon.

[12]After the deportation to Babylon, Jeconiah had a son, Shealtiel. Shealtiel was the father of Zerubbabel; [13]Zerubbabel was the father of Abiud; Abiud was the father of Eliakim; Eliakim was the father of Azor; [14]Azor was the father of Zadok; Zadok was the father of Achim; Achim was the father of Eliud; [15]Eliud was the father of Eleazar; Eleazar was the father of Matthan; Matthan was the father of Jacob; [16]Jacob was the father of Joseph, who married a woman named Mary. It was Mary who gave birth to Jesus, and it is Jesus who is *the Savior, the Anointed One*, the Liberating King.

[17]Abraham and David were linked with 14 generations, 14 generations link David to the Babylonian exile, and 14 more take us from the exile to the birth of the Liberator.

I've told you this long genealogy for a good reason: to show you how this Jesus fulfills the prophecies that tell us the Liberator will be a descendant of Abraham and of David.

And I've told you about some of the women in Jesus' line so you'll know God is gracious to everyone, even to prostitutes and adulterers. Because some of the women I listed weren't Israelites, but were strangers and foreigners, they foreshadow all the foreigners God will adopt into His church through Jesus. I've told you about these women so you know that the children in God's family are often conceived under strange circumstances (like Tamar's twins being conceived as she played the harlot, and like King Solomon being born to adulterous parents). Now that you know about this unusual family, you won't be surprised

at what happens next—because what happens next is the conception of a baby under very strange circumstances.

[18]So here, *finally*, is the story of the Liberator's* birth *(it is quite a remarkable story)*:

Mary was engaged to marry Joseph, *son of David*. They hadn't married. And yet, some time well before their wedding date, Mary learned that she was pregnant by the Holy Spirit. [19]Joseph, because he was kind and upstanding and honorable, wanted to spare Mary shame. He did not wish to cause her more embarrassment than necessary.

*T*his was remarkable, because Mary had never had sex. She and Joseph had not even spent very much time alone, but they were pledged to each other and their wedding feast was planned.

She had never even kissed a man. She was a virgin, yet she was pregnant. Miraculous! On the other hand, Joseph suspected that Mary had cheated on him and had sex with another man. He knew he would have to break their engagement, but he decided to break their engagement quietly. Mary understood that it was God, in the Person of the Holy Spirit, who had made her pregnant.

[20]Now when Joseph had decided to act on his instincts, a messenger of the Lord came to him in a dream.

Messenger of the Lord: Joseph, son of David, do not be afraid to wed Mary *and bring her into your home and family* as your wife. *She did not sneak off and sleep with someone else*—rather, she conceived the baby she now carries through the miraculous wonderworking of the Holy Spirit.

* 1:18 "Christ" and "Messiah" are translated as "Liberator" or the "Liberating King."

21She will have a son, and you will name Him Jesus, *which means "the Lord saves,"* because this Jesus is the person who will save all of His people from sin.

24Joseph woke up from his dream and did exactly what the messenger had told him to do: he married Mary and brought her into his home as his wife 25(though he did not consummate their marriage until after her son was born). *And when the baby was born,* Joseph named Him Jesus, *Savior.**

22*This is a remarkable and strange story. But it is not wholly surprising because years and years ago, Isaiah,* a prophet of Israel, foretold the story *of Mary, Joseph, and Jesus:*

> 23A virgin will conceive and bear
>   a Son,
>   and His name will be Emmanuel

(which is a Hebrew name that means "God with us").*

*M*ary and Joseph named their baby Jesus, but sometimes we refer to Him as Emmanuel, because by coming to dwell with us, living and dying among us, He was able to save us from our sin.

2 Jesus was born in the town of Bethlehem, in the province of Judea, at the time when King Herod reigned. *Not long after Jesus was born,* magi, wise men or seers from the East, *understood that the One who would save His people from sin had been born, so they set off to find the baby Savior.* Making their way from the East to Jerusalem, these wise men made inquiries.

Wise Men: 2Where is this newborn, who is the King of the Jews? When we were far away in the East we saw His star, and we have followed its glisten and gleam all this way to worship Him.

3King Herod began to hear rumors of the wise men's quest, and he, and all of his followers in Jerusalem, were worried. 4So Herod called all of the leading Jewish teachers, the chief priests and head scribes, and he asked them where *Hebrew tradition claimed* the long-awaited Liberator would be born.

Scribes and Priests: 5*An ancient Hebrew prophet, Micah,* said this:

> 6But you, Bethlehem, in the land of
>   Judah,
>   are no poor relation—
> For from your people will come a
>   Ruler
>   who will be the shepherd of My
>   people Israel.*

*F*rom that prophecy we learn that the Savior would be born in the town of Bethlehem, in the province of Judea. This information in hand, Herod ordered the wise men to come to his chambers in secret, and when they arrived, Herod quizzed them.

7Herod called the wise men to him, demanding to know the exact time the special star had appeared to them. 8Then Herod sent them to Bethlehem.

Herod: Go *to Bethlehem* and search high and low for this *Savior* child, and as soon as you know where He is, report it to me so that I may go and worship Him.

*H*erod, of course, didn't really want to worship the baby Jesus. He wanted to kill Him. He was being crafty, trying to trick the magi into betraying the One they sought. But it didn't work.

* 1:25 Verses 24 and 25 have been moved before verse 22 to help the reader understand the continuity of the passage.
* 1:23 Isaiah 7:14
* 2:6 Micah 5:2

9-10The wise men *left Herod's chambers* and went on their way. The star they had first seen in the East reappeared—a miracle that, of course, overjoyed and enraptured the wise men. The star led them to the house where Jesus lay; 11and as soon as the wise men arrived, they saw Him with His mother Mary, and they bowed down and worshiped Him. They unpacked their satchels and gave Jesus gifts of gold, frankincense, and myrrh.

*T*hese were exceptionally good gifts, for gold is what you give a king, and Jesus is the King of kings; incense is what you give a priest, and Jesus is the High Priest of all high priests; myrrh ointment is used to heal, and Jesus is a healer. But myrrh is also used to embalm corpses—and Jesus was born to die.

12And then, *just as Joseph did a few months before*, the wise men had a dream warning them not to go back to Herod. *The wise men heeded the dream. Ignoring Herod's instructions*, they returned to their homes in the East by a different route.
    13After the wise men left, a messenger of the Lord appeared to Joseph in a dream.

Messenger of the Lord *(to Joseph)*: Get up, take the child and His mother, and head to Egypt. Stay there until I tell you *it is safe to leave. For Herod understands that Jesus threatens him and all he stands for.* He is planning to search for the child and kill Him. *But you will be safe in Egypt.*

14So Joseph got up in the middle of the night; he bundled up Mary and Jesus, and they left for Egypt.*
    16*After a few months had passed*, Herod realized he'd been tricked. The wise men *were not coming back; they weren't going to lead him to the infant King.* Herod, *of course*, was furious, *but he was not to be outdone.* He simply ordered that all boys who lived in or near Bethlehem and were two years of age and younger be killed. *He*

knew the baby King was this age *because of what the wise men told him.

*H*erod knew ordinary babies would die in this purge, but he didn't care—Herod was not so much cold-blooded as pragmatic, willing to do whatever was necessary to kill this new supposed King. And so all those other baby boys died. But, of course, Herod's plan ultimately failed. He didn't know the baby Savior had been whisked to safety in Egypt.

17This *sad event* had long been foretold by the prophet Jeremiah:

18A voice will be heard in Ramah,
    weeping *and wailing* and mourning
        out loud all day and night.
    The voice is Rachel's, weeping for
        her children,
        her children who have been killed;
        she weeps, and she will not be
            comforted.*

15Joseph, Mary, and Jesus stayed *in Egypt* until Herod died. This fulfilled yet another prophecy. The prophet *Hosea* once wrote, "Out of Egypt I called My Son."*
    19And after Herod died, a messenger of the Lord appeared in a dream to Joseph in Egypt:

Messenger of the Lord: 20*You may go home now.* Take the child and His mother and go back to the land of Israel, for the people who were trying to take the child's life are now dead.

21So Joseph got up and took Mary and Jesus and returned to the land of Israel. 22Soon he learned that Archelaus, Herod's *oldest and notoriously brutal son*, was ruling Judea. *Archelaus, Joseph knew, might not be*

* 2:14 Verse 15 has been moved to follow verse 18 to help the reader understand the continuity of the passage.
* 2:18 Jeremiah 31:15
* 2:15 Hosea 11:1

any friendlier to Joseph and his family than Herod had been. Joseph was simply afraid. He had another dream, and in this dream, he was warned *away from Judea*; so Joseph *decided* to settle *up north* in a district called Galilee, [23]in a town called Nazareth. And this, too, fulfilled what the prophets have taught, *"The Savior* will be a Nazarene."*

"Nazarene," as you may know, means, "tender branch, green branch, the branch that is living." And that, of course, is what this Jesus is. He is the living Branch, the branch of David that extends the reach of the tree of Israel eventually to foreigners and outsiders.

---

3 Around the same time, a man called John* began to travel, preach, and ritually wash people in the wilderness of Judea. *John preached a stern but exciting message.*

John: [2]Repent! For the kingdom of heaven is near.

[3]John's proclamation fulfilled a promise made by the *ancient* prophet Isaiah, who had said, "There will be a voice calling from the desert, saying,

Prepare the road for the Eternal
    One's journey;
repair and straighten out *every
    mile of* our God's highway."*

[4]John *was all about wilderness. He preached in the wilderness. He* wore *wild* clothes made from camel hair with a leather belt around his waist—*the clothes of an outcast, a rebel—clothes just like the prophet Elijah had worn.* He ate locusts and wild honey.

Sometimes when people saw John they were reminded of the last time God's people had wandered in a wilderness—after the exodus from Egypt. They thought perhaps John was

---

inaugurating a new exodus. Actually, that is a pretty good way to think of it. The Liberator, whose way John came to prepare, would call us away from comfort and status; He would call us all to challenge our assumptions and the things we take for granted.

---

[5]People from Jerusalem, all of Judea, and indeed from all around the river Jordan came to John. [6]They confessed their sins, and they were dunked* by him in the Jordan.

[7]*But John was—well, he was not exactly warm to all those who came to him seeking cleansing.** He told some Pharisees and Sadducees who came for the ritual,

John: *You children of serpents! You brood of vipers! Did someone suggest you flee from the wrath that is upon us?* [8-9]*If you think that simply hopping in the Jordan will cleanse you, then you are sorely mistaken.* Your life must bear the fruits of turning toward righteousness. Nor are you correct if you think that being descended from Abraham is enough to make you holy and right with God. *Yes, the children of Abraham are God's chosen children,* but God can adopt as daughters and sons *anyone He likes—He can turn* these stones *into sons if He likes.*

To be made right with God, you must truly repent. Living for God must overtake your whole life, your whole being. Don't you know what "repent" means? It means to turn completely away from sin and completely toward God.

John: [10]Even now there is an ax poised at the root of every tree, and every tree that does not bear good fruit will be cut down

---

* 2:23 Isaiah 11:1
* 3:1 Literally, John who immersed, to show repentance
* 3:3 Isaiah 40:3
* 3:6 Literally, immersed, to show repentance
* 3:7 Literally, immersion, an act of repentance

and tossed into the fire. ¹¹I ritually cleanse* you as a mark of turning your life around. But someone is coming after me, someone whose sandals I am not fit to carry, someone who is more powerful than I. He will wash* you *not in water* but in fire and with the Holy Spirit. ¹²He carries a winnowing fork in His hand, and He will clear His threshing floor; He will gather up the good wheat in His barn, and He will burn the chaff with a fire that cannot be put out.

¹³And then, *the One of whom John spoke— the all-powerful One, the One who carried that winnowing fork—that One, of course, was* Jesus—He came to the Jordan from Galilee to be washed* by John. ¹⁴At first, John demurred.

John: I need to be cleansed* by You. Why do You come to me?
Jesus: ¹⁵It will be right, true, and faithful to God's chosen path for you to cleanse Me *with your hands in the Jordan River.*

John agreed, and he ritually cleansed Jesus, dousing Him in the waters of the Jordan. ¹⁶Jesus emerged from the water,* and at that moment heaven was opened, and Jesus saw the Spirit of God descending like a dove and coming upon Him, *alighting on His very body.*

A Voice from Heaven: ¹⁷This is My Son, whom I love; *this is the Apple of My eye*; with Him I am well pleased.

4 The Spirit then led Jesus into the desert to be tempted by the devil. ²Jesus fasted for 40 days and 40 nights. After this fast, He was, *as you can imagine,* hungry. ³But He was also curiously *stronger because of His fast. And so He was able to withstand the devil,* the tempter, when he came to Jesus.

The Devil: If You are the Son of God, tell these stones to become bread.
Jesus *(quoting Deuteronomy)*: ⁴It is written, "Man does not live by bread alone. Rather,

he lives on every word that comes from the mouth of the Eternal One."*

The point, of course, is not that Jesus couldn't have turned these stones to bread. As you will see a little later in our story, He can make food appear when He needs to. But Jesus doesn't work miracles out of the blue, for no reason, for show or proof or spectacle. He works them in intimate, close places; He works them to meet people's needs and to show them the way to the Kingdom.

⁵Then the devil took Jesus to the holy city, *Jerusalem,* and he had Jesus stand at the very highest point in the holy temple.

The Devil: ⁶If You are the Son of God, jump! *And then we will see if You fulfill* the Scripture that says,

He will command His heavenly
  messengers concerning You,
and the messengers will buoy
  You in their hands
So that You will not *crash, or fall,
  or even* graze Your foot on a
  stone.*

Jesus: ⁷That is not the only thing Scripture says. It also says, "Do not put the Eternal One, your God, to the test."*

⁸And still the devil *subjected Jesus to a third test. He* took Jesus to the top of a very high mountain, and he showed Jesus all the kingdoms of the world in all their *splendor and* glory, *their power and pomp.*

* 3:11 Literally, immerse, to show repentance
* 3:11 Literally, immerse, in a rite of initiation and purification
* 3:13 Literally, immersed, to show repentance
* 3:14 Literally, immersed, in a rite of initiation and purification
* 3:16 Literally, after being immersed, Jesus came up from the water.
* 4:4 Deuteronomy 8:3
* 4:6 Psalm 91:11-12
* 4:7 Deuteronomy 6:16

The Devil: [9]If You bow down and worship me, I will give You all these kingdoms.

Jesus: [10]Get away from Me, Satan. *I will not serve you. I will instead follow* Scripture, which tells us to "worship the Eternal One, your God, and serve only Him."*

[11]Then the devil left Jesus. And heavenly messengers came and ministered to Him.

[12]*It was not long until powerful people put* John in prison. When Jesus learned this, He went back to Galilee. [13]He moved from Nazareth to Capernaum, a town by the sea in the regions of Zebulun and Naphtali— [14]He did this to fulfill one of the prophecies of Isaiah:

[15]In the land of Zebulun and the
land of Naphtali,
the road to the sea along the
Jordan in Galilee, the land of
the outsiders—
[16]*In these places*, the people who had
been living in darkness
saw a great light.
The light of life will overtake those
who dwelt in the shadowy
darkness of death.*

[17]From that time on, preaching was part of Jesus' work. *His message was not dissimilar from John's.*

Jesus: *Turn away from sin; turn toward God.* Repent, for the kingdom of heaven is at hand.

*B*y now Jesus desired a community around Him, friends and followers who would help Him carry this urgent, precious message to people. And so He called a community around Him. We call these first beloved followers "disciples," which means "apprentices." The first disciples were two brothers, Simon and Andrew. They were fishermen.

[18]*One day* Jesus was walking along the Sea of Galilee when He saw Simon (also called Peter) and Andrew throwing their nets into the water. They were, of course, fishermen.

Jesus: [19]*Come*, follow Me, and I will make you fishers of men.

[20]Immediately Peter and Andrew left their fishnets and followed Jesus.

[21]Going on from there, Jesus saw two more brothers, James the son of Zebedee and his brother John. *They, too, were fishermen.* They were in a boat with their father Zebedee getting their nets ready to fish. Jesus summoned them, *just as He had called to Peter and Andrew,* [22]and immediately they left their boat and their father to follow Jesus.

[23]And so Jesus went throughout Galilee. He taught in the synagogues. He preached the good news of the Kingdom, and He healed people, ridding their bodies of sickness and disease. [24]*People talked about this Jesus, this Preacher and Healer,* and word *of His charisma and wisdom and power and love* spread all over Syria, as more and more sick people came to Him. *People who were too sick to walk persuaded their friends and relatives to carry them to Jesus.* The innumerable ill who came before Him had all sorts of diseases—they were in crippling pain; they were possessed by demons; they had seizures; they were paralyzed. But Jesus healed them *all.* [25]Large crowds from Galilee, from Jerusalem, from *the ten cities called* the Decapolis, from Judea, and from the region across the Jordan—*these cripples and demonized and ill and paralytics came to Jesus, and He healed them, and they followed Him.*

[5] Now when He saw the crowds, He went up on a mountain (*as Moses had done before Him*) and He sat down (*as Jewish teachers of His day usually did*). His disciples gathered around Him.

* 4:10 Deuteronomy 6:13
* 4:15-16 Isaiah 9:1-2

*T*here on the mountain Jesus taught them all. And as He was teaching, crowds gathered around and overheard His teachings, listened in, and were captivated, just as you who now hear this story are invited to come around and listen in and hear and be taught and be captivated.

And He began to teach them.

Jesus: ³Blessed are the spiritually poor—
the kingdom of heaven is theirs.
⁴Blessed are those who mourn, *who
weep about sin and long for
how things are supposed to be—*
they will be comforted.
⁵Blessed are the *meek and* gentle—
they will inherit the earth.
⁶Blessed are those who hunger
and thirst for righteousness—
they will be filled.
⁷Blessed are the merciful—
they will be shown mercy.
⁸Blessed are those who are pure in
heart—they will see God.
⁹Blessed are the peacemakers—
they will be called children
of God.
¹⁰Blessed are those who are
persecuted because of
righteousness—the kingdom of
heaven is theirs.

¹¹And blessed are you, *blessed are all of
you,* when people persecute you or deni-
grate you or despise you or tell lies about
you on My account. ¹²*But when this happens,* rejoice. Be glad. Remember that
God's prophets have been persecuted in
the past. And know that in heaven, you
have a great reward.

*A*nd be sure, you will be despised because of Jesus. You will be persecuted and tarred and targeted and tarnished and cursed because you have loved and followed Him.

Jesus continued by teaching about salt. Just as salt draws out the good flavors subtly hidden in our food, you help creation be its truest self. As salt preserves food that would otherwise spoil, you help preserve the goodness of creation. So, too, those who claim to be children of God, but live selfish, small lives, have no part in the king-dom of heaven. They will be thrown out and trampled.

Jesus: ¹³You, *beloved,* are the salt of the earth. But if salt becomes bland and loses its saltiness, can anything make it salty again? *No.* It is useless. *It just lies there, white and bland and grainy.* It is tossed out, thrown away, or trampled.

¹⁴And you, *beloved,* are the light of the world. A city built on a hilltop cannot be hidden. ¹⁵Similarly it would be silly to light a lamp and then hide it under a bowl. When someone lights a lamp, she puts it on a table or a desk or a chair, and the light illumines the entire house. ¹⁶*You are like that illuminating light.* Let your light shine everywhere you go, *that you may illumine creation,* so men and women everywhere may see your good actions, *may see creation at its fullest, may see your devotion to Me,* and may turn and praise your Father in heaven *because of it.*

¹⁷Do not think that I have come to overturn or do away with the law or the words of our prophets. *To the contrary:* I have not come to overturn them but to fulfill them. *I ask you not merely to follow the Commandments, but to give Me your heart, your body, and your very life.*

¹⁸This, *beloved,* is the truth: until heaven and earth disappear, not one let-ter, not one pen stroke, will disappear from the sacred law—for everything, everything in the sacred law will be ful-filled and accomplished. *Our community is not about destroying the law.* ¹⁹Anyone who breaks even the smallest, most obscure commandment—not to mention teaches others to do the same—will be called small *and obscure* in the kingdom

of heaven. Those who practice the law and teach others how to live the law will be called great in the kingdom of heaven. ²⁰For I tell you this: you will not enter the kingdom of heaven unless your righteousness goes deeper than the Pharisees, even more righteous than the most learned learner of the law. *And this is one reason I have come to you, beloved—to make you righteous, through and through.*

²¹*And then Jesus began to interpret the law of Scripture for the people:*

Jesus: As you know, long ago God instructed *Moses to tell* His people, "Do not murder;* those who murder will be judged *and punished.*" ²²*But here is the even harder truth*: anyone who is angry with his brother will be judged for his anger. Anyone who *taunts his friend, speaks contemptuously toward him, or* calls him "Loser" or "Fool" or "Scum," will have to answer to the high court. And anyone who calls his brother a fool may find himself in the fires of hell.

²³Therefore, if you are bringing an offering to God and you remember that your brother is angry at you or holds a grudge against you, ²⁴then leave your gift before the altar, go to your brother, *repent and forgive one another*, be reconciled, and then return to the altar to offer your gift to God. *It does not matter if it took you three days to get to the temple— go home and reconcile with your brother before you make your offering to God.*

²⁵If someone sues you, settle things with him quickly. Talk to him as you are walking to court—otherwise, he may turn matters over to the judge, and the judge may turn you over to an officer, and you may land in jail. ²⁶I tell you this: you will not emerge from prison until you have paid your last penny.

²⁷As you know, long ago God forbade His people to commit adultery.* ²⁸*You may think you have abided by this Commandment, walked the straight and narrow*, but I tell you this: any man who looks at a woman with lust has already committed adultery in his heart. ²⁹If

your right eye leads you into sin, gouge it out and throw it *in the garbage*—for better you lose one part of your body than march your entire body *through the gates of sin and* into hell. ³⁰And if your right hand leads you into sin, cut it off and throw it away—for better you lose one part of your body than march your entire body *through the gates of sin and* into hell.

³¹And here is something else: *you have read in Deuteronomy that* anyone who divorces his wife *must do so fairly*—he must give her the requisite certificate of divorce *and send her on her way, free and unfettered.** ³²But I tell you this: unless your wife cheats on you, you must not divorce her, period. Nor are you to marry someone who has been married and divorces, for a divorced person who remarries commits adultery.

³³You know that God expects us to abide by the oaths we swear and the promises we make. ³⁴But I tell you this: do not ever swear an oath. *What is an oath?* You cannot say, "I swear by heaven"—*for heaven is not yours to swear by;* it is God's throne. ³⁵And you cannot say, "I swear by this good earth," *for the earth is not yours to swear by;* it is God's footstool. And you cannot say, "I swear by *the holy city* Jerusalem," for *it is not yours to swear by;* it is the city *of God, the capital* of the King of kings. ³⁶You cannot even say that you swear by your own head, *for God has dominion over your hands, your lips, your head.* It is He who determines if your hair be *straight or curly*, white or black; *it is He who rules over even this small scrap of creation, one lock of straight hair, one cutting of curls.* ³⁷*You need not swear an oath*—any impulse to do so is of evil. Simply let your "yes" be "yes," and let your "no" be "no."

³⁸You know that *Hebrew Scripture* sets this standard *of justice and punishment*: take an eye for an eye and a tooth

* 5:21 Exodus 20:13
* 5:27 Exodus 20:14
* 5:31 Deuteronomy 24:1

for a tooth.* ³⁹But I say this, don't fight against the one who is working evil against you: *do not gouge the eye of one who gouges your eye, and do not crush the tooth of one who makes you toothless.* If someone strikes you on the right cheek, you are to turn and offer him your left cheek. ⁴⁰If someone connives to get your shirt, give him your jacket as well. ⁴¹If someone forces you to walk with him for a mile, walk with him for two instead. ⁴²If someone asks you for something, give it to him. If someone wants to borrow something from you, do not turn away.

⁴³You have been taught to love your neighbor and hate your enemy.* ⁴⁴But I tell you this: love your enemies. Pray for those who torment you and persecute you— ⁴⁵in so doing, you become children of your Father in heaven. *He, after all, loves each of us—good and evil, kind and cruel.* He causes the sun to rise *and shine* on evil and good alike. He causes the rain *to water the fields* of the righteous and *the fields* of the sinner. ⁴⁶It is easy to love those who love you—even a tax collector can love those who love him. ⁴⁷And it is easy to greet your friends—even outsiders do that! ⁴⁸*But you are called to something higher:* "Be perfect, as your Father in heaven is perfect."

6 **Jesus:** *Part of imitating the perfection of God is acting charitably and generously, doing good deeds, working for justice,* and praying. But when you do these righteous acts, *do not do them in front of spectators.* Don't do them where you can be seen, *let alone lauded,* by others. If you do, you will have no reward from your Father in heaven. ²When you give to the poor, *do not boast about it,* announcing your donations with blaring trumpets as the play actors do. Do not brazenly give your charity in the synagogues and on the streets; *indeed, do not give at all* if you are giving because you want to be praised by your neighbors. Those people who give in order to reap praise have already received their

reward. ³⁻⁴When you give to the needy, do it in secret—even your left hand should not know what your right hand is doing. Then your Father, who sees in secret, will reward you.

⁵Likewise, when you pray, do not be as hypocrites who love to pray loudly at synagogue or on street corners—their concern is *not meant to be heard by God (who can hear even the softest of whispers) but* to be seen by men. *Those people who sing their prayers with bravado and show, so that their neighbors might see them and be impressed with their piety*—they have already earned their reward. ⁶When you pray, go into a private room, close the door, and pray unseen to your Father who is unseen. Then your Father, who sees in secret, will reward you. ⁷And when you pray, do not go on and on, excessively and strangely like the outsiders—they think their verbosity will let them be heard *by their deities.* ⁸Do not be like them. *Your prayers need not be labored or lengthy or grandiose*—for your Father knows what you need before you ever ask Him.

⁹Your prayers, rather, should be *simple,* like this:

Our Father in heaven,
  let Your name remain holy.
¹⁰Bring about Your kingdom.
  Manifest Your will here on earth,
    as it is manifest in heaven.
¹¹Give us each day that day's bread,
    no more, no less,
¹²And forgive us our debts
    as we forgive those who owe us
      something.
¹³Lead us not into temptation,
    but deliver us from evil.
[But let Your kingdom be,
    and let it be powerful
    and glorious forever. Amen.]*

* 5:38 Exodus 21:24; Leviticus 24:20; Deuteronomy 19:21
* 5:43 Leviticus 19:18
* 6:13 Some early manuscripts omit this portion.

*Y*ou will notice that in this prayer, you are told to declare your forgiveness of those who have wronged you—you forgive them their sins, and you forgive them their debts. This is because your forgiveness of other people emulates God's forgiveness of you.

Jesus: ¹⁴If you forgive people when they sin against you, then your Father will forgive you *when you sin against Him and when you sin against your neighbor*. ¹⁵But if you do not forgive your neighbors' sins, your Father will not forgive your sins.

¹⁶And when you fast, do not look miserable as *the actors and* hypocrites do when they are fasting—*they walk around town putting on airs about their suffering and weakness, complaining about how hungry they are.* So everyone will know they are fasting, they don't wash or anoint themselves with oil, *pink their cheeks, or wear comfortable shoes. Those who show off their piety,* they have already received their reward. ¹⁷When you fast, wash your face and beautify yourself with oil, ¹⁸so no one who looks at you will know about your discipline. Only your Father, who is unseen, will see your fast. And your Father, who sees in secret, will reward you.

¹⁹Some people store up treasures *in their homes* here on earth. *This is a shortsighted practice*—don't undertake it. Moths and rust will eat up any treasure you may store here. Thieves may break into *your homes* and steal *your precious trinkets*. ²⁰Instead, put up your treasures in heaven where moths do not attack, where rust does not corrode, and where thieves are barred at the door. ²¹For where your treasure is, there your heart will be also.

²²The eye is the lamp of the body. *You draw light into your body through your eyes, and light shines out to the world through your eyes.* So if your eye is well *and shows you what is true*, then your whole body will be filled with light. ²³But if your eye is clouded *or evil*, then

your body will be filled with *evil and dark clouds*. And the darkness that takes over the body *of a child of God who has gone astray*—that is the deepest, darkest darkness there is.

*W*hen Jesus speaks of eyes and light, He means keep your eyes on God because your eyes are the windows of your soul. And do not look at trash—at pornography, at filth, at expensive baubles you will soon lust after. And this is what He means when He says, "Where your treasure is, there your heart will be also": where your eyes are, there your treasure will be.

Jesus: ²⁴No one can serve two masters. *If you try*, you will wind up loving the first master and hating the second, or vice versa. People try to serve both God and money—but you can't. *You must choose one or the other.*

²⁵Here is the bottom line: do not worry about your life. Don't worry about what you will eat or what you will drink. Don't worry about how you clothe your body. Living is about more than merely eating, and the body is about more than dressing up. ²⁶Look at the birds in the sky. They do not store food for winter. *They don't plant gardens.* They do not sow or reap—and yet, they are always fed because your heavenly Father feeds them. And you are even more precious to Him than a beautiful bird. *If He looks after them, of course He will look after you.* ²⁷*Worrying does not do any good*—who here can claim to add even an hour to his life by worrying?

²⁸Nor should you worry about clothes. Consider the lilies of the field and how they grow. They do not work or weave or sew, *and yet their garments are stunning.* ²⁹Even King Solomon, dressed in his most regal garb, was not as lovely as these lilies. ³⁰*And think about grassy fields*—the grasses are here now, but they will be dead by winter. And yet God

adorns them so radiantly. How much more will He clothe you, you of little faith, *you who have no trust?* [31]So do not consume yourselves with questions: What will we eat? What will we drink? What will we wear? [32]Outsiders make themselves frantic over such questions—*they don't realize that* your heavenly Father knows exactly what you need. [33]Seek first the kingdom of God and His righteousness, and then all these things will be given to you *too.* [34]So do not worry about tomorrow. Let tomorrow worry about itself. Living faithfully is a large enough task for today.

7 Jesus: If you judge *other people*, then you will find that you, too, are being judged. [2]Indeed, you will be judged by the very standards to which you hold other people.

So when you are tempted to criticize your neighbor because her house isn't clean enough, she seems ill-tempered, or she is a bit flighty—remember those same standards and judgments will come back to you. Don't criticize your neighbor for being short-tempered one morning, when you yourself are snippish and snappish and waspish all the time.

Jesus: [3]Why is it that you see the dust in your brother's or sister's eye, but you can't see what is in your own eye? [4]Don't ignore the wooden plank in your eye, but criticize the speck of sawdust in your brother's eyelashes. [5]That type of criticism and judgment is a sham! Remove the plank from your own eye, and then perhaps you will be able to see clearly how to help your brother flush out his sawdust.

[6]Don't give precious things to dogs. Don't cast your pearls before swine. If you do, the pigs will trample the pearls with their *little pigs'* feet, and then they will turn back and attack you.

Now Jesus returns to the topic of prayer. Prayer is so very important and sometimes so hard, but He helps us focus here by giving us the very essence of prayer.

Jesus: [7]Just ask and it will be given to you; seek after it and you will find. *Continue to* knock and the door will be opened for you. [8]All who ask receive. Those who seek, find what they seek. And he who knocks, will have the door opened.

[9]Think of it this way: if your son asked you for bread, would you give him a stone? *Of course not—you would give him a loaf of bread.* [10]If your son asked for a fish, would you give him a snake? *No, to be sure, you would give him a fish—the best fish you could find.* [11]So if you, who are sinful, know how to give your children good gifts, how much more so does your Father in heaven, who is perfect, know how to give great gifts to His children!

[12]This is what our Scriptures come to teach: in everything, in every circumstance, do to others as you would have them do to you.

[13]*There are two paths before you; you may take only one path.* One doorway is narrow. *And one door is wide.* Go through the narrow door. For the wide door leads to a wide path, and the wide path is broad; the wide, broad path is easy, and the wide, broad, easy path has many, many people on it; but the wide, broad, easy, crowded path leads to death. [14]Now then that narrow door leads to a narrow road that in turn leads to life. It is hard to find that road. Not many people manage it.

[15]Along the way, watch out for false prophets. They will come to you in sheep's clothing, but underneath *that quaint and innocent wool, they* are hungry wolves. [16]But you will recognize them by their fruits. You don't find *sweet, delicious* grapes growing on thorny bushes, do you? You don't find *delectable* figs growing in the midst of

prickly thistles. [17]*People and their lives are like trees.* Good trees bear beautiful, tasty fruit, but bad trees bear ugly, bitter fruit. [18]A good tree cannot bear ugly, bitter fruit; nor can a bad tree bear fruit that is beautiful and tasty. [19]And what happens to the rotten trees? They are cut down. They are used for firewood. [20]*When a prophet comes to you and preaches this or that,* look for his fruits: *sweet or sour? rotten or ripe?*

[21]Not everyone who says to Me, "Lord, Lord," will enter the kingdom of heaven. *Simply calling Me "Lord" when you reach heaven will not be enough.* Only those who do the will of My Father who is in heaven *will join Me in heaven.* [22]*At the end of time, on the day of judgment—* on that day, many will say to Me, "Lord, Lord, did we not prophesy in Your name? Did we not drive demons out *of the possessed* in Your name? Did we not perform miracles in Your name?" [23]But I will say to them, "I never knew you. And now, you must get away from Me, you evildoers!"

[24]Those people who are listening to Me, those people who *hear what I say and* live according to My teachings—you are like a wise man who built his house on a rock, *on a firm foundation.* [25]*When storms hit,* rain pounded down and waters rose, *levies broke* and winds beat all the walls of that house. But the house did not fall because it was built upon rock. [26]Those of you who are listening and do not hear, *those who are listening and ignore My teachings, and those who take the wider, easier path, keeping company with false prophets:* you are like a fool who builds a house on sand. [27]When a storm comes to his house, *what will happen?* The rain will fall, the waters will rise, the wind will blow, and his house will collapse with a great crash. *Because it is built on nothing, on ephemera, on shifty, shifting sands.*

[28]With that Jesus finished His teaching, and the crowds were amazed by all He had said. [29]But Jesus taught in His own name, on His own authority, not like the scribes.

In some ways, He had taught like the rabbis of old; in other ways, this teaching was new and different. For usually rabbis cited other rabbis, generations of rabbis before them. He honored the law, but He was clear and insistent—this is the way we must read the law now.

8 Large crowds followed Jesus when He came down from the mountain. [2]*And as Jesus was going along,* a leper approached Him and knelt down before Him.

Leper: Lord, if You wish to, *please* heal me and make me clean!

Jesus *(stretching out His hand):* [3]Of course I wish to. Be clean.

Immediately the man was healed.

Jesus: [4]Don't tell anyone *what just happened.* Rather, go to the priest, show yourself to him, and give a wave offering as Moses commanded. Your actions will tell the story of what happened here today.

[5]Eventually Jesus came to *the little town of* Capernaum. In Capernaum a military officer came to Him and asked Him for help.

Officer: [6]Lord, I have a servant who is lying at home in agony, paralyzed.

Jesus: [7]I will come *to your house,* and I will heal him.

Officer: [8]Lord, I don't deserve to have You in my house. *And, in truth, I know You don't need to be with my servant to heal him.* Just say the word, and he will be healed. [9]That, after all, is how authority works. My troops obey me whether I am next to them or not—*similarly, this sickness that is plaguing my servant will obey You, whether You heal him from his bedside or from across an ocean.*

[10]Jesus was stunned by the depth of the officer's faith.

Jesus (to His followers): This is the plain truth: I have not met a single person in Israel with as much faith *as this officer.* [11]It will not be just the children of Abraham and Isaac and Jacob who celebrate at their heavenly banquet at the end of time. No, people will come from the East and the West—*and those who recognize Me, regardless of their lineage, will sit with Me at that feast.* [12]But those who have feigned their faith will be cast out into outer darkness where people weep and gnash their teeth.

[13]Then Jesus turned to the Centurion.*

Jesus: You may go home, *and when you get home, you will see that your servant is just fine.* For it is as you say it is; it is as you believe.

And the officer's servant was healed, right then.

*W*hat happened next seemed to embody the officer's wise opinion about authority: over and over Jesus showed just what His authority meant.

[14]Jesus went to Peter's house, and there He saw Peter's mother-in-law lying in bed, sick and burning up with a fever. [15]Jesus touched her hand, and *then she was healed*—the fever vanished. She got up from bed and began to wait on Him. [16]Toward nighttime many people who were possessed by demons were brought to Jesus, and He said one word of command and drove the demons out, healing everyone who was sick. [17]These miraculous healings fulfilled what the prophet Isaiah had predicted:

He took up our infirmities upon Himself,
and He bore our diseases.*

[18]Jesus saw that a crowd had gathered around Him, and He gave orders to go to the other side *of the sea.* [19]A scribe came up to Him.

Scribe: Teacher, I will follow You wherever You go.
Jesus: [20]Foxes have dens *in which to sleep,* and the birds have nests. But the Son of Man has no place to lay His head.
Disciple: [21]Jesus, before I do the things You've asked me to do, I must first bury my father.
Jesus: [22]Follow Me! And let the dead bury their own dead.

*D*id Jesus say, "Fair enough, you must of course bury your father. Just catch up with Me when you are done"? No. You see, this is one of the strange and radical things Jesus brought about—our families are no longer our families. Our deepest bonds are not those of blood. Our family now is found in the bonds of fellowship made possible by this Jesus.

[23]And then Jesus got into a boat, and His disciples followed Him. [24]Out of nowhere, a vicious storm blew over the sea. Waves were lapping up over the boat, threatening to overtake it! Yet Jesus was asleep. [25]*Frightened (not to mention confused—how could anyone sleep through this?), the disci*ples woke Him up.

Disciples: Lord, save us! We're going to drown!
Jesus: [26]Please! What are you so afraid of, you of little faith?

And these, remember, were Jesus' close disciples! Jesus got up, told the wind and the waves to calm down, and they did. The sea became still and calm, *pacific once again.* [27]The disciples were astonished. *This Jesus was no ordinary miracle worker.*

* 8:13 A Roman military officer in charge of about 100 foot soldiers
* 8:17 Isaiah 53:4

Disciples: Who is this? What sort of man is He, that the sea and the winds listen to Him?

28Eventually Jesus came to the other side *of the sea,* to the region of the Gadarenes. There, two men *who lived* near the tombs and were possessed by demons came out *to the seaside* and met Jesus. They were flailing about, so violent that they obstructed the path of anyone who came their way.

Demons *(screaming at Jesus):* 29Why are You here? Have You come to torture us even before the judgment day, O Son of God?

30A ways off—*though still visible, not to mention odoriferous*—was a large herd of pigs, eating.

Demons: 31If You cast us out *of the bodies of these two men,* do send us into that herd of pigs!
Jesus: 32*Very well then,* go!

And the demons flew out of the bodies *of the two flailing men,* they set upon the pigs, and every last pig rushed over a steep bank into the sea and drowned. 33The pig herders *(totally undone, as you can imagine)* took off; they headed straight for town, where they told everyone what they'd just seen—even about the demon-possessed men. 34And so the whole town came out to see Jesus for themselves. And when they saw Him, they begged Him to leave their area.

> *S*ome people recognized that Jesus was powerful, but they wanted nothing to do with His kind of power. As in this case, it cost them dearly.

9 *And so Jesus decided to go home.* He got back in the boat, crossed *the sea,* and returned to His own town. 2When He got there, some men approached Him carrying a mat. On the mat was another man, a paralytic. *The men believed fervently*

that Jesus could heal the paralytic, and Jesus saw their faith, how much faith they had in His authority and power.

Jesus: Rest assured, My son; your sins are forgiven.

3Now some scribes *and teachers of the law had been watching this whole scene.*

Scribes and Teachers *(to themselves):* This man is blaspheming!

4*Though they had only spoken in low whispers among themselves,* Jesus knew their thoughts.

Jesus: Why do you hold such hardness and wickedness in your hearts? 5Look, is it easier to say, "Your sins are forgiven," or "Get up and walk"? 6To make clear that the Son of Man has the authority on earth to forgive sins (turning to the paralytic man *on the mat),* Get up, pick up your mat, and go home.

7And the man did. 8When the crowd saw this, they were amazed, *even a little scared,* and they praised God who had given humans the authority *to do such miraculous things.*
9Later Jesus was walking along and He saw a man named Matthew sitting in the tax collector's office.

Jesus *(to Matthew):* Follow Me.

Matthew got up and followed Him.
10*It was not, in fact, unusual for Jesus to hang out with tax collectors.* Once when He ate a meal at home with His disciples, a whole host of tax collectors and other sinners joined them. 11When the Pharisees saw this, they asked Jesus' disciples,

Pharisees: Why does your Teacher eat with tax collectors and sinners?
Jesus *(overhearing this):* 12Look, who needs a doctor—healthy people or sick people? 13I am not here to attend to people who are already right with God; I am here to attend to sinners. *In the book of the*

prophet Hosea, we read, "It is not sacrifice I want, but mercy."* Go and meditate on that for a while—*maybe you'll come to understand it.*

[14]And then some of the disciples of John *the Teacher who ritually washed people* came.

John's Disciples: *What's the story with fasting?* We fast and the Pharisees fast, but Your disciples do not fast!

Jesus: [15]When you celebrate—as at a wedding when one's dearest friend is getting married—you do not fast. The time will come when the bridegroom will be taken from them. Then My friends and followers will fast. [16]You would begin by washing and shrinking a patch you would use to mend a garment—otherwise, the patch would shrink later, pull away from the garment, and make the original tear even worse. [17]You wouldn't pour new wine into old wineskins. If you did, the skins would burst, the wine would run out, and the wineskins would be ruined. No, you would pour new wine into new wineskins—and both the wine and the wineskins would be preserved.

[18]As He was saying these things, a certain official came before Jesus and knelt in front of Him.

Official: My daughter just died. Would You come and lay Your hands on her? Then, I know, she would live again.

[19]Jesus got up, and He and His disciples went with the man. [20-21]*But as they were heading to the man's house, a woman who had been hemorrhaging and bleeding for 12 years—12 years!—crept up behind Jesus. She had been listening to Him teach and watching Him, so she knew that if she so much as touched the fringes of His cloak, she would be healed. And so she came up behind Him and touched His cloak.* [22]Jesus turned around and saw her.

Jesus: Take heart, daughter. Your faith has healed you.

And indeed, from that moment, the woman was healed. [23]Then Jesus went to the official's house. He saw flute players and mourners; *He saw the girl's family weeping and shocked; He saw neighbors bringing food and trying to bring comfort.*

Jesus (to the crowd): [24]Go away, *and do your ministering somewhere else.* This girl is not dead. She is merely asleep.

The crowd—*who knew with certainty that the girl was dead*—laughed at Him. [25]*But they obeyed Him and left the house, and once they were gone,* Jesus went to the girl. *She was lying on a mat on the floor.* When He took her hand, she *opened her eyes and stood up.* [26]When the crowds outside learned that the girl was indeed alive, they spread throughout the town and the surrounding country telling everyone what had happened.

[27]Jesus left the official's house. And as He was walking, two blind men began to follow Him.

Blind Men: Son of David! Have mercy on us!

[28]Jesus went to their house, and the blind men sat in front of Him.

Jesus: Do you believe that I am able to do this?
Blind Men: Yes, Lord.

> *B*y now you know that faith in Jesus and His power is essential for healing. So you will not be surprised to learn that all it took was Jesus' touch to heal these men.

Jesus (touching their eyes): [29]According to your faith, it will be done to you.

[30]And they could see. Then Jesus spoke to them *as He had spoken to the leper.*

Jesus: Don't tell anyone about this.

* 9:13 Hosea 6:6

31But when the men (*who could now see everything perfectly; everything was sharp and colorful*) left, they told everyone in the area they met what had happened.

32Later a man who was possessed by demons and could not talk was brought to Jesus. 33Jesus drove out the demons, and the mute man spoke. The crowds were amazed.

Crowd: Nothing like this has ever been seen in Israel.

Pharisees: 34It must be the prince of demons who gives Him the power to cast out demons.

35Jesus went through many towns and villages. He taught in their synagogues. He preached the good news of the kingdom of God. He healed every disease and sickness. 36Whenever crowds came to Him, He had compassion for them because they were so deeply distraught, malaised, and heartbroken. They seemed to Him like lost sheep without a shepherd. 37*Jesus understood what an awesome task was before Him,* so He said to His disciples, "The harvest is plentiful but the workers are few. 38Ask the Lord of the harvest to send more workers into His harvest field."

10 Jesus called His twelve disciples to Him. He endowed them with the authority to heal sickness and disease and to drive demons out of those who were possessed.

*U*p to this point, the disciples had been, mostly, following Jesus around, listening to Him teach, watching Him heal. And so now we call these twelve beloved men not merely "disciples," or "apprentices," but "apostles," which means "those who are sent as representatives, emissaries." Jesus was preparing to send them into the harvest field to do His Father's work.

2These are the names of the twelve apostles: Simon (who is called Peter, *which*

means "the rock") and his brother Andrew; James, son of Zebedee, and his brother John; 3Philip and Bartholomew; Thomas and Matthew (the tax collector); James, son of Alphaeus, and Thaddaeus; 4Simon the Zealot and Judas Iscariot (who would betray Him).

5Jesus sent out these twelve with clear instructions.

Jesus: Don't go to the outsiders or to the towns inhabited by Samaritans. 6Go instead to find *and heal* the lost sheep of Israel. 7As you go, preach this message: "The kingdom of heaven is at hand." 8Heal the sick, raise the dead, and cleanse those who have leprosy. Drive out demons *from the possessed.* You received *these gifts* freely, so you should give *them* to others freely. 9Do not take money with you: don't take gold, silver, or even small, worthless change. 10Do not pack a bag with clothes. Do not take sandals or a walking stick. *You must embody simplicity.* Be fed and sheltered by those who show you hospitality, *but never let it be said that you are working wonders in order to get rich.* 11When you enter a town or village, look for someone who is trustworthy and stay at his house as long as you are visiting that town. 12When you enter this home, greet the household kindly. 13And if the home is indeed trustworthy, let your blessing of peace rest upon it; if not, keep your blessing to yourself. 14If someone is inhospitable to you or refuses to listen to your testimony, leave that house or town and shake the dust from your feet. 15This is the truth: Sodom and Gomorrah, *those ancient pits of inhospitality,* will fare better on judgment day than towns *who ignore you tomorrow or next week.*

16Listen: I am sending you out to be sheep among wolves. You must be as shrewd as serpents and as innocent as doves. 17You must be careful. You must be discerning. You must be on your guard. There will be men who try to hand you over to their town councils and have you flogged in their synagogues. 18Because of Me, naysayers and doubters will try to make an example out of you by trying you before rulers and kings. *They will try to show people from all nations that they, not I, have all authority and power.* ¹⁹When this happens—*when you are arrested, dragged to court, handed over for flogging*—don't worry about what to say or how to say it. The words you should speak will be given to you. For at that moment, ²⁰it will not be you speaking; it will be the Spirit of your Father speaking through you.

²¹*Your task will be fraught with betrayal*: brother will betray brother, even to the point of death; fathers will betray their children, and children will rebel against their fathers, even to the point of death. ²²⁻²³When you are persecuted in one town, flee to the next town. This is the truth: you will not be able to witness to every town in Israel before the Son of Man comes. Everyone will hate you because of Me. But remember: he who stays on the narrow path until the end will be saved.

²⁴A student is no greater than his teacher, and a servant is never greater than his master. ²⁵It is sufficient if the student is like his teacher and the servant like his master. If people call the head of a house "Beelzebul," *which means "devil,"* just imagine what they're calling the members of his household.

²⁶Do not be afraid of those *who may taunt or persecute you.* Everything they do—even if they think they are hiding behind closed doors—will come to light. All their secrets will eventually be made known. ²⁷And you should proclaim in the bright light of day everything that I have whispered to you in the dark. Whatever whispers you hear—shout them from the rooftops of houses.

²⁸Don't fear those who *aim to* kill just the body but are unable to touch the soul. The one to fear is he who can destroy you, soul and body, in the fires of hell. ²⁹Look, if you sold a few sparrows, *how much money would you get*? A copper coin apiece, perhaps? And yet your Father in heaven knows when those small sparrows fall to the ground.

³⁰⁻³¹You, beloved, are worth so much more than a whole flock of sparrows. God knows *everything about you*, even the number of hairs on your head. So do not fear.

³²*Whoever knows Me here on earth, I will know him in heaven.* And whoever proclaims faith in Me here on earth, I will proclaim *faith in* him before My Father in heaven. ³³But whoever disowns Me here, I will disown before My Father in heaven.

³⁴Do not imagine that I have come to bring peace to the earth. I did not come to bring peace, but a sword. ³⁵I have come to turn men against their fathers, daughters against their mothers, and daughters-in-law against their mothers-in-law. ³⁶You will find you have enemies even in your own household.* ³⁷If you love your father or mother more than you love Me, then you are not worthy of Me. If you love your son or daughter more than you love Me, then you are not worthy of Me. ³⁸If you refuse to take up your cross and follow Me *on the narrow road*, then you are not worthy of Me. ³⁹To find your life, you must lose your life—and whoever loses his life for My sake will find it.

⁴⁰Anyone who welcomes you welcomes Me, and anyone who welcomes Me welcomes the One who sent Me. ⁴¹Anyone who welcomes a prophet and surrenders to his prophecy will receive a prophet's reward, and anyone who welcomes a righteous person and conforms to the righteousness that surrounds him and proceeds from him will receive a righteous man's reward. ⁴²And anyone who has so much as given a cup of cold water to one of the little ones, because he is My disciple, I tell you, that person will be well rewarded.

11 With that, Jesus finished instructing His disciples, and He went on to preach and teach in the towns *of Galilee.* ²John *the Teacher who dipped*

* 10:36 Micah 7:6

people,* meanwhile, was still in prison. But stories about the Liberating King's teachings and healing reached him.

> *Q*uite frankly, John was perplexed. He had been awaiting the Liberating King, but he believed the Liberator would be a great political ruler, a king, or a military hero. Jesus seemed to be all about healing people and insisting that the poor and the meek were blessed.

So John sent his followers ³to question Jesus.

John's Followers: Are You the One we have been expecting as Savior for so long? *Are You the One Scripture promised would come?* Or should we expect someone else?

Jesus: ⁴Go back and tell John the things you have heard and the things you have seen. ⁵*Tell him you have seen* the blind receive sight, the lame walk, the lepers cured, the deaf hear, the dead raised, and the good news preached to the poor. ⁶Blessed are those who *understand what is afoot and* stay on My narrow path.

⁷John's disciples left, and Jesus began to speak to a crowd about John. *He wanted to make sure people understood who they had seen when they saw John.*

Jesus: What did you go into the desert to see? Did you expect to see a reed blowing around in the wind? ⁸No? Were you expecting to see a man dressed in the finest silks? No, of course not—you find silk in the sitting rooms of palaces and mansions, not in the middle of the wilderness. ⁹So what did you go out to see? A prophet? Yes. Yes, a prophet and more than a prophet. ¹⁰When you saw John, you saw the one whom the prophet *Malachi envisioned when he* said,

I will send My messenger ahead of You,
and he will prepare the way for You.*

¹¹This is the truth: no one who has ever been born to a woman is greater than John the Immersing Teacher.* And yet the most insignificant person in the kingdom of heaven is greater than he. ¹²⁻¹³All of the prophets of old, all of the law—that was all prophecy leading up to the coming of John. *Now, the time for that sort of prophecy is through. All of that prophecy and teaching was to prepare us to come to this very point, right here and now.* When John the Teacher who ritually cleansed* came, the kingdom of heaven began to break in upon us, and those in power are trying to clamp down on it—*why do you think John is in jail?* ¹⁴If only you could see it—John is the Elijah, the prophet we were promised would come *and prepare the way.* ¹⁵He who has ears *for the truth,* let him hear.

> *I*n this way, Jesus invited His followers to understand who John the Teacher was, and, in turn, who He must be.

Jesus: ¹⁶What is this generation like? You are like children sitting in the marketplace and calling out, ¹⁷"When we played the flute, you did not dance; and when we sang a dirge, you did not mourn." ¹⁸*What I mean is this:* When John came, *he came from a place of the wilderness. He dressed in the clothes of a prophet, and* he did not eat and drink *like others but lived on honey and wild locusts. And people wondered if he was crazy,* if he had been possessed by a demon. ¹⁹Then the Son of Man appeared—*He didn't fast, as John had,* but ate *with sinners* and drank *wine.* And the people said, "This man is a glutton! He's a drunk! And He hangs around with tax collectors and sinners, to boot."

---

* 11:2 Literally, immersed, to show repentance
* 11:10 Malachi 3:1
* 11:11 Literally, John who immersed, to show repentance
* 11:12-13 Literally, John who immersed, to show repentance

Well, Wisdom will be vindicated by her actions—*not by your opinions.*

20Then Jesus began to preach about the towns He'd visited. He'd performed some of His most fantastic miracles *in places like Chorazin and Bethsaida*, but still the people in those places hadn't turned to God.

Jesus: 21Woe to you, Chorazin! And woe to you, Bethsaida! Had I gone to Tyre and Sidon and performed miracles there, they would have repented immediately, taking on sackcloth and ashes. 22But I tell you this: the people from Tyre and Sidon will fare better on the day of judgment than you will. 23And Capernaum! Do you think you will reign exalted in heaven? *No*, you'll rot in hell. Had I gone to Sodom and worked miracles there, *the people would have repented, and* Sodom would still be standing, *thriving, bustling.* 24*Well, you know what happened to Sodom.* But know this—the people from Sodom will fare better on the day of judgment than you will.

25And then Jesus began to pray:

Jesus: I praise You, Father—Lord of heaven and earth. You have revealed Your truths to the lowly *and the ignorant, the children and the crippled, the lame and the mute.* You have hidden wisdom from those who pride themselves on being so wise and learned. 26You did this, simply, because it pleased You. 27The Father has handed over everything to My care. No one knows the Son except the Father, and no one knows the Father except the Son—and those to whom the Son wishes to reveal the Father. 28Come to Me, all who are weary and burdened, and I will give you rest. 29Put My yoke upon your shoulders—*it might appear heavy at first, but it is perfectly fitted to your curves.* Learn from Me, for I am gentle and humble of heart. *When you are yoked to Me,* your weary souls will find rest. 30For My yoke is easy, and My burden is light.

12 The Sabbath came, and Jesus walked through a field. His disciples, who were hungry, began to pick some of the grain and eat it.

> *T*he Sabbath is a day of rest when one creates nothing, breaks nothing, gives nothing, makes no contracts, cuts no flowers, and boils no water; it is a day set aside by the Lord to remember the creative work of God and to experience the peace of the Lord.

2When the Pharisees saw this, they reacted.

Pharisees: Look! Your disciples are breaking the law of the Sabbath!
Jesus: 3Haven't you read what David did? When he and his friends were hungry, 4they went into God's house and they ate the holy bread, even though neither David nor his friends, but only priests, were allowed that bread. 5*Indeed,* have you not read that on the Sabbath priests themselves do work in the temple, breaking the Sabbath law yet remaining blameless? 6Listen, One who is greater than the temple is here.
   7Do you not understand *what the prophet Hosea recorded*, "I desire mercy, not sacrifice"?* If you understood *that snippet of Scripture*, you would not condemn these innocent men *for ostensibly breaking the law of the Sabbath.* 8For the Son of Man *has not only the authority to heal and cast out demons, He also* has authority over the Sabbath.

9Jesus left the field and went to the synagogue, 10and there He met a man with a shriveled hand. The Pharisees wanted to set up Jesus.

Pharisees: Well, is it lawful to heal on the Sabbath too?

* 12:7 Hosea 6:6

Jesus: [11]Look, imagine that one of you has a sheep that falls into a ditch on the Sabbath—*what would you do?*

*J*esus—who could see that the Pharisees were testing Him and basically missed the point—was growing a little testy. The Pharisees said nothing. Each was secretly thinking that he, of course, would dive in and get his sheep.

Jesus (*to the Pharisees*): You would dive in and rescue your sheep. [12]Now what is more valuable, a person or a sheep? *So what do you think—should I heal this man on the Sabbath?* Isn't it lawful to do good deeds on the Sabbath? [13](to the man *with the shriveled hand*) Stretch out your hand.

As the man did so, his hand was completely healed, as good as new. [14]The Pharisees went and mapped out plans to destroy Jesus. [15]Jesus knew *that the Pharisees were plotting to kill Him—so He followed His own advice (the advice He had given the apostles)* and left the area. Many people followed Him, and He healed them all, [16]always insisting that they tell no one about Him. [17]He did this in keeping with the prophecy Isaiah made so long ago:

[18]This is My servant, whom I have
  well chosen;
    this is the One I love, the One in
      whom I delight.
  I will place My Spirit upon Him;
    He will proclaim justice to all the
      world.
[19]He will not fight or shout
    or talk loudly in the streets.
[20]He will not crush a reed under
      His heel
    or blow out a smoldering candle
  until He has led justice *and
    righteousness* to final victory.
[21]All the world will find its hope in
    His name.*

[22]Some of the faithful brought Jesus a man who was possessed by a demon, who was blind and mute, and Jesus healed him. The man could see and talk, *and demons no longer crawled around in him.*

People (*astonished*): [23]Could this be the Son of David?
Pharisees: [24]It is only through Beelzebul, the prince of demons, that this Jesus can cast out demons.

*W*hat they were thinking simply made no sense. Satan glories in every demoniac, every possessed mute, every incubus who corrupts a righteous person. Why would Satan wish to drive demons out of the possessed?

[25]Jesus knew what the Pharisees were thinking.

Jesus: That would be like a father splitting his own household down the middle or a king cutting his kingdom in half—the household and the kingdom would fall apart. [26]So, too, if Satan *imbued people with the power to* drive out demons, Satan's kingdom would collapse. [27]And you should think about this too: you have friends who drive out demons. If I am working as a tool of Beelzebul, who are your people working for? [28]When I come to you and drive out demons by the Spirit of your Father in heaven—*for the glory of your Father in heaven—you should recognize and rejoice that* the kingdom of God has come to you.
[29]Imagine you wanted to break into the house of your neighbor, a strong brawny man, and steal his furniture. First, you'd have to tie up your neighbor, *yes?* Once he was bound and tied, you could take whatever you wanted. [30]*Similarly*—he who is not with Me is against Me, and he who is not doing the Father's work of gathering *up the flock* may as well be scattering *the flock.*

* 12:18-21 Isaiah 42:1-4

31-32It is one thing for you to speak ill of the Son of Man. People will be forgiven for every sin they commit and blasphemy they utter. *But those who call the work of God the work of Satan utterly remove themselves from God, and* those who blaspheme God's Spirit will not be forgiven, neither in this world nor in the world to come.

33Good trees produce good fruits; bad trees produce bad fruits. You can always tell a tree by its fruits.

34You children of snakes, you who are evil—how could you possibly say anything good? For the mouth simply shapes the heart's impulses into words. 35And so the good man (who is filled with goodness) speaks good words, while the evil man (who is filled with evil) speaks evil words. 36I tell you this: on the day of judgment, people will be called to account for every careless word they have ever said. 37*The righteous* will be acquitted by their own words, and you *evildoers* will be condemned by your own words.

Scribes and Pharisees: 38Teacher, we want to see some miraculous sign from You.

Jesus: 39You wicked and promiscuous generation—you are looking for signs, *are you*? The only sign you will be given is the sign of the prophet Jonah. 40Jonah spent three days and three nights in the belly of a great fish, as the Son of Man will spend three days and three nights in the belly of the earth. 41One day, the people of Nineveh will rise up in judgment and will condemn your present generation—for the Ninevites turned from sin to God when they heard Jonah preach, and now One far greater than Jonah is here. 42The Queen of the South will also stand in judgment and condemn this generation—for she came from the ends of the earth to listen to Solomon's wisdom. And today One greater *and wiser* than Solomon is among you.

43*Let Me tell you what will happen to this wicked generation:* When an evil spirit comes out of a man, it rattles around through *deserts and other* dry places looking for a place to rest—but it does not find anywhere to rest. 44So the spirit says, "I will return to the house I left." And it returns to find that house unoccupied, tidy, swept, and sparkling clean. 45Well, then not only does one spirit set up shop in that sparkling house, but it brings seven even more wicked spirits along. And the poor man—the house—is worse off than he was before. This evil generation will suffer a similar fate.

46While Jesus was speaking to the crowd, His mother and brothers came up and wanted to speak to Him.

Someone in the Crowd: 47Your mother and brothers are waiting outside to speak to You.

Jesus: 48Who is My mother? And who are My brothers? 49(pointing to His disciples) These are My mother and brothers. 50Anyone who does the will of My Father in heaven is My mother and brother and sister.

13

That same day, Jesus left the house and went to sit by the sea.

*Y*ou're probably sensing that by now, large crowds flocked to Jesus wherever He went. This was quickly becoming the case. Sometimes these large groups made it difficult for Him to teach.

2Large crowds gathered around Him, and He got into a boat on the sea and sat there. The crowd stood on the shore *waiting for His teaching*.

3And so Jesus began to teach. *On this day*, He spoke in parables. *Here is His first parable:*

Jesus: Once there was a sower who scattered seeds. 4One day he walked in a field scattering seeds as he went. Some seeds fell beside a road, and a flock of birds came and ate all those seeds. [5]So the sower scattered seeds *in a field,* one with shallow soil and strewn with rocks. But the seeds grew quickly amid all the rocks, [6]without rooting themselves in the shallow soil. Their roots got tangled up in all the stones. The sun scorched these seeds, and they died. [7]And so the sower scattered seeds *near a path,* this one covered with thorny vines. *The seeds fared no better there*—the thorns choked them, *and they died.* [8]*And so finally* the sower scattered his seeds in a patch *of* good earth. *At home in the good earth, the seeds grew and grew. Eventually* the seeds bore fruit, *and the fruit grew ripe and was harvested. The harvest was immense*—30, 60, 100 times what was sown.

[9]He who has ears to hear, let him hear.

Disciples: [10]Why do You speak to the people in parables?

Jesus: [11]The knowledge of the secrets of heaven has been given to you, but it has not been given to them. [12]Those who have something will be given more—and they will have abundance. Those who have nothing will lose what they have—*they will be destitute.* [13]I teach in parables so the people may look but not see, listen but not hear or understand.* [14]They are fulfilling Isaiah's prophecy:

You will listen, but you will not
   understand;
   you will look, but you will not see.
[15]The people's hearts have turned
   to flab;
   their ears are clogged;
   their eyes are shut.
They will try to see, but they will
   not see;
   they will try to hear, but they
   will not hear;
   they will try to understand, but
   they will not comprehend.
*If they, with their blindness and
   deafness, so choose,* then I will
   heal them.*

[16-17]Many holy prophets and righteous men and women *and people of prayer*

and doers of good have wanted to see but did not see, and have wanted to hear but did not hear. Your eyes and ears are blessed.

[18]This is what the parable of the sower means. [19]*It is about the kingdom of heaven.* When someone hears the story of the Kingdom and cannot understand it, the evil one comes and snatches away whatever *goodness and holiness* had been sown in the heart. This is like the seeds sown beside the road. [20-21]*You know* people who hear the word of God and receive it joyfully—but then, somehow, the word fails to take root in their hearts. It is temporary. As soon as God's word causes trouble for those people, they trip: *your friend who left her husband as soon as things got rocky; your friend who listened rapturously to a teaching about trusting God, but refused to take a risk when a risk was called for*—those people are the seeds strewn on the rocky soil. [22]And you know people who hear the word, but it is choked inside them because they constantly worry and prefer the wealth and pleasures of the world: *they prefer drunken dinner parties to prayer, power to piety, and riches to righteousness.* Those people are like the seeds sown among thorns. [23]The people who hear the word and receive it and grow in it—those are like the seeds sown on good soil. They produce a bumper crop, 30 or 60 or 100 times what was sown. *Your Father in heaven must plant many seeds in order to ensure that some seeds bear fruit. The final harvest, however, is worth whatever the toil.*

[24]Jesus told them another parable.

Jesus: The kingdom of heaven is like this: Once there was a farmer who sowed good seeds in his field. [25]While the farmer's workers were sleeping, his enemy crept into the field and sowed weeds among all the wheat seeds. Then

---

* 13:13 Psalm 78:2
* 13:14-15 Isaiah 6:9-10

he snuck away again. 26Eventually the crops grew—wheat, but also weeds. 27So the farmer's workers said to him, "Sir, why didn't you sow good seeds in your field? Where did these weeds come from?"

28"My enemy must have done this," replied the farmer.

"Should we go pull up all the weeds?" asked his workers.

29"No," said the farmer. "It's too risky. As you pull up the weeds, you would probably pull up some wheat as well. 30We'll let them both grow until harvesttime. I will tell the harvesters to collect the weeds and tie them in bundles to be burned, and only then to harvest the wheat and bring it to my barn."

31Jesus told them another parable.

Jesus: The kingdom of heaven is like a mustard seed, which a sower took and planted in his field. 32Mustard seeds are minute, tiny—but the seeds grow into trees. Flocks of birds can come and build their nests in the branches.

33And Jesus told a *fourth* parable about *a baker adding leaven to change what would be flat and uninteresting into a valuable commodity.*

Jesus: *Imagine a woman preparing a loaf of bread.* The kingdom of heaven is like the leaven she folds into her dough. She kneads and kneads until the leaven is worked into all the dough. *Without the leaven, the dough remains flat. But the secret is the almost invisible leaven making her loaves fluff and rise.*

34Jesus gave all these teachings to the crowd in parables. Indeed, He spoke only in parables 35in fulfillment of the prophetic words *of the Psalms:*

I will open My mouth in parables;
   I will tell them things that have
      been hidden and obscure since
     the very beginning of the
     world.*

36Then Jesus left the crowds and returned to His house. His disciples followed Him.

Disciples: Explain to us the story You told about the weeds.

Jesus: 37The one who sowed the good seed is the Son of Man. 38The field is the world; the good seed represents the children of the Kingdom. The weeds—*who do you think the weeds are?* They are the children of the evil one, 39and the enemy who threw the weeds among the wheat is the devil. The harvest is the end of the age, and the workers are God's heavenly messengers. 40*In the parable,* I told you the weeds would be pulled up and burned— well, that is how it will be at the end of this age. 41The Son of Man will send His messengers out into the world, and they will root out from His kingdom everything that is poisonous, ugly, and malicious, and everyone who does evil. 42They will throw all that wickedness into the fiery furnace where there will be weeping and grinding of teeth. 43And the righteous will shine like the sun in their Father's kingdom. He who has ears to hear, let him hear.

44The kingdom of heaven is like a treasure that is hidden in a field. A *crafty* man found the treasure buried there and buried it again *so no one would know where it was.* Thrilled, he went off and sold everything he had, and then he came back and bought the field *with the hidden treasure part of the bargain.*

45Or the kingdom of heaven is like a jeweler on the lookout for the finest pearls. 46When he found a pearl more beautiful and valuable than any jewel he had ever seen, the jeweler sold all he had and bought that pearl, *his pearl of great price.*

47Or *think of it this way:* the kingdom of heaven is like a net that was cast into the sea, a net that caught a world of flickering fish. 48When the net was full, the fishermen hauled it to shore. They separated the good fish from the bad, placing

* 13:35 Psalm 78:2

the good fish in a bucket and throwing out the inedible fish. 49That is what the end of time will be like. The heavenly messengers will separate *the good from the bad,* the righteous from the wicked, *the repentant from the prideful, the faithful from the hard-hearted.* 50*The bad, the wicked, the prideful, and the hard-hearted* will be thrown into the fiery furnace where there will be weeping and grinding of teeth.

51Do you understand?

Disciples: Yes, *we understand.*

Jesus: 52Every scribe *and teacher of the law* who has become a student of the ways of the Kingdom is like the head of the household who brings some new things and some old things, both out of the storeroom.

53With that Jesus finished teaching His parables, and He moved on. 54-56He came to *Nazareth,* the town where He had grown up. He taught at the local synagogue, and the people were astonished.

People: *Is this our little Jesus? Is this Mary's son? Is this the carpenter's son? Is this Jesus, brother of James, Joseph, Simon, and Judas? Didn't we just see His sisters yesterday at the market?* Where did He learn all this? Whence His power?

57They were offended by Him—by His teachings, by His presumptuousness, by His bearing, by His very self.

Jesus: Prophets are respected—except in their hometowns and in their own households. *There the prophet is dishonored.*

58Jesus didn't bother to work wondrous miracles there *in Nazareth* because the people did not believe.

14 At this time, the ruler *of Galilee* was Herod *Antipas.* He began to hear reports about all that Jesus was doing.

2*Like the people of Nazareth,* Herod wondered where Jesus' power came from.

Herod (*to his servants*): He must be John the Teacher who ritually cleansed,* raised from the dead; thus His power.

*H*erod was quite concerned with the attention that John the Teacher was receiving, but he didn't want to spend precious political capital killing a reputed holy man. On top of that, Jesus was beginning to create an even greater problem for Herod.

3-5Herod's brother Philip had married a woman named Herodias, *who eventually married Herod.* John denounced Herod's marriage to her as adulterous. Herod was incensed (*not to mention a little fearful*) and wanted to kill John, but he knew the people considered John a prophet. Instead, he bound John and put him in jail.

6-7*There John sat until* Herod's birthday. On that night, *Salome,* Herodias's daughter *by Philip,* came and danced for her stepfather and all his birthday guests. Herod so enjoyed her dancing that he vowed to give her whatever she wanted.

Salome (*after whispering with her mother*): 8Bring me the head of John the Teacher and Prophet,* displayed on a platter.

*T*his was not what Herod had expected—he'd imagined his stepdaughter might ask for a necklace or maybe a slave.

9Herod still thought it unwise to kill John, but *because he had made such a show of his promise*—because he had actually sworn an oath and *because the scene was playing out in front of the watchful eyes* of so many guests—Herod felt bound *to give his stepdaughter what she wanted.* 10And so he sent

---

* 14:2 Literally, John who immersed, to show repentance
* 14:8 Literally, John who immersed, to show repentance

orders to the prison to have John beheaded, [11]and there was his head, displayed on a platter, given first to *Salome* and then passed on to her mother.

[12]John's disciples went to the prison, got John's body, and buried him. Then they went to tell Jesus.

[13]When Jesus learned what had happened, He got on a boat and went away to spend some time in a private place. The crowds, of course, followed Jesus on foot from their cities. [14]*Though Jesus wanted solitude,* when He saw the crowds, He had compassion on them, and He healed the sick *and the lame.* [15]At evening-time, Jesus' disciples came to Him.

Disciples: We're in a fairly remote place, and it is getting late; *the crowds will get hungry for supper.* Send them away so they have time to get back to the villages and get something to eat.
Jesus: [16]They don't need to go back to the villages in order to eat supper. Give them something to eat here.
Disciples: [17]*But we don't have enough food.* We only have five rounds *of flatbread* and two fish.
Jesus: [18]Bring the bread and the fish to Me.

So the disciples brought Him the five rounds of flatbread and the two fish, [19]and Jesus told the people to sit down on the grass. He took the bread and the fish, He looked up to heaven, He gave thanks, and then He broke the bread. Jesus gave the bread to the disciples, and the disciples gave the bread to the people; [20]everyone ate and was satisfied. *When everyone had eaten,* the disciples picked up 12 baskets *of crusts and broken pieces of bread and crumbs. Not only was there enough, but there was an abundance.* [21]There were 5,000 men there, not to mention all the women and children.

[22]Immediately Jesus made the disciples get into the boat and go on to the other side of the sea while He dismissed the crowd. [23]Then, after the crowd had gone, Jesus went up to a mountaintop alone (*as He had intended from the start*). As evening descended, He stood alone on the mountain, praying. [24]The boat was in the water, some distance from land, buffeted and pushed around by waves and wind.

[25]Deep in the night, *when He had concluded His prayers,* Jesus walked out on the water to His disciples *in their boat.* [26]The disciples saw a figure moving toward them and were terrified.

Disciple: It's a ghost!
Another Disciple: A ghost? *What will we do?*
Jesus: [27]Be still. It is I. You have nothing to fear.
Peter: [28]Lord, if it is really You, then command me to meet You on the water.
Jesus: [29]*Indeed,* come.

Peter stepped out of the boat onto the water and began walking toward Jesus. [30]But when he remembered how strong the wind was, his courage caught in his throat and he began to sink.

Peter: Master, save me!

[31]Immediately Jesus reached for Peter and caught him.

Jesus: O you of little faith. Why did you doubt *and dance back and forth between following* Me *and heeding fear*?

[32]Then Jesus and Peter climbed in the boat together, and the wind became still. [33]And the disciples worshiped Him.

Disciples: Truly You are the Son of God.

[34]All together, Jesus and the disciples crossed *to the other side of the sea.* They landed at Gennesaret, *an area famous for its princely gardens.* [35]The people of Gennesaret recognized Jesus, and they spread word of His arrival all over the countryside. People brought the sick *and wounded* to Him [36]and begged Him for permission to touch the fringes of His robe. Everyone who touched Him was healed.

15 Some Pharisees and scribes came from Jerusalem to ask Jesus a question.

Scribes and Pharisees: ²The law of Moses has always held that one must ritually wash his hands before eating. Why don't Your disciples observe this tradition?

³Jesus—*who was developing a reputation as One who gave as good as He got*—turned the Pharisees' question back on them.

Jesus: Why do you violate God's command because of your tradition? ⁴God said, "Honor your father and mother."* Anyone who curses his father or mother must be put to death."* ⁵⁻⁶But you say that one need no longer honor his parents so long as he says to them, "What you might have gained from me, I now give to the glory of God." Haven't you let your tradition trump the word of God? ⁷You hypocrites! Isaiah must have had you in mind when he prophesied,

⁸People honor Me with their lips,
   but their hearts are nowhere
      near Me.
⁹Because they elevate mere human
      ritual to the status of law,
   their worship of Me is a
      meaningless sham.*

¹⁰(to the multitude) Hear and understand this: ¹¹What you put into your mouth cannot make you *clean or unclean*—it is what comes out of your mouth that can make you unclean.

¹²Later the disciples came to Him.

Disciples: Do You realize the Pharisees were shocked by what You said?
Jesus: ¹³Every plant planted by someone other than My heavenly Father will be plucked up by the roots. ¹⁴So let them be. They are blind guides. What happens when one blind person leads another? Both of them fall into a ditch.
Peter: ¹⁵Explain that riddle to us.
Jesus: ¹⁶Do you still not see? ¹⁷Don't you

understand that whatever you take in through your mouth makes its way to your stomach and eventually out *of the bowels* of your body? ¹⁸But the things that come out of your mouth—*your curses, your fears, your denunciations*—these come from your heart, and it is the stirrings of your heart that can make you unclean. ¹⁹For your heart harbors evil thoughts—fantasies of murder, adultery, and whoring; fantasies of stealing, lying, and slandering. ²⁰These make you unclean—not eating with a hand you've not ritually purified with a splash of water *and a prayer.*

²¹Jesus left that place and withdrew to Tyre and Sidon. ²²A Canaanite woman—*a non-Jew*—came to Him.

Canaanite Woman (*wailing*): Lord, Son of David, have mercy on me! My daughter is possessed by a demon. *Her body is wracked! Her mind is senseless! Have mercy, Lord!*

²³Jesus said nothing. *And the woman continued to wail.* His disciples came to Him.

Disciples: Do something—she keeps crying after us!
Jesus: ²⁴I was sent here only to gather up the lost sheep of Israel.

²⁵The woman came up to Jesus and knelt before Him.

Canaanite Woman: Lord, help me!
Jesus: ²⁶It is not right to waste your children's bread feeding dogs.
Canaanite Woman: ²⁷But, Lord, even dogs eat the crumbs that fall by the table as their master is eating.

²⁸Jesus—*whose ancestors included Ruth and Rahab*—spoke *with kindness and insight.*

Jesus: Woman, you have great faith. And your request is done.

* 15:4 Exodus 20:12; Deuteronomy 5:16
* 15:4 Leviticus 20:9
* 15:8-9 Isaiah 29:13

And her daughter was healed, right then and from then on.

²⁹Jesus left and went to the Sea of Galilee. He went up on a mountaintop and sat down. ³⁰Crowds thronged to Him there, bringing the lame, *the maimed,* the blind, the crippled, the mute, and many other *sick and broken* people. They laid them at His feet, and He healed them. ³¹The people saw the mute speaking, the lame walking, *the maimed made whole,* the crippled dancing, and the blind seeing; and the people were amazed, and they praised the God of Israel.

Jesus *(to His disciples)*: ³²*We must take pity on* these people for they have touched My heart—they have been with Me for three days, and they don't have any food. I don't want to send them home this hungry—they might collapse on the way!
Disciples: ³³We'll never find enough food for all these people, out here in the middle of nowhere!
Jesus: ³⁴How much bread do you have?
Disciples: Seven *rounds of flatbread* and a few small fish.

³⁵He told the crowd to sit down. ³⁶He took the bread and the fish, He gave thanks, and then He broke the bread and divided the fish. He gave the bread and fish to the disciples, the disciples distributed them to the people, ³⁷and everyone ate and was satisfied. When everyone had eaten, the disciples picked up seven baskets *of crusts* and *broken pieces and crumbs. Not only was there enough, but there was an abundance.* ³⁸There were 4,000 men there, not to mention all the women and children. ³⁹Then Jesus sent the crowd away. He got into His boat and went to Magadan.

16 They came to Him together, a band of Pharisees and a band of Sadducees, trying to trick and trap Him.

N ow at this time in Judea, the Jews, the children of Israel,

were a diverse bunch. One group of Jews, which you have already read about, was called the Pharisees. Another family of Jews was called the Sadducees. The two groups did not agree about how to read Scripture; they did not see eye-to-eye, and they did not get along. They rarely partnered with each other. But here we find them partnering—because they were so perplexed, befuddled, and panicked about this Jesus.

They asked Him for a sign from heaven.

Jesus: ²At evening time, you read the sky as a sign—you say, "The weather will be fine because the sky is shading red," ³and in the morning, *you read the sky as a sign, saying,* "The red, stormy sky tells me that today we will have storms." So you are skilled at interpreting the sky, but you cannot interpret the signs of the times? ⁴Only a cheating and evil generation *such as this* would beg for a miraculous sign *from heaven.* The only sign you will get will be the sign of Jonah.

And then Jesus left them and went away. ⁵When next the disciples crossed *the Sea of Galilee,* they forgot to bring any bread with them.

Jesus: ⁶Be careful; avoid the leaven of the Pharisees and Sadducees.

⁷The disciples *were not quite sure what Jesus meant, so they* discussed His warning among themselves.

Disciples: *He must mean not to buy any bread from a baker who associates with the Pharisees or Sadducees. He must have* given us this warning because we showed up here without any bread.

⁸Jesus knew what the disciples were saying among themselves, *and He took them to task.*

Jesus: You men of little faith, *do you really think that I care which baker you patronize? After spending so much time with Me, do you still not understand what I mean?* So you showed up without bread; why talk about it? 9-10Don't you remember that we fed 5,000 men with five rounds of flatbread? Don't you remember that we fed 4,000 men with seven rounds of bread? Don't you remember what excess, what abundance there was—*how many broken pieces and crusts you collected after everyone had eaten and was sated?* 11So when I speak about leaven, I am not talking about what we will eat for dinner. I say again, avoid the leaven of the Pharisees and Sadducees.

12And then the disciples understood: Jesus was not talking about the bread you eat, *but about the food that feeds your soul. He was speaking in metaphor;* He was warning them against imbibing the teachings of the Pharisees and Sadducees.

13Jesus then went to Caesarea Philippi.

Jesus (to His disciples): Who do people say the Son of Man is?
Disciples: 14Some say John who ritually cleansed people.* And some say Elijah. And some say Jeremiah or one of the other prophets.
Jesus: 15And you? Who do you say that I am?
Simon Peter: 16You are the Liberating King. You are the Son of the living God.
Jesus: 17Simon, son of Jonah, your knowledge is a mark of blessing. For you didn't learn this truth from your friends or from teachers or from sages you've met on the way. You learned it from My Father in heaven. 18This is why I have called you Peter (*rock*): for on this rock I will build My church. The church will reign triumphant even at the gates of hell. 19Peter, I give you the keys to the kingdom of heaven. Whatever you bind on earth will be bound in heaven, and whatever you loose on earth will be loosed in heaven.

*W*ith Peter's confession that Jesus is the Liberating King, the foundation of the church is laid. In the days ahead, the church will storm the gates of hell and nothing will be able to stop it. No darkness, no doubt, no deception—not even death will be able to stand against it.

20And Jesus ordered His disciples *to keep these teachings secret.*

Jesus: You must tell no one that I am the Liberator.

21Then Jesus began to tell the disciples *about what would happen to Him. He said* He would have to go to Jerusalem. There the elders, chief priests, and scribes would meet Him; He would suffer at their hands; and He would be killed. But three days later, He would be raised *to new life.*
22*As Jesus spoke of the things to come,* Peter took Him aside. *Sad and confused, and maybe a little bit prideful,* Peter chastised Jesus.

Peter: No, Lord! Never! These things that You are saying—they will never happen to You!
Jesus (*turning to Peter*): 23Get away from Me, Satan!

*T*his, you will recall, was the very thing He said to the devil during those wilderness temptations.

Jesus: You are a stumbling block before Me! You are not thinking about God's story— you are thinking about *some distorted story of fallen, broken people.* 24(to His disciples) If you want to follow Me, you must deny yourself *the things you think you want.* You must pick up your cross and follow Me. 25The person who wants to save his life must lose it, and she who loses her life for Me will find it. 26Look,

* 16:14 Literally, John who immersed, to show repentance

does it make sense to truly become suc-
cessful, but then to hand over your very
soul? What is your soul really worth?
27The Son of Man will come in His
Father's glory, with His heavenly messengers, and then He will reward each
person for what has been done. 28I tell
you this: some of you standing here, you
will see the Son of Man come into His
kingdom before you taste death.

*J*esus is providing an entirely different perspective on success
and happiness. The new Kingdom is
breaking in, and the new community is
coming together. This is the logic of
that Kingdom and that community: if
you want to inhabit God's story, this is
what you must do. To accrue fame and
comfort and riches is counter to this
new community. In the mathematics
and logic of this new community,
real success is measured spiritually
and the promised rewards are
immense.

17 Six days later, Jesus went up to
the top of a high mountain with
Peter, James, and John. 2There,
something spectacular happened: Jesus' face
began to glow and gleam and shine like the
morning sun. His clothes gleamed too—
bright white, like sunlight *mirroring off a
snowfall.* He was, *in a word,* transfigured.
3Suddenly there at the top of the mountain
were Moses and Elijah, *those icons of the
faith, beloved of God.* And they talked to
Jesus. *The three men stood at the intersection
of heaven and earth; they were gleaming,
talking.*

Peter: 4Lord, how amazing that we are here
*to see these heroes of our faith, these men
through whom God spoke.* Should I
quickly build some shelter, three *small*
tabernacles, for You, for Moses, and for
Elijah?

5As Peter spoke, a bright cloud enveloped
all of them.

Voice from the Cloud: This is My beloved Son.
With Him I am well pleased. Listen to
Him.

*Y*ou will remember: this was but
an echo of the Voice that spoke
at Jesus' ritual cleansing. It is an echo
of what God said through Moses during his final sermon on the mount. God
promised that although Moses could
not enter the promised land, He would
send His people another prophet.
Moses' very last wish for his beloved
people was that they would listen to
this new prophet when He came.

6This voice from heaven terrified the three
disciples, and they fell prostrate on the
ground. 7But Jesus—*who was, by this time,
used to His disciples being plagued by fear*—
touched them.

Jesus: Get up. Don't be afraid.

8And when the disciples got up, they saw
they were alone with their Lord. *Moses
and Elijah had returned from where they
came.*
9The four men hiked back down the
mountain, and Jesus told His disciples to
stay silent.

Jesus: Don't tell anyone what happened
here, not until the Son of Man has been
raised from the dead.

*W*hy did Jesus often instruct His
disciples to keep secrets? In
this case, perhaps He did because He
realized they would not understand the
meaning of the transfiguration until they
had lived through that other hilltop event,
the death of Jesus on the cross. We,
like the disciples, will better understand
this bath of light and revelation when
we come to Golgotha and the cross.

Disciples: 10Master, why do the scribes teach
that the prophet Elijah must come
before the Liberating King?

Jesus: ¹¹*The teachers of the law are not wrong: our sacred Scripture tells us clearly that indeed* Elijah will come to restore all things. ¹²But see this: Elijah has come already. No one recognized him for who he was, so he was arrested and killed. *That is part of the preparation of which our Scripture speaks*: for the Son of Man, too, will be arrested and killed at the hands of people *who do not see Him for who He is.*

¹³And then the disciples realized the man they knew as John the Teacher from the wilderness* was the one Jesus was speaking of *as the fulfillment of the prophet Elijah's role—he who prepared the way for the coming of the Lord.*

¹⁴*They had come down from the mountain, and as they headed toward town,* they came to a crowd. As they approached the crowd, a man rushed up to Jesus and knelt before Him.

Man from the Crowd: ¹⁵Lord, have mercy on my son. He has seizures. *They are uncontrollable, unpredictable, wholly unmanageable, and* sometimes when they come on, my son falls into the fire or into a pond. *We are sure he will one day be burned to a crisp or will drown in the sea or will shake to death.* ¹⁶I brought him to Your disciples, but they could not heal him.
Jesus: ¹⁷This generation *is no better than the generation who wandered in the desert,* who lost faith and bowed down *to golden idols as soon as Moses disappeared upon Mount Sinai!* How long will I have to shepherd these unbelieving sheep? *(turning to the man)* Bring the boy to Me.

¹⁸*The man did, and* Jesus castigated the demon who had taken up residence in the boy. And the demon fled the boy's body *at the sound of Jesus' voice,* and the boy was healed from that moment on. *No more shaking. No more falling into fires.*
¹⁹*Later,* when they were away from the crowds, the disciples asked Jesus why they hadn't been able to drive out the demon themselves.

Jesus: ²⁰Because you have so little faith. I tell you this: *if you had even a faint spark of faith,* even faith as *tiny as* a mustard seed, you could say to this mountain, "Move from here to there," and *because of your faith,* the mountain would move. *If you had just a sliver of faith,* you would find nothing impossible. [²¹But this kind is not realized except through much prayer and fasting.]*

²²Jesus and the disciples came to Galilee.

Jesus: The Son of Man is going to be betrayed into the hands of men. ²³They will kill Him, and on the third day, He will be resurrected, *vindicated, newly alive.*

The disciples were filled with grief.
²⁴Then Jesus and His disciples went toward Capernaum, and when they arrived there, some people who had collected the two-drachma tax *that went for the upkeep of the temple* came up to Peter.

Temple Tax Collectors: Does your Teacher not pay the *temple* tax?
Peter: ²⁵He does pay the tax.

*J*esus knew that He and His followers were the true temple, and yet Jesus was canny. It was not quite time to shake the foundations of the temple or of the old way of doing things. And so He would pay the tax and bide His time.

So when Peter came into the house where they were staying, Jesus explored the subject.

Jesus: Simon, what do you think? When kings collect taxes and duties and tolls,

* 17:13 Literally, John who immersed, to show repentance
* 17:21 The earliest manuscripts omit verse 21.

from whom do they collect—do they levy taxes on their own people or on strangers and foreigners?

Peter: ²⁶The foreigners, my Lord.

Jesus: Well, then, we children of the King should be exempt from this two-drachma tax. ²⁷But all in all, it's better not to make any waves; *we'd better go on and pay the tax.* So do this: go out to the lake and throw out your line. And when you catch a fish, open its jaws and you will find a four-drachma coin. Take this to the tax collectors, and pay your taxes and Mine.

18 Around that same time, the disciples came to Jesus and questioned Him about the kingdom of heaven.

A Disciple: In the kingdom of heaven, who is the greatest?

*T*he disciples struggled with the concept of the kingdom of heaven. They did not yet understand that in the arithmetic of the new Kingdom to even consider who was most important or most powerful was a contradiction in terms.

²Jesus called over a little child. *He put His hand on the top of the child's head.*

Jesus: ³This is the truth: unless you change and become like little children, you will never enter the kingdom of heaven. ⁴In that kingdom, the most humble who are most like this child are the greatest. ⁵And whoever welcomes a child, *whoever welcomes the weak and the friendless, the small and the frail, the mute and the poor, the ugly and disfigured—whoever welcomes those* in My name welcomes Me. ⁶And do not lead astray one of the weak and friendless who believes in Me. *Do not plant doubt or tempt or in any way lure her from Me.* If you do, it would be better for you to be dragged down with a

millstone and drowned in the bottom of the sea.

⁷Beware indeed of those in a world filled with obstacles and temptations *that cause people to turn away from Me.* Those temptations are woven into the fabric of a world *not yet redeemed,* but beware to anyone who lures righteous women and men off the narrow path. ⁸If your hand constantly grasps at the things of this world rather than serves the Kingdom—cut it off and throw it away. If your foot is always leading you to wander, then cut it off and throw it away; it is better for you to hobble, crippled, into *the kingdom of* life than to burn in hell with two hands and two feet. ⁹And if your eye always focuses on things that cause you to sin, then pull your eye out and throw it away. It is better for you to see *the kingdom of* life with one eye than to see the fires of hell with perfect sight.

¹⁰Make sure that you do not look down on the little ones, *on those who struggle, on those who are further behind you on the path of righteousness.* For I tell you: they are watched over by those *most beloved* messengers who are always in the company of My Father in heaven. [¹¹The Son of Man has come to save all those who are lost.]* ¹²A shepherd in charge of 100 sheep notices that one of his sheep has gone astray. What do you think he should do? Should the shepherd leave the flock on the hills unguarded to search for the lost sheep? *God's shepherd goes to look for that one lost sheep,* ¹³and when he finds her, he is happier about her return than he is about the 99 who stayed put. ¹⁴Your Father in heaven does not want a single one of the *tripped, waylaid, stumbling* little ones to be lost.

*T*he wisdom of the world would say that the shepherd should forget that one missing sheep and chalk it up as a loss because the sheep was not

* 18:11 The earliest manuscripts omit verse 11.

worth the time he'd spend chasing her down. The arithmetic of heaven's value works differently. In God's economy, each soul has its own value apart from all others.

Jesus: [15]This is what you do if one of your brothers or sisters sins against you: go to him, in private, and tell him just what you perceive the wrong to be. If he listens to you, you've won a brother. [16]*But sometimes he will not listen.* And if he does not listen, go back, taking a friend or two friends with you (*for, as we have learned in Deuteronomy*, every matter of communal import should be testified to by two or three witnesses).* [17]Then, if your brother or sister still refuses to heed, you are to share what you know with the entire church; and if your brother or sister still refuses to listen to the entire church, you are to cast out your unrepentant sibling and consider him no different from outsiders and tax collectors.

What God desires most is not the rebuke of sin for the sake of the rebuke, but loving chastisement for the sake of bringing the sinful back to God. Casting out an unrepentant member is only a last resort.

Jesus: [18]Remember this: whatever you bind on earth will be bound in heaven, and whatever you loose on earth will be loosed in heaven. [19]And this: if two *or three* of you come together as a community *and discern clearly* about anything, My Father in heaven will bless that discernment. [20]For when two or three gather together in My name, I am there in the midst of them.

Peter: [21]Lord, when someone has sinned against me, how many times ought I forgive him? *Once? Twice?* As many as seven times?

Jesus: [22]You must forgive not seven times, but seventy times seven.

The response of Jesus is like the story of Lamech in Genesis. Lamech was Adam and Eve's great-great-great-great-grandson. He had two wives. And one day he said to his wives, "Wives, listen to me: once a young man wounded me, and I killed him. You see, I will be avenged seventy-seven times."* In this new Kingdom of forgiveness, we reverse and invert Lamech's plan. As Christians, we should forgive others' transgressions more readily than the world would avenge them.

Jesus: [23]If you want to understand the kingdom of heaven, think about a king who wanted to settle accounts with his servants. [24]Just as the king began to get his accounts in order, his assistants called his attention to a slave who owed a huge sum to him—what 100,000 laborers might earn if they worked for 100 days.* [25]The slave, *maybe an embezzler,* had no way to make restitution, so the king ordered that he, his wife, their children, and everything the family owned be sold *on the auction block*; the proceeds from the slave sale would go toward paying back the king. [26]Upon hearing this judgment, the slave fell down, prostrated himself before the king, and begged for mercy: "Have mercy on me, and I will somehow pay you everything." [27]The king was moved by the pathos of the situation, so indeed he took pity on the servant, told him to stand up, and then forgave the debt.

[28]But the slave went and found a friend, another slave, who owed him about a hundred days' wages.* "Pay me back that money," shouted the slave, throttling his friend and shaking him with threats and violence. [29]The slave's friend fell down prostrate and begged for mercy: "Have mercy on me, and I will somehow pay you everything." [30]But the first slave *cackled and was hard-hearted*

* 18:16 Deuteronomy 19:15
* **Note:** Genesis 4:23-24
* 18:24 Literally, 10,000 talents
* 18:28 Literally, denarii, Roman coins

and refused *to hear his friend's plea*. He *found a magistrate and* had his friend thrown into prison "where," he said, "you will sit until you can pay me back." [31]The other servants saw what was going on. They were upset, so they went to the king and told him everything that had happened.

[32]The king summoned the slave, *the one who had owed so much money, the one whose debt the king had forgiven. The king was livid*. "You slovenly scum," he said, *seething with anger*. "You begged me to forgive your debt, and I did. [33]What would be the faithful response to such latitude and generosity? Surely*—you should have shown the same charity to a friend who was in your debt."

[34]The king turned over the unmerciful slave to his brigade of torturers, *and they had their way with him* until he should pay his whole debt. [35]And that is what My Father in heaven will do to you, unless you forgive each of your brothers *and each of your sisters* from *the very cockles of* your heart.

[19]After Jesus had finished His teaching about forgiveness, He left Galilee and He went to the section of Judea on the other side of the Jordan River. [2]Large crowds followed Him, *and when He got to Judea*, He set about healing them. [3]Some Pharisees—*eyeing the crowds and watching the healings—decided that it was again time to try to trip up Jesus*. So they approached Jesus and asked Him this tricky question *about divorce*:

Pharisees: Is it ever lawful for a man to divorce his wife?

Jesus: [4]Haven't you read that in the beginning God created humanity male and female?* *Don't you remember what the story of our creation tells us about marriage?* [5]"For this reason, a man will leave his mother and father and cleave to his wife, and the two shall become one flesh."* *If a husband and wife are indeed one flesh, how can they divorce?* [6]If a husband and wife are one flesh, *divorce*

would be a bloody amputation, would it not?* "What God has brought together, let no man separate."

Pharisees: [7]Why did Moses explain that if a man leaves his wife, then he must give her a certificate of divorce and send her away, free and clear of him?

Jesus: [8]Moses permitted you to divorce your wives because your hearts were hard. *But divorce was an innovation, an accommodation to a fallen world*. There was no divorce at creation. [9]Listen, friends: if you leave your wife, unless there is adultery, and then marry another woman, you yourself are committing adultery. *Only if there is adultery can you divorce your wife*.

*W*hy? Because adultery itself is the divorce. Adultery is the thing that breaks the bond of marriage. Just as an excommunication merely recognizes the fact that someone has already been removed from the people, a divorce merely legalizes what harlotry has created. But should someone leave his wife for any other reason—because he has nothing to say to her, because she continually burns his food, because she is profligate with the household resources, because he simply cannot stand the sight of her—this is outside of the message Jesus offered here. You may behave as if a marriage has been undone—indeed, you may believe that a marriage has been undone—but you are deluding yourselves. In the eyes of God, the marriage bonds still hold a man to his wife.

The disciples, who had listened and heard every word of this exchange, were shaken.

Disciples: [10]If this is how it is, then it is better to avoid marrying in the first place.

Jesus: [11]Not everyone can hear this teaching, only those to whom it has been

* 19:4 Genesis 1:27
* 19:5 Genesis 2:24

given. ¹²*Some people do not marry, of course.* Some people are eunuchs because they are born that way, others have been made eunuchs by men, and others have renounced marriage for the sake of the kingdom of heaven. Anyone who can embrace that call should do so.

¹³At this, some *of Jesus' followers* brought their children before Jesus; they wanted Him to place His hands on the children and pray *for them.* Some of the disciples, *mistakenly thinking that Jesus wouldn't want to be bothered with the likes of children,* began to rebuke the crowd.

Jesus: ¹⁴Let the little children come to Me; do not get in their way. For the kingdom of heaven belongs to children like these.

¹⁵He laid His hands on them, *He prayed with them,* and then He left that spot *and went elsewhere.* ¹⁶Then a *young* man came up to Jesus.

Young Man: Teacher, what good deed can I do to assure myself eternal life?
Jesus: ¹⁷Strange that you should ask Me what is good. There is only One who is good. If you want to participate in His *divine* life, obey the Commandments.
Young Man: ¹⁸Which Commandments *in particular?*
Jesus: *Well, to begin with,* do not murder, do not commit adultery, do not steal, do not give false testimony, ¹⁹honor your father and mother, and love your neighbor as yourself.*
Young Man: ²⁰I've kept those Commandments faithfully. What else do I need to do?

*J*esus looked at the man and could see that he was very earnest, wanted to be taught, and wanted to know what he needed to do to participate in God's reality. Jesus knew his shoulders would sag under the weight of the next hard instruction.

Jesus: ²¹If you want to be perfect, go and sell all your possessions and give all your money to the poor; then you will have treasure in heaven. And then come, follow Me.

²²The young man's *shoulders did indeed sag, and he* went away sad because he was very wealthy indeed.

Jesus: ²³This is the truth: it is hard for a rich man to enter the kingdom of heaven. ²⁴Yes, it is easier for a camel to go through the eye of a needle than for a rich man to enter the kingdom of God.

²⁵The disciples, hearing this, were stunned.

Disciples: Who then can be saved?
Jesus: ²⁶People cannot save themselves. But with God, all things are possible.
Peter: ²⁷*You just told that man to leave everything and follow You.* Well, all of us have done just that. So what should we be expecting?
Jesus: ²⁸I tell you this. When *creation is consummated and* all things are renewed, when the Son of Man sits on His throne in glory, you who have followed Me will also sit on thrones. There will be twelve thrones, and you will sit and judge the twelve tribes of Israel. ²⁹You who have left your house and your fields, or your brothers and sisters, or your father and mother, or even your children in order to follow Me, *at that time when all is renewed, you will receive so much more*: you will receive 100 times what you gave up. You will inherit eternal life. ³⁰Those who are the first will be last, and those who are the last will be first.

20 Jesus: The kingdom of heaven is like a wealthy landowner who got up early in the morning and went out, first thing, to hire workers to tend his vineyard. ²He agreed to pay them a

* 19:19 Exodus 20:12-17; Deuteronomy 5:16-20; Leviticus 19:18

day's wage* for the day's work. The workers headed to the vineyard *while the landowner headed home to deal with some paperwork.* ³About three hours later, he went back to the marketplace. He saw *some unemployed* men standing around with nothing to do.

Landowner: ⁴*Do you need some work?* Go over to my vineyard *and join the crew there.* I'll pay you well.

So off they went *to join the crew at the vineyard.* ⁵About three hours later, and then three hours after that, *the landowner went back to the market and saw another crew of men and hired them, too, sending them off to his vineyard and promising to pay them well.* ⁶Then finally late in the afternoon, *at the cusp of night,* the landowner walked again *through the marketplace,* and he saw other *workers* still standing around.

Landowner: Why have you been standing here all day, doing nothing?
Workers: ⁷Because no one has hired us.
Landowner: Well, you should go over to my vineyard *and put in a few moments of work.*

And off the workers went. ⁸When quitting time arrived, the landowner called to his foreman.

Landowner: Pay the workers their day's wages, beginning with the workers I hired most recently and ending with the workers who have been here all day.

⁹So the workers who had been hired just a short while before came to the foreman, and he paid them each a day's wage.* ¹⁰*Then the workers who had arrived midday came to the foreman, and he paid each of them a day's wage too.* Finally, the workers who'd been toiling since early morning came thinking they'd be paid more, but the foreman paid each of them a day's wage.* ¹¹As they received their pay, this last group of workers began to protest.

First Workers: ¹²*We've been here since the crack of dawn!* And you're paying us the exact same wage you paid the crew that just showed up. *We deserve more than they do.* We've been slogging in the heat of the sun all day—*these others haven't worked nearly as hard as we have!*

¹³*The landowner heard these protests.*

Landowner *(to a worker)*: Friend, no one has been wronged here today. *This isn't about what you deserve.* You agreed to work for a day's wage,* did you not? ¹⁴So take your money and go home. *I can give my money to whomever I please, and* it pleases me to pay everyone the same amount of money. ¹⁵Do you think I don't have the right to dispose of my money as I wish? Or does my generosity somehow prick at you?

¹⁶*And that is your picture:* The last will be first and the first will be last.

God's glory and kingdom are His, so He is free to lavish goodness on anyone He pleases. If you feel jealous because your friend's husband seems nicer than your husband, or because your brother works no harder than you but somehow earns far more money, or because your classmate who has the intelligence of a sponge always seems to get better grades than you do, then God's generosity will indeed undo all you have come to know and expect.

¹⁷As Jesus was making His way to Jerusalem, He took His twelve disciples aside and *once again* told them *what was about to happen.*

* 20:2 Literally, denarius, a Roman coin
* 20:9 Literally, denarius, a Roman coin
* 20:10 Literally, denarius, a Roman coin
* 20:13 Literally, denarius, a Roman coin

Jesus: ¹⁸We are going to Jerusalem. The Son of Man will be betrayed to the chief priests and to the teachers of the law. He will be condemned to death, ¹⁹and the priests and teachers will turn Him over to the Romans, who will mock Him and flog Him and crucify Him. But on the third day, He will be raised from the dead *to new resurrected life.*

²⁰*As Jesus was speaking about the things that were to come,* Zebedee's wife, whose sons were among Jesus' disciples, came to Jesus with her sons and knelt down before Him to ask a favor.

Jesus: ²¹What do you want?
Zebedee's Wife: When the kingdom of God is made manifest, I want one of my boys to sit at Your right hand, and one to sit at Your left hand.

*A*pparently the wife of Zebedee secretly thought her sons had worked harder and sacrificed more for Jesus than the other disciples, and she probably suspected that Jesus loved them best. She thought He would at least do the right thing and reward their hardest work and most loyal service. She also hoped that if her sons were there on the nearest, closest thrones, she could spend eternity near and close, too, clutching onto their coattails.

Jesus *(to all three)*: ²²You don't understand what you are asking. Can you drink the cup I am going to drink?
Zebedee Brothers: Of course!
Jesus: ²³Yes, you will drink from My cup, but the thrones to My right and My left are not Mine to grant. My Father has already given those seats to those for whom they were created.

²⁴The other ten disciples learned what the Zebedee brothers had asked of Jesus, and they were upset.

*T*he conversation probably went something like this:
"How sneaky!" said one disciple.
"And, really, drawing your mother into the deal . . . that's just plain low-down," said another disciple.
"Pathetic, really," said a third, who pretended to have known all along that those thrones weren't up for grabs.

²⁵So Jesus called the disciples together.

Jesus: *You need some perspective here.* Do you want the Kingdom run like the Romans run their kingdom? Their rulers have great power over the people, *but God the Father doesn't play by the Romans' rules.* ²⁶*This is the Kingdom's logic:* whoever wants to become great must first make himself a servant; ²⁷whoever wants to be first must bind himself as a slave— ²⁸just as the Son of Man did not come to be served, but to serve and to give His life as the ransom for many.

²⁹So finally Jesus and His disciples left Jericho and headed for Jerusalem; and, *of course,* a large crowd followed them. ³⁰Two blind men, sitting on the roadside, heard the crowd approaching with Jesus.

Two Blind Men: Lord, have mercy on us, Son of David!

³¹The crowd rebuked them and told them to be quiet, but they shouted louder.

Two Blind Men: Lord, Son of David, have mercy on us!
Jesus *(taking the two blind men aside)*: ³²What is it that you want, *brothers*?
Two Blind Men: ³³Lord, we want to see.

³⁴Jesus had compassion on them and touched their eyes. Immediately they could see, and so they followed Him.

21 Jesus, the disciples, and the great crowds were heading toward Jerusalem when they came to Bethphage on the Mount of Olives. Jesus stopped and beckoned to two of the disciples.

Jesus: ²Go to the village over there. There you'll find a donkey tied *to a post* and a foal beside it. Untie them and bring them to Me. ³If anyone tries to stop you, then tell him, "The Master needs these," and he will send the donkey and foal immediately.

⁴*He sent the disciples on ahead so His entry into Jerusalem could* fulfill what the prophet *Zechariah* had *long since* foretold:

⁵Tell this to Zion's daughter,
"Look—your King is
    approaching,
        seated humbly on a donkey,
a young foal, a beast of burden."*

⁶So the disciples went off and followed Jesus' instructions. ⁷They brought the donkey and foal *to Jesus*, they spread their cloaks on the animals, and Jesus sat down on them. ⁸The great crowd followed suit, laying their cloaks on the road. Others cut leafy branches from the trees and scattered those *before Jesus*. ⁹And the crowds went before Jesus, *walked alongside Him*, and processed behind—all singing.

Crowd: Hosanna, praises to the Son of David! Blessed is He who comes in the name of the Eternal One! Hosanna in the highest!*

¹⁰*And that is how* Jesus entered Jerusalem: *on a lowly donkey, with crowds surrounding Him singing praises.* The people of Jerusalem, *to say the least*, noticed this strange parade. They wondered who this could be, *this humble bearded man on a donkey who incited such songs.*

Crowd: ¹¹This is Jesus, the prophet, from Nazareth in Galilee.

After a great parade, Jesus and His disciples walked into the temple area, and what He saw enraged Him. He saw moneychangers, buying and selling. He saw men sitting on benches, hawking doves to those who had come from the countryside to make a sacrifice. He saw that the salesmen and teachers had turned a sanctuary of worship into a place of spiritual prostitution. This was the place where Jesus came as a boy to sit with the great teachers. It was a place where His Father received the offerings of His people. It was more than Jesus could take.

¹²Jesus came to the temple. He drove out all those who were buying and selling. He upended the moneychangers' tables and the dove-sellers' benches.

Jesus: ¹³It is written, "My house will be a house of prayer *for all people*," but you have turned this house of prayer into a den of robbers.*

Could anyone be surprised at this other side to Jesus? He has turned out to be not just a kindly teacher as we expected. Instead He is the Liberating King, not to be taken lightly. In the midst of this scene filled with joy and chaos, there were extremes. Some were beginning to understand who this man from Galilee was—the Liberator—but the rulers were having great difficulty with the disruption to their orderly world.

¹⁴Then the blind and the lame came to the temple, and Jesus healed them. ¹⁵Rings of children circled round and sang, "Hosanna to the Son of David." But the priests and scribes didn't understand. When they saw

* 21:5 Zechariah 9:9
* 21:9 Psalm 118:26
* 21:13 Isaiah 56:7; Jeremiah 7:11

the upturned tables, the walking paralytics, and the singing children, they were shocked, indignant, and angry, and they did not understand.

Priests and Scribes: [16]Do you hear what these children are saying?

Jesus: Yes. Haven't you read *your own psalter*? "From the mouths *and souls* of infants and toddlers, *the most innocent,* You have decreed praises for Yourself."*

[17]At that, Jesus left *Jerusalem*. He went to Bethany, where He spent the night.

[18]The next morning, Jesus went back to the city. *It was early and* He was wanting breakfast, so [19]He stopped at a lone fig tree by the road. The fig tree, *disappointingly,* had no figs, only leaves.

Jesus: May you never bear fruit again!

Immediately the tree shriveled up. [20]The disciples were amazed.

Disciples: How did that fig tree wither so quickly?

Jesus: [21]I tell you this: if you have faith and do not doubt, then you will be able to wither a fig tree with one glance. You will be able to tell mountains to throw themselves into the ocean, and they will obey.

As Jesus said this, one or two disciples probably glanced around the shadows of the early morning, confused and afraid. Jesus had just paraded into Jerusalem and upset the vendors and leaders with His bold talk. Now He was challenging His disciples to expect the physical creation to respond to their commands and faith. But Jesus wasn't finished.

Jesus: [22]If you believe, whatever you ask for in prayer will be granted.

[23]Jesus returned to the temple and began to teach. The chief priests and elders came to Him and wanted to know who had given Him permission to disturb the temple precincts and to teach *His crazy notions in this most sacred of spots.*

Chief Priests and Elders: Who gave You the authority to do these things?

Jesus: [24]I will answer your questions if first you answer one of Mine: [25]You saw John ritually cleansing* people *for the redemption of their sins*. Did John's cleansing come from heaven, or was he simply washing people of his own whim?

The elders knew that this question was tricky—there was no simple answer. If they acknowledged that John's ritual cleansing was from heaven, Jesus would ask why they had not accepted John's authority. [26]But if they said he had dipped people simply by his own accord, they would outrage the people who believed John was a prophet.

Chief Priests and Elders: [27]We don't know.

Jesus: Then neither will I tell you about the authority under which I am working. [28]*But I will tell you a story, and* you can tell Me what you make of it: There was a man who had two sons. He said to his first son,

Father: Go and work in the vineyard today.

First Son: [29]No, I will not.

But later the first son changed his mind and went. [30]Then the father went to his second son.

Father: Go and work in the vineyard today.

Second Son: Of course, Father.

But then he did not go. [31]So which of the sons did what the father wanted?

Chief Priests and Elders (*answering at once*): The first.

Jesus: I tell you this: the tax collectors and prostitutes will enter the kingdom of God ahead of you. [32]John came to show

---

* 21:16 Psalm 8:2
* 21:25 Literally, immersing, an act of repentance

you *the straight path*, the path to righteousness. You did not believe him, but the tax collectors and the prostitutes did. Even as you saw *the prostitutes and the tax collectors forgiven and washed clean, finding their footing on the straight path to righteousness,* still you did not change your ways and believe.

³³Here is another story: A landowner planted a vineyard, put a wall around it, fitted it with a winepress, and built a watchtower. Then he rented the vineyard and left town. ³⁴When harvesttime came, the landowner sent his servants to collect rent—in the form of grapes—*from his tenants.* ³⁵The tenants attacked these rent-collecting servants. They killed one, stoned another, and beat a third. ³⁶The *dismayed* landowner sent another band of servants *to try to collect his due,* a larger group of servants this time, but the tenants did the same thing—*capturing, beating, killing.* ³⁷Finally the landowner sent his son to the tenants, thinking, "They will at least respect my son." ³⁸*But the tenants knew the son was the best way to get to the landowner,* so when they saw the son approaching they said,

Tenants: This is the landowner's heir apparent! Let's kill him and take his inheritance.

³⁹And so they did—they threw him out of the vineyard and killed him. ⁴⁰What do you think the landowner will do when he comes and sees those tenants?

Chief Priests and Elders: ⁴¹He will eviscerate them, *to be sure!* Then he will rent the vineyard to other tenants who will pay him at harvesttime.

Jesus: ⁴²I wonder if any of you has ever opened your own psalter:

The stone that the builders
    rejected
  has become the very stone that
    holds together the entire
    foundation.
This is the work of the Eternal One,
  and it is marvelous in our eyes.*

⁴³Therefore, the kingdom of God will be taken away from you and given to people who will tend its *sweet* fruit *and who will give the Creator His due.* [⁴⁴He who falls on the stone will be broken to pieces, and he on whom the stone falls will be crushed.]*

> *J*esus had just confronted the spiritual leaders of the land with hard reality. They had two choices: they could believe Him and repent, or they could disbelieve Him and call His stories rabble-rousing and craziness. In their minds, the cost of believing was just too high. Everything they had—their positions and standings in the community, their worldviews, their own images of themselves—was at stake. But they couldn't openly condemn this popular teacher of the people.

⁴⁵And so the chief priests and the Pharisees, *the teachers and the elders,* knew that when Jesus told these stories He was speaking about them. ⁴⁶*Not believing,* they looked for a way to arrest Him—*a stealthy way, though.* They were afraid *to make too bold a move against Him* because all the people believed He was a prophet.

22 Jesus went on speaking in parables.

Jesus: ²The kingdom of heaven is like a king whose son was getting married. The king organized a great feast, *a huge wedding banquet.* ³*He invited everyone he knew. The day of the wedding arrived, and* the king sent his servants into town to track down his guests—but *when the servants approached them with the king's message,* they refused to come. ⁴So the king sent out another batch of servants.

King: Tell those people I've invited to come to the wedding banquet! *Tell them* I have prepared a great feast!—everything is ready!—the oxen and

* 21:42 Psalm 118:22-23
* 21:44 Some manuscripts omit verse 44.

fattened cattle have all been butchered, *the wine is decanted, and the table is laid out just so.*

⁵*And off the servants went, and they carried the king's message to the errant guests*—who still paid not a whit of attention. One guest headed into his field *to do a little surveying; one slammed the door in the servant's face and* sat at his desk to attend to his accounts. ⁶The rest of the guests actually turned on the servants, brutalizing them and killing them. ⁷*When he learned of this*, the king was furious. He sent his army to kill the murderers and burn their towns. ⁸*But there was, of course, still a wedding to celebrate.*

King *(to his remaining servants)*: The wedding banquet is ready, but those I invited didn't rise to the occasion. ⁹So go into the streets and invite anyone you see; invite everyone you meet.

¹⁰And the servants did just that—they went into the streets and invited everyone they met, *rich and poor*, good and bad, *high and low, sick and well.* Everyone who was invited came, and the wedding hall practically burst with guests.

¹¹The king looked around the wedding party *with glee. It was a fine way to celebrate his son's marriage.* But he spotted one man who was not dressed *appropriately. In fact, he was dressed rather plainly*, in clothes not at all fitting for a fine nuptial feast.

King: ¹²Kind sir, how did you get in here without a proper suit of wedding clothes?

The man was speechless. *(He had been invited in off the street, after all! The king's question was confusing, even impertinent!)* ¹³*Getting no response*, the king told his servants,

King: Tie him up, and throw him out into the outer darkness, where there is weeping and grinding of teeth.

¹⁴For many are invited, but few are chosen.

¹⁵At that, the Pharisees left. They determined to trap this Jesus with His own words—*hang Him by His own rope, you*

might say. ¹⁶They sent a batch of students to Him, along with a group that was loyal to Herod.

Students: Teacher, we know You are a man of integrity and You tell the truth about the way of God. We know You don't cotton to public opinion. ¹⁷*And that is why we trust You and want You to* settle something for us: should we, *God's chosen people*, pay taxes to Caesar or not?

¹⁸Jesus knew these men were out to trap Him.

Jesus: You hypocrites! Why do you show up here with such a transparent trick? ¹⁹Bring Me a coin you would use to pay tax.

Someone handed Him a denarius.* ²⁰*Jesus fingered the coin.*

Jesus: Of whom is this a portrait, and who owns this inscription?
Students: ²¹Caesar.
Jesus: Well then, render to Caesar what is Caesar's and to God what is God's.

²²And those *who had come hoping to trick Jesus* were confounded and amazed. And they left Him and went away.

²³That same day, a band of Sadducees— *a sect of Jewish aristocrats who, among other things,* did not expect a resurrection *or anticipate any sort of future life at all*— put their own question to Jesus.

Sadducees: ²⁴Teacher, *the law of* Moses teaches that if a *married* man dies with no children, then his brother must marry the widow and father children in his brother's name. ²⁵Now we knew a family of seven brothers. The eldest brother married and died, and since he had no children, the next brother married his widow. ²⁶*And shortly thereafter*, that second brother *died, still having fathered no children. And on and on it happened—that poor widow kept marrying these brothers,*

---

* 22:19 A Roman coin, equivalent to a day's wage

and they kept dying, and there were no children from any of the seven marriages. ²⁷Eventually the wife died. ²⁸So now, *Teacher,* whose wife will she be at the resurrection? *Will she have seven husbands,* since they were each married to her?

Jesus: ²⁹You know neither God's Scriptures nor God's power—and so your assumptions are all wrong. ³⁰At the resurrection, people will neither marry nor be given in marriage. They will be like the messengers in heaven. *They will be kith and kin, sister and brother to everyone. They will devote themselves to praise.* ³¹A key to this resurrected life can be found *in the words of Moses,* which you do claim to read: ³²"I am the God of Abraham, the God of Isaac, and the God of Jacob."* Our God is not the God of the dead. He is the God of the living.

³³And again the crowd was amazed. They were astonished at His teaching.

³⁴Hearing that Jesus had silenced the Sadducees, *a group of* Pharisees met *to consider new questions that might trip up Jesus.* ³⁵A legal expert thought of one that would certainly stump Him.

Pharisees: ³⁶Teacher, of all the laws, which commandment is the greatest?

Jesus *(quoting Scripture)*: ³⁷"Love the Eternal One your God with all your heart and all your soul and all your mind."* ³⁸This is the first and greatest commandment. ³⁹And the second is nearly as important, "Love your neighbor as yourself."* ⁴⁰The rest of the law, and all the teachings of the prophets, are but variations on these themes.

⁴¹Since the Pharisees were gathered together there, Jesus *took the opportunity to* pose a question of His own.

Jesus: ⁴²What do you think about the Liberating King, *the Anointed One?* Whose Son is He?

Pharisees: *But, of course,* He is the Son of David.

Jesus: ⁴³Then how is it that David—*whose words were surely shaped* by the Spirit— calls Him "Lord"? *For in his psalms—or perhaps you haven't opened your psalter recently—*David writes,

⁴⁴The Master said to my master
"Sit here at My right hand,
in the place of honor and power,
And I will gather Your enemies together,
lead them in on hands and knees,
and You will rest Your feet on their backs."*

⁴⁵How can David call his own Son "Lord"?

⁴⁶No one had an answer to Jesus' question. And from that day forward, no one asked Him anything.

23

Jesus spoke to His disciples and to the crowds that had gathered around.

Jesus: ²The Pharisees and the scribes occupy the seat of Moses. ³So you should do the things they tell you to do—but don't do the things they do. *Mind their words, not their examples. For they talk about righteousness and faithfulness, but they are a faithless and unrighteous crew.* ⁴They heap heavy burdens upon their neighbors' backs, and they prove unwilling to do anything to help shoulder the load. ⁵They are interested, above all, in presentation: they wrap their heads and arms in the accoutrements of prayer, they cloak themselves with flowing tasseled prayer garments, ⁶they covet the seats of honor at fine banquets and in the synagogue, ⁷and they love it when people recognize them in the marketplace, call them "Teacher," and beam at them.

⁸But you: do not let anyone call you "Rabbi." For you are all brothers, and you

* 22:32 Exodus 3:6
* 22:37 Deuteronomy 6:5
* 22:39 Leviticus 19:18
* 22:44 Psalm 110:1

have only one teacher. ⁹Indeed, do not call anyone on earth "Father," for you have only one father, and He is in heaven. ¹⁰Neither let anyone call you "leader," for you have one leader—the Liberating King. ¹¹If you are recognized at all, let it be for your service. *Delight in the one who calls you servant. Delight in the one who does not notice you at all.* ¹²For whoever exalts himself will be humbled, and whoever humbles himself will be exalted.

¹³Woe to you, you teachers of the law and Pharisees. *There is such a gulf between what you say and what you do. There is such a gulch between the beauty of the sacred Scripture you claim to love and the shape of your daily lives.* You will stand before a crowd and lock the door of the kingdom of heaven *right in front of everyone*; you won't enter the Kingdom yourselves, and you prevent others from doing so.

[¹⁴Woe to you, you teachers of the law and Pharisees. What you say is not what you do. You steal the homes from under the widows while you pretend to pray for them. You will suffer great condemnation for this.]*

¹⁵Woe to you Pharisees, woe to you who teach the law, hypocrites! You traverse hills and mountains and seas to make one convert, and then when he does convert, you make him much more a son of hell than you are.

¹⁶Woe to you who are blind but deign to lead others. You say, "Swearing by the temple means nothing—but he who swears by the gold in the temple is bound by his oath." ¹⁷Are you fools? You must be blind! For which is greater: the gold or the temple that makes the gold sacred? ¹⁸You also say, "Swearing by the altar means nothing, but he who swears by the sacrifice on the altar is bound by his oath." ¹⁹You must be blind! Which is greater: the sacrifice or the altar that makes it sacred? ²⁰So anyone who swears by the altar swears by it and by the sacrifices and gifts laid upon it. ²¹And anyone who swears by the temple swears by it and by the God who sanctifies it. ²²And

when you swear by heaven, you are swearing by God's throne and by Him who sits upon it.

²³So woe to you, teachers of the law and Pharisees. You hypocrites! You tithe from *your luxuries and your spices, giving away a tenth of* your mint, your dill, and your cumin. But you have ignored the essentials of the law: justice, mercy, faithfulness. It is practice of the latter that makes sense of the former. ²⁴You *hypocritical*, blind leaders. You spoon a fly from your soup and swallow a camel.

²⁵Woe to you, teachers of the law and Pharisees, you hypocrites! You remove fine layers of film and dust from the outside of a cup or bowl, but you leave the inside full of *greed and* covetousness and self-indulgence. ²⁶You blind Pharisee—can't you see that if you clean the inside of the cup, the outside will be clean too?

²⁷Woe to you, teachers of the law and Pharisees, you hypocrites! You are like a grave that has been whitewashed. You look beautiful on the outside, but on the inside you are full of moldering bones and decaying rot. ²⁸You appear, at first blush, to be righteous, *selfless, and pure*; but on the inside you are *polluted*, sunk in hypocrisy *and confusion* and lawlessness.

²⁹Woe to you, teachers of the law and Pharisees, you hypocrites! You build monuments to your dead, *you mouth pieties over the bodies of prophets,* you decorate the graves of your righteous ancestors. ³⁰And you say, "If we had lived when our forefathers lived, *we would have known better*—we would not have joined them when they rose up against the prophets." ³¹*Even when you are preening*, you make plain that you descended from those who murdered our prophets. ³²So why don't you finish what your forefathers started? ³³You are children of vipers, you *belly-dragging* snakes. You won't escape the judgment of hell.

³⁴That is why I am sending you prophets and wise men, teachers *of*

---

* 23:14 The earliest manuscripts omit verse 14.

breadth and depth and substance. You will kill some of them and crucify others. You will flog others in your synagogues. You will pursue them from town to town. 35And on your heads, *stained through your hands and drenching your clothes, my friends,* will be all the righteous blood ever shed on this earth, from the blood of innocent Abel to the blood of Zechariah son of Berechiah whom you murdered *in the house of the Lord* between the sanctuary and the altar. 36I tell you: this generation will bear the blood of all that has gone before.

37O Jerusalem, Jerusalem. You kill the prophets *whom God gives you*; you stone those God sends you. I have longed to gather your children the way a hen gathers her chicks under her wings, but you refuse to be gathered. 38Surely you can see that God has already removed His blessing from the house *of Israel.* 39I tell you this: you will not see Me again until you say, *with the psalmist,* "Anyone who comes in the name of the Eternal One will be blessed."*

24 Jesus left the temple. As He was walking away, His disciples came up to Him and asked what He thought about the temple buildings.

Jesus: 2Look around you. All of it will become rubble. I tell you this: not one stone will be left standing.

3*Later,* as Jesus was sitting on the Mount of Olives, the disciples came to Him privately.

Disciples: *You have been making these wild predictions.* Tell us, when will these things happen: *When will the temple be destroyed?* What will be the sign that You are returning? How will we know that the end of the age is upon us?

*T*he disciples have been listening to the prophetic judgment that Jesus issued on the religious leaders.

They have images of collapsing temple buildings, of prophets pursued from town to town, of floggings, and of blood-soaked garments. They can imagine themselves blood-soaked. When will this all happen, and what does it mean?

Jesus: 4Take care that you are not deceived. 5For many will come in My name claiming they are the Liberating King, and many poor souls will be taken in. 6You will hear of wars, and you will hear rumors of wars, but you should not panic. It is inevitable, *this violent breaking apart of the sinful world, but remember,* the wars are not the end. *The end is still unfolding.* 7Nations will do battle with nations, and kingdoms will fight neighboring kingdoms, and there will be famines and earthquakes. 8*But these are not the end.* These are the birth pangs, the beginning. *The end is still unfolding.*

9They will hand you over to your enemies, who will torture you and then kill you, and you will be hated by all nations because of Me. 10And many *who have followed Me and claimed to love Me and sought God's kingdom* will turn away—*they will abandon the faith and* betray and hate one another. 11-12The love that they had for one another will grow cold because few will obey the law. False prophets will appear, many will be taken in by them, and the only thing that will grow is wickedness. *There will be no end to the increase of wickedness.* 13But those who do not waver from our path and do not follow those false prophets—those *among you* will be saved. 14And this good news of God's kingdom will be preached throughout the whole world, a testimony to *all people and* all nations. Then, *beloved,* the end, *the consummation of all things,* will come.

15You will remember that the prophet Daniel predicted this—predicted the abomination that causes desolation*—

* 23:39 Psalm 118:26
* 24:15 Daniel 9:27; 11:31; 12:11

when you see the prophesied desolation of the holy place. (Reader, take notice; it is important that you understand this.) [16]*When you see this,* let those in Judea flee to the mountains. [17]If you are *relaxing* on your rooftop *one evening and the signs of the temple's destructions come,* don't return to your house *to rescue a book or a pet or a scrap of clothing.* [18]If you are in the field *when the great destruction begins,* don't return home for a cloak. [19]Pregnant women and nursing mothers will have the worst of it. [20]*And as for you,* pray that your flight *to the hills* will not come on the Sabbath or in the cold of winter. [21]For the tribulation will be unparalleled—hardships of a magnitude that has not been seen since creation and that will not be seen again. [22]*Indeed the Lord God your merciful judge* will cut this time of trial short, and this will be done for the benefit of the elect *that some might indeed be saved—* for no one could survive *the depravity* for very long.

[23]*I cannot say this clearly enough: during this time,* someone will say to you, "Look, here is the Liberating King!" or *"Aren't you relieved?* Haven't you seen the Savior *down there, around the bend, over the hill and dale?"* Do not believe them. [24]False liberators and false prophets will appear, and *they will know a few tricks*—they will perform great miracles, *and they will make great promises.* If it were possible, they would even deceive God's elect. [25]But I am warning you ahead of time: *remember—do not fall for their lies or lines or promises. Don't let their tricks and miracles distract you.* [26]If someone says, "He's out there in the desert"—do not go. And if someone says, "He's here at our house, *at our table"*— do not believe him. [27]When the Son of Man comes, *He will be as visible* as lightning in the East is visible even in the West. [28]And where the carcass is, there will always be vultures.

[29]*And as the prophets have foretold it:* after the distress of those days,

The sun will grow dark,
    and the moon will be hidden.
The stars will fall from the sky,
    and all the powers in the heavens
    will be dislodged and shaken
    *from their places.**

[30]That is when the sign of the Son of Man will appear in the sky. All the nations of the earth will mourn. They will see the Son of Man coming; they will see Him powerful and glorious, *riding on chariots* of clouds in the sky. [31]With a loud trumpet call, He will send out *battalions of* heavenly messengers; and they will gather His *beloved faithful* elect from the four corners of creation, from one end of heaven to the other.

[32]Now think of the fig tree. As soon as its twigs get tender *and greenish,* as soon as it begins to sprout leaves, you know to expect summer. [33]In the same way, when you see *the wars and the suffering and the false liberators and the desolations,* you will know the Son of Man is near—right at the door. [34]I tell you this: this generation will see all these things take place before it passes away. [35]*My words are always true and always here with you, and you can unfurl them like a banner and chant them to yourself when you think you might forget.* Heaven and earth will pass away, but My words will never pass away.

[36]*You can't predict exactly when the beginning of the end will be unleashed.* No one knows the hour or the day, not even the messengers in heaven, not even the Son. Only the Father knows. [37]As it was at the time of Noah, so it will be with the coming of the Son of Man. [38]In the days before the flood, people *were busy making lives for themselves: they* were eating and drinking, marrying and giving in marriage, *making plans and having children and growing old,* until the day Noah entered the ark. [39]Those people *had no*

* 24:29 Isaiah 13:10; 34:4

idea what was coming; they knew nothing *about the floods* until the floods were upon them, sweeping them all away. That is how it will be with the coming of the Son of Man. ⁴⁰Two men will be plowing a field: one will be taken, and the other will be left *in the field.* ⁴¹Two women will be *somewhere* grinding at a mill: one will be taken, and the other will be left *at the mill.*

⁴²So keep watch. You don't know when your Lord will come. ⁴³But you should know this: If the owner of a house had known his house was about to be broken into, *he would have stayed up all night, vigilantly.* He would have kept watch, and he would have thwarted the thief. ⁴⁴So you must be ready because you know the Son of Man will come, but you can't know precisely when.

⁴⁵The trustworthy servant is the one whom the master puts in charge of *all the servants of* his household; it is the trustworthy servant who *not only oversees all the work, but also* ensures the servants are properly fed and cared for. ⁴⁶*And it is, of course, crucial that a servant who is given such responsibility performs his responsibility to his master's standards*—so when the master returns he finds his trust has been rewarded. ⁴⁷For then the master will put that good servant in charge of all his possessions. ⁴⁸But imagine *that the master's trust was misplaced,* that the supposedly responsible servant is actually a thief who says to himself, "My master has been gone so long, *he is not possibly coming back.*" ⁴⁹Then he beats his fellow servants and dines and drinks with drunkards. ⁵⁰*Well, when the master returns—as certainly he will—the servant will be caught unawares.* The master will return on a day and at an hour when he isn't expected. ⁵¹And he will cut his worthless servant into pieces and throw him out *into darkness* with the hypocrites, where there is weeping and grinding of teeth.

25 Jesus: *Or picture the kingdom of heaven this way.* The kingdom of heaven will be like ten brides-maids who each picked up a lantern and went out to meet a certain bridegroom. ²⁻⁴Five of these women were sensible, *good with details,* and remembered to bring small flasks of oil for their lanterns. But five of them were flighty, *too caught up in the excitement of their jaunt,* and forgot to bring oil with them. ⁵The bridegroom did not turn up right away. Indeed, all the women, *while waiting,* found themselves falling asleep. ⁶And then in the middle of the night, they heard someone call, "The bridegroom is here, finally! Wake up and greet him!" ⁷The women got up and trimmed the wicks of their lanterns *and prepared to go greet the groom.* ⁸The five women who had no oil turned to their friends for help.

Ill-prepared Bridesmaids: Please give us some of your oil! Our lanterns are flickering and will go out soon.

⁹But the five women who'd come prepared with oil said they didn't have enough.

Prepared Bridesmaids: If we give you some of our oil, we'll all run out too soon! You'd better go wake up a dealer and buy your own supply.

¹⁰So the five *ill-prepared* women went in search of oil to buy, and while they were gone, the groom arrived. The five who stood ready *with their lanterns* accompanied him to the wedding party, and *after they arrived,* the door was shut.

¹¹Finally the rest of the women turned up *at the party.* They knocked on the door.

Ill-prepared Bridesmaids: Master, open up and let us in!

Bridegroom *(refusing):* ¹²I certainly don't know you.

And the door remained shut. ¹³So stay awake; you neither know the day nor hour [when the Son of Man will come].* ¹⁴*This is how it will be.* It will be like a landowner who is going on a trip. He instructed his slaves about caring for his property. ¹⁵He gave five talents to one slave, two to the next, and then one

* 25:13 The earliest manuscripts omit this portion.

talent to the last slave—each according to his ability. Then the man left.

¹⁶Promptly the man who had been given five talents went out and bartered and sold and turned his five talents into ten. ¹⁷And the one who had received two talents *went to the market and* turned his two into four. ¹⁸And the slave who had received just one talent? He dug a hole in the ground and buried his master's money there.

¹⁹Eventually the master came back from his travels, *found his slaves,* and settled up with them. ²⁰The slave who had been given five talents came forward and told his master how he'd turned five into ten; *then he handed the whole lot over to his master.*

Master: ²¹Excellent. *You've proved yourself not only clever but loyal.* You've executed a rather small task masterfully, so now I am going to put you in charge of something larger. *But before you go back to work,* come join my great feast and celebration.

²²Then the slave who had been given two talents came forward and told his master how he'd turned two into four, *and he handed all four talents to his master.*

Master: ²³Excellent. *You've proved yourself not only clever but loyal.* You've executed a rather small task masterfully, so now I am going to put you in charge of something larger. *But before you go back to work,* come join my great feast and celebration.

²⁴Finally the man who had been given one talent came forward.

Servant: Master, I know you are a hard man, *difficult in every way. You can make a healthy sum when others would fail.* You profit when other people are doing the work. You grow rich on the backs of others. ²⁵So I was afraid, *dug a hole,* and hid the talent in the ground. Here it is. You can have it.

²⁶*The master was furious.*

Master: You are a pathetic excuse for a servant! *You have disproved my trust in you and squandered my generosity. It would be better for you if you were utterly ignorant, but you don't have that*

excuse. You know I am interested in making profit! ²⁷You could have at least put this talent in the bank—then I could have earned a little interest on it! ²⁸Take that one talent away, and give it to the servant who doubled my money from five to ten.

²⁹You see, everything was taken away from the man who had nothing, but the man who had something got even more. ³⁰*And as for the slave who had buried his talent in the ground?* His master ordered his slaves to tie him up and throw him outside into the utter darkness where there is miserable mourning and great fear.

³¹When the Son of Man comes in all His majesty accompanied by throngs of heavenly messengers, His throne will be wondrous. ³²All the nations will assemble before Him, and He will judge them, distinguishing them from one another as a shepherd isolates the sheep from the goats. ³³He will put some, the sheep, at His right hand and some, the goats, at His left. ³⁴Then the King will say to those to His right,

King: Come here, *you beloved,* you people whom My Father has blessed. Claim your inheritance, the Kingdom prepared for you from the beginning of creation. ³⁵*You shall be richly rewarded,* for when I was hungry, you fed Me. And when I was thirsty, you gave Me something to drink. I was alone as a stranger, and you welcomed Me *into your homes and into your lives.* ³⁶I was naked, and you gave Me clothes to wear; I was sick, and you tended to My needs; I was in prison, and you comforted Me.

³⁷Even then the righteous *will not have achieved perfect understanding and will say that they don't recall visiting Him in prison or clothing Him.*

Righteous: Master, when did we find You hungry and give You food? When did we find You thirsty and slake Your thirst? ³⁸When did we find You a stranger and welcome You in, or find You naked and clothe You? ³⁹When did we find You sick *and nurse You to health*? When did we visit You when You were in prison?

King: ⁴⁰I tell you this: whenever you saw a brother *or sister hungry or cold,* whatever you did to the least of these, so you did to Me.

⁴¹At that He will turn to those on His left hand.

King: Get away from Me, *you despised* people whom My Father has cursed. *Claim your inheritance*—the pits of flaming hell where the devil and his minions suffer. ⁴²For I was starving, and you left Me with no food. When I was *dry and* thirsty, you left Me *to struggle with* nothing to drink. ⁴³When I was *alone as* a stranger, you turned away from Me. When I was *pitifully* naked, you left Me unclothed. When I was sick, *you gave Me no care.* When I was in prison, you did not comfort Me.

Unrighteous: ⁴⁴Master, when did we see You hungry and thirsty? When did we see You friendless *or homeless or excluded*? When did we see You without clothes? When did we see You sick or in jail? *When did we see You in distress* and fail to respond?

King: ⁴⁵I tell you this: *whenever you saw a brother hungry or cold, when you saw a sister weak and without friends,* when you saw the least of these and ignored their suffering, so you ignored Me.

⁴⁶So these, *the goats,* will go off to everlasting punishment. But the beloved, *the sheep* (the righteous), will go into everlasting life.

26

And so this is what happened, *finally.* Jesus finished all His teaching, and He said to His disciples,

Jesus: ²The feast of Passover begins in two days. That is when the Son of Man is handed over to be crucified.

³*And almost as He spoke,* the chief priests were getting together with the elders at the home of the high priest, Caiaphas. ⁴They schemed *and mused* about how they could *trick Jesus,* sneak around and capture Him, and then kill Him.

Chief Priests: ⁵We shouldn't try to catch Him at the great public festival. The people would riot *if they knew what we were doing.*

⁶Meanwhile Jesus was at Bethany staying at the home of Simon the leper. ⁷*While He was at Simon's house,* a woman came to see Him. She had an alabaster flask of very valuable ointment with her, and as Jesus reclined at the table, she poured the ointment on His head. ⁸The disciples, seeing this scene, were furious.

Disciples: This is an absolute waste! ⁹The woman could have sold that ointment for lots of money, and then she could have given it to the poor.

¹⁰Jesus knew what the disciples were saying among themselves, *so He took them to task.*

Jesus: Why don't you leave this woman alone? She has done a good thing. ¹¹*It is good that you are concerned about the poor,* but the poor will always be with you—I will not be. ¹²In pouring this ointment on My body, she has prepared Me for My burial. ¹³I tell you this: the good news *of the kingdom of God* will be spread all over the world, *and wherever the good news travels,* people will tell the story of this woman and her good discipleship. And people will remember her.

¹⁴At that, one of the twelve, Judas Iscariot, went to the chief priests.

Judas Iscariot: ¹⁵What will you give me to turn Him over to you?

They offered him 30 pieces of silver. ¹⁶And from that moment, he began to watch for a chance to betray Jesus.

¹⁷On the first day of the Festival of Unleavened Bread, the disciples said to Jesus,

Disciples: Where would You like us to prepare the Passover meal for You?

Jesus: [18]Go into the city, find a certain man, and say to him, "The Teacher says, 'My time is near, and I am going to celebrate Passover at your house with My disciples.' "

[19]So the disciples *went off and* followed Jesus' instructions. *They found the man's house, secured the owner's permission,* and got the Passover meal ready. [20]When evening came, Jesus sat down with the twelve. [21]*They praised God for redeeming His people from bondage in Egypt,* and they ate their dinner.

Jesus: I tell you this: one of you here will betray Me.

[22]The disciples, *of course,* were horrified.

A Disciple: Not me!
Another Disciple: *It's not me, Master, is it?*
Jesus: [23]It's the one who shared this dish of food with Me. That is the one who will betray Me. [24]Just as our sacred Scripture has taught, the Son of Man is on His way. But there will be nothing but misery for he who hands Him over. That man will wish he had never been born.

[25]At that, Judas, who was indeed planning to betray Him, said,

Judas: It's not me, Master, is it?
Jesus: I believe you've just answered your own question.

[26]As they were eating, Jesus took some bread. He offered a blessing *over the bread,* and then He broke it and gave it to His disciples.

Jesus: Take this and eat; it is My body.

[27]And then He took the cup *of wine,* He made a blessing over it, and He passed it around the table.

Jesus: Take this and drink, all of you: [28]this is My blood of the new covenant, which is poured out for many for the forgiveness of sins. [29]But I tell you: I will not drink of the fruit of the vine again until I am with you once more, drinking in the kingdom of My Father.

[30]*The meal concluded.* Together, all the men sang a hymn *of praise and thanksgiving,* and then they took a late evening walk to the Mount of Olives.

Jesus: [31]Scripture says,

I shall strike the shepherd,
    and the sheep of the flock will
        scatter.*

Just so, each of you will stumble tonight, *stumble and fall,* on account of Me. [32]Afterward I will be raised up. And I will go before you to Galilee.

Peter: [33]*Lord,* maybe everyone else will *trip and* fall tonight, but I will not. *I'll be beside You. I won't falter.*
Jesus: [34]*If only that were true.* In fact, this very night, before the cock crows *in the morning,* you will deny Me three times.
Peter: [35]*No!* I won't deny You. Even if that means I have to die with You!

And each of the disciples echoed Peter.

Disciples: *We won't deny You, Lord. We'd rather cut off our right hands, or slice out our tongues, or even go with You to death.*

All of the disciples and Peter especially were sad and confused, and maybe a little bit prideful. They couldn't stand what they were hearing. Peter could not believe that he could ever betray his Lord. It was indeed a dark, bitter night.

[36]At that, Jesus led His disciples to the place called Gethsemane.

Jesus: I am going over there to pray. You sit here *while I'm at prayer.*

* 26:31 Zechariah 13:7

37Then He took Peter and the two sons of Zebedee with Him, and He grew sorrowful and deeply distressed.

Jesus: 38My soul is overwhelmed with grief, to the point of death. Stay here and keep watch with Me.

39He walked a little farther and finally fell prostrate and prayed.

Jesus: Father, *this is the last thing I want.* If there is any way, please take this *bitter* cup from Me. Not My will, but Yours be done.

40When He came back to the disciples, He saw that they were asleep. *Peter awoke a little less confident and slightly chagrined.*

Jesus (to Peter): So you couldn't keep watch with Me for just one short hour? 41*Now maybe you're learning:* the spirit is willing, but the body is weak. Watch and pray and take care that you are not pulled down during a time of testing.

42With that, Jesus returned *to His secluded spot* to pray again.

Jesus: Father, if there is no other way for this cup to pass without My drinking it— *then not My will,* but Yours be done.

43Again Jesus returned to His disciples and found them asleep. Their eyes were heavy-lidded, *and their bodies were curled like children who've fallen asleep in their parents' laps.* 44So Jesus left them again and returned to prayer, praying the same sentiments with the same words. 45Again He returned to His disciples.

Jesus: Well, you are still sleeping—are you getting a good long rest? Now the time has come; the Son of Man is just about to be given over to *the betrayers and* the sinners. 46Get up; we have to be going. Look, here comes the one who's going to betray Me.

47There he was, Judas, one of the twelve leading a crowd of people from the chief priests and elders with swords and clubs; the chief priests and the elders were right there, *ready to arrest* Jesus. 48*And Judas,* the one who intended to betray Him, had said *to the elders and the chief priests* that he would give them a sign.

Judas: *I'll greet Him with a kiss.* And you will know that the One I kiss is the One you should arrest.

49So at once, he went up to Jesus.

Judas: Greetings, Teacher (he kisses Him).
Jesus: 50My friend, do what you have come to do.

And at that, the company came and seized Him. 51One of the men with Jesus grabbed his sword and swung toward the high priest's slave, slicing off his ear.

Jesus: 52Put your sword back. People who live by the sword die by the sword. 53Surely you realize that if I called on My Father, He would send 12 legions of messengers to rescue Me. 54But if I were to do that, I would be thwarting the scriptural story, wouldn't I? *And we must allow the story of God's kingdom to unfold.* 55(to the crowds) Why did you bring these weapons, these clubs and bats? Did you think I would fight you? That I would try to dodge and escape like a common criminal? You could have arrested Me any day when I was teaching in the temple, but you didn't. 56This scene has come together just so, so that the prophecies in the sacred Scripture could be fulfilled.

And at that, all the disciples ran away and abandoned Him. 57The crowd that had arrested Jesus took Him to Caiaphas, the high priest. The scribes and elders had gathered *at Caiaphas's house and were waiting for Jesus to be delivered.* 58Peter followed Jesus (though at some distance *so *as not to be seen*). He slipped into Caiaphas's house and attached himself to a group of servants. And he sat watching, waiting to see how things would unfold.

⁵⁹The high priest and his council of advisors first produced false evidence against Jesus—*false evidence meant to justify some charge and Jesus' execution.* ⁶⁰But even though many men were willing to lie, the council couldn't come up with the evidence it wanted. Finally, two men stood up.

Two Men: ⁶¹Look, He said, "I can destroy God's temple and rebuild it in three days." *What more evidence do you need?*

⁶²Then Caiaphas the high priest stood up and addressed Jesus.

Caiaphas: Aren't You going to respond to these charges? What exactly are these two men accusing You of?

⁶³Jesus remained silent.

Caiaphas (*to Jesus*): Under a sacred oath before the living God, tell us plainly: are You the Liberating King, the Son of God?
Jesus: ⁶⁴So you *seem to be* saying. I will say this: beginning now, you will see the Son of Man sitting at the right hand of God's power and glory and coming on heavenly clouds.

⁶⁵The high priest tore his robes *and screeched.*

Caiaphas: Blasphemy! We don't need any more witnesses—we've all just witnessed this most grievous blasphemy, *right here and now.* ⁶⁶So, gentlemen, what's your verdict?
Gentlemen: He deserves to die.

⁶⁷Then they spat in His face and hit Him. Some of them smacked Him, slapped Him across the cheeks, ⁶⁸and jeered.

Some of the Men: Well, Liberator. Prophesy for us, *if You can*—who hit You? *And who is about to hit You next?*

⁶⁹*As all this was going on in Caiaphas's chamber,* Peter was sitting in the courtyard with some servants. One of the servant girls came up to him.

Servant Girl: You were with Jesus the Galilean, *weren't you?*

⁷⁰*And just as Jesus had predicted,* Peter denied it before everyone.

Peter: Not me! I don't know what you're talking about.

⁷¹He went out to stand by the gate. And as he walked past, another servant girl recognized him.

Another Servant Girl (*speaking to those standing around*): That man over there—he was here with Jesus the Nazarene!

⁷²Again, *just as Jesus had predicted,* Peter denied it, swearing an oath.

Peter: I don't know Him!

⁷³Peter then went to chat with a few of the servants. A little while later, some other servants approached him:

Other Servants: Look, we know that you must be one of Jesus' followers. You speak like you are from the same area as His followers. You've got that tell-tale Galilean accent.

⁷⁴Cursing and swearing, *agitated veins popping up in his forehead and his shoulders growing tense, Peter denied Him again.*

Peter: I do not know Him!

As the exclamation point left his mouth, a cock crowed. ⁷⁵And Peter remembered. He remembered that Jesus had *looked at him with something like pity and* said, "This very night, before the cock crows in the morning, you will deny Me three times." And Peter went outside, *sat down on the ground,* and wept.

27 Eventually the chief priests and the elders looked around and saw that it was morning. They convened a council meeting whose sole purpose was to hand down Jesus' death sentence. ²They tied Jesus up, took Him away, and handed Him over to the governor *of Judea,* a man called Pilate.

³Judas—the one who had betrayed Him *with a kiss for 30 pieces of silver*—saw that Jesus had been condemned, and suddenly Judas regretted what he had done. He took the silver back to the chief priests and elders *and tried to return it to them.*

Judas: ⁴*I can't keep this money! I've sinned! I've betrayed an innocent man! His blood will be on my hands.*

> he priests and elders wanted nothing to do with Judas, and they refused to take his money.

Chief Priests and Elders: *We're through with you, friend. Feel remorseful if you like, or dance on His grave if you want*—the state of your soul is really none of our affair.

⁵Judas threw down the money in the temple, went off, and hanged himself.
⁶The chief priests looked at the silver coins and picked them up.

Chief Priests and Elders: You know, according to the law, we can't put blood money in the temple treasury.

⁷After some deliberation, they took the money and bought a plot of land called Potter's Field—they would use it to bury foreigners, *suicides, and others who were unfit for a full Jewish burial.* ⁸(To this day, the field is called Blood Field, *because it was bought with blood money.*) ⁹*And when the priests bought Potter's Field,* they *unwittingly* fulfilled a prophecy made long ago by the prophet Jeremiah: "They took 30 pieces of silver, the price set on the head of the man by the children of Israel, ¹⁰and they gave them for the Potter's Field as the Eternal One instructed."*

¹¹Jesus was standing before the governor, *Pilate.*

Pilate: Are You the King of the Jews?
Jesus: So you say.

¹²The chief priests and the elders *stood and poured out their accusations: that Jesus was a traitor, a seditious rebel, a crazy, a would-be Savior, and a would-be king.* Jesus stood in the stream of accusations, but He did not respond.

Pilate: ¹³Do You hear these accusations they are making against You?

¹⁴Still Jesus said nothing, which Pilate found rather astounding—*no protests, no defense, nothing.*
¹⁵Now the governor had a custom. During the *great Jewish* festival *of* Passover, he would allow the crowd to pick one of the condemned men, and he, *Pilate,* would set the man free. *Just like that. Gratuitous, gracious freedom.* ¹⁶At this time, they had a notorious prisoner named Barabbas. ¹⁷So when the crowd gathered, Pilate offered them a choice:

Pilate: Whom do you want me to free? Barabbas or Jesus, whom some call the Liberating King?

> ilate could have called our Jesus, "Jesus of Nazareth" or "Jesus the Carpenter," but said, "whom some call the Liberating King." It is significant that Pilate was in a position where he would pass judgment. He could determine who would live and who would die, and he was now preparing to hold court.

¹⁸Pilate knew the chief priests and elders hated Jesus and had delivered Him up because they envied Him.
¹⁹Then Pilate sat down on his judgment seat, and he received a message from his wife: "Distance yourself utterly from *the*

* 27:10 Zechariah 11:12-13; Jeremiah 32:6-9

proceedings against this righteous man. I have had a dream about Him, a dream full of twisted sufferings—*He is innocent, I know it, and we should have nothing to do with Him."*

²⁰But the chief priests and the elders convinced the crowd to demand that Barabbas, not Jesus-*whom-some-call-the-Liberating King*, be freed and that Jesus be put to death.

Pilate (*standing before the crowd*): ²¹Which of these men would you have me free?

Crowd (*shouting*): Barabbas!

Pilate: ²²What would you have me do with this Jesus?

Crowd (*shouting*): Crucify Him!

> *P*ilate found himself arguing with the crowd.

Pilate: ²³Why? What crime has this man committed?

Crowd (*responding with a shout*): Crucify Him!

²⁴Pilate saw *that he had laid his own trap. He realized that he had given the crowd a choice, the crowd had chosen, and*—unless he wanted a riot on his hands—he now had to bow to their wishes. So he took *a pitcher of* water, stood before the crowd, and washed his hands.

Pilate: You will see to this crucifixion, for this man's blood will be *upon you* and not upon me. *I wash myself of it.*

Crowd: Indeed, let His blood be upon us— upon us and our children!

²⁶So Pilate released Barabbas, and he had Jesus flogged and handed over to be crucified.

²⁷The governor's soldiers took Jesus into a great hall, gathered a great crowd, ²⁸and stripped Jesus of His clothes, draping Him in a bold scarlet cloak, *the kind that soldiers sometimes wore.* ²⁹They gathered some thorny vines, wove them into a crown, and perched that crown upon His head. They stuck a reed in His right hand,

and then they knelt before Him, *this inside-out, upside-down King.* They mocked Him *with catcalls.*

Soldiers: Hail, the King of the Jews!

³⁰They spat on Him and whipped Him on the head with *His scepter of* reeds, ³¹and when they had their fill, they pulled off the bold scarlet cloak, dressed Him in His own simple clothes, and led Him off to be crucified.

³²As they were walking, they found a man called Simon of Cyrene and forced him to carry the cross. ³³Eventually they came to a place called Golgotha, which means "Place of the Skull." ³⁴There they gave Him a drink—wine mixed with bitter herbs. He tasted it but refused to drink it.

³⁵And so they had Him crucified.

> *L*et me tell you what the soldiers did as Jesus hung on the cross, what they did with those clothes that once gleamed the whitest white on a transfiguration mountaintop:

They divided the clothes off His back by drawing lots,* ³⁶and they sat on the ground and watched Him *hang.* ³⁷They placed a sign over His head: "This is Jesus, King of the Jews." ³⁸And then they crucified two thieves next to Him, one at His right hand and one at His left hand. *These thieves were King Jesus' retinue.*

³⁹Passersby shouted curses and blasphemies at Jesus. They wagged their heads *at Him and hissed.*

Passersby: ⁴⁰You're going to destroy the temple and then rebuild it in three days? Why don't You start with saving Yourself? Come down from the cross if You can, if You're God's Son.

Chief Priests, Scribes, and Elders (*mocking Him*): ⁴¹⁻⁴²He saved others, but He can't save Himself. If He's really the King of Israel, then let Him climb down from the cross—then we'll believe Him. ⁴³He

* 27:35 Psalm 22:18

claimed communion with God—well, let God save Him, if He's God's beloved Son.

[44]Even the thieves hanging to His right and left poured insults upon Him. [45]And then, starting at noon, the entire land became dark. It was dark for three hours. [46]In the middle of the dark afternoon, Jesus cried out in a loud voice.

Jesus: Eli, Eli, lama sabachthani—My God, My God, why have You forsaken Me?*
Bystanders: [47]He's calling on Elijah.

[48]One bystander grabbed a sponge, steeped it in vinegar, stuck it on a reed, and gave Jesus the vinegar to drink.

Others: [49]We'll see—we'll see if Elijah is going to come and rescue Him.

[50]And then Jesus cried out once more, loudly, and then He breathed His last breath. [51]At that instant, the temple curtain was torn in half, from top to bottom. The earth shook; rocks split in two; [52]tombs burst open, and bodies of many sleeping holy women and men were raised up. [53]After Jesus' resurrection, they came out of their tombs, went into the holy city of Jerusalem, and showed themselves to people. [54]When the Centurion and soldiers who had been charged with guarding Jesus felt the earthquake *and saw the rocks splitting and the tombs opening*, they were, of course, terrified.

Soldiers: He really was God's Son.

[55]A number of women, who had been devoted to Jesus and followed Him from Galilee, were present, too, watching from a distance. [56]Mary Magdalene was there, and Mary the mother of James and Joseph, and the mother of the sons of Zebedee.
[57]At evening time, a rich man from Arimathea arrived. His name was Joseph, and he had become a disciple of Jesus. [58]He went to Pilate and asked to be given Jesus' body; Pilate assented and ordered his servants to turn Jesus' body over to

Joseph. [59]So Joseph took the body, wrapped Jesus in a clean sheath of white linen, [60]and laid Jesus in his own new tomb, which he had carved from a rock. Then he rolled a great stone in front of the tomb's opening, and he went away. [61]Mary Magdalene was there, and so was the other Mary. They sat across from the tomb, *watching, remembering.*
[62]The next day, which is the day after the Preparation Day, the chief priests and the Pharisees went together to Pilate. [63]They reminded him that when Jesus was alive He had claimed that He would be raised from the dead after three days.

Chief Priests and Pharisees: [64]So please order someone to secure the tomb for at least three days. Otherwise His disciples might sneak in and steal His body away, and then claim that He has been raised from the dead. If that happens, then we would have been better off just leaving Him alive.
Pilate: [65]You have a guard. Go and secure the grave.

[66]So they went to the tomb, sealed the stone in its mouth, and left the guard to keep watch.

28 After the Sabbath, as the light of the next day, the first day of the week, crept over Palestine, Mary Magdalene and the other Mary came to the tomb *to keep vigil.* [2]Earlier there had been an earthquake. A messenger of the Lord had come down from heaven and had gone to the grave. He rolled away the stone and sat down on top of it. [3]He *veritably* glowed. He was vibrating with light. *His clothes were light,* white *like transfiguration,* like fresh snow. [4]The soldiers guarding the tomb were terrified. They froze like stone.
[5]The messenger spoke to the women, *to Mary Magdalene and the other Mary.*

Messenger of the Lord: Don't be afraid. I know you are here keeping watch for

* 27:46 Psalm 22:1

Jesus who was crucified. ⁶But Jesus is not here. He was raised, just as He said He would be. Come over to the grave, and see for yourself. ⁷And then go straight to His disciples, and tell them He's been raised from the dead and has gone on to Galilee. You'll find Him there. Listen carefully to what I am telling you.

⁸The women were both terrified and thrilled, and they quickly left the tomb and went to find the disciples and give them this *outstandingly good* news. ⁹But while they were on their way, they saw Jesus Himself.

Jesus *(greeting the women)*: Rejoice.

The women fell down before Him, kissing His feet and worshiping Him.

Jesus: ¹⁰Don't be afraid. Go and tell My brothers to go to Galilee. Tell them I will meet them there.

¹¹As the women were making their way to the disciples, some of the soldiers who had been standing guard *by Jesus' tomb recovered themselves*, went to the city, and told the chief priests everything that had happened—*the earthquake just after dawn, the heavenly messenger, and his commission to the Marys.* ¹²The chief priests gathered together all the elders, *an emergency conference of sorts. They needed a plan. They decided the simplest course was bribery:* they would pay off the guards ¹³and order them to say that the disciples had come in the middle of the night and had stolen Jesus' corpse while they slept. ¹⁴The chief priests promised the soldiers they would run interference with the governor so that the soldiers wouldn't be punished *for falling asleep when they were supposed to be keeping watch.* ¹⁵The guards took the bribe and spread the story around town—and indeed, you can still find people today who will tell you *that Jesus did not really rise from the dead, that it was a trick, some sort of sleight of hand.*

¹⁶The eleven disciples, *having spoken to the Marys*, headed to Galilee, to the mountain where they were to meet Jesus. ¹⁷When the disciples saw Jesus there, many of them fell down and worshiped, *as Mary and the other Mary had done. But a few hung back. They were not sure (and who can blame them?). They did not know, not for sure, what to do or how to be.* ¹⁸Jesus came forward and addressed *His beloved disciples.*

Jesus: I am here speaking with all the authority of God, *who has commanded Me to give you this commission*: ¹⁹Go out and make disciples in all the nations. Wash them ceremonially* in the name of the *triune God*: Father, Son, and Holy Spirit. ²⁰Then disciple them. *Form them in the practices and postures that* I have taught you, and show them how to follow the commands I have laid down for you. And I will be with you, day after day, to the end of the age.

---

* 28:19 Literally, immerse, in a rite of initiation and purification

Mark

Record of the servant of God
By Mark, a follower of Jesus

This Gospel is probably the first written account of the life of Jesus. It focuses on Jesus as the Servant of God who works miracles, makes disciples, and suffers on the way to bring salvation to the world. Tradition has it that Mark accompanied Paul on some of his missionary journeys and later became Peter's associate in his ministry, hearing and writing down his eyewitness accounts. Apparently Mark was a Jewish Christian who grew up in Jerusalem with his mother, Mary. The audience for his Gospel was likely Roman Christians who were not Jews. That's why he explains Jewish words, phrases, and customs. That may also be why he does not often appeal to the Hebrew Scriptures to explain Jesus' words and deeds.

For Mark, the life of Jesus—from His ritual cleansing by John in the Jordan River to His resurrection in Jerusalem—is the beginning of the good news. It is "the mustard seed stage" of the kingdom of God. Ultimately God's reign is destined to fill the world and become a place where the nations come to find shelter and salvation. So Mark invites his readers to understand that, in following Jesus, their lives make up the next part of the story. As the people of the Kingdom, they are the next step in preparing the way for God's salvation. So when Jesus invites His disciples to "follow Me," Mark takes that as an invitation to imitate His life and follow His teachings.

Mark's Gospel is the shortest of the New Testament Gospels. It is especially fast-paced and action-oriented. It moves quickly from episode to episode as Jesus demonstrates that He has authority over nature, disease, death, and evil. For Mark, Jesus' miracles are more than powerful acts done by a good man; they are manifestations of God's coming reign. They show us what the world will be like when God's kingdom comes finally and completely. But until then, Jesus and His followers are locked in conflict with powerful forces— religious and political. Ultimately these forces join together to oppose and crucify Him, but even this is God's plan; His torturous death is not the last word. Instead, the last word is God's, and it is a word of life and resurrection. Implicitly Mark's story of Jesus is a promise that those who suffer on their journey as His disciples will one day share in the resurrection. While the way of Jesus may well lead to suffering, it will ultimately lead to glory.

When Mark writes in the first chapter about a mysterious man entering the scene, instantly you know there's something very different about Him. He comes into the picture not as a rock star but rather as someone humble, kind, and yet, still kingly. Soon after we meet the protagonist of the story, Mark begins sharing about the people who are drawn toward this man—regular people like you and me who have become affected by the character, passion, and light of this strange Galilean.

Maybe that's why Mark jumps right into the action of Jesus' story. He offers little by way of introduction. He writes nothing about Jesus' family tree. Unlike Matthew and Luke, he doesn't mention His birth. Mark's retelling begins with Scripture and the preaching of John, the wandering prophet. Like all the greats of history, Jesus doesn't just arrive—He is announced—and who better than John to do that? Right before Jesus makes His entrance into Mark's narrative, John says, "I've washed you here with water, *but when He gets here*, He will wash you in the Spirit of God."

1 This is the beginning of the good news of Jesus, the Liberating King, the Son of God.
2 Isaiah the prophet told us *what would happen before the Liberator came when he delivered the words of God*:

Watch, I will send My messenger in front of You
to prepare Your way and make it clear *and straight.**
3 *You'll hear him*, a voice crying in the wilderness,
"Prepare the way of the Eternal One,
a straight way in the wandering desert, a highway for our God."*

4 *That messenger was* John the Prophet,* who appeared in the desert *near the Jordan River* preaching that people should be ritually cleansed* *with water as a sign of* both their changed hearts* and God's forgiveness of their sins. 5 People from across the countryside of Judea and from the city of Jerusalem came to him and confessed that they were deeply flawed and needed help, so he cleansed* them with the waters of the Jordan.

According to Luke's Gospel, John was the only child of a Jewish priest named Zacharias and his wife Elizabeth, who was a cousin to Mary, the mother of Jesus. Zacharias and Elizabeth didn't think they could have children, so when Elizabeth became pregnant with John very late in life, it was quite surprising. In fact, Zacharias doubted; he didn't believe his wife could bear a child. Then one day Gabriel, the messenger of the Lord, visited him at the temple. The heavenly messenger not only announced John's birth, but also told Zacharias what the baby should be named and what his role in the Liberating King's story would be. However, because of Zacharias's unbelief, he lost his ability to speak until the day of John's circumcision—six months prior to Jesus' birth.

6 John dressed *as some of the Hebrew prophets had,* in clothes made of camels' hair with a leather belt around his waist. He made his meals *in the desert* from locusts and wild honey. 7 He preached a message *in the wilderness*.

John the Prophet: Someone is coming who is a lot more powerful than I am—One

* 1:2 Malachi 3:1
* 1:3 Isaiah 40:3
* 1:4 Literally, John who immersed, to show repentance
* 1:4 Literally, immersed, to show repentance
* 1:4 Literally, repentance
* 1:5 Literally, immersed, to show repentance

whose sandals I'm not worthy to bend down and untie. ⁸I've washed* you here with water; *but when He gets here,* He will wash* you in the Spirit of God.

> *T*he Jordan River is the setting of some of the most memorable miracles in the Old Testament. On their journey through the wilderness to the promised land, the Israelites walked across the Jordan River on dry ground because God parted its waters. Elisha, one of the prophets of God, healed Naaman by telling him to bathe seven times in its waters. Partly because of miracles like these and partly because of a growing wilderness spirituality, many of the Jews in John's day went out to hear him and be dipped in its cool, cleansing waters. They were looking for God to intervene miraculously in their lives as He had done in the past. What they didn't know was that God was about to intervene, for at that time, Jesus left Nazareth and headed south.

⁹It was in those days that Jesus left Nazareth (*a village in the region* of Galilee) and came down to the Jordan, and John cleansed* Him there *in the same way all the others were ritually cleansed.* ¹⁰But as Jesus was coming out of the waters, He looked up and saw the sky split open. The Spirit *of God* descended upon Him like a dove, ¹¹and a voice echoed in the heavens.

Voice: You are My Son,* My beloved One, and I am very pleased with You.

¹²After that the Spirit compelled Him to go into the wilderness, ¹³and there in the desert He stayed for 40 days. He was tested by Satan himself and surrounded by wild animals; *but through these trials,* heavenly messengers *cared for Him and* ministered to Him.
¹⁴After John was arrested *by Herod, who ruled the Jewish lands on behalf of Roman interests,* Jesus went back into *the region of*

Galilee and began to proclaim the good news of God.

Jesus: ¹⁵It's time! The kingdom of God is near! Seek forgiveness, change your actions,* and believe this good news!

¹⁶As Jesus walked along the *shore of the* Sea of Galilee, He met *the first of His disciples,* two brothers, Simon and Andrew, both fishermen who were casting their fishing net into the shallow waters.

Jesus: ¹⁷*Come and* follow Me, and I'll send you to catch people *instead of fish.*

¹⁸Simon and Andrew left their nets and followed Jesus at once.
¹⁹When He had walked a little farther, He saw the sons of Zebedee, James and John, in their boat repairing their nets. ²⁰Right away He called to them, and they dropped what they were doing and left their father Zebedee and the hired men aboard the boat to follow Him *as His disciples.*
²¹They came *at last* to the village of Capernaum *on the Sea of Galilee;* and on the Sabbath Day, Jesus went straight into a synagogue, *sat down,* and began to teach. ²²The people *looked at each other,* amazed, because this strange teacher acted as One authorized *by God, and what He taught affected them* in ways their own scribes' teachings could not.

> *J*esus was no stranger to the synagogue; His parents were faithful Jewish folk who taught their children the traditions of their faith. When He was 12 years old, His parents took Him to Jerusalem for the Passover celebration. When the family made the trip home, Jesus' parents realized He wasn't with them; so they returned to Jerusalem to find Him sitting with the

* 1:8 Literally, immersed, to show repentance
* 1:8 Literally, immerse, in a rite of initiation and purification
* 1:9 Literally, immersed
* 1:11 Psalm 2:7
* 1:15 Literally, repent

Jewish teachers, teaching them about God. Here we read about Jesus teaching at the synagogue as an adult.

23 Just then a man in the gathering who was overcome by an unclean spirit shouted.

Unclean Spirit: 24 What are You doing here, Jesus of Nazareth? Have You come to destroy us? I can see who You are! You're the Holy One of God.

Jesus (*rebuking him*): 25 Be quiet, and come out of him now!

26 The man's body began to shake and shudder; and then, howling, the spirit flew out of the man. 27 The people couldn't stop talking about what they had seen.

People: *Who is this Jesus?* This is a new teaching—and it has such authority! Even the unclean spirits obey His commands!

28 It wasn't long before news of Jesus spread over the countryside of Galilee.
29 Right after they left the synagogue, Jesus went with James and John to the home of Simon and Andrew. 30 They told Him about Simon's mother-in-law who was there in bed, sick and feverish. 31 Jesus went to her side, took her hand, and lifted her up. As soon as He touched her, the fever left her *and she felt well again— strong enough to bustle around the house* taking care of her visitors.
32 Just before night fell, others had gathered all the sick, *diseased,* and demon-infested people *they could find.* 33 *It seemed as if* the whole town had gathered at Simon and Andrew's door. 34 Jesus was kept busy healing people of every sort of ailment and casting out unclean spirits. He was very careful not to let the demons speak because they knew Him *and could reveal to the people who He really was.*
35 Early in the morning, Jesus got up, left the house while it was still dark outside, and went to a deserted place to pray.
36 Simon and the others traveling with

Jesus looked for Him. 37 They finally tracked Him down.

Whenever possible, Jesus sought out solitude so He could pray and meditate. Perhaps this was just one of the ways Jesus revealed His humanity. In these silent and reflective moments, He seemed to refuel mentally, physically, and spiritually because Jesus heard His Father speak during His time alone. Throughout Jesus' ministry on earth, hearing from His Father seemed to help Him focus on the mission at hand: redemption.

People: Everybody wants to know where You are!
Jesus: 38 It's time we went somewhere else— the next village, maybe—so I can tell more people *the good news about the kingdom of God.* After all, that's the reason I'm here.

39 So He traveled *to the next village and the one after that,* throughout the region of Galilee, teaching in the synagogues and casting out unclean spirits *as His students trailed along and watched.*
40 *During that time, Jesus met a man stricken with leprosy—a skin disease that many people thought made him ritually unclean.* The leper walked right up to Jesus, dropped to his knees, and begged Him for help.

Leper: If You want to, You can make me clean.

41 Jesus was powerfully moved. He reached out and actually touched the leper.

Jesus: I do want to. Be clean.

42 And at that very moment, the disease left him; the leper was cleansed *and made whole once again.* 43 Jesus sent him away, but first He warned him strongly.

Jesus: 44 Don't tell anybody how this happened. Just go and show yourself to the priest *so that he can certify you're clean.* Perform the ceremony prescribed by Moses as proof of your cleansing, *and then you may return home.*

45*But, of course, good news is hard to keep quiet.* The man talked everywhere about how Jesus had healed him, until Jesus could no longer come into a town openly *without the risk of being mobbed.* So He remained on the outskirts. Even so, people still sought Him out from far and wide.

2 1-2Some days later when Jesus came back to Capernaum, people heard that Jesus was back in town and many gathered at the house where He was staying. Soon the crowd overflowed from the house into the streets, *and still more people pressed forward* to hear Jesus teaching the message *of God's kingdom.* 3Four men tried to bring a crippled friend to Him; 4but since the crowd prevented their carrying him close enough to get Jesus' attention, they climbed up onto the roof, opened a hole in it, and lowered the paralyzed man on his mat down to Jesus.

5Jesus recognized the faith of these men.

Jesus *(to the paralyzed man):* Son, your sins are forgiven.

6Some scribes were sitting in the crowd, *and they didn't like what they were hearing.*

Scribes *(reasoning to themselves):* 6-7What does this Jesus think He is doing? This kind of talk is blasphemy, *an offense against the Most High!* Only God can forgive sins.

8At once Jesus realized what they were thinking. He turned to them.

Jesus: Why do My words trouble you so? 9*Think about this:* is it easier to tell this paralyzed man, "Your sins are forgiven," or to tell him, "Get up, pick up your mat, and walk"? 10Still, I want to show you

that the Son of Man has been given the authority on earth to forgive sins. (to the paralytic) 11Get up, pick up your mat, and go home.

12The man rose to his feet, immediately rolled up his mat, and walked out *into the streets.* Everyone in the crowd was amazed. All they could do was *shake their heads,* thank God for this miracle, and say to each other, "We've never seen anything like that!"

To some who believed wholeheartedly in God's laws, Jesus was a troublemaker, a mere man who had a bad habit of making statements that took away from the honor due to the one true God. The "scribes" who made these kinds of accusations against Jesus were usually connected to the Pharisees (a Jewish sect popular with the people, mostly middle class and religiously strict when it came to following God's laws) or the Sadducees (a smaller Jewish sect made up of priests and aristocrats from Jerusalem). While the two groups often clashed with each other politically and theologically, they did find common ground—and sometimes even worked together—in opposing Jesus.

13Another time Jesus was out walking alongside the Sea *of Galilee* teaching the gathering crowd as He went. 14He saw Levi, the son of Alphaeus, sitting at the booth where he collected taxes.

Jesus *(calling out to him):* Follow Me.

Levi left the booth and went along with Him.

Jesus' invitation to follow Him, like His invitations to all the disciples, involved a lot more than joining the caravan; Jesus' invitation was for sinners to change their way of life. Jesus makes it clear, despite the criticisms of some observers, that this invitation is indeed open to all—especially to the sinners who need it most. Jesus grants to those who choose Him not just companionship and forgiveness but the ability to truly receive a new identity and live a new life.

¹⁵At Levi's house, many tax collectors and other sinners—*Jews who did not keep the strict purity laws of the Jewish holy texts*—were dining with Jesus and His disciples. Jesus had attracted such a large following that all kinds of people surrounded Him. ¹⁶When the Pharisees' scribes saw who shared the table with Jesus, they were quick to criticize:

Scribes (*to His disciples*): *If your master is such a righteous person,* then why does He eat and drink with tax collectors and sinners, *the worst among us?*

¹⁷Jesus heard them.

Jesus (*to the scribes*): People who have their health don't need to see a doctor. Only those who are sick do. I'm not here to call those already in good standing with God; I'm here to call sinners to turn back to Him.*

¹⁸The disciples of John *the Prophet* and the Pharisees made a practice of fasting.

*I*t was common for religious Jews to fast twice a week and pray three times daily, but Jesus would have a different set of practices for His followers. Since many believed that conformity to these traditions was the measure of holiness, some of the pious were disturbed by the actions, or we might say the inaction, of Jesus and His disciples.

Some People (*to Jesus*): Why is it that John's followers and the Pharisees' followers

fast, but Your disciples are eating and drinking *like it was any other day?*
Jesus: ¹⁹Guests at the wedding can't fast when the bridegroom is with them. It would be wrong to do anything but feast. ²⁰When the bridegroom is snatched away from them, then the time will come to fast *and mourn.*

²¹*These are new things I'm teaching, and they can't be reconciled with old habits.* Nobody would ever use a piece of new cloth to patch an old garment because when the patch shrinks, it pulls away and makes the tear even worse. ²²And nobody puts new, *unfermented* wine into old wineskins because if he does, the wine will burst the skins; they would lose both the wineskins and the wine. No, the only appropriate thing is to put new wine into new wineskins.

²³One Sabbath Jesus and His disciples were walking through a field of grain; as they walked, His disciples *grew hungry.* They began to pull from the stalks *and eat.*
²⁴The Pharisees *saw a chance to attack Jesus because of the actions of His followers, so they* confronted Him.

Pharisees: Did You see that? Why are Your disciples doing what our law forbids on the Sabbath?
Jesus (*turning toward the Pharisees*): ²⁵Do you remember the story about what *King* David and his followers did when they were hungry and had nothing to eat?

They said nothing, so He continued.

Jesus: ²⁶David went into the house of God, when Abiathar was the high priest, and ate the bread that was consecrated to God. Now our laws say no one but the priests can eat that holy bread; *but when David was hungry, he ate* and also shared the bread with those who followed him.*
²⁷The Sabbath was made for *the needs of* human beings, and not the other way around. ²⁸So the Son of Man is Lord even over the Sabbath.

* 2:17 Literally, repentance
* 2:26 1 Samuel 21:3-6

3 *Soon the Pharisees had another chance to confront Jesus. On the Sabbath,* Jesus had come into a synagogue where He saw a man with a withered hand.

²The Pharisees held their breath: would Jesus cure this man on the Sabbath, *right there in front of everyone*? If so, they could charge Him *with breaking the Sabbath law.* ³*Jesus knew their hearts.* He called to the man with the withered hand.

Jesus: Come to Me.

⁴Then He turned to the Pharisees with a question.

Jesus: Do our laws tell us to do good or evil on the Sabbath? To save life, or to snuff it out?

They remained silent. ⁵Jesus was furious as He looked out over the crowd, and He was grieved by their hard hearts. *How could anyone care so much about the words of the law and so little about the spirit of it?*

Jesus (*to the man with the withered hand*): *So be it.* Stretch out your hand.

The man stretched forth his hand; and as he did, it was completely healed. ⁶The Pharisees *didn't say anything to Jesus, but their actions spoke loudly. They* went directly from the synagogue to consult with the supporters of Herod, *the Romans' puppet ruler,* about how they could get rid of this dangerous dreamer.

⁷Meanwhile Jesus and His followers traveled to *the shore of* the Sea *of Galilee; as always,* a huge crowd from Galilee and Judea gathered. ⁸People had come *from miles* to see this man they were hearing so much about. They came from *the big cities, including* Jerusalem *of Judea,* Tyre and Sidon *of Phoenicia,* and from the region of Idumea, south of Judea. ⁹⁻¹⁰Since Jesus had healed so many, the sick and the infirm pushed forward constantly to touch Him, *to be healed, and to ask His blessing.* The crowd pressed so closely around Jesus that He asked His disciples to get a boat He could board if the crush became too great.

¹¹*Everyone wanted to be near Him, except for those possessed by* unclean spirits. Those people fell down before Him.

Unclean Spirits: You are the Son of God.

¹²But He ordered them not to reveal His true identity. ¹³Jesus called together a select group *of His followers* and led them up onto a mountain. ¹⁴There He commissioned them the twelve. [*Later* He calls them His emissaries.]* He wanted them to be with Him. He sent them out to spread the good news ¹⁵and to cast out evil spirits [and heal diseases].* ¹⁶Here are the names of the original twelve: Simon (whom Jesus called Peter, *meaning "the rock"*), ¹⁷James and John (the sons of Zebedee, whom Jesus called "the Sons of Thunder"), ¹⁸Andrew, Philip, Bartholomew, Matthew (*the tax collector, also called Levi*), Thomas, James (the son of Alphaeus), Thaddaeus, Simon of Canaan (who was also called "the Zealot"), ¹⁹and Judas Iscariot (who one day would betray Jesus *to the authorities in Jerusalem so God's purpose could be fulfilled*). ²⁰Jesus *and His disciples* went into a house to eat, but so many people pressed in to see Jesus that they could not be served. ²¹When Jesus' family heard *about this craziness,* they went to drag Him out of that place.

Jesus' Family (*to one another*): This is dangerous. Jesus has lost His mind.

²²The scribes, *for their part,* came down from Jerusalem *and spread the slander that Jesus was in league with the devil.*

Scribes: That's how He casts out demons. He's casting them out by the power of Beelzebul—*the ancient Philistine god*—the prince of demons.

* 3:14 Most manuscripts omit this portion.
* 3:15 Most manuscripts omit this portion.

²³When Jesus heard this, He tried to reason with them using parables.

Jesus: *Listen.* How can Satan drive out Satan? *Darkness drive out darkness?* ²⁴A kingdom that makes war against itself will collapse. ²⁵A household divided against itself cannot stand. ²⁶If Satan opposes himself, he cannot stand and is finished.

²⁷If you want to break into the house of a strong man and plunder it, you have to bind him first. Then you can do whatever you want with his possessions. ²⁸Listen, the truth is that people can be forgiven of almost anything. *God forgives all sorts of nonsense,* any kind of blasphemy. ²⁹But speaking evil of the Spirit of God is an unforgivable sin that will follow you into eternity.

³⁰He said this because the scribes were telling people that Jesus got His power from dark forces instead of from God.

*P*opularity is often a dangerous thing, particularly in a land occupied by Roman soldiers. As Jesus' ministry grew, some of His friends and family started to get nervous: they wondered if He had "lost His mind" entirely. Surrounded by crowds wanting to hear His teaching and to experience His healing touch, His family just couldn't understand what was happening and why He was so important. It must not have seemed right—the kid from Nazareth setting Himself up like that. In fact, they were so uncomfortable with it that they decided to intervene and take Him home.

But Jesus' family wasn't the only group trying to undermine Him. The Pharisees were doing their best to spread doubt about His authority with the worst accusations possible: His power to heal came from the devil himself. When the Pharisees accused Him of getting His power from demonic sources, they were attacking Him publicly and questioning His identity as the Liberating King.

³¹When Jesus' mother and brothers arrived, *they couldn't break through the crowd,* so they sent word in to Jesus that He should come out to them. ³²The crowd was pressed in tight around Him when He received the message, "Your mother and brothers [and sisters]* are waiting outside for You."

³³*Jesus looked around.*

Jesus (*answering them*): Who are My mother and brothers?

He called into the silence. No one spoke.
³⁴At last His gaze swept across those gathered close, *and Jesus smiled.*

Jesus: You, here, are My mother and My brothers! ³⁵Whoever does the will of God is My true family, *a family that's formed not of blood but of spirit. You are My family.*

4 ¹⁻²Jesus went out again to teach by the Sea *of Galilee.* When the crowd became unmanageable, He climbed aboard a boat and sat down to teach the people listening on the shore by telling them parables. One of His teachings went like this:

Jesus: ³Listen! A farmer went out and sowed his seed, *broadcasting it left and right out of a pouch he wore around his neck.* ⁴As he scattered it, one seed fell along the *hardened* path, and a bird flapped down and snapped it up. ⁵One seed fell onto rocky places where the soil was thin, so it sprang up quickly. ⁶But when the hot sun scorched *the fragile stems and leaves,* the seedling withered because its roots didn't go deep in the soil. ⁷One of the seeds fell among the *weeds and* thorns, which crowded the seedling out of producing a crop. ⁸And

* 3:32 Some manuscripts omit this portion.

the rest of the seeds fell in good, rich soil. When they sprouted, the plants grew and produced 30, 60, even 100 seeds for every one that the farmer had sown.

⁹All who have ears to hear, let them listen.

¹⁰When they were alone, the twelve and others close to Him asked why He always taught in parables *instead of explaining His teachings clearly.*

Jesus: ¹¹God has let you in on the inside story regarding the workings of the Kingdom—the hidden meanings. But the crowds—I teach them in parables ¹²*as the prophet Isaiah predicted,*

So that when they look, they see
    and yet do not understand.
When they hear, they listen and
    yet do not comprehend.
Otherwise, they might really turn
    and be forgiven.*

*T*his made the disciples scratch their heads. They themselves were already puzzled by the parables. Why would He want to hide the truth from some people? His teachings were hard enough without putting them into parables.

Jesus: ¹³Do you mean to say that you didn't understand My parable of the sower? *That was the key parable. If you don't see what I was trying to teach there,* how will you be able to understand any of the others?

¹⁴The seed the farmer is sowing is *the good news,* God's word. ¹⁵Some people are the seed thrown onto the path, and the tempter snaps up the word *before it can even take root.* ¹⁶Others are the seed thrown among the rocks. Those people hear the word and receive it immediately with joy and enthusiasm; ¹⁷but without deep roots, *doubt,* trouble, or persecution instantly withers their faith. ¹⁸Still others are the seed tossed among *weeds and*

brambles. The word has reached them, ¹⁹but the things of this life—the worries, the drive for more and more, the desire for other things—those things *cluster around close and* choke the life of God out of them until they cannot produce. ²⁰But those last seeds—those sown into good soil? Those people hear the word, accept it, *meditate on it, act on it,* and bear fruit—a crop 30, 60, or 100 times larger *than the farmer dropped to earth.*

*J*esus' teaching often included parables: stories that explain the truth about the Kingdom with examples from the everyday lives of His hearers. Considering that most of His listeners knew about farming, it's no wonder that most of Jesus' parables were based on agricultural realities: sowing seeds, pulling weeds, harvesting crops. The farmers in His audience that day would have had no trouble picturing this story as He described it; it was something they did every season. They had seen firsthand the birds landing in the field gobbling up their seed. They had seen how some seed sprang up on the rocky edges of the field only to have them bake in the hot sun. They had seen how weeds choked out the tender seedlings and produced nothing. But—and this was the good news—they knew that most of their seed fell into good, rockless, weed-free soil and produced a crop that would feed them and their families this year and the next.

Parables like this forced Jesus' listeners to think about the reality of the kingdom of God differently. He challenged their ideas and wishes for the future. As a master teacher, He also knew that they were unlikely to forget it. Every season when they saw farmers broadcasting their seeds, they would remember this parable and ponder the mysteries of the Kingdom just as Jesus

* 4:12 Isaiah 6:9-10

wanted. It never seemed to bother Him that people were confused by His teaching. He didn't expect them to understand everything; He didn't even want them to. Instead, He wanted them to wrestle with His teachings so His words would sit in their hearts and simmer—much like the seed sitting in good soil that eventually grows to bear fruit.

Jesus: ²¹When you bring a lamp *into the house,* do you put it under a box or *stuff it* under your bed? Or do you set it on top of a table *or chest*? ²²Those things that are hidden are meant to be revealed, and what is concealed is meant to be brought out where its light can shine.

²³All who have ears to hear, let them listen.

²⁴*That's why I do what I do.* So consider carefully the things you're hearing. If you put it to use, you'll be given more to wrestle with—much more. ²⁵Those who have *listened* will receive more, but those who don't hear will forget even the little they've failed to understand.

²⁶Here is what the kingdom of God is like: a man who throws seeds onto the earth. ²⁷Day and night, as he works and as he sleeps, the seeds sprout and climb out into the light, even though he doesn't understand how it works. ²⁸*It's as though* the soil itself produced the grain *somehow*—from a sprouted stalk to ripened fruit. ²⁹But *however it happens,* when he sees that the grain has grown and ripened, he gets his sickle and begins to cut it because the harvest has come.

³⁰What else is the kingdom of God like? What earthly thing can we compare it to? ³¹The kingdom of God is like a mustard seed, the tiniest seed you can sow. ³²But after that seed is planted, it grows into the largest plant in the garden, a plant so big that birds can build their nests in the shade of its branches.

³³Jesus spoke many parables like these to the people who followed Him. ³⁴This was the only way He taught them, although when He was alone with His chosen few, He interpreted all the stories *so the disciples truly understood.*

³⁵The same evening, Jesus suggested they cross over to the other side *of the lake.* ³⁶With Jesus already in the boat, they left the crowd behind and set sail along with a few other boats that followed. ³⁷*As they sailed,* a storm formed. *The winds whipped up* huge waves that broke over the bow, filling the boat *with so much water that even the experienced sailors among them were sure they were going to sink.*

³⁸Jesus was back in the stern of the boat, sound asleep on a cushion, when the disciples shook Him awake.

Disciples *(shouting over the storm)*: Jesus, Master, don't You care that we're going to die?

³⁹He got up, shouted words into the wind, and commanded the waves.

Jesus: That's enough! Be still!

And immediately the wind died down to nothing, the waves stopped, *and the surface of the sea was as smooth as a sheet of glass.*

Jesus: ⁴⁰How can you be so afraid? *After all you've seen,* where is your faith?

⁴¹The disciples were still afraid, *looking about them in every direction, slowly coming to grips with what they had seen.*

Disciples *(to one another)*: Who is this *Jesus*? How can it be that He has power over even the wind and the waves?

For most of Jesus' miracles, the disciples were observers: they watched Him heal the sick, raise dead bodies, and cast demons out of strangers. But they were merely watching, there to record the events instead of being part of them. This time, however, it was the disciples—and even Jesus Himself—who were in danger. Maybe that's why they had such a hard time trusting that His power was greater than their situation.

They had seen Him cast out demons. They knew He had powers that were not of natural origin. But they had never seen—or even heard of—anything like this. It's one thing to heal human sickness or even to order demons around. But to order the waves and the wind? To command the sea and the storm? That's a miracle of an entirely different order.

5 They traveled across the sea to the land of Gerasa* *in Galilee, where the people were outsiders who had not seen Jesus before.* 2-3When Jesus came ashore there, He was immediately met by a man who was tortured by an evil spirit. This man lived in the cemeteries, and no one could control him—not even those who tried to tie him up or chain him. 4He had often been bound in chains, but his strength was so great that he could break the chains and tear the irons loose *from his feet and hands.* No one *and nothing* could subdue him. 5Day and night, he lurked among the tombs or *ran mad* in the hills, and *the darkness* made him scream or cut himself with *sharp-edged* stones. 6When this man saw Jesus coming in the distance, he ran to Him and fell to his knees in front of Him. 7-8Jesus started commanding the unclean spirit.

Jesus: Come out of that man, you wicked spirit!
Unclean Spirit (*shouting*): What's this all about, Jesus, Son of the Most High? In the name of God, I beg You—don't torture me!
Jesus: 9What is your name?
Unclean Spirit: They call me "Legion," for there are thousands of us *in this body.*

10And then Legion begged Jesus again *to leave them alone,* not to send them out of the country. 11*Since the Gerasenes were not Jews (who considered pigs to be unclean),* there hap-

pened to be a large herd of swine, *some 2,000 of them,* feeding on the hill nearby.

Unclean Spirit (*begging*): 12Send us into those pigs *if You have to,* so that we may enter into them.

13Jesus granted the request. The darkness swept up out of the man and into the herd of pigs. And then they thundered down the hill into the water; and there they drowned, all 2,000 of them. 14The swineherds ran away, telling everybody they met what had happened. Eventually a crowd of people came to see for themselves. 15When they reached Jesus, they found the man Legion had afflicted sitting quietly, sane and fully clothed; when they saw this, they were overwhelmed with fear *and wonder.* 16Those who had witnessed everything told the others what had happened: how Jesus had healed the man, how the pigs had rushed into the sea, and how they had destroyed themselves. 17*When they had heard the whole story,* the Gerasenes turned to Jesus and begged Him to go away. 18When Jesus climbed back into the boat, the cured demoniac asked if he could come and be with Him, but Jesus said no.

Jesus: 19Stay here; I want you to go back home to your own people and let them see what the Lord has done—how He has had mercy on you.

20So the man went away and began telling this news in the Ten Cities* region; wherever he went, people were amazed by what he told them.

*T*wo things stand out in this story: how Jesus dealt with the demons and how the people responded to Jesus.

Although Jesus healed many people of demon possession during His

* 5:1 The earliest manuscripts read "Gerasenes"; others read "Gadarenes."
* 5:20 Literally, the Decapolis

ministry, this healing was unique. You see, this is the only time in the Gospels when Jesus seemed to listen to the pleading of a demon or a demon-possessed person. The demons immediately acknowledged Jesus as all-powerful; the possessed man's first reaction on seeing Jesus was to fall at His feet and call Him the "Son of the Most High." So it's unlikely that Jesus is negotiating with them in order to convince them to obey His orders. Although we can't assume to know why Jesus listened to their pleading, the effect was clear: the people in that region saw firsthand the power of evil and its ultimate destiny, namely, destruction.

The people's reaction to Jesus' decision to transfer the demons from the man into the herd of swine never could have been predicted. Instead of being pleased that they were now free from the terror of the demon-possessed man, the people in the town asked Jesus to leave. After all, the local economy took a pretty big hit when 2,000 of their choicest pigs rushed into the sea. But Kingdom priorities are always different from ours. Where God rules, people matter more than possessions.

²¹After Jesus returned across the sea, a large crowd quickly found Him, so He stayed by the sea. ²²One of the leaders of the synagogue—a man named Jairus—came and fell at Jesus' feet, ²³begging Him to heal his daughter.

Jairus: My daughter is dying, *and she's only 12 years old.* Please come to my house. Just place Your hands on her. I know that if You do, she will live.

²⁴Jesus began traveling with Jairus toward his home.

In the crowd pressing around Jesus, ²⁵there was a woman who had suffered continuous bleeding for 12 years, *bleeding that made her ritually unclean and an out-cast according to the purity laws.* ²⁶She had suffered greatly; and although she spent all her money on her medical care, she had only gotten worse. ²⁷She had heard of this *Miracle-Man,* Jesus, so she snuck up behind Him in the crowd and reached out her hand to touch His cloak.

Woman (*to herself*): ²⁸Even if all I touch are His clothes, I know I will be healed.

²⁹*As soon as her fingers brushed His cloak,* the bleeding stopped. She could feel that she was whole again.

³⁰Lots of people were pressed against Jesus at that moment, but He immediately felt her touch; He felt healing power flow out of Him.

He stopped. Everyone stopped. He looked around.

Jesus: Who just touched My robe?

³¹His disciples broke the uneasy silence.

Disciples: Jesus, the crowd is so thick that everyone is touching You. Why do You ask, "Who touched Me?"

³²*But Jesus waited.* His gaze swept across the crowd to see who had done it. ³³At last, the woman—knowing He was talking about her—pushed forward and dropped to her knees. She was shaking with fear *and amazement.*

Woman: *I touched You.*

Then she told Him the reason why. ³⁴*Jesus listened to her story, and He nodded.*

Jesus: Daughter, you are well because you *dared to* believe. Go in peace, and stay well.

*J*esus occasionally instigated His own miracles: He would go up to someone, like a paralyzed man, and offer to heal him. More often, as in the case of Jairus's daughter, people would come to Jesus and ask for healings. But the woman in this story is unique because she received her healing without asking for it—simply by touching Jesus in faith. He was surrounded by crowds pressing in on every side, and crowds in first-century Palestine weren't particularly concerned about personal space. But Jesus knew that one person's touch was different, in a way that only He could perceive: one woman was touching Him deliberately, in hope and faith, knowing that He had the power to heal her.

35While He was speaking, some members of Jairus's household pushed through the crowd.

Jairus's Servants (to Jairus): Your daughter is dead. There's no need to drag the Teacher any farther.

36Jesus overheard their words. Then He turned to look at Jairus.

Jesus: *It's all right.* Don't be afraid; just believe.

37-38Jesus asked everyone but Peter, James, and John (James's brother) to remain outside when they reached Jairus's home. Inside the synagogue leader's house, the mourning had already begun; the weeping and wailing carried out into the street.
39Jesus *and His three disciples* went inside.

Jesus: Why are you making all this sorrowful noise? The child isn't dead. She's just sleeping.

40The mourners laughed *a horrible, bitter laugh and went back to their wailing.* Jesus cleared the house so that only His three disciples, Jairus, and Jairus's wife were left inside with Him. They all went to where the child lay. 41Then He took the child's hand.

Jesus: Little girl, it's time to wake up.

42Immediately the 12-year-old girl opened her eyes, arose, and began to walk. Her parents could not believe their eyes.

Jesus (to the parents): 43Don't tell anybody what you've just seen. Why don't you give her something to eat? *I know she is hungry.*

*J*esus at last arrived at the miracle He was asked to perform: the healing of Jairus's daughter. But He was too late—the girl was already dead. Although Jesus would later raise other dead people back to life, up to that point He had not yet performed such a powerful miracle. His ability to heal sickness was common knowledge, and the disciples had glimpsed His power over the natural world; but no one yet had an inkling of His power over the forces of life and death. He allowed only His closest disciples to see this first miracle of resurrection, and He urged everyone who did see it to keep it quiet. Nevertheless, it was this miracle that first demonstrated to those who saw it that He did indeed have power over death itself.

6 Jesus went back into His own hometown where He had grown up, and His disciples followed Him there. 2When the Sabbath came, He went into the synagogue *in Nazareth* and began to teach *as He had done elsewhere,* and many of those who heard Him were astonished.

Those in the Synagogue: Where did He gain this wisdom? And what are all these stories we've been hearing about the signs and healings He's performed? *Where did He get that kind of power?* 3Isn't this *Jesus, the little boy we used to see in Joseph's carpenter shop?* Didn't He grow up to be a carpenter *just like His father?* Isn't He the son of Mary *over there* and the brother of James, Joses, Judas,

Simon, and their sisters? *Who does He think He is?*

And when they had thought about it that way, they became indignant and closed themselves to His message.

Jesus (*seeing this*): [4]A prophet can find honor anywhere except in his hometown, among his own people, and in his own household.

[5]He could not do any of His great works among them except with a few of the sick, whom He healed by laying His hands upon them. [6]He was amazed by the stubbornness of their unbelief.

Jesus went out among the villages teaching, [7]and He called the twelve to Him and began to send them out in pairs. He gave them authority over unclean spirits [8]and instructed them to take nothing with them but a staff: no money, no bread, no bag, [9]nothing but the sandals on their feet and the coat* on their back.

Jesus: [10]When you go into a house, stay there until it is time for you to leave that town. [11]And if someone will not accept you and your message, when you leave, shake off the dust of that place from your feet as a judgment against it. [On the day of judgment, that city will wish for the punishment of Sodom and Gomorrah.]*

[12]And so His disciples went out *into the countryside,* preaching the changed life* *as Jesus had taught them,* [13]casting out unclean spirits and anointing the sick with oil to heal them.

[14]Jesus had become so well known that King Herod received reports of all that Jesus was doing. Some were saying* that John the Prophet* had been raised from the dead and that these mighty works were the fruits of his resurrection. *Herod was stunned and shaken by this thought.*

Others (*disagreeing*): [15]No, this Jesus is Elijah, *returned to work on the earth.*

And still others said He was another of the prophets.

Herod (*to himself*): [16]No, it is John, the prophet I beheaded, risen from the dead.

For the blood of John was on his hands. [17-18]Herod had imprisoned John *in the days before Jesus began His teaching.* John had preached to Herod that he should not have married his own brother's wife, Herodias, for *so it is written in the Hebrew Scriptures:* "It is not lawful for one to marry his brother's wife."*

[19]Herodias held a grudge against John and would have had him killed, but she couldn't. [20]Herod feared John as a holy and righteous man and did what he could to protect him. John taught hard truths,* and yet Herod found he usually liked hearing them.

So Herod had put John in prison instead of executing him; [21-22]*and there John sat until* Herod's birthday, when the governor held a great state dinner. That night, Herod's stepdaughter danced beautifully for the state officials; and the king proclaimed a solemn vow in the presence of *his honored guests,* military officers, and some of the leading men of Galilee.

Herod: Ask me whatever you wish, and I will grant it. [23]Whatever you want, I will give you—up to half my province.

[24]She went out and consulted with her mother, *Herodias, who had only one great desire* and told her daughter what she must say.

* 6:9 Literally, "not to wear two tunics"
* 6:11 Some of the earliest manuscripts omit this portion.
* 6:12 Literally, repentance
* 6:14 Some of the earliest manuscripts read "He was saying."
* 6:14 Literally, John who immersed, to show repentance
* 6:17-18 Leviticus 18:16; 20:21
* 6:20 Some early manuscripts read "he did many things."

Herod's Stepdaughter (*immediately, in response to Herod*): 25There is only one thing I desire. I want the head of John the Prophet*—right now—delivered to me on a platter.

26Herod was horrified, but he had sworn an oath and could not break his word in front of his invited guests. 27So immediately he sent an executioner to the prison to behead John and bring them the head. 28It was brought to the girl upon a platter, and she took it to her mother.

29When John's disciples were told of this, they came for his body and gave it a proper burial.

30Now the twelve returned from their travels and told Him what they had done, *who they had seen,* and how they had spread the news of God's kingdom.

Jesus (*to the disciples*): 31Let us go out into the wilderness for a while and rest ourselves.

The crowds gathered as always, and Jesus and the twelve couldn't eat because so many people came and went. 32They could get no peace until they boarded a boat and sailed toward a deserted place.

33*But the people would not be put off so easily.* Those *along the shore* who recognized Jesus followed *along the coast.* People pushed out of all the cities and gathered ahead of Him 34so that when Jesus came ashore and saw this crowd of people waiting for Him *in a place that should have been relatively deserted,* He was moved with compassion. They were like sheep without a shepherd.

He began to teach them many things 35as the day passed; at last the disciples came to Jesus.

Disciples: It is getting late, and there is nothing around for miles. 36Send these people to the surrounding villages so they can buy something to eat.

Jesus: 37Why don't you give them something to eat?

Disciples (*looking at Him*): What? It would cost a fortune* to buy bread for these people!

Jesus: 38Does anyone have any bread? Go and see.

Disciples (*returning from the crowd*): There are five *pieces of flatbread* and two fish, *if that makes any difference.*

Jesus: 39-40*Listen,* tell them to gather in smaller groups and sit on that green patch of grass.

And so the disciples gathered the people in groups of 100 or of 50, and they sat down.

41Jesus took the five pieces *of flatbread* and the two fish, looked up to heaven, thanked God for the food, and broke it. He gave the pieces to the disciples to distribute, 42and all of the people ate until no one was hungry. 43Then they gathered twelve baskets full of leftovers.

44*That day,* 5,000 men ate their fill of the bread *when Jesus fed the hungry crowd.*

The disciples must have felt like they spent a lot of their time trying to bring Jesus back to earth. In the middle of His heavenly teachings, they were frequently reminding Him of ordinary concerns. In this case, their worries were especially mundane: they were out in a deserted place with thousands of people, and nobody had eaten anything all day. The disciples probably spent a long time discussing the problem among themselves before they finally decided to bother Jesus. Feeling irritable from hunger, with their stomachs growling loudly, they finally pulled Jesus aside to point out the obvious: everyone needed to go and eat something.

But Jesus, as usual, wasn't about to be distracted by the obvious. His

---

* 6:25 Literally, John who immersed, to show repentance
* 6:37 Literally, 200 denarii, Roman coins

answer must have irritated them even further: "Why don't you give them something to eat?" The disciples must have been dumbfounded. But Jesus was seeing a much bigger reality. He was deliberately creating a turning point in His ministry: He wanted to make them a part of His miracles. From recorders and observers, they would become participants. And so the disciples, not Jesus, told the people to sit down, passed out the food, and collected the leftovers after everyone had eaten until they were stuffed. The disciples must have felt pretty sheepish as they experienced how Jesus was making them a part of the miracle—despite their mundane concerns and their frustration with Him.

45Not long after, He sent His disciples out onto their boat to sail to Bethsaida on the other shore, and He sent the crowd away. 46After everyone had gone, He slipped away to pray on a mountain *overlooking the sea.*

47When evening came, the boat was out on the sea and He was alone on the land. 48He saw that the disciples were making little progress because they were rowing against a stiff wind. Before daylight He came near them, walking on the water, and would have passed by them. 49Some of them saw Him walking on the surface of the water, thought He was a ghost, and cried out. 50When they all saw Him, they were terrified.

Jesus (*immediately calling out*): Don't be frightened. Do you see? It is I.

51*He walked across the water to the boat;* and as soon as He stepped aboard, the contrary wind ceased its blowing. They were greatly astonished; 52although they had just witnessed the miracle of Jesus feeding 5,000 with bread *and fish, and other signs besides,* they didn't understand *what it all meant* and their hearts remained hard.

How could the disciples still be in doubt about Jesus after having been part of so many miracles? Like the Israelites in the Old Testament, the disciples were discovering the truth that miracles don't produce faith. As Jesus so often pointed out in His healings, the process works the other way around: it's faith that produces miracles. Miracles are only signs—evidence of truth that you have to know before you can understand the miracle. As long as the disciples were still in doubt about who Jesus was, they would find their faith constantly challenged and frequently wavering, no matter how many miracles they witnessed or even participated in. It wouldn't be until after the resurrection, the greatest miracle of all, that they would come to recognize and believe in Jesus for who He was; and then their hearts would at last become open.

53When they finished their journey, they landed the boat in Gennesaret. 54People at once recognized Jesus *as the Healer.* 55Immediately they hurried to collect the sick and infirm—bringing them to Him in beds if they had to— 56laying them out in the markets of any village, city, or field where He might pass.

Gennesarites: Just let us touch the fringe of Your robe.

Even people who touch only it are made whole again.

7 Then the Pharisees returned to talk with Jesus, and with them came some of the scribes *and scholars* from Jerusalem.

Scribes and Scholars (*seeing the disciples eating*): 2Your disciples are eating bread with defiled, unwashed hands.

3Now *you need to know that* the Pharisees, and all Jews *for that matter,* held the tradition of their ancestors that hands must be washed before eating to avoid being ritually unclean. ⁴Likewise, they washed when they returned from the market and followed similar purity teachings as well, from the washing of their food to the washing of their bowls, cups, and kettles.

Scribes and Pharisees: ⁵Why don't Your disciples follow the traditions passed down to us? Why do they eat their bread with defiled hands?

Jesus: ⁶Isaiah prophesied wisely about your religious pretensions when he wrote,

> These people honor Me *with words off their lips;*
> meanwhile their hearts are far from Me.
> ⁷Their worship is empty, *void of true devotion.*
> They teach a human commandment, *memorized and practiced by rote.**

⁸When you cling blindly to your own traditions [such as washing utensils and cups],* you completely miss God's command. ⁹Then, indeed, you have perfected setting aside God's commands for the sake of your tradition. ¹⁰Moses gave you God's commandment: "Honor your father and your mother."* And also, "If you curse your father or your mother, you will be put to death."* ¹¹But *I hear one of* you say to your *aged* parents, "I've decided that the support you were expecting from me will now be the holy offering set aside for God." ¹²After that he is not allowed to do anything for his parents. ¹³Do you think God wants you to honor your traditions that you have passed down *or His commandment of mercy, passed down directly from Him?* This is only one of many places where you are blind. ¹⁴(to the crowd that had gathered) Listen, all of you, to this teaching. I want you to understand. ¹⁵There is nothing outside someone that can corrupt him. Only the things that come out of a person can corrupt him. [¹⁶All who have ears to hear, let them listen.]*

¹⁷When they had come in from the road, His disciples asked Him what He meant by this teaching.

Jesus: ¹⁸Do you mean you don't understand this one either? Whatever goes into people from outside can't defile them ¹⁹because it doesn't go into their hearts. Outside things go through their guts and back out, thus making all foods pure.* ²⁰No, it's what comes from within that corrupts. ²¹⁻²²It's what grows out of the hearts of people that leads to corruption: evil thoughts, immoral sex, theft, murder, adultery, greed, wicked acts, treachery, sensuality, jealousy, slander, pride, and foolishness. ²³All of these come from within, and these are the sins that truly corrupt a person.

> Although Mark specifically states that Jesus was overriding the Old Testament dietary laws and declaring all foods pure, it would be a long time before the disciples were willing to act on that message. One of the biggest controversies in the early church was the question of dietary restrictions and how the Old Testament laws ought to be observed by Jewish and non-Jewish Christian believers. However, Jesus made it clear in this passage that His main concern had nothing to do with what people ate. Instead, He was concerned about the hearts of His followers.

²⁴From there Jesus and His followers traveled to the region of Tyre [and Sidon]* *on the Mediterranean coast.* He hoped to slip unnoticed into a house, but people

---

* 7:6-7 Isaiah 29:13
* 7:8 Some of the earliest manuscripts omit this portion.
* 7:10 Exodus 20:12; Deuteronomy 5:16
* 7:10 Exodus 21:17; Leviticus 20:9
* 7:16 Some manuscripts omit verse 16.
* 7:19 The earliest texts say "Jesus declared all foods pure."
* 7:24 Some manuscripts omit this portion.

discovered His presence. 25*Shortly after He arrived,* a woman whose daughter was filled with an unclean spirit heard that He was there, so she came directly to Him and prostrated herself at His feet.

26The woman was *not a Jew, but* a Syrophoenician (a Greek) by birth. *All the same,* she came to Jesus and begged Him to cast the unclean spirit out of her daughter.

Jesus (*shaking His head*): 27I must feed the children first. It would do no good to take the children's bread and throw it to the dogs.

Syrophoenician Woman: 28Yes, Lord, but even the dogs under the table may eat of the children's crumbs.

Jesus (*smiling and nodding*): 29This is a wise saying. Go back home. Your daughter is free of the spirit that troubled her.

30And when she returned to her house, *she discovered that it was as Jesus had told her.* Her daughter lay on her bed, in her right mind, *whole and healthy.*

*A*lthough Jesus at first answered the Greek woman harshly, He ultimately responded to her request. By healing her daughter, He demonstrated that God's loving presence has come to all people and not just to Jews. It's one of the first glimpses in this Gospel of the truth that would become clearer later—the truth that, through Jesus, God is making all people, and not just one chosen nation, clean and whole.

31Jesus traveled on His way through Tyre and Sidon, eventually returning to the region of the Sea of Galilee. From there He pressed on to the area of the Ten Cities.* 32*Among the sick* who were brought to Him was a man who was deaf and could barely speak at all, and those who brought him begged Jesus to lay His hands on the man. 33Jesus took him aside from the crowd, alone, touched his ears with His fingers, and after spitting on His fingers, Jesus touched the man's tongue. 34Looking heavenward to God, Jesus sighed and commanded,

Jesus: Open up* *and let this man speak.*

35[Immediately]* the man could hear, his tongue was loosed, and he spoke plainly. 36Jesus ordered those *who had witnessed this* to tell no one; but the more He insisted, the more zealously people spread the word.

People (*astonished*): 37He does everything so well! He even returns sound to the deaf and mute.

*O*n His journey back from Tyre and Sidon, Jesus returned to an area where earlier He had performed an impressive miracle: the healing of the demon-possessed man.* Although the people of that town were eager to get rid of Him the first time, the testimony of the formerly possessed man had some effect because now the people of the Ten Cities were eager to bring a sick man to Jesus for healing.

Most of Jesus' healings took place with a simple word: He would speak, and the sick person would be well. But for this healing, He went through a series of actions. Why did Jesus, who could so easily heal without even seeing or touching a person, suddenly touch the man's ears and tongue and look up dramatically toward heaven before the man could be cured? Jesus wanted the man to have the chance to experience faith—the faith that Jesus often said was so important for all His healings. Since the man was deaf, Jesus communicated with him through signs so that the man could know what Jesus was doing. By touching the man's ears and tongue, Jesus demon-

---

* 7:31 Literally, the Decapolis
* 7:34 Aramaic *Ephphatha*
* 7:35 Some of the earliest manuscripts omit this word.
* **Note** Mark 5:1-20

strated His intention to heal the parts that were broken. By looking up toward God, Jesus showed the man where His power came from. Only then, once the man had plenty of opportunity to anticipate the healing, did Jesus open his ears and free his tongue.

8 Once again a huge crowd had followed them, and they had nothing to eat. So Jesus called His disciples together.

Jesus: [2]These people have been with Me for three days without food. They're hungry, and I am concerned for them. [3]If I try to send them home now, they'll faint along the way because many of them have come a long, long way *to hear and see Me.*
Disciples: [4]Where can we find enough bread for these people in this desolate place?
Jesus: [5]How much bread do we have left?
Disciples: Seven rounds of flatbread.

[6]*So, as before,* He commanded the people to sit down; and He took the rounds of flatbread, gave thanks for them, and broke them. His disciples took what He gave them and fed the people. [7]They also had a few small fish, which, after He had spoken a blessing, He likewise gave His followers to pass to the people. [8]When all had eaten their fill and they had gathered up the food that remained, seven baskets were full.

[9]*On this occasion,* there were about 4,000 people who had eaten the food *that Jesus provided.* Jesus sent the crowd home; [10] then, immediately, He got into a boat with His disciples and sailed away. Upon their arrival in Dalmanutha *in the district of Magdala,* [11]they were met by Pharisees—ready with their questions and tests—seeking some sign from heaven *that His teaching was from God.*

Jesus *(sighing with disappointment)*: [12]Why does this generation ask for a sign *that will cause them all to believe?* Believe Me when I say that you will not see one.

[13]He left the Pharisees and sailed across to the other shore.
[14]The disciples had forgotten to buy provisions, so they had only one round of flatbread among them. [15]Jesus took this moment to warn them.

Jesus: Beware of the yeast of the Pharisees and the leaven of Herod.

The disciples *didn't understand what Jesus was talking about and* discussed it among themselves.

Some Disciples: [16]What?
Other Disciples: He's saying this because we have run out of bread.
Jesus *(overhearing them)*: [17-19]Why are you focusing on bread? Don't you see yet? Don't you understand? You have eyes—why don't you see? You have ears—why don't you hear? Are you so hard-hearted?
   Don't you remember when I broke the five rounds of flatbread among the 5,000? *Tell Me,* how many baskets of scraps were left over?
Disciples: Twelve.
Jesus: [20]And how many were left when I fed the 4,000 with seven rounds?
Disciples: Seven.
Jesus: [21]And still you don't understand?

[22]When they came into Bethsaida, a group brought a blind man to Jesus, and they begged Him to touch the man *and heal him.* [23]So Jesus guided the man out of the village, *away from the crowd;* and He spat on the man's eyes and touched them.

Jesus: What do you see?
Blind Man *(opening his eyes)*: [24]I see people, but they look like trees—walking trees.

[25]Jesus touched his eyes again; and when the man looked up, he could see everything clearly.
[26]Jesus sent him away to his house.

Jesus (to the healed man): Don't go into town yet. [And don't tell anybody in town what happened here.]*

> Bethsaida was the hometown of at least three of Jesus' emissaries—Peter, Andrew, and Philip—and possibly James and John as well. Jesus performed many miracles there, most notably the feeding of the 5,000. However, this miracle—the healing of the blind man—is the only miracle recorded in all the Gospels that was done in stages instead of instantly.
>
> Of course, there's no way to know for sure why Jesus chose to heal this man partly before He healed him entirely. Jesus frequently linked faith, or lack of faith, with the healings. Bethsaida, too, was a town He criticized for its lack of faith.*
>
> Since Jesus had just rebuked His disciples for not understanding the meaning of His miracles, it's likely He wanted to demonstrate to them that their inability to see His purpose could be healed, too, even if it took time.

27As He traveled with His disciples into the villages of Caesarea Philippi, He posed an *important* question to them.

Jesus: Who are the people saying I am?

28They told Him *about the great speculation in the land concerning His identity.*

Disciples: Some of them say *You are* John the Prophet,* others say Elijah, while others say one of the prophets *of old.*
Jesus (pressing the question): 29And who do you say that I am?
Peter: You are the Liberating King, *God's Anointed One.*
Jesus: 30Don't tell anyone. *It is not yet time.*

31And He went on to teach them many things *about Himself*: how the Son of Man would suffer, how He would be rejected by the elders, chief priests, and scribes, how He would be killed, and how, after three days, *God would* raise Him from the dead. 32He said all these things in front of them all, but Peter took Jesus aside.

Peter (rebuking Him): Lord, don't say this. *This can't be true.*

> Peter represents the best and worst in humanity. One day, Peter drops everything to become a follower of Jesus; the next, he's busy putting his foot in his mouth. Peter is always responding to his Liberator, frequently making mistakes, but never drifting far from Jesus' side. In this passage, Peter verbalizes God's word and Satan's temptation—almost in the same breath. Peter thought he understood who Jesus was, but he still had a lot to learn about what Jesus came to do.

Jesus (seeing His disciples surrounding them): 33Get behind Me, you tempter! You're thinking only of human things, not of the things God has planned.

34He gathered the crowd and His disciples alike.

Jesus: If any one of you wants to follow Me, you will have to give yourself up to God's plan, take up your cross, and do as I do. 35For any one of you who wants to be rescued will lose your life, but any one of you who loses your life for My sake and for the sake of this good news will be liberated. 36Really, what profit is there for you to gain the whole world and lose yourself *in the process*? 37What can you give in exchange for your life? 38If you are ashamed of Me and of what I came to teach to this adulterous and sinful generation, then the Son of Man will be ashamed of you when He comes in the glory of His Father along with the holy messengers *at the final judgment.*

* 8:26 Some manuscripts omit this portion.
* **Note** Matthew 11:21-22
* 8:28 Literally, John who immersed, to show repentance

9 Jesus *(continuing)*: Truly, some of you who are here now will not experience death before you see the kingdom of God coming in *glory and* power.

[2]Six days after saying this, Jesus took Peter, James, and John and led them up onto a high mountaintop by themselves. There He was transformed [3]so that His clothing became intensely white, brighter than any earthly cleaner could bleach them. [4]Elijah and Moses appeared to them and talked with Jesus.

Peter *(to Jesus)*: [5]Teacher, it's a great thing that we're here. We should build three shelters here: one for You, one for Moses, and one for Elijah.

[6]He *was babbling and* did not know what he was saying because they were terrified *by what they were witnessing.*

[7]Then a cloud surrounded them, and they heard a voice within that cloud.

Voice: This is My beloved Son. Listen to Him.

[8]All of a sudden, they looked about and all they had seen was gone. They stood alone on the mountain with Jesus.

[9]On their way back down, He urged them not to tell anyone what they had witnessed until the Son of Man had risen from the dead, [10]so they kept it all to themselves.

*I*n what was probably one of the most spectacular events of their lives, Jesus' three closest disciples—Peter, James, and John—were given a glimpse of His divine nature. Mark doesn't usually record events with much attention to chronology; but in this case, he is careful to tell us that the transfiguration took place six days after Peter's confession of Jesus' identity. In a dramatic confirmation of the truth Peter had spoken then, the three disciples saw that Jesus is indeed the Anointed One of God. The veil of Jesus' human nature was pulled away, and the glory of His divinity shone through.

Alongside Jesus, the disciples saw two people whom they had never met but instantly recognized: Moses and Elijah. Moses, who liberated the Hebrew slaves and received God's covenant atop Mount Sinai, represented God's law. Elijah represented all the prophets throughout history, since he was one of the greatest of them. The appearance of these two famous figures from the past showed that Jesus was the fulfillment of the law and the answer to all the promises of the prophets.

Finally the disciples heard a voice from heaven—God's own voice—commanding them to listen to Jesus as His beloved Son. What an incredible confirmation of the truth that Peter had spoken in faith only six days before!

Disciples *(to one another)*: What does He mean, "Until the Son of Man is risen"? [11](to Jesus) Master, why do the scribes say that Elijah must come first?

Jesus *(thinking of John the Prophet)*: [12]Elijah does come first to restore all things. *They have it right.* But there is something else written in the Scriptures about the Son of Man: He will have to suffer and be rejected. [13]*Here's the truth:* Elijah has come; *his enemies treated him with contempt* and did what they wanted to him, just as it was written.

[14]When they reached the rest of the disciples, Jesus saw that a large crowd had gathered and that among them the scribes were asking questions. [15]Right when the crowd saw Jesus, they were overcome with awe and surged forward immediately, *nearly running over the disciples.*

Jesus *(to the scribes)*: [16]What are you debating with My disciples? *What would you like to know?*

Father *(in the crowd)*: [17]Teacher, I have brought my son to You. He is filled with an unclean spirit. He cannot speak, [18]and when the spirit takes control of him, he is thrown to the ground *to wail and moan*, to foam at the mouth, to grind his teeth, and to stiffen up. I brought him to Your followers, but they could do nothing with him. *Can You help us?*

Jesus: [19]Oh, faithless generation, how long must I be among you? How long do I have to put up with you? Bring the boy to Me.

[20]They brought the boy toward Jesus; but as soon as He drew near, the spirit took control of the boy and threw him on the ground, where he rolled, foaming at the mouth.

Jesus *(to the father)*: [21]How long has he been like this?

Father: Since he was a baby. [22]This spirit has thrown him often into the fire and sometimes into the water, trying to destroy him. *I have run out of options; I have tried everything.* But if there's anything You can do, please, have pity on us and help us.

Jesus: [23]*What do you mean, "if there's anything"*—all things are possible, if you only believe.

Father *(crying in desperation)*: [24]I believe, Lord. Help me to believe!

[25]Jesus noticed that a crowd had gathered around them now. He issued a command to the unclean spirit.

Jesus: Listen up, you no-talking, no-hearing demon. I Myself am ordering you to come out of him now. Come out, and don't ever come back!

[26]The spirit shrieked and caused the boy to thrash about; then it came out of the boy and left him lying as still as death. Many of those in the crowd whispered that he was dead. [27]But Jesus took the boy by the hand and lifted him to his feet.

[28]Later He and His disciples gathered privately in a house.

Disciples *(to Jesus)*: Why couldn't we cast out that unclean spirit?

Jesus: [29]That sort *of powerful spirit* can only be conquered with much prayer [and fasting].*

> *T*he father of the possessed boy had some faith to begin with—enough to bring his son to Jesus and enough to ask for Jesus to heal him. But his faith was incomplete: this man asked hesitantly whether there was anything Jesus could do. In his desperation, the father recognized the limits of his faith. He believed—but was his faith strong enough for a healing? He wasn't sure, and that's why he begged for help. Perhaps that very desperation was enough faith; at any rate, Jesus immediately healed his son.
>
> But later the disciples showed the limitations of their faith when they drew Jesus aside for a private conversation. Having successfully healed many demon-possessed people when Jesus sent them out earlier, they were at a loss to know why they were completely unable to heal this little boy. Jesus' reply is cryptic and surprising: "That sort *of powerful spirit* can only be conquered with much prayer [and fasting]." It seems that although the disciples had faith that they could heal the boy, they were spiritually unprepared for the depth of evil that resides in the world. They needed to be saturated in the presence of God to face the challenge.

[30]When they left that place, they passed secretly through Galilee.

Jesus *(to the disciples as they traveled)*: [31]The Son of Man will be delivered into the hands of the people, and they will kill Him. And after He is killed, He will rise on the third day.

* 9:29 The earliest manuscripts omit this portion.

³²But again they did not understand His meaning, and they were afraid to ask Him *for an explanation.*

³³At last, they came to Capernaum where they gathered in a house.

Jesus: What was it I heard you arguing about along the way?

³⁴They *looked down at the floor and* wouldn't answer, for they had been arguing among themselves about who was the greatest *of Jesus' disciples.*

*I*t was only natural for them to wonder which of them would be His right-hand man. And although it's hard to believe that the three disciples who had just seen Jesus' glory revealed in the transfiguration would be part of such a petty discussion, how could they have resisted it? After all, who had a better claim than they did to being the greatest of Jesus' disciples?

Fortunately Jesus overheard what they were talking about, and He was quick to respond in mercy to correct their mistake. Greatness in His eyes doesn't consist of seeing wonders or performing miracles or even fasting and praying. Instead, greatness is about humility and service. This is why He came. These are the heart of the kingdom of heaven.

³⁵He sat down with the twelve to teach them.

Jesus: Whoever wants to be first must be last, and *whoever wants to be the greatest* must be the servant of all.

³⁶He then called forward a child, set the child in the middle of them, and took the child in His arms.

Jesus: ³⁷Whoever welcomes a child like this in My name welcomes Me; and whoever welcomes Me is welcoming not Me, but the One who sent Me.

John *(to Jesus)*: ³⁸Master, we saw another man casting out unclean spirits in Your name, but he was not one of our group. So we told him to stop what he was doing.

Jesus: ³⁹You shouldn't have said that. Anyone using My name to do a miracle cannot turn quickly to speak evil of Me. ⁴⁰Anyone who isn't against us is for us. ⁴¹The truth of the matter is this: anyone who gives you a cup of *cool* water to drink because you carry the name of your Liberator will be rewarded.

⁴²But if anyone turns even the smallest of My followers away from Me, it would be better for him if someone had hung a millstone around his neck and flung him into the deepest part of the sea.

⁴³If your hand turns you away from the things of God, then you should cut it off. It's better to come into *eternal* life maimed than to have two hands and be flung into hell— [⁴⁴where the worm will not die and the fire will not be smothered.]*

⁴⁵If your foot trips you on the path, you should cut it off. It's better to come into *eternal* life crawling than to have two feet and be flung into hell— [⁴⁶where the worm will not die and the fire will not be smothered.]*

⁴⁷And if your eye keeps you from seeing clearly, then you should pull it out. It's better to come into the kingdom of God with one eye than to have two eyes and be flung into hell, ⁴⁸where the worm will not die and the fire will not be smothered.* ⁴⁹Everyone will be salted with fire[, and every sacrifice will be seasoned with salt].* ⁵⁰Salt is a good thing; but if it has lost its zest, how can it be seasoned again? You should have salt within yourselves and peace with one another.

* 9:44 The earliest manuscripts omit verse 44, a quote from Isaiah 66:24.
* 9:46 The earliest manuscripts omit verse 46, a quote from Isaiah 66:24.
* 9:48 Isaiah 66:24
* 9:49 Some of the earliest manuscripts omit this portion.

10 From there Jesus traveled to Judea and beyond the Jordan River; He taught the crowds who gathered as was His custom.

²Some Pharisees came to Him to test Him *on His adherence to the law of Moses.*

Pharisees: Is it lawful for a husband to divorce his wife?

Jesus: ³What did Moses say to you?

Pharisees: ⁴Moses permitted us to write a certificate of dismissal and divorce her.*

Jesus: ⁵Moses gave you this law *as a concession* because of the hardness of your hearts. ⁶But truly, God created humans male and female in the beginning.* ⁷*As it is written in the Hebrew Scriptures,* "For this, a man will leave his father's and mother's *house* [to marry his wife],* ⁸and the two of them will become one flesh *and blood."** So they are no longer two people, but one. ⁹What God has joined together in this way, no one may sever.

¹⁰In the privacy of their dwelling that evening, the disciples asked Him about this teaching, ¹¹and He went even further.

Jesus: If any husband divorces his wife and then marries another woman, he commits adultery against her. ¹²And if a wife should divorce her husband and marry another, then she commits adultery *against him.*

---

*T*he Pharisees hoped to trip Jesus on a rather controversial question. His answer, however, is unusually straightforward. Instead of answering as they expected and taking a side in the popular debate, Jesus went back to the purpose and meaning of marriage—not just from a social perspective, but from a spiritual one.

---

¹³*When the crowd gathered again,* parents *and grandparents* had brought their children *and grandchildren* to see Jesus, hoping that He might *grant them His blessing* through His touch.

His disciples turned them all away; ¹⁴but when Jesus saw this, He was incensed.

Jesus (to the disciples): Let the children come to Me, and don't ever stand in their way, for this is what the kingdom of God is all about. ¹⁵Truly anyone who doesn't accept the kingdom of God as a little child does can never enter it.

¹⁶Jesus gathered the children in His arms, and He laid His hands on them to bless them.

¹⁷When He had traveled on, a *young* man came and knelt *in the dust of the road* in front of Jesus.

Young Man: Good Teacher! What must I do to gain life in the world to come?

Jesus: ¹⁸You are calling Me good? *Don't you know that* God and God alone is good? ¹⁹*Anyway, why ask Me that question?* You know the Commandments *of Moses:* "Do not murder, do not commit adultery, do not steal, do not slander, do not defraud, and honor your father and mother."*

Young Man: ²⁰Yes, Teacher, I have done all these since I was a child.

²¹Then Jesus, looking at the young man, *saw that he was sincere* and responded out of His love for him.

Jesus: *Son,* there is still one thing you have not done. Go now. Sell everything you have and give the proceeds to the poor so that you will have treasure in heaven. After that, come, follow Me.

²²The young man went away sick at heart at these words because he was very wealthy, ²³and Jesus looked around *to see if His disciples were understanding His teaching.*

* 10:4 Deuteronomy 24:1
* 10:6 Genesis 1:27; 5:2; the Hebrew name for the Book of Genesis is "In the beginning."
* 10:7 Some of the earliest manuscripts omit this portion.
* 10:7-8 Genesis 2:24
* 10:19 Exodus 20:12-16; Deuteronomy 5:16-20

Jesus (*to His disciples*): Oh, it is hard for people with wealth to find their way into God's kingdom!

Disciples (*amazed*): 24What?

Jesus: *You heard Me.* How hard it is to enter the kingdom of God [for those who trust in their wealth]!* 25I think you'll see camels squeezing through the eye of a needle before you'll see the rich *celebrating and dancing as they* enter into *the joy of* God's kingdom!

26The disciples looked around at each other, whispering.

Disciples (*aloud to Jesus*): Then who can be liberated?

Jesus (*smiling and shaking His head*): 27For human beings it is impossible, but not for God: God makes everything possible.

Peter: 28Master, we have left behind everything we had to follow You.

Jesus: 29That is true. And those who have left their houses, their lands, their parents, or their families for My sake, and for the sake of this good news 30will receive all of this 100 times greater than they have in this time—houses and farms and brothers, sisters, mothers, and children, along with persecutions—and in the world to come, they will receive eternal life. 31But many of those who are first *in this world* shall be last *in the world to come*, and the last, first.

*T*his young man, like many wealthy people, was confident in his own abilities. He wanted to make sure that he would live well in the coming world, but he was not convinced that he was falling that short of the mark. And without humbly recognizing his own sinfulness and need in the face of God's goodness and perfection, it was indeed very hard for him to find the Kingdom.

This unnamed seeker was the only person in the Gospels outside of the twelve whom Jesus personally invited to follow Him. He was also the only person in the Gospels to walk away from that invitation.

Jesus now moved on. He was being drawn toward the holy city. Something wonderful and dangerous was ahead.

32At length, they made their way toward Jerusalem. Jesus was walking ahead of them. As they neared the city, wonder and amazement filled them. But soon those who were following began to tremble.

Jesus (*taking the twelve aside*): 33Look, we are going up to Jerusalem, and there the Son of Man is going to be delivered to the chief priests and the scribes. They shall seek His death and deliver Him to the outsiders *to carry out that sentence.* 34Then people will mock Him, spit upon Him, whip Him, and kill Him. But on the third day, He will rise again.

Two of the twelve—the sons of Zebedee *as they were known*—approached Jesus and pulled Him aside.

James and John: 35Teacher, will You do something for us if we ask it of You?

Jesus: 36What is it that you want?

James and John: 37*Master,* grant that we might sit on either side of You, one at Your right hand and one at Your left, when You come into the glory *of Your kingdom.*

Jesus: 38You don't know what it is you're asking. Can you drink from the cup I have to drink from or be washed* with the baptism that awaits Me?

James and John: 39We can.

Jesus: You will indeed drink from the cup I drink from and follow Me in what I must endure.* 40But to sit at My right or at My left is an honor I cannot grant. That will be given to those for whom it has been prepared.

* 10:24 Some manuscripts omit this portion.
* 10:38 Literally, immersed
* 10:39 Literally, be immersed with the immersion

⁴¹When the other ten heard about this request, they were angry with James and John; ⁴²but Jesus stopped them.

Jesus: You know that among the nations of the world the great ones lord it over the little people and act like tyrants. ⁴³But that is not the way it will be among you. Whoever would be great among you must serve and minister. ⁴⁴Whoever wants to be great among you must be slave of all. ⁴⁵Even the Son of Man came not to be served but to be a servant—to offer His life as a ransom for others.

> Jesus' disciples were so convinced that He would rule as the conquering Liberator and King that they simply couldn't hear what He was saying about His trial and death. None of the disciples understood what He was telling them, and none of His predictions would become clear to them until after His resurrection.
>
> In the meantime, several of His disciples were not only failing to understand His warnings about the things to come; they were missing His message on things right before their eyes. Jesus had already told them that to be great among His followers meant to become humble like a child; but James and John still thought that as two of His closest disciples, they could win worldly fame and power.

⁴⁶*By that time,* they had reached Jericho; as they passed through the town, a crowd of people followed along. They came to a blind beggar, Bartimaeus, the son of Timaeus, who sat beside the *main* road. ⁴⁷When he was told that Jesus of Nazareth was passing in that throng, he called out in a loud voice.

Bartimaeus: Jesus, Son of David, take pity on me and help me!

Disgusted by the blind man's public display, others in the crowd tried to silence him *until the Master passed.*

Some of the Crowd: ⁴⁸Be quiet. Shush.
Bartimaeus (*still louder*): Jesus, Son of David, have pity on me!

⁴⁹Jesus stopped where He stood. *The crowd stopped with Him.* He told those *near the front of the crowd* to call the blind man forward.

Some of the Crowd (*to Bartimaeus*): Good news! *Jesus has heard you. Listen*—He calls for you. Get up *and go to Him.*

⁵⁰Bartimaeus cast aside his *beggar's* robe and stepped forward, *feeling his way* toward Jesus.

Jesus: ⁵¹*Why did you call out to Me?* What do you want?
Bartimaeus: Teacher, I want to see.
Jesus: ⁵²Your faith has made you whole. Go in peace.

In that moment, Bartimaeus could see again; and from that time on, he followed Jesus.

> Few people in the Gospels showed as much persistence and eagerness in their desire to be healed as blind Bartimaeus. It took courage for him to ask Jesus to go out of His way for someone as seemingly unimportant as a blind beggar. Bartimaeus was not about to be swayed from his efforts to attract Jesus' attention. The discouragement from everyone around him only made him shout louder, determined to get the attention of the healer he'd heard about.
>
> Jesus told the crowd to bring Bartimaeus to Him, and the blind man's actions demonstrated his faith. Beggars in first-century Palestine would spread a cloak on the ground in front of them to collect donations from compassionate passersby. It probably wasn't much, but for Bartimaeus, his cloak was everything he had. He threw it aside without a thought—probably

along with the coins he had collected that day—because he was certain that once he'd met Jesus, he wouldn't need to be a beggar anymore.

11 When they had gotten close to Jerusalem, near the two villages of Bethphage and Bethany and the Mount of Olives, Jesus sent two of His followers *ahead of them.*

Jesus: ²Go to that village over there. As soon as you get into the town, you'll see a young colt tied that nobody has ever ridden. Untie it and bring it back *to Me.* ³If anybody *stops you and* asks what you're doing, just say, "The Lord needs it, and He will send it back right after He's done."

⁴*Everything happened just as Jesus had told them.* They found the colt in the street tied near a door, and they untied it.

Bystanders: ⁵What are you doing?

⁶They answered as Jesus had instructed and were allowed to take it, ⁷so they brought the colt back to Jesus, piled garments on its back *to make a comfortable seat,* and Jesus rode the animal *toward Jerusalem.* ⁸*As they traveled,* people cast their cloaks onto the road and spread out leafy branches, which they had brought from the fields *along the way.* ⁹People walked ahead of them, and others followed behind.

People (*shouting*): Hosanna! *Rescue us now, Lord!*

*T*his impromptu parade fulfilled the Hebrew Scriptures. "Hosanna" means, "Rescue us, Lord." The people sang this and other words out of the Psalms to praise and honor Jesus.

People (*singing*): Hosanna!

Blessed be the One who comes in the name of the Eternal One!*
¹⁰And blessed is the kingdom of our father David, which draws closer *to us today!*
Hosanna in the highest heavens!

*L*ess than a week before He would be crucified, Jesus entered Jerusalem for the last time and acted in ways His followers expected of the Liberating King. But as He accepted the praise of the crowds, He radically redefined their every expectation. His description to His disciples of where they would find the colt He would ride, and how they should get it, had an air of prophecy and supernatural knowledge. More overtly He rode a donkey instead of being carried into town on the backs of servants (in a litter as a conquering king would have done), fulfilling the prophecy that the King would come riding a donkey.* After all, donkeys were a poor man's mount, and Jesus wanted to identify with the poor. Even in this triumphal entry, Jesus made it clear that He did not intend to conquer and rule in a worldly way.

However, the grandeur of His entrance was augmented by the response of the crowds who followed Him. For most of His ministry, Jesus avoided crowds and suppressed rumors and praise about the miracles He had done. Now, for the first time, He allowed the crowds to voice their excitement about who He was and all that He'd been doing.

¹¹*To the sound of this chanting,* Jesus rode through the gates of Jerusalem and up to the temple. He looked around, *taking note;* but because evening was coming, He and

* 11:9 Psalm 118:26
* **Note** Zechariah 9:9

the twelve went back to Bethany *to spend the night.*

¹²The next morning, when they departed Bethany *and were traveling back to the city,* Jesus was hungry. ¹³Off in the distance, He saw a fig tree fully leafed out, so He headed toward it to see if it might have any ripe fruit. But when He reached it, He found only leaves because the fig season had not yet come.

¹⁴As the disciples listened, *Jesus pronounced a curse on the tree.*

Jesus: No one will ever eat fruit from your branches again.

> *T*his is the only time in the Gospels when Jesus used His supernatural power to destroy rather than to heal; and on the surface, He seems to have done so mostly out of irritation.
>
> The tree was "fully leafed out"— a stage that usually would come after figs were ripe and not before. So the tree was already barren: its leaves had grown profusely before their time, without the tree having produced fruit. Because the tree looked as though it ought to have fruit but didn't, it was a perfect illustration of people who believed they had the good fruit of righteousness even though their actions were void of true compassion and love, as empty and useless as leaves. And so Jesus cursed the fig tree, not out of anger with the tree itself, but as a warning to hypocrites who thought their appearance was more important than the fruit of their actions.

¹⁵They continued into Jerusalem *and made their way up to the temple.*

Upon reaching the temple *that morning,* Jesus dealt with those who were selling and buying *animals for sacrifices* and drove them out of the area. He turned over the tables of those who exchanged money *for* *the temple pilgrims* and the seats of those selling birds, ¹⁶and He *physically* prevented anyone from carrying anything through the temple.

Jesus *(to those who were listening)*: ¹⁷Didn't the prophets write, "My house will be called a house of prayer, for all the people,"* but you have made it into a "haven for thieves"*?

> *A*t the temple, Jesus was confronted with a scene that shocked Him. So He made a scene Himself. But He wasn't merely acting out; He had a message and, like the prophets of old, this message was better seen than heard. He acted decisively and with great emotion against those who had turned God's house into a place where pilgrims were exploited. You see, the temple leadership had allowed profiteers and merchants to set up shop in the court of the Gentiles, and they were making ridiculous profits. For the people who came long distances to worship, it was a normal practice to have merchants selling animals for them to sacrifice. What was not normal and what was immoral was where and how they transacted business. Jesus took issue with robbers profiteering in His Father's house.

¹⁸The chief priests and the scribes heard these words *and knew Jesus was referring to them,* so they plotted His destruction. They had grown afraid of Him because His teachings struck the crowds into astonishment.

¹⁹When evening came, [Jesus and His followers]* left the city again. ²⁰The next morning *on the way back to Jerusalem,* they passed a tree that had withered down to its very roots.

* 11:17 Isaiah 56:7
* 11:17 Jeremiah 7:11
* 11:19 Some of the earliest manuscripts read "He."

Peter (*remembering*): ²¹That's the fig tree, Teacher, the one You cursed *just yesterday morning.* It's withered away *to nothing!*

Jesus: ²²Trust in God. ²³*If you do,* honestly, you can say to this mountain, "Mountain, uproot yourself and throw yourself into the sea." If you don't doubt, but trust that what you say will take place, then it will happen. ²⁴So listen to what I'm saying: Whatever you pray for or ask *from God,* believe that you'll receive it and you will. ²⁵When you pray, if you remember anyone who has wronged you, forgive him so that God above can also forgive you. [²⁶If you don't forgive others, don't expect God's forgiveness.]*

²⁷As they arrived in Jerusalem and were walking in the temple, the chief priests, scribes, and elders came to Jesus ²⁸and asked Him a question.

Leaders: Tell us, who has given You the authority to say and do the things You're saying and doing?

Jesus: ²⁹I will answer your question, if you will answer one for Me. Only then will I tell you who gives Me authority to do these things. ³⁰Tell Me, when John was ritually cleansing* *for the forgiveness of sins,* was his authority from heaven or was it merely human?

³¹The priests, scribes, and elders huddled together to think through an answer.

Leaders (*to themselves*): If we say, "It must have been from heaven," *then Jesus will jump on us.* He'll ask, "Then why didn't you listen to him and follow him?" ³²But if we say, "John's cleansing was only human," the people will be up in arms because they think John was a prophet *sent by God.* ³³(responding to Jesus) We don't know what to tell You.

Jesus: *All right,* then don't expect Me to tell you where I get the authority to say and do these things.

The question that the religious leaders asked Jesus—where His authority came from—is, in many ways, the central question about Jesus. They were probably referring to His overturning the tables in the temple and subsequently challenging a business practice that was perfectly acceptable to all the religious leaders. But there was more! What gave Him the right to heal people on the Sabbath or teach people about God? What gave Him the right to do all those miracles and cast out demons? Who exactly did He think He was—and where did His authority come from? Was He, as people were saying, the Liberating King? Did He plan to become king? They thought they could trap Him with this question: if He claimed His authority was from God, then they could argue that God would not endorse someone who broke His laws; but if He said His authority was His own, then it would be easy to get Him in trouble with the crowds that followed Him and perhaps even with the Roman governor.

Jesus, however, had a better idea. He issued a challenge: I'll tell you what you want to know if you'll answer this question for Me first. But He asked them an impossible question—impossible not because they didn't know the answer, but because they couldn't say the answer.

12 Then He told a story.

Jesus: There was a man who established a vineyard. *He planted and staked the grapes;* he put up a wall around it to fence it in; he dug a pit for a winepress; he built a watchtower. *When he had finished this work,* he leased the vineyard to some tenant farmers and went away to a distant land.

* 11:26 Some of the earliest manuscripts omit verse 26.
* 11:30 Literally, immersing, to show repentance

²When the grapes were in season, he sent a slave to the vineyard to collect *his rent*—his share of the fruit. ³But the farmers grabbed the slave, beat him, and sent him back to his master empty-handed. ⁴The owner sent another slave, and this slave the farmers beat over the head and sent away dishonored. ⁵A third slave, the farmers killed. This went on for some time, with the farmers beating some of the messengers and killing others *until the owner had lost all patience.* ⁶He had a son whom he loved above all things, and he said to himself, *"When these thugs see my son, they'll know he carries my authority. They'll have to respect him."*

⁷*But when the tenant farmers saw the owner's son coming,* they said among themselves, "Look at this! It's the son, the heir to this vineyard. If we kill him, then the land will be ours!" ⁸So they seized him and killed him and threw him out of the vineyard.

⁹Now what do you suppose the owner will do *when he hears of this*? He'll come and destroy these farmers, and he'll give the land to others.

¹⁰Haven't you read the Scriptures? *As the psalmist says,*

The stone that the builders rejected
    has become the very stone that
      holds together the entire
      foundation.
¹¹This is the work of the Eternal One,
    and it is marvelous in our eyes.*

¹²The priests, scribes, temple leaders, and elders knew the story was directed against them. They couldn't figure out how to lay their hands on Jesus then because they were afraid the people *would rise up against them.* So they left Him alone, and they went away *furious.*

*S*tunning. In their minds, judgment would come upon their enemies, and they would be justified. The implication that they themselves would face judgment, not to mention

the imminent threat the ending of the story conveys, went against everything they believed about themselves and about God. And so, blinded by their own anger, they acted exactly as He said they would, despite the warning He gave them about what the ultimate consequence would be.

¹³Then some Pharisees and some of Herod's supporters banded together to try to entrap Jesus. ¹⁴They came to Him and complimented Him.

Pharisees: Teacher, we know You are truthful *in what You say* and that You don't play favorites. You're not worried about what anyone thinks of You, so You teach with total honesty what God would have us do. *So tell us:* is it lawful that we Jews should pay taxes to the Roman emperor or not? ¹⁵Should we give or not?

Jesus (*seeing through their ruse*): Why do you test Me like this? Listen, bring Me a coin* so that I can take a look at it.

¹⁶When they had brought it to Him, He asked them another question.

Jesus: *Tell Me,* whose picture is on this coin? And of whom does this inscription speak?
Pharisees: Caesar, of course.
Jesus: ¹⁷Then give to the emperor what belongs to the emperor. And give God what belongs to God.

They could not think of anything to say to His response.

*J*esus answered their question. But since He knew the spiritual state of their hearts, He turned the question back on them. It wasn't about taxes or loyalty to the emperor. It was about knowing and living faithfully to the one true God.

* 12:10-11 Psalm 118:22-23
* 12:15 Literally, denarius, a Roman coin

[18]Later a group of Sadducees, *Jewish religious leaders* who didn't believe the dead would be resurrected, came to test Jesus.

Sadducees: [19]Teacher, the law of Moses tells us, "If a man's brother dies, leaving a widow without sons, then the man should marry his sister-in-law and *try to have children with her* in his brother's name."*

[20]Now here's the situation: there were seven brothers. The oldest took a wife and left her a widow with no children. [21]So the next oldest married her, left her a widow, and again there were no children. So the next brother married her and died, and the next, *and the next.* [22]Finally all seven brothers had married her, but none of them had conceived children with her, and at last she died also.

[23]Tell us then, in the resurrection [when humans rise from the dead],* whose wife will she be? For all seven of them married her.

Jesus: [24]You can't see the truth because you don't know the Scriptures well and because you don't really believe that God is powerful. [25]The answer is this: when the dead rise, they won't be married or given in marriage. They'll be like the messengers in heaven, *who are not united with one another in marriage.* [26]But how can you fail to see the truth of resurrection? Don't you remember in the Book of Moses how God talked to Moses out of a burning bush and what God said to him then? "I am the God of Abraham, the God of Isaac, and the God of Jacob."* *"I am," God said. Not "I was."* [27]So God is not the God of the dead but of the living. You are sadly mistaken.

[28]One of the scribes *who studied and copied the Hebrew Scriptures* overheard this conversation and was impressed by the way Jesus had answered.

Scribe: Tell me, Teacher. What is the most important thing that God commands *in the law*?

Jesus: [29]The most important commandment is this: "Hear, O Israel, the Eternal One is our God, and the Eternal One is the only God. [30]You should love the Eternal, your God, with all your heart, with all your soul, with all your mind, and with all your strength."* [31]The second *great commandment* is this: "Love others in the same way you love yourself."* There are no commandments more important than these.

*A*lthough Jesus was asked for only the single most important commandment, He answered by naming two commands: love God and love others. He included both because these two teachings can never be really separated from each other. Some people think they can love God and ignore the people around them, but Jesus frequently made it clear that loving God apart from His people is completely impossible.

Scribe: [32]Teacher, You have spoken the truth. For there is one God and only one God, [33]and to love God with all our heart and soul and mind and strength and to love our neighbors as ourselves are more important than any burnt offering or sacrifice *we could ever give.*

[34]Jesus heard that the man had spoken with wisdom.

Jesus: *Well said; if you understand that,* then the kingdom of God is closer than you think.

Nobody asked Jesus any more questions after that.

[35]Later Jesus was teaching in the temple.

* 12:19 Deuteronomy 25:5
* 12:23 Some manuscripts omit this portion.
* 12:26 Exodus 3:6,15
* 12:30 Deuteronomy 6:4-5
* 12:31 Leviticus 19:18

Jesus: Why do the scribes say that the Liberating King is the son of David? ³⁶*In the Psalms,* David himself was led by the Holy Spirit to sing,

> The Master said to my master,
>   "Sit at My right hand,
>   *in the place of power and honor,*
> And I will gather Your enemies together,
>   *lead them in on hands and knees,*
>   and You will rest Your feet on their backs."*

³⁷If David calls the Liberator "Master," how can He be his son?

The crowd listened to Him with delight.

Jesus: ³⁸Watch out for the scribes *who act so religious*—who like to be seen in pious clothes and to be spoken to respectfully in the marketplace, ³⁹who take the best seats in the synagogues and the place of honor at every dinner, ⁴⁰who spend widows' inheritances and pray long prayers to impress others. These are the kind of people who will be condemned above all others.

⁴¹Jesus sat down opposite the treasury, where people came to bring their offerings, and He watched as they came and went. Many rich people threw in large sums of money, ⁴²but a poor widow came and put in only two small coins* worth only a fraction of a cent.*

Jesus (*calling His disciples together*): ⁴³Truly this widow has given a greater gift than any other contribution. ⁴⁴All the others gave a little out of their great abundance, but this poor woman has given God everything she has.

13 As Jesus left the temple *later that day,* one of the disciples noticed *the grandeur of Herod's temple.*

Disciple: Teacher, I can't believe the size of these stones! Look at these magnificent buildings!
Jesus: ²Look closely at these magnificent buildings. *Someday* there won't be one of these great stones left on another. Everything will be thrown down.

³They took a seat on the Mount of Olives, across *the valley* from the temple; and Peter, James, John, and Andrew asked Jesus to explain His statement to them privately.

Peter, James, John, and Andrew: ⁴Don't keep us in the dark. When will the temple be destroyed? What sign will let us know that it's about to happen?
Jesus: ⁵Take care that no one deceives you. ⁶Many will come claiming to be Mine, saying, "I am the One," and they will fool lots of people. ⁷You will hear of wars, or that war is coming, but don't lose heart. These things will have to happen, although it won't mean the end yet. ⁸Tribe will rise up against tribe, nation against nation, and there will be earthquakes in place after place and famines. These are a prelude to "labor pains" *that precede the temple's fall.*

⁹Be careful, because you will be delivered to trial and beaten in the places of worship. Kings and governors will stand in judgment over you as you speak in My name. ¹⁰The good news *of the coming kingdom of God* must be delivered first in every land and every language. ¹¹When people bring you up on charges and it is your time to defend yourself, don't worry about what message you'll deliver. Whatever comes to your mind, speak it, because the Holy Spirit will inspire it.

¹²*But it will get worse.* Brothers will betray each other to death, and fathers will betray their children. Children will turn against their parents and cause them to be executed. ¹³Everyone will

---

* 12:36 Psalm 110:1
* 12:42 Literally lepta, a Roman coin worth an insignificant amount
* 12:42 Literally, kodrantes, a Roman penny

hate you because of your allegiance to Me. But if you're faithful until the end, you will be rescued.

¹⁴On the day that you see the desecration of our most holy place* [described by Daniel the prophet]* where it is out of place,

Let the one who reads *and hears* understand,

Jesus: Whoever is in Judea should flee for the mountains. ¹⁵The person on the rooftop shouldn't reenter the house to get anything, ¹⁶and the person working in the field shouldn't turn back to grab his coat. ¹⁷It will be horrible for women who are pregnant or who are nursing their children when those days come. ¹⁸And pray that you don't have to run for your lives in the winter. ¹⁹When those days come, there will be suffering like nobody has seen from the beginning of the world that God created until now, and it never will be like this again. ²⁰And if the Lord didn't shorten those days for the sake of the ones He has chosen, then nobody would survive them.

²¹If anyone tells you in those days, "Look, there is the Liberating King!" or "Hey, that must be Him!" don't believe them. ²²False liberators and prophets will pop up *like weeds,* and they will work signs and perform miracles that would entice even God's chosen people, if that were possible. ²³So be alert, and remember how I have warned you.

²⁴⁻²⁵*As Isaiah said* in the days after that great suffering,

The sun will refuse to shine,
 and the moon will hold back its
  light.
The stars in heaven will fall,
 and the powers in the heavens
  will be shaken.*

²⁶Then you will see (*as Daniel predicted*) "the Son of Man coming in the clouds,"* *clothed* in power and majesty. ²⁷And He will send out His heavenly messengers and gather together to Himself those He has chosen from the four corners of the world, from every direction and every land.

*E*ven though the disciples had never understood Jesus' warnings about His coming death, they couldn't help but notice that something was in the air during this week between His entry into Jerusalem and His crucifixion. Surely the moment they'd been waiting for—the moment when Jesus would reveal Himself as the Liberating King—couldn't be far off.

As the disciples were asking about the temple, they were also thinking of promises about the Liberator. But for Jesus, everything now was connected to His imminent death and resurrection. Even as He predicted the temple's fall—an event that did occur about 40 years later—and spoke of His second coming, He was still thinking about His death. After all, resurrection can't happen unless something dies first. And the old world, too, will have to die before the world is made new.

Jesus: ²⁸Learn this lesson from the fig tree: When its branch is new and tender and begins to put forth leaves, you know that summer must be near. ²⁹In the same way, when you see *and hear* the things I've described to you taking place, you'll know the time is drawing near. ³⁰It's true—this generation will not pass away before all these things have happened. ³¹Heaven and earth may pass away, but these words of Mine will never pass away.

³²*Take heed:* no one knows the day or hour when the end is coming. The messengers in heaven don't know, nor does the Son. Only the Father knows.

---

* 13:14 Literally abomination of desolation, Daniel 9:27; 11:31; 12:11
* 13:14 The earliest manuscripts omit this portion.
* 13:24-25 Isaiah 13:10; 34:4
* 13:26 Daniel 7:13

³³So be alert. Watch for it [and pray,]* for you never know when that time might approach.

³⁴This situation is like a man who went on a journey; when he departed, he left his servants in charge of the house. Each of them had his own job to do; and the man left the porter to stand at the door, watching. ³⁵So stay awake, because no one knows when the master of the house is coming back. It could be in the evening or at midnight or when the rooster crows or in the morning. ³⁶*Stay awake;* be alert so that when he suddenly returns, the master won't find you sleeping.

³⁷The teaching I am giving *the four of you* now is for everyone *who will follow Me:* stay awake, *and keep your eyes open.*

*M*any Christians have tried to use this chapter to predict exactly when Jesus will come and how the world will end. But to do that is to do exactly the opposite of what Jesus intended when He spoke these words. He made it very clear that He doesn't want anyone to use this description of signs to predict an exact time and date for His coming; even He Himself doesn't know that time and date, and no one else needs to know either. In fact, it's probably to our benefit not to know. Instead, the purpose was to warn them—and us—to stay ready and alert.

14 The Passover and the Feast of Unleavened Bread were two days away.

*F*or the Jews, no time of the year was more important than the Passover. Anyone who could make the journey came to Jerusalem during this celebration of the rescue of the Hebrew slaves from Egypt. As the city of Jerusalem filled with Jewish pilgrims and as the Roman soldiers stationed in Jerusalem stood ready to keep order, excitement and tension began to build.

The Jewish leaders—the chief priests and the scribes—gathered to discuss how they might secretly arrest Jesus and kill Him. But some were cautious.

Jewish Leaders: ²We can't do it during the festivals. It might create an uproar. *There is too much potential for trouble.*

³While Jesus was eating dinner in Bethany at the house of Simon the leper, a woman came into the house carrying an alabaster flask filled with a precious, sweet-smelling ointment made from spikenard. She came to Jesus, broke the jar, and gently poured out the perfume onto His head.

⁴Some of those around the table were troubled by this and grumbled to each other.

Dinner Guests: Why did she waste this precious ointment? ⁵We could have sold this ointment for almost a year's wages,* and the money could have gone to the poor!

Their *private concerns* turned to public criticism against her.

Jesus: ⁶Leave her alone. Why are you attacking her? She has done a good thing. ⁷The poor will always be with you, and you can show kindness to them whenever you want. But I won't always be with you. ⁸She has done what she could for Me—she has come to anoint My body and prepare it for burial. ⁹Believe Me when I tell you that this act of hers will be told in her honor as long as there are people who tell the good news.

*L*ike many people today, the disciples couldn't see any value in something apart from its practical purpose, and pouring so much perfume on Jesus was obviously a waste. We as

* 13:33 Some manuscripts omit this portion.
* 14:5 Literally, more than 300 denarii, Roman coins

Christians need to be careful about what we call wasteful or useless because in God's kingdom, small and apparently useless actions may have great meaning. Clearly this experience was a meaningful one for Jesus. The woman was demonstrating her love for Him with an abandon and an emotional commitment that few people had ever shown, and He appreciated her love and her faith. To Him, it was more than a gesture; it was a practical preparation for His imminent death and burial. No one else there could see what use her action was; but to Jesus, it was incredibly precious—so much so that He promised to make sure her action was never forgotten.

[10]It was after this that Judas Iscariot, one of the twelve, went to meet the chief priests with the intention of betraying Jesus to them. [11]When they heard what he proposed, they were delighted and promised him money. So from that time on, Judas *thought and waited and* sought an opportunity to betray Jesus.
[12]On the first day of the Feast of Unleavened Bread, the customary day when the Passover lamb is sacrificed, His disciples wondered *where they would celebrate the feast.*

Disciples: Where do You want us to go and make preparations for You to eat the Passover meal?

[13]So *again* He sent two of His disciples ahead and told them to watch for a man carrying a jar of water.

Jesus: Follow that man; [14]and wherever he goes in, say to the owner of the house, "The Teacher asks, 'Where is the guest room where I can eat the Passover meal with My disciples?'" [15]He will take you upstairs and show you a large room furnished and ready. Make our preparations there.

[16]So the two left and went into the city. All was as Jesus had told them, and they prepared the meal in the upper room. [17]That evening Jesus and the twelve arrived *and went into the upper room*; [18]and each reclined around the table, *leaning upon an elbow* as he ate.

Jesus: I tell you in absolute sincerity, one of you eating with Me tonight is going to betray Me.

[19]The twelve were upset. *They looked around at each other.*

Disciples (*one by one*): Lord, it's not I, is it?
Jesus: [20]It is one of you, the twelve—one of you who is dipping your bread in the same dish that I am.
[21]The Son of Man goes *to His fate.* That has already been predicted in the Scriptures. But still, it will be terrible for the one who betrays Him. It would have been better for him if he had never been born.

[22]As they ate, Jesus took bread, offered a blessing, and broke it. He handed the pieces to His disciples.

Jesus: Take this [and eat it].* This is My body.

[23]He took a cup *of wine*; and when He had given thanks *for it*, He passed it to them, and they all drank from it.

Jesus: [24]This is My blood, a covenant* poured out on behalf of many. [25]Truly I will never taste the fruit of the vine again until the day when I drink it new in the kingdom of God.

*T*he church has always regarded this moment of the Last Supper, a moment commemorated in services all over the world for thousands of years, as one of the most important

* 14:22 Some manuscripts omit this portion.
* 14:24 Some manuscripts read "the new covenant."

moments in Jesus' life. Exactly what Jesus meant by calling the bread and wine His body and blood has been debated over the centuries; the full meaning of that statement remains a mystery. Still, Christians have always agreed that whenever this moment is remembered and celebrated, the Liberating King is present with His people. By eating the bread and drinking the wine, we as believers participate not only in this supper but also in His death and resurrection because the bread is torn and the wine is poured, just as His body was torn and His blood poured out.

Sometimes it's easier for us to understand these mysteries in a spiritual and allegorical sense. But to do that too much is to forget the incarnation. Just as Jesus' physical body housed the Spirit of God, the physicality of the bread and wine has a spiritual significance. Otherwise, we wouldn't need to eat the bread and drink the wine to celebrate this moment—it would be enough for us to read the story and remember what happened. But we, too, are physical as well as spiritual; and our physical actions can have spiritual importance.

²⁶*After the meal,* they sang a psalm and went out *of the city* to the Mount of Olives.

Jesus: ²⁷All of you will desert Me tonight. It was written *by Zechariah,*

I will strike the shepherd,
and the sheep will scatter.*

²⁸But when I am raised up, I will go ahead of you to Galilee.

Peter (*protesting*): ²⁹It doesn't matter who else turns his back on You. I will never desert You.

Jesus: ³⁰Peter, mark My words. This very night before the cock crows twice, you will have denied Me three times.

Peter (*insisting*): ³¹*No, Teacher.* Even if it means that I have to die with You, I'll never deny You.

All the other disciples said similar things.

³²They came *at length* to a garden called Gethsemane.

Jesus: Stay here. I'm going *a little farther* to pray *and to think.*

³³He took Peter, James, and John with Him; *and as they left the larger group behind,* He became distressed and filled with sorrow.

Jesus: ³⁴My heart is so heavy; I feel as if I could die. Wait here for Me, and *stay awake to* keep watch.

³⁵He walked on a little farther. Then He threw Himself on the ground and prayed for deliverance from what was about to come.

Jesus: ³⁶Abba, Father, I know that anything is possible for You. Please take this cup away so I don't have to drink from it. But whatever happens, let Your will be done—not Mine.

³⁷He got up, went back *to the three,* and found them sleeping.

Jesus (*waking Peter*): Simon, are you sleeping? Couldn't you wait with Me for just an hour? ³⁸Stay awake, and pray that you aren't led into a trial of your own. *It's true*—even when the spirit is willing, the body can betray it.

³⁹He went away again, *threw Himself on the ground,* and prayed again the same prayer as before—*pleading with God but surrendering to His will.*

⁴⁰He came back and found the three asleep; *and when He woke them,* they didn't know what to say to Him.

* 14:27 Zechariah 13:7

⁴¹After He had gone away and prayed for a third time, *He returned to find them slumbering.*

Jesus: Again? Still sleeping and getting a good rest? Well, that's enough sleep. The time has come; the Son of Man is betrayed into the hands of sinners. ⁴²Get up now, and let's go. The one who is going to betray Me is close by.

*I*n the moments before Jesus' death, Mark gives us an intimate glimpse into Jesus' humanity. For anyone who's ever wondered whether Jesus really knew what it felt like to be human and afraid, this story proves He did. Jesus knew exactly what was about to happen to Him and exactly how bad it would be. We all know to some extent what it is like to face pain and suffering. We can't help but be afraid and plead with God to take it away. So, too, Jesus had been anticipating this suffering for a long time. And now that the time for it had come, He felt all the natural human emotions.

Most amazing of all is the prayer Jesus said in that moment: "Please take this cup away *so I don't have to drink from it.*" Even though, in His divine nature, He knew what was going to happen—what must happen—He still asked, in His human nature, for a reprieve. At the same time, He submitted His human desires and will to the plan of His Father: in order to experience fully what it means to be human, He had to go through even this—denying Himself and what He wanted to face certain torture and death.

⁴³Before He had finished talking, Judas (one of the twelve) approached with a large group of people—agents of the chief priests, scribes, and elders in Jerusalem armed with swords and clubs.
⁴⁴The signal they had arranged *was a kiss.* "Watch to see whom I kiss; He's the One," Judas had told them. "Arrest Him, and take Him into secure custody."

⁴⁵As soon as they arrived, Judas stepped forward.

Judas *(kissing Jesus)*: My Teacher.*

⁴⁶*Immediately* the soldiers grabbed Jesus and took Him into custody.
⁴⁷Now one *of the disciples* standing close by drew his sword and swung, cutting off the ear of a slave of *Caiaphas,* the high priest.

Jesus *(calling out)*: ⁴⁸Am I a thief or a bandit that you have to come armed with swords and clubs to capture Me? ⁴⁹I sat teaching in the temple every day with you. You could have taken Me at any time, but you never did. Let the Scriptures be fulfilled; *it will be as it was predicted.*

⁵⁰*When they saw the armed crowd take Jesus into custody,* the disciples fled. ⁵¹One of those following Jesus was a young man who was wearing nothing but a linen cloth. When people from the mob grabbed for him, ⁵²*he wriggled out of their grasp,* left them holding the cloth, and ran naked *into the night.*
⁵³They led Jesus off to see the high priest, *who had gathered a council of religious and civic leaders,* scribes, chief priests, and elders *to hear the evidence and render some decision regarding Jesus.*
⁵⁴Peter followed, at a safe distance, all the way into the courtyard of the high priest, and he sat down with the guards to warm himself at their fire. *He hoped no one would notice.*
⁵⁵The chief priests and other religious leaders called for witnesses against Jesus so they could execute Him, but things didn't turn out the way they had planned. ⁵⁶There were plenty of people willing to get up and accuse Jesus falsely, *distorting what Jesus had said or done*; but their testimonies disagreed with each other, *and the leaders were left with nothing.* ⁵⁷Some gave the following distorted testimony:

* 14:45 Literally, Rabbi

Witnesses: [58]We heard Him say, "I will destroy this temple that has been made by human hands, and in three days, I will build another that is not made by human hands."

[59]But even here the witnesses could not agree on exactly what He had said.
    [60]The high priest stood up and turned to Jesus.

High Priest: Do You have anything to say *in Your own defense*? What do You think of what all these people have said about You?

[61]But Jesus *held His peace and* didn't say a word.

> *T*he Liberator had come not as a conquering king but as a sacrificial lamb who would die without defending Himself.
>   He was accused of setting Himself in the place of God, but He was innocent of that accusation because He is God. But He does not defend Himself because His death protects from punishment the sinners who have made themselves like God ever since Adam ate the fruit in the garden—every single one of us.

High Priest: Are You the Liberating King, the Son of the Blessed One?
Jesus: [62]I am. *One day* you will see the Son of Man "sitting at His right hand, *in the place of honor and* power,"* and "coming in the clouds of heaven."*

[63]Then the high priest, *hearing Jesus quote the Scriptures supporting His authority,* tore his clothes.

High Priest (*to the council*): What else do we need to hear? [64]You have heard the blasphemy from His own lips. What do you have to say about that?

The verdict was unanimous—Jesus was guilty of a capital crime.

[65]*So the people began to humiliate Him.* Some even spat upon Him. Then He was blindfolded, and they slapped and punched Him.

People: *Come on, Prophet,* prophesy for us! *Tell us who just hit You.*

Then the guards took Him, beating Him as they did so.
    [66-67]While Peter was waiting by the fire outside, one of the servant girls of the high priest saw him.

Servant Girl: You were one of those men with Jesus of Nazareth.
Peter: [68]Woman, I don't know what you're talking about.

He left the fire, and as he went out into the gateway, [a cock crowed.]*
    [69]The servant girl saw him again.

Servant Girl: Hey, this is one of them. *One of those who followed Jesus.*
Peter: [70]No, I'm not one of them.

A little later, some of the other bystanders turned to Peter.

Bystander: Surely you're one of them. You're a Galilean. [We can tell by your accent.]*

[71]And then he swore an oath that if he wasn't telling the truth that he would be cursed.

Peter: *Listen,* I don't even know the man you're talking about.

[72]And as he said this, a cock crowed [a second time];* and Peter remembered what Jesus had told him: "Before the cock crows [twice],* you will have denied Me three times."
    He began to weep.

* 14:62 Psalm 110:1
* 14:62 Daniel 7:13
* 14:68 Some early manuscripts omit this portion.
* 14:70 Some early manuscripts omit this portion.
* 14:72 Some early manuscripts omit this portion.
* 14:72 Some early manuscripts omit "twice."

15 When morning came, the chief priests met in council with all the Jewish leaders. They bound Jesus, led Him away, and turned Him over to *the Roman governor,* Pilate.

Pilate *(after hearing them)*: [2]Are You the King of the Jews?
Jesus: You have said so.

[3]The chief priests went on to accuse Jesus of many things, but Jesus simply stood quietly.

Pilate: [4]Do You have anything to say? How do You respond to all these charges that have been made against You?

[5]But Jesus said nothing more, and Pilate was astonished.
    [6]Now it was his custom at that feast that Pilate should release one prisoner from custody, whomever the people most desired. [7]There was one rebel from those imprisoned for insurrection *against the Roman occupation.* He had committed murder during an uprising. His name was Barabbas. [8]A crowd had gathered *in front of Pilate's judgment seat* to request that Pilate follow his usual custom.
    [9]Pilate turned to them.

Pilate: Why don't I release to you the King of the Jews?

[10]He knew that the chief priests had delivered Jesus because they were threatened by Him, *not because Jesus was a criminal.*
    [11]But priests moved among the crowd and persuaded them to call for Barabbas instead.

Pilate: [12]Then what do you want me to do with the King of the Jews?
Crowd: [13]Crucify Him, *crucify Him!*

*C*rucifixion was a painful method of capital punishment often used by the Romans to publicly humiliate and make an example of rabble-rousers, and Pilate had sentenced many to die on Roman crosses.

[14]But now he called to them.

Pilate: Why? What has He done to deserve such a sentence?
Crowd *(crying all the louder)*: Crucify Him, *crucify Him!*

*B*arabbas was active and militant, a Jewish leader against the Roman occupiers. In one sense, the choice that the crowd was offered— to have either Jesus or Barabbas released—could be seen as a choice between two types of revolutions. Did they want a revolution of power, a revolution that was easily visible, a revolution that would conquer their enemies in a way they could understand? Or did they want a revolution of healing, a revolution of love, a revolution that brought the kingdom of God to earth in a mystical, transcendental, no less real way? In the heat of the moment, it's no wonder they made the choice they did. Who wants a gentle revolution in a time of war?

[15]When Pilate saw that he could not persuade the crowd to change its mind, he released Barabbas to them and had Jesus publicly whipped, *which was the normal prelude to crucifixion.* Then he had Jesus led away to be crucified. [16]The soldiers took Him into the headquarters of the governor; and the rest of the soldiers in the detachment gathered there, *hundreds of them.* [17]They put a purple robe on Him and made a crown of thorns that they forced onto His head, [18]and they began to cry out in mock salute.

Soldiers: Hail to the King of the Jews!

[19]For a long while they beat Him on the head with a reed, spat upon Him, and knelt down *as if to honor Him.* [20]When they had finished mocking Him, they stripped off His purple robe and put His own clothes back on Him. Then they took Him away to be executed.

²¹Along the way, they met a man from Cyrene, Simon (the father of Rufus and Alexander), who was coming in from the fields; and they ordered him to carry *the heavy crossbar of* the cross. ²²And so they came at last to *the execution site,* a hill called Golgotha, which means the "Place of a Skull."

²³The soldiers offered Jesus wine mixed with myrrh *to dull His pain,* but He refused it. ²⁴And so they crucified Him, divided up His clothes, and cast lots (*an ancient equivalent of rolling dice*) to see who would keep the clothes *they had stripped from Him.*

²⁵His crucifixion began about nine o'clock in the morning. ²⁶Over His head hung a sign that indicated the charge for which He was being crucified. It read, "THE KING OF THE JEWS." ²⁷On either side of Him were two insurgents *who also had received the death penalty.* [²⁸And the Hebrew Scripture was completed that said, "He was considered *just another* criminal."]*

²⁹Those passing by on their way into or out of Jerusalem insulted and ridiculed Him.

Some in the Crowd: So You're the One who was going to destroy the temple and rebuild it in three days? ³⁰Well, *if You're so powerful,* then why don't You rescue Yourself? Come on down from the cross!

Chief Priests and Scribes (*mocking Jesus among themselves*): ³¹He rescued others, but He can't rescue Himself. ³²Let the Liberator—the King of Israel—come down from the cross now, and we will see it and believe.

Even the insurgents who were being crucified next to Him taunted Him and reviled Him.

³³At noon, the day suddenly darkened for three hours across the entire land. ³⁴Sometime around three o'clock Jesus called out in a loud voice.

Jesus: Eloi, Eloi, lama sabachthani?

Jesus was speaking, as in the Psalms, "My God, My God, why have You turned Your back on Me?"*

³⁵Some of those standing nearby misunderstood Him.

Bystanders: Hey, He's calling for Elijah.

Many Jews believed that Elijah would return someday. ³⁶One of them filled a sponge with wine that had turned to vinegar and lifted it to Jesus' lips on a stick so He could drink.

Bystander: Let's see if Elijah will come to take Him down.

³⁷Then Jesus cried out with a loud voice, and He took His last breath.

³⁸At that moment, the curtain in the temple *that separated the most holy place from the rest of the temple* was torn in two from top to bottom.

*T*he tearing of the temple veil was tremendously significant as a sign of what Jesus' death had accomplished. The heart of the temple sanctuary was divided into two sections: the holy place and the most holy place. The most holy place was a chamber so sanctified that only the high priest could enter—and then only once a year. There God's presence lived on earth.

A long curtain or veil divided the two areas. The veil allowed access to God, and in some ways, protected an unholy people from a truly holy God. And so, when the veil in the temple ripped, it signified a complete and utter transformation in the relationship between God and humanity. It meant that impure people could now approach God—because they were protected by a better veil now, the veil of the Liberator's blood. It meant, too, that God was free to enter again and rule the world He made. Only God Himself could have ripped the curtain in two, opening the way for people to come into His presence.

* 15:28 Some manuscripts omit verse 28, a quote from Isaiah 53:12.
* 15:34 Psalm 22:1

³⁹The Roman Centurion, *the soldier in charge of the executions,* stood in front of Jesus, [heard His words,]* and saw the manner of His death.

Centurion: Surely this man was the Son of God!

⁴⁰Off in the distance, *away from the crowds,* stood some women *who knew and had followed Jesus,* including Mary Magdalene and Mary the mother of the younger James, Joses, and Salome. ⁴¹These were women who used to care for Him when He was in Galilee, and many other women who had followed Jesus to Jerusalem joined them.

⁴²Evening came. The crucifixion had taken place on preparation day, Friday, before the Jewish Sabbath began *at sundown.* ⁴³Joseph of Arimathea, a member of the ruling council who was also *a believer anxiously* waiting for the kingdom of God, went to Pilate and boldly asked for the body of Jesus.

⁴⁴Pilate could not believe Jesus was already dead, so he sent for the Centurion, ⁴⁵who confirmed it. Then Pilate gave Joseph permission to take the body.

⁴⁶Joseph had the body wrapped in a linen burial cloth he had purchased and laid Him in a tomb that had been carved out of rock. Then he had a stone rolled over the opening *to seal it.* ⁴⁷Mary Magdalene and Mary the mother of Joses were watching as the body was interred, *so they knew where His resting place was.*

16 ¹⁻²At the rising of the sun, after the Sabbath on the first day of the week, the two Marys and Salome brought sweet-smelling spices they had purchased to the tomb to anoint the body of Jesus. ³Along the way, they wondered to themselves how they would roll the heavy stone away from the opening. ⁴But when they arrived, *they were filled with wonder and awe; the tomb was open, and* the stone was already rolled away in spite of its weight and size.

⁵Stepping through the opening, they were startled to see a young man in a white robe seated inside and to the right.

Man in White: ⁶Don't be afraid. You came seeking Jesus of Nazareth, the One who was crucified. He is gone. He has risen. See the place where His body was laid. ⁷Go back, and tell Peter and His disciples that He goes before you into Galilee, just as He said. You will see Him there *when you arrive.*

⁸The women went out quickly; and when they were outside the tomb, they ran away trembling and astonished. Along their way, they didn't stop to say anything to anyone because they were too afraid.

*M*ark finishes his Gospel in the same way he begins it—quickly, without commentary or explanation. He also finishes it in a very humble way: it is the lowly women who take center stage in this greatest miracle of Jesus. The heavenly messenger sends the women with a commission to tell the disciples what has happened, making them the first preachers of the resurrection.

[⁹After He rose from the dead early on Sunday,* Jesus appeared first to Mary Magdalene, a woman out of whom He had cast seven demons. ¹⁰She brought this news back to all those who had followed Him and were still mourning and weeping, ¹¹but they refused to believe she had seen Jesus alive.

¹²After that, Jesus appeared in a different form to two of them as they walked through the countryside, ¹³and again the others did not believe it.

¹⁴The eleven did not believe until Jesus appeared to them all as they sat at dinner. He rebuked them for their hard hearts—for their lack of faith—because they had failed

---

* 15:39 Some early manuscripts omit this portion.
* 16:9 Literally, "the first day of the week." The new creation was underway.

to believe those witnesses who had seen Him after He had risen.

Jesus: ¹⁵Go out into the world and share the good news with all of creation. ¹⁶Anyone who believes this good news and is ceremonially washed* will be rescued, but anyone who does not believe it will be condemned. ¹⁷And these signs will follow those who believe: they will be able to cast out demons in My name, speak with new tongues, ¹⁸take up serpents, drink poison without being harmed, and lay their hands on the sick to heal them.

¹⁹After the Lord Jesus had charged the disciples in this way, He was taken up into heaven and seated at the right hand of God. ²⁰The disciples went out proclaiming the good news; and the risen Lord continued working through them, confirming every word they spoke with the signs He performed through them.]*

[And the women did everything they had been told to do, speaking to Peter and the other disciples. Later Jesus Himself commissioned the disciples to take this sacred and eternal message of salvation far to the East and the West.]*

The remaining eleven disciples took this command as their life's mission. According to tradition, all but one of them (John) were killed for their refusal to stop proclaiming the truth that Jesus was the Liberating King who had been crucified and who had arisen from the dead.

Perhaps the most compelling piece of evidence for the reality of Jesus' resurrection is the lives of the disciples themselves. They dedicated their lives—and their deaths—to the proclamation of this reality. If they hadn't been absolutely certain of the truth of Jesus' resurrection, then they wouldn't have dedicated their lives to announcing it to the world.

Their lives make up the next chapter in the good news of Jesus, the Liberating King.

* 16:16 Literally, immersed, to show repentance
* 16:9-20 are not contained in the earliest manuscripts. However, many manuscripts do contain these verses. It is likely the original Gospel ended in 16:8 or that the original ending was lost.
* 16:20 One manuscript concludes with these bracketed words.

Luke

Carefully researched account of God's Anointed
By Luke, the physician

This Third Gospel account was written by a physician named Luke. Unlike Matthew and John, Luke was not one of the twelve or an eyewitness to any of the life of Jesus. However, he was a close friend and traveling companion of the most influential missionary of the early church—Paul, the emissary.

Luke writes with a highly advanced literary style; his is the only Gospel that begins with a formal, literary introduction, a feature characteristic of many books written in his day. Luke clearly states the method and purpose for writing his Gospel. He has researched the life of Jesus thoroughly in order to correct the misinformation being spread about Him and to provide the most historically accurate report of Jesus' ministry possible. He wants to ensure believers that the Christian faith is rooted in fact, not fiction.

Luke addresses his Gospel to Theophilus, a Roman official, but it's clear that he also writes with a broader audience in mind. In fact, the name "Theophilus" means "one who loves God," suggesting his account is for anyone who loves God. Luke himself may have been an outsider to the Jewish faith. If so, he would be the only Gentile author in the New Testament. Luke traces Jesus' genealogy all the way back to Adam (rather than starting with Abraham, as Matthew does) in order to emphasize that Jesus is the Savior of all humanity, not just the Jewish Messiah. Connecting Jesus with Adam also emphasizes the humanity of Jesus, which is repeatedly stressed in this Gospel. Luke, of course, does not deny Jesus' divinity; he just shows how Jesus exemplified the perfect human being. Luke also focuses on the compassion of Jesus toward the disadvantaged members of society, including women, outcasts, and the poor. The Gospel according to Luke turns the world upside down and exalts the humble while humbling the exalted.

Luke's story of Jesus is the most comprehensive we have. It begins with the announcement of the birth of John the wandering prophet. It continues through Jesus' life, death, resurrection, and ascension into heaven. But Luke's story does not end there. After showing his readers how Jesus welcomed all people to follow Him, Luke gives the next chapter in his account of this movement Jesus began—the book known as the Acts of the Apostles. There he describes how the followers of Jesus moved beyond Jerusalem and the Jews and took the message of Jesus to the outsider nations across the known world.

We must try to imagine Luke's world. Fortunately, we have Luke's sequel to this Gospel to help us understand more about him. (It's called the Acts of the Apostles in many Bibles, and the two documents shed light on each other.) Tradition tells us that Luke is a physician, active in the early church in the years around A.D. 60. He travels widely with the Lord's emissary, Paul; so he is a sort of cosmopolitan person, multicultural in his sensitivities, understanding both Jewish culture and the broader Greco-Roman culture of the Roman Empire. As a physician, he is more educated than the average person of his day and has an impressive ability to relate to common people. Luke is especially skilled as a storyteller. Remember that Luke isn't presenting us with a theological treatise (as good and important as theological treatises may be); he's telling us the story of Jesus, gathered from many eyewitnesses. Based on the intended audience of his book (Theophilus—literally, God-lover, translated here as "those who love God"), presumably he wants to help people who love God to love Him even more by knowing what He has done through Jesus.

1 ¹⁻³For those who love God, several other people have already written accounts of what God has been bringing to completion among us, using the reports of the original eyewitnesses, those who were there from the start to witness the fulfillment of prophecy. Like those other servants who have recorded the messages, I present to you my carefully researched, orderly account of these new teachings. ⁴I want you to know that you can fully rely on the things you have been taught *about Jesus, God's Anointed One.*

⁵*To understand the life of Jesus, I must first give you some background history, events that occurred when* Herod ruled Judea *for the Roman Empire.* Zacharias was serving as a priest *in the temple in Jerusalem* those days as his fathers had before him. He was a member of the priestly division of Abijah (*a grandson of Aaron who innovated temple practices*), and his wife, Elizabeth, was of the priestly lineage of Aaron, *Moses' brother.* ⁶They were good and just people in God's sight, walking with integrity in the Lord's ways and laws. ⁷Yet they had this sadness. Due to Elizabeth's infertility, they were childless, and at this time, they were both quite old—*well past normal childbearing years.*

In the time of Jesus, Jewish life was centered in the temple in Jerusalem. The temple was staffed by religious professionals, what we might refer to as "clergy" today, called priests. They were responsible for the temple's activities—which included receiving religious pilgrims and their sacrifices (cattle, sheep, goats, and doves). Animal sacrifices sound strange to us—we often associate them with some kind of extremist cult. But in the ancient world, they were quite common. It may help, in trying to understand animal sacrifices, to remember that the slaughter of animals was a daily experience in the ancient world; it was part of any meal that included meat. So perhaps we should think of the sacrifice of animals as, first and foremost, a special meal. This meal brings together the Jewish family from near and far, seeking to affirm their connection to the one true and living God. Their gift of animals was their contribution to the meal. (The priests, by the way, were authorized to use the meat for the sustenance of their families.)

The presentation of the blood and meat of these sacrifices was accompanied by a number of prescribed rituals, performed by priests wearing pre-scribed ornamental clothing, according to a prescribed schedule. As the story continues, we see these solemn rituals interrupted in a most unprecedented way.

⁸One day Zacharias was chosen to perform his priestly duties in God's presence, according to the temple's normal schedule and routine. ⁹He had been selected from all the priests by the customary procedure of casting lots *for a once-in-a-lifetime oppor-tunity* to enter the sacred precincts of the temple. There he burned sweet incense, ¹⁰while outside a large crowd of people prayed. ¹¹*Suddenly Zacharias realized he was not alone:* a messenger of the Lord was there with him. The messenger stood just to the right of the altar of incense. ¹²Zach-arias was shocked and afraid, ¹³but the messenger reassured him.

Messenger: Zacharias, calm down! Don't be afraid!

Again and again, when people encounter God (or when they receive a message from God, often through a vision of a heavenly messen-ger), their first response is terror, and so they need to be calmed down before they can receive the message. We might think Zacharias shouldn't be surprised to hear from God; after all, he's a priest working in the temple. But priests didn't normally hear from God. Those who heard from God were called prophets, not priests.

Priests worked "the family busi-ness," so to speak. One became a priest by being born in a priestly family line. Prophets, on the other hand, arose unpredictably. Prophets had no special credentials except the message they carried. So Zacharias had no reason to believe his duties would be interrupted in this way.

Often in the biblical story, when people receive a message from God, after getting over the initial shock, they start asking questions. They push back; they doubt. However, when the word of the Lord comes to people, it doesn't turn them into unthinking zom-bies or robots; it doesn't override their individuality or capacity to think. Perhaps many of us in some way hear the voice of the Lord, but we don't realize it because we're expecting lightning flashes and a voice with a lot of reverb, a voice so overpowering that we are incapable of questioning and doubting it.

Messenger: Zacharias, your prayers have been heard. Your wife is going to have a son, and you will name him John. ¹⁴He will bring you great joy and happiness—and many will share your joy at John's birth.

¹⁵This son of yours will be a great man in God's sight. He will not drink alcohol in any form;* *instead of alcoholic spirits,* he will be filled with the Holy Spirit from the time he is in his mother's womb. ¹⁶*Here is his mission: he will stop many of the children of Israel in their misguided paths, and* he'll turn them around to follow the path to the Lord their God instead. ¹⁷Do you remember the prophecy about someone to come in the spirit and power of the prophet Elijah; someone who will turn the hearts of the parents back to their chil-dren;* someone who will turn the hearts of the disobedient to the mind-set of the just and good? Your son is the one who will fulfill this prophecy: he will be the Lord's forerunner, the one who will pre-pare the people and make them ready for God.

Zacharias: ¹⁸How can I be sure of what you're telling me? I am an old man, and

* 1:15 Numbers 6:3; Leviticus 10:9
* 1:17 Malachi 4:5-6

my wife is far past the normal age for women to bear children. *This is hard to believe!*

Messenger (*sternly*): [19]I am Gabriel, the messenger who inhabits God's presence. I was sent here to talk with you and bring you this good news. [20]Because you didn't believe my message, you will not be able to talk—not another word—until you experience the fulfillment of my words.

[21]Meanwhile the crowd at the temple wondered why Zacharias hadn't come out of the sanctuary yet. It wasn't normal for the priest to be delayed so long. [22]When at last he came out, *it was clear from his face something had happened in there.* He was making signs with his hands to give the blessing, but he couldn't speak. They realized he had seen some sort of vision. [23]When his time on duty at the temple came to an end, he went back home to his wife. [24]Shortly after his return, Elizabeth became pregnant. She avoided public contact for the next five months.

Elizabeth: [25]I have lived with the disgrace of being barren for all these years. Now God has looked on me with favor. When I go out in public *with my baby,* I will not be disgraced any longer.

[26]Six months later in Nazareth, a city in *the rural province of* Galilee, the heavenly messenger Gabriel made another appearance. This time the messenger was sent by God [27]to meet with a virgin named Mary, who was engaged to a man named Joseph, a descendant of King David himself. [28]The messenger entered her home.

Messenger: Greetings! You are favored, and the Lord is with you! [Among all women on the earth, you have been blessed.]*

[29]The heavenly messenger's words baffled Mary, and she wondered what type of greeting this was.

Messenger: [30]Mary, don't be afraid. You have found favor with God. [31]Listen, you are going to become pregnant. You will have a son, and you must name Him "Liberation," *or* Jesus.* [32]Jesus will become the greatest among men. He will be known as the Son of the Highest God. God will give Him the throne of His ancestor David, [33]and He will reign over the covenant family of Jacob forever.

Mary: [34]But I have never been with a man. How can this be possible?

Messenger: [35]The Holy Spirit will come upon you. The Most High will overshadow you. That's why this holy child will be known, *as not just your son, but also* as the Son of God. [36]*It sounds impossible,* but listen—you know your relative Elizabeth has been unable to bear children and is now far too old to be a mother. Yet she has become pregnant, *as God willed it.* Yes, in three months, she will have a son. [37]So the impossible is possible with God.

Mary (*deciding in her heart*): [38]Here I am, the Lord's humble servant. As you have said, let it be done to me.

> *L*uke is very interested in the ways that disadvantaged people of his day—the poor, the sick, and women—respond to God. Already we see a fascinating interplay between Zacharias's response to God and Mary's. If you compare them, you'll see how their responses are similar in some ways but very different in others.

And the heavenly messenger was gone. [39]Mary immediately got up and hurried to the hill country, in the province of Judah, [40-41]where her cousins Zacharias and

---

* 1:28 The earliest manuscripts omit this portion.
* 1:31 Through the naming of Jesus, God is speaking prophetically about the role Jesus will play in our salvation.

Elizabeth lived. When Mary entered their home and greeted Elizabeth, who felt her baby leap in her womb, Elizabeth was filled with the Holy Spirit.

Elizabeth (*shouting*): ⁴²You are blessed, *Mary*, blessed among all women, and the child you bear is blessed! ⁴³And blessed I am as well, that the mother of my Lord has come to me! ⁴⁴As soon as I heard your voice greet me, my baby leaped for joy within me. ⁴⁵How fortunate you are, Mary, for you believed that what the Lord told you would be fulfilled.

> *M*ary is deeply moved by these amazing encounters—first with the messenger and then with her cousin, Elizabeth. Mary's response can't be contained in normal prose; her noble soul overflows in poetry. And this poetry isn't simply religious; it has powerful social and political overtones. It speaks of a great reversal—what we might call a social, economic, and political revolution. To people in Mary's day, there would be little question as to what she was talking about. The Jewish people were oppressed by the Roman Empire, and to speak of a Liberator who would demote the powerful and rich and elevate the poor and humble would mean one thing: God was moving toward setting them free! Soon we'll hear Zacharias overflowing in poetry of his own.

Mary: ⁴⁶My soul lifts up the Lord!
⁴⁷My spirit celebrates God, my
    Liberator!
⁴⁸For though I'm God's humble
    servant,
    God has noticed me.
Now and forever,
    I will be considered blessed
        by all generations.
⁴⁹For the Mighty One has done
    great things for me;
    holy is God's name!

⁵⁰From generation to generation,
    God's lovingkindness endures
    for those who revere Him.

⁵¹God's arm has accomplished
        mighty deeds.
    The proud in mind and heart,
    God has sent away in disarray.
⁵²The rulers from their high
        positions of power,
    God has brought down low.
    And those who were humble and
        lowly,
    God has elevated with dignity.
⁵³The hungry—God has filled with
        fine food.
    The rich—God has dismissed
        with nothing in their hands.
⁵⁴To Israel, God's servant,
    God has given help,
⁵⁵As promised to our ancestors,
    remembering Abraham and his
        descendants in mercy forever.

⁵⁶Mary stayed with Elizabeth *in Judea* for the next three months and then returned to her home *in Galilee*.

⁵⁷When the time was right, Elizabeth gave birth to a son. ⁵⁸News about the Lord's special kindness to her had spread through her extended family and the community. Everyone shared her joy, *for after all these years of infertility, she had a son!* ⁵⁹*As was customary,* eight days after the baby's birth the time came for his circumcision *and naming.* Everyone assumed he would be named Zacharias, like his father.

Elizabeth (*disagreeing*): ⁶⁰No. We will name him John.

Her Relatives (*protesting*): ⁶¹That name is found nowhere in your family.

⁶²They turned to Zacharias and asked him what he wanted the baby's name to be.

⁶³He motioned for a tablet, and he wrote, "His name is John." Everyone was shocked *by this breach of family custom.* ⁶⁴*They were even more surprised when,* at that moment, Zacharias was able to talk again, and he shouted out praises to God.

65A sense of reverence spread through the whole community. In fact, this story was spread throughout the hilly countryside of Judea. 66People were certain that God's hand was on this child, and they wondered what sort of person John would turn out to be when he became a man.

67When Zacharias's voice was restored to him, he sang from the fullness of the Spirit a prophetic blessing.

Zacharias:

68May the Lord God of Israel be
    blessed indeed!
For God's intervention has
    begun,
and He has moved to rescue us,
    the people of God.
69And the Lord has raised up a
    powerful sign of liberation for
    us
from among the descendants of
    God's servant, *King* David.
70As was prophesied through the
    mouths of His holy prophets
    in ancient times:
71*God will* liberate us from our
    enemies
and from the hand of our
    oppressors!*

72-74God will show mercy promised to
    our ancestors,
upholding the abiding covenant
    He made with them,
Remembering the original vow He
    swore to Abraham,
from whom we are all
    descended.
God will grant us liberation from
    the grasp of our enemies
so that we may serve Him
    without fear all our days
75In holiness and justice, in the
    presence of the Lord.

76And you, my son, will be called the
    prophet of the Most High.
For you will be the one to
    prepare the way for the Lord*

77So that the Lord's people will
    receive knowledge of their
    liberation
through the forgiveness of their
    sins.

78All this will flow from the kind
    and compassionate mercy of
    our God.
A new day is dawning:
the Sunrise from the heavens
    will break through in our
    darkness,
79And those who huddle in night,
    those who sit in the shadow of
    death,
Will be able to rise and walk in the
    light,*
    guided in the pathway of peace.

80And John grew up and became strong in spirit. He lived in the wilderness, *outside the cities,* until the day came for him to step into the public eye in Israel.

2 Around the time *of Elizabeth's amazing pregnancy and John's birth, the emperor in Rome,* Caesar Augustus, required everyone in the Roman Empire to participate in a massive census— 2the first census since Quirinius had become governor of Syria. 3Each person had to go to his or her ancestral city to be counted.

Remember—for the original hearers of this story, this political background wasn't incidental: it was crucial to the story. Conquering nations in the ancient world worked in various ways. Some brutally destroyed and plundered the nations they conquered. Some took conquered people as slaves or servants. Other empires allowed the people to remain in their

* 1:71 Psalm 106:10
* 1:76 Isaiah 40:3
* 1:79 Isaiah 9:2

land and work as before, but with one major change: the conquered people would have to pay taxes to their rulers. The purpose of a census like the one Luke describes was to be sure that everyone was appropriately taxed and knew ultimately who was in charge.

4-5Mary's fiancé Joseph, from Nazareth in Galilee, had to participate in the census in the same way *everyone else did*. Because he was a descendant of *King* David, his ancestral city was Bethlehem, David's birthplace. Mary, who was now late in her pregnancy *which the messenger Gabriel had predicted*, 6accompanied Joseph. While in Bethlehem, she went into labor 7and gave birth to her firstborn son. She wrapped the baby in a blanket and laid Him in a feeding trough because the inn had no room for them.

8Nearby, in the fields outside of Bethlehem, a group of shepherds were guarding their flocks *from predators* in the darkness of night. 9Suddenly a messenger of the Lord stood in front of them, and the darkness was replaced by a glorious light—the shining light of God's glory. They were terrified!

Messenger: 10Don't be afraid! Listen! I bring good news, news of great joy, news that will affect all people everywhere. 11Today, in the city of David, a Liberator has been born for you! He is the promised Liberating King, the Supreme Authority! 12You will know you have found Him when you see a baby, wrapped in a blanket, lying in a feeding trough.

13At that moment, the first heavenly messenger was joined by thousands of other messengers—a vast heavenly choir. They praised God.

Heavenly Choir:
14To the highest heights of the universe, glory to God!
And on earth, peace among all people who bring pleasure to God!

15As soon as the heavenly messengers disappeared into heaven, the shepherds were buzzing with conversation.

Shepherds: Let's rush down to Bethlehem right now! Let's see what's happening! Let's experience what the Lord has told us about!

16So they ran into town, and *eventually* they found Mary and Joseph and the baby lying in the feeding trough. After they saw the baby, 17they spread the story of *what they had experienced and* what had been said to them about this child. 18Everyone who heard their story couldn't stop thinking about its meaning. 19Mary, too, pondered all of these events, treasuring each memory in her heart.

20The shepherds returned *to their flocks*, praising God for all they had seen and heard, and they glorified God for the way the experience had unfolded just as the heavenly messenger had predicted.

*R*emember what we said about Luke's fascination with disadvantaged people? Here we have it again. Jesus' first visitors were not ambassadors, dignitaries, or wealthy landowners. The first to pay Him homage were simple shepherds, minimum-wage workers in the ancient agrarian economy. They had little to no status in the world. They were the humble and the poor whom God was now raising up to receive heavenly messages and an audience with the great King. Watch for this theme as the story continues.

21Eight days after His birth, the baby was circumcised *in keeping with Jewish religious requirements,* and He was named Jesus, the name the messenger had given Him before His conception in Mary's womb. 22After Mary had observed the ceremonial days of *postpartum* purification required by Mosaic law, she and Joseph brought Jesus to the temple in Jerusalem to present Him to the Lord. ²³They were fulfilling the Lord's requirement that "every firstborn *Israelite* male will be dedicated to the Eternal One as holy."* ²⁴They also offered the sacrifice required by the law of the Lord, "two turtledoves or two young pigeons."*

²⁵*While fulfilling these sacred obligations at the temple,* they encountered a man in Jerusalem named Simeon. He was a just and pious man, anticipating the liberation of Israel from her troubles. He was a man in touch with the Holy Spirit. ²⁶The Holy Spirit had revealed to Simeon that he would not die before he had seen the Lord's Liberating King. ²⁷The Spirit had led him to the temple that day, and there he saw the child Jesus in the arms of His parents, who were fulfilling their sacred obligations. ²⁸Simeon took Jesus into his arms and blessed God.

Simeon:

²⁹Now, Lord *and King,* You can let me,
Your humble servant, die in peace.
³⁰You promised me that I would see with my own eyes
what I'm seeing now: Your liberation,
³¹Raised up in the presence of all peoples.
³²He is the light who reveals Your message to the other nations,
and He is the shining glory of Your *covenant* people, Israel.

³³His father and mother were stunned to hear Simeon say these things. ³⁴Simeon went on to bless them both, and to Mary in particular he gave predictions.

Simeon: Listen, this child will make many in Israel rise and fall. He will be a significant person whom many will oppose. ³⁵*In the end,* He will lay bare the secret thoughts of many hearts. And a sword will pierce even your own soul, Mary.

³⁶At that very moment, an elderly woman named Anna stepped forward. Anna was a prophetess, the daughter of Phanuel, of the tribe of Asher. She had been married for seven years *before her husband died* ³⁷and a widow to her current age of 84 years. She was *deeply devoted to the Lord,* constantly in the temple, fasting and praying. ³⁸When she approached *Mary, Joseph, and Jesus,* she began speaking out thanks to God, and she continued spreading the word about Jesus to all those who shared her hope for the liberation of Jerusalem.

³⁹After fulfilling their sacred duties according to the law of the Lord, Mary and Joseph returned *with Jesus* to their own city of Nazareth in the province of Galilee. ⁴⁰There Jesus grew up, maturing in physical strength and increasing in wisdom, and the grace of God rested on Him.

⁴¹Every year *during Jesus' childhood,* His parents traveled to Jerusalem for the Passover celebration. ⁴²When Jesus was 12, He made the journey with them. ⁴³They spent several days there, participating in the whole celebration. When His parents left for home, Jesus stayed in Jerusalem, but Joseph and Mary were not aware. ⁴⁴They assumed Jesus was elsewhere in the caravan *that was traveling together.* After they had already traveled a full day's journey *toward home,* they began searching for Him among their friends and relatives. ⁴⁵When no one had seen the boy, Mary and Joseph rushed back to Jerusalem and searched for Him.

⁴⁶After three days of separation, they finally found Him—sitting among a group of religious teachers in the temple, *deep in the give-and-take of serious conversation—* asking them questions, listening to their answers, *and answering the questions they asked Him.* ⁴⁷Everyone was surprised and impressed that a 12-year-old boy could have such deep understanding and could answer questions *with such wisdom.*

⁴⁸His parents, of course, had a different reaction.

Mary: Son, why have You treated us this way? Listen, Your father and I have been

* 2:23 Exodus 13:2,12,15
* 2:24 Leviticus 5:11; 12:8

sick with worry *for the last three days, wondering where You were,* looking everywhere for You.

Jesus: [49]Why did you need to look for Me? Didn't you know that I must be working for My Father?

$\mathcal{W}$e are told so little about Jesus' life between His birth and the age of 30. But this one episode tells us so much. First, it tells us that Jesus' family life was a lot like our own—full of mishaps and misunderstandings. Second, it tells us that as Jesus entered young adulthood, He began manifesting an extraordinary sense of identity. (Remember, a 12-year-old wasn't "just a kid" in those days—he was becoming a man.) He wasn't just "Mary's boy" or "Joseph's stepson." He had a direct relationship with God as His Father, and He knew that His life would follow a path of working for God.

[50]Neither Mary nor Joseph really understood what He meant by this. [51]Jesus went back to Nazareth with them and was obedient to them. His mother continued to store these memories like treasures in her heart. [52]And Jesus kept on growing—in wisdom, in physical stature, in favor with God, and in favor with others.

3 Our story continues 15 years after Tiberius Caesar had begun his reign over the empire. Pilate was governor of Judea, Herod ruled Galilee, his brother Philip ruled Ituraea and Trachonitis, and Lysanias ruled Abilene.

$\mathcal{M}$ore than any other Gospel writer, Luke wants to situate the story of the Liberating King in what we might call "secular history." In particular, he gives us details of the emperor, governor, and other client rulers. With a toxic mixture of cruelty and might, these authorities lorded it over the common people. Yet these high and mighty are—if you remember Mary's poem—destined to be brought down in the presence of a new kind of king and a new kind of kingdom. Jesus will exercise His authority in a radically different way—not through domination and violence, but through love, healing, compassion, and service.

[2]*In Jerusalem* Annas and Caiaphas were high priests in the temple. And in those days, out in the wilderness, John (son of Zacharias) received a message from God.

[3]John brought this divine message to all those who came to the Jordan River. He preached that people should be ritually cleansed* as an expression of changed lives for the forgiveness of sins. [4]As Isaiah the prophet had said,

A solitary voice is calling:
"Go into the wilderness;
    prepare the road for the Eternal
        One's journey.
In the desert, repair and straighten
    every mile of our True God's
        highway.
[5]Every low place will be lifted
    and every high mountain,
    every hill will be humbled;
The crooked road will be
        straightened out
    and rough places ironed out
        smooth;
[6]Then the radiant glory of the Eternal
    One will be revealed.
All flesh together will take it in."*

[7]In fulfillment of those words, crowds streamed out *from the villages and towns* to be ritually washed* by John *at the Jordan.*

$\mathcal{Y}$ou'll remember that Zacharias was a priest who served in Jerusalem at the temple. Among their other duties, priests would perform

---

* 3:3 Literally, immersed, to show repentance
* 3:4-6 Isaiah 40:3-5
* 3:7 Literally, immersed, to show repentance

ritual cleansings necessary for Jewish worshipers who had become ceremonially unclean—perhaps through contact with outsiders (non-Jewish people), perhaps through contact with blood or a dead body, perhaps through a physical illness. Near the temple, archaeologists have found many of the baths or pools that were used for these ritual cleansings. But notice that when John appears on the scene, he hasn't followed in his father's footsteps. He's not fulfilling the role of the priest, but rather of the prophet. He works far outside of Jerusalem, and he baptizes people in the Jordan River, not near the temple. It's as if John is performing a symbolic drama: If you want to be in tune with God, the temple and its normal routines can't help you anymore. Instead of being cleansed there, you should come out to this radical preacher and let him cleanse you in the river. And his message, as you're about to see, isn't a polite, tame message. It's fiery and intense! God isn't interested in just routine religion. He wants changed lives!

John the Preacher: You bunch of venomous snakes! Who told you that you could escape God's coming wrath? [8]Don't just talk of turning to God; you'd better bear the authentic fruit of a changed life. Don't take pride in your religious heritage, saying, "We have Abraham for our father!" Listen—God could turn these rocks into children of Abraham!

[9]*Face the facts, people! God is fed up with religious talk. God wants you to bear fruit!* If you don't produce good fruit, then you'll be chopped down like a fruitless tree and made into firewood. God's ax is taking aim and ready to swing!

People: [10]What shall we do *to perform works from changed lives*?

John the Preacher: [11]The person who has two shirts must share with the person who has none. And the person with food must share with the one in need.

[12]Some tax collectors were among those in the crowd seeking ritual washing.*

Tax Collectors: Teacher, what kind of fruit is God looking for from us?

John the Preacher: [13]Stop overcharging people. Only collect what you must turn over to the Romans.

Soldiers: [14]What about us? What should we do *to show true change*?

John the Preacher: Don't extort money from people by throwing around your power or making false accusations, and be content with your pay.

[15]John's bold message seized public attention, and many began wondering if John might himself be the Liberating King *promised by God*.

John the Preacher: [16]*I am not the One.* I ritually cleanse* you with water, but One is coming—One far more powerful than I, One whose sandals I am not worthy to untie—who will radically purify* you with the Holy Spirit and with fire. [17]He is coming *like a farmer at harvesttime*, tools in hand to separate the wheat from the chaff. He will burn the chaff with unquenchable fire, and He will gather the genuine wheat into His barn.

[18]He preached with many other provocative figures of speech and so conveyed God's message to the people—*the time had come to rethink everything.* [19]*But John's public preaching ended when* he confronted Herod, the ruler of Galilee, for his many corrupt deeds, including *taking* Herodias, the ruler's sister-in-law, *as his own wife*. [20]Herod responded by throwing John into prison.

[21]*But before John's imprisonment, when he was still preaching and* ritually cleansing* the people in the Jordan River, Jesus

---

* 3:12 Literally, immersion, an act to show repentance
* 3:16 Literally, immerse, to show repentance
* 3:16 Literally, immerse
* 3:21 Literally, immersing, to show repentance

also came to him to be ritually cleansed. As Jesus prayed, the heavens opened, 22and the Holy Spirit came upon Him in a physical manifestation that resembled a dove. A voice echoed out from heaven.

Voice from Heaven: You are My Son,* the Son I love, and in You I take great pleasure.

*W*hat would it mean for Jesus to be baptized by John? If John's baptism symbolizes a rejection of the religious establishment centered in the temple in Jerusalem, then Jesus' choice to be baptized by John would symbolize that He was aligned with this radical preacher. Jesus wasn't simply coming to strengthen or even renew the centers of power. Instead, He was joining John at the margins to be part of something wild and new that God was doing. And the vivid manifestation of God's pleasure—the dovelike appearance and the voice from heaven—would suggest that even though Jesus was in a sense aligning Himself with John, John was simply the opening act and Jesus was the main attraction. The choreography between John's work and Jesus' work will continue, but from this point on, Jesus is in the center of the story.

23At this, the launch of Jesus' ministry, Jesus was about 30 years old.

He was assumed to be the son of Joseph, the son of Eli, 24the son of Matthat, the son of Levi, the son of Melchi, the son of Jannai, the son of Joseph, 25the son of Mattathias, the son of Amos, the son of Nahum, the son of Hesli, the son of Naggai, 26the son of Maath, the son of Mattathias, the son of Semein, the son of Josech, the son of Joda, 27the son of Joanan, the son of Rhesa, the son of Zerubbabel, the son of Shealtiel, the son of Neri, 28the son of Melchi, the son of Addi, the son of Cosam, the son of Elmadam, the son of Er, 29the son of Joshua, the son of Eliezer, the son of Jorim, the son of Matthat, the son of Levi, 30the son of Simeon, the son of Judah, the son of Joseph, the son of Jonam, the son of Eliakim, 31the son of Melea, the son of Menna, the son of Mattatha, the son of Nathan, the son of David, 32the son of Jesse, the son of Obed, the son of Boaz, the son of Salmon, the son of Nahshon, 33the son of Amminadab, the son of Admin, the son of Ram, the son of Hezron, the son of Perez, the son of Judah, 34the son of Jacob, the son of Isaac, the son of Abraham, the son of Terah, the son of Nahor, 35the son of Serug, the son of Reu, the son of Peleg, the son of Heber, the son of Shelah, 36the son of Cainan, the son of Arphaxad, the son of Shem, the son of Noah, the son of Lamech, 37the son of Methuselah, the son of Enoch, the son of Jared, the son of Mahalaleel, the son of Cainan, 38the son of Enosh, the son of Seth, the son of Adam, the son of God.

*W*hile genealogies may seem tedious to us, for people in many cultures (including Luke's), genealogies are important and meaningful. They remind us where we come from and give us a sense of identity and history. Luke places Jesus in the mainstream of biblical history, connected to King David, Abraham, Noah, and Adam. Since all humanity is seen as Adam's descendants, Luke shows how Jesus is connected to and relevant for all people. By connecting Jesus with Adam, and ultimately with God, Luke may also be suggesting that in Jesus God is launching a new creation and a new humanity, with Jesus as the new Adam. Unlike the first Adam, though, Jesus will be completely faithful to God, as the next episode will make clear. Perhaps echoing Adam and Eve being tempted by the serpent in the garden,* Luke moves from the stories of Jesus' beginnings to His temptation.

* 3:22 Psalm 2:7
* **Note** Genesis 3:1-7

4 When Jesus returned from the Jordan River, He was full of the Holy Spirit, and the Holy Spirit led Him away *from the cities and towns* and out into the desert.

²For 40 days, the Spirit led Him from place to place in the desert, and while there, the devil tempted Jesus. Jesus was fasting, eating nothing during this time, and at the end, He was terribly hungry. ³At that point, the devil came to Him.

Devil: Since You're the Son of God, You don't need to be hungry. Just tell this stone to transform itself into bread.

Jesus: ⁴It is written *in the Hebrew Scriptures,* "People need more than bread to live."*

⁵Then the devil gave Jesus a vision. It was as if He traveled around the world in an instant and saw all the kingdoms of the world at once.

Devil: ⁶All these kingdoms, all their glory, I'll give to You. They're mine to give because this whole world has been handed over to me. ⁷If You just worship me, then everything You see will all be Yours. All Yours!

Jesus: ⁸[Get out of My face, Satan!]* The Hebrew Scriptures say, "Worship and serve the Eternal One your God—only Him—and nobody else."*

⁹Then the devil led Jesus to Jerusalem, and he transported Jesus to stand upon the pinnacle of the temple.

Devil: Since You're the Son of God, just jump. Just throw Yourself into the air. ¹⁰You keep quoting the Hebrew Scriptures. They themselves say,

He will put His heavenly
    messengers in charge of You,
    to keep You safe in every way.

¹¹And,

They will hold You up in their hands
    so that You do not smash Your
    foot against a stone.*

Jesus: ¹²Yes, but the *Hebrew* Scriptures also say, "You will not presume on God; you will not test the Lord, the One True God."*

¹³The devil had no more temptations to offer *that day,* so he left Jesus, preparing to return at some other opportune time.

¹⁴Jesus returned to Galilee in the power of the Holy Spirit, and soon people across the region had heard news of Him. ¹⁵He would regularly go into their synagogues and teach. His teaching earned Him the respect and admiration of everyone who heard Him.

¹⁶He eventually came to His hometown, Nazareth, and did there what He had done elsewhere *in Galilee*—entered the synagogue and stood up to read *from the Hebrew Scriptures.*

¹⁷The *synagogue attendant* gave Him the scroll of the prophet Isaiah, and Jesus unrolled it to the place where Isaiah had written these words:

¹⁸The Spirit of the Lord the Eternal
        One is on Me.
Why? Because the Eternal
        designated Me
    to be His representative to the
        poor, to preach good news to
        them.
He sent Me to tell those who are
        held captive that they can now
        be set free,
    and to tell the blind that they can
        now see.
He sent Me to liberate those held
        down by oppression.

---

* 4:4 Deuteronomy 8:3
* 4:8 Many early manuscripts omit this portion.
* 4:8 Deuteronomy 6:13; 10:20
* 4:10-11 Psalm 91:11-12
* 4:12 Deuteronomy 6:16

[19]*In short, the Spirit is upon Me to proclaim that now is the time; this is the jubilee season of the Eternal One's grace.**

> *L*uke's original hearers didn't divide the world into sacred/secular, religious/political as we often do. For them, life was integrated. And for them, these words from Isaiah would have a powerful and (in our terminology) "political" meaning: because they saw themselves as oppressed by the Roman occupation, Jesus' words would suggest that His "good news" described a powerful change about to come—a change that would liberate the people from their oppression. His fellow Jews had long been waiting for a liberator (or savior) to free them from Roman oppression. Jesus' next words would tell them that their hopes were about to be fulfilled. But then, just as people speak well of Jesus, you'll see how He lets them know that their expectations aren't in line with God's plans. He tells them not to expect God to fit into their boxes and suggests the unthinkable: that God cares for the Gentiles, the very people who are oppressing them! They aren't too pleased by this, as you'll soon see.

[20]Jesus rolled up the scroll and returned it to the synagogue attendant. Then He sat down, *as a teacher would do,* and all in the synagogue focused their attention on Jesus, *waiting for Him to speak.* [21]He told them that these words from the Hebrew Scriptures were being fulfilled then and there, in their hearing. *His purpose was to fulfill what Isaiah had described.*

[22]At first everyone was deeply impressed with the gracious words that poured from Jesus' lips. Everyone spoke well of Him and was amazed that He could say these things.

Everyone: Wait. This is only the son of Joseph, right?

Jesus: [23]You're about to quote the old proverb to Me, "Doctor, heal yourself!" Then you're going to ask Me to prove Myself to you by doing the same miracles I did in Capernaum. [24]But face the truth: hometowns always reject their homegrown prophets.

[25]Think back to the prophet Elijah. There were many needy Jewish widows in *his homeland,* Israel, when a terrible famine persisted there for three and a half years. [26]Yet the only widow God sent Elijah to help was *an outsider* from Zarephath in Sidon.*

[27]It was the same with the prophet Elisha. There were many Jewish lepers in his homeland, but the only one he healed—Naaman—*was an outsider* from Syria.*

[28]The people in the synagogue became furious when He said these things. [29]They seized Jesus, took Him to the edge of town, and pushed Him right to the edge of the cliff on which the city was built. They would have pushed Him off and killed Him, [30]but He passed through the crowd and went on His way.

[31-33]Next He went to Capernaum, another Galilean city. Again He was *in the synagogue* teaching on the Sabbath, and as before, the people were enthralled by His words. He had a way of saying things— a special authority, *a unique power.*

In attendance that day was a man with a demonic spirit.

Demon-Possessed Man *(screaming at Jesus)*: [34]*Get out of here!* Leave us alone! What's Your agenda, Jesus of Nazareth? Have You

* 4:18-19 Isaiah 61:1-2
* 4:26 1 Kings 17:8-16
* 4:27 2 Kings 5:1-14

come to destroy us? I know who You are: You're the Holy One, the One sent by God!

Jesus (*firmly rebuking the demon*): ³⁵Be quiet. Get out of that man!

Then the demonic spirit immediately threw the man into a fit, and he collapsed right there in the middle of the synagogue. It was clear the demon had come out, and the man was completely fine after that. ³⁶Everyone was shocked to see this, and they couldn't help but talk about it.

Synagogue Members: What's this about? What's the meaning of this message? Jesus speaks with authority, and He has power to command demonic spirits to go away.

³⁷The excitement about Jesus spread into every corner of the surrounding region.

³⁸*Picture this:*

Jesus then leaves that synagogue and goes over to Simon's place. Simon's mother-in-law is there. She is sick with a high fever. Simon's family asks Jesus to help her.

³⁹Jesus stands over her, *and just as He had rebuked the demon,* He rebukes the fever, and the woman's temperature returns to normal. She feels so much better that she gets right up and cooks them all a big meal.

⁴⁰By this time, it's just before nightfall, and as the sun sets, *groups of families, friends, and bystanders come* until a huge crowd has gathered. Each group has brought along family members or friends who are sick with any number of diseases. One by one, Jesus lays His hands on them and heals them. ⁴¹On several occasions, demonic spirits are expelled from these people, after shouting at Jesus, "You are the Son of God!"

Jesus always rebukes them and tells them to be quiet. They know He is the Liberating King, *but He doesn't want to be acclaimed in this way.*

⁴²The next morning, Jesus sneaks away. He finds a place away from the crowds, but soon they find Him. The crowd tries their best to keep Him from leaving.

Jesus: ⁴³No, I cannot stay. I need to preach the kingdom of God to other cities too. This is the purpose I was sent to fulfill.

⁴⁴So He proceeds from synagogue to synagogue across Judea,* preaching His message *of the kingdom of God.*

The essential message of Jesus can be summed up this way: the kingdom of God is available to everyone, starting now. When Jesus refers to the kingdom of God, He doesn't mean something that happens after we die, far off in heaven; He equates the kingdom of God with God's will being done on earth as it is in heaven. So the kingdom of God is life as God intends it to be—life to the full, life in peace and justice, life in abundance and love. Individuals enter the Kingdom when they enter into a relationship with the Liberating King, when they trust Him enough to follow His ways. But make no mistake, the Kingdom is about more than our individual lives; it is about the transformation and renewal of all God has created. It may start with our individual responses, but it doesn't stop there.

Jesus describes His purpose as proclaiming this message. But Jesus not only expresses His message of the kingdom of God in words, He also dramatizes it in deeds. Luke calls these amazing deeds "signs and wonders," suggesting that these actions have symbolic meaning, which is *sign*ificant, and are *wonder*ful, which means they fill people with awe and *wonder*. In the coming chapters, as you encounter these signs and wonders, try to feel the wonder that the original eyewitnesses would have felt, and then ponder their significance as signs of the kingdom of God.

* 4:44 Other early manuscripts read "Galilee."

5 *Picture this scene:*
On the banks of Gennesaret Lake, a huge crowd, Jesus in the center of it, presses in to hear His message from God. ²Off to the side, fishermen are washing their nets, leaving their boats unattended on the shore.

³Jesus gets into one of the boats and asks its owner, Simon, to push off *and anchor* a short distance from the beach. Jesus sits down and teaches the people standing on the beach.

⁴After speaking for a while, Jesus speaks to Simon.

Jesus: Move out into deeper water, and drop your nets to see what you'll catch.
Simon *(perplexed):* ⁵Master, we've been fishing all night, and we haven't caught even a minnow. But . . . all right, I'll do it if You say so.

⁶Simon then gets his fellow fishermen to help him let down their nets, *and to their surprise,* the water is bubbling with thrashing fish—*a huge school.* The strands of their nets start snapping under the weight of the catch, ⁷so the crew shouts to the other boat to come out and give them a hand. They start scooping fish out of the nets and into their boats, and before long, their boats are so full of fish they almost sink!

⁸⁻¹⁰Simon's fishing partners, James and John (two of Zebedee's sons), along with the rest of the fishermen, see this incredible haul of fish. They're all stunned, especially Simon. He comes close to Jesus and kneels in front of His knees.

Simon: I can't take this, Lord. I'm a sinful man. You shouldn't be around the likes of me.
Jesus: Don't be afraid, Simon. From now on, I'll ask you to bring Me people instead of fish.

¹¹The fishermen haul their fish-heavy boats to land, and they leave everything to follow Jesus.

¹²Another time in a city nearby, a man covered with skin lesions comes along. As soon as he sees Jesus, he prostrates himself.

Leper: Lord, if You wish to, You can heal me of my disease.

¹³Jesus reaches out His hand and touches the man, *something no one would normally do for fear of being infected or of becoming ritually unclean.*

Jesus: I want to heal you. Be cleansed!

Immediately the man is cured. ¹⁴Jesus tells him firmly not to tell anyone about this.

Jesus: Go, show yourself to the priest, and do what Moses commanded by making an appropriate offering to celebrate your cleansing. This will prove to everyone what has happened.

¹⁵Even though Jesus said not to talk about what happened, soon every conversation was consumed by these events. The crowds swelled even larger as people went to hear Jesus preach and to be healed of their many afflictions. ¹⁶Jesus repeatedly left the crowds, though, stealing away into the wilderness to pray.

¹⁷One day Jesus was teaching *in a house,* and the healing power of the Lord was with Him. Pharisees and religious scholars were sitting and listening, having come from villages all across the regions of Galilee and Judea and from *the holy city of* Jerusalem.

¹⁸Some men came *to the house,* carrying a paralyzed man on his bed pallet. They wanted to bring him in and present him to Jesus, ¹⁹but the house was so packed with people that they couldn't get in. So they climbed up on the roof and pulled off some roof tiles. Then they lowered the man *by ropes* so he came to rest right in front of Jesus.

²⁰In this way, their faith was visible to Jesus.

Jesus *(to the man on the pallet):* My friend, all your sins are forgiven.

21The Pharisees and religious scholars were offended at this. They turned to one another and asked questions.

Pharisees and Religious Scholars: Who does He think He is? Wasn't that blasphemous? Who can pronounce that a person's sins are forgiven? Who but God alone?

Jesus (*responding with His own question*): 22Why are your hearts full of questions? 23Which is easier to say, "Your sins are forgiven," or, "Get up and walk"? 24Just so you'll know that the Son of Man is fully authorized to forgive sins on earth (He turned to the paralyzed fellow *lying on the pallet*), I say, get up, take your mat, and go home.

25Then, right in front of their eyes, the man stood up, picked up his bed, and left to go home—full of praises for God! 26Everyone was stunned. They couldn't help but feel awestruck, and they praised God too.

People: We've seen extraordinary things today.

*T*he miracles Jesus performs come in all types. As we've seen, He heals the sick. He frees the oppressed. He shows His power over nature. He will even raise the dead. But as this story shows, one of the greatest miracles of all is forgiveness. To have our sins forgiven—to start over again, to have God separate us from our mistakes and moral failures, to lift the weight of shame and guilt—this may well be the weightiest evidence that the Liberating King is on the move. The kingdom of God doesn't throw all guilty people in jail; it doesn't execute every one of us who have made mistakes or tell us we're just getting what we deserve. Instead, it brings us forgiveness, reconciliation, a new start, a second chance. In this way, it mobilizes us so we can have a new future.

We've seen how Jesus communicates the message of the Kingdom through words and through signs and wonders. Now we'll also see how Jesus embodies the message in the way He treats people, including outcasts like Levi. As a tax collector, Levi is a Jew who works for the Romans, the oppressors, the enemies. No wonder tax collectors were despised! Notice how Jesus treats this compromiser: He doesn't leave him paralyzed in his compromised position; He invites him—like the paralyzed man we just met—to get up and walk, and to walk in a new direction toward a new King and Kingdom.

27Some time later, Jesus walked along the street and saw a tax collector named Levi sitting in his tax office.

Jesus: Follow Me.

28And Levi did. He got up from his desk, left everything (*just as the fishermen had*), and followed Jesus.

29Shortly after this, Levi invited his many friends and associates, including many tax collectors, to his home for a *large* feast in Jesus' honor. Everyone sat at a table together.

*W*hen Jesus healed the paralyzed man, we had our first encounter with a group called the Pharisees. Now they're back again, and they'll be with us through the rest of the story. Pharisaism was a religious movement, consisting of lay people (not clergy) who shared a deep commitment to the Hebrew Scriptures and traditions. They felt that the Jewish people had not yet been liberated from the Romans because of their tolerance of sin. There were too many drunks, too many prostitutes, and too many gluttons. "If we could just get these sinners to change their ways," they felt, "then God would send the One who will liberate us." You can imagine how angry they would be at Jesus for not just forgiving sins (as He did with the paralyzed man) but also for eating with sinners! After all, to eat with people meant that you accepted them. The kind of Liberator they expected would hate and destroy sinners, not forgive them and enjoy their company!

30The Pharisees and their associates, the religious scholars, got the attention of some of Jesus' disciples.

Pharisees (in low voices): What's wrong with you? Why are you eating and drinking with tax collectors and other immoral people?

Jesus (answering for the disciples): 31Healthy people don't need a doctor, but sick people do. 32I haven't come for the pure and upstanding; I've come to call *notorious* sinners to rethink their lives and turn to God.

Pharisees: 33Explain to us why You and Your disciples are so commonly found partying like this, when our disciples—and even the disciples of John—are known for fasting rather than feasting, and for saying prayers rather than drinking *wine*.

Jesus: 34Imagine there's a wedding going on. Is that the time to tell the guests to ignore the bridegroom and fast? 35Sure, there's a time for fasting—when the bridegroom has been taken away. 36Look, nobody tears up a new garment to make a patch for an old garment. If he did, the new patch would shrink and rip the old, and the old garment would be worse off than before. 37And nobody takes freshly squeezed juice and puts it into old, stiff wineskins. If he did, the fresh wine would make the old skins burst open, and both the wine and the wineskins would be ruined. 38New demands new—new wine for new wineskins. 39Anyway, those who've never tasted the new wine won't know what they're missing; they'll always say, "The old wine is good enough for me!"

6 1-2One Sabbath Day,* some Pharisees confronted Jesus again. This time, they saw the disciples picking some grain as they walked through the fields. The disciples would dehusk the grain by rubbing the kernels in their hands, and then they would eat it raw.

Pharisees: Don't You know the sacred law says You can't harvest and mill grain on the Sabbath Day—the day on which all work is forbidden? Why do You think You can ignore the sacred law?

Jesus, as was His habit, responded to their question with a question of His own. The Pharisees think they have God all figured out. They claim to be experts in the sacred writings—the Scriptures. But Jesus doesn't fit in with their assumptions and expectations, and He doesn't submit to their presumed expertise. So they are constantly criticizing Him and trying to trap Him in some obvious wrongdoing or unorthodoxy. But notice how Jesus responds. He doesn't answer their questions; instead, He asks them questions. He seems to decide that the best way to help them is simply by trying to challenge them to think, to question their assumptions, to open them up to new possibilities, to see things from a higher or deeper perspective. For example, they argue about what is permissible on the Sabbath Day (the seventh day, the day of rest); Jesus gets them thinking about the deeper purpose of the Sabbath Day, as you'll see in the next episode.

Jesus: 3Speaking of the sacred law, haven't you ever read about the time when David and his companions were hungry? 4Don't you remember how he went into the

* 6:1 Other manuscripts read "On the second Sabbath after the first."

house of God and took the sacred bread of the presence—which, you may recall, only the priests were lawfully permitted to eat? Remember that he not only ate it, but he also gave it to his companions?* ⁵Likewise, the Son of Man has authority over the Sabbath.

⁶On another Sabbath, Jesus entered the synagogue and taught there. In the congregation was a man who had a deformed right hand. ⁷The religious scholars and Pharisees watched Jesus; they suspected that He might try to perform a healing on that day, which they would use as evidence to convict Him of Sabbath-breaking.

⁸Jesus knew about their plan, and He told the man with the deformed hand to come and stand in front of everyone. The man did so. ⁹Then Jesus spoke directly to the religious scholars and Pharisees.

Jesus: Here's a question for you: On the Sabbath Day, is it lawful to do good or to do harm? Is it lawful to save life or to destroy it?

¹⁰He turned His gaze to each of them, *one at a time.* Then He spoke to the man.

Jesus: Stretch your hand out.

As the man did, his deformed hand was made normal again. ¹¹This made the Pharisees and religious scholars furious. They began discussing together what they would do to Jesus.

So as you can see, Jesus had His detractors. They watched Him closely and voiced their opposition to His words and actions. Sometimes they would even try to stump Him with questions or publicly humiliate Him. But Jesus refused to be intimidated. For every charge they leveled, He had an answer. To the charge of blasphemy, He responded: "I have the authority to forgive sins." To the charge that He befriended sinners and partied too much, He answered:

"These are My people; I've come for them." To the accusation that He broke Sabbath law, He quipped: "The Sabbath is a great servant, but it's not your master. I am Lord of the Sabbath." The crowds were amazed at the tense give-and-take between Jesus and His opponents. They seemed to respect the Pharisees for their strict observance of God's law, or perhaps they feared them because they didn't want to become the target of Pharisaic criticism. Yet they were attracted to Jesus because of the peculiar moral authority He exhibited. As time went on, Jesus crossed more and more lines drawn in the sand. The tension between Jesus and the Pharisees now becomes a major plotline of Luke's story.

¹²Around this time, Jesus went outside the city to a nearby mountain, *along with a large crowd of His disciples.* He prayed through the night to God. ¹³The next morning, He chose 12 of them and gave each a new title—*they were no longer simply disciples, which means "learners";* now they were also *apostles, which means "emissaries."* ¹⁴They included Simon (Jesus called him Peter) and Andrew (Simon's brother); James and John; Philip and Bartholomew; ¹⁵Matthew and Thomas; James (son of Alphaeus) and Simon (known as the Zealot); ¹⁶Judas (son of James) and the other Judas (Judas Iscariot, who later betrayed *Jesus*).

¹⁷The whole crowd of disciples (*including the 12 now designated as His emissaries*) came down together, and they stood on a level area nearby. They were joined by an even greater crowd of people who had come from across the whole region—from all of Judea, from Jerusalem, from the coastal areas of Tyre and Sidon. ¹⁸These people came to hear Jesus teach and to be healed by Jesus of their diseases. Those who were troubled by demonic spirits were liberated.

* 6:4 1 Samuel 21:2-6

¹⁹Everyone wanted to touch Jesus because when they did, power emanated from Him and they were healed. ²⁰He looked across the faces of His disciples.

Jesus: All you who are poor, you are blessed
for the kingdom of God belongs
to you.
²¹All you who are hungry now, you
are blessed
for your hunger will be
satisfied.
All you who weep now, you are
blessed
for you shall laugh!
²²When people hate you,
when they exclude you
and insult you
and write you off as evil
on account of the Son of Man,
you are blessed.
²³When these things happen,
rejoice! Jump for joy!
Then you have a great reward
in heaven
For at that moment, you are
experiencing what the
ancient prophets did when
they were similarly treated
by the ancestors of your
detractors.
²⁴All you who are rich now, you are
in danger
for you have received your
comfort in full.
²⁵All you who are full now, you are
in danger
for you shall be hungry.
All you who laugh now, you are in
danger
for you shall grieve and cry.
²⁶And when everyone speaks well
of you, you are in danger
for their ancestors spoke well of
the false prophets too.

*E*arlier we met the Pharisees, those who set themselves up as Jesus' antagonists. Now we've met the disciples, those who place themselves not against Jesus but with Him, following Him. Here we have Luke's most concentrated summary of Jesus' teachings for His followers. Here He describes what life in the kingdom of God looks like.

Jesus: ²⁷If you're listening, here's My message: Keep loving your enemies no matter what they do. Keep doing good to those who hate you. ²⁸Keep speaking blessings on those who curse you. Keep praying for those who mistreat you. ²⁹If someone strikes you on one cheek, offer the other cheek too. If someone steals your coat, offer him your shirt too. ³⁰If someone begs from you, give to him. If someone robs you of your valuables, don't demand them back. ³¹Think of the kindness you wish others would show you; do the same for them.

³²Listen, what's the big deal if you love people who already love you? Even scoundrels do that much! ³³So what if you do good to those who do good to you? Even scoundrels do that much! ³⁴So what if you lend to people who are likely to repay you? Even scoundrels lend to scoundrels if they think they'll be fully repaid.

³⁵If you want to be extraordinary—love your enemies! Do good *without restraint*! Lend *with abandon*! Don't expect anything in return! Then you'll receive the truly great reward—you will be children of the Most High—for God is kind to the ungrateful and those who are wicked. ³⁶So imitate God and be truly compassionate, the way your Father is.

³⁷If you don't want to be judged, don't judge. If you don't want to be condemned, don't condemn. If you want to be forgiven, forgive. ³⁸Don't hold back—give freely, and you'll have plenty poured back into your lap—a good measure, pressed down, shaken together, brimming over. You'll receive in the same measure you give.

³⁹Jesus told them this parable:

Jesus: What happens if a blind man leads a blind man? Won't both of them fall into a pit? 40You can't turn out better than your teacher; when you're fully taught, you will resemble your teacher.

41Speaking of blindness: Why do you focus on the speck in your brother's eye? Why don't you see the log in your own? 42How can you say to your brother, "Oh, brother, let me help you take that little speck out of your eye," when you don't even see the big log in your own eye? What a hypocrite! First, take the log out of your own eye. Then you'll be able to see clearly enough to help your brother with the speck in his eye.

43*Count on this:* no good tree bears bad fruit, and no bad tree bears good fruit. 44You can know a tree by the fruit it bears. You don't find figs on a thorn bush, and you can't pick grapes from a briar bush. 45*It's the same with people.* A person full of goodness in his heart produces good things; a person with an evil reservoir in his heart pours out evil things. The heart overflows in the words a person speaks; your words reveal what's within your heart.

46*But it's not just words that matter.* What good is it to mouth the words, "Lord! Lord!" if you don't live by My teachings? 47What matters is that you come to Me, hear My words, and actually live by them. 48If you do that, you'll be like the man who wanted to build a sturdy house. He dug down deep and anchored his foundation to solid rock. During a violent storm, the floodwaters slammed against the house, but they couldn't shake it because of solid craftsmanship. [It was built upon rock.]*

49On the other hand, if you hear *My teachings* but don't put them into practice, you'll be like the careless builder who didn't bother to build a foundation under his house. The floodwaters barely touched that pathetic house, and it crashed in ruins in the mud.

As Jesus traveled through Galilee, He taught and healed the crowds in public, but that's not all He did. He also gathered disciples. The word "disciple" means simply a student or an apprentice. So Jesus was the master-teacher, and His disciples were His students. Their classroom was the world—hillsides and beaches, homes and country roads, fields and city streets. Their subject was life—life in the kingdom of God. Jesus had many students, both men and women. But He formed a special inner circle known as "the twelve." The number "twelve" was highly symbolic because the Jewish people were originally composed of twelve tribes. However, over the centuries, some of the tribes had been decimated. By calling together a new twelve, Jesus seemed to be dramatizing a new beginning for the people of God. The original twelve tribes found their identity in the law of Moses, but now Jesus is giving a new way of life for His twelve to learn and follow.

7 Jesus shared all these sayings with the crowd that day on the plain. When He was finished, He went into the town of Capernaum. 2There, a Centurion had a slave he loved dearly. The slave was sick—about to die— 3so when the Centurion heard about Jesus, he contacted some Jewish elders. He sent them to ask Jesus to come and heal his dear slave. 4With great emotion and respect, the elders presented their request to Jesus.

Jewish Elders: This man is worthy of Your help. *It's true that he's a Centurion,* 5but he loves our nation. In fact, he paid for our synagogue to be built.

6So Jesus accompanied them. When they approached the Centurion's home, the Centurion sent out some friends to bring a message to Jesus.

Message of the Centurion: Lord, don't go to the trouble of coming inside. I am not worthy to have You come under my roof.

* 6:48 The earliest manuscripts omit this portion.

⁷That's why I sent others with my request. Just say the word, and that will be enough to heal my servant. ⁸I understand how authority works, being under authority myself and having soldiers under my authority. I command to one, "Go," and he goes. I say to another, "Come," and he comes. I say to my slave, "Do this," and he obeys me.

⁹Jesus was deeply impressed when He heard this. He turned to the crowd that followed Him.

Jesus: Listen, everyone. *This outsider, this Roman,* has more faith than I have found even among our own Jewish people.

¹⁰The friends of the Centurion returned home, and they found the slave was completely healed.

¹¹It wasn't long after this when Jesus entered a city called Nain. Again all of His disciples accompanied Him, along with a huge crowd. ¹²He was coming near the gate of the city as a corpse was being carried out. This man was the only child *and support* of his widowed mother, and she was accompanied by a large funeral crowd.

¹³As soon as the Lord saw her, He felt compassion for her.

Jesus: Don't weep.

¹⁴Then He came to the stretcher, and those carrying it stood still.

Jesus: Young man, listen! Get up!

¹⁵The dead man immediately sat up and began talking. Jesus presented him to his mother, ¹⁶and everyone was both shocked and jubilant. They praised God.

Funeral Crowd: A tremendous prophet has arisen in our midst! God has visited His people!

¹⁷News of Jesus spread across the whole province of Judea and beyond to the surrounding regions. ¹⁸When these reports reached John's disciples, they brought

news to John himself, *who was known for his preaching and ritual cleansing.** ¹⁹John sent two of his disciples to ask the Lord, "Are You the Promised One, or shall we keep looking for someone else?"

²⁰They came to Jesus and asked their question exactly as directed by John.

²¹Before He answered John's messengers, Jesus cured many from various diseases, health conditions, and evil spirits. He even caused many blind people to regain their sight.

Jesus *(to John's disciples)*: ²²Go and tell John what you've witnessed with your own eyes and ears: the blind are seeing again, the lame are walking again, the lepers are clean again, the deaf hear again, the dead live again, and good news is preached to the poor.* ²³Whoever is not offended by Me is blessed indeed.

*J*ohn, it seems, is having second thoughts. Is Jesus really the One we have expected? Is He the Liberating King? But who can blame John for these doubts? After all, John is in prison, unjustly held by a corrupt, immoral ruler. Ultimately the desert prophet will have his head severed from his body when the drunken, lusty king makes a silly promise in front of dinner guests. So who can blame John for wondering out loud: *Are You the One? Shouldn't John be free to preach, free to ritually cleanse his followers? Shouldn't Jesus be setting up court, fielding an army, and repelling the Roman occupiers?* Jesus, realizing fully the kinds of expectations others had, gently reminds John and his disciples of the Scriptures: "the blind see, the lame walk, the lepers are cleansed, the deaf hear, the dead live, and the poor receive the good news." We don't know how John responded to the report as he neared his own end. What is clear is that Jesus had the utmost

* 7:18 Literally, immersing, to show repentance
* 7:22 Isaiah 29:18; 35:5-6

respect for His colleague and friend. He didn't reject him for his doubts but tried to send him reassurance.

[24]When John's messengers left, Jesus talked to the crowds about John.

Jesus: When you went out into the wilderness to see John, what were you expecting? A reed shaking in the wind? [25]What were you looking for? A man in expensive clothing? Look, if you were looking for fancy clothes and luxurious living, you went to the wrong place—you should have gone to the kings' courts, *not to the wilderness!* [26]What were you seeking? A prophet? Ah yes, that's what John is, and even more than a prophet. [27]*The prophet Malachi was talking about John when he wrote,*

> I will send My messenger *before You,*
>   to clear Your path in front of You.*

[28]Listen, there is no human being greater than this man John. Yet even the least significant person in the coming kingdom of God is greater than John.

[29]*These words elicited two opposite reactions among the people.* The common people and tax collectors heard God's own wisdom in Jesus' assessment of John because they had been ritually cleansed* by John. [30]But the Pharisees and religious scholars hardened their hearts and turned their backs on God's purposes for them because they had refused John's ritual cleansing.

Jesus: [31]The people of this generation— what are they like? To what can they be compared? [32]*I'll tell you:* they're like spoiled kids sitting in the marketplace *playing games,* calling out,

> We played the pipes for you,
>   but you didn't dance to our tune!
> We cried like mourners,
>   but you didn't cry with us!

[33]*You can't win with this generation.* John the Preacher comes along, fasting and abstaining from wine, and you say, "This guy is demon-possessed!" [34]The Son of Man comes along, feasting and drinking *wine,* and you say, "This guy is a glutton and a drunk, a friend of scoundrels and tax collectors!" [35]Well, wisdom's true children know wisdom when they hear it.

[36-40]Once a Pharisee named Simon invited Jesus to be a guest for a meal.

Picture this:

Just as Jesus enters the man's home and takes His place at the table, a woman from the city—notorious as a woman of ill repute—follows Him in. She has heard that Jesus will be at the Pharisee's home, so she comes in and approaches Him, carrying an alabaster flask of perfumed oil. Then she begins to cry, she kneels down so her tears fall on Jesus' feet, and she starts wiping His feet with her own hair. Then she actually kisses His feet, and she pours the perfumed oil on them.

Simon *(thinking)*: Now I know this guy is a fraud. If He were a real prophet, He would have known this woman is a sinner and He would never let her get near Him, much less touch Him . . . *or kiss Him!*

Jesus *(knowing what the Pharisee is thinking)*: Simon, I want to tell you a story.

Simon: Tell me, Teacher.

Jesus: [41]Two men owed a certain lender a lot of money. One owed 100 weeks' wages, and the other owed 10 weeks' wages. [42]Both men defaulted on their loans, but the lender forgave them both. Here's a question for you: which man will love the lender more?

Simon: [43]Well, I guess it would be the one who was forgiven more.

Jesus: Good answer.

---

* 7:27 Malachi 3:1
* 7:29 Literally, immersed, to show repentance

44-46Now Jesus turns around so He's facing the woman, although He's still speaking to Simon.

Jesus: Do you see this woman here? *It's kind of funny.* I entered your home, and you didn't provide a basin of water so I could wash the road dust from My feet. 45You didn't give Me a customary kiss of greeting and welcome. You didn't offer Me the common courtesy of providing oil to brighten My face. But this woman has wet My feet with her own tears and washed them with her own hair. She hasn't stopped kissing My feet since I came in. And she has applied perfumed oil to My feet. 47This woman has been forgiven much, and she is showing much love. But the person who has shown little love shows how little forgiveness he has received.

48(to the woman) Your sins are forgiven.

Simon and Friends (*muttering among themselves*): 49Who does this guy think He is? He has the audacity to claim the authority to forgive sins?

Jesus (*to the woman*): 50Your faith has liberated you. Go in peace.

8 Soon after this incident, Jesus preached from city to city, village to village, carrying the good news of the kingdom of God. He was accompanied by a group called "the twelve," 2and also by a larger group including some women who had been liberated from evil spirits and healed of diseases. There was Mary, called Magdalene, who had been released from seven demons. 3There were others like Susanna and Joanna, who was married to Chuza, a steward of King Herod. And there were many others too. *These women played an important role in Jesus' ministry,* using their wealth to provide for Him and His other companions.

4While a huge crowd gathered with people from many surrounding towns streaming to hear Jesus, He told them a parable.

*P*arables are works of art, specifically, works of short fiction. They are intricately constructed and complex in their intent. In some ways, they are intended to hide the truth; they don't reduce truth to simple statements or formulae. Instead, they force the reader to take things to a deeper level, to engage the imagination, to think and think again. In this way, they invite people to ask questions; they stir curiosity; they create intrigue.

Jesus: 5Once a farmer went out to scatter seed *in his fields.* Some seeds fell along a trail where they were crushed underfoot by people walking by. Birds flew in and ate those seeds. 6Other seeds fell on gravel. Those seeds sprouted but soon withered, depleted of moisture *under the scorching sun.* 7Still other seeds landed among thorns where they grew for a while, but eventually the thorns stunted them so they couldn't thrive or bear fruit. 8But some seeds fell into good soil—*soft, moist, free from thorns.* These seeds not only grew, but they also produced *more seeds,* a hundred times what the farmer originally planted. If you have ears, hear My meaning!

9His disciples heard the words, but the deeper meaning eluded them.

Disciples: What were You trying to say?

Jesus: 10The kingdom of God contains many secrets.
> They keep listening, but do not comprehend;
> keep observing, but do not understand.*

I want you to understand, so 11here's the interpretation: The voice of God falls on human hearts like seeds scattered across a field. 12Some people hear that message, but the devil opposes the liberation that would come to them by believing. So he swoops in and steals the

* 8:10 Isaiah 6:9

message from their hard hearts like birds stealing the seeds from the footpath. [13]Others receive the message enthusiastically, but their vitality is short-lived because the message cannot be deeply rooted in their shallow hearts. In the heat of temptation, their faith withers, like the seeds that sprouted in gravelly soil. [14]A third group hears the message, but as time passes, the daily anxieties, the pursuit of wealth, and life's addicting delights outpace the growth of the message in their hearts. Even if the message blossoms and fruit begins to form, the fruit never fully matures because the thorns choke out the plants' vitality.

[15]But some people hear the message and let it take root deeply in receptive hearts made fertile by honesty and goodness. With patient dependability, they bear good fruit.

[16]If you light a lamp, you're not going to cover it with a clay pot. You're not going to hide it under your bed. If you light a lamp, you're going to put it out in the open so your guests *can feel welcome and* see where they're going.

[17]Hidden things will always come out into the open. Secret things will come to light and be exposed. [18]*I hope you're still listening.* And I hope you're listening carefully. If you get what I'm saying, you'll get more. If you miss My meaning, even the understanding you think you have will be taken from you.

[19]Around this time, Jesus was speaking to a crowd of people gathered in a house. His mother and brothers arrived to see Him, but the crowd around Him was so huge that they couldn't even get through the door. [20]Word spread through the crowd.

Someone from the Crowd: Jesus, Your mother and brothers are outside the house hoping to see You.

Jesus: [21]Do you want to know who My mother and brothers are? They're the ones who truly understand God's message and obey it.

[22]*Picture this:*

One day Jesus and His disciples get into a boat.

Jesus: Let's cross the lake.

So they push off from shore and begin sailing to the far side. [23]As they progress across the lake, Jesus falls sound asleep. Soon a raging storm blows in. The waves wash over the sides of the boat, and the boat starts filling up with water. Every second the situation becomes more dangerous.

[24]The disciples *shake Jesus and* wake Him.

Disciples (shouting): Master! Master! We're all going to die!

Jesus wakes up and tells the wind to stop whipping them around, and He tells the furious waves to calm down. They do just that. [25]Then Jesus turns to the disciples.

Jesus: What happened to your faith?

The disciples had been terrified during the storm, but now they're afraid in another way. They turn to each other and start whispering, chattering, and wondering.

Disciples: Who is this man? How can He command wind and water so they do what He says?

[26]When they get to the other side of the lake, in the Gerasene country opposite Galilee, [27]a man from the city is waiting for Jesus when He steps out of the boat. The man is full of demonic spirits. He's been running around for a long time stark naked, and he's homeless, sleeping among the dead in a cemetery. [28-29]This man has on many occasions been tied up and chained and kept under guard, but each time he has broken free and the demonic power has driven him back into remote places *away from human contact.* Jesus commands the demonic force to leave him.

The man looks at Jesus and starts screaming. He falls down in front of Jesus.

Possessed Man (*shouting*): Don't torment me, Jesus, Son of the Most High God! Why are You here?
Jesus (*calmly and simply*): ³⁰What's your name?
Possessed Man: Battalion.

He says this because an army of demons is inside of him. ³¹The demons start begging Jesus not to send them into the bottomless pit. ³²They plead instead to enter into a herd of pigs feeding on a steep hillside near the shore. Jesus gives them permission to do so. ³³Suddenly the man is liberated from the demons, but the pigs—they stampede, squealing down the hill and into the lake where they drown themselves.

³⁴The pig owners see all this. They run back to their town and tell everyone in the region about it. ³⁵Soon a crowd rushes from the town to see what's going on out by the lake. There they find Jesus seated *to teach* with the newly liberated man sitting at His feet *learning in the posture of a disciple*. This former madman is now properly dressed and completely sane. This frightens the people. ³⁶The pig owners tell them the whole story—the healing, *the pigs' mass suicide, everything.*

³⁷The people are scared to death, and they don't want this scary abnormality happening in their territory. They ask Jesus to leave immediately. *Jesus doesn't argue.* He prepares to leave, ³⁸but before they embark, the newly liberated man begs to come along and join the band of disciples.

Jesus: ³⁹No. Go home. Tell your people this amazing story about how much God has done for you.

The man does so. In fact, he tells everyone in the whole city how much Jesus did for him that day *on the shore.*

⁴⁰When Jesus and His disciples crossed the lake, another crowd was waiting to welcome Him. ⁴¹A man made his way through the crowd. His name was Jairus, and he was a synagogue official. *Like the man on the other side of the lake,* this dignified man also fell at Jesus' feet, begging Jesus to visit his home ⁴²where his only daughter, a girl of 12, lay dying. Jesus set out with Jairus. The crowd came along, too, pressing hard against Him.

⁴³In the crowd was a woman. She had suffered from an incurable menstrual disorder for 12 years [and had spent her livelihood on doctors with no effect].* *It had kept her miserable and ritually unclean, unable to participate fully in Jewish life.* ⁴⁴*She followed Jesus, working her way through the crowd closer to Him* until she could reach Him. She touched the fringe of the robe Jesus wore, and at that moment the bleeding stopped.

Jesus (*stopping and looking about*): ⁴⁵Who touched Me?
Crowd (*everyone speaking at once*): Not me. It wasn't me either.
Peter [and those with him]* (*intervening*): Master, what kind of question is that, with this huge crowd all around You and many people touching You on all sides?
Jesus: ⁴⁶*I felt something.* I felt power going out from Me. I know that somebody touched Me.

⁴⁷The woman now realized her secret was going to come out sooner or later, so she stepped out of the crowd, shaking with fear, and she fell down in front of Jesus. Then she told her story in front of everyone—why she touched Him, what happened as a result.

Jesus: ⁴⁸Your faith has made you well again, daughter. Go in peace.

⁴⁹Right at that instant, one of *Jairus's* household servants arrived.

Servant: Sir, your daughter is dead. It's no use bothering the Teacher with this anymore.

* 8:43 This portion is omitted in some early manuscripts.
* 8:45 The earliest manuscripts omit this portion.

Jesus *(interrupting Jairus before he could speak)*: [50]Don't be afraid. Just believe. She'll be well again.

[51-52]As they approached the house, the whole neighborhood was full of the sound of mourning—weeping, wailing, loud crying. Jesus told everyone to stay outside—everyone except Peter, John, James, and, of course, the girl's father and mother.

Jesus *(to the mourners)*: Please stop weeping. The girl isn't dead. She's only asleep.

[53]They knew for certain that she was dead, *so their bitter tears now mixed* with mocking laughter *at what they thought was the naïveté or stupidity of Jesus' remark.*
    [54]Meanwhile, inside, Jesus took the girl's hand.

Jesus: Child, get up!

[55]She started breathing again, and she sat right up.

Jesus: Get her something to eat.

[56]Her parents were amazed, but Jesus sternly told them to keep what had happened a secret.

*W*e've just completed an almost breathtaking succession of encounters between Jesus and people in need. Each story is unique; Jesus responds to each person as an individual, and there is no detectable formula to His way of treating people—except that in every case, His interactions are characterized by love and compassion.

9 Jesus convened a gathering of the twelve. He gave them power and authority to free people from all demonic spirits and to heal them of diseases.

*N*ow Jesus takes His ministry of teaching the kingdom of God in word and deed to a new level: He sends out His disciples to do what they have seen Him do. Jesus commissions the twelve to multiply His ministry. So in the coming episodes, we see them go out from and then return to report to Jesus what they've experienced and learned. But as you'll see, it's hard for them to get any time alone to talk. There are so many people who want time with Jesus!

[2]He sent them out to preach the kingdom of God and to heal the sick. These were His instructions:

[3]1. Travel light on your journey: don't take a staff, backpack, bread, money, or even an extra change of clothes.
[4]2. When you enter a house, stay there until you leave that city.
[5]3. If a town rejects you, shake the dust from your feet as you leave as a witness against them.

[6]The disciples left on their journeys from village to village. They preached the good news, and they healed the sick everywhere they went.
    [7-8]*Their mission didn't go unnoticed.* The local official installed by Rome, Herod, was especially anxious about the news because rumors were flying *that something unprecedented was occurring.* Some people said that Elijah or one of the other ancient prophets had been resurrected, while others said that John, *famous for his ritual cleansing,** was alive *and preaching again.*

Herod: [9]I am the one who beheaded John. So who is this man who is causing such a stir?

Herod *was curious about Jesus and* wanted to see Him.
    [10]The emissaries* whom Jesus had sent out returned, and Jesus took them away from the crowds for a time of retreat in a

---

* 9:7-8 Literally, immersion, an act to show repentance
* 9:10 Literally, apostles

city called Bethsaida. They gave Jesus a full report of their accomplishments and experiences. [11]But soon the crowds discovered where they were and pursued Him. Jesus didn't turn them away; He welcomed them, spoke of the kingdom of God to them, and brought health to those who needed healing.

[12]*Picture what happened* while in Bethsaida, where Jesus and His disciples were spending time with the crowds:

The sun is low in the sky, and soon it will be dusk. The twelve come to Jesus with advice.

Disciples: Send the crowd away so they can find lodging and food in the nearby villages and countryside. We're out here in the middle of nowhere.

Jesus: [13-14]No. You give them something to eat.

Disciples: *Are You kidding?* There are at least 5,000 men here, *not to mention women and children*. All we have are five loaves and two fish. The only way we could provide for them would be to go to a nearby city and buy cartloads of food. *That would cost a small fortune.*

Jesus: Just do this: organize them in little communities of about 50 people each and have them sit down.

[15]They do what Jesus says, and soon groups of 50 are scattered across the landscape.

[16]Then Jesus takes the five loaves and two fish, and He looks up to heaven. He praises God for the food, takes each item, and breaks it into fragments. Then He gives fragments to the twelve disciples and tells them to distribute the food to the crowd.

[17]Everyone eats. Everyone is satisfied. Nobody goes away hungry. In fact, when the disciples recover the leftovers, they have 12 baskets full of broken pieces.

[18]Once Jesus was praying in solitude. The disciples were nearby, and He came to them with a question.

Jesus: What are the people saying about Me?

Disciples: [19]Some people think You're John the Preacher. Others say You're the prophet Elijah, or else one of the other ancient prophets who has come back from the dead.

Jesus: [20]Ah, but what about you? Who do you say that I am?

Peter: You are the Liberating King sent by God.

Jesus (*sternly*): [21]Don't tell anyone this. [22]The Son of Man must suffer intensely. He must be rejected by the religious establishment—the elders, the chief priests, the religious scholars. Then He will be killed. And then, on the third day He will be raised.

[23]If any of you want to walk My path, you're going to have to deny yourself. You'll have to take up your cross every day and follow Me. [24]If you try to avoid danger and risk, then you'll lose everything. If you let go of your life and risk all for My sake, then your life will be liberated, *healed, made whole and full*. [25]Listen, what good does it do you if you gain everything—if the whole world is in your pocket—but then your own life slips through your fingers and is lost to you?

[26]If you're ashamed of who I am and what I teach, then the Son of Man will be ashamed of you when He comes in all His glory, the glory of the Father, and the glory of the holy messengers. [27]*Are you ready for this?* I'm telling you the truth: some of you will not taste death until your eyes see the kingdom of God.

*I*n this section of Luke, Jesus is working hard with the disciples. They have a lot to learn and not much time left to learn it. But their "not-getting-it-factor" is quite amazing. We can almost see Luke shaking his head and chuckling as he writes, thinking about how foolish the disciples can be at times. And, of course, he's probably thinking of himself too . . . just as we do when we read about the stupid things the disciples say and do—one moment seeing and hearing glorious things, the next moment missing the point entirely.

28Those words had about eight days *to settle in with the disciples.* Then, once again, Jesus went away to pray. This time He took along only Peter, John, and James. They climbed a mountainside *and came to a place of solitude.*

29-32Jesus began to pray and the disciples tried to stay awake, but their eyes grew heavier and heavier and finally they all fell asleep. When they awakened, they looked over at Jesus and saw something inexplicable happening. Jesus was changing before their eyes, beginning with His face. It seemed to glow. The glow spread, and even His clothing took on a blinding whiteness. Then, two figures appeared in the glorious radiance emanating from Jesus. The three disciples somehow knew that these figures were Moses and Elijah. Peter, James, and John overheard the conversation that took place among Jesus, Moses, and Elijah—a conversation that centered on Jesus' "departure"* and how He would accomplish this departure from the capital city, Jerusalem.

33*The glow began to fade, and* it was clear that Moses and Elijah were about to disappear.

Peter (*to Jesus*): Please, Master, it is good for us to be here *and see this.* Can we make three structures—one to honor You, one to honor Moses, and one to honor Elijah, *to try to capture what's happening here*?

Peter had no idea what he was saying. 34While he spoke a cloud descended, and they were enveloped in it, and fear fell on them. 35Then a voice came out of everywhere and nowhere at once.

Voice from Heaven: This is My Son!* This is the One I have chosen! Listen to Him!*

36Then the voice was silent, *the cloud disappeared,* and Moses and Elijah were gone. Peter, James, and John were left speechless, *stunned, staring at* Jesus who now stood before them alone. For a long time, they did not say a word about this whole experience.

37They came down the mountain, and the next day yet another huge crowd gathered around Jesus. There was a man in the crowd who shouted out.

Man in Crowd: 38Teacher! Please come and look at my son here, my only child. 39From time to time, a demonic spirit seizes him. It makes him scream and go into convulsions. He foams at the mouth. It nearly destroys him and only leaves after causing him great distress. 40*While You were up on the mountain,* I begged Your disciples to liberate him from this spirit, but they were incapable of helping us.

Jesus: 41O generation faithless, twisted, and crooked, how long can I be with you? How much can I bear? Bring your boy here.

42The boy had taken a few steps toward Jesus when suddenly the demon seemed to rip into the boy, throwing him into convulsions. Jesus spoke sternly to the demonic spirit, and the boy was healed. Jesus presented the boy to his father.

43*The crowd began cheering and* discussing this amazing healing and the power of God, but Jesus turned to His disciples.

Jesus: 44Listen. Listen hard. Let these words get down deep: the Son of Man is going to be turned over to the authorities and arrested.

45They had no idea what He meant by this; they heard the words but missed the meaning, and they felt too afraid to ask Him to explain further.

* 9:32 Literally, His exodus
* 9:35 Psalm 2:7; Luke 3:22
* 9:35 Deuteronomy 18:15; Isaiah 42:1

⁴⁶Later the close followers of Jesus began to argue over the *stupid and vain* question, "Which one of us is the greatest disciple?"

⁴⁷Jesus saw what was going on—*not just the argument, but* the deeper heart issues—so He found a child and had the child stand beside Him.

Jesus: ⁴⁸*See this little one?* Whoever welcomes a little child in My name welcomes Me. And whoever welcomes Me welcomes the One who sent Me. The smallest one among you is therefore the greatest.

John: ⁴⁹Master, we found this fellow casting out demons. He said he was doing it in Your name, but he's not one of our group. So we told him to stop.

Jesus: ⁵⁰*What?* No! Don't think like that! Whoever is not working against you is working with you.

⁵¹The time approached for Him to be taken back up *to the Father*; so strong with resolve, Jesus made Jerusalem His destination. ⁵²He sent some people ahead of Him into the territory of the Samaritans, *a minority group at odds with the Jewish majority*. He wanted His messengers to find a place for them to stay in a village *along the road to Jerusalem*. ⁵³But because the Samaritans realized Jesus was going to Jerusalem, they refused to welcome them. ⁵⁴*James and John were outraged.*

James and John: Lord, do You want us to call down fire from heaven to destroy these people who have rejected You?* [Just as Elijah did.]*

Jesus (*turning toward them and shaking His head*): ⁵⁵You just don't get it. [⁵⁶The Son of Man didn't come to ruin the lives of people, but He came to liberate them.]*

He led them on toward another village. ⁵⁷Farther along on the road, a man volunteered to become a disciple.

Volunteer: I'll follow You to any destination.
Jesus: ⁵⁸Foxes are at home in their burrows. Birds are at home in their nests. But the Son of Man has no home. ⁵⁹You (to another person)—I want you to follow Me!

Another Volunteer: *I'd be glad to,* Teacher, but let me first attend to my father's funeral.

Jesus: ⁶⁰Let the dead bury their dead. I'm giving you a different calling—to go and proclaim the kingdom of God.

A Third Volunteer: ⁶¹I'll come, Jesus. I'll follow You. But just let me first run home to say good-bye to my family.

Jesus: ⁶²Listen, if your hand is on the plow but your eyes are looking backwards, then you're not fit for the kingdom of God.

10 The Lord then recruited and deployed 70* more disciples. He sent them ahead, in teams of two, to visit all the towns and settlements between them and Jerusalem. ²This is what He ordered.

Jesus: There's a great harvest waiting in the fields, but there aren't many good workers to harvest it. Pray that the Harvest Master will send out good workers to the fields.

³It's time for you *70* to go. I'm sending you out *armed with vulnerability*, like lambs walking into a pack of wolves. ⁴Don't bring a wallet. Don't carry a backpack. I don't even want you to wear sandals. Walk along *barefoot, quietly,* without stopping for small talk. ⁵When you enter a house seeking lodging, say, "Peace on this house!" ⁶If a child of peace—one who welcomes God's message of peace—is there, your peace will rest on him. If not, don't worry; nothing is wasted. ⁷Stay where you're welcomed. *Become part of the family,* eating and drinking whatever they give you. You're My workers, and you deserve to be cared for. Again, don't go from house to house,

* 9:54 2 Kings 1:10,12
* 9:54 Most early manuscripts omit this portion.
* 9:56 The earliest manuscripts omit this portion.
* 10:1 Other early manuscripts read "72."

8but settle down in a town and eat whatever they serve you. 9Heal the sick and say to the townspeople, "The kingdom of God has come near to you."

10Of course, not every town will welcome you. If you're rejected, walk through the streets and say, 11*"We're leaving this town. We'll wipe off the dust that clings to our feet in protest against you. But even so, know this: the kingdom of God has come near."* 12I tell you the truth, on *judgment* day, Sodom will have an easier time of it than the town *that rejects My messengers.*

13It's going to be bad for you, Chorazin! It's going to be bad for you, Bethsaida! If the mighty works done in your streets had been done in the cities of Tyre and Sidon, they would have been moved to turn to God and cry out in sackcloth and ashes. 14On judgment day, Tyre and Sidon will have an easier time of it than you. 15It's going to be bad for you too, Capernaum! Will you be celebrated to heaven? No, you will go down to the place of the dead.

16*Listen, disciples:* if people give you a hearing, they're giving Me a hearing. If they reject you, they're rejecting Me. And if they reject Me, they're rejecting the One who sent Me. *So—go now!*

17When the 70* *completed their mission and* returned *to report on their experiences,* they were elated.

Seventy: It's amazing, Lord! When we use Your name, the demons do what we say!
Jesus: 18*I know. I saw it happening.* I saw Satan falling from above like a lightning bolt. 19I've given you true authority. You can smash vipers and scorpions under your feet.* You can walk all over the power of the enemy. You can't be harmed. 20But listen—that's not the point. Don't be elated that evil spirits leave when you say to leave. Rejoice that your names are written in heaven.

21Then Jesus Himself became elated. The Holy Spirit was on Him, and He began to pray with joy.

Jesus: Thank You, Father, Lord of heaven and earth. Thank You for hiding Your mysteries from the wise and intellectual, instead revealing them to little children. Your ways are truly gracious. 22My Father has given Me everything. No one knows the full identity of the Son except the Father, and nobody knows the full identity of the Father except the Son, and the Son fully reveals the Father to whomever He wishes. 23(then almost in a whisper to the disciples) How blessed are your eyes to see what you see! 24Many prophets and kings dreamed of seeing what you see, but they never got a glimpse. They dreamed of hearing what you hear, but they never heard it.

25Just then a scholar *of the Hebrew Scriptures* tried to trap Jesus.

Scholar: Teacher, what must I do to experience the eternal life?
Jesus (*answering with a question*): 26What is written in the *Hebrew* Scriptures? How do you interpret their answer to your question?
Scholar: 27You shall love—"love the Eternal One your God with everything you have: all your heart, all your soul, all your strength, and all your mind"*—and "love your neighbor as yourself."*
Jesus: 28*Perfect.* Your answer is correct. Follow these commands and you will live.

29The scholar *was frustrated by this response because he* was hoping to make himself appear smarter than Jesus.

Scholar: Ah, but who is my neighbor?
Jesus: 30This fellow was traveling down from Jerusalem to Jericho when some robbers mugged him. They took his clothes, beat him to a pulp, and left him naked and bleeding and in critical condition. 31By chance, a priest was going down that same road, and when he saw

* 10:17 Other early manuscripts read "72."
* 10:19 Psalm 91:13
* 10:27 Deuteronomy 6:5
* 10:27 Leviticus 19:18

the wounded man, he crossed over to the other side and passed by. ³²Then a Levite *who was on his way to assist in the temple* also came and saw the victim lying there, and he too kept his distance. ³³Then a *despised* Samaritan journeyed by. When he saw the fellow, he felt compassion for him. ³⁴The Samaritan went over to him, stopped the bleeding, applied some first aid, and put the poor fellow on his donkey. He brought the man to an inn and cared for him through the night.

³⁵The next day, the Samaritan took out *some money*—two days' wages*—to be exact—and paid the innkeeper, saying, "Please take care of this fellow, and if this isn't enough, I'll repay you next time I pass through."

³⁶Which of these three proved himself a neighbor to the man who had been mugged by the robbers?

Scholar: ³⁷The one who showed mercy to him.

Jesus: Well then, go and behave like that Samaritan.

*T*his story brings together many themes from Jesus' teaching of the Kingdom. Samaritans in Jesus' day were seen as "half-breeds" by Jesus' fellow Jews—racially mixed and also religiously compromised. By making a Samaritan the hero of the story, Jesus is once again tweaking assumptions and breaking out of conventional boxes: "In the kingdom of God," Jesus is saying, "the outcasts and last can move to the front of the line." The focus for Jesus is not on the kinds of sophisticated arguments preferred by the religious scholar; for Jesus the kingdom of God is about living life, and in particular, living a life of love for God and for neighbor—whoever that neighbor may be.

³⁸Jesus continued from there *toward Jerusalem* and came to another village. Martha, a resident of that village, welcomed Jesus into her home. ³⁹Her sister, Mary, went and sat at Jesus' feet, listening

to Him teach. ⁴⁰Meanwhile Martha was anxious about all the hospitality arrangements.

Martha (*interrupting Jesus*): Lord, why don't You care that my sister is leaving me to do all the work by myself? Tell her to get over here and help me.

Jesus: ⁴¹Oh Martha, Martha, you are so anxious and concerned about a million details, ⁴²but really, only one thing matters. Mary has chosen that one thing, and I won't take it away from her.

11 Another time Jesus was praying, and when He finished, one of His disciples approached Him.

Disciple: Teacher, would You teach us Your way of prayer? John taught his disciples his way of prayer, *and we're hoping You'll do the same.*

Jesus: ²Here's how to pray:

Father [in heaven], may Your name
    be revered.
  May Your kingdom come.
  [May Your will be accomplished on
    earth
    as it is in heaven.]
³Give us the food we need for
    tomorrow,
⁴And forgive us for our wrongs,
    for we forgive those who wrong us.
  And lead us away from temptation.
  [And save us from the evil one.]*

⁵Imagine that one of your friends comes over at midnight. He bangs on the door and shouts, "Friend, will you lend me three loaves of bread? ⁶A friend of mine just showed up unexpectedly from a journey, and I don't have anything to feed him." ⁷Would you shout out from your bed, "I'm already in bed, and so are the kids. I already locked the door. I can't be bothered"? ⁸You know this as well as I do: even if you didn't care that

* 10:35 Literally, denarii, Roman coins
* 11:2-4 The earliest manuscripts omit the bracketed text.

this fellow was your friend, if he keeps knocking long enough, you'll get up and give him whatever he needs simply because of his brash persistence!

9So listen: Keep on asking, and you will receive. Keep on seeking, and you will find. Keep on knocking, and the door will be opened for you. 10All who keep asking will receive, all who keep seeking will find, and doors will open to those who keep knocking.

11Some of you are fathers, so ask yourselves this: if your son comes up to you and asks for a fish for dinner, will you give him a snake instead? 12If your boy wants an egg to eat, will you give him a scorpion? 13Look, all of you are flawed in so many ways, yet in spite of all your faults, you know how to give good gifts to your children. How much more will your Father in heaven give the Holy Spirit to all who ask!

14*Picture this:*

Jesus is exorcising a demon that has long kept a man from speaking. When the demon is expelled, the man starts talking and the people are amazed. 15*But then controversy erupts.*

Some People: Do you know why He can cast out demons? It's because He's in league with the demon prince, Beelzebul.

16Other people want to see more, so they challenge Jesus to give them another miraculous sign. 17Jesus knows what they're thinking.

Jesus: *People, be logical.* If a kingdom is divided against itself, it will collapse. If a ruling family is divided against itself, it will fall apart. 18So if Satan's kingdom is divided against itself, won't his whole enterprise collapse? Does it make any sense to say I'm casting out demons by Beelzebul? 19Besides, if you're saying it takes satanic power to cast out Satan, by whose power do your own exorcists work? If you condemn Me for an exorcism, you'll have to condemn them; *do you really want to do*

that? 20But if I by the power of God cast out demonic spirits, then *face this fact:* the kingdom of God is here, *just as I've been saying.*

21When a man of power with his full array of weapons guards his own palace, everything inside is secure. 22But when a new man who is stronger *and better armed* attacks the palace, the old ruler will be overcome, his weapons and trusted defenses will be removed, and his treasures will be plundered. *Can you see Satan as that old man of power and Me as the new man of power?* 23Can you see that I'm asking you to choose whose side you're on—working with Me or fighting against Me?

24*You seem to think you're experts on demonic spirits, but let Me instruct you:* When a demonic spirit is expelled from someone, he wanders through waterless wastelands seeking rest. But there is no rest for him anywhere, so he says, "I'm going back to my old house." 25He returns and finds the old house has been swept clean and fixed up again. 26So he goes and finds seven other spirits even worse than he is, and they make themselves at home in the man's life so that he's worse off now than he was before.

27As He is speaking, a woman shouts out from the crowd and interrupts Him.

Woman: How blessed is Your mother's womb for bearing You! How blessed are her 28breasts for nursing You!
Jesus: No, how blessed are those who hear God's voice and make God's message their way of life.

29*Jesus was becoming more and more popular,* and the crowds swelled wherever He went. *He wasn't impressed.*

Jesus: This generation is evil. These people are seeking signs *and spectacles, but I'm not going to play their game.* The only sign they will be given is the sign of Jonah. 30Just as Jonah became a sign to the people of Nineveh, so will the Son of Man be to this generation.

31The queen of Ethiopia will stand to condemn the people of this generation on the day of judgment. She, *an outsider,* came from so far away to hear the wisdom given to Solomon, but now, something greater than Solomon is here: *how are the people of this generation responding?*

32Similarly, the people of Nineveh will stand to condemn the people of this generation on the day of judgment. They, *outsiders,* responded and changed because of the preaching of Jonah, but now, something greater than Jonah is here: *how are the people of this generation responding?*

33*You need a light to see.* Only an idiot would light a lamp and then put it beneath the floor or under a bucket. No, any intelligent person would put the lamp on a table so everyone who comes in the house can see. 34Listen, your eye, *your outlook, the way you see*—is your lamp. If your way of seeing is functioning well, then your whole life will be enlightened. But if your way of seeing is darkened, then your life will be a dark, dark place. 35So be careful, people, because your light may be malfunctioning. 36If your outlook is good, then your whole life will be bright, with no shadowy corners, as when a radiant lamp brightens your home.

*I*n the next several episodes, Jesus engages in tense conversation with the Pharisees and other religious scholars. Jesus is fearless in His engagement with them. But the series of episodes begins with Jesus agreeing to eat in the home of a Pharisee where a religious scholar has also been invited—a sign that underneath their conflict, Jesus loved them and wanted to get through to them.

37A Pharisee interrupted His speech with an invitation to dinner. Jesus accepted the invitation and took His place at his table. 38The Pharisee was offended that Jesus didn't perform the ceremonial hand-washing before eating—*something Pharisees were fastidious about doing.*

Jesus: 39You Pharisees *are a walking contradiction.* You are so concerned about external things—like someone who washes the outside of a cup and bowl but never cleans the inside, *which is what counts!* Beneath your fastidious exterior is a mess of extortion and filth.

40You guys don't get it. Did the potter make the outside but not the inside too? 41*If you were full of goodness within,* you could overflow with generosity from within, and if you did that, everything would be clean for you.

42Woe to you, Pharisees! *Judgment will come on you!* You are fastidious about tithing—keeping account of every little leaf of mint and herb, but you neglect what really matters: justice and the love of God! If you'd get straight on what really matters, then your fastidiousness about little things would be worth something.

43Woe to you, Pharisees! *Judgment will come on you!* What you really love is having people fawn over you when you take the seat of honor in the synagogue or when you are greeted in the public market.

44*Wake up! See what you've become!* Woe to you; you're like a field full of unmarked graves. People walk on the field and have no idea of the corruption that's a few inches beneath their feet.

Scholar (*sitting at Jesus' table*): 45Rabbi, if You insult the Pharisees, then You insult us too.

Jesus: 46Well, *now that you mention it,* watch out, all you religious scholars! *Judgment will come on you too!* You load other people down with unbearable burdens *of rules and regulations,* but you don't lift a finger to help others. 47-48Woe to you; *you don't fool anybody! You seem very religious*—honoring the prophets by building them elaborate memorial tombs. Come to think of it, that's very fitting, since you're so much like the people who killed the prophets! They killed the prophets; you build their tombs—*you're all in the same family business!*

⁴⁹This is why the Wisdom of God said, "I will send these people My prophets and emissaries,* and these people will kill and persecute many of them." ⁵⁰As a result, this generation will be held accountable for the blood of all the prophets shed from the very beginning of time, ⁵¹from Abel's blood to Zechariah's blood, who was killed in the temple itself between the altar and the holy place. I'm serious: this generation will be held accountable.

⁵²So, religious scholars, judgment will come on you! *Don't think you'll evade the consequences of your behavior. You're supposed to be teachers, unlocking the doorway of knowledge and guiding people through it.* But the fact is, you've never even passed through the doorway yourselves. You've taken the key, left the door locked tight, and stood in the way of everyone who sought entry.

⁵³After that dinner, things were never the same. The religious scholars and Pharisees put constant pressure on Jesus, ⁵⁴trying to trap Him and trick Him into saying things they could use to bring Him down.

12 The crowds at this time were packed in so tightly that thousands of people were stepping on each other. Jesus spoke to His disciples, *knowing that the crowds could overhear.*

Jesus: Guard yourselves from the yeast that puffs up the Pharisees—hypocrisy, *false appearance, trying to look better than you really are.*

²Nothing is covered up that won't be discovered; nothing is hidden that won't be exposed. ³Whatever a person says in the dark will be published in the light of day, and whatever a person whispers in private rooms will be broadcast from the housetops.

⁴Listen, My friends, if people are trying to kill you, why be afraid? After you're dead, what more can they do? ⁵⁻⁶Here's whose opinion you should be concerned about: the One who can take your life and then throw you into hell! He's the only One you should fear! *But don't misunderstand: you don't really need to be afraid of God,* because God cares for every little sparrow. How much is a sparrow worth—don't five of them sell for a few cents?* ⁷*Since God never loses track of even one little sparrow,* and since you are so much more precious to God than a thousand flocks of sparrows, *and since God knows you in every detail*—down to the number of hairs on your head *at this moment*—you can be secure and unafraid *of any person, and* you have nothing to fear from God *either.*

⁸*That's why I keep telling you not to be intimidated.* If you identify unashamedly with Me before others, I, the Son of Man, will affirm you before God and all the heavenly messengers. ⁹But if you deny Me before others, you will be denied before God and all the heavenly messengers. ¹⁰People can speak a word against Me, the Son of Man, and the sin is forgivable. *But they can go too far,* slandering the testimony of the Holy Spirit by rejecting His message about Me, and they won't be forgiven for that.

¹¹So you can anticipate that you will be put on trial before the synagogues and religious officials. Don't worry how you'll respond, and don't worry what you should say. ¹²The Holy Spirit will give you the words to say at the moment when you need them.

*J*esus has a lot to say about money. In the kingdom of God, money is valued in a very different way. In fact, concern for money can easily turn the spiritual life into a lukewarm, halfhearted affair.

¹³A person in the crowd got Jesus' attention.

Person in the Crowd: Teacher, intervene and tell my brother to share the family inheritance with me.

* 11:49 Literally, apostles
* 12:5-6 Two small coins

Jesus: ¹⁴Since when am I your judge or arbitrator?

¹⁵Then He used that opportunity to speak to the crowd.

Jesus: You'd better be on your guard against any type of greed, for a person's life is not about having a lot of possessions.

¹⁶(then, beginning another parable) A wealthy man owned some land that produced a huge harvest. ¹⁷He often thought to himself, "I have a problem here. I don't have anywhere to store all my crops. What should I do? ¹⁸I know! I'll tear down my small barns and build even bigger ones, and then I'll have plenty of storage space for my grain and all my other goods. ¹⁹Then I'll be able to say to myself, 'I have it made! I can relax and take it easy for years! So I'll just sit back, eat, drink, and have a good time!' "

²⁰Then God interrupted the man's conversation with himself. "Excuse Me, Mr. Brilliant, but your time has come. Tonight you will die. Now who will enjoy everything you've earned and saved?"

²¹This is how it will be for people who accumulate huge assets for themselves but have no assets in relation to God.

²²(then, to His disciples) This is why I keep telling you not to worry about anything in life—about what you'll eat, about how you'll clothe your body. ²³Life is more than food, and the body is more than fancy clothes. ²⁴Think about those crows flying over there: do they plant and harvest crops? Do they own silos or barns? *Look at them fly.* It looks like God is taking pretty good care of them, doesn't it? Remember that you are more precious to God than birds! ²⁵Which one of you can add a single hour to your life or 18 inches* to your height by worrying really hard? ²⁶If worry can't change anything, why do you do it so much?

²⁷Think about those beautiful wild lilies growing over there. They don't work up a sweat toiling for needs or wants—they don't worry about clothing. Yet the great King Solomon never had an outfit that was half as glorious as theirs!

²⁸Look at the grass growing over there. One day it's thriving in the fields. The next day it's being used as fuel. *If God takes such good care of such transient things,* how much more you can depend on God to care for you, weak in faith as you are. ²⁹Don't reduce your life to the pursuit of food and drink; don't let your mind be filled with anxiety. ³⁰People of the world who don't know God pursue these things, *but you have a Father caring for you,* a Father who knows all your needs.

³¹*Since you don't need to worry—about security and safety, about food and clothing*—then pursue God's kingdom *first and foremost,* and these other things will come to you as well.

³²My little flock, don't be afraid. *God is your Father, and* your Father's great joy is to give you His kingdom.

³³That means you can sell your possessions and give generously to the poor. You can have a different kind of savings plan: one that never depreciates, one that never defaults, one that can't be plundered by crooks or destroyed by natural calamities. ³⁴*Your treasure will be stored in the heavens,* and since your treasure is there, your heart will be lodged there as well.

³⁵⁻³⁶*I'm not just talking theory. There is urgency in all this.* If you're apathetic and complacent, then you'll miss the moment of opportunity. You should be wide awake and on your toes like servants who are waiting for their master to return from a big wedding reception. They'll have their shoes on and their lamps lit so they can open the door for him as soon as he arrives home. ³⁷How fortunate those servants will be when the master knocks and they open the door immediately! You know what the master will do? He'll put on an apron, sit them down at the kitchen table, and he'll serve them a midnight snack. ³⁸The later he comes home—whether it's at midnight or even later, just before dawn—the more fortunate the alert servants will be.

* 12:25 Literally, one cubit

³⁹*In contrast, imagine a complacent, apathetic household manager who has no sense of urgency. He wanders out one night and leaves the door unlocked, and some thieves sneak in and empty the place.* If he had been aware that thieves *were waiting in the bushes* and what hour they were coming, [he would have watched and]* he never would have left the house! ⁴⁰I'm trying to tell you that these are times for alertness, times requiring a sense of urgency and intensity, because *like the master in the first story or the thief in the second,* the Son of Man shows up by surprise.

Peter: ⁴¹Lord, I'm not sure if this parable is intended only for us disciples or if this is for everyone else too.

Jesus: ⁴²Imagine the stories of two household managers, and decide for yourself which one is faithful and smart. Each household manager is told by his master *to take good care of all his possessions and* to oversee the other employees—*the butlers, cooks, gardeners, and so on.* ⁴³One servant immediately busies himself in doing just what he was told. His master eventually comes to check on him ⁴⁴and rewards him with a major promotion and with more responsibility and trust. ⁴⁵The other household manager thinks, "Look, my boss is going to be gone for a long time. *I can be complacent; there's no urgency here.*" So he beats the other employees—the women as well as the men. He sits around *like a slob,* eating and getting drunk. ⁴⁶Then the boss comes home unexpectedly and catches him by surprise. One household manager will be fortunate indeed, and the other will be cut into pieces and thrown out.

⁴⁷Now if a servant who is given clear instructions by his master doesn't follow those instructions but instead is complacent and apathetic, then he will be punished severely. ⁴⁸But if a servant doesn't know what his master expects and behaves badly, then he will receive a lighter punishment. If you are given much, much will be required of you. If much is entrusted to you, much will be expected of you.

⁴⁹*This is serious business we're involved in.* My mission is to send a purging fire on the earth! In fact, I can hardly wait to see the smoke rising. ⁵⁰I have a kind of ceremonial washing* to go through, and I can't relax until My mission is accomplished! ⁵¹Do you think I've come with a nice little message of peace? No way. Believe Me, My message will divide. ⁵²It will divide a household of five into three against two or two against three. ⁵³It will divide father against son and son against father; mother against daughter and daughter against mother; mother-in-law against daughter-in-law and daughter-in-law against mother-in-law.

⁵⁴(speaking to the crowd) You see a cloud arise *from the sea* in the west, and you can say, "Here comes a shower!" And you're right. ⁵⁵Or you feel the hot wind blowing in from *the desert in* the south and you say, "It's going to be really hot!" And you're right. ⁵⁶Listen, hypocrites! You can predict the weather by paying attention to the sky and the earth, but why can't you interpret the urgency of this present moment? ⁵⁷Why don't you see it for yourselves?

⁵⁸Imagine you're being sued. You and your accuser are on your way to court. Wouldn't you do everything in your power to settle out of court before you stand before the magistrate? After all, he might drag you to stand before the judge, and the judge might hand you over to the police, and they might throw you in jail. ⁵⁹Once you're in jail, it's too late: you're not going anywhere until you've paid in full.

13 As He said this, some people told Him the latest news about a group of Galilean pilgrims *in Jerusalem—a group not unlike Jesus' own entourage.* Pilate butchered them *while they were at*

* 12:39 The earliest manuscripts omit the bracketed portion.
* 12:50 Literally, immersion

worship, their own blood mingling with the blood of their sacrifices.

Jesus: [2]Do you think these Galileans *were somehow being singled out for their sins,* that they were worse than any other Galileans, because they suffered this terrible death? [3]Of course not. But listen, if you do not consider God's ways and truly change, then friends, you should prepare to face His judgment and eternal death.

[4]*Speaking of current events,* you've all heard about the 18 people killed *in that building accident* when the tower in Siloam fell. Were they extraordinarily bad people, worse than anyone else in Jerusalem, *so that they would deserve such an untimely death?* [5]Of course not. *But all the buildings of Jerusalem will come crashing down on you* if you don't wake up and change direction now.

[6](following up with this parable) A man has a fig tree planted in his vineyard. One day he comes out looking for fruit on it, but there are no figs. [7]He says to the vineyard keeper, "Look at this tree. For three years, I've come hoping to find some fresh figs, but what do I find? Nothing. So just go ahead and cut it down. Why waste the space with a fruitless tree?"

[8]The vineyard keeper replies, "Give it another chance, sir. Give me one more year working with it. I'll cultivate the soil and heap on some manure to fertilize it. [9]If it surprises us and bears fruit next year, that will be great, but if not, then we'll cut it down."

[10]Around this time, He was teaching in a synagogue on the Sabbath, *the Jewish day of rest.* [11]A woman there had been sick for 18 years; she was weak, hunched over, and unable to stand up straight. [12-13]Jesus placed His hands on her and suddenly she could stand straight again. She started praising God, [14]but the synagogue official was indignant because Jesus had not kept their Sabbath regulations by performing this healing.

Synagogue Official: Look, there are six other days when it's appropriate to get work done. Come on those days to be healed, not on the Sabbath!

Jesus: [15]You *religious leaders* are such hypocrites! Every single one of you unties his ox or donkey from its manger every single Sabbath Day, and then you lead it out to get a drink of water, right? [16]Do you care more about your farm animals than you care about this woman, one of Abraham's daughters, oppressed by Satan for 18 years? Can't we untie her from her oppression on the Sabbath?

[17]As the impact of His words settled in, His critics were humiliated, but everyone else loved what Jesus said and celebrated everything He was doing.

Jesus (explaining): [18]Do you want to understand the kingdom of God? Do you want Me to tell you what it's like? [19]It's like a single mustard seed that someone took and planted in his garden. That tiny seed grew and became a tree so large that the birds could fly in and make their nests in its branches.

[20]Do you want Me to tell you what the kingdom of God is like? [21]It's like some yeast which a woman hid within a huge quantity of flour; soon the whole batch of dough was rising.

[22]He was pressing toward Jerusalem, His journey taking Him through various towns and villages. In each one, He taught the people. [23]Once a person asked this question:

Inquiring Individual: Lord, will only a few people be rescued?

Jesus: [24]Strive to enter through the narrow door now, because many people—hear Me on this—will try to enter *later on* and will not be able to. [25]Imagine you want to enter someone's home, but you wait until after the homeowner has shut the door. Then you stand outside and bang on the door, and you say, "Sir, please open the door for us!" But he will answer, "I don't know where you're from."

[26]Then you'll say, "Just a minute. We ate and drank with you, and you taught in our streets." [27]But he'll say, "Sorry, I have

no idea where you're from. Leave me, all of you evildoers." [28]Then you'll see something that will make you cry and grind your teeth together—you'll see Abraham and Isaac and Jacob and all the prophets in the kingdom of God, but you yourselves will be on the outside looking in. [29]And then you'll see people streaming in from east and west, from north and south, gathering around the table in the kingdom of God, *but you'll be on the outside looking in.* [30]That's how it will be; some are last now who will be first then, and some are first now who will be last then.

[31]Right then some Pharisees came and warned Him.

Pharisees: You'd better get out of here because Herod is plotting Your murder.

Jesus: [32]You can give that sly fox this message: "Watch as I cast out demons and perform healings today and tomorrow, and on the third day I'll reach My destination. [33]But for today and tomorrow and the next day, I have to continue My journey, for no prophet should perish outside of Jerusalem."

[34]O Jerusalem! O Jerusalem! You kill the prophets and you stone the messengers who are sent to you. How often I wanted to gather in your children as a hen gathers in her chicks under her wings, but you were not willing to come to Me. [35]Look now, your house is abandoned and empty. You won't see Me until you welcome Me with the words *of the Psalms,* "Anyone who comes in the name of the Eternal One will be blessed!"*

14 Another Sabbath Day came and Jesus was invited to an official's home for a meal. This fellow was a leader of the Pharisees, and Jesus was still under close surveillance by them. [2]Jesus noticed a man suffering from a swelling disorder. [3]He questioned the religious scholars and Pharisees.

Jesus: Is it permitted by traditions and the Hebrew Scriptures to heal people on the Sabbath, or is it forbidden?

[4]They didn't reply. Then Jesus healed the man and sent him on his way.

Jesus: [5]Would any single one of you leave his son* or even his ox in a well on the Sabbath if he had fallen into it, or would you pull him out immediately?

[6]They still didn't reply.

[7]Then He noticed how the guests were jockeying for places of honor at the dinner, so He gave them advice.

Jesus: [8]Whenever someone invites you to a wedding dinner, don't sit at the head table. Someone more important than you might also have been invited, [9]and your host will have to humiliate you publicly by telling you to give your seat to the other guest and to go find an open seat in the back of the room. [10]Instead, go and sit in the back of the room. Then your host may find you and say, "My friend! Why are you sitting back here? Come up to this table near the front!" Then you will be publicly honored in front of everyone. [11]Listen, if you lift yourself up, you'll be put down, but if you humble yourself, you'll be honored.

[12]Jesus still wasn't finished. Now He turned to the host who had invited Him to this gathering.

Jesus: When you host a dinner or banquet, don't invite your friends, your brothers, your relatives, or your rich neighbors. If you do, they might invite you to a party of their own, and you'll be repaid for your kindness. [13]Instead, invite the poor, the amputees, the cripples, the blind. [14]Then you'll be blessed because they can

* 13:35 Psalm 118:26
* 14:5 Some manuscripts read "donkey."

never repay you. Your reward will come from God at the resurrection of the just and good.

Guest: ¹⁵Blessed is everyone who will eat bread in the kingdom of God!

Jesus: ¹⁶A man once hosted a huge banquet and invited many guests. ¹⁷When the time came, he sent his servant to tell the guests who had agreed to come, "We're ready! Come now!" ¹⁸But then every single guest began to make excuses. One said, "Oh, *I'm sorry*. I just bought some land, and I need to go see it. Please excuse me." Another said, "*So sorry*. I just bought five pairs of oxen. I need to go check them out. Please excuse me." Another said, "I just got married, so I can't come."

²¹The servant returned and reported their responses to his master. His master was angry and told the servant, "Go out quickly to the streets and alleys around town and bring the poor, the amputees, the blind, and the cripples."

²²The servant came back again: "Sir, I've done as you said, but there is still more room." ²³And the host said, "Well then, go out to the highways and hedges and bring in the complete strangers you find there, until my house is completely full. ²⁴One thing is for sure, not one single person on the original guest list shall enjoy this banquet."

²⁵Great crowds joined Him on His journey, and He turned to them.

Jesus: ²⁶If any of you come to Me without hating your own father, mother, wife, children, brothers, sisters, and yes, even your own life, you can't be My disciple. ²⁷If you don't carry your own cross *as if to your own execution* as you follow Me, you can't be part of My movement. ²⁸Just imagine that you want to build a tower. Wouldn't you first sit down and estimate the cost to be sure you have enough to finish what you start? ²⁹If you lay the foundation but then can't afford to finish the tower, everyone will mock you: ³⁰"Look at that guy who started something that he couldn't finish!"

³¹Or imagine a king gearing up to go to war. Wouldn't he begin by sitting down *with his advisors* to determine whether his 10,000 troops could defeat the opponent's 20,000 troops? ³²If not, he'll send a peace delegation quickly and negotiate a peace treaty. ³³In the same way, if you want to be My disciple, it will cost you everything. *Don't underestimate that cost!*

³⁴Don't be like salt that has lost its taste. How can its saltiness be restored? *Flavorless salt is absolutely worthless.* ³⁵You can't even use it as fertilizer, so it's worth less than manure! Don't just listen to My words here. Get the deeper meaning.

15 Jesus became increasingly popular among *notorious* sinners—tax collectors and other social outcasts. ²The Pharisees and religious scholars noticed this.

Pharisees and Religious Scholars: This man welcomes immoral people and enjoys their company over a meal!

Jesus (*with another parable*): ³⁻⁴Wouldn't every single one of you, if you have 100 sheep and lose one, leave the 99 in their grazing lands and go out searching for the lost sheep until you find it? ⁵When you find the lost sheep, wouldn't you hoist it up on your shoulders, feeling wonderful? ⁶And when you go home, wouldn't you call together your friends and neighbors? Wouldn't you say, "Come over and celebrate with me, because I've found my lost sheep"? ⁷This is how it is in heaven. They're happier over one sinner who changes his way of life than they are over 99 good and just people who don't need to change their ways of life.

⁸Or imagine a woman who has 10 silver coins. She loses one. Doesn't she light a lamp, sweep the whole house, and search diligently until that coin is found? ⁹And when she finds it, doesn't she invite her friends and neighbors and say, "Celebrate with me! I've found that

silver coin that I lost"? ¹⁰Can't you understand? There is joy in the presence of all God's messengers over even one sinner who changes his way of life.

¹¹Once there was this man who had two sons. ¹²One day the younger son came to his father and said, "Father, eventually I'm going to inherit my share of your estate. Rather than waiting until you die, I want you to give me my share now." And so the father *liquidated assets and* divided them. ¹³A few days passed and this younger son gathered all his wealth and set off on a journey to a distant land. Once there he wasted everything he owned on wild living. ¹⁴He was broke, a terrible famine struck that land, and he felt desperately hungry and in need. ¹⁵He got a job with one of the locals, who sent him into the fields to feed the pigs. ¹⁶The young man felt so miserably hungry that he wished he could eat the slop the pigs were eating. Nobody gave him anything.

¹⁷So he had this moment of self-reflection: *"What am I doing here?* Back home, my father's hired servants have plenty of food. Why am I here starving to death? ¹⁸I'll get up and return to my father, and I'll say, "Father, I have done wrong—wrong against God and against you. ¹⁹I have forfeited any right to be treated like your son, but I'm wondering if you'd treat me as one of your hired servants?" ²⁰So he got up and returned to his father. The father looked off in the distance and saw the young man returning. He felt compassion for his son and ran out to him, enfolded him in an embrace, and kissed him.

²¹The son said, "Father, I have done a terrible wrong in God's sight and in your sight too. I have forfeited any right to be treated as your son."

²²But the father turned to his servants and said, "Quick! Bring the best robe we have and put it on him. Put a ring on his finger and shoes on his feet. ²³Go get the fattest calf and butcher it. Let's have a feast and celebrate ²⁴because my son was dead and is alive again. He was lost and has been found." So they had this huge party.

²⁵Now the man's older son was still out in the fields working. He came home at the end of the day and heard music and dancing. ²⁶He called one of the servants and asked what was going on. ²⁷The servant said, "Your brother has returned, and your father has butchered the fattest calf to celebrate his safe return."

²⁸The older brother got really angry and refused to come inside, so his father came out and pleaded with him to join the celebration. ²⁹But he argued back, "Listen, all these years I've worked hard for you. I've never disobeyed one of your orders. But how many times have you even given me a little goat to roast for a party with my friends? Not once! *This is not fair!* ³⁰So this son of yours comes, this wasteful delinquent who has spent your hard-earned wealth on loose women, and what do you do? You butcher the fattest calf from our herd!"

³¹The father replied, "My son, you are always with me, and all I have is yours. ³²Isn't it right to join in the celebration and be happy? This is your brother we're talking about. He was dead and is alive again; he was lost and is found again!"

The parable ends. Jesus never tells us how it comes out. Did the older brother join the party and reconcile with his younger, wayward brother? Or did he stay outside, fuming over the seeming injustice of his father's extravagant love? The story remains unresolved because it is, in fact, an invitation—an invitation to the Pharisees and other opponents of Jesus to join Him in welcoming sinners and other outsiders into the joyful party of the Kingdom.

16

Here's a parable He told the disciples:

Jesus: Once there was a rich *and powerful* man who had an asset manager. One day, the man received word that his asset manager was squandering his assets.

2The rich man brought in the asset manager and said, "You've been accused of wrongdoing. I want a full and accurate accounting of all your financial transactions because you are really close to being fired."

3The manager said to himself, "*Oh, no!* Now what am I going to do? I'm going to lose my job here, and I'm too weak to dig ditches and too proud to beg. 4I have an idea. This plan will mean that I have a lot of hospitable friends when I get fired."

5So the asset manager set up appointments with each person who owed his master money. He said to the first debtor, "How much do you owe my boss?" 6The debtor replied, "A hundred barrels* of oil." The manager said, "I'm discounting your bill by half. Just write 50 on this contract." 7Then he said to the second debtor, "How much do you owe?" This fellow said, "A hundred bales* of wheat." The manager said, "I'm discounting your debt by 20 percent. Just write down 80 bales on this contract."

8When the manager's boss realized what he had done, he congratulated him for at least being clever. That's how it is: those attuned to this evil age are more clever in dealing with their affairs than the enlightened are in dealing with their affairs!

9*Learn some lessons from this crooked but clever asset manager.* Realize that the purpose of money is to strengthen friendships, to provide opportunities for being generous and kind. Eventually money will be useless to you—but if you use it generously to serve others, you will be welcomed joyfully into your eternal destination.

10If you're faithful in small-scale matters, you'll be faithful with far bigger responsibilities. If you're crooked in small responsibilities, you'll be no different in bigger things. 11If you can't even handle a small thing like money, who's going to entrust you with spiritual riches that really matter? 12If you don't manage well someone else's assets that are entrusted to you, who's going to give over to you important spiritual and personal relationships to manage?

13Imagine you're a servant and you have two masters giving you orders. *One tells you to do one thing, and the other tells you to do the opposite. What are you going to do?* You can't serve both, so you'll either hate the first and love the second, or you'll faithfully serve the first and despise the second. One master is God and the other is money. You can't serve them both.

14The Pharisees overheard all this, and they started mocking Jesus because they really loved money.

Jesus (to the Pharisees): 15*You've made your choice.* Your ambition is to look good in front of other people, not God. But God sees through to your hearts. He values things differently from you. The goals you and your peers are reaching for God detests.

16The law and the prophets had their role until the coming of John *the Preacher.* Since John's arrival, the good news of the kingdom of God has been taught while people are clamoring to enter it. 17*That's not to say that God's rules for living are useless.* The stars in the sky and the earth beneath your feet will pass away before one letter of God's rules for living become worthless.

18*Take God's rules regarding marriage for example.* If a man divorces his wife and marries somebody else, then it's still adultery *because that man has broken his vow to God.* And if a man marries a woman divorced from her husband, he's committing adultery *for the same reason.*

* 16:6 About 600-800 gallons
* 16:7 About 700 bushels

19There was this rich man who had everything—purple clothing of fine quality and high fashion, gourmet meals every day, and a large house. 20Just outside his front gate lay this poor *homeless* fellow named Lazarus. Lazarus was covered in ugly skin lesions. 21He was so hungry he wished he could scavenge scraps from the rich man's trash. Dogs would come and lick the sores on his skin. 22The poor fellow died and was carried on the arms of the heavenly messengers to the embrace of Abraham. Then the rich fellow died and was buried 23and found himself in the place of the dead. In his torment, he looked up and off in the distance he saw Abraham, with Lazarus in his embrace.

24He shouted out, "Father Abraham! Please show me mercy! Would you send *that beggar* Lazarus to dip his fingertip in water and cool my tongue? These flames are hot, and I'm in agony!"

25But Abraham said, "Son, you seem to be forgetting something: your life was full to overflowing with comforts and pleasures, and the life of Lazarus was just as full with suffering and pain. So now is his time of comfort, and now is your time of agony. 26Besides, a great canyon separates you and us. Nobody can cross over from our side to yours, or from your side to ours."

27"Please, Father *Abraham,* I beg you," the formerly rich man continued, "send Lazarus to my father's house. 28I have five brothers there, *and they're on the same path I was on.* If Lazarus warns them, they'll choose another path and won't end up here in torment."

29But Abraham said, *"Why send Lazarus?* They already have the law of Moses and the writings of the prophets to instruct them. Let your brothers hear them."

30"No, Father Abraham," he said, *"they're already ignoring the law and the prophets.* But if someone came back from the dead, then they'd listen for sure; then they'd change their way of life."

31Abraham answered, "If they're not listening to Moses and the prophets, they won't be convinced even if someone comes back from the dead."

You've noticed, no doubt, how the theme of money and wealth has come up again and again. It's what really motivates the Pharisees, it turns out. We might say that money is God's top competitor. In the previous parable, Jesus turns the tables. The rich man, who represents what most people wish they could become, turns out to be the one who is hopeless in God's judgment; he was rich in possessions but poor in compassion, and compassion is what God was measuring, not wealth. The kingdom of God, Jesus is making clear, calls rich people to stop working to increase their personal wealth portfolio; instead, it challenges them to join God by using their wealth and power on behalf of the poor.

17 Jesus *(to His disciples)*: 1You can't stop temptations to do wrong from coming. But how tragic it will be for the person who becomes the source of the temptation! 2It would be better if a millstone were hung around his neck and he were thrown into the sea, than that he should offend one of these little ones.

3So each of you needs to be careful. *Instead of encouraging wrongdoing in any way, be a person who overcomes wrongdoing.* If your brother sins [against you],* confront him about it, and if he has a change of mind and heart, then forgive him. 4Even if he wrongs you seven times in a single day, if he turns back to you each time and says he's sorry and will change, you must forgive him.

The Lord's Emissaries: 5*We don't have enough faith for this!* Help our faith to grow!

Jesus *(pointing to a nearby mulberry tree)*: 6*It's not like you need a huge amount of faith. If you just had faith the size of a single, tiny mustard seed, you could say to this huge tree, "Pull up your roots and*

---

* 17:3 The earliest manuscripts omit this portion.

replant yourself in the sea," and it would *fly through the sky and* do what you said. *So even a little faith can accomplish the seemingly impossible.*

7Imagine this scenario. You have a servant—say he's been out plowing a field or taking care of the sheep—and he comes in hot and sweaty from his work. Are you going to say, *"You poor thing!* Come in and sit down right away"? Of course not! 8Wouldn't you be more likely to say, "First, cook my supper and set the table, and then after I've eaten, you can get something to eat and drink for yourself"? 9And after your servant has done everything you told him to do, are you going to make a big deal about it and thank him? [I don't think so!]* 10Now apply this situation to yourselves. When you've done everything I'm telling you to do, just say, "We're servants, unworthy of extra consideration or thanks; we're just doing our duty."

11Jesus was still pressing toward Jerusalem, taking a road that went along the border between Samaria *(considered undesirable territory)* and Galilee. 12On the outskirts of a border town along this road, He was greeted from a distance by a group of 10 people who were under quarantine because of an ugly and disgusting skin disease known as leprosy.

Lepers *(shouting across the distance)*:
13Jesus, Master, show mercy to us!
Jesus: 14Go now and present yourselves to the priests *for inspection of your disease.*

They went, and before they reached the priests, their skin disease was healed, *leaving no trace of the disease that scarred them and separated them from the community.*

15One of them, the instant he realized he had been healed, turned and ran back to Jesus, shouting praises to God. 16He prostrated himself facedown at Jesus' feet.

Leper: Thank You! Thank You!

Now this fellow happened to be, *not a Jew, but a Samaritan.*

Jesus: 17Didn't all ten receive the same healing this fellow did? Where are the other nine? 18Was the only one who came back to give God praise an outsider? 19(to the Samaritan man) Get up, and go your way. Your faith has made you healthy again.

20Some Pharisees asked Jesus when the kingdom of God would come.

Jesus: The kingdom of God comes—but not with signs that you can observe. 21People are not going to say, "Look! Here it is!" They're not going to say, "Look! It's over there!" You want to see the kingdom of God? The kingdom of God is already here among you.
   22(to His disciples) Days are coming when you will wish you could see just one of the days of the Son of Man, but you won't see it. 23People will say, "Look, it's there!" or "Look! It's here!" Don't even bother looking. Don't follow their lead. 24You know how lightning flashes across the sky, bringing light from one horizon to the other. That's how the Son of Man will be when His time comes.
   25But first, He must face many sufferings. He must be rejected by this generation. 26The days of the Son of Man will be like the days of Noah. 27People were eating, drinking, marrying, and being given in marriage. *Everything seemed completely normal* until the day Noah entered the ark. Then it started raining, and soon they were all destroyed by the flood.
   28It was just the same in the days of Lot. People were eating, drinking, buying, selling, planting, building, *and carrying on business as usual.* 29But then came the day when Lot left Sodom—a different kind of rain began to fall, and they were all destroyed by fire and sulfur falling from the sky.* 30That's how it will be on the day when the Son of Man is revealed.
   31When that day comes, if you're on the housetop, don't run inside to try to save any of your belongings. If you're in

* 17:9 The earliest manuscripts omit this portion.
* 17:29 Genesis 19:24

the field, don't bother running back *to the house.* [32]Remember Lot's wife. *Turning back is fatal for those who do so.* [33]If you try to hold on to your life, it will slip through your fingers; if you let go of your life, you'll keep it. [34]Listen, on the day of the Son of Man, two people will be asleep in bed; destruction will take one and the other will be left to survive. [35]Two women will be grinding grain together; destruction will take one and the other will survive. [[36]Two men will be working out in the field; destruction will overtake one and the other will survive.]*

Disciples: [37]Where, Lord?

Jesus: Where vultures circle over rotting corpses.

18 He told them a parable, urging them to keep praying and never grow discouraged. The parable went like this:

Jesus: [2]There was a judge living in a certain city. He showed no respect for God or humanity. [3]In that same city there was a widow. Again and again she kept coming to him seeking justice: "Clear my name from my adversary's false accusations!" [4]He paid no attention to her request for a while, but then he said to himself, "I don't care about what God thinks of me, much less what any mere human thinks. [5]But this widow is driving me crazy. She's never going to quit coming to see me unless I hear her case and provide her legal protection."

[6]Did you catch what this self-assured judge said? [7]*If he can be moved to act justly,* won't God bring justice for His chosen people when they cry to Him day and night? Will He be slow to bring them justice? [8]Mark My words: God will intervene fast with vindication. But here's the question: when the Son of Man comes, will He find anyone who still has faith?

*T*hroughout His life and teachings, Jesus emphasizes the importance of persistence and humility

in prayer. Why is prayer so important for Jesus? It's clear that the kingdom of God will not come through valiant efforts or foolproof strategies. It will come as people pray, "may Your kingdom come," with persistence and with humility.

[9]He told another parable—this one addressed to people who were confident in their self-righteousness and looked down on other people with disgust.

Jesus: [10]Imagine two men *walking up a road,* going to the temple to pray. One of them is a Pharisee and the other is a *despised* tax collector. [11]Once inside the temple, the Pharisee stands up and prays this prayer in honor of himself: "God, how I thank You that I am not on the same level as other people—crooks, cheaters, the sexually immoral—like this tax collector over here. [12]*Just look at me!* I fast *not once but* twice a week, and I faithfully pay my tithes on every penny of income." [13]Over in the corner, the tax collector begins to pray, but he won't even lift his eyes to heaven. He pounds on his chest *in sorrow* and says, "God, be merciful to me, a sinner!"

[14]*Now imagine these two men walking back down the road to their homes.* Listen, it's the tax collector who walks home clean before God, and not the Pharisee, because whoever lifts himself up will be put down and whoever takes a humble place will be lifted up.

[15]Some people brought infants to Jesus, hoping He would touch them *in blessing.* The disciples rebuked them for doing so, [16]but Jesus called to the people.

Jesus: Let the little children come to Me. Never hinder them! Don't you realize—the kingdom of God belongs to those who are like children? [17]You can depend on this: if you don't receive the Kingdom as a child would, you won't enter it at all.

* 17:36 Most manuscripts omit verse 36.

Public Official: [18]Good Teacher, what do I need to do to inherit the life of the age to come?

Jesus: [19]Why did you just call Me good? No one is good but God—only God. [20]You know what the *Hebrew* Scriptures command: "Do not commit adultery; do not murder; do not steal; do not bear false witness; honor your father and mother."*

Public Official: [21]I've already been doing these things—since I came of age.

Jesus: [22]One thing you still lack—one thing; sell all your possessions and distribute the proceeds to the poor. Then you will have treasure in heaven. Then you can come and follow Me.

[23]The man heard these words and sadness came over his face, for his wealth was considerable.

Jesus: [24]What a hard thing it is for those with much wealth to enter the kingdom of God! [25]In fact, it would be easier for a camel to squeeze through the eye of a needle than it would be for a rich person to enter the kingdom of God!

Listeners: [26]Then who can be liberated?

Jesus: [27]Remember, what is humanly impossible is possible with God.

Peter: [28]We have left our homes and followed You.

Jesus: [29]I'm telling you the truth: there is nobody who leaves his house or wife or siblings or parents or children for the sake of the kingdom of God [30]who will not receive more than he has given up—much more—in this age and in the age to come. He will receive eternal life.

[31]He took the twelve aside and spoke privately to them.

Jesus: Look, *my friends,* we are going up to Jerusalem. Everything the prophets have written about the Son of Man will be fulfilled. [32]He will be handed over to the outsiders. They will mock Him, disgrace Him, and spit on Him; [33]they will scourge Him, and they will kill Him. And on the third day, He will rise from death.

[34]But they had no comprehension of what He was talking about. The meaning was hidden from them, and they couldn't grasp it.

[35]*Picture this:*

Jesus is nearing the city of Jericho. A blind man is sitting there, begging by the roadside. [36]He can hear the sounds of the crowd *accompanying Jesus*, and he asks what's going on.

Crowd: [37]Jesus of Nazareth is passing this way.

[38]Then the man starts shouting.

Blind Man: Jesus, Son of *King* David, show mercy to me!

[39]The people in the front of the crowd reprimand him and tell him to be quiet, but he just shouts louder.

Blind Man: Son of *King* David, show mercy to me!

[40]Jesus stops and tells the people to bring the man over to Him. The man stands in front of Jesus.

Jesus: [41]What do you want Me to do for you?

Blind Man: Lord, let me receive my sight.

Jesus: [42]Receive your sight; your faith has made you well.

[43]At that very instant, the man is able to see. He begins following Jesus, shouting praises to God; and everyone in the crowd, when they see what has happened, starts praising God too.

19

Jesus enters Jericho and seems only to be passing through. [2]Living in Jericho is a man named Zaccheus. He's the head tax collector and is very rich. [3]He is also very short. He wants to see Jesus as He passes through

* 18:20 Exodus 20:12-16; Deuteronomy 5:16-20

the center of town, but he can't get a glimpse because the crowd blocks his view. [4]So he runs ahead of the crowd and climbs up into a sycamore tree so he can see Jesus when He passes beneath him.

[5]Jesus comes along and looks up into the tree[, and there He sees Zaccheus].*

Jesus: Zaccheus, hurry down from that tree because I need to stay at your house *tonight*.

[6]Zaccheus scrambles down and joyfully brings Jesus back to his house. [7]Now the crowd sees this, and they're upset.

Crowd (*grumbling*): Jesus has become the houseguest of this fellow who is a notorious sinner.

Zaccheus: [8]Lord, I am giving half of my goods to the poor, and whomever I have cheated I will pay back four times what I took.

Jesus: [9]Today liberation has come to this house, since even Zaccheus is living as a son of Abraham. [10]For the Son of Man came to seek and to liberate the lost.

[11]The crowd has been listening to all this, and everyone assumes that the kingdom of God is going to appear at any moment, since He's nearing Jerusalem. So He tells them this parable:

Jesus: [12]A ruler once planned a journey to a distant country to take the throne of that country and then return home. [13]Before his departure, he called 10 of his servants and gave them each about three months of wages.* "Use this money to buy and sell until I return." [14]After he departed, the people under his rule despised him and sent messengers with a clear message: "We do not want this man to rule over us."

[15]He successfully assumed kingship *of the distant country* and returned home. He called his 10 servants together and told them to give an account of their success in doing business with the money he had entrusted to them.

[16]The first came before him and said, "Lord, I have made 10 times the amount you entrusted to me." [17]The ruler replied, "Well done! You're a good servant indeed! Since you have been faithful in handling a small amount of money, I'll entrust you with authority over 10 cities *in my new kingdom*."

[18]The second came and said, "Lord, I've made five times the original amount." [19]The ruler replied, "I'll entrust you with authority over five cities."

[20]A third came and said, "Lord, I have successfully preserved the money you gave me. I wrapped it up in a napkin and hid it away [21]because I was afraid of you. After all, you're a tough man. You have a way of taking a profit without making an investment and harvesting when you didn't plant any seed."

[22]The ruler replied, "I will condemn you using your very own words, you worthless servant! So I'm a severe man, am I? So I take a profit without making an investment and harvest without planting seed? [23]Then why didn't you invest my money in the bank so I could have at least gained some interest on it?" [24]The ruler told the onlookers, "Take the money I gave him, and give it to the one who multiplied my investment by 10."

[25]Then the onlookers replied, "Lord, he already has 10 times the original amount!"

[26]The ruler responded, "Listen, whoever has some will be given more, and whoever doesn't have anything will lose what he thinks he has. [27]And these enemies of mine who didn't want me to rule over them—bring them here and execute them in my presence."

*I*n Jesus' day, as today, many people want to speculate about when the kingdom of God will fully arrive. But Jesus, through the previous parable, makes it clear that such speculation is a waste of time. Instead, people should be busy investing their lives in

* 19:5 The earliest manuscripts omit this portion.
* 19:13 Literally, mina, Roman coins

the kingdom of God. And Luke has made clear what that means in some earlier episodes. In His encounter with the rich young ruler, Jesus invited the man to stop collaborating with the Roman Empire for his own benefit and to switch sides—so he could start working with the kingdom of God for the sake of the poor. The man refused; but soon after, a man named Zaccheus volunteered to do that very thing: to stop working for his own wealth by collaborating with Caesar's kingdom and to start working for justice for the poor by collaborating with God's kingdom. Speculation about the dates and times of the coming of the Kingdom can make us miss the point—we should live, starting now, in the way of the Kingdom.

28When He finished the parable, He pushed onward, climbing the steep hills toward Jerusalem.

29He approached the towns of Bethphage and Bethany, which are near Mount Olivet. He sent two of the disciples ahead.

Jesus: 30Go to the next village. When you enter, you will find a colt tied—a colt that has never been ridden before. Untie it and bring it here. 31If anyone asks you why you're untying it, just say, "The Lord needs it."

32So the two disciples found things just as He had told them. 33When its owners did indeed ask why they were untying the colt, 34the disciples answered *as they had been instructed.*

Disciples: The Lord needs it.

35They brought the colt to Jesus, threw their coats on the colt's back, and then sat Jesus on it. 36As Jesus rode along, some people began to spread their garments on the road *as a carpet.* 37When they passed the crest of Mount Olivet and began descending toward Jerusalem, a huge crowd of disciples began to celebrate and praise God with loud shouts, glorifying God for the mighty works they had witnessed.

Crowd of Disciples: 38The King who comes in the name of the Eternal One is blessed!*
    Peace in heaven! Glory in the highest!
Pharisees *(who were in the crowd)*:
    39Teacher, tell these people to stop making these wild claims and acting this way!
Jesus: 40Listen—if they were silent, the very rocks would start to shout!

41When Jerusalem came into view, He looked intently at the city and began to weep.

Jesus: 42How I wish you knew today what would bring peace! But you can't see. 43Days will come when your enemies will build up a siege ramp, and you will be surrounded and contained on every side.* 44Your enemies will smash you into rubble and not leave one stone standing on another, and they will cut your children down too, because you did not recognize the day when God's Anointed One visited you.

*I*n this powerful scene as Jesus comes into the city, echoing the words of Zechariah 9:9, Jesus shows how His kingdom is upside down compared to the kingdoms of this world. Caesar would enter a town riding a white stallion, accompanied by dignitaries and soldiers with weapons. Jesus comes on a little donkey, cheered by common people waving branches and coats. The contrast between the two ways, He suggests through tears, is the difference between peace and violent destruction.

* 19:38 Psalm 118:26
* 19:43 Ezekiel 4:2; 26:8

⁴⁵He entered *Jerusalem* and went into the temple. He began driving out the temple merchants.

Jesus: ⁴⁶The *Hebrew* Scriptures say, "My house shall be a house of prayer,"* but you have turned it into a shelter for thieves.*

⁴⁷He came back day after day to teach in the temple. The chief priests, the religious scholars, and the leading men of the city wanted to kill Him, ⁴⁸but because He was so popular among the people—who hung upon each word He spoke—they were unable to do anything.

20 One day when He was teaching the people in the temple and proclaiming the good news, the chief priests, religious scholars, and elders came up and questioned Him.

Elders: ²Tell us by what authority You march into the temple and disrupt our worship. Who gave You this authority?

Jesus: ³Let Me ask you a question first. Tell Me this: ⁴was the ritual cleansing* of John *the Preacher* from God, or was it merely a human thing?

Chief Priests, Religious Scholars, and Elders (*conferring together*): ⁵If we say it was from God, then He'll ask us why we didn't believe John. ⁶If we say it was merely human, all the people will stone us because they are convinced that John was a true prophet.

⁷So they said they didn't know where John's ritual washing came from.

Jesus: ⁸Well then, if you won't answer My question, I won't tell you by what authority I have acted.

⁹He told the people another parable:

Jesus: A man planted a vineyard. He rented it to tenants and went for a long trip to another country. ¹⁰At the harvesttime, he sent a servant to the tenants so he could be paid his share of the vineyard's fruit, but the tenants beat the servant and sent him away empty-handed. ¹¹The man sent another servant, and they beat him and treated him disgracefully and sent him away empty-handed too. ¹²He sent a third servant who was injured and thrown out. ¹³Then the vineyard owner said, "Now what am I going to do? I'll send my much-loved son. They should treat him with respect."

¹⁴But when the tenants recognized the owner's son, they said, *"Here's our chance to actually own this vineyard!* Let's kill the owner's heir so we can claim this place as our own!" ¹⁵So they threw him out of the vineyard and murdered him. What do you think the owner will do to these scoundrels?

¹⁶*I'll tell you what he'll do;* he'll come and wipe those tenants out, and he'll give the vineyard to others.

Crowd: No! God forbid that this should happen!

Jesus: ¹⁷Why then do the *Hebrew* Scriptures contain these words:

The stone that the builders rejected
        has become the very stone
        that holds together the entire
            foundation?*

¹⁸Everyone who falls on that stone will be broken to fragments, and if that stone falls on anyone, he will be ground to dust.

¹⁹*That was the last straw for* the religious scholars and the chief priests; they were ready to attack Him right then and there. But they couldn't for fear of public opinion, and they realized that Jesus, through this parable, had exposed their violent intentions.

²⁰*Since they couldn't use overt violence against Him, they developed a covert plan.* They would keep Him under constant surveillance. They would send spies, pretending to ask sincere questions, listening for

* 19:46 Isaiah 56:7
* 19:46 Jeremiah 7:11
* 20:4 Literally, immersion, an act to show repentance
* 20:17 Psalm 118:22

something they could seize upon that would justify His arrest and condemnation under the governor's authority.

Chief Priests, Religious Scholars, and Elders: 21Teacher, we respect You because You speak and teach only what is right, You show no partiality to anyone, and You truly teach the way of God. 22So—is it lawful for us to pay taxes to Caesar's *occupying regime*, or should we refuse?

23He saw through their transparent trick.

Jesus: [Why are you trying to trick Me?]* 24Show Me a coin. Whose image and name are on this coin?

Chief Priests, Religious Scholars, and Elders: Caesar's.

Jesus: 25Well then, you should give to Caesar whatever is Caesar's, and you should give to God whatever is God's.

26Once again they failed to humiliate Him in public or catch Him in a punishable offense. They were confounded by His reply and couldn't say anything in response.
    27Another group came to test Him—this time from the Sadducees, a *rival party of the Pharisees*, who believe that there is no resurrection.

*I*n addition to the Pharisees, there was a religious sect in Jesus' day called the Sadducees. They were religious conservatives holding to an ancient tradition in Judaism that didn't believe in an afterlife. Their disbelief in an afterlife seemed to make them conclude, "There's only one life, and this is it, so you'd better play it safe." That meant that they were very happy to collaborate with the Romans—and make a healthy profit—rather than risk any kind of rebellion or revolt. For this reason, they were closely allied with another group called the Herodians, allies of Caesar's puppet king Herod. Their contemporaries, the Pharisees, who believed in an afterlife, were more

prone to risk their lives in a rebellion since they believed martyrs would be rewarded with resurrection. For this reason, the Pharisees were closely allied with the Zealots, who were more overtly revolutionary. But the Pharisees too were very fond of money. It's interesting to see each group try to trap Jesus and then to watch Jesus turn the tables on them, using each encounter to shed more light on the message of the kingdom of God. In case after case, as we've seen already and as you'll see again shortly, Jesus brings His hearers to the heart of the matter; and again and again, the bottom-line issue is money.

Sadducees: 28Teacher, Moses wrote *in the Hebrew Scriptures* that a man must marry his brother's wife and the new couple should bear children for his brother if his brother dies without heirs.* 29Well, once there were seven brothers, and the first took a wife and then died without fathering children. 30The second [took her as his wife and then he died childless,]* 31and then the third, and so on through the seven. They all died leaving no children. 32Finally the woman died too. 33*Here's our question:* in the resurrection, whose wife will she be, since all seven had her for a while? *Will she be the wife of seven men at once?*

Jesus: 34The children of this era marry and are given in marriage, 35but those who are considered worthy to attain the resurrection of the dead in the coming era do not marry and are not given in marriage. 36They are beyond mortality; they are on the level of heavenly messengers; they are children of God and children of the resurrection. 37*Since you brought up the issue of resurrection,* even Moses made clear in the passage about the burning bush that the dead are, in fact, raised. After all, he calls the Lord the

* 20:23 The earliest manuscripts omit this portion.
* 20:28 Deuteronomy 25:5
* 20:30 The earliest manuscripts omit this portion.

God of Abraham, Isaac, and Jacob.* [38]*By Moses' time, they were all dead,* but God isn't God of the dead, but of the living. So all live to God.

Religious Scholars: [39]Teacher, that was a good answer.

[40]After this no one had the courage to ask Him any more questions. [41]But He asked them a question.

Jesus: How is it that people say the Liberating King is David's descendant? [42]Don't you remember how David himself wrote in the Psalms,

The Master said to my master:
  "Sit here at My right hand,
  in the place of honor and power.
[43]And I will gather Your enemies together,
  lead them in on hands and knees,
  and You will rest Your feet on their backs."*

Did you hear that? David calls his son "Lord." Elders don't respect their younger that way. How is David's son also "Lord"?

[45]Jesus turned to His disciples, speaking loud enough for the others to hear.

Jesus: [46]Beware of the religious scholars. They like to parade around in long robes. They love being greeted in the marketplaces. They love taking the best seats in the synagogues. They adore being seated around the head table at banquets. [47]But *in their greed* they rob widows of their houses and *cover up their greed* with long pretentious prayers. Their condemnation will be all the worse *because of their hypocrisy.*

21 And then He turned His attention from the religious scholars to some wealthy people who were depositing their donations in the offering boxes. [2]A widow, obviously poor, came up and dropped two copper coins in one of the boxes.

Jesus: [3]I'm telling you the truth, this poor widow has made a bigger contribution than all of those rich fellows. [4]They're just giving from their surplus, but she is giving from her poverty—she's giving all she has to give.

[5]Some people were impressed with the temple's opulence—the precious stones and expensive decorations—but Jesus countered their observations.

Jesus: [6]Go ahead, look around, and be impressed; but days are coming when one stone will not be left standing on another. Everything here will be demolished.

Crowd: [7]When will this happen, Teacher? What signs will tell us this is about to occur?

Jesus: [8]Be careful. It's easy to be deceived. Many people will come claiming to have My authority. They'll shout, "I'm the One!" or "The time is now!" Don't take a step in their direction. [9]You'll hear about wars and conflicts, but don't be frightened at all because these things must surely come, although they don't signify the immediate coming of the end. [10]*You can count on this:* nation will attack nation, and kingdom will make war on kingdom. [11]There will be disturbances around the world—from great earthquakes to famines to epidemics. Terrifying things will happen, and there will be shocking signs from heaven. [12]But before any of this happens, they will capture you and persecute you. They'll send you to synagogues *for trial* and to prisons *for punishment*; you'll stand before kings and government officials for the sake of My name. [13]This will be your opportunity—your opportunity to tell your story. [14]Make up your mind in advance not to plan your strategy for answering their questions, [15]for when the time comes, I will give you the words to say—wise words—which none of your adversaries will be able to answer or argue against.

* 20:37 Exodus 3:6,15
* 20:42-43 Psalm 110:1

¹⁶Your own parents, brothers, relatives, and friends will turn on you and turn you in. Some of you will be killed, ¹⁷and all of you will be hated by everyone for the sake of My name.

¹⁸But whatever happens, not a single hair of your heads will be harmed. ¹⁹By enduring all of these things, you will find *not loss but gain*—not death but authentic life.

²⁰Here's how you will know that the destruction of Jerusalem *and her temple* is imminent: Jerusalem will be surrounded by armies. ²¹When that happens, *there's only one thing to do:* if you're in Judea, flee to the mountains; and if you're inside the city, escape; and if you're outside the city, stay there—don't enter— ²²because the time has come for the promised judgment to fall. ²³How sad it will be for all the pregnant women, for all the nursing mothers in those days! All the land of Israel and all her people will feel the distress, the anger, falling on them *like rain.* ²⁴The sword will cut some down, the outsider nations will take others captive, and this holy city, this Jerusalem, will be trampled upon by the outsiders until their times are fulfilled.

²⁵*There will be earth-shattering events*—the heavens themselves will seem to be shaken with signs in the sun, in the moon, and in the stars. And across the earth the *outsider* nations will feel powerless and terrified in the face of a roaring flood *of fear and foreboding,* crashing like tidal waves upon them. ²⁶"What's happening to the world?" people will wonder. The cosmic order will be destabilized. ²⁷And then, at that point, they will see the Son of Man coming in a cloud with power and blazing glory. ²⁸So when the troubles begin, *don't be afraid.* Look up—raise your head high, because the truth is that your liberation is fast approaching.

²⁹(continuing with a parable) Look over there at that fig tree—and all the trees surrounding it. ³⁰When the leaves break out of their buds, nobody has to tell you that summer is approaching; it's obvious to you. ³¹*It's the same in the larger scheme of things.* When you see all these things happening, you can be confident that the kingdom of God is approaching. ³²I'm telling you the truth: this generation will not pass from the scene before everything I'm telling you has occurred. ³³Heaven and earth will cease to exist before My words ever fail.

³⁴So be careful. Guard your hearts. They can be made heavy with moral laxity, with drunkenness, with the hassles of daily life. Then the day I've been telling you about might catch you unaware and trap you. ³⁵Because it's coming—nobody on earth will escape it. ³⁶So you have to stay alert, praying that you'll be able to escape the coming trials so you can stand tall in the presence of the Son of Man.

³⁷⁻³⁸Through this whole period of time, He taught in the temple each day. People would arrive at the temple early in the morning to listen. Then, at day's end, He would leave the city and sleep on Mount Olivet.

22 *This daily pattern continued* as they came closer to the holiday of Unleavened Bread, also known as the Passover.

> *J*esus taught of a judgment to come and the destruction of the temple. The crowds were intrigued with His teaching, but the religious leaders were increasingly nervous. All things moved toward a collision of ideas and faith at the most important feast of the year.

²The chief priests and religious scholars continued looking for a way to kill Jesus; they hadn't been able to act yet due to their fear of the people's reaction. ³At this point, Satan entered into one of the twelve, Judas (also called Iscariot). ⁴Judas set up a private meeting with the chief priests and the captains of the temple police to discuss a plan for betraying Jesus and putting Him

in their hands. ⁵*This was just the kind of break they had been waiting for,* so they were thrilled and agreed to a handsome payment. ⁶Everything was settled, and Judas simply waited for the right moment, when the crowds weren't around, to betray Jesus into their custody.

⁷They came to the Day of Unleavened Bread, a holy day when a special lamb (called the Passover lamb) had to be sacrificed. ⁸Jesus chose Peter and John and gave them instructions.

Jesus: Go and make all the necessary preparations for the Passover meal so we can eat together.

Peter and John: ⁹Where do You want us to make preparations?

Jesus: ¹⁰When you enter the city, you'll encounter a man carrying a jar of water. Just follow him *wherever he goes,* and when he enters a house, ¹¹tell the homeowner, "The Teacher has this question for you: 'Where is the guest room where I can share the Passover meal with My disciples?'" ¹²He'll show you a spacious second-story room that has all the necessary furniture. That's where you should prepare our meal.

¹³They did as He said and found everything just as He said it would be, and they prepared the Passover meal. ¹⁴When the meal was prepared, Jesus sat at the table, joined by His emissaries.*

The meal that Jesus and His disciples shared is still celebrated today among followers of Jesus. We surround it with varied rituals and music, but the original meal took place in the midst of great drama and tension. Next you'll hear the disciples arguing and Jesus teaching them yet another lesson about life in the kingdom of God. Jesus will speak of His own suffering and their betrayal and denial. Yet through it all, Jesus' focus remains on the central theme of His life and mission: the coming of the kingdom of God.

Jesus: ¹⁵It has been My deep desire to eat this Passover meal with you before My suffering begins. ¹⁶Know this: I will not eat another Passover meal until its meaning is fulfilled in the kingdom of God.

¹⁷He took a cup *of wine* and gave thanks for it.

Jesus: Take this; share it among yourselves. ¹⁸Know this: I will not drink another sip of wine until the kingdom of God has arrived in fullness.

¹⁹Then He took bread, gave thanks, broke it, and shared it with them.

Jesus: This is My body, My body given for you. Do this to remember Me.

²⁰And similarly, after the meal had been eaten, He took the cup.

Jesus: This cup, which is poured out for you, is the new covenant, made in My blood. ²¹But even now, the hand of My betrayer is with Me on this table. ²²As it has been determined, the Son of Man, *that firstfruit of a new generation of humanity,* must be betrayed, but how pitiful it will be for the person who betrays Him.

²³They immediately began questioning each other.

Disciples: Which one of us could do such a horrible thing?

²⁴Soon they found themselves arguing about the opposite question.

Disciples: Which one of us is the most faithful, the most important?

Jesus (*interrupting*): ²⁵The authority figures of the outsiders play this game, flexing their muscles in competition for power over one another, masking their quest for domination behind words like "benefactor" or "public servant." ²⁶But you must

* 22:14 Literally, apostles

not indulge in this charade. Instead, among you, the greatest must become like the youngest and the leader must become a true servant. ²⁷Who is greater right here as we eat this meal—those of us who sit at the table, or those who serve us? Doesn't everyone normally assume those who are served are greater than those who serve? But consider My role among you. I have been with you as a servant.

²⁸You have stood beside Me faithfully through My trials. ²⁹I give you a kingdom, just as the Father has given Me a kingdom. ³⁰You will eat and drink at My table in My kingdom, and you will have authority over the twelve tribes of Israel.

³¹Simon, Simon, how Satan has pursued you, that he might make you part of his harvest. ³²But I have prayed for you. I have prayed that your faith will hold firm and that you will recover from your failure and become a source of strength for your brothers here.

Peter: ³³*Lord, what are You talking about? I'm going all the way to the end with You—to prison, to execution—I'm prepared to do anything for You.*

Jesus: ³⁴No, Peter, the truth is that before the rooster crows at dawn, you will have denied that you even know Me, not just once, but three times. ³⁵Remember when I sent you out with no money, no pack, not even sandals? Did you lack anything?

Disciples: Not a thing.

Jesus: ³⁶It's different now. If you have some savings, take them with you. If you have a pack, *fill it and* bring it. If you don't have a sword, sell your coat and buy one. ³⁷Here's the truth: what the Hebrew Scriptures said, "And He was taken as one of the criminals,"* must come to fruition in Me. These words must come true.

Disciples: ³⁸Look, Lord, we have two swords here.

Jesus: That's enough.

³⁹Once again He left the city as He had been doing during recent days, returning to Mount Olivet along with His disciples.

There is a powerful consistency in Jesus' life. Again and again, we see Him withdraw from the crowds to pray in solitude. Now, at this dramatic moment, Jesus again withdraws to pray—in a solitude made more intense by the fact that He has asked His disciples to pray too; but they have fallen asleep. And in this moment of anguished emotion, we also hear on Jesus' lips a prayer that resonates with His consistent message of the Kingdom. He has taught His disciples to pray, "May Your kingdom come," which is a request for God's will to be done on earth as it is in heaven. Now, drenched in sweat, Jesus Himself prays simply for God's will to be done, even if it means that He must drink the cup of suffering that awaits Him in the hours ahead. We often speak of having faith *in* Jesus; but we seldom speak of the faith *of* Jesus, a faith that is demonstrated consistently throughout His life and now, here, in this place. In a moment of agony, Jesus still trusts God, still yields His will to God, and still approaches God as "Father," placing Himself in the position of a child, in trust—profound, tested, sincere.

⁴⁰And He came to a certain place.

Jesus: Pray for yourselves, that you will not sink into temptation.

⁴¹He distanced Himself from them about a stone's throw and knelt there, ⁴²praying.

Jesus: Father, if You are willing, take this cup away from Me. Yet not My will, but Your will, be done.

[⁴³Then a messenger from heaven appeared to strengthen Him. ⁴⁴And in His anguish, He prayed even more intensely, and His sweat was like drops of blood

* 22:37 Isaiah 53:12

falling to the ground.]* ⁴⁵When He rose from prayer and returned to the disciples, He found them asleep, weighed down with sorrow. ⁴⁶He roused them.

Jesus: Why are you sleeping? Wake up and pray that you will not sink into temptation.

⁴⁷Even as He said these words, *the sound of a crowd could be heard in the distance,* and as the crowd came into view, it was clear that Judas was leading them. He came close to Jesus and gave Jesus *the traditional greeting of* a kiss.

Jesus: ⁴⁸Ah, Judas, is this how you betray the Son of Man—with a kiss?
Disciples (*realizing what was going on*): ⁴⁹Lord, is this why You told us to bring the swords? Should we attack?

⁵⁰Before Jesus could answer, one of them had swung his sword at the high priest's slave, cutting off his right ear.

Jesus: ⁵¹Stop! No more of this!

Then He reached out to touch—and heal—the man's ear. ⁵²Jesus turned to the chief priests, the captains of the temple, and the elders and spoke.

Jesus: Do you think I'm some sort of violent criminal? Is that why you came with swords and clubs? ⁵³*I haven't been hard to find*—each day I've been in the temple in broad daylight, and you never tried to seize Me there. But this is your time—*night*—and this is your power—the power of darkness.

⁵⁴They grabbed Him at this point and took Him away to the high priest's home. Peter followed—at a distance. ⁵⁵*He watched from the shadows as* those who had seized Jesus made a fire in the center of the courtyard and sat down around it. Then Peter *slipped in quietly and* sat with them. ⁵⁶But a young servant girl saw his face in the firelight. She stared for a while and then spoke.

Servant Girl: This fellow here was with Jesus. *I recognize him.*
Peter (*denying it*): ⁵⁷Woman, I don't even know the man.

⁵⁸A little later, a man also recognized him.

Man: *I recognize you.* You're one of Jesus' followers.
Peter: Man, you're wrong. I'm not.

⁵⁹An hour or so passed, and then another person pointed to Peter.

Another Person: This fellow is obviously Galilean. He must be a member of Jesus' group.
Peter: ⁶⁰Look, I have no idea what you're talking about.

And he hadn't even finished the sentence when a nearby rooster crowed. ⁶¹The Lord turned toward Peter, and their eyes met. Peter remembered Jesus' words about his triple denial before the rooster would crow, ⁶²so he left the courtyard and wept bitter tears.
    ⁶³At this point, the men who were holding Jesus began to mock Him and beat Him. ⁶⁴They put a blindfold on Him.

Men Holding Jesus: *Hey, Prophet!* Use Your prophetic powers to tell us who just whacked You!

⁶⁵They kept on with this sort of insulting, degrading treatment for quite some time. ⁶⁶When dawn had given way to full day, the Sanhedrin council assembled, consisting of religious leaders *of the Sadducean party*, along with the chief priests and religious scholars. They took Him to their headquarters *for interrogation*.

Sanhedrin: ⁶⁷If you are the Liberating King whom God promised us, tell us plainly.
Jesus: If I give you an answer, you won't believe it. ⁶⁸And if I ask you a question, you won't answer it. ⁶⁹But *this I will say*

* 22:43-44 Some early manuscripts omit these verses.

to you: from now on, the Son of Man will take His seat at the right hand of the power of God.

Sanhedrin: ⁷⁰So You are the Son of God, then?

Jesus: It's as you say.

Sanhedrin: ⁷¹What more evidence do we need? We've heard it with our own ears from His own lips.

23 So the whole council got up and took Jesus to Pilate. ²They brought accusations against Him.

Sanhedrin: We have observed this man leading our nation astray. He even forbade us to pay our taxes to Caesar. He claims to be the Liberator and a King Himself.

Pilate: ³Are You the King of the Jews?

Jesus: It's as you say.

Pilate (to the chief priest and crowd): ⁴I find this man guilty of no crime.

Sanhedrin (growing more intense): ⁵He has been stirring up discontent among the people all over Judea. He started up in Galilee, and now He's brought His brand of trouble all the way to Jerusalem!

Pilate: ⁶*Just a minute.* Is this man a Galilean?

⁷When Pilate learned *that Jesus was indeed Galilean*—which meant He was officially under Herod's jurisdiction—Pilate sent Him over to Herod, who was currently in Jerusalem. ⁸Herod was fascinated to meet Jesus for he had heard about Him for a long time. He was hoping he might be treated to a miracle or two. ⁹He interrogated Jesus for quite a while, but Jesus remained silent, refusing to answer his questions. ¹⁰Meanwhile the chief priests and religious scholars had plenty to say—angrily hurling accusations at Jesus.

¹¹Eventually Herod and his soldiers began to insult Jesus, mocking and degrading Him. They put expensive clothing on Him and sent Him back to Pilate. ¹²This ended a long-standing rift between Herod and Pilate; they became friends from that day forward.

¹³Pilate assembled the chief priests and other Jewish authorities.

Pilate: ¹⁴You presented this man to me as a rabble-rouser, but I examined Him in your presence and found Him not guilty of the charges you have leveled against Him. ¹⁵Herod also examined Him and released Him to my custody. So He hasn't done anything deserving the death penalty. ¹⁶I'll see to it that He is properly whipped and then let Him go.

[¹⁷It was the custom for Pilate to set one prisoner free during the holiday festivities.]*

Crowd (all shouting at once): ¹⁸Away with this man! Free Barabbas instead!

¹⁹Barabbas had been imprisoned after being convicted of an insurrection he had led in Jerusalem. He had also committed murder. ²⁰Pilate argued with them, wishing he could release Jesus, ²¹but they wouldn't be silenced.

Crowd (shouting): Crucify Him! Crucify Him!

Pilate (countering a third time): ²²Why? What has He done that is so evil? I have found in Him no offense worthy of capital punishment. As I said, I will punish Him and then release Him.

²³But they would not relent. They shouted louder and louder that He should be crucified, and eventually Pilate capitulated. ²⁴So he pronounced the punishment they demanded.

²⁵He released the rebel and murderer *Barabbas*—the insurrectionist they had pleaded for in His place—and he handed Jesus over to them to do with as they desired.

²⁶On the way to the place of crucifixion, they pulled a man from the crowd—his name was Simon of Cyrene, a person from the countryside who happened to be entering the city at that moment. They put Jesus' cross on Simon's shoulders, and he followed behind Jesus. ²⁷Along with Him was a huge crowd of common people,

* 23:17 The earliest manuscripts omit verse 17.

including many women shrieking and wailing in grief.

Jesus (*to the people in the crowd*):

²⁸Daughters of Jerusalem, do not weep for Me. Weep instead for yourselves and weep for your children. ²⁹Days are coming when people will say, "Blessed are the infertile; blessed are the wombs that never bore *a child*; blessed are the breasts that never nursed *an infant.*" ³⁰People will beg the mountains, "Surround us!" They'll plead with the hills, "Cover us!"* ³¹For if they treat Me like this when I'm like green unseasoned wood, what will they do to a nation that's ready to burn like seasoned firewood?

³²*Jesus wasn't the only one being crucified that day.* There were two others, criminals, who were also being led to their execution. ³³When they came to the place known as "The Skull," they crucified Jesus there, in the company of criminals, one to the right of Jesus and the other to His left.

*H*istorians tell us that crucifixion was often used for insurrectionists. Anyone who dared to defy the power and authority of Caesar would be executed in this public and humiliating way. The cross, then, became a symbol of the invincible and dominating power of Caesar and his empire; and Jesus is crucified as a revolutionary, between two other revolutionaries. The ironies are powerful.

First, Jesus indeed was a revolutionary. He didn't come to proclaim a new religion, but a new kingdom—a new way of life. He was indeed a threat to Caesar's way of doing things, a way that had co-opted the religious leaders. But Jesus wasn't a threat in the way His neighbors on the other two crosses were a threat, which brings us to the second irony: Jesus' revolution was a peaceful revolution.

Jesus didn't advocate the use of violence—in fact, a few hours earlier, when one of His disciples used the sword to try to protect Jesus from arrest, Jesus healed the "enemy" and rebuked His disciple. So Jesus doesn't support the regime of Caesar on the one hand, but on the other hand, He doesn't follow the usual violent path of revolution: He leads a revolutionary revolution—in a path of love, healing, justice, and reconciliation.

Third, instead of being humiliated and defeated by the cross, Jesus appropriates the cross from Rome. He transforms the symbol of their power into a symbol of His greater power. He makes it, not the icon of violent domination, but the reverse. By hanging on the cross and speaking of forgiveness, Jesus shows that there is a greater power at work in the world than the power of domination: it's the power of God's saving and reconciling love.

Jesus: ³⁴[Father, forgive them, for they don't know what they're doing.]*

Meanwhile they were drawing lots to see who would win Jesus' clothing. ³⁵The crowd of people stood, watching.

Authorities (*mocking Jesus*): So He was supposed to rescue others, was He? He was supposed to be the big Liberator from God, God's special Messenger? Let's see Him start by liberating Himself!

³⁶The soldiers joined in the mockery. First, they *pretended to offer Him a soothing drink*—but it was sour wine.

Soldiers: ³⁷Hey, if You're the King of the Jews, why don't You free Yourself!

³⁸Even the inscription they placed over Him was intended to mock Him—"This is the King of the Jews!" [This was written in Greek, Latin, and Hebrew.]*

* 23:30 Hosea 10:8
* 23:34 The earliest manuscripts omit this portion.
* 23:38 Some early manuscripts omit this portion.

39One of the criminals joined in the cruel talk.

Cynical Criminal: You're supposed to be the Liberator, right? *Well—do it!* Rescue Yourself and us!

40But the other criminal told him to be quiet.

Believing Criminal: Don't you have any fear of God at all? You're getting the same death sentence He is! 41We're getting what we deserve since we've committed crimes, but this man hasn't done anything wrong at all! 42(turning to Jesus) Jesus, when You come into Your kingdom, please remember me.

Jesus: 43I promise you that this very day you will be with Me in paradise.

44At this point, it was about noon, and a darkness fell over the whole region. The darkness persisted until about three in the afternoon, 45and at some point during this darkness, the curtain in the temple was torn in two.

*T*he tearing of this heavy curtain in the temple is highly symbolic. Because this curtain separated the holiest place in the temple from the rest of the temple, some have seen in this act a symbol of God opening the way for unholy humans to enter into His holy presence: Jesus' death has brought forgiveness and opened the way for all to come to God. Others have seen in the curtain's being torn the opposite meaning: God's presence can no longer be confined to any single geographical place. The suffering and death of Jesus ended one age of human history, and now a new era has begun. Now God is on the move, at large, invading the whole world. Or perhaps this graphic image could mean both.

Jesus (*shouting out loudly*): 46Father, I entrust My spirit into Your hands!*

And with those words, He exhaled—and breathed no more.

47The Centurion*—*one of the soldiers who performed the execution*—saw all this, and he praised God.

Centurion: No doubt, this man must have been innocent.

48The crowds of common people who had gathered and watched the whole ordeal through to its conclusion left for their homes, pounding on their own chests *in profound grief.* 49And all who knew Jesus personally, including the group of women who had been with Him *from the beginning* in Galilee, stood at a distance, watching all of these things unfold.

50Meanwhile a man named Joseph *had been at work.* He was a member of the council, a good and fair man, 51from a Judean town called Arimathea. He had objected to the plans and actions of the council; he was seeking the kingdom of God. 52He had gone to Pilate and asked for the body of Jesus. 53He removed the body from the cross and wrapped it in a shroud made of *fine* linen. He then laid the body in a cavelike tomb cut from solid rock, a tomb that never had been used before. 54It was Preparation Day—*the day before the holy* Sabbath—and it was about to begin *at sundown.* 55The women who had accompanied Jesus *from the beginning* in Galilee now came, took note of where the tomb was and how His body had been prepared, 56then left to prepare spices and ointments *for His proper burial.* They ceased their work on the Sabbath so they could rest as the *Hebrew* Scriptures required.

24 Early on Sunday morning, even before the sun had fully risen, these women made their way back to the tomb with the spices *and ointments* they had prepared. 2When they arrived, they found the stone was rolled away from the tomb entrance, 3and when they looked

* 23:46 Psalm 31:5
* 23:47 A Roman military officer in charge of 100 soldiers

inside, the body of the Lord Jesus was nowhere to be seen. ⁴They didn't know what to think. As they stood there in confusion, two men suddenly appeared standing beside them. These men seemed to glow with light. ⁵The women were so terrified that they fell to the ground facedown.

Two Men: Why are you seeking the living One in the place of the dead? ⁶He is not here. He has risen *from the dead.* Don't you remember what He told you way back in Galilee? ⁷He told you that the Son of Man must be handed over to wicked men, He must be crucified, and then on the third day He must rise.

This phrase, "Son of Man," is very important in Luke's story, but scholars struggle to capture its many layers of meaning. It could mean "epitome of humanity" or "prime example of what a human can be." But it also evokes a specific passage of Scripture that was very important to Jewish people of Jesus' day, Daniel 7:13–27. There the phrase "Son of Man" refers to a king who receives an eternal and universal kingdom, and it also represents "the saints of the Most High"—the people of God. In light of Jesus' central message about the kingdom of God, it seems likely that the phrase should suggest to us that Jesus is the long-awaited Liberating King who launches a new era in human history and who creates a community of people who will represent the eternal and universal kingdom of God. In this way, "Son of" suggests "new generation of," and "Man" suggests "humanity." Jesus is Himself the new generation of humanity (a second Adam, a new beginning), and the community He creates will also share this identity (a new creation, a new humanity in the Liberator). The two messengers here use this pregnant phrase in a way that would have shocked everyone: The way this long-awaited Liberating King would receive

His kingdom would not be through conventional military victory where enemies were defeated and killed. No, this King would receive His kingdom by suffering, dying, and rising again Himself. Amazing news—good news!

⁸The women did remember Jesus' words about this, ⁹so they returned from the tomb and found the eleven and recounted for them—and others with them—everything they had experienced. ¹⁰⁻¹¹The Lord's emissaries* heard their stories as fiction, a lie; they didn't believe a word of it. (By the way, this group of women included Mary Magdalene, Joanna, and Mary the mother of James, along with a number of others.) ¹²Peter, however, got up and ran to the tomb. *When he reached the opening,* he bent down, looked inside, and saw the linen burial cloths lying there. But the body was gone. He walked away, full of wonder about what had happened.

¹³*Picture this:*

That same day, two other disciples (*not of the eleven*) are traveling the seven miles from Jerusalem to Emmaus. ¹⁴As they walk along, they talk back and forth about all that has transpired during recent days. ¹⁵While they're talking, discussing, and conversing, Jesus catches up to them and begins walking with them, ¹⁶but for some reason they don't recognize Him.

Jesus: ¹⁷*You two seem deeply engrossed in conversation.* What are you talking about as you walk along this road?

They stop walking and just stand there, looking sad. ¹⁸One of them—Cleopas is his name—speaks up.

Cleopas: You must be the only visitor in Jerusalem who hasn't heard about what's been going on over the last few days.

Jesus: ¹⁹What are you talking about?

* 24:10-11 Literally, apostles

Two Disciples: It's all about the man named Jesus of Nazareth. He was a mighty prophet who did amazing miracles and preached powerful messages in the sight of God and everyone around. 20Our chief priests and authorities handed Him over to be executed—crucified, in fact.

21We had been hoping that He was the One—you know, the One who would liberate all Israel *and bring God's promises.* Anyway, on top of all this, just this morning—the third day after the execution— 22some women in our group really shocked us. They went to the tomb early this morning, 23but they didn't see His body anywhere. Then they came back and told us they did see something—a vision of heavenly messengers—and these messengers said that Jesus was alive. 24Some people in our group went to the tomb to check it out, and just as the women had said, it was empty. But they didn't see Jesus.

Jesus: 25Come on, men! Why are you being so foolish? Why are your hearts so sluggish when it comes to believing what the prophets have been saying all along? 26Didn't it have to be this way? Didn't the Liberating King have to experience these sufferings in order to come into His glory?

27Then He begins with Moses and continues, prophet by prophet, explaining the meaning of the Hebrew Scriptures, showing how they were talking about the very things that had happened to Jesus. 28About this time, they are nearing their destination. Jesus keeps walking ahead as if He has no plans to stop there, 29but they convince Him to join them.

Two Disciples: Please, be our guest. It's getting late, and soon it will be too dark to walk.

So He accompanies them to their home. 30When they sit down at the table for dinner, He takes the bread in His hands, He gives thanks for it, and then He breaks it and hands it to them. 31At that instant, *two things happen simultaneously:* their eyes are suddenly opened so they recognize Him, and He instantly vanishes—just disappears before their eyes.

Two Disciples (*to each other*): 32Amazing! Weren't our hearts on fire within us while He was talking to us on the road? *Didn't you feel it all coming clear* as He explained the meaning of the Hebrew Scriptures?

33So they get up immediately and rush back to Jerusalem—*all seven miles*—where they find the eleven gathered together—the eleven plus a number of others. 34*Before Cleopas and his companion can tell their story,* the others have their own story to tell.

Other Disciples: The Lord has risen indeed! It's true! He appeared to Simon!

35Then the two men report their own experience—their conversation along the road, their moment of realization and recognition as He broke the bread. 36At that very instant, as they're still telling the story, Jesus is there, standing among them!

Jesus: May you have peace!

37*You might expect them to be overjoyed, but they aren't.* They're startled and terrified; they think they're seeing a ghost.

Jesus: 38Why are you upset? Why are your hearts churning with questions? 39Look— look at My hands and My feet! See that it's Me! Come on; touch Me; see for yourselves. A ghost doesn't have flesh and bones, as you can see that I have!

[40Then He shows them His hands and His feet.]*

41Now their fear gives way to joy; but it seems too good to be true, and they're still unsure.

---

* 24:40 Some manuscripts omit verse 40.

Jesus: Do you have anything here to eat?

[42]They hand Him a piece of broiled fish, [43]and He takes it and eats it in front of them.

Jesus: [44]I've been telling you this all along, that everything written about Me in the Hebrew Scriptures must be fulfilled— everything from the law of Moses to the prophets to the psalms.

[45]Then He opens their minds so they can comprehend the meaning of the Hebrew Scriptures.

Jesus: [46]This is what the Scriptures said: that the promised Liberating King should suffer and rise from the dead on the third day, [47]that in His name a radical change of thought and life should be preached, and that in His name the forgiveness of sins should be preached, beginning in Jerusalem and extending to all nations. [48]You have witnessed the fulfillment of these things. [49]So I am sending My Father's promise to you. Stay in the city until you receive it—until power from heaven comes upon you.

[50]Then He leads them out to Bethany. He lifts up His hands and blesses them, [51]and at that moment, with His hands raised in blessing, He leaves them and is carried up into heaven. They worship Him, then they return to Jerusalem, filled with intense joy, [53]and they return again and again to the temple to celebrate God.

Luke has told his story. It ends with joy and praise. The crucified Jesus has been resurrected and has ascended to heaven to take His place at God's right hand just as the ancient prophets predicted. For the band of disciples, Easter joy has eclipsed Good Friday sorrow.

This ending point becomes the starting point for Luke's sequel, known to us as "The Acts of the Apostles." You see, the story isn't really over; it's just begun. The life and ministry of Jesus that Luke has just recounted is the mustard-seed stage of the kingdom of God that continues to grow and grow and grow. Now it's time for this Kingdom to fill the world. If the Gospel we have just read is about what Jesus began to do and teach, then Luke's sequel will tell us what the risen Jesus continued to do and teach through His followers. And, of course, that story continues to today. In fact, Luke writes in hope that our lives can be taken up into this beautiful story that will never, ever end.

John

Visitation of God's Son
By John, the apostle

According to tradition, this Gospel was written by John the apostle toward the end of his life while in Ephesus of Asia Minor after the destruction of Jerusalem in A.D. 70. Along with Peter and James, John was part of an inner circle of disciples closest to Jesus. Many interpreters believe that "the beloved disciple," a unique description for one of Jesus' disciples, referred to John. So John had a special relationship with Jesus that allowed him to write this uniquely insightful account of Jesus' life.

John was likely the last eyewitness to the life, death, and resurrection of Jesus. So he composes a Gospel that is distinct from the other New Testament Gospels. Matthew, Mark, and Luke present the life of Jesus from a similar perspective. They share a great number of parallel accounts, arrange them in a similar order, and use many of the same words and expressions. Because of their similarities, Matthew, Mark, and Luke are often called the Synoptic Gospels. "Synoptic" means "with the same eye" or "seeing together." The Gospel of John, on the other hand, contains only a little of the material found in the other Gospels. John takes us behind the scenes into Jesus' conversations with people and into long, often private talks He has with His disciples. Jesus is clearly a miracle worker in this Fourth Gospel, but His miracles are interpreted as "signs" because they point to a greater reality, the reality of life—abundant and eternal—that has entered our world. Further, John makes many bold claims to Jesus' deity. For example, John includes a number of "I am" sayings spoken by Jesus (for example, "I am the bread of life," "I am the light of the world," "I am the resurrection and the life"). These statements associate Jesus with God's holy, unspeakable name and are implicit claims to His divinity. Plus, in John's theological prologue (John 1:1-18), he calls Jesus the Logos ("the Word") that preexists with God, is the agent of creation, and is made flesh for our salvation.

Another unique feature of this Gospel is its simplicity. Its language and grammar are easily grasped. Its ideas, while deeply symbolic and evocative, can be understood by people young and old. It is filled with dualisms that contrast the difference eternal life makes when it enters into the world: life and death, belief and unbelief, light and darkness, to name a few. For many people, the simplicity of this Gospel, with its deeply personal and intimate look at Jesus' life, makes it their favorite story of the Liberating King.

In John's Gospel and Epistles, the notes are written in first person. Who better to comment on this inspired story of Jesus' life than the one who had walked so closely with Him?

My name is John. My father's name was Zebedee. We made our living by fishing on the Sea of Galilee. I am the last eyewitness to the life of Jesus. All the rest are gone; some long gone. Many died years ago, tragically young, the victims of Roman cruelty and persecution. For some reason, Jesus chose me to live to be an old man. In fact, some in my community have taken to calling me "the elder."

I am the inspiration behind the Fourth Gospel. These are my stories, recorded, told to you by my disciples. I'm proud of what they have done. Me? I've never done much writing. But the story is truly mine.

You see my hands. They've been hurting for the past 20 years now. I couldn't hold a pen even if I wanted to. Not that I was ever good at writing. I was a fisherman, so my hands were calloused. I could tie ropes, mend nets, and pull the oars, but never make a decent *xi* (Greek letter). So we used secretaries when we wanted to write. There was always a bright young man around it seems, ready to take a letter or help us put pen to papyrus.

My eyes are too weak to read anymore. I can't remember the last time I could see well enough to read a letter or even see the inscriptions. So one of the brothers (I call them my "little children") reads to me. They are all very gracious to me in my old age, compiling my stories, bringing me food, laughing at my jokes, and caring for my most intimate needs. Time is taking its toll on me though. I rarely have the energy to tell the old stories and preach entire sermons. Instead, I simply remind them of the Liberating King's most vital command, saying as loudly as I can, "Little children, love one another."

I've outlived all the rest of the twelve and His other followers. I can't tell you how lonely it is to be the last person with a memory, some would even say a fuzzy memory, of what Jesus looked like, the sound of His voice, the manner of His walk, the penetrating look in His eyes. All I can do is tell my story.

Now I want to be very clear. This is my story, but unlike what you hear from most storytellers, this is completely true. I am giving you the testimony of an eyewitness. And like my brother disciples, I will swear upon my life that it is true.

1 Before time itself was measured, the Voice was speaking. The Voice was and is God. [2]This *celestial* Voice remained ever present with the Creator; [3]His speech shaped the entire cosmos. *Immersed in the practice of creating,* all things that exist were birthed in Him. [4]His breath filled all things with a living, breathing light— [5]light that thrives in the depths of darkness, *blazing through murky bottoms.* It cannot, and will not, be quenched.

[6]A man named John, who was sent by God, *was the first to clearly articulate the source of this unquenchable Light.* [7]This wanderer, *John who ritually cleansed,** put in plain words the *elusive mystery of the Divine* Light that all might believe through him. *Because John spoke with power, many believed in the Light. Others wondered whether he might be the Light,* [8]but John was not the Light. He merely pointed to the Light, *and in doing so, he invited the entire creation to hear the Voice.*

[9]The true Light, who shines upon the heart of everyone, was coming into the cosmos. [10]*He does not call out from a distant place but draws near.* He enters our world, a world He made, *and speaks clearly;* yet His creation did not recognize Him. [11]*Though the Voice utters only truth,* His own people, *who have heard the Voice before,* rebuff this inner calling and refuse to listen. [12]But those who *hear and* trust the beckoning of the Divine Voice and embrace Him, they shall be reborn as children of God; [13]He bestows this birthright not by human power or initiative but by

* 1:7 Literally, immersed, to show repentance

God's will. *Because we are born of this world, we can only be reborn to God by accepting His call.*

[14]The Voice *that had been an enigma in the heavens chose to* become human and live surrounded by His creations. We have seen Him. Undeniable splendor enveloped Him—the one true Son of God—*evidenced in* the perfect balance of grace and truth. [15]John, *the wanderer* who testified of the Voice, introduced Him. "This is the one I've been telling you is coming. He is much greater than I because He existed *long* before me." [16]Through this man we all receive *gifts of* grace beyond our imagination. *He is the Voice of God.* [17]You see, Moses gave us rules to live by, but Jesus, the Liberating King, offered the gifts of grace and truth *which make life worth living.* [18]God, unseen until now, is revealed in the Voice, God's only Son, *straight from* the Father's heart.

*B*efore Jesus came along, many thought John the Immerser might be the Liberating King. But when Jesus appeared in the wilderness, John pointed us to Him. The Immerser knew his place in God's redemptive plan. John the Immerser was a man sent from God, but Jesus is the Voice of God. John rejected any messianic claim outright. Jesus, though, accepted it with a smile, but only from a few of us—at least at first. Don't get me wrong, John was important, but he wasn't the Liberating King. He preached repentance. He told everybody to get ready for One greater to come along. The One who comes will immerse us in fire and power, he said. John even told some of his followers to leave him and go follow Jesus.

[19]The words of the Immerser were *gaining attention*, and many had questions, including Jewish religious leaders from Jerusalem. [28]Their entourage approached John in Bethany just beyond the Jordan River while he was cleansing* followers in water, *and bombarded him with questions:**

Religious Leaders: Who are you?
John the Immerser: [20]I'm not the Liberator, *if that is what you are asking.*
Religious Leaders: [21]*Your words sound familiar, like a prophet's.* Is that how we should address you? Are you the Prophet Elijah?
John the Immerser: No, I am not Elijah.
Religious Leaders: Are you the Prophet *Moses told us would come?*
John the Immerser: No.

They continued to press John, unsatisfied with the lack of information.

Religious Leaders: [22]Then tell us who you are and what you are about because everyone is asking us, *especially the Pharisees,* and we must prepare an answer.

[23]John replied with the words of Isaiah:

John the Immerser:
> *Listen!* I am a voice calling out in the wilderness.
> Straighten out the road for the Lord. *He's on His way.**

[24-25]Then some priests who were sent by the Pharisees started in on him again.

Religious Leaders: How can you *travel the countryside* cleansing* people of their sins if you are not the Liberator or Elijah or the Prophet?
John the Immerser: [26]Cleansing* with water is what I do, but the One *whom I speak of, whom we all await,* is standing among you and you have no idea who He is. [27]Though He comes after me, I am not even worthy to unlace His sandals.*

---

* 1:28 Literally, immersing, to show repentance
* 1:28 Verse 28 has been inserted here to help retain the continuity of events.
* 1:23 Isaiah 40:3
* 1:24-25 Literally, immersing, to show repentance
* 1:26 Literally, immersing, to show repentance
* 1:27 Verse 28 has been moved before verse 20 to retain the continuity of events.

*T*he mystery of Jesus' identity occupied us and will occupy generations of believers for centuries to come. As we journeyed with Him, it gradually became clearer who this man was, where He came from, and how His existence would profoundly affect the rest of human history. The question of "Who is this man?" was not answered overnight.

²⁹The morning after *this conversation, as John is going about his business,* he sees *the Voice,* Jesus, coming toward him. *In eager astonishment,* he shouts out:

John the Immerser: Look! *This man is more than He seems!* He is the Lamb sent from God, *the sacrifice* to erase the sins of the world! ³⁰He is the One I have been saying will come after me, who existed long before me and is much greater than I. ³¹*No one here* recognized Him—myself included. I came ritually cleansing* with water so that He might be revealed to Israel. ³²⁻³³And, just as the One who sent me told me, I knew who He was the moment I saw the Spirit come down upon Him as a dove and seal itself to Him. Now He will cleanse* with the Holy Spirit. ³⁴I give my oath that everything I have seen is true. *If you don't believe now, keep listening.* He is *the Voice,* the Son of God!

³⁵⁻³⁶The day after, John *saw Him again as* he was visiting with two of his disciples. As Jesus walked by, he announced again:

John the Immerser: Do you see Him? This man is the Lamb of God; *He will be God's sacrifice to cleanse our sin.*

³⁷At that moment, the two disciples began to follow Jesus, ³⁸⁻³⁹who turned back to them, saying:

Jesus: What is it that you want?
Two Disciples: We'd like to know where You are staying. Teacher, *may we remain at Your side today?*

Jesus: Come and see. *Follow Me, and we will camp together.*

It was about four o'clock in the afternoon *when they met Jesus.* They came and they saw where He was staying, *but they got more than they imagined.* They remained with Him the rest of the day *and followed Him for the rest of their lives.* ⁴⁰⁻⁴¹One of these new disciples, Andrew, rushed to find his brother Simon and tell him they had found the Christ, the Liberating King, *the One who will heal the world.* ⁴²As Andrew approached with Simon, Jesus looked into him.

Jesus: Your name is Simon, and your father is called John. But from this day forward you will be known as Peter,* the rock.

⁴³⁻⁴⁴The next day Jesus set out to Galilee; and when He came upon Philip, He invited him to join them.

Jesus: Follow Me.

Philip, like Andrew and Peter, came from a town called Bethsaida, *and he decided to make the journey with Him.* ⁴⁵Philip found Nathanael, *a friend,* and burst in with *excitement:*

Philip: We have found the One. Moses wrote about Him in the Law; all the prophets spoke of the day when He would come, and now He is here—His name is Jesus, son of Joseph *the carpenter,* and He comes from Nazareth.
Nathanael: ⁴⁶How can anything good come from *a place like* Nazareth?
Philip: Come with me. See *and hear* for yourself.

⁴⁷As they approached, Jesus saw Nathanael coming.

Jesus: Look closely and you will see an Israelite who is a truth-teller.

* 1:31 Literally, immersing, to show repentance
* 1:32-33 Literally, immerse
* 1:42 Literally, Cephas

Nathanael: [48]How would You know this about me? *We have never met.*

Jesus: *I have been watching you* before Philip invited you here. *Earlier in the day, you were enjoying the shade and fruit of* the fig tree. I saw you then.

Nathanael: [49]Teacher, *I am sorry—forgive me.* You are the One—God's own Son and Israel's King.

Jesus: [50]Nathanael, if all it takes for you to believe is My telling you I saw you under the fig tree, then what you will see later shall astound you. *The miracles you will witness are greater than your imagination can comprehend.* [51]I tell you the truth: *before our journey is complete,* you will see the heavens standing open while heavenly messengers ascend and descend, *swirling* around the Son of Man.

2 [1-2]Three days after *the disciples encountered Jesus for the first time*, they were all invited to celebrate a wedding feast in Cana of Galilee together with Mary, the mother of Jesus. [3]While they were celebrating, the wine ran out and Jesus' mother hurried over to her son.

Mary: *The host stands on the brink of embarrassment; there are many guests, and* there is no more wine.

Jesus: [4]Dear woman, is it our problem *they miscalculated when buying wine and inviting guests?* My time has not arrived.

[5]*But Mary sensed the time was near. So in a way that only a mother can,* she turned to the servants.

Mary: Do whatever my son tells you.

[6]In that area were six *massive* stone water pots that could each hold 20 to 30 gallons.* They were typically used for Jewish purification rites. [7]Jesus' instructions *were clear:*

Jesus: Fill each water pot with water until it's ready to spill over the top; [8]then fill a cup and deliver it to the headwaiter.

They did exactly as they were instructed. [9]After tasting the water that had become wine, the headwaiter couldn't figure out where such wine came from (even though the servants knew), and he called over the bridegroom *in amazement.*

Headwaiter: [10]*This wine is delectable.* Why would you save the most exquisite fruit of the vine? A host would generally serve the good wine first and, when his inebriated guests don't notice or care, he would serve the inferior wine. You have held back the best for last.

[11]Jesus performed this miracle, the first of His signs, in Cana of Galilee. *They did not know how this happened,* but when the disciples *and the servants* witnessed this miracle, their faith blossomed.

[12]Jesus then gathered His clan—His family members and disciples—for a journey to Capernaum where they lingered several days. [13]The time was near to celebrate the Passover, *the festival commemorating when God rescued His children from slavery in Egypt,* so Jesus went to Jerusalem *for the celebration.* [14]*Upon arriving,* He entered the temple *to worship and honor the Father. But it did not have the appearance of a holy place. The porches and colonnades* were filled with merchants selling *sacrificial animals, such as* doves, oxen, and sheep, and exchanging money. [15]*In a display that can only be described as a righteous anger,* Jesus fashioned a whip of cords and used it *with skill* driving out animals; He scattered the money and overturned the tables, emptying profiteers from the house of God. [16]There were dove merchants *still standing around,* and Jesus reprimanded them.

Jesus: *What are you still doing here?* Get all your stuff, and haul it out of here! Stop making My Father's house a place for your own profit!

* 2:6 Literally, two to three measures

17*The disciples were astounded*, but they remembered that the Hebrew Scriptures said "jealous devotion for God's house consumes me."* 18Some of the Jews cried out to Him *in unison*.

Jews: Who gave You the right to shut us down? *If it is God, then* show us a sign.
Jesus: 19*You want a sign? Here it is.* Destroy this temple, and I will rebuild it in 3 days.
Jews: 20*Three days?* This temple took more than 46 years to complete. You think You can replicate that feat in 3 days?

21*Jesus was planting seeds of truth in them.* The true temple was His body, *which would be destroyed on the cross and rebuilt in the resurrection.* 22His disciples remembered this bold prediction after He was resurrected. *Because of this knowledge, their faith in the Hebrew Scriptures and in Jesus' teachings grew.*

23During the Passover feast in Jerusalem, *the crowds were watching Jesus closely,* and many began to believe in Him because of the signs He was doing. 24-25But Jesus saw through to the heart of humankind, and He chose not to give them what they requested. He didn't need anyone to prove to Him the character of humanity. He knew what man was made of—*the dust of the earth*—and they needed the seeds He was planting.

3 Nicodemus was one of the Pharisees, a man with some clout among his people. 2He came to Jesus under the cloak of darkness to question Him.

Nicodemus: Teacher, some of us have been talking. You are obviously a teacher who has come from God. The signs You are doing are proof that God is with You.

*A*t this time, our Roman occupiers had given a small group of Pharisees limited powers to rule, and Nicodemus was one of those Pharisees. He held a seat on the ruling council known as the Sanhedrin, and surprisingly Nicodemus was among those who sought out Jesus for His teaching. It appeared that he believed more about Jesus than he wanted others to know. So he came at night.

Jesus: 3I tell you the truth: only someone who experiences birth for a second time* can *hope to* see the kingdom of God.
Nicodemus: 4*I am a grown man.* How can someone be born again when they are old *like me*? Am I to crawl back into my mother's womb for a second birth? *That's impossible!*
Jesus: 5I tell you the truth, if someone does not experience water and Spirit birth, there's no chance he will make it into God's kingdom. 6*Like from like.* Whatever is born from flesh is flesh; whatever is born from Spirit is spirit. 7Don't be shocked by My words, *but I tell you the truth.* Even you, *an educated and respected man among your people,* must be reborn *by the Spirit to enter the kingdom of God.* 8The wind* blows all around us as if it has a will of its own; we *feel and* hear it, but we do not understand where it has come from or where it will end up. Life in the Spirit is as if it were the wind of God.
Nicodemus: 9I still do not understand how this can be.
Jesus: 10Your responsibility is to instruct Israel *in matters of faith,* but you do not comprehend *the necessity of life in the Spirit?* 11I tell you the truth: we speak about the things we know, and we give evidence about the things we have seen, and you choose to reject *the truth of* our witness. 12If you do not believe when I talk to you about ordinary, earthly realities, then heavenly realities will certainly elude you. 13No one has ever journeyed to heaven above except the One who has come down from heaven—the Son of

* 2:17 Psalm 69:9
* 3:3 Other manuscripts read "from above."
* 3:8 "Wind" and "spirit" are the same word in Greek.

Man, who is of heaven. [14]Moses lifted up the serpent in the wilderness. In the same way, the Son of Man must be lifted up; [15]then all those who believe in Him will experience everlasting life.

[16]For God expressed His love for the world in this way: He gave His only Son so that whoever believes in Him will not face everlasting destruction, but will have everlasting life. [17]Here's the point. God didn't send His Son into the world to judge it; instead, He is here to rescue a world *headed toward certain destruction.*

[18]No one who believes in Him has to fear condemnation, yet condemnation is already the reality for everyone who refuses to believe. *Whoever embraces unbelief swims in a sea of judgment* because he *chooses to ignore the Voice, and in doing so,* he rejects the name of the only Son of God. [19]Why does God allow for judgment *and condemnation?* Because the Light, *sent from God,* pierced through the world's darkness *to expose ill motives, hatred, gossip, greed, violence, and the like.* Still some people preferred the darkness over the light because their actions were dark. [20]Some of humankind hated the light *and so avoided its warm glow.* They *scampered hurriedly* back into the darkness where vices thrive and wickedness flourishes. [21]Those who *abandon deceit and* embrace what is true, they will enter into the light where it will be clear that all their deeds come from God.

*J*esus made the point clear: stay connected to Him, and you will have no reason to fear. Jesus doesn't mean that the instant you have faith fear simply vanishes or only good things happen in your life. In fact, the blessings that come with eternal life often have nothing to do with present or future circumstances, but they have everything to do with our connections to God and one another. That is my message to all of you. God came to earth wrapped in flesh, and then He reached His greatest acclaim through a torturous death. If this is all true, then we will find strength and beauty in places we never imagined. Abiding in Jesus, the Liberator, is the good life, regardless of the external circumstances.

[22]Not long after, Jesus and His disciples traveled to the Judean countryside where they could enjoy one another's company and ritually cleanse* *new followers.* [23-24]About the same time, *Jesus' cousin John—the wandering prophet* who had not yet been imprisoned—was *upriver* at Aenon near Salim ritually cleansing* *scores of* people in the abundant waters there. [25]John's activities raised questions about the nature of purification among his followers and a religious leader, [26]so they approached him with their questions.

John's Followers: Teacher, the One who was with you *earlier* on the other side of the Jordan, the One whom you have been pointing to, is ritually washing* the multitudes who are coming to Him.

John the Immerser: [27]Apart from the gifts that come from heaven, no one can receive anything at all. [28]I have said it many times, and you have heard me—I am not the Liberating King; I am the one who comes before Him. [29]If you are confused, consider this: the groom is the one with the bride. The best man takes his place close by and listens for him. When he hears the voice of the groom, he is swept up in the joy *of the moment.* So hear me. My joy could not be more complete. [30]He, *the groom,* must take center stage, and I, *the best man,* must step to His side.

[31]If someone comes from heaven above, he ranks above it all *and speaks of heavenly things.* If someone comes from the earth, he speaks of earthly things. The One from the heavens is superior; He is over all. [32]He

* 3:22 Literally, immerse, to show repentance
* 3:23-24 Literally, immersing, to show repentance
* 3:26 Literally, immersing, to show repentance

reveals the mysteries seen and *realities heard of the heavens above*, but no one below is listening. [33]Those who are listening and accept His witness *to these truths* have gone on record. They acknowledge the fact that God is true! [34]The One sent from God speaks with the very words of God and abounds with the very Spirit and essence of God. [35]The Father loves the Son and withholds nothing from Him. [36]Those who believe in the Son will bask in eternal life, but those who disobey the Son will never experience life. They will know only God's lingering wrath.

4 [1-3]The picture was becoming clear to the Pharisees that Jesus, whose disciples were busy ritually cleansing* many new disciples, had gained a following much larger than that of John, *the wandering prophet*. Because the Lord could see *that the Pharisees were beginning to plot against Him*, He chose to leave Judea *where most Pharisees lived* and return to *a safer location in* Galilee, [4]a trip that would take them through Samaria.

*F*or us, Samaria was a place to be avoided. Before Solomon's death 1,000 years earlier, the regions of Samaria and Judea were part of a united Israel. After the rebellion that divided the kingdom, Samaria became a hotbed of idol worship. The northern kings made alliances that corrupted the people by introducing foreign customs and strange gods. They even had the nerve to build a temple to the true God on Mt. Gerizim to rival the one in Jerusalem. By the time we were traveling with Jesus, it was evident that the Samaritans had lost their way. By marrying outsiders, they had polluted the land. We considered them to be half-breeds—mongrels—and we knew we had to watch out for them or else we might be bitten.

[5-8]In a *small* Samaritan town known as Sychar, Jesus *and His entourage* stopped to

rest at the historic well that Jacob gave his son Joseph. It was about noon when Jesus found a spot to sit close to the well while the disciples ventured off to find provisions. *From His vantage, He watched as* a Samaritan woman approached to draw some water. *Unexpectedly* He spoke to her.

Jesus: Would you *draw water and* give Me a drink?

Woman: [9]I cannot believe that You, a Jew, would associate with me, a Samaritan woman, much less ask me to give You a drink.

Jews, you see, have no dealings with Samaritans. *Besides, a man would never approach a woman like this in public. Jesus was breaking accepted social barriers with this confrontation.*

Jesus: [10]You don't know the gift of God or who is asking you for a drink *of this water from Jacob's well*. Because if you did, you would have asked Him *for something greater* and He would have given you the living water.

Woman: [11]Sir, You sit by this deep well *a thirsty man* without a bucket in sight. Where does this living water come from? *Do You believe You can draw water and share it with me?* [12]Are You claiming superiority to our father Jacob who labored long and hard to dig *and maintain* this well so that he could share clean water with his sons, *grandchildren,* and cattle?

Jesus: [13]Drink this water, and your thirst is quenched only for a moment. *You must return to this well again and again.* [14]I offer water that will become a wellspring within you that gives life throughout eternity. You will never be thirsty again.

Woman: [15]*Please*, Sir, give me some of this water, so I'll never be thirsty and never again have to make the trip to this well.

Jesus: [16]Then bring your husband to Me.

Woman: [17-18]I do not have a husband.

Jesus: Technically you are telling the truth. But you have had five husbands and are

---

* 4:1-3 Literally, immersing, to show repentance

currently living with a man you are not married to.

Woman: [19]Sir, it is obvious to me that You are a prophet. *Maybe You can explain to me why our peoples disagree about how to worship:* [20]Our fathers worshiped here on this mountain, but Your people say that Jerusalem is the only place for all to worship. *Which is it?*

Jesus: [21-24]Woman, I tell you that neither *is so.* Believe this: a new day is coming—in fact, it's already here—when the importance will not be placed on the time and place of worship but on the truthful hearts of worshipers. You worship what you don't know while we worship what we do know, for God's salvation is coming through the Jews. The Father is spirit, and He is seeking followers whose worship is sourced in truth and deeply spiritual as well. Regardless of whether you are in Jerusalem or on this mountain, if you do not seek the Father, then you do not worship.

Woman: [25]These mysteries will be made clear by the coming Liberator, the Anointed One.

*J*esus is often called "Christ." But "Christ" is not a name; it is the Greek translation of the Hebrew title "Messiah," which means in English "Liberating King." To call Jesus "the Christ" is to confess "Jesus is the Liberating King" or "the Anointed." The term "Liberating King" refers to a human being, God's end-time agent destined to bring universal peace and justice to our world. Jesus did just that when He spoke with the Samaritan woman. As the Liberating King, He could speak with her regardless of her heritage, lifestyle, or gender and offer her freedom from sin and peace.

Jesus: [26]The Liberating King speaks to you. I am the One you have been looking for.

[27]The disciples returned to Him *and gathered around Him* in amazement that He would *openly break their customs* by speaking to this woman, but none of them would ask Him what He was looking for or why He was speaking with her. [28]The woman went back to the town, leaving her water pot behind. She stopped men *and women* on the streets and told them about what had happened.

Woman: [29]*I met* a stranger who knew everything about me. Come and see for yourselves; can He be the Liberating King?

[30]A crowd came out of the city and approached Jesus. [31]During all of this, the disciples were urging Jesus to eat the food they gathered.

Jesus: [32]I have food to eat that you know nothing about.

Disciples *(to one another)*: [33]Is it possible someone else has brought Him food while we were away?

Jesus: [34]I receive My nourishment by serving the will of the Father who sent Me and completing His work. [35]You have heard others say, *"Be patient; we have four more months to wait until the crops are ready for the harvest."* I say, take a closer look and you will see that the fields are ripe and ready for the harvest. [36]The harvester is collecting his pay, harvesting fruit ripe for eternal life. So even now, he and the sower are celebrating *their fortune.* [37]The saying *may be old, but it* is true: "One person sows, and another reaps." [38]I sent you to harvest where you have not labored; someone else took the time to plant and cultivate, and you feast on the fruit of their labor.

[39]Meanwhile, because one woman shared with her neighbors how Jesus exposed her past and present, the village *of Sychar* was transformed—many Samaritans heard and believed. [40]The Samaritans approached Jesus and repeatedly invited Him to stay with them, so He lingered there for two days *on their account.* [41]With the words that came from His mouth, there were many more believing Samaritans. [42]They began their faith journey because of the testimony of the woman *beside the well,*

but when they heard for themselves, they were convinced the One they were hearing was and is the Savior sent to rescue the entire world.

⁴³⁻⁴⁵After two days *of teaching and conversation*, Jesus proceeded to Galilee, where His countrymen received Him *with familiar smiles. These old friends should have been the first to believe;* after all, they witnessed His miracle at the feast in Jerusalem. But Jesus understood and often quoted *the maxim:* "No one honors a hometown prophet." *It took outsiders like the Samaritans to recognize Him.*

⁴⁶⁻⁴⁷As Jesus traveled to Cana (the village in Galilee where He transformed the water into *fine* wine), He was met by a government official *at one o'clock in the afternoon.* This man heard *a rumor that* Jesus left Judea and was heading to Galilee, and he came *in desperation* begging for Jesus' help because his young son was near death. *He was fearful that unless* Jesus would go with him to Capernaum, his son would have no hope.

Jesus (*to the official*): ⁴⁸My word is not enough; you only believe when you see miraculous signs.
Official: ⁴⁹Sir, this is my son; please come with me before he dies.
Jesus (*interrupting him*): ⁵⁰Go home and *be with your son; you have My word that* he will live.

When he heard the voice of Jesus, faith took hold of him and he turned to go home. ⁵¹Before he reached his village, his servants met him on the road celebrating his son's miraculous recovery.

Servants (*to the official*): One moment your son was hunched over burning with fever; then suddenly every sign of illness was gone.
Official: ⁵²What time did this happen?
Servants: Yesterday about one o'clock in the afternoon.

⁵³At that moment, it dawned on the father the exact time that Jesus spoke the words "he will live." After that, he believed; and

when he told his family *about his amazing encounter with the Liberating King,* they believed too. ⁵⁴This was the second sign-miracle Jesus performed when He came back to Galilee from Judea.

5 When these events were completed, Jesus led His followers to Jerusalem where they would celebrate a Jewish feast* together.

*J*esus took our little group of disciples into one of the most miserable places I have ever seen. It was a series of pools where the crippled and diseased would gather hoping to be healed. The stench was unbearable, and no sane person would willingly march into an area littered with such wretched and diseased bodies. We knew what could happen, what they had could have easily rubbed off on us. That kind of impurity was frightening, but we followed Him as He approached a crippled man on his mat.

²⁻³In Jerusalem they came upon a pool by the sheep gate surrounded by five covered porches. In Hebrew this place is called Bethesda.

Crowds of people lined the area, lying around the porches. *As they walked among the crowds, it became clear that* all of these people were *disabled in some way;* some were blind, lame, paralyzed, or plagued by diseases[, and they were waiting for the waters to move. ⁴From time to time, a heavenly messenger would come to stir the water in the pool. Whoever reached the water first and got in after it was agitated would be healed of his or her disease.]*
⁵⁻⁶In the crowd, Jesus noticed one particular man who had been living with his disability for 38 years. He knew this man had been waiting here a long time.

* 5:1 Perhaps Passover
* 5:4 Some early manuscripts omit the end of verse 3 and all of verse 4.

Jesus (to the disabled man): Are you *here in this place* hoping to be healed?

Disabled Man: [7]Kind Sir, I wait, *like all of these people,* for the waters to stir, *but I cannot walk. If I am to be healed in the waters,* someone must carry me into the pool. *So the answer to Your question is yes—but I cannot be healed here unless someone will help me.* Without a helping hand, someone else beats me to the water's edge each time it is stirred.

Jesus: [8]Stand up, carry your mat, and walk.

[9]At the moment Jesus uttered these words, a healing energy coursed through the man and returned life to his limbs—he stood and walked *for the first time in 38 years.* But this was the Sabbath Day, *and any work, including carrying a mat, was prohibited on this day.*

*Y*ou can't even begin to imagine this man's excitement. His entire life had been defined by his illness. Now he was free from it. Free from the pain and weakness. Free from the depression that gripped his soul. Free, too, from the shame he had always known. Now he did not just walk—he ran and celebrated with friends and family. Everyone was rejoicing with him, except for some of the Jewish leaders. Instead, they drilled him with questions as if they could disregard this miracle.

Jewish Leaders (to the man who had been healed): [10]Must you be reminded that it is the Sabbath? You are not allowed to carry your mat today!

Formerly Disabled Man: [11]The man who healed me gave me specific instructions to carry my mat and go.

Jewish Leaders: [12]Who is the man who gave you these instructions? *How can we identify Him?*

[13]The man genuinely did not know who it was that healed him. In the midst of the crowd *and the excitement of his renewed health,* Jesus had slipped away. [14]Some time later, Jesus found him in the temple and again spoke to him.

Jesus: Take a look at your body; it has been made whole and strong. So avoid a life of sin or else a calamity greater than any disability may befall you.

[15]The man went immediately to tell the Jewish leaders that Jesus was the mysterious healer. [16]So they began pursuing and attacking Jesus because He performed these miracles on the Sabbath.

Jesus (to His attackers): [17]My Father is at work. So I, too, am working.

*T*his issue kept arising from the Jewish leaders. They did not appreciate the good things that Jesus did on the Sabbath. But Jesus was very clear about this. He cared for the poor, the sick, the marginalized more than He cared for how some people might interpret and apply God's law. You see, it is easy to turn law into a set of rules; it is much harder to care for the things of the heart. He also made it clear to us who followed His path—we were here to serve. Our service came out of love for our Liberator. All who followed Him were to love and to serve, especially on the Sabbath.

[18]Most Jews cowered at the rebuke from these men, but Jesus did not. In fact, He was justifying the importance of His work on the Sabbath, claiming God as His Father in ways that suggested He was equal to God. These pious religious leaders sought an opportunity to kill Jesus, and these words fueled their hatred.

Jesus: [19]The truth is that the Son does nothing on His own; *all these actions are led by the Father.* The Son watches the Father closely and then mimics the work of the Father. [20]The Father loves the Son, so He does not hide His actions. Instead, He shows Him everything, and the things not yet revealed by the Father will dumbfound you. ²¹The Father can give life to those who are dead; in the same way, the Son can give the gift of life to those He chooses.

²²The Father does not *exert His power to* judge anyone. Instead, He has given the authority as Judge to the Son. ²³So all of creation will honor *and worship* the Son as they do the Father. If you do not honor the Son, then you dishonor the Father who sent Him.

²⁴I tell you the truth: eternal life belongs to those who hear My voice and believe in the One who sent Me. These people have no reason to fear judgment because they have already left death and entered life.

²⁵I tell you the truth: a new day is imminent—in fact, it has arrived—when the voice of the Son of God will penetrate death's domain and everyone who hears will live. ²⁶⁻²⁷You see, the Father radiates with life, and He also animates the Son *of God* with the same life-giving *beauty and* power to exercise judgment *over all of creation*. Indeed, the Son of God is also the Son of Man. ²⁸If this sounds amazing to you, what is even more amazing is that when the time comes, those buried long ago will hear His voice *through all the rocks, sod, and soil* ²⁹and step out *of decay into resurrection. When this hour arrives,* those who did good will be resurrected to life, and those who did evil will be resurrected to judgment.

³⁰I have not ever acted, and will not in the future act, on My own. I listen *to the directions of the One who sent Me* and act *on these divine instructions. For this reason*, My judgment is always fair and never self-serving. I'm committed to pursuing God's agenda and not My own.

³¹If I stand as the lone witness to My true identity, then I can be dismissed as a liar. ³²But *if you listen,* you will hear another testify about Me, and I know what He says about Me is genuine and true. ³³You sent *messengers* to John, and he told the truth *to everyone who would listen.* ³⁴Still his message about Me *originated in heaven,* not in mortal man. I am

telling you these things *for one reason—* so that you might be rescued. ³⁵*The voice of* John, *the wandering prophet,* is like a light in the darkness; and for a time, you took great joy and pleasure in the light he offered.

³⁶There's another witness standing in My corner who is greater than John, *or any other man.* The mission that brings Me here, and the things I am called to do, demonstrate the authenticity of My calling, which comes directly from the Father. ³⁷In the act of sending Me, the Father has endorsed Me. *None of you knows the Father.* You have never heard His voice or seen His profile. ³⁸His word does not abide in you because you do not believe in the One sent by the Father.

³⁹Here you are scouring through the Scriptures, hoping that you will find eternal life among a pile of scrolls. *What you don't seem to understand is that* the Scriptures point to Me. ⁴⁰*Here I am with you,* and still you reject the truth *contained in the law and prophets* by refusing to come to Me so that you can have life. *I am the source of life, the animating energy of creation that you desperately lack.*

⁴¹This kind of glory does not come from mortal men. ⁴²*I stand before you with eyes that penetrate your soul,* and I see that you do not possess the love of God. ⁴³I have *pursued you,* coming here in My Father's name, and you have turned Me away. If someone else were to approach you with a different set of credentials, you would welcome him. ⁴⁴*That's why it is hard to see* how true faith is even possible for you: you are consumed by the approval of other men, *longing to look good in their eyes,* and yet you disregard the approval of the one true God. ⁴⁵Don't worry that I might bring you up on charges before My Father. Moses is your accuser even though you've put your hope in him ⁴⁶because if you believed *what* Moses had to *say,* then you would believe in Me because he wrote about Me. ⁴⁷But if you ignore Moses and the deeper meaning of his writings, then how will you ever believe what I have to say?

6Once this had transpired, Jesus made His way to the other side of the Sea of Galilee (which some these days call the Sea of Tiberias). ²As Jesus walked, a large crowd pursued Him hoping to see new signs *and miracles*; His healings of the sick and lame were garnering great attention. ³Jesus went up a mountain and found a place to sit down *and teach*. His disciples gathered around. ⁴The celebration of the Passover, one of the principal Jewish feasts, would take place soon. ⁵But when Jesus looked up, He could see an immense crowd coming toward Him. Jesus approached Philip.

Jesus *(to Philip)*: Where is a place to buy bread so these people may eat?

⁶Jesus knew what He was planning to do, but He asked Philip nonetheless. He had something to teach, and it started with a test.

Philip: ⁷I could work for more than half of a year* and still not have the money to buy enough bread to give each person a very small piece.

⁸Andrew, the disciple who was Simon Peter's brother, spoke up.

Andrew: ⁹I met a young boy in the crowd carrying five barley loaves and two fish, but that is practically useless in feeding a crowd this large.
Jesus: ¹⁰Tell the people to sit down.

They all sat together on a large grassy area. *Those counting the people reported* approximately 5,000 men—*not counting the women and children*—sitting in the crowd. ¹¹Jesus picked up the bread, gave thanks to God, and passed it to everyone. He repeated this ritual with the fish. *Men, women, and children* all ate to their heart's content. ¹²When the people had all they could eat, He told the disciples *to gather the leftovers.*

Jesus: Go and collect the leftovers, so we are not wasteful.

¹³They filled 12 baskets with fragments of the five barley loaves. ¹⁴After witnessing this sign-miracle that Jesus did, the people stirred in conversation.

Crowd: This man must be the Prophet *God said was* coming into the world.

¹⁵Jesus sensed the people were planning to mount a revolution *against Israel's Roman occupiers* and make Him king, so He withdrew further up the mountain by Himself.

You have to remember what we had experienced as a people. Since the Babylonians seized Judah in 586 B.C., we, the Jews, had one foreign occupier after another in our land. As conquerors go, the Romans weren't all that bad. They allowed us to worship God in His temple, and they appointed certain ones of us to govern. Of course, we still longed to rule ourselves and throw the Roman rulers out. Some of our people thought Jesus was just the man to lead that revolution. But political upheaval wasn't what He was teaching, and it wasn't why He came to earth.

¹⁶Later that evening the disciples walked down to the sea, ¹⁷boarded a boat, and set sail toward Capernaum. Twilight gave way to darkness. Jesus had not yet joined them. ¹⁸*Suddenly,* the waves rose and a fierce wind began *to rock the boat.* ¹⁹After rowing three or four miles* *through the stormy seas*, they spotted Jesus approaching the boat walking mysteriously upon the deep waters that surrounded them. They panicked.

Jesus *(to the disciples)*: ²⁰I am the One. Don't be afraid.

²¹They welcomed Jesus aboard their small vessel; and when He stepped into the boat,

* 6:7 Literally, 200 denarii
* 6:19 Literally, 25 or 30 stadia

the next thing they knew, they were ashore at their destination.

22The following day some people gathered on the other side of the sea and saw that only one boat had been there; *they were perplexed.* They remembered seeing the disciples getting into the boat without Jesus, *but somehow Jesus was gone. How did He cross the sea without a boat?*

23Other boats were arriving from Tiberias near the grassy area where the Lord offered thanks and passed out bread. 24When this crowd could not find Him or His disciples, they boarded their small boats and crossed the sea to Capernaum looking for Him. 25When they found Jesus across the sea, they questioned Him.

Crowd: Teacher, when did You arrive at Capernaum?

Jesus: 26I tell you the truth—you are tracking Me down because I fed you, not because you saw signs from God. 27Don't spend your life chasing food that spoils and rots. Instead, seek the food that lasts into all the ages and comes from the Son of Man, the One on whom God the Father has placed His seal.

Crowd: 28What do we have to do to accomplish the Father's works?

Jesus: 29If you want to do God's work, then believe in the One He sent.

Crowd: 30Can You show us a miraculous sign? *Something spectacular?* If we see something like that, it will help us to believe. 31Our fathers ate manna when they wandered in the desert. The Hebrew Scriptures say, "He gave them bread from heaven to eat."*

Jesus: 32I tell you the truth: Moses did not give you bread from heaven; it is My Father who offers you true bread from heaven. 33The bread of God comes down out of heaven and breathes life into the cosmos.

Crowd: 34Master, we want a boundless supply of this bread.

Jesus: 35I am the bread that gives life. If you come to My table and eat, you will never go hungry. Believe in Me, and you will never go thirsty. 36Here I am standing in front of you, and still you don't believe.

37All that My Father gives to Me comes to Me. I will receive everyone; I will not send away anyone who comes to Me. 38And here's the reason: I have come down from heaven not to pursue My own agenda but to do what He desires. I am here on behalf of the Father who sent Me. 39He sent Me to care for all He has given Me so that nothing *and no one* will perish. *In the end,* on the last day, He wants everything to be resurrected *into new life.* 40So if you want to know the will of the Father, know this: everyone who sees the Son and believes in Him will live eternally; and on the last day, I am the One who will resurrect him.

41Some of the Jews began to *quietly* grumble against Him because He said "I am the bread that came down from heaven." *Wasn't He a human just like everyone else?*

Crowd: 42Isn't Jesus the son of Joseph? We know His parents! *We know where He came from,* so how can He claim to have "come down from heaven"?

Jesus: 43Stop grumbling *under your breaths.* 44If the Father who sent Me does not draw you, then there's no way you can come to Me. But I will resurrect everyone who does come on the last day. 45Among the prophets, it's written, "Everyone will be taught of God."* So everyone who has heard and learned from the Father finds Me. 46No one has seen the Father, except the One sent from God. He has seen the Father. 47I am telling you the truth: the one who accepts these things has eternal life. 48I am the life-bread. 49Your fathers ate manna in the wilderness, and they died *as you know.* 50But there is another bread that comes from heaven; if you eat this bread, you will not die. 51I am the living bread that has come down from heaven *to rescue those who eat it.* Anyone who eats this bread will live forever. The bread that I will give breathes life into the cosmos. This bread is My flesh.

* 6:31 Exodus 16:4
* 6:45 Isaiah 54:13

⁵²*The low whispers of* some of Jesus' detractors turned into an out-and-out debate.

Crowd: *What is He talking about?* How is He able to give us His flesh to eat?
Jesus: ⁵³I tell you the truth; unless you eat the flesh of the Son of Man and drink His blood, you will not know life. ⁵⁴If you eat My flesh and drink My blood, then you will have eternal life, and I will raise you up at the end of time. ⁵⁵My flesh and blood provide true nourishment. ⁵⁶If you eat My flesh and drink My blood, you will abide in Me and I will abide in you. ⁵⁷The Father of life who sent Me has given life to Me; and as you eat My flesh, I will give life to you. ⁵⁸This is bread that came down from heaven; I am not like the manna that your fathers ate and then died! If you eat this bread, your life will never end.

*H*ow is it that we can follow this path and believe these truths? To be honest, it is not easy. In fact, some found this so hard that they left Jesus for good. The rest of us would readily admit that we're still working on what it means to follow Him. So Jesus left behind a number of practices to help us. One of these is known as the Lord's Supper. Jesus instructed us to break bread and share wine to remember how He allowed His body to be broken for all humankind. In some beautiful, mysterious way, Jesus is present for us in the simple elements of bread and wine. Touch Him; taste His richness; remember His most glorious hour on the cross. In that moment, He embraced all darkness and shame and transformed them into light. As I come to the table with my community and we feast on His light, life seems more hopeful and complete. As you take the bread and the wine, you affirm the reality that the Liberating King is among and within you.

⁵⁹He spoke these words in the synagogue as part of His teaching mission in Capernaum. ⁶⁰Many disciples heard what He said, and they had questions *of their own.*

Disciples: How are we supposed to understand all of this? It is a hard teaching.

⁶¹Jesus was aware that even His disciples were murmuring about this.

Jesus: Has My teaching offended you? ⁶²What if you were to see the Son of Man ascend *to return* to where He came from? ⁶³The Spirit brings life. The flesh has nothing to offer. The words I have been teaching you are spirit and life. ⁶⁴But some of you do not believe.

From the first day *Jesus began to call disciples*, He knew those who did not have genuine faith. He knew, too, who would betray Him.

Jesus: ⁶⁵This is why I have been telling you that no one comes to Me without the Father's blessing and guidance.

⁶⁶After hearing these teachings, many of His disciples walked away and no longer followed Jesus.

Jesus *(to the twelve)*: ⁶⁷Do you want to walk away too?
Simon Peter: ⁶⁸Lord, if we were to go, who would we follow? You speak the words that give everlasting life. ⁶⁹We believe and recognize You as the Holy One of God.
Jesus: ⁷⁰I chose each one of you, the twelve, Myself. But one of you is a devil.

⁷¹This cryptic comment referred to Judas the son of Simon Iscariot, for he was the one of the twelve who was going to betray Him.

7 After these events, *it was time for Jesus to move on.* He began a long walk through the Galilean countryside. He was purposefully avoiding Judea because of *the violent threats made against*

Him by the Jews there who wanted to kill Him. [2]*It was fall,* the time of year when the Jews celebrated the Festival of Booths.

> *W*e always looked forward to this week-long festival filled with food, worship, prayer, and celebration. On this holiday, everyone moved out of their homes and camped in temporary quarters, called booths, to remember that God was with us as our ancestors wandered for 40 years without a home. It was common for us to celebrate these holidays with family, so the brothers of Jesus were with us as we discussed our destination. Where would we celebrate?

Brothers of Jesus *(to Jesus)*: [3]Let's get out of here and go *south* to Judea so You can show Your disciples there what You are capable of doing. [4]No one who seeks the public eye is content to work in secret. If You want to perform these signs, then step forward on the world's stage; *don't hide up here in the hills, Jesus.*

[5]Jesus' own brothers *were speaking contemptuously*; they did not yet believe in Him, *just as the people in His hometown did not see Him as anything more than Joseph's son.*

Jesus: [6]My time has not yet arrived, but for you My brothers, *by all means,* it is always the right time. [7]*You have nothing to worry about because* the world doesn't hate you, but it despises Me because I am always exposing the dark evil in its works. [8]Go on to the feast without Me; I am not going *right now* because My time is not yet at hand.

[9]This conversation came to an *abrupt* end, and Jesus stayed in Galilee [10]until His brothers were gone. Then He, too, went up to Jerusalem. But He traveled in secret to avoid drawing any public attention. [11]Some Jewish leaders were searching for Him at the feast and asking the crowds where they could find Him. [12]The crowds would talk in groups: some favored Jesus and thought He was a good man; others disliked Him and thought He was leading people astray. [13]*All of these conversations took place in whispers.* No one was willing to speak openly about Jesus for fear of the religious leaders.

[14]In the middle of the festival, Jesus marched directly into the temple and started to teach. [15]Some of the Jews *who heard Him* were amazed at Jesus' ability, and people questioned repeatedly:

Jews: How can this man be so wise *about the Hebrew Scriptures*? He has never had a formal education.
Jesus: [16]I do not claim ownership of My words; they are *a gift* from the One who sent Me. [17]If anyone is willing to act according to His purposes *and is open to hearing truth,* he will know the source of My teaching. Does it come from God or from Me? [18]If a man speaks his own words, *constantly quoting himself,* he is after adulation. But I chase only after glory for the One who sent Me. My intention is *authentic and* true. You'll find no wrong *motives* in Me.
[19]Moses gave you the law, didn't he? Then how can you *blatantly* ignore the law and look for an opportunity to murder Me?

> *N*otice how Jesus changed in tone and subject. This shift seemed abrupt to us because we didn't know anything about the Pharisees' plotting.

Crowd: [20]You must be possessed with a demon! Who is trying to kill You?
Jesus: [21]*Listen,* all it took was for Me to do one thing, *heal a crippled man,* and you all were astonished. [22]Don't you remember how Moses passed down circumcision as a tradition of our ancestors? When you pick up a knife to circumcise on the Sabbath, *isn't that work?* [23]If a male is circumcised on the Sabbath to keep the law of Moses intact, how can making one man whole on the Sabbath

be a cause for your violent rage? [24]You should not judge by outward appearance. When you judge, search for what is right and just.

Some People of Jerusalem: [25]There is the man they are seeking to kill; surely He must be the one. [26]But here He is, speaking out in the open to the crowd, while they have not spoken a word to *stop or challenge* Him. *Do you think they've changed their minds? Do these leaders now* believe He is the Liberating King? [27]But He can't be; we know where this man comes from, but the true origin of the Liberator will be a mystery to all of us.

Jesus (*speaking aloud as He teaches on the temple's porch*): [28]*You think* you know Me and where I have come from, but I have not come here on My own. I have been sent by the One who embodies truth. You do not know Him. [29]I know Him because I came from Him. He has sent Me.

[30]Some were trying to seize Him because of His words, but no one laid as much as a finger on Him—His time had not yet arrived. [31]In the crowd, there were many in whom faith was taking hold.

Believers in the Crowd: When the Liberator arrives, will He perform any more signs than this man has done?

[32]Some Pharisees *were hanging back in the crowd*, overhearing the gossip about Him. The temple authorities and the Pharisees *took action and* sent officers to arrest Jesus.

Jesus: [33]I am going to be with you for a little while longer; then I will return to the One who sent Me. [34]You will look for Me, but you will not be able to find Me. Where I am, you are unable to come.

Some Jews in the Crowd (*to each other*): [35]Where could He possibly go that we could not find Him? You don't think He's about to go into the Dispersion* and teach our people scattered among the Greeks, do you? [36]What do you think He means, "You will look for Me, but not be able to find Me," and "Where I am, you are not able to come"?

[37]On the last day, the biggest day of the festival, Jesus stood again and spoke aloud.

Jesus: If any of you is thirsty, come to Me and drink. [38]If you believe in Me, the Hebrew Scriptures say that rivers of living water will flow from within you.*

[39]Jesus was referring to *the realities of life in* the Spirit made available to everyone who believes in Him. But the Spirit had not yet arrived because Jesus had not been glorified.

*T*he Holy Spirit connects us to the Father and His Son, the Liberating King. So lay down any fear you have about being disconnected from God; the Creator of the Universe dwells within you, sustains you, and will accomplish the impossible through you.

After Jesus' exit, we, the church, take on our most important role as we become His body here on earth. We are intimately connected to the living God individually, but it also is important to remember our journey is to be shared in community.

The church is a redeeming force in the world: His hands, His feet, His body. If you want to know the Liberator, then you must know His body. Life in Him is not just about embracing and loving God; it's about being the living body of the church. We will find strength, passion, and comfort in our collective mission.

Some of the Crowd (*speaking aloud as He teaches on the temple's porch*): [40]This man is definitely the Prophet.
Others: [41]This is the Liberating King!
Still Others: Is it possible for the Liberator to come from Galilee? [42]Don't the Hebrew Scriptures say that He will come

* 7:35 Literally, the Diaspora (Greek for "scattering"). The Diaspora refers to those Jews who were exiled or settled outside the traditional lands of Israel.
* 7:38 Isaiah 44:3; 55:1; 58:11

from Bethlehem,* King David's village, and be a descendant of King David?

⁴³*Rumors and* opinions about the true identity of Jesus divided the crowd. ⁴⁴Some wanted to arrest Him, but no one dared to touch Him.

⁴⁵The officers *who had been sent by* the chief priests and Pharisees *to take Jesus into custody* returned *empty-handed,* and they faced some hard questions.

Chief Priest and Pharisees: *Where is Jesus?* Why didn't you capture Him?
Officers: ⁴⁶*We listened to Him.* Never has a man spoken like this man.
Pharisees: ⁴⁷So you have also been led astray? ⁴⁸Can you find one leader or educated Pharisee who believes this man? *Of course not. Anyone who has studied the Scriptures knows His words are wrong and a threat to our people.* ⁴⁹This crowd is plagued by ignorance about the teachings of the law; *that is why they will listen to Him.* That is also why they are under God's curse.

⁵⁰Nicodemus, *the Pharisee* who approached Jesus *under the cloak of darkness,* was present when the officers returned empty-handed. He addressed the leaders.

Nicodemus: ⁵¹Does our law condemn someone without first giving him a fair hearing and learning something about him?
Pharisees *(ignoring Nicodemus's legal point)*: ⁵²Are you from Galilee too? Look it up for yourself; no real prophet is supposed to come from Galilee.

[⁵³The time came for everyone to go home.

8 Jesus went to the Mount of Olives. ²He awoke early in the morning to return to the temple. *When He arrived,* the people surrounded Him, so He sat down and began to teach them. ³*While He was teaching,* the scribes and Pharisees brought in a woman who was caught in the act of adultery, and stood her before Jesus.

Pharisees: ⁴Teacher.

*I*magine the tension in that moment. You can sense the sarcasm in the air as these men threatening Jesus are now calling Him "Teacher." Jesus knew this was a test.

Pharisees: This woman was caught in the act of adultery. ⁵Moses says in the law that we are to kill such women by stoning. What do You say about it?

⁶This was all set up as a test for Jesus; His answers would give them grounds to accuse Him *of crimes against Moses' law.* Jesus bent over and wrote something in the dirt with His finger. ⁷They persisted in badgering Jesus, so He stood up straight.

Jesus: Let the first stone be thrown by the one among you who has not sinned.

⁸Once again Jesus bent down to the ground and resumed writing with His finger. ⁹The Pharisees who heard Him *stood still for a few moments and then* began to leave slowly, one by one, beginning with the older men. *Even the pious Pharisees knew they had sinned, so there would be no stones thrown this day.* Eventually only Jesus and the woman remained, ¹⁰and Jesus looked up.

Jesus: *Dear* woman, where is everyone? *Are we alone?* Did no one step forward to condemn you?
Woman Caught in Adultery: ¹¹Lord, no one *has condemned me.*
Jesus: Well, I do not condemn you either; *all I ask is that you* go and from now on avoid the sins that plague you.]*

¹²*On another occasion,* Jesus spoke to the crowds again.

* 7:42 Micah 5:1-2
* 7:53–8:11 Many early manuscripts omit these verses.

Jesus: I am the light that shines through the cosmos; if you walk with Me, you will thrive in the *nourishing* light that gives life and will not know darkness.

Pharisees: ¹³Jesus, what You are claiming about Yourself cannot possibly be true. The only person bearing witness is You.

Jesus: ¹⁴Even if I am making *bold* claims about Myself—*who I am, what I have come to do*—I am speaking the truth. You see, I know where I came from and where I will go *when I am done here*. You know neither where I come from nor where I will go. ¹⁵You spend your time judging *by the wrong criteria*, by human standards, but I am not here to judge anyone. ¹⁶If I were to judge, then My judgment would be based on truth, but I would not judge anyone alone. I act in harmony with the One who sent Me. ¹⁷Your law states that if the testimonies of two witnesses agree, their testimony is true. ¹⁸Well, I testify about Myself, and so does the Father who sent Me here.

Pharisees: ¹⁹Where is the Father *who testifies on Your behalf*?

Jesus: You don't know the Father or Me. If you knew Me, then you would also know the Father.

²⁰Jesus said all of these things in the treasury while He was teaching in the temple; *followers and opponents alike gathered to hear Him,* but none of His enemies tried to seize Him because His time had not yet come.

Jesus (*to the crowds*): ²¹I am leaving this place, and you will look for Me and die in your sin. For where I am going, you are not able to come.

Jews: ²²Is He suicidal? He keeps saying, "Where I am going, you are not able to come." *Surely He does not have plans to kill Himself.*

Jesus: ²³You originate from *the earth* below, and I have come from *the heavens* above. You are from this world, and I am not. ²⁴That's why I told you that you will die here as a result of your sins. Unless you believe I am who I have said I am, your sins will lead to your death.

Jews: ²⁵Who exactly are You?

Jesus: From the beginning of My mission, I have been telling you who I am. ²⁶I have so much to say about you, so many judgments to render, *but if you hear one thing,* hear that the One who sent Me is true, and all the things I have heard from Him I speak into the world.

²⁷The people had not understood that Jesus was teaching about the Father.

Jesus: ²⁸Whenever *the day comes and* you lift up the Son of Man, then you will know that I am He. *It will be clear then* that I am not acting alone, but that I am speaking the things I have learned directly from the Father. ²⁹The One who sent Me is with Me; He has not abandoned Me because I always do what pleases Him.

³⁰As Jesus was speaking, many in the crowd believed in Him. *But they could not imagine what He meant about the lifting up of the Son of Man.*

Jesus (*to the new Jewish believers*): ³¹If you *hear My voice and* abide in My word, you are truly My disciples; ³²you will know the truth, and that truth will give you freedom.

Jewish Believers: ³³We are Abraham's children, and we have never been enslaved to anyone. How can You say to us, "You will be set free"?

Jesus: ³⁴I tell you the truth: everyone who commits sin surrenders his freedom to sin. *He is a slave to sin's power.* ³⁵Even a household slave does not live in the home like a member of the family, but a son belongs there forever. ³⁶So *think of it this way,* if the Son comes to make you free, you will really be free.

Jesus noticed that some of His opponents were listening, so He spoke louder and turned His remarks to them.

Jesus: ³⁷I know you are descendants of Abraham, but here you are plotting to murder Me. *You want Me dead, and for what reason?* Because you do not welcome My voice into your lives. [38]As I speak, I am painting you a picture of what I have seen with My Father; here you are repeating the things you have seen from your father.

Jews: [39]Abraham is our father.

Jesus: If you are truly Abraham's children, then act like Abraham! [40]From what I see you are trying to kill Me, a man who has told you the truth that comes from the Father. This is not something Abraham would do, [41]but you are doing what you have learned from your father.

Jews: We were not born from adulterous parents; we have one Father: God.

Jesus: [42]I come from the one true God, and I'm not here on My own. He sent Me *on a mission.* If God were your Father, you would *know that and you would* love Me. [43]You don't even understand what I'm saying. *Do you?* Why? It is because You cannot stand to hear My voice. [44]You are just like your true father, the devil, and you spend your time pursuing the things your father loves. He started out as a killer, and he cannot tolerate truth because he is void of anything true. At the core of his character, he is a liar; everything he speaks originates in these lies because he is the father of lies. [45]So when I speak truth, you don't believe Me. [46-47]If I speak the truth, why don't you believe Me? If you belong to God's family, then why can't you hear God speak? The answer is clear; you are not in God's family. *I speak truth, and you don't believe Me.* Can any of you convict Me of sin?

Jews: [48]We were right when we called You a demon-possessed Samaritan.

Jesus: [49-50]I'm not taken by demons. You dishonor Me, but I give *all glory and honor to* the Father. But I am not pursuing My own fame. There is only One who pursues and renders justice. [51]I tell you the truth, anyone who *hears My voice and* keeps My word will never experience death.

Jews: [52]We are even more confident now that You are demon-possessed. *Just go down the list:* Abraham died, the prophets all died. Yet You say, "If you keep My word, you won't taste death." [53]Are you greater than our father Abraham? He died; *remember?* Prophets—are any of them still alive? No. Who do You think You are?

Jesus: [54]If I were trying to make Myself somebody important, *it would be a waste of time.* That kind of fame is worth nothing. It is the Father who *is behind Me, urging Me on,* giving Me praise. You say, "He is our God," [55]but you are not in relationship with Him. I know Him *intimately;* even if I said anything other than the truth, I would be a liar, like you. I know Him, and I do as He says. [56]Your father Abraham anticipated the time when I would come, and he celebrated My coming.

Jews: [57]You aren't even 50 years old, yet You have seen *and talked with* Abraham?

Jesus: [58]I tell you the truth; I AM before Abraham was born.

[59]The people picked up stones to hurl at Him, but Jesus slipped out of the temple. *Their murderous rage would have to wait.*

I have had a few things to say about "the Jews." You all seem to cringe every time the subject arises. People are overly sensitive about that. The fact is: I am a Jew. I am a son of Abraham, as are many in my community, so when I criticize certain Jewish leaders I am not criticizing a whole people. I'm not stereotyping or making generalizations. When I use the term "the Jews," I am talking about a corrupt group of power brokers who conspired against Jesus with the Romans to have Him crucified and who later had my people expelled from the synagogue. They are members of my family, and I can't stand what they did to Jesus and what they are doing to my other family, my faith family. Don't you remember the prophets? Men like Micah, Isaiah, and Amos? Prophets have the duty—Jeremiah said he had "a fire in his bones"*—to speak for God and condemn hypocrisy and unbelief wherever it is found. When injustice and unbelief are found close to home, prophets must speak. That's my call. That's what I'm doing.

9 While walking *together* along the road, Jesus saw a man who was blind since his birth.

Disciples: ²Teacher, who sinned? *Who is responsible for this man's blindness?* Did he commit sins that merited this punishment? If not his sins, is it the sins of his parents?

Jesus: ³Neither. His blindness cannot be *explained or* traced to any particular person's sins. He is blind so the deeds of God may be put on display. ⁴While it is daytime, we must do the works of the One who sent Me. But when the *sun sets and* night falls, this work is impossible. ⁵Whenever I am in the world, I am the light of the world.

*C*ertainly Jesus knew the Pharisees frowned on His Sabbath healings, but their opinions were not His motivation to finish before sunset. Jesus used the sunset to make a point to us: just as the sun illuminates the world, He brings enlightenment; just as the sun is up for a short time each day, His time on earth is short.

⁶After He said these things, He spat on the ground and mixed saliva and dirt to form mud, which He smeared across the blind man's eyes.

Jesus (to the blind man): ⁷Go, wash yourself in the pool of Siloam.

Siloam means "sent," *and its name reminded us that his healing was sent by God.* The man went, washed, and returned to Jesus, his eyes now alive with sight. ⁸Then neighbors and others who knew him were confused to see a man so closely resembling the blind beggar running about.

Townspeople: Isn't this the man we see *every day* sitting and begging *in the streets*?
Others: ⁹This is the same man.
Still Others: This cannot be him. But this fellow bears an uncanny resemblance to the blind man.
Formerly Blind Man: I am the same man. *It's me!*
Townspeople: ¹⁰How have your *lifeless* eyes been opened?
Formerly Blind Man: ¹¹A man named Jesus *approached me and* made mud from the ground and applied it to my eyes. He then said to me, "Go, wash yourself in the pool of Siloam." I went and washed, and suddenly I could see.
Townspeople: ¹²Where is this man *who healed you*?
Formerly Blind Man: I don't know.

¹³⁻¹⁴The townspeople brought the formerly blind beggar to appear before the Pharisees *the same day Jesus healed him*, which happened to be on the Sabbath Day. ¹⁵The Pharisees began questioning him, looking for some explanation for how he could now see.

Formerly Blind Man: He smeared mud on my eyes, and I washed; now I see.
Some Pharisees: ¹⁶God can't possibly be behind this man because He is breaking the rules of the Sabbath.
Other Pharisees: How can such a lawbreaking scoundrel do something like this?

The Pharisees were at odds with one another about Jesus and could not agree *whether His power came from God or the devil.*

Pharisees (to the formerly blind man): ¹⁷What do you say about this man, about the fact He opened your eyes so you could see?
Formerly Blind Man: *I have no doubt*—this man is a prophet.

¹⁸Some of the Jews suspected the whole situation was a charade, that this man was

* **Note** Jeremiah 20:9

never blind. So they summoned the man's parents to testify about his condition.

Pharisees: ¹⁹Is this man your son? Do you testify that he has been blind from birth? How therefore does he now see?

Parents: ²⁰We can tell you this much: he is our son, and he was born blind. ²¹But his new sight is a complete mystery to us! We do not know the man who opened his eyes. Why don't you ask our son? He is old enough to speak for himself.

²²The man's parents were a bit evasive because they were afraid of the Jewish leaders. It had been rumored that anyone who spoke of Jesus as the Liberating King would be expelled from the synagogue. ²³So they deferred the thorny question to their son, ²⁴and the Pharisees called on him a second time.

Pharisees: Give God the credit. *He's the One who healed you.* All glory belongs to God. We are persuaded this man you speak of is a sinner *who defies God.*

Formerly Blind Man: ²⁵If this man is a sinner, I don't know. *I am not qualified to say.* I only know one thing: I was blind and now I see.

Pharisees: ²⁶What did He do to you? How did He give you sight?

Formerly Blind Man: ²⁷*Listen,* I've already answered all these questions, and you don't like my answers. Do you really need me to say it all over again? Are you thinking about joining up with Him and becoming His followers?

Pharisees (*berating him*): ²⁸You're one of His followers, but we follow Moses. ²⁹We have confidence that God spoke to Moses, but this man *you speak of is a mystery;* we don't even know where He comes from.

Formerly Blind Man: ³⁰Isn't it ironic that you, *our religious leaders,* don't even know where He comes from; yet He gave me sight! ³¹We know that God does not listen to sinners, but He does respond and work through those who worship Him and do His will. ³²No one has ever heard of someone opening the eyes of any per-

son blind from birth. ³³This man must come from God; otherwise, this miracle would not be possible. *Only God can do such things.*

Pharisees: ³⁴You were born under a cloud of sin. How can you, *of all people,* lecture us?

The religious leaders banished him from their presence. ³⁵Jesus heard what had happened and sought out the man.

Jesus: Do you believe in the Son of Man?

Formerly Blind Man: ³⁶I want to believe, Lord. Who is He?

Jesus: ³⁷You have seen His face *with your new eyes,* and you are talking to Him now.

Formerly Blind Man: ³⁸Lord, I do believe.

The man bowed low to worship Jesus.

Jesus: ³⁹I have entered this world to announce a verdict *that changes everything.* Now those without sight may begin to see, and those who see may become blind.

Some Pharisees (*who overheard Jesus*): ⁴⁰Surely we are not blind, are we?

Jesus: ⁴¹If you were blind, you would be without sin. But because you claim you can see, your sin is ever present.

*I*t seemed like the Pharisees were frequently around to challenge whatever Jesus would say and do. But He would always get the better of them. Once again, Jesus turned what the Pharisees said inside out. They thought blindness was a curse that evidenced sin, and they thought vision ensured knowledge and understanding—even concerning spiritual matters. Instead, the Pharisees' confidence in their vision and discernment made them unable to see the truth about Jesus. Ironically, they had a blind trust in their sighted leaders. By refusing to believe in Him, they were the sinners—not the blind man.

10

Jesus: I tell you the truth: the man who crawls through the fence of the sheep pen, rather than walking through the gate, is a thief or a vandal. ²The shepherd walks openly through the entrance. ³The guard who is posted to protect the sheep opens the gate for the shepherd, and the sheep hear his voice. He calls his own sheep by name and leads them out. ⁴When all the sheep have been gathered, he walks on ahead of them, and they follow him because they know his voice. ⁵The sheep would not be willing to follow a stranger; they run because they do not know the voice of strangers. *But they know and follow the shepherd's voice.*

⁶Jesus explained a profound truth through this metaphor, but they did not understand His teaching. ⁷So He explained further.

Jesus: I tell you the truth: I am the gate of the sheep. ⁸All who approached the sheep before Me came as thieves and robbers, and the sheep did not listen to their voices. ⁹I am the gate; whoever enters through Me will be liberated, will go in and go out, and will find pastures. ¹⁰The thief approaches *with malicious intent*, looking to steal, slaughter, and destroy; I came to give life with joy and abundance.

¹¹I am the good shepherd. The good shepherd lays down His life for the sheep *in His care*. ¹²The hired hand is not like the shepherd caring for His own sheep. When a wolf attacks, snatching and scattering the sheep, he runs for his life, leaving them *defenseless*. ¹³The hired hand runs because he works only for wages and does not care for the sheep. ¹⁴I am the good shepherd; I know My sheep, and My sheep know Me. ¹⁵As the Father knows Me, I know the Father; I will give My life for the sheep. ¹⁶There are many more sheep than you can see here, and I will bring them as well. They will hear My voice, and the flock will be united. One flock. One shepherd. ¹⁷The Father loves Me because I *am willing to* lay down My life—but I will take it up

again. ¹⁸My life cannot be taken away by anybody else; I am giving it of My own free will. My authority allows Me to give My life and to take it again. All this has been commanded by My Father.

*J*esus loved to explain truth through the everyday things we encountered. He spoke of vines, fruit, fishing, building, and shepherding. He was a master communicator. In this metaphor, Jesus is the shepherd. Eventually He would become the sheep as well. On the cross, He was destined to become the innocent sacrifice that would make all future sin sacrifices and burnt offerings unnecessary.

¹⁹When He spoke these words, some of the Jews began to argue.

Many Jews: ²⁰He has a demon and is a raving maniac. Why are you people listening to Him?

Other Jews: ²¹No demon-possessed man ever spoke like this. Do demons give sight to the blind?

²²⁻²³It was winter and time for the Festival of Dedication.* While in Jerusalem, Jesus was walking through the temple in an area known as Solomon's porch, ²⁴and Jews gathered around Him.

Jews: How long are You going to keep us guessing? If You are the Liberating King, announce it clearly.

Jesus: ²⁵I have told you, and you do not believe. The works I am doing in My Father's name tell the truth about Me. *You do not listen;* ²⁶you lack faith because you are not My sheep. ²⁷My sheep *respond as they* hear My voice; I know them *intimately*, and they follow Me. ²⁸I give them a life that is unceasing, and death will not have the last word. *Nothing or* no one can steal them from My hand. ²⁹My Father has given the

* 10:22-23 The Festival of Lights or Hanukkah

flock to Me, and He is superior to all *beings and things.* No one is powerful enough to snatch the flock from My Father's hand. ³⁰The Father and I are one.

³¹The Jews gathered stones to execute Jesus right then and there.

Jesus: ³²I have performed many beautiful works before you in the name of the Father. Which of these can be judged as an offense that merits My execution?

Jews: ³³You are not condemned for performing miracles. We demand Your life because You are a man, yet you claim to be God. This is blasphemy!

Jesus: ³⁴*You know* what is written in the Scriptures. Doesn't it read, "I said, you are gods"?* ³⁵If the Scriptures called your ancestors *(mere mortals)* gods to whom the word of God came—and the Scriptures cannot be set aside— ³⁶what should you call One *who is unique,* sanctified by and sent from the Father into the world? I have said, "I am God's Son." How can you call that blasphemy? ³⁷*By all means,* do not believe in Me, if I am not doing the things of the Father. ³⁸But examine My actions, *and you will see that My work is the work of the Father.* Regardless of whether you believe in Me—believe the miracles. Then you will know that the Father is in Me, and I am in the Father.

³⁹Once again, *some of* the Jews tried to capture Him, but He slipped away, eluding their grasp. ⁴⁰Jesus crossed the Jordan River and returned to the place where John was ritually cleansing* the people in the early days. He lingered in the area, ⁴¹and scores of people gathered around Him.

Crowds: John never performed any miracles, but every word he spoke about this man has come to pass. It is all true!

⁴²In that place, many believed in Him.

There was a certain man who was very ill. He was known as Lazarus from Bethany, which is the hometown of Mary and her sister Martha. ²Mary *did a beautiful thing for Jesus. She* anointed the Lord with a pleasant-smelling oil and wiped His feet with her hair. Her brother Lazarus became deathly ill, ³so the sisters immediately sent a message to Jesus which said, "Lord, the one You love is very ill." ⁴Jesus heard the message.

Jesus: His sickness will not end in his death but will bring great glory to God. As these events unfold, the Son of God will be exalted.

⁵Jesus *dearly* loved Mary, Martha, and Lazarus. ⁶However, after receiving this news, He waited two more days where He was.

Jesus *(speaking to the disciples):* ⁷It is time to return to Judea.

Disciples: ⁸Teacher, the last time You were there, some Jews attempted to execute You by crushing You with stones. Why would You go back?

Jesus: ⁹There are 12 hours of daylight, correct? If anyone walks in the day, that person does not stumble because he or she sees the light of the world. ¹⁰If anyone walks at night, he will trip and fall because he does not have the light within. ¹¹(Jesus briefly pauses.) Our friend Lazarus has gone to sleep, so I will go to awaken him.

Disciples: ¹²Lord, if he is sleeping, then he will be all right.

¹³Jesus used "sleep" *as a metaphor* for death, but the disciples took Him literally *and did not understand.* ¹⁴Then Jesus spoke plainly.

---

* 10:34 Psalm 82:6
* 10:40 Literally, immersing, to show repentance

Jesus: Lazarus is dead, [15]and I am grateful for your sakes that I was not there when he died. Now you will *see and* believe. *It does not matter if the people there want to kill Me.* Gather yourselves, and let's go to him.

Thomas, the Twin (*to the disciples*): [16]Let's go so we can die with Him.

[17-18]As Jesus was approaching Bethany (which is about two miles east of Jerusalem), He heard that Lazarus had been in the tomb four days. [19]Now many people had come to comfort Mary and Martha as they mourned the loss of their brother. [20]Martha went to meet Jesus when word arrived that He was approaching Bethany, but Mary stayed behind at the house.

Martha: [21]Lord, if You had been with us, my brother would not have died. [22]Even so I still believe that anything You ask of God will be done.

Jesus: [23]Your brother will rise to life.

Martha: [24]I know. He will rise again when everyone is resurrected on the last day.

Jesus: [25]I am the resurrection and the source of all life; those who believe in Me will live even in death. [26]Everyone who lives and believes in Me will never truly die. Do you believe this?

Martha: [27]Yes, Lord, I believe that You are the Liberating King, God's own Son who *we have heard* is coming into the world.

[28]After this Martha ran home to Mary.

Martha (*whispering to Mary*): Come with me. The Teacher is here, and He has asked for you.

[29]Mary did not waste a minute. She got up and went [30]to the same spot where Martha had found Jesus outside the village. [31]The people gathered in her home offering support and comfort assumed she was going back to the tomb to cry and mourn, so they followed her. [32]Mary approached Jesus, saw Him, and fell at His feet.

Mary: Lord, if only You had been here, my brother would still be alive.

[33]When Jesus saw Mary's *profound grief and the moaning and* weeping of her companions, He was deeply moved *by their pain* in His spirit and was intensely troubled.

Jesus: [34]Where have you laid his body?

Jews: Come and see, Lord.

[35]*As they walked,* Jesus wept; [36]and everyone noticed how much Jesus must have loved Lazarus. [37]But others were skeptical.

Others: If this man can give sight to the blind, He could have kept him from dying. *Why wasn't He here sooner if He loved Lazarus so much?*

[38]Then Jesus, who was intensely troubled by all of this, approached the tomb— a *small* cave covered by a *massive* stone.

Jesus: [39]Remove the stone.

Martha: Lord, he has been dead four days; the stench will be unbearable.

Jesus: [40]Remember, I told you that if you believe, you will see the glory of God.

[41]They removed the stone, and Jesus lifted His eyes toward heaven.

Jesus: Father, I am grateful that You have heard Me. [42]I know that You are always listening, but I proclaim it loudly so that everyone here will believe You have sent Me.

[43]After these words, He called out in a thunderous voice.

Jesus: Lazarus, come out!

[44]Then, the man who was dead walked out of his tomb bound from head to toe in a burial shroud.

Jesus: Untie him, and let him go.

Once again Jesus amazed us. How could He raise Lazarus? What kind of man was this who could speak life into death's darkness? Throughout His time with us, we were continually surprised by Jesus. He was obviously unique. He was unlike anyone we had met before. I remember the time Jesus was awakened from a peaceful rest and rose to face a fierce gale of wind and the stinging spray that came off the Sea of Galilee. Even the seasoned sailors among us were panicking. Jesus rebuked the storm and said, "That's enough! Be still!" Immediately the wind subsided. The rough sea became calm. Jesus turned to us and rebuked us for our lack of faith. In the wake of that storm, we talked among ourselves, asking, "Who is this Jesus? How can it be that He has power over even the wind and the waves? And how could He have power over death?"* It took us a while, but more and more we became convinced this was no ordinary man.

45As a result, many of the Jews who had come with Mary saw what happened and believed in Him. 46But some went to the Pharisees to report what they witnessed Jesus doing. 47As a result of these reports—*and on short notice*—the chief priests and Pharisees called a meeting of the high council.

Pharisees: What are we going to do about this man? He is performing many miracles. 48If we don't stop this now, every man, woman, and child will believe in Him. *You know what will happen next?* The Romans *will think He's mounting a revolution and* will destroy our temple. It will be the end of our nation.

Caiaphas, the High Priest That Year: 49You have no idea what you are talking about; 50what you don't understand is that it's better for you that one man should die for the people so the whole nation won't perish.

51*His speech was more than it seemed.* As high priest that year, Caiaphas prophesied (without knowing it) that Jesus would die on behalf of the entire nation, 52and not just for the *children of* Israel—He would die so all God's children could be gathered from the four corners of the world into one people. 53In that moment, they cemented their intentions to have Jesus executed.

54From that day forward, Jesus refrained from walking publicly among the people in Judea. He withdrew to a small town known as Ephraim, a rural area near the wilderness, where He set up camp with His disciples.

55The Passover was approaching, and Jews everywhere traveled to Jerusalem early so they could purify themselves and prepare for Passover. 56People were looking for Jesus, hoping to catch a glimpse of Him in the city. All the while, some Jews were discussing Him in the temple.

Some Jews: Do you think He will decide not to come *to Jerusalem this year* for the feast?

57*In the midst of this confusion,* the Pharisees and the chief priests ordered that if anyone knew the whereabouts of Jesus *of Nazareth*, it must be reported immediately so they could arrest Him.

12 Six days before the Passover feast, Jesus journeyed to the village of Bethany, to the home of Lazarus, who had recently been raised from the dead, 2where they hosted Him for dinner. Martha was busy serving *as the hostess*, Lazarus reclined at the table with Him, 3and Mary took a pound of fine ointment, pure nard (which is *both rare and* expensive), and anointed Jesus' feet with it, and then wiped them with her hair. As the pleasant fragrance of this extravagant ointment filled the entire house, 4Judas Iscariot, one of His disciples (who was plotting to betray Jesus), began to speak.

Judas Iscariot: 5*How could she pour out* this vast amount of fine oil? Why didn't she

* **Note** Mark 4:35-41

sell it? It is worth nearly a year's wages;* the money could have been given to the poor.

[6]This had nothing to do with Judas's desire to help the poor. The truth is he served as the treasurer, and he helped himself to the money from the common pot at every opportunity.

Jesus: [7]Leave her alone. She has observed this custom in anticipation of the day of My burial. [8]The poor are ever present, but I will be leaving.

[9]Word spread of Jesus' presence, and a large crowd was gathering to see Jesus and the formerly deceased Lazarus, whom He had brought back from the dead. [10]The chief priests were secretly plotting Lazarus's murder since, [11]because of him, many Jews were leaving their teachings and believing in Jesus.
[12]The next day, a great crowd of people who had come to the festival heard that Jesus was coming to Jerusalem, [13]so they gathered branches of palm trees to wave as they celebrated His arrival.

Crowds (shouting):
Hosanna!
He who comes in the name of the
Lord is truly blessed*
and is King of all Israel.

[14]Jesus found a young donkey, sat on it, *and rode through the crowds mounted on this small beast.* The Scriptures foretold of this day:

[15]Daughter of Zion, do not be afraid.
Watch! Your King is coming.
You will find Him seated on the
colt of a donkey.*

[16]The disciples did not understand any of this at the time; these truths did not sink in until Jesus had been glorified. As they reflected on their memories of Jesus, they realized these things happened just as they were written. [17]Those who witnessed the resurrection of Lazarus enthusiastically spoke of Jesus to all who would listen, [18]and that is why the crowd went out to meet Him. They had heard of the miraculous sign He had done.

*W*e suspected during our time with Jesus that He was more than a man, but it took the power and glory of the resurrection to convince us completely that Jesus was divine. When we saw Him, when we touched Him, when the sound of His voice thundered in our souls, we knew we were face-to-face with God's immense glory, the unique Son of God. As we read and reread the Scriptures in light of our experience of Him, we found that Jesus' life and story were the climax of God's covenants with His people.

Pharisees (to one another): [19]Our efforts to squelch Him have not worked, *but now is not the time for action.* Look, the world is following after Him.

[20]Among the crowds traveling to Jerusalem were Greeks seeking to *follow God and* worship at the great feast. [21-22]Some of them came to Philip with an important request.

Greek Pilgrims (to Philip): Sir, we are hoping to meet Jesus.

Philip, a disciple from the Galilean village of Bethsaida, told Andrew *that these Greeks were wanting to see Jesus.* Together Andrew and Philip approached Jesus to inform Him about the request.

Jesus (to Philip and Andrew): [23]The time has come for the Son of Man to be glorified. [24]I tell you the truth: unless a grain of wheat is planted in the ground and dies, it remains a solitary seed. But when it is planted, it produces in death a great

* 12:5 Literally, 300 denarii, Roman coins
* 12:13 Psalm 118:26
* 12:15 Zechariah 9:9

harvest. 25The one who loves this life will lose it, and the one who despises it in this world will have life forevermore. 26Anyone who serves Me must follow My path; anyone who serves Me will want to be where I am, and he will be honored by the Father. 27My spirit is low and unsettled. How can I ask the Father to save Me from this hour? This hour is the purpose for which I have come *into the world. But what I can say is this:* 28"Father, glorify Your name!"

Suddenly a voice echoed from the heavens.

The Father: I have glorified My name. And again I will bring glory *in this hour that will resound throughout time.*

29The crowd of people surrounding Jesus were confused.

Some in the Crowd: It sounded like thunder.
Others: A heavenly messenger spoke to Him.
Jesus: 30The voice you hear has not spoken for My benefit, but for yours. 31Now judgment comes upon this world, *and everything will change.* The tyrant of this world, *Satan,* will be thrown out. 32When I am lifted up from the earth, then all of humanity will be drawn to Me.

33These words foreshadowed the nature of His death.

Crowd: 34The law teaches that the Liberating King is the One who will remain without end. How can You say it is essential that the Son of Man be lifted up? Who is this Son of Man *You are talking about*?
Jesus: 35Light is among you, but very soon it will flicker out. Walk as you have the light, and then the darkness will not surround you. Those who walk in darkness don't know where they are going. 36While the light is with you, believe in the light and you will be reborn as sons *and daughters* of the light.

After speaking these words, Jesus left the people to go to a place of seclusion.

37Despite all the signs He performed, they still did not believe in Him. 38Isaiah spoke of this reality, saying,

> Lord, who could accept what we've
>   been told?
> And who has seen the awesome
>   power of the Lord revealed?*

39This is the reason they are unable to believe. 40Isaiah also said,

> God has blinded their eyes,
>   and hardened their hearts
> So that their eyes cannot see
>   *properly*
>   and their hearts cannot
>   understand
>   *and be persuaded*
>   *by the truth* to turn to Me
>   and be reconciled by My healing
>   hand.*

41Isaiah could say this because he had seen the glory of the Lord *with his own eyes* and declared His beauty aloud. 42Yet many leaders secretly believed in Him but would not declare their faith because the Pharisees continued their threats to expel all His followers from the synagogue; 43here's why: they loved to please men more than they desired to glorify God.

Jesus (*crying out before the people*):
44Anyone who believes in Me is not placing his faith in Me, but in the One who sent Me here. 45If one sees Me, he sees the One who sent Me. 46I am here to bring light in this world, freeing everyone who believes in Me from the darkness *that blinds him.* 47If anyone listening to My teachings chooses to ignore them, so be it: I have come to liberate the world, not to judge it. 48However, those who reject Me and My teachings will be judged: in the last day, My words will be their judge. 49Because I am not speaking *of My own volition and* from My own authority, but the Father who sent Me has

* 12:38 Isaiah 53:1
* 12:40 Isaiah 6:10

commanded Me what to say and speak. ⁵⁰I know His command is eternal life, so every word I utter originates in Him.

13 Before the Passover festival began, Jesus was keenly aware that His hour had come to depart from this world and to return to the Father. From beginning to end, Jesus' days were marked by His love for His people. ²Before Jesus and His disciples gathered for dinner, the adversary filled Judas Iscariot's heart with plans of deceit and betrayal. ³Jesus, knowing that He had come from God and was going away to God, ⁴stood up from dinner and removed His outer garments. He then wrapped Himself in a towel, ⁵poured water in a basin, and began to wash the feet of the disciples, drying them with His towel.

Simon Peter (as Jesus approaches): ⁶Lord, are You going to wash my feet?

Jesus: ⁷Peter, you don't realize what I am doing, but you will understand later.

Peter: ⁸You will not wash my feet, now or ever!

Jesus: If I don't wash you, you will have nothing to do with Me.

Peter: ⁹Then wash me but don't stop with my feet. Cleanse my hands and head as well.

Jesus: ¹⁰Listen, anyone who has bathed is clean all over except for the feet. But I tell you this, not all of you are clean.

*M*y life changed that day; there was a new clarity about how I was supposed to live. I saw the world in a totally new way. The dirt, grime, sin, pain, rebellion, and torment around me were no longer impediments to the spiritual path.

Where I saw pain and filth, I found an opportunity to extend God's kingdom through an expression of love, humility, and service. This simple act of washing feet is a metaphor for the lens that Jesus gives us to see the world. He sees the people, the world He created—which He loves. He also sees the filth, the corruption in the world that torments us. His mission is to cleanse those whom He loves from the horrors that torment them. This is His redemptive work with feet, families, disease, famine, and our hearts.

When Jesus saw disease, He saw the opportunity to heal. When He saw sin, He saw a chance to forgive and redeem. When He saw dirty feet, He saw a chance to wash them.

What do you see when you wander through the market, along the streets, on the beaches, and through the slums? Are you disgusted? Or do you seize the opportunity to expand God's reign of love in the cosmos? This is what Jesus did. The places we avoid, Jesus seeks.

¹¹He knew the one with plans of betraying Him, which is why He said, "not all of you are clean." ¹²After washing their feet and picking up His garments, He reclined at the table again.

Jesus: Do you understand what I have done to you? ¹³You call Me Teacher and Lord, and truly, that is who I am. ¹⁴So if your Lord and Teacher washes your feet, then you should wash one another's feet. ¹⁵I am your example; keep doing what I do. ¹⁶I tell you the truth: an emissary* is not greater than the master. Those who are sent are not greater than the One who sends them. ¹⁷If you know these things, and if you put them into practice, you will find happiness. ¹⁸I am not speaking about all of you. I know whom I have chosen, but let the Hebrew Scripture be fulfilled that says, "The very same man who eats My bread with Me will stab Me in the back."* ¹⁹Assuredly, I tell you these truths before they happen so that when it all transpires you will believe that I am. ²⁰I tell you the truth: anyone who accepts the ones I send accepts Me.

* 13:15 Literally, apostle
* 13:18 Psalm 41:9

In turn, the ones who accept Me also accept the One who sent Me.

[21]Jesus was becoming visibly distressed.

Jesus: I tell you the truth: one of you will betray Me.

[22]The disciples began to stare at one another, wondering who was the unfaithful disciple. [23]One disciple in particular, who was loved by Jesus, reclined next to Him at the table. [24]Peter motioned to the disciple at Jesus' side.

Peter (to the beloved disciple): Find out who the betrayer is.
Beloved Disciple (leaning in to Jesus): [25]Lord, who is it?
Jesus: [26]I will dip a piece of bread in My cup and give it to the one who will betray Me.

He dipped one piece in the cup and gave it to Judas, the son of Simon Iscariot. [27]After this occurred, Satan entered into Judas.

Jesus (to Judas): Make haste, and do what you are going to do.

[28]No one understood Jesus' instructions to Judas. [29]Because Judas carried the money, some thought he was being instructed to buy the necessary items for the feast or give some money to the poor. [30]So Judas took his piece of bread and departed into the night.
[31]Upon Judas's departure, Jesus spoke:

Jesus: Now the Son of Man will be glorified as God is glorified in Him. [32]If God's glory is in Him, His glory is also in God. The moment of this astounding glory is imminent. [33]My children, My time here is brief. You will be searching for Me, and as I told the Jews, "You cannot go where I am going." [34]So I give you a new command: Love each other *deeply and fully*. Remember the ways that I have loved you, and demonstrate your love for others in those same ways. [35]Everyone will know you as My followers if you demonstrate your love to others.

Simon Peter: [36]Lord, where are You going?
Jesus: Peter, you cannot come with Me now, but later you will join Me.
Peter: [37]Why can't I go now? I'll give my life for You!
Jesus: [38]Will you really give your life for Me? I tell you the truth: you will deny Me three times before the rooster crows.

*U*ltimately Peter was telling the truth. He was more than willing to lay down his life. But none of us understood the magnitude of the persecution and hatred that was about to be unleashed on all of us.

Even Peter, dear Peter, was afraid. He protested any inference to Jesus' impending departure. We all would have done the same. Jesus calmed our fears over and over again with stories, metaphors, and outright promises, saying, "I will never abandon you like orphans; I will return to be with you."*

14 Jesus: Don't get lost in despair; believe in God and keep on believing in Me. [2]My Father's home is designed to accommodate all of you. If there were not room for everyone, I would have told you that. I am going to make arrangements for your arrival. [3]I will be there to personally greet you and welcome you home, where we will be together. [4]You know where I am going and how to get there.
Thomas: [5]Lord, we don't know where You are going, so how can we know the path?
Jesus: [6]I am the path, the truth, and the *energy of* life. No one comes to the Father except through Me. [7]If you know Me, you know the Father. Rest assured now; you know Him and have seen Him.
Philip: [8]Lord, all I am asking is that You show us the Father.
Jesus (to Philip): [9]I have lived with you all this time, and you still don't know who I

* **Note** John 14:18

am? If you have seen Me, you have seen the Father. How can you keep asking to see the Father? [10]Don't you believe Me when I say I abide in the Father and the Father dwells in Me? I'm not making this up as I go along. The Father has given Me these truths that I have been speaking to you, and He empowers all My actions. [11]Accept these truths: I am in the Father, and the Father is in Me. If you have trouble believing based on My words, believe because of the things I have done. [12]I tell you the truth: whoever believes in Me will be able to do what I have done, but they will do even greater things, because I will return to be with the Father. [13]Whatever you ask for in My name, I will do it so that the Father will get glory from the Son. [14]*Let Me say it again:* if you ask for anything in My name, I will do it. [15]If you love Me, obey the commandments I have given you. [16]I will ask the Father to send you another Helper, *the Spirit of truth,* who will remain constantly with you. [17]The world does not recognize the Spirit of truth, because it does not know the Spirit and is unable to receive Him. But you do know the Spirit because He lives with you, and He will dwell in you. [18]I will never abandon you like orphans; I will return to be with you. [19]In a little while, the world will not see Me, but I will not vanish completely from your sight. Because I live, you will also live. [20]At that time, you will know that I am in the Father, you are in Me, and I am in you. [21]The one who loves Me will do the things I have commanded. My Father loves everyone who loves Me, and I will love you and reveal My heart, will, and nature to you.

We are here as redeeming forces on this earth; our time here is about reclaiming the things He has created. We believe that God has created the entire cosmos; our work here is to say, "This belongs to God," and to help point out the beauty of creation to everyone we know, everyone we meet. And most of all, to live in it ourselves.

The Other Judas: [22]Lord, why will You reveal Yourself to us, but not to the world?

Jesus: [23]Anyone who loves Me will listen to My voice and obey. The Father will love him, and We will draw close to him and make a dwelling place within him. [24]The one who does not love Me ignores My message, which is not from Me, but from the Father who sent Me.

[25]I have spoken these words while I am here with you. [26]The Father is sending a great Helper, the Holy Spirit, in My name to teach you everything and to remind you of all I have said to you. [27]My peace is the legacy I leave to you. I don't give gifts like those of this world. Do not let your heart be troubled or fearful. [28]You were listening when I said, "I will go away, but I will also return to be with you." If you love Me, celebrate the fact that I am going to be with the Father because He is far greater than I am. [29]I have told you all these things in advance so that your faith will grow as these things come to pass. [30]I am almost finished speaking to you. The one who rules the world is stepping forward, and he has no part in Me; [31]but to demonstrate to the cosmos My love for the Father, I will do just as He commands. Stand up. It is time for us to leave this place.

God became flesh and lived among us, not just to have a transaction with us and ultimately die, but to continue to be with us even when He didn't have to and to send His Spirit to be present with us. So, in that, God calls us to something greater, something more significant:

The Holy Spirit planted the teachings of our Lord into our very beings. God would now dwell in the hearts of all true believers, and the chasm between God and humanity would be bridged. As you can imagine, the idea of Jesus leaving us created a whirlwind of fear and doubt. But once again, Jesus reached in gently and calmed our storms when He said, "I will now dwell inside of you." A connection is made between God and us, much like the first days in the garden—God the Creator strolling in paradise with Adam. God is, once again in Jesus and the Holy Spirit, present amid suffering, hope, sin, and friendship.

15 Jesus: I am the true vine, and My Father is the keeper of the vineyard. ²My Father examines every branch in Me and cuts away those who do not bear fruit. He leaves those bearing fruit and carefully prunes them so that they will bear more fruit; ³already you are clean because you have heard My voice. ⁴Abide in Me, and I will abide in you. A branch cannot bear fruit if it is disconnected from the vine, and neither will you if you are not connected to Me.

⁵I am the vine, and you are the branches. If you abide in Me and I in you, you will bear great fruit. Without Me, you will accomplish nothing. ⁶If anyone does not abide in Me, he is like a branch that is tossed out and shrivels up and is later gathered to be tossed into the fire to burn. ⁷If you abide in Me and My voice abides in you, anything you ask will come to pass for you. ⁸Your abundant growth and your faithfulness as My followers will bring glory to the Father.

At a time when all of us were feeling as if we were about to be uprooted, Jesus sketched out a picture for us of this new life as a flourishing vineyard—a labyrinth of vines and strong branches steeped in rich soil, abundant grapes hanging from their vines ripening in the sun. Jesus sculpted out a new garden of Eden in our imaginations—one that was bustling with fruit, sustenance, and satisfying aromas. This is the Kingdom life. It is all about connection, sustenance, and beauty.

Jesus: ⁹I have loved you as the Father has loved Me. Abide in My love. ¹⁰Follow My example in obeying the Father's commandments and receiving His love. If you obey My commandments, you will stay in My love. ¹¹I want you to know the delight I experience, to find ultimate satisfaction, which is why I am telling you all of this.

¹²My commandment to you is this: love others as I have loved you. ¹³There is no greater way to love than to give your life for your friends. ¹⁴You celebrate our friendship if you obey this command. ¹⁵I don't call you servants any longer; servants don't know what the master is doing, but I have told you everything the Father has said to Me. I call you friends. ¹⁶You did not choose Me. I chose you, and I orchestrated all of this so that you would be sent out and bear great and perpetual fruit. As you do this, anything you ask the Father in My name will be done. ¹⁷This is My command to you: love one another.

¹⁸If you find that the world despises you, remember that before it despised you, it first despised Me. ¹⁹If you were a product of the world order, then it would love you. But you are not a product of the world because I have taken you out of it, and it despises you for that very reason. ²⁰Don't forget what I have spoken to you: "a servant is not superior to the master." If I was mistreated, you should expect nothing less. If they accepted what I have spoken, they will also hear you. ²¹Everything they do to you they will do on My account because they do not know the One who has sent Me. ²²If I had not spoken within their hearing, they would not be guilty of sin, but now they have no excuse for ignoring My voice.

²³If someone despises Me, he also despises My Father. ²⁴If I had not demonstrated things for them that have never been done, they would not be guilty of sin. But the reality is they have stared Me in the face, and they have despised Me and the Father nonetheless.

²⁵Yet, their law, which says, "They despised Me without any cause,"* has again been proven true.

²⁶I will send a great Helper to you from the Father, one known as the Spirit of truth. He comes from the Father and will point to the truth as it concerns Me. ²⁷But you will also point others to the truth about My identity, because you have journeyed with Me since this all began.

> As Jesus warns us of the mistreatment we can expect, He disarms our fears by reminding us of the most important things. If the Spirit is in us, we have no reason to fear. In fact, the church will thrive under persecution. Yet we are obsessed with power and political prominence as a means to influence the culture. As Christian citizens, we have an obligation to actively strive for justice and freedom. But how will that happen?
>
> Listen carefully, for this is the wisdom God has given to each generation. Lasting justice and morality cannot be lobbied for or legislated. It is a result of the Holy Spirit's work in the lives of those of us who learn that God loves us. So take heed, lest we forget these important labors are always secondary to the gospel and at times even affect the cause of the Liberating King negatively. True Christianity, the real work of the Kingdom, often thrives under fierce attack and opposition. Jesus announced this coming persecution to us, His followers, believing this will lead to our finest hour.

16 Jesus: I am telling you all of this so that you may avoid the offenses that are coming. ²The time will come when they will kick you out of the synagogue because some believe God desires them to execute you as an act of faithful service. ³They will do this because they don't know the Father, or else they would know Me. ⁴I'm telling you all this so that when it comes to pass

you will remember what you have heard. It was not important for Me to give you this information in the beginning when I was with you. ⁵But now, I am going to the One who has sent Me, and none of you ask Me, "Where are You going?"

⁶I know that hearing news like this is overwhelming and sad. ⁷But the truth is that My departure will be a gift that will serve you well, because if I don't leave, the great Helper will not come to your aid. When I leave, I will send Him to you. ⁸⁻⁹When He arrives, He will uncover the sins of the world, expose unbelief as sin, and allow all to see their sins in the light of righteousness for the first time. ¹⁰This new awareness of righteousness is important because I am going to the Father and will no longer be present with you. ¹¹The Spirit will also carry My judgment because the one who rules in this world has already been defeated.

¹²I have so much more to say, but you cannot absorb it right now. ¹³⁻¹⁵The Spirit of truth will come and guide you in all truth. He will not speak His own words to you; He will speak what He hears, revealing to you the things to come and bringing glory to Me. The Spirit has unlimited access to Me, to all that I possess and know, just as everything the Father has is Mine. That is the reason I am confident He will care for My own and reveal the path to you. ¹⁶For a little while you will not see Me, but after that, a time will come when you will see Me again.

Some of His Disciples: ¹⁷What does He mean? "I'll be here, and then I won't be here, because I'll be with the Father"?

Other Disciples: ¹⁸What is He saying? "A little while"? We don't understand.

> The promise of eternity is a reminder that we were made for another world. We found great comfort amid our fear, knowing we would be reunited with our Liberating King and joined with the Father. As we labor

* 15:25 Psalm 35:19

together in this world—enduring pain, loss, and unfulfilled desires—be encouraged that in eternity all our needs will be fulfilled in the presence of God.

[19] Jesus knew they had questions to ask of Him, so He approached them.

Jesus: Are you trying to figure out what I mean when I say you will see Me in a little while? [20] I tell you the truth, a time is approaching when you will weep and mourn while the world is celebrating. You will grieve, but that grief will give birth to great joy. [21-22] In the same way that a woman labors in great pain during childbirth, only to forget the intensity of the pain when she holds her child, when I return, your labored grief will also change into a joy that cannot be stolen.

[23] When all this transpires, you will finally have the answers you have been seeking. I tell you the truth, anything you ask of the Father in My name, He will give to you. [24] Until this moment, you have not sought after anything in My name. Ask and you will receive so that you will be filled with joy.

[25] I have been teaching you all of these truths through stories and metaphors, but the time is coming for Me to speak openly and directly of the Father. [26] The day is coming when you will make a request in My name, but I will not represent you before the Father. [27] *You will be heard directly by the Father.* The Father loves you because you love Me and know that I come from the Father. [28] I came from the Father into the cosmos, but soon I will leave it and return to the Father.

All of us disciples mourned Jesus' refusal to take His rightful place as a king and lead a revolution. Jesus knew that political might, brute force, and earthly governments are not helpful tools in a battle for hearts. Spiritual revolutions are subversive. They are led by defiant acts of love (e.g., healing, foot washing, and martyrdom). Laws do not change hearts, and violence induces hatred and fear. But a sincere community of faith in which love and hope are demonstrated even in the darkest hours will lead a spiritual revolution. It is time we go forward with open eyes and continue to labor as Christian citizens, placing our hope only in the redemptive work of the gospel.

Disciples: [29] We hear You speaking clearly and not in metaphors. *How could we misunderstand?* [30] We see now that You are aware of everything and You reveal things at the proper time. So we do not need to question You, because we believe You have come from God.

Jesus: [31] So you believe now? [32] Be aware that a time is coming when you will be scattered *like seeds.* You will return to your own way, and I will be left alone. But I will not be alone, because the Father will be with Me. [33] I have told you these things so that you will be *whole and* at peace. In this world, you will be plagued with times of trouble, but you need not fear; I have triumphed over this corrupt world order.

Generations from now, believers will struggle to understand how they are connected to God and one another. They will see themselves as autonomous individuals, free agents who choose whatever allegiances suit them. Those of us who walked with Jesus had a different perspective. Maybe it came from our culture. Maybe it came from our faith. Probably both. We already saw ourselves as dependent on and connected to other people. We belonged to a family, a tribe, a people. To know who we were, we didn't look inside ourselves; we looked to others because they knew us and we were part of them. No one needed to "find himself" because he already knew. Our identities were tied up completely with others. As humans we inherit the characteristics of our parents and their parents before them going back hundreds of generations. While as Christ followers we still have those characteristics, something new changes everything. With Jesus at the center of our lives, we have new perspective and power.

17 Jesus (lifting His face to the heavens): Father, My time has come. Glorify Your Son, and I will bring You great glory 2-3because You have given Me total authority over humanity. *I have come bearing the plentiful gifts of God*, and all that receive Me will experience everlasting life, a new intimate relationship with You, the one true God, and Jesus, the Liberating King (the One You have sent). 4I have glorified You on earth and fulfilled the mission You set before Me.

5In this moment, Father, fuse Our collective glory and bring Us together as We were before creation existed. 6You have entrusted Me with these men who have come out of this corrupt world order. I have told them about Your nature and declared Your name to them, and they have held on to Your words and understood that these words, 7like everything else You have given Me, come from You. 8It is true that these men You gave Me have received the words that come from You and not only understood them but also believed that You sent Me. 9I am now making an appeal to You on their behalf. This request is not for the entire world; it is for those whom You have given to Me because they are Yours. 10Yours and Mine, Mine and Yours, for all that are Mine are Yours. Through them I have been glorified.

11I will no longer be physically present in this world, but they will remain in this world. As I return to be with You, holy Father, remain with them through Your name, *the name You have given Me*. May they be one even as We are one.

12While I was physically present with them, I protected them through Your name, *which You have shared with Me*. I watched over them closely; and only one was lost, the one the Scriptures said was the son of destruction. 13Now I am returning to You. I am speaking this prayer here in the created cosmos *alongside friends and foes* so that in hearing it they might be consumed with joy. 14I have given them Your word; and the world has despised them because they are not products of the world, in the same way that I am not a product of the corrupt world order. 15Do not take them out of this world; protect them from the evil one.

16Like Me, they are not products of the corrupt world order. 17Immerse them in the truth, the truth Your voice speaks. 18In the same way You sent Me into this world, I am sending them. 19It is entirely for their benefit that I have set Myself apart so that they may be set apart by truth. 20I am not asking solely for their benefit; this prayer is also for all the believers who will follow them and hear them speak. 21Father, may they all be one as You are in Me and I am in You; may they be in Us, for by this unity the world will believe that You sent Me.

22All the glory You have given to Me, I pass on to them. May that glory unify them and make them one as We are one, 23I in them and You in Me, that they may be refined so that all will know that You sent Me, and You love them in the same way You love Me.

24Father, I long for the time when those You have given Me can join Me in My place so they may witness My glory, which comes from You. You have loved Me before the foundations of the cosmos were laid. 25Father, You are just; though this corrupt world order does not know You, I do. These followers know that You have sent Me. 26I have told them about Your nature; and I will continue to speak of Your name, in order that Your love, which was poured out on Me, will be in them. And I will also be in them.

18

When Jesus finished praying, He began a brief journey with His disciples to the other side of the Kidron Valley, a deep ravine that floods in the winter rains, then farther on to a garden where He gathered His disciples.

2-3Judas Iscariot (who had already set his betrayal in motion and knew that Jesus often met with the disciples in this olive grove) entered the garden with an entourage of Roman soldiers and officials sent by the chief priests and Pharisees. They brandished their weapons under the light of torches and lamps. 4Jesus stepped forward. It was clear He was not surprised because He knew all things.

Jesus: Whom are you looking for?
Judas's Entourage: 5Jesus the Nazarene.
Jesus: I am the One.

Judas, the betrayer, stood with the military force. 6As Jesus spoke "I am the One," the forces fell back on the ground. 7Jesus asked them a second time:

Jesus: Whom are you searching for?
Judas's Entourage: Jesus the Nazarene.
Jesus: 8I have already said that I am the One. If you are looking for Me, then let these men go free.

9This happened to fulfill the promise He made that none of those entrusted to Him will be lost.* 10Suddenly Peter lunged toward Malchus, one of the high priest's servants, and, with his sword, severed the man's right ear.

Jesus (to Peter): 11Put down your sword and return it to the sheath. Am I to turn away from the cup the Father has given Me to drink?

12So the Roman commander, soldiers, and Jewish officials arrested Jesus, cuffed His hands and feet, 13and brought Him to Annas (the father-in-law of Caiaphas the high priest). 14You may remember that Caiaphas counseled to the Jews that one should die for all people. 15-16Simon Peter and another disciple followed behind Jesus. When they arrived, Peter waited in the doorway while the other disciple was granted access because of his relationship with the high priest. That disciple spoke to the woman at the door, and Peter was allowed inside.

Servant Girl (to Peter): 17You are one of this man's disciples, aren't you?
Peter: I am not.

18All the servants and officers gathered around a charcoal fire to keep warm. It was a cold day, and Peter made his way into the circle to warm himself.

Annas (to Jesus): 19Who are Your disciples, and what do You teach?
Jesus: 20I have spoken in public where the world can hear, always teaching in the synagogue and in the temple where the Jewish people gather. I have never spoken in secret. 21So why would you need to interrogate Me? Many have heard Me teach. Why don't you question them? They know what I have taught.

22While Jesus offered His response, an officer standing nearby struck Jesus with his hand.

Officer: Is that how You speak to the high priest?
Jesus: 23If I have spoken incorrectly, why don't you point out the untruths that I speak? Why do you hit Me if what I have said is correct?

24Annas sent Jesus to Caiaphas bound as a prisoner. 25As this was happening, Peter was still warming himself by the fire.

Servants and Officers: You, too, are one of His disciples, aren't you?
Peter: No, I am not.

26One of the high priest's servants was related to the one assaulted by Peter.

* 18:9 John 6:39

High Priest's Servant, a Relative of Malchus:
Didn't I see you in the garden with Him?

²⁷Peter denied it again, and instantly a rooster crowed.

²⁸Before the sun had risen, Jesus was taken from Caiaphas to the governor's palace. The Jewish leaders would not enter the palace because their presence in a Roman office would defile them and cause them to miss the Passover feast. Pilate, the governor, met them outside.

*N*ow Caiaphas was high priest at this time. The sacred office he occupied had been corrupted for more than a century by Jewish collaboration with Greeks and Romans. Reformers were few, and they had been unable to cleanse the high office from its pollutants. Because of this, many Jews had stopped coming to the temple. How could God's holy habitation on earth be pure if its primary representative was coddling the enemies of Israel? Caiaphas knew he needed friends in high places to put an end to Jesus. So he turned to Pilate, the Roman governor. It was his job to look out for Roman interests in Judea. History records that he was an irritable man, unnecessarily cruel and intentionally provocative. Many Jews died on his watch. For Pilate, Jesus would be just one more.

Pilate: ²⁹What charges do you bring against this man?
Priests and Officials: ³⁰If He weren't a lawbreaker, we wouldn't have brought Him to you.
Pilate: ³¹Then judge Him yourselves, by your own law.
Jews: Our authority does not allow us to give Him the death penalty.

³²All these things were a fulfillment of the words Jesus had spoken indicating the way that He would die. ³³So Pilate reentered the governor's palace and called for Jesus to follow him.

*I*nitially, Pilate told the Jewish leaders to take Jesus and try Him according to our own laws, but when they hinted at capital charges, Pilate agreed to interrogate Jesus. Rome reserved the right to decide who lived and died in the provinces. They didn't delegate that to the Jewish high council. The charge of blasphemy carried no weight in Roman jurisprudence for it was a matter of our Jewish religious law. Rome had no opinion on such matters. So a new charge must be concocted, a charge that Rome did care about. Rome did care about taxes, of course, and took a dim view of anyone making royal claims under their noses.

Pilate agreed to hear the charge, not wasting a Roman minute. He took Jesus inside and began asking Him about these charges.

Pilate: Are You the King of the Jews?
Jesus: ³⁴Are you asking Me because you believe this is true, or have others said this about Me?
Pilate: ³⁵I'm not a Jew, am I? Your people, including the chief priests, have arrested You and placed You in my custody. What have You done?
Jesus: ³⁶My kingdom is not recognized in this world. If this were My kingdom, My servants would be fighting for My freedom. But My kingdom is not in this physical realm.
Pilate: ³⁷So You are a king?
Jesus: You say that I am king. For this I have been born, and for this I have come into the cosmos, to demonstrate the power of truth. Everyone who seeks truth hears My voice.
Pilate *(to Jesus)*: ³⁸What is truth?

Pilate left Jesus to go and speak to the Jewish people.

Pilate *(to the Jews)*: I have not found any cause for charges to be brought against this man. ³⁹Your custom is that I should release a prisoner to you each year in honor of the Passover celebration; shall I release the King of the Jews to you?

Jews: [40]No, not this man! Give us Barabbas!

You should know that Barabbas was a terrorist.

I'd like to have been a fly on the wall when Pilate had that private moment with Jesus. Pilate was interrogating Jesus like the man he was: an insecure and cruel power broker representing Roman interests in our land. Jesus, though, was doing His typical mustard seed bit, speaking right over the head of the man who later would show Him no mercy. Pilate couldn't handle the truth when he asked, "Are You the King of the Jews?" Jesus was the King of the Jews. And that was the truth. Although Pilate wouldn't recognize it, He was his King too. But as Jesus knew, the world didn't recognize His kingdom. That's because it was sourced in heaven above, not in Rome. His authority came from God the Father, Creator, Sustainer—not from the Roman senate.

19 Pilate took Jesus and had Him flogged. [2]The soldiers twisted thorny branches together as a crown and placed it onto His brow and wrapped Him in a purple cloth. [3]They drew near to Him, shouting:

Soldiers (*striking at Jesus*): Bow down, everyone! This is the King of the Jews!

Pilate (*going out to the crowd*): [4]Listen, I stand in front of you with this man to make myself clear: I find this man innocent of any crimes.

[5]Then Jesus was paraded out before the people, wearing the crown of thorns and the purple robe.

Pilate: Here is the man!

Chief Priests and Officers (*shouting*): [6]Crucify, crucify!

Pilate: You take Him and crucify Him; I have declared Him not guilty of any punishable crime!

Jews: [7]Our law says that He should die because He claims to be the Son of God.

[8]Pilate was terrified to hear the Jews making their claims for His execution, [9]so he retired to his court, the Praetorium.

Pilate (*to Jesus*): Where are You from?

Jesus did not speak.

Pilate: [10]How can You ignore me? Are You not aware that I have the authority to either free You or crucify You?

Jesus: [11]Any authority you have over Me comes from above, not from your political position. Because of this, the one who handed Me to you is guilty of the greater sin.

[12]Pilate listened to Jesus' words; and, taking them to heart, he attempted to release Jesus, but the Jews opposed him, shouting:

Jews: If you release this man, you have betrayed Caesar. Anyone who claims to be a king threatens Caesar's throne.

[13]After Pilate heard these accusations, he sent Jesus out and took his seat in the place where he rendered judgment. This place was called the Pavement, or Gabbatha in Hebrew. [14]All this occurred at the sixth hour on the day everyone prepares for the Passover.

Pilate (*to the Jews*): Look, here is your King!

Jews: [15]Put Him away; crucify Him!

Pilate: You want me to crucify your King?

Chief Priests: We have no king but Caesar!

[16]Pilate handed Him over to his soldiers, knowing that He would be crucified. [17]They sent Jesus out carrying His own instrument of execution, the cross, to a hill known as the place of the skull, or Golgotha in Hebrew. [18]In that place, they crucified Him along with two others. One

was on His right and the other on His left. [19]Pilate ordered that a plaque be placed above Jesus' head. It read, "Jesus of Nazareth, King of the Jews." [20]Because the site was near an urban region, it was written in three languages (Greek, Latin, and Hebrew) so that all could understand.

Chief Priests (to Pilate): [21]Don't write, "The King of the Jews." Write, "He said, 'I am King of the Jews'!"

Pilate: [22]I have written what I have written.

[23]As Jesus was being crucified, the soldiers tore His outer garments into four pieces, one for each of them. They wanted to do the same with His tunic, but it was seamless—one piece of fabric woven from the top down. [24]So they said,

Soldier (to other soldiers): Don't tear it. Let's cast lots, and the winner will take the whole thing.

This happened in keeping with the Hebrew Scriptures, which said, "They divided My outer garments and cast lots for My clothes."* These soldiers did exactly what was foretold in the Hebrew Scriptures. [25]Jesus' mother was standing next to His cross along with her sister, Mary the wife of Clopas, and Mary Magdalene. [26]Jesus looked to see His mother, and the disciple He loved, standing nearby.

Jesus (to Mary, His mother): Dear woman, this is your son (motioning to the beloved disciple)! [27]This is now your mother (to His mother and to John, His disciple).

*N*ow you know who "the beloved disciple" is, the last eyewitness to the life, death, and resurrection of Jesus. Mary became family to me, fulfilling the dying wish of Jesus, my Savior. For those of us who gathered at the foot of the cross, family was less about blood kinship than it was about covenant obedience.

Caring for her was never a burden, and the reality is that she has always been a simple and private woman. God made her the vessel to bring His Son into the world, and her love for Him was warm and beautiful. Part of me is protective of her, as a son naturally is of his mother. Still I can see why those who didn't know her would want to learn more about this remarkable woman, especially those grieving over their own losses. Surely they are looking for answers to how to move forward in their own lives. The mother of our Lord served the redemptive purposes of her son and the Savior of us all until her last day on earth.

When I would feel sorry for myself, I just had to think about Jesus. He spent all this time before His death, and through His death, showing us how to love and how to serve. He was asking me to do no more in serving Mary than He did in serving us.

From that moment, the disciple treated her like his own mother and welcomed her into his house. [28]Jesus knew now that His work had been accomplished, and the Hebrew Scriptures were being fulfilled.

Jesus: I am thirsty.

[29]A jar of sour wine had been left there, so they took a hyssop branch with a sponge soaked in the vinegar and put it to His mouth. [30]When Jesus drank, He spoke:

Jesus: It is finished!

In that moment, His head fell, and He gave up the spirit. [31]The Jews asked Pilate to have their legs broken so the bodies would not remain on the crosses on the Sabbath. It was the day of preparation for the Passover, and that year the Passover fell on the Sabbath. [32]The soldiers came and broke the legs of both the men crucified

* 19:24 Psalm 22:18

next to Jesus. [33]When they came up to Jesus' cross, they could see that He was dead, so they did not break His legs. [34]Instead, one soldier took his spear and pierced His abdomen, which brought a gush of blood and water.

[35]This testimony is true; in fact, it is an eyewitness account, and he has reported what he saw so that you also may believe. [36]It happened this way to fulfill the Hebrew Scriptures that "not one of His bones shall be broken";* [37]and the Hebrew Scriptures also say, "they will look upon Him whom they pierced."*

[38]After all this, Joseph of Arimathea, a disciple who kept his faith a secret for fear of the Jewish officials, made a request to Pilate for the body of Jesus. Pilate granted his request, and Joseph retrieved the body. [39]Nicodemus, who first came to Jesus under the cloak of darkness, brought over 100 pounds of myrrh and ointments for His burial. [40]Together, they took Jesus' body and wrapped Him in linens soaked in essential oils and spices, according to Jewish burial customs.

[41]Near the place He was crucified, there was a garden with a newly prepared tomb. [42]Because it was the day of preparation, they arranged to lay Jesus in this tomb so they could rest on the Sabbath.

*A*s the lifeless body of Jesus was laid into the virgin tomb, those of us who witnessed the spectacle retreated into the city that had claimed the lives of so many prophets. All of us were crushed that our teacher and friend had died such a horrible death. Our hopes were dashed against the rocks of Golgotha. In the first hours of our grief, we huddled together in secret in the city, hoping to avoid our own arrests and executions. We mourned. We grieved. We remembered. Three days later, some of us ventured outside the city and returned to the place where He was buried. Miraculously, the stone was rolled back and the rock-hewn tomb was empty. Had someone taken His body? Were His enemies laying a trap for us? Or perhaps—could it be—that the last days were here?

Now I want you to know what I remember of that glorious day.

20 Before the sun had risen on Sunday morning, Mary Magdalene made a trip to the tomb where His body was laid to rest. In the darkness, she discovered the covering had been rolled away. [2]She darted out of the garden to find Simon Peter and the dearly loved disciple to deliver this startling news.

Mary Magdalene: They have taken the body of our Lord, and we cannot find Him!

[3]Together, they all departed for the tomb to see for themselves. [4]They began to run, and Peter could not keep up. The beloved disciple arrived first [5]but did not go in. There was no corpse in the tomb, only the linens and cloths He was wrapped in. [6]When Simon Peter finally arrived, he went into the tomb and observed the same: [7]the cloth that covered His face appeared to have been folded carefully and placed, not with the linen cloths, but to the side. [8]After Peter pointed this out, the other disciple (who had arrived long before Peter) also entered the tomb and, based on what he saw, faith began to well up inside him! [9]Before this moment, none of them understood the Scriptures and why He must be raised from the dead. [10]Then they all went to their homes.

[11]Mary, however, stood outside the tomb, sobbing, crying, and kneeling at the entrance of the tomb. [12]As she cried, two heavenly messengers appeared before her sitting where Jesus' head and feet had been laid.

Heavenly Messengers: [13]Dear woman, why are you weeping?

* 19:36 Exodus 12:46; Numbers 9:12; Psalm 34:20
* 19:37 Zechariah 12:10

Mary Magdalene: They have taken away my Lord, and I cannot find Him.

¹⁴After uttering these words, she turned around to see Jesus standing before her, but she did not recognize Him.

Jesus: ¹⁵Dear woman, why are you sobbing? Who is it you are looking for?

She still had no idea who it was before her. Thinking He was the gardener, she muttered:

Mary Magdalene: Sir, if you are the one who carried Him away, then tell me where He is and I will retrieve Him.
Jesus: ¹⁶Mary!
Mary Magdalene (*she turns to Jesus and tries to hug Him, speaking in Hebrew*): Rabboni, my Teacher!
Jesus: ¹⁷Mary, you cannot hold Me. I must rise above this world to be with My Father, who is also your Father; My God, who is also your God. Go tell this to all My brothers.

¹⁸Mary Magdalene obeyed and went directly to His disciples.

*T*he hope of resurrection had often been a topic on the lips of Jesus. Now it was taking shape in our time. Confusion gave way to conviction as Jesus appeared to us alive over the next few Sundays. One by one He convinced us that God had raised Him from the dead.

Mary Magdalene (*announcing to the disciples*): I have seen the Lord, and this is what He said to me . . .

¹⁹On that same evening (Resurrection Sunday), the followers gathered together behind locked doors in fear that some of the Jewish leaders in Jerusalem were still searching for them. Out of nowhere, Jesus appeared in the center of the room.

Jesus: May each one of you be at peace.

²⁰As He was speaking, He revealed the wounds in His hands and side. The disciples began to celebrate as it sank in that they were really seeing the Lord.

Jesus: ²¹I give you the gift of peace. In the same way the Father sent Me, I am now sending you.

²²Now He drew close enough to each of them that *they could feel His breath.* He breathed on them:

Jesus: Welcome the Holy Spirit of the living God. ²³You now have the mantle of God's forgiveness. As you go, you are able to share the life-giving power to forgive sins, or withhold forgiveness.

²⁴All of the eleven were present with the exception of Thomas. ²⁵He heard the accounts of each brother's interaction with the Lord.

The Other Disciples: We have seen the Lord!
Thomas: Until I see His hands, feel the wounds of the nails, and put my hand to His side, I won't believe what you are saying.

²⁶Eight days later, they gathered again behind locked doors and Jesus reappeared. This time Thomas was with them.

Jesus: May each one of you be at peace.

²⁷He drew close to Thomas and said:

Jesus: Reach out and touch Me. See the punctures in My hands; reach out your hand and put it to My side; leave behind your faithlessness and believe.
Thomas (*filled with emotion*): ²⁸You are the one true God and Lord of my life.
Jesus: ²⁹Thomas, you have faith because you have seen Me. Blessed are all those who never see Me and yet they still believe.

³⁰Jesus performed many other wondrous signs that are not written in this book. ³¹The accounts are recorded so that you,

too, might believe that Jesus, the Liberating King, is the Son of God, because believing grants you the life He came to share.

21 There was one other time when Jesus appeared to the disciples—this time by the Sea of Tiberias.

> After Jesus' death, we didn't know what to do with ourselves. What we all knew was fishing. So—we went fishing. Jesus never taught us how to turn two fish into a mound of food that could feed thousands, and we had no money. So, if we wanted to eat, then we had to go catch some fish. Grief has a way of stripping you down to basic survival skills. We were still trying to wrap our brains around what had happened and why. We couldn't even catch our own bait!

This is how it happened: ²Simon Peter, Thomas (called Didymus), Nathanael (the Galilean from Cana), the sons of Zebedee, and two other disciples were together.

Simon Peter (*to disciples*): ³I am going fishing.
Disciples: Then we will come with you.

> We were a band of fishermen who were lost and lonely. But just when we thought things couldn't become stranger, Jesus showed up. He told us to fish on the other side of the boat. We did, and we were suddenly overwhelmed with fish. The nets were bulging.
>
> What He showed us here is that not only would our old ways of living leave us as empty as our nets, but our old habits were not going to work for us anymore. He had impacted our lives in a way that changed us forever. We couldn't go back. And He knew we didn't know how to go forward.

They went out in the boat and caught nothing through the night. ⁴As day was breaking, Jesus was standing on the beach, but they did not know it was Jesus.

Jesus: ⁵My sons, you haven't caught any fish, have you?
Disciples: No.
Jesus: ⁶Throw your net on the starboard side of the boat, and your net will find the fish.

They did what He said, and suddenly they could not lift their net because of the massive weight of the fish that filled it. ⁷The disciple loved by Jesus turned to Peter and said:

Beloved Disciple: It is the Lord.

Immediately, when Simon Peter heard these words, he threw on his shirt (which he would take off while he was working) and dove into the sea. ⁸The rest of the disciples followed him, bringing in the boat and dragging in their net full of fish. They were close to the shore, fishing only about 100 yards out. ⁹When they arrived on shore, they saw a charcoal fire laid with fish on the grill. *He had* bread too.

Jesus (*to disciples*): ¹⁰Bring some of the fish you just caught.

¹¹Simon Peter went back to the boat to unload the fish from the net. He pulled 153 large fish from the net. Despite the number of the fish, the net held without a tear.

Jesus: ¹²Come and join Me for breakfast.

> After spending time with Jesus, I realize there are no coincidences. He revealed to me a world where God is intimately involved, the main actor in the drama of history. It was no accident that we caught the fish. It was no accident the nets didn't break. These fish, all 153, were a sign

from God representing the community of believers, men and women transformed by faith. Some of us sat down and didn't say a word as we pondered all of this. Others busied themselves in work, their hands moving quickly to stack the catch in baskets and untangle the net. Each in his own way thought, wondered, and prayed. I have to admit, the prospect of it all still makes me smile.

That's how I always begin and end my stories of Jesus. I remind my little children that through faith He gives us the authority to become the sons of God. Brother Paul said it's all grace. He's right. We are what we are because of His wonderful work in us. The challenge we face every day is to become what we are—His loving, devoted children. To do that, we have to strip away every vestige of our old lives. Like worn-out clothes, we find our former lives aren't able to contain the beauty of this new creation. Before we can put on the new life and take up our new calling, we have to set aside every ugly and broken aspect of our lives. Repentance, Jesus told us, is not just about what you put off. It's about what you put on. In the human spirit, there is no vacuum. Something will always occupy you and fill your life. It is either life from above or death from below. If the resurrection of Jesus taught us anything, it's that He is the resurrection and the life. I'm not talking about life after death. What I mean is that through Jesus we can have abundant life, a full and meaningful life, here and now.

Not one of the disciples dared to ask, "Who are You?" They knew it was the Lord. [13]Jesus took the bread and gave it to each of them, and then He did the same with the fish. [14]This was the third time the disciples had seen Jesus since His death and resurrection. [15]They finished eating breakfast.

Jesus: Simon, son of John, do you love Me more than these other things?
Simon Peter: Yes, Lord. You know that I love You.
Jesus: Take care of My lambs.

[16]Jesus asked him a second time . . .

Jesus: Simon, son of John, do you love Me?
Simon Peter: Yes, Lord. You must surely know that I love You.
Jesus: Shepherd My sheep.
    [17](for the third time!) Simon, son of John, do you love Me?

Peter was hurt because He asked him the same question a third time, "Do you love Me?"

Simon Peter: Lord, You know everything! You know that I love You.
Jesus: Look after My sheep. [18]I tell you the truth, when you were younger, you would pick up and go wherever you pleased; but when you grow old, someone else will help you and take you places you do not want to go.

When Jesus took Simon Peter off to the side to speak to him, the rest of us knew what was about to happen. He felt small. He felt he had betrayed Jesus. Up to that point, neither Simon nor Jesus had brought it up. They sat far enough away that the rest of us couldn't hear what was said. We tried to look busy, like we didn't notice. But we did. Simon told us later how it went, what Jesus said. I think that conversation on the beach that day affected him profoundly. From then on, Simon was one of the most humble men I knew.

What got everyone's attention was that Jesus called him "Simon." He hadn't done that in years. From the time that Jesus gave him the nickname "Peter" ("the Rock"), He had always referred to him by that name. But

"Peter" hadn't felt like "the Rock" ever since the night Judas betrayed us. For days he felt miserable, like a complete traitor. Jesus knew that, so when it came time to give him "the talk," He called him "Simon."

19 Jesus said all this as an indicator of the nature of Peter's death, which would glorify God. After this conversation, Jesus said,

Jesus: Follow Me!

20 Peter turned around to see the disciple loved by Jesus following the two of them, the one who leaned back on Jesus' side during their supper and asked, "Lord, who is going to betray You?"

What Jesus did was nothing short of brilliant. Three times He asked Simon whether he loved Him. Simon was perturbed that Jesus asked him the same question three times. But later he figured it out—with my help, I might add. Three times Simon denied Him. Now Jesus gave him three chances to repent, confess his love, and be restored. Face-to-face with His Lord, he declared his love, and as he did, he felt the burden of his betrayal lift. He began to feel more like the rock he was. Jesus forgave him and then commissioned him to take care of His people. We all took notice. Our Master put Peter, the Rock, in charge.

We all learned a lesson that day. No matter what we have done, no matter the weight of our burden and sin, our Master wants the miracle of forgiveness to restore us to be the people He made us and called us to be. Something happens when we confess our love for Jesus. We are transformed. Our burdens lift. The positive confession of our love for God, hearing His voice, and doing what He asks are as important as confessing our faults.

Peter: 21 Lord, and what will happen to this man?

Jesus: 22 If I choose for him to remain till I return, what difference will this make to you? You follow Me!

23 It is from this exchange with Jesus that some thought this disciple would not die. But Jesus never said that. He said, "If I choose for him to remain till I return, what difference will this make to you?" 24 That very same disciple is the one offering this truthful account written just for you. 25 There are so many other things that Jesus said and did; and if these accounts were also written down, the books could not be contained in the entire cosmos.

Initially all of us stayed in Jerusalem, basking in the glow of the Spirit and the power of His presence. It took a wave of persecution to dislodge us from David's capital and take the message to Judea, Samaria, and the ends of the earth. We really didn't know what to expect. The suffering we faced was a surprise, but we should have anticipated it. Jesus suffered, so why would it be any different for us? What He is showing us is that the fruits of our labor will be so much sweeter when they are rooted in His mission.

He lays out this choice as He did on the beach when He laid fish on the grill: "You can stay here if you want, and drown in grief, spending the rest of your days trying to feed your own hunger. Or you can follow Me, serve My people, and feast on My endless love." What He is saying is that our lives are about more than just feeding ourselves; they're about feeding the world.

I've reached the end of my story. This old man is tired and ready for a rest. It will come soon enough. You'll go on without me, but not without my words. My voice is added to the voices of the prophets and the witnesses.

God has become flesh. Somehow this man, Jesus, manifested God's life in our midst. Now that's a pretty big idea for a fisherman. I'll let people smarter than I am figure that one out, but I'll go to my grave bearing witness that it is true.

Now it is your turn to pass along the faith to your children and grandchildren. It's your turn to leave behind your former ways, as we all did, to receive a new life. You have everything you need. You have the Scriptures. You have my account of the good news. You have the church. And you have the Holy Spirit to empower and guide you. You are not alone.

As Jesus prayed for all of us, I pray to God the Father that you will enter into God's kingdom, that faith will grow deep inside you, and that you will experience eternal life. I invite you to join me in this marvelous journey.

Acts

History of the early church
By Luke, the physician

The Acts of the Apostles, written by Luke as a sequel to his Gospel, presents a selective history of the early church from Jesus' resurrection and ascension to the dispersion of the good news from Jerusalem to Rome, the center of the known world. Luke writes in the manner of an apologist, describing how the amazing growth of this Kingdom movement could have come only through the power of God. He presents it as an outgrowth of the Jewish faith and not a new religion in the Roman Empire. It begins in Jerusalem, the center of Jewish life, and fulfills the promises spoken centuries earlier by Israel's poets and prophets. Acts shows us how the gospel message moved culturally from the Jews to the Samaritans to the non-Jews. The message moved geographically from Jerusalem to Asia Minor to Greece and, finally, to Rome.

As with his Gospel, Luke dedicates Acts to Theophilus, likely a high-ranking Roman official. He describes this account as the continuing story of what Jesus began to do and teach. Now the risen Jesus was working through people He chose to carry the message of redemption to the ends of the earth. Despite the name of this book, not all the apostles or emissaries of the Liberating King are discussed in this history. Luke focuses his account on the contributions of two men: Simon Peter, one of "the twelve," and Paul (also called Saul), a Pharisee who persecuted the movement until he encountered the risen Jesus on his way to Damascus. Luke also traces the history of two churches: the church in Jerusalem, the mother church consisting mainly of Jewish Christians, and the church in Antioch, consisting of both Jewish and non-Jewish believers. It was the church in Antioch that helped to launch Paul's missionary efforts to Asia and Greece, and it was there that believers were first called Christians. At the heart of Luke's story are the conflicts and changes that took place as Jesus' kingdom message went from place to place and people to people. Jesus had been a polarizing figure in His day, so it's no wonder that Jesus' followers also created controversy as they carried on His message.

In spite of persecution by the Romans and disagreements within the church, the early church grew rapidly. When believers were forced out of Jerusalem and into other cities, they took the good news with them. Believers used their suffering as a catalyst to spread the message of Jesus, which is a lesson that continues to inspire the church today.

1 To *a lover of God,* Theophilus: In my first book I recounted the events of Jesus' life—His actions, His teachings— ²⁻³*from the beginning of His life* until He was taken up into heaven. After His great suffering *and vindication,* He showed His apostles that He was alive—appearing to them repeatedly over a period of 40 days, giving them many convincing proofs of His resurrection. *As before,* He spoke constantly of the kingdom of God. During these appearances, He had instructed His chosen messengers through the Holy Spirit, ⁴prohibiting them from leaving Jerusalem, but rather requiring them to wait there until they received what He called "the promise of the Father."

Jesus: This is what you heard Me teach— ⁵that just as John ritually cleansed* people with water, so you will be washed with the Holy Spirit very soon.

*S*cripture doesn't preserve Jesus' teachings during those mysterious meetings with the apostles after His death. We can only imagine the joy, curiosity, and amazement of the disciples as they hung on every word. What we do know is that His presence proved the reality of His bodily resurrection beyond any doubt and that He primarily wanted to talk to them about the kingdom of God. These words were undoubtedly intended to prepare each of them for this journey, a journey with a clear destination in sight—the kingdom of God.

In the actions and teachings of Jesus, the kingdom of God was breaking into the world. But now His followers must embody this reality and extend His mission to the ends of the earth. The kingdom of God is essentially the rule of God. As Jesus taught us, it is the time and place when God's will is done on earth as it is in heaven. It started in the hearts and lives of a few, but it will not stop until all creation is redeemed and every creature bows before Him in love and adoration.

Already the ragtag group of Jesus-followers had seen the Kingdom turn their worlds upside down, but the transformation of the cosmos will not be complete until the second Advent. In Jesus the kingdom of God is born, and the Holy Spirit is the midwife.

⁶When they had gathered *just outside Jerusalem at the Mount of Olives,* they asked Jesus,

Disciples: Is now the time, Lord—the time when You will reestablish Your kingdom in *our land of* Israel?

Jesus: ⁷The Father, on His own authority, has determined the ages and epochs *of history,* but you have not been given this knowledge. ⁸*Here's the knowledge you need:* you will receive power when the Holy Spirit comes on you. And you will be My witnesses, first here in Jerusalem, then beyond to Judea and Samaria, and finally to the farthest places on earth.

⁹As He finished this commission, He began to rise from the ground before their eyes until the clouds obscured Him from their vision. ¹⁰As they strained to get one last glimpse of Him going into heaven, the Lord's emissaries* realized two men in white robes were standing among them.

Two Men: ¹¹You Galileans, why are you standing here staring up into the sky? This Jesus who is leaving you and ascending to heaven will return in the same way you see Him departing.

¹²Then the disciples returned to Jerusalem—their short journey from the Mount of Olives was an acceptable Sabbath Day's walk.
¹³⁻¹⁴Back in the city, they went to the room where they were staying—a second-floor room. This whole group devoted themselves to constant prayer with one

---

* 1:5 Literally, immersed, to show repentance
* 1:10 Literally, apostles

accord: Peter, John, James, Andrew, Philip, Thomas, Bartholomew, Matthew, James (son of Alphaeus), Simon (the Zealot), Judas (son of James), a number of women including Mary (Jesus' mother), and some of Jesus' brothers.

¹⁵As the disciples prayed, Peter stood among the group of about 120 people and made this proposal:

Peter: ¹⁶⁻¹⁷My friends, everything in the Hebrew Scriptures had to be fulfilled, including what the Holy Spirit foretold through David about Judas. *As you know,* Judas was one of us and participated in our ministry until he guided the authorities to arrest Jesus. ¹⁸(He was paid handsomely for his betrayal, and he bought a field with the blood money. But he died *on that land*—falling so that his abdomen burst and his internal organs gushed out. ¹⁹News of this death spread to everyone in Jerusalem, so Judas's property is known as Hakeldama, which means "field of blood.") ²⁰In this way, one of *David's* psalms was fulfilled: "May their camps be bleak, with not one left in any tent."* But the psalms also include these words: "Let his position of oversight be given to another."* ²¹So we need *to determine his replacement* from among the men who have been with us during all of the Lord Jesus' travels among us— ²²from His ritual cleansing* by John until His ascension. We need someone to join us as a witness of Jesus' resurrection.

²³The group put forward two men: Joseph (who was also known as Barsabbas or Justus) and Matthias.

Disciples: ²⁴Lord, You know everyone's heart. Make it clear to us which of these two is Your choice ²⁵to take on this ministry as your apostle, replacing Judas who went his own way to his own destination.

²⁶Then they drew lots, and the lot fell to Matthias, so he was added to the eleven apostles *to reconstitute the twelve.*

*T*he Creator of heaven and earth is orchestrating a redemptive story that will radically change the course of history. The most significant supernatural event in the history of this newly formed church will be the filling of the Holy Spirit. Through the Holy Spirit, God will direct the church's growth. But how did the early church make important decisions before the Holy Spirit descended on them?

The company of disciples turned to the practice of "drawing lots," a practice used by many saints to discover God's providential leading. After much prayer, Joseph and Matthias most likely wrote their names on scraps; then someone drew the replacement's name out of a bag. What seems to us like a 50/50 chance was, in fact, God's way of imparting His will. You see, the disciples weren't putting their faith in "chance." They were putting their faith in a God who lives. And this living God wasn't distant; He was a player in their lives, active when His people sought Him and His will. They believed that God directed the process, start to finish, and determined whose name was drawn to join the eleven. When they drew lots, these early believers were using a centuries-old method to discern God's will.

2 When the holy day of Pentecost came *50 days after Passover*, they were gathered together in one place.

²*Picture yourself among the disciples:*

A sound roars from the sky without warning, the roar of a violent wind, and the whole house where you are gathered reverberates with the sound. ³Then a flame appears, dividing into smaller flames and spreading from one person to the next. ⁴All

---

* 1:20 Psalm 69:25-26
* 1:20 Psalm 109:8
* 1:22 Literally, immersion, an act to show repentance

the people present are filled with the Holy Spirit and begin speaking in languages they've never spoken, as the Spirit empowers them.

⁵*Because of the holiday,* there are devout Jews staying as pilgrims in Jerusalem from every nation under the sun. ⁶They hear the sound, and a crowd gathers. They are amazed because each of them can hear the group speaking in their native languages. ⁷They are shocked and amazed by this.

Pilgrims: Just a minute. Aren't all of these people Galileans? ⁸How in the world do we all hear our native languages being spoken? ⁹*Look*—there are Parthians here, and Medes, Elamites, Mesopotamians, and Judeans, residents of Cappadocia, Pontus, and Asia, ¹⁰Phrygians and Pamphylians, Egyptians and Libyans from Cyrene, Romans including both Jews *by birth* and converts, ¹¹Cretans, and Arabs. We're each, in our own languages, hearing these people talk about God's powerful deeds.

¹²Their amazement becomes confusion as they wonder,

Pilgrims: What does this mean?
Skeptics: ¹³It doesn't mean anything. They're all drunk on some fresh wine!

*N*o matter who you were or what you may have seen, this miraculous sign of God's kingdom would have astounded you. The followers of Jesus were not known as people who drank too much wine with breakfast, but this unusual episode required some kind of explanation. Unfortunately we can't comprehend or express what transpired on Pentecost. But this was not a novelty performance; rather, it was a taste of the kingdom of God.

¹⁴As the twelve stood together, Peter shouted to the crowd,

Peter: Men of Judea and all who are staying here in Jerusalem, listen. I want you to understand: ¹⁵these people aren't drunk as you may think. Look, it's only nine o'clock in the morning! ¹⁶No, *this isn't drunkenness;* this is the fulfillment of the prophecy of Joel. ¹⁷Hear what God says!

In the last days,
I will offer My Spirit to humanity
as a libation.
Your children will boldly speak *the word of the Lord.*
Young warriors will see visions,
and your elders will dream dreams.
¹⁸Yes, in those days I shall offer My Spirit to all servants,
both male and female, and they will boldly speak My word.
¹⁹And in the heaven above and on the earth below,
I shall give signs *of impending judgment*: blood, fire, and clouds of smoke.
²⁰The sun will become a void of darkness,
and the moon will become blood.
Then the great and dreadful day of the Lord will arrive,
²¹And everyone who calls on the name of the Lord
will be liberated *into God's freedom and peace.**

²²All of you Israelites, listen to my message: it's about Jesus of Nazareth, a man whom God authenticated for you by performing in your presence powerful deeds, wonders, and signs through Him, just as you yourselves know. ²³This man, *Jesus,* who came into your hands by God's sure plan and advanced knowledge, you nailed to a cross and killed in collaboration with lawless outsiders. ²⁴But God raised Jesus and unleashed Him from the agonizing birth-pains of death, for death could not possibly keep

* 2:17-21 Joel 2:28-32

Jesus in its power. ²⁵David spoke of Jesus' *resurrection*, saying:

> I see the Lord is ever present with
>   me.
> I will not live in fear *or abandon*
>   *my calling* because He guides
>   my right hand.
> ²⁶My heart is glad; my soul rejoices;
>   my body is safe. *Who could hope*
>   *for more?*
> ²⁷You will not abandon me to
>   experience the suffering of a
>   miserable afterlife,
>   nor leave Your Holy One to rot
>   *alone.*
> ²⁸*Instead*, You direct me on a path
>   that leads to a beautiful life.
> As I walk with You, the pleasures
>   are never-ending, and I know
>   true joy and contentment.*

²⁹My fellow Israelites, I can say without question that David our ancestor died and was buried, and his tomb is with us today. ³⁰*David wasn't speaking of himself;* he was speaking as a prophet. He saw *with prophetic insight* that God had made a solemn promise to him: God would put one of his descendants on His throne. ³¹Here's what David was seeing in advance; here's what David was talking about—the Liberating King would be resurrected. Think *of David's words* about Him not being abandoned to the place of the dead nor being left to decay in the grave. ³²*He was talking about* Jesus, the One God has raised, whom all of us have seen with our own eyes *and announce to you today.* ³³Since Jesus has been lifted to the right hand of God—*the highest place of authority and power*—and since Jesus has received the promise of the Holy Spirit from the Father, He has now poured out what you have seen and heard here today. ³⁴*Remember:* David couldn't have been speaking of himself rising to the heavens when he said,

> The Master said to my master,
> "Sit here at My right hand,
>   *in the place of honor and power,*

> ³⁵And I will gather Your enemies
>   together,
>   *lead them in on hands and knees,*
> and You will rest Your feet on
>   their backs."*

³⁶Everyone in Israel should now realize with certainty *what God has done*: God has made Jesus both Lord and Liberating King—this same Jesus whom you crucified.

³⁷When the people heard this, their hearts were pierced and they said to Peter and his fellow apostles,

Pilgrims: Our brothers, what should we do?
Peter: ³⁸Reconsider your lives; change your direction. Participate in the ceremonial washing* in the name of Jesus, the Liberating King. Then your sins will be forgiven, and the gift of the Holy Spirit will be yours. ³⁹For the promise *of the Spirit* is for you, for your children, for all people—even those considered outsiders and outcasts—the Lord our God invites everyone to come to Him. *Let God liberate you from this decaying culture!*

⁴⁰Peter was pleading and offering many logical reasons to believe. ⁴¹Whoever made a place for his message in their hearts received the ceremonial washing;* in fact, that day alone, about 3,000 people joined the disciples.

⁴²The community continually committed themselves to learning what the apostles taught them, gathering for fellowship, breaking bread, and praying. ⁴³Everyone felt a sense of awe because the apostles were doing many signs and wonders among them. ⁴⁴There was an intense sense of togetherness among all who believed; they shared all their material possessions in trust. ⁴⁵They sold any possessions and

---

* 2:25-28 Psalm 16:8-11
* 2:34-35 Psalm 110:1
* 2:38 Literally, immersion, a rite of initiation and purification
* 2:41 Literally, immersion, a rite of initiation and purification

goods *that did not benefit the community* and used the money to help everyone in need. ⁴⁶They were unified as they worshiped at the temple day after day. In homes, they broke bread and shared meals with glad and generous hearts. ⁴⁷The new disciples praised God, and they enjoyed the goodwill of all the people *of the city*. Day after day the Lord added to their number everyone who was experiencing liberation.

Although this young and thriving church had no political influence, property, fame, or wealth, it was powerful. Its power was centered in living the gospel. The people valued one another more than any possessions. They came together as a large, passionate, healthy family where it was natural to pray and share all of life together. The kingdom of God was blossoming on earth as these lovers of God embraced the teachings of the Liberator. In the days ahead, the church will lose much of the beauty and appeal we see in this story. It will become consumed with a desire for material possessions, cultural influence, and power.

3 One day at three o'clock in the afternoon, a customary time for daily prayer, Peter and John walked to the temple. ²Some people were carrying in a man who had been paralyzed since birth. Every day they brought him to a place near the Beautiful Gate (*one of the temple entrances*) so he could beg for money from people entering *to worship*. ³He saw Peter and John coming and asked them for a contribution. ⁴Peter gazed intensely at him—so did John.

Peter: Look at us.

⁵The man looked up at them, assuming they were about to give him some money.

Peter: ⁶I want to give you something, but I don't have any silver or gold. Here's what I can offer you: stand up and walk in the name of Jesus of Nazareth, the Liberating King.

⁷Then Peter took the man's right hand and lifted him to his feet. Instantly the man's feet and ankles grew strong. ⁸He jumped and walked, accompanying Peter and John into the temple where he walked, jumped for joy, and shouted praises to God. ⁹⁻¹¹A crowd ran to the commotion, and they gathered around this man in an open area called Solomon's Porch. There he was, standing on his own two feet, holding on to Peter and John. They knew exactly who he was—the beggar they passed at the Beautiful Gate every day. Everyone was absolutely amazed at this wonderful miracle; they were speechless, stunned.

Peter (*to the crowd*): ¹²Why are you so amazed, my fellow Israelites? Why are you staring at my friend and me as though we did this miracle through our own power or made this fellow walk by our own holiness? ¹³*We didn't do this— God did!* The God of Abraham, the God of Isaac, the God of Jacob—the God of our ancestors has glorified Jesus, God's servant—the same Jesus whom you betrayed and rejected in front of Pilate, even though Pilate was going to release Him. ¹⁴He is the Holy and Righteous One, but you rejected Him and asked for a murderer to be released to you instead. ¹⁵*You not only rejected Him,* but you killed Him—the very Author of life! But God raised Jesus from the dead, whom my friend John and I have seen with our own eyes. ¹⁶So that's how this miracle happened: we have faith in the name of Jesus, and He is the power that made this man strong—this man who is known to all of you. It is faith in Jesus that has given this man his complete health here today, in front of all of you.

¹⁷Listen, friends, I know you didn't fully realize what you were doing *when you rejected and betrayed Jesus.* I know that you, and your rulers as well, were acting in ignorance. ¹⁸God was at work in all this, fulfilling what He had predicted

through all the prophets—that His Liberating King would suffer. ¹⁹So now you need to rethink everything and turn to God so your sins will be forgiven and a new day can dawn, days of refreshing times flowing from the Lord. ²⁰Then God may send the Liberating King—Jesus, whom God has chosen for you. ²¹He is in heaven now and must remain there until the day of universal restoration comes—the restoration which in ancient times God announced through the holy prophets. ²²Moses, *for example,* said, "The Eternal One your God will raise up from among your people a prophet who will be like me. You must listen to Him. ²³And whoever does not listen to His words will be completely uprooted from among the people."*

²⁴*It wasn't just Moses who predicted what is happening these days.* Every prophet, from Samuel through all of his successors, agreed. ²⁵You are the descendants of these prophets, and you are the people of God's covenant to your ancestors. God's word to Abraham includes you: "Because of your descendants, all the *families* of the earth will be blessed."* ²⁶So when God raised up His Servant, God sent Him first to you, to begin blessing you by calling you to change your path from evil ways *to God's ways.*

4 The conversation continued *for a few hours there in Solomon's Porch.* Suddenly, the head of the temple police and some members of the Sadducean party interrupted Peter and John. ²They were annoyed because Peter and John were *enthusiastically* teaching that in Jesus, resurrection of the dead is possible—*an idea the Sadducees completely rejected.* ³So they arrested Peter, John, *and the man who was healed* and kept them in jail overnight. ⁴*But during these few afternoon hours between the man's miraculous healing and their arrest,* Peter and John already had convinced about 5,000 more people to believe their message about Jesus!

⁵The next morning, *the Jewish leaders—*their officials, elders, and scholars—called a meeting in Jerusalem ⁶presided over by Annas (the patriarch of the ruling priestly clan), along with Caiaphas *(his son-in-law),* John, Alexander, and other members of their clan. ⁷They made their prisoners stand in the middle of the assembly and questioned them.

Jewish Leaders: Who gave you the authority to create that spectacle in the temple yesterday?

Peter *(filled with the Spirit)*: ⁸Rulers and elders of the people, ⁹yesterday a good deed was done. Someone who was sick was healed. If you're asking us how this happened, ¹⁰I want all of you and all of the people of Israel to know this man standing in front of you—obviously in good health—was healed by the authority of Jesus, the Liberating King from Nazareth. This is the same Jesus whom you crucified and whom God raised from the dead. ¹¹He is "the stone that you builders rejected who has become the very stone that holds together the entire foundation"* *on which a new temple is being built.* ¹²There is no one else who can rescue us, and there is no other name under heaven given to any human by whom we may be rescued.

¹³Now the leaders were surprised and confused. They looked at Peter and John and realized they were *typical peasants*—uneducated, utterly ordinary fellows—with extraordinary confidence. The leaders recognized them as companions of Jesus, ¹⁴then they turned their attention to the third man standing beside them—recently lame, now standing tall and healthy. What could they say in response to all this?

¹⁵*Because they were at a loss about what to do,* they excused the prisoners so the council could deliberate in private.

* 3:23 Deuteronomy 18:15,18-19
* 3:25 Genesis 22:18; 26:4
* 4:11 Psalm 118:22

Jewish Leaders: [16]What do we do with these fellows? Anyone who lives in Jerusalem will know an unexplainable sign has been performed through these two preachers. We can't deny their story. [17]The best we can do is try to keep it from spreading. So let's warn them to stop speaking to anybody in this name.

[18]The leaders brought the prisoners back in and prohibited them from doing any more speaking or teaching in the name of Jesus. [19]Peter and John *listened quietly and then* replied,

Peter and John: You are the judges here, so we'll leave it up to you to judge whether it is right in the sight of God to obey your commands or God's. [20]*But one thing we can tell you:* we cannot possibly restrain ourselves from speaking about what we have seen and heard *with our own eyes and ears.*

[21-22]The council threatened them again, but finally let them go because public opinion strongly supported Peter and John and this man who had received this miraculous sign. He was over 40 years old, *so his situation was known to many people,* and they couldn't help but glorify God for his healing. [23]Peter and John, upon their release, went right to their friends and told the story—including the warning from the council. [24]The whole community responded with this prayer to God:

Community of Believers: God, our King, You made the heaven and the earth and the sea and everything they contain.* [25]You are the One who, by the Holy Spirit, spoke through our ancestor David, Your servant, with these words:

> Why did the nations rage?
> Why did they imagine useless things?
> [26]The kings of the earth took their stand;

their rulers assembled in opposition against the Eternal One and His Liberating King.*

[27]This is exactly what has happened among us, here in this city. *The foreign ruler* Pontius Pilate and *the Jewish ruler* Herod, along with their respective peoples, have assembled in opposition to Your holy servant Jesus, the One You chose. [28]They have done whatever Your hand and plan predetermined should happen. [29]And now, Lord, take note of their intimidations *intended to silence us.* Grant us, Your servants, the courageous confidence we need to go ahead and proclaim Your message [30]while You reach out Your hand to heal people, enabling us to perform signs and wonders through the name of Your holy servant Jesus.

[31]They finished their prayer, and immediately the whole place where they had gathered began to shake. All the disciples were filled with the Holy Spirit, and they began speaking God's message with courageous confidence.

*T*he Holy Spirit changed everyone and everything. If there is any doubt about the power of the Spirit, just take a look at Peter. When the Liberator was captured, Peter cowered in fear that he might be fingered as a man who loved Jesus. Now this same man is preaching, healing, and pointing his finger in the face of Jewish officials who have captured him and John. With a boldness that is not his own, he blames them for the death of Jesus, the Liberating King, and does not cower at their show of violence.

* 4:24 A prayer inspired by other biblical prayers: 2 Kings 19:15; Nehemiah 9:6; Psalm 146:6; Isaiah 37:16
* 4:25-26 Psalm 2:1-2

32During those days, the entire community of believers was deeply united in heart and soul to such an extent that they stopped claiming private ownership of their possessions. Instead, they held everything in common. 33The apostles with great power gave their eyewitness reports of the resurrection of the Lord Jesus. Everyone was surrounded by an extraordinary grace. 34Not a single person in the community was in need because those who had been affluent sold their houses or lands and brought the proceeds 35to the emissaries* of the Lord. They then distributed the funds to individuals according to their needs. 36-37One fellow, a Cyprian Levite named Joseph, earned a nickname *because of his generosity* in selling a field and bringing the money to the apostles *in this way.* From that time on, they called him Barnabas, which means "son of encouragement."

This portrait of the early church as an unselfish community is captivating and inspiring. But, how does this translate into future cultures? How do we, in our time, respond as they did in theirs? How do we speak boldly? How do we bring healing and miracles in God's name? How do we join together with one heart and mind? How do we relinquish our possessions?

5 1-2*The life of the community was wonderful in those days, but it wasn't perfect.* Once a man named Ananias, with his wife Sapphira fully cooperating, *committed fraud.* He sold some property and kept some of the proceeds, but he pretended to make a full donation to the Lord's emissaries.*

Peter: 3Ananias, have you allowed Satan to influence your lies to the Holy Spirit and hold back some of the money? 4Look, it was your property before you sold it, and the money was all yours after you sold it. Why have you concocted this scheme in

your heart? You weren't just lying to us; you were lying to God.

5Ananias heard these words and immediately dropped to the ground, dead; fear overcame all those who heard of the incident. 6Some young men came, wrapped the body, and buried it immediately. 7About three hours had passed when Sapphira arrived. She had no idea what had happened.

Peter: 8Did you sell the land for such-and-such a price?
Sapphira: Yes, that was the price.
Peter: 9Why did the two of you conspire to test the Spirit of the Lord? Do you hear those footsteps outside? Those are the young men who just buried your husband, and now they will carry you out as well.

10She—*like her husband*—immediately fell dead at Peter's feet. The young men came in and carried her corpse outside and buried it beside her husband. 11The whole church was terrified by this story, as were others who heard it.

In these formative days, God chose to send some strong messages about His work in the church: the power to heal, the beauty of life in the Spirit, and His hatred for arrogant religion. If God had not rebuked the married couple who chose to make a show of their supposed generosity, Christianity would have drifted in the wrong direction. The Jewish leaders were using religion as a means to gain power and increase their reputations. The teachings of the true Liberator, Jesus, lead us down a path toward the kingdom of God rather than toward our own advancement. God chose to expose these bad motives quickly, so that the church throughout history

* 4:35 Literally, apostles
* 5:1-2 Literally, apostles

would give out of pure motives rather than out of a desire to appear righteous.

[12]*Those were amazing days*—with many signs and wonders being performed through the apostles among the people. The church would gather as a unified group in Solomon's Porch, [13]enjoying great respect by the people of the city—though most people wouldn't risk publicly affiliating with them. [14]Even so, record numbers of believers—both men and women—were added to the Lord. [15]*The church's popularity was so great that* when Peter walked down the street, people would carry out their sick relatives hoping his shadow would fall on some of them as he passed. [16]Even people from towns surrounding Jerusalem would come, bringing others who were sick or tormented by unclean spirits, all of whom were cured.

[17]*Of course, this popularity elicited a response:* the high priest and his affiliates in the Sadducean party were jealous, [18]so they arrested the apostles and put them in the public prison. [19]But that night, a messenger of the Lord opened the doors of the prison and led them to freedom.

Messenger of the Lord: [20]Go to the temple, and stand up to tell the people the whole message about this way of life *from Jesus.*

[21]At dawn they did as they were told; they returned to their teaching in the temple.

Meanwhile the council of Jewish elders was gathering—convened by the high priest and his colleagues. They sent the temple police to the prison to have the Lord's emissaries* brought *for further examination,* [22]but, of course, the temple police soon realized they weren't there. They returned and reported,

Temple Police: [23]The prison was secure and locked, and the guards were standing in front of the doors, but when we unlocked the doors, the cell was empty.

[24]The captain of the temple police and the senior priests were completely mystified when they heard this. They had no idea what had happened. [25]Just then, someone arrived with this news:

Temple Messenger: You know those men you put in prison last night? *Well, they're free.* At this moment, they're *at it again,* teaching our people in the temple!

[26]The temple police—this time, accompanied by their captain—rushed over *to the temple* and brought the emissaries* of the Lord to the council. They were careful not to use violence, because the people were so supportive of them that the police feared being stoned by the crowd *if they were too rough.* [27]Once again the men stood before the council. The high priest began the questioning.

High Priest: [28]Didn't we give you strict orders to stop teaching in this name? But here you are, spreading your teaching throughout Jerusalem. And you are determined to blame us for this man's death.

Peter and the Apostles: [29]If we have to choose between obedience to God and obedience to any human authority, then we must obey God. [30]The God of our ancestors raised Jesus from death. You killed Jesus by hanging Him on a tree, [31]but God has lifted Him high, to God's own right hand, as the Prince, as the Liberator. God intends to bring Israel to a radical rethinking of our lives and to a complete forgiveness of our sins. [32]We are witnesses to these things. There is another witness too—the Holy Spirit—whom God has given to all who choose to obey Him.

[33]*Peter's speech didn't go over very well.* The council was furious and would have killed them, [34]but Gamaliel, a Pharisee in the council respected as a teacher of the

* 5:21 Literally, apostles
* 5:26 Literally, apostles

Hebrew Scriptures, stood up and ordered the men to be sent out *so the council could confer privately.*

Gamaliel: [35]Fellow Jews, you need to act with great care in your treatment of these fellows. [36]Remember when a man named Theudas rose to notoriety? He claimed to be somebody important, and he attracted about 400 followers. But when he was killed, his entire movement disintegrated and nothing came of it. [37]After him came Judas, that Galilean fellow, at the time of the census. He also attracted a following, but when he died, his entire movement fell apart. [38]So here's my advice: in this case, just let these men go. Ignore them. If this is just another movement arising from human enthusiasm, it will die out soon enough. [39]But then again, if God is in this, you won't be able to stop it—unless, of course, you're ready to fight against God!

[40]The council was convinced, so they brought the apostles back in. They were flogged, again told not to speak in the name of Jesus, and then released. [41]As they left the council, they *weren't discouraged at all. In fact, they* were filled with joy over being considered worthy to suffer disgrace for the sake of His name. [42]And constantly, *whether in public,* in the temple, or in their homes, they kept teaching and proclaiming Jesus as the Liberating King.

*T*hese emissaries of Jesus inspire us with their passion to serve Jesus and advance the gospel in the face of torture and abuse. After a night in prison and a public flogging, they move forward with smiles on their faces. We are often crippled by mere criticism or the fear that we might be criticized. What would happen to the church if we embraced their boldness and risked our own safety to see the captives rescued and the oppressed freed?

6 *Things were going so well,* and the number of disciples was growing. But a problem arose. The Greek-speaking believers became frustrated with the Hebrew-speaking believers. The Greeks complained that the Greek-speaking widows were being discriminated against in the daily distribution of food. [2]The twelve convened the entire community of disciples.

The Twelve: We could solve this problem ourselves, but that wouldn't be right. We need to focus on proclaiming God's message, not on distributing food. [3]So, friends, find seven respected men from the community of faith. These men should be full of the Holy Spirit and full of wisdom. Whomever you select we will commission to resolve this matter [4]so we can maintain our focus on praying and serving—*not meals*—but the message.

[5]The whole community—*Greek-speaking and Hebrew-speaking*—was very pleased with this plan, so they chose *seven men:* Stephen (a man full of faith and full of the Holy Spirit), Philip, Prochorus, Nicanor, Timon, Parmenas, and Nicolas (a Greek-speaking convert from Antioch). [6]These men were presented to the apostles, who then prayed for them and commissioned them by laying their hands on them. [7]The message of God continued to spread, and the number of disciples continued to increase significantly there in Jerusalem. Even priests in large numbers became obedient to the faith.

[8]Stephen continually overflowed with extraordinary grace and power, and he was able to perform a number of miraculous signs and wonders in public view. [9]But eventually a group arose to oppose Stephen *and the message to which his signs and wonders pointed.* (These men were from a group called the Free Synagogue and included Cyrenians, Alexandrians, Cilicians, and Asians.) [10]The Holy Spirit gave Stephen such wisdom in responding

to their arguments that they were humiliated; [11]*in retaliation,* they spread a vicious rumor: "We heard Stephen speak blasphemies against Moses and God."

[12]Their rumor prompted an uprising that included common people, religious officials, and scholars. They surprised Stephen, grabbed him, and hauled him before the council. [13]They convinced some witnesses to give false testimony.

False Witnesses: This fellow constantly degrades the holy temple and mocks our holy law. [14]*With our own ears,* we've heard him say this Jesus fellow, this Nazarene *he's always talking about,* will actually destroy the holy temple and will try to change the sacred customs we received from Moses.

[15]The entire council turned its gaze on Stephen *to see how he would respond.* They *were shocked to* see his face radiant *with peace*—as if he were a heavenly messenger.

High Priest: *What do you have to say for yourself?* Are these accusations accurate?

Stephen: [2]Brothers, fathers, please listen to me. Our glorious God revealed Himself to our common ancestor Abraham, when he lived far away in Mesopotamia before he immigrated to Haran. [3]God gave him this command: "Leave your country. Leave your family *and your inheritance.* Move into unknown territory, where I will show you a new homeland."* [4]First, he left Chaldea *in southern Mesopotamia* and settled in Haran until his father died. Then God led him still farther from his original home—until he settled here, in our land. [5]*But at that point,* God still hadn't given him any of this land as his permanent possession—not even the footprint under his sandal actually belonged to him yet. But God did give Abraham a promise—a promise that yes, someday, the entire land would indeed belong to him and his descendants. *Of course, this promise was all the more*

amazing because at that moment, Abraham had no descendants at all.

[6]God said that Abraham's descendants would first live in a foreign country as resident aliens, *as refugees,* for 400 years. During this time, they would be enslaved and treated horribly. *But that would not be the end of the story.* [7]God promised, "I will judge the nation that enslaves them,"* and "I will bring them to this mountain to serve Me."* [8]God gave him the covenant ritual of circumcision *as a sign of His sacred promise.* When Abraham fathered his son, Isaac, he performed this ritual of circumcision on the eighth day. Then Isaac fathered Jacob, and Jacob fathered the twelve patriarchs.

[9]The patriarchs were jealous of *their brother* Joseph, so they sold him as a slave into Egypt. Even so, God was with him, [10]and *time after time,* God rescued Joseph from whatever trials befell him. God gave Joseph the favor and wisdom *to overcome each adversity* and eventually to win the confidence and respect of *his captors, including* Pharaoh, the king of Egypt himself. So Pharaoh entrusted his whole nation and his whole household to Joseph's stewardship. [11]*Some time later,* a terrible famine spread through the entire region—from Canaan down to Egypt—and everyone suffered greatly. Our ancestors, *living here in the region of Canaan,* could find nothing to eat. [12]Jacob heard that Egypt had stores of grain, so he sent our forefathers, *his sons, to procure food* there. [13]Later, when they returned to Egypt a second time, Joseph revealed his true identity to them. He also told Pharaoh his family story.

[14-16]Joseph then invited his father Jacob and all his clan to come and live with him in Egypt. So Jacob came, along with 75 extended family members. After their deaths, their remains were brought

* 7:3 Genesis 12:1
* 7:7 Genesis 15:14
* 7:7 Exodus 3:12

back to this land so they could be buried in the same tomb where Abraham *had buried Sarah* (he had purchased the tomb for a certain amount of silver from the family of Hamor in *the town of* Shechem).

[17]Still God's promise to Abraham had not yet been fulfilled, but the time for that fulfillment was drawing very near. In the meantime, our ancestors living in Egypt rapidly multiplied. [18]Eventually a new king came to power—one who had not known Joseph *when he was the most powerful man in Egypt.* [19]This new leader *feared the growing population of our ancestors and* manipulated them for his own benefit, eventually seeking to control their population by forcing them to abandon their infants so they would die. [20]Into this horrible situation *our ancestor* Moses was born, and he was a beautiful child in God's eyes. He was raised for three months in his father's home, [21]and then he was abandoned *as the brutal regime required.* However, Pharaoh's daughter found, adopted, and raised him as her own son. [22]So Moses learned the culture and wisdom of the Egyptians and became a powerful man—both as an intellectual and as a leader. [23]When he reached the age of 40, his heart drew him to visit his kinfolk, our ancestors, the Israelites. [24]During his visit, he saw one of our people being wronged, and he took sides with our people by killing an Egyptian. [25]He thought his kinfolk would recognize him as their God-given liberator, but they didn't realize *who he was and what he represented.*

[26]The next day Moses was walking among the Israelites again when he observed a fight—but this time, it was between two Israelites. He intervened and tried to reconcile the men. "You two are brothers," he said. "Why do you attack each other?" [27]But the aggressor pushed Moses away and responded *with contempt*: "Who made you our prince and judge? [28]Are you going to slay me *and hide my body* as you did with the Egyptian yesterday?"* [29]Realizing this murder had not gone unnoticed, he

quickly escaped Egypt and lived as a refugee in the land of Midian. He *married there and* had two sons.

[30]Forty more years passed. One day while Moses was in the desert near Mount Sinai, a heavenly messenger appeared to him in the flames of a burning bush. [31]The phenomenon intrigued Moses, and as he approached for a closer look, he heard a voice—the voice of the Lord: [32]"I am the God of your own fathers, the God of Abraham, Isaac, and Jacob."* This terrified Moses—he began to tremble and looked away in fear. [33]The voice continued: "Take off your sandals *and stand barefoot on the ground in My presence,* for this ground is holy ground. [34]I have avidly watched how My people are being mistreated by the Egyptians. I have heard their groaning *at the treatment of their oppressors.* I am descending *personally* to rescue them. So get up. I'm sending you to Egypt."*

[35]*Now remember:* this was the same Moses who had been rejected by his kinfolk when they said, "Who made you our prince and judge?" This man, *rejected by his own people,* was the one God had truly sent, commissioned by the heavenly messenger who appeared in the bush, to be their leader and liberator.

[36]*You remember what happened next.* Moses indeed led our ancestors to freedom, and he performed miraculous signs and wonders in Egypt, at the Red Sea, and in the wilderness over a period of 40 years. [37]This Moses promised our ancestors, "The Eternal One your God will raise up from among your people a Prophet who will be like me."* [38]This is the same one who led the people to Mount Sinai, where a heavenly messenger spoke to him and our ancestors, and who received the living message of God to give to us.

[39]But our ancestors still resisted. They again pushed Moses away and

* 7:28 Exodus 2:13-14
* 7:32 Exodus 3:6
* 7:34 Exodus 3:5,7-8,10
* 7:37 Deuteronomy 18:15

refused to follow him. In their hearts, they were ready to return to *their former slavery in* Egypt. ⁴⁰*While Moses was on the mountain communing with God,* they begged Aaron to make idols to lead them—*they actually preferred idols to following Moses in the way of the Lord.* "We have no idea what happened to this fellow, Moses, who brought us from Egypt,"* they said. ⁴¹So they made a calf as their new god, and they even sacrificed to it and celebrated an object they had fabricated *as if it were their God.*

⁴²*And you remember what God did next:* He let them go. He turned from them and let them follow their idolatrous path—worshiping sun, moon, and stars *just as their unenlightened neighbors did.* The prophet *Amos* spoke for God *about this horrible betrayal*:

Did you offer Me sacrifices or give
        Me offerings
    during your 40-year wilderness
        journey, you Israelites?
⁴³*No, but* you have taken along your
        sacred tent for the worship of
        Moloch,
    and you honored the star of
        Rompha, your false god.
So, if you want to worship your
        man-made images,
    you may do so—beyond
        Babylon.*

⁴⁴Now recall that our ancestors had a sacred tent in the wilderness, the tent God directed Moses to build according to the pattern revealed to him. ⁴⁵When Joshua led our ancestors to dispossess the nations God drove out before them, our ancestors carried this sacred tent. It remained here in the land until the time of David. ⁴⁶David found favor with God and asked Him for permission to build a permanent structure (*rather than a portable tent*) to honor Him. ⁴⁷It was, of course, Solomon who actually built God's house. ⁴⁸Yet we all know the Most High God doesn't actually dwell in structures made by human hands, as the prophet *Isaiah* said,

⁴⁹"Since My throne is heaven
        and since My footstool is earth—
    What kind of structure can you
        build to contain Me?
    What *man-made* space could
        provide Me a resting place?"
    asks the Eternal One.
⁵⁰"Didn't I make all things with My
        own hand?"*

⁵¹You stubborn, stiff-necked people! Sure, you are physically Jews, but you are no different from outsiders in your hearts and ears! You are just like your ancestors, constantly fighting against the Holy Spirit. ⁵²Didn't your ancestors persecute the prophets? First, they killed those prophets who predicted the coming of the Just One, and now you have betrayed and murdered the Just One Himself! ⁵³Yes, you received the law as given by heavenly messengers, but you haven't kept the law which you received.

⁵⁴Upon hearing this, *his audience could contain themselves no longer*; they boiled in fury at Stephen; they clenched their jaws and ground their teeth. ⁵⁵But Stephen *didn't seem to notice. Instead of being filled with fear,* he was filled with the Holy Spirit. Gazing upward into heaven, he saw *something they couldn't see:* the glory of God, and Jesus standing at His right hand.

Stephen: ⁵⁶Look, I see the heavens opening! I see the Liberator standing at the right hand of God!

⁵⁷At this, they covered their ears and started shouting. The whole crowd rushed at Stephen, converged on him, ⁵⁸dragged him out of the city, and stoned him.

They laid their coats at the feet of a young man named Saul, ⁵⁹while they were pelting Stephen with rocks.

Stephen (*as rocks fell upon him*): Lord Jesus, receive my spirit.

* 7:40 Exodus 32:1
* 7:42-43 Amos 5:26-27
* 7:49-50 Isaiah 66:1-2

⁶⁰Then he knelt *in prayer,* shouting at the top of his lungs,

Stephen: Lord, do not hold this evil against them!

Those were his final words; then he fell asleep *in death.*

---

*S*tephen's sermon is one of the most profound ever preached. He weaves together the story of the Jews and the life of Jesus. The point of the message is that God pursues us despite our constant failure. The crucifixion of Jesus is the greatest of all of these failures.

Stephen affirms that through circumcision they have made themselves look like Jews, but their hearts and ears need circumcising as well. As you might expect, telling the Jewish leaders of the day to get their hearts and ears circumcised elicits a rather violent response. Stephen speaks the truth so that all might hear, including a man named Saul.

---

8 ¹⁻²Some devout men buried Stephen and mourned his passing with loud cries of grief. But Saul, *this young man who seemed to be supervising the whole violent event,* was pleased by Stephen's death. That very day, the *whole* church in Jerusalem began experiencing severe persecution. All *of the followers of Jesus*—except for the emissaries* themselves—fled to the countryside of Judea and Samaria *(the very places, you remember, where Jesus said His disciples would be His witnesses).* ³*Young* Saul went on a rampage—hunting the church, house after house, dragging both men and women to prison.

⁴All those who had been scattered *by the persecution* moved from place to place, *and wherever they went, they weren't afraid or silent. Instead,* they spread the message of Jesus.

⁵Philip, *for example,* headed north to the city of Samaria, and he told them the news of the Liberating King. ⁶The crowds were united in their desire to understand Philip's message. They not only listened with their ears, but they witnessed miraculous signs with their eyes. ⁷Unclean spirits cried out with loud screams as they were exorcised from people. Paralyzed people and lame people moved and walked in plain view. ⁸So the city was swept with joy.

⁹⁻¹¹There was a fellow named Simon who had a widespread and long-standing reputation as a sorcerer in Samaria. Everyone—not just poor or uneducated people, but also the city's elite—paid him great respect. Because he had amazed them with his magic, they thought, "This is a truly great man, full of the power of the God of Greatness." ¹²But they were even more impressed with Philip as he proclaimed the good news of the kingdom of God and the name of Jesus, the Liberating King. Both men and women received ceremonial washing*— ¹³and even Simon himself became a believer. After his ceremonial washing,* he shadowed Philip constantly, and he was as amazed as everyone else when he saw great and miraculous signs taking place.

¹⁴Meanwhile word had reached the Lord's emissaries* in Jerusalem that the message of God was welcomed in Samaria—*a land of half-breeds and heretics in the minds of many Judeans.* They sent Peter and John ¹⁵to pray for the Samaritans. They were especially eager to see if the new believers would receive the Holy Spirit ¹⁶because until this point they had been ceremonially washed* in the name of the Lord Jesus but had not experienced the Holy Spirit. ¹⁷When Peter and John laid hands on the people, the Holy Spirit did indeed come upon them *all.*

---

* 8:1-2 Literally, apostles
* 8:12 Literally, immersion, a rite of initiation and purification
* 8:13 Literally, immersion, a rite of initiation and purification
* 8:14 Literally, apostles
* 8:16 Literally, immersed, in a rite of initiation and purification

18Simon *watched all this closely.* He saw the Holy Spirit coming to the people when the apostles laid hands on them. So he *came to Peter and John and* offered them money.

Simon: 19I want to purchase this ability to confer the Holy Spirit on people through the laying on of my hands.

Peter: 20May your silver rot right along with you, Simon! To think the Holy Spirit is some kind of magic that can be procured with money! 21You aren't even close to being ready for this kind of ministry; your heart is not right with God. 22You need to turn from your past, and you need to pray that the Lord will forgive the evil intent of your heart. 23I can see deep bitterness has poisoned you, and wickedness has locked you in chains.

Simon: 24*Please*—you must pray to the Lord for me. I don't want these terrible things to be true of me.

25Peter and John preached to and talked *with the Samaritans* about the message of the Lord, and then they returned to Jerusalem, stopping in many other Samaritan villages along the way to proclaim the good news.
26A heavenly messenger brought this *short* message from the Lord to Philip *during his time preaching in Samaria:*

Messenger of the Lord: Leave Samaria. Go south to the Jerusalem-Gaza road.

That was the whole message. It was especially unusual because this road runs through the middle of uninhabited desert. 27But Philip got up, *left the excitement of Samaria,* and did as he was told to do. *Along this road, Philip saw a chariot in the distance. In the chariot was* a dignitary from Ethiopia (the treasurer for Queen Candace), *an African man* who had been castrated. He had gone north to Jerusalem to worship *at the Jewish temple,* 28and he was now *heading southwest* on his way home. He was seated in the chariot and was reading aloud from a scroll of the prophet Isaiah.
29Philip received another prompting from the Holy Spirit:

Holy Spirit: Go over to the chariot and climb on board.

30So he started running until he was even with the chariot. Philip heard the Ethiopian reading aloud and recognized the words from the prophet Isaiah.

Philip: Do you understand the meaning of what you're reading?

The Ethiopian: 31How can I understand it unless I have a mentor?

Then he invited Philip to sit in the chariot. 32Here's the passage he was reading from the Hebrew Scriptures:

Like a sheep, He was led to be slaughtered.
Like a lamb about to be shorn of its wool,
He was completely silent.
33He was humiliated, and He received no justice.
Who can describe His peers? *Who would treat Him this way?*
For they snuffed out His life.*

The Ethiopian: 34*Here's my first question.* Is the prophet describing his own situation, or is he describing someone else's *calamity?*

35That began a conversation in which Philip used the passage to explain the good news of Jesus. 36Eventually the chariot passed a body of water beside the road.

The Ethiopian: Since there is water here, is there anything that might prevent me

* 8:32-33 Isaiah 53:7-8

from being ceremonially washed* *and identified as a disciple of Jesus?*

Philip: [37If you believe in your heart that Jesus is the Liberating King, then nothing can stop you.

The Ethiopian said that he believed.]*

38He commanded the charioteer to stop the horses. Then Philip and the Ethiopian official walked together into the water. There Philip washed him ceremonially,* *initiating him as a fellow disciple.* 39When they came out of the water, Philip was immediately caught up by the Holy Spirit and taken from the sight of the Ethiopian, who climbed back into his chariot and continued on his journey, overflowing with joy. 40Philip found himself at a town called Azotus (*formerly the Philistine capital city of Ashdod, on the Mediterranean*), and from there he traveled north again, proclaiming the good news in town after town until he came to Caesarea.

9 Back to Saul—this fuming, raging, hateful man who wanted to kill every last one of the Lord's disciples: he went to the high priest *in Jerusalem* 2for authorization to purge all the synagogues in Damascus of followers of the way of Jesus.* His plan was to arrest and chain any of Jesus' followers—women as well as men—and transport them back to Jerusalem. 3He traveled north toward Damascus *with a group of companions.*

Imagine this: A light flashes from the sky around you. 4Saul falls to the ground at the sound of a voice.

The Lord: Saul, Saul, why are you attacking Me?
Saul: 5Lord, who are You?

Then he hears these words—*shocking, unexpected words that will change his life forever*—

The Lord: I am Jesus. I am the One you are attacking. 6Get up. Enter the city. You will learn there what you are to do.

7His other traveling companions just stand there, *paralyzed,* speechless because they too heard the voice, but there is nobody in sight. 8Saul rises to his feet, his eyes wide open, but he can't see a thing. So his companions lead their blind friend by the hand and take him into Damascus. 9He waits for three days—completely blind—and does not eat a bite or drink a drop of anything.

10Meanwhile, in Damascus a disciple named Ananias had a vision in which the Lord Jesus spoke to him.

The Lord: Ananias.
Ananias: Here I am, Lord.
The Lord: 11Get up and go to Straight Boulevard. Go to the house of Judas and inquire about a man from Tarsus, Saul by name. He is praying *to Me at this very instant.* 12He has had a vision—a vision of a man by your name who will come, lay hands on him, and heal his eyesight.
Ananias: 13Lord, *I know whom You're talking about.* I've heard rumors about this fellow. He*'s an evil man and* has caused great harm for Your special people in Jerusalem. 14I've heard that he has been authorized by the religious authorities to come here and chain everyone who associates with Your name.
The Lord: 15*None of that matters anymore!* Go! I have chosen him to be My instrument to bring My name far and wide—to outsiders, to kings, and to the people of Israel as well. 16I have much to show him, including how much he must suffer for My name.

17So Ananias went and entered the house *where Saul was staying.* He laid his hands on Saul and called to him.

* 8:36 Literally, immersed, in a rite of initiation and purification. The official may have been referring to the prohibition in Judaism from full participation in temple worship against men like himself, ones who had been castrated—a prohibition he would likely have encountered in this very visit to Jerusalem.
* 8:37 The earliest manuscripts omit verse 37.
* 8:38 Literally, immersed, in a rite of initiation and purification
* 9:2 The Christian movement

Ananias: Brother Saul, the Lord Jesus, who appeared to you on your way here, sent me so you can regain your sight and be filled with the Holy Spirit.

[18]At that instant, something like scales fell from Saul's eyes, and he could see. So he got up, received the ceremonial washing* *identifying him as a disciple,* [19]ate some food *(remember, he had not eaten for three days),* and regained his strength. He spent a lot of time with the disciples in Damascus over the next several days—*as their brother, not their persecutor.* [20]Then he went into the very synagogues he had intended to purge, proclaiming,

Saul: Jesus is God's Son, *our Liberating King*!

[21]Obviously this amazed everybody, and the buzz spread.

The People: Isn't he the man who caused so much trouble in Jerusalem for everyone identified with Jesus? Didn't he come here to arrest followers of Jesus and bring them in chains to the religious authorities? *Now he's switched sides and is preaching Jesus?*

[22]As time passed, Saul's confidence grew stronger and stronger, so much so that he debated with the Jews of Damascus and made an irrefutable case that Jesus is, in fact, the Liberating King.

[23]*They didn't like being confounded like this,* so, after several days, the Jews plotted to assassinate Saul. [24]But he learned of the plot. He knew they were keeping the city gates under constant surveillance, so they could follow and kill him when he left. [25]*To save Saul, the disciples came up with a plan of their own.* During the night, they put Saul in a basket and lowered him by ropes from an opening in the wall of the city *so he never even passed through the gates. Their plan worked,* [26]and he returned to Jerusalem.

Things didn't go well for Saul in Jerusalem, though. He tried to join the disciples there, but they didn't think he was sincere.

[27]*Only one person accepted Saul as a genuine disciple, and he was Barnabas, who, you remember, received this nickname because of his encouraging spirit.* Barnabas became Saul's advocate to the apostles. He told the whole story of what happened in Damascus, from Saul's vision and message from the Lord to his transformation into a confident proclaimer of the name of Jesus. [28]Finally they accepted Saul and gave him access to their community, and he continued to speak confidently in the name of the Lord. [29]He dialogued—and argued—with a group of Greek-speaking Jews. *That didn't go well either, because soon* they were plotting to kill him also. [30]His fellow believers helped him escape by bringing him to Caesarea and sending him to *his hometown,* Tarsus.

[31]And so the church enjoyed a period of peace and growth throughout the regions of Judea, Galilee, and Samaria. The disciples lived in deep reverence for the Lord, they experienced the strong comfort of the Holy Spirit, and their numbers increased.

[32]*Peter hadn't been idle during all this time.* He was having a number of amazing experiences of his own, traveling from group to group and visiting the various communities of believers. Once he came to a town called Lydda, *a border town between Samaria and Judea,* and met with God's special people there. [33]He visited a man named Aeneas. This poor fellow had been paralyzed for eight years, unable to leave his bed.

Peter: [34]Aeneas, Jesus the Liberating King heals you. Get up! Now you can make your own bed!

And immediately—he got up! [35]All the local residents—both of Lydda and nearby Sharon—saw Aeneas *healthy and strong again,* so they turned to the Lord.

[36]In *a nearby coastal city,* Joppa, there lived a disciple whose *Aramaic* name was Tabitha, or Dorcas in Greek. She was a good woman—devotedly doing good and

---

* 9:18 Literally, immersion, a rite of initiation and purification

giving to the poor. ³⁷While Peter was in Lydda, she fell sick and died. Her fellow disciples washed her body and laid her in an upstairs room. ³⁸They had heard Peter was nearby, so two of them went with an urgent message, "Please come to Joppa as soon as possible."

³⁹Peter went with them and immediately entered the room where the corpse had been placed. *It was quite a scene*—the widows *of the community* were crowded in the room, weeping, showing the various items of clothing that Dorcas had made for them.

⁴⁰Peter asked them to leave the room; then he got on his knees. He prayed *for a while* and then turned to her body.

Peter: Tabitha, get up!

She opened her eyes, saw Peter, and sat up. ⁴¹Giving her his hand, Peter lifted her up. Then he called in the other disciples—including the widows—and reintroduced them to their beloved friend. ⁴²The news of this miracle spread throughout the city, and many believed in the Lord. ⁴³Peter stayed in Joppa for some time as the guest of Simon, a tanner by profession.

10 *While Peter was in Joppa, another story was developing a day's journey to the north along the Mediterranean coast* in Caesarea. Cornelius, a Roman Centurion and a member of *a unit called* the Italian Cohort, lived there. ²Cornelius was *an outsider, but he was* a devout man—a God-fearing fellow with a God-fearing family. He consistently and generously gave to the poor, and he practiced constant prayer to God. ³About three o'clock one afternoon, he had a vision of a messenger of God. *Everything in the vision seemed so distinct, so real.*

Messenger of God: Cornelius!
Cornelius *(terrified)*: ⁴What is it, sir?
Messenger of God: God has heard your prayers, and He has seen your kindness to the poor. *God has taken notice of you.* ⁵⁻⁶Send men *south* to Joppa, to the house of a tanner named Simon. Ask to speak to a guest of his named Simon, but also called Peter. You'll find this house near the waterfront.

⁷After the messenger departed, Cornelius immediately called two of his slaves and a soldier under his command—an especially devout soldier. ⁸He told them the whole story and sent them to Joppa.

⁹Just as these men were nearing Joppa about noon the next day, Peter went up on the flat rooftop *of Simon the tanner's house.* He planned to pray, ¹⁰but he soon grew hungry. While his lunch was being prepared, Peter had a vision of his own—*a vision that linked his present hunger with what was about to happen:* ¹¹A rift opened in the sky and a wide container—something like a huge sheet suspended by its four corners—descended through the torn opening toward the ground. ¹²This container teemed with four-footed animals, creatures that crawl, and birds—*pigs, bats, lizards, snakes, frogs, toads, and vultures.*

A Voice: ¹³Get up, Peter! Kill! Eat!
Peter: ¹⁴No way, Lord! *These animals are disgusting! They're forbidden in the dietary laws of the Hebrew Scriptures! I've never eaten non-kosher foods like these before—not once in my life!*
A Voice: ¹⁵If God calls something permissible and clean, you must not call it forbidden and dirty!

¹⁶Peter saw this vision three times, but the third time, the container of animals flew up through the rift in the sky, *the rift healed,* ¹⁷and Peter was confused and unsettled as he tried to make sense of this strange vision.

At that very moment, *Peter heard the voices of* Cornelius's delegation, who had asked for directions to Simon's house, coming from the front gate.

Delegation: ¹⁸Is there a man named Simon, also called Peter, staying at this house?

19-20 Peter's mind was still racing about the vision when the voice of the Holy Spirit broke through his churning thoughts.

Holy Spirit: The three men who are searching for you have been sent by Me. So get up! Go with them. Don't hesitate *or argue.*

21Peter rushed downstairs to the men.

Peter: I'm the one you're seeking. Can you tell me why you've come?
Delegation: **22**We've been sent by *our commander and master,* Cornelius. He is a Centurion, and he is a good, honest man who worships your God. All the Jewish people speak well of him. A holy messenger told him to send for you so you would come to his home and he could hear your message.

23Peter extended hospitality to them and gave them lodging overnight. When they departed together the next morning, Peter brought some believers from Joppa.

24They arrived in Caesarea the next afternoon *just before three o'clock.* Cornelius had anticipated their arrival and had assembled his relatives and close friends *to welcome them.* **25**When Peter and Cornelius met, Cornelius fell at Peter's feet in worship, **26**but Peter helped him up.

Peter: Stand up, man! I am just a human being!

27They talked and entered the house to meet the whole crowd inside.

Peter: **28**You know *I am a Jew. I would never enter the home of outsiders like yourselves.* We Jews consider it a breach of divine law to associate, much less share hospitality, with outsiders. But God has shown me something in recent days: I should no longer consider any human beneath me or unclean. **29**That's why I made no objection when you invited me; rather, I came willingly. Now let me hear the story of why you invited me here.
Cornelius: **30**It was about this time of day

four days ago when I was here, in my house, praying the customary mid-afternoon prayer. Suddenly a man appeared out of nowhere. His clothes were dazzling white, and he stood directly in front of me **31**and addressed me: "Cornelius, your prayer has been heard and your kindness to the poor has been noticed by God. **32**God wants you to find a man in Joppa, Simon who is also called Peter, who is staying at the home of a tanner named Simon, near the seaside." **33**I wasted no time, *did just as I was told,* and you have generously accepted my invitation. So here we are, in the presence of God, ready to take in all that the Lord has told you to tell us.
Peter: **34**It is clear to me now that God plays no favorites, **35**that God accepts every person whatever his or her culture or ethnic background, that God welcomes all who revere Him and do right. **36***You already know that* God sent a message to the people of Israel; it was a message of peace, peace through Jesus, the Liberating King—who is King of all people. **37**You know this message spread through Judea, beginning in Galilee where John called people to be ritually cleansed.* **38**You know God identified Jesus as the uniquely chosen One by pouring out the Holy Spirit on Him, by empowering Him. You know Jesus went through the land doing good *for all* and healing all who were suffering under the oppression of the evil one, for God was with Him. **39**My friends and I stand as witnesses to all Jesus did in *the region of* Judea and *the city of* Jerusalem. The people of our capital city killed Him by hanging Him on a tree, **40**but God raised Him up on the third day and made it possible for us to see Him. **41**Not everyone was granted this privilege, only those of us whom God chose as witnesses. We actually ate and drank with Him after His resurrection. **42**He told us to spread His message to everyone and to tell them that He is the One whom God has chosen to be Judge, *to make a*

---

* 10:37 Literally, immersed, to show repentance

just assessment of all people—both living and dead. ⁴³All the prophets tell us about Him and assert that every person who believes in Jesus receives forgiveness of sins through His name.

> *T*he true gospel was becoming increasingly clear as the church spread and developed. What happened that day in Caesarea changed the face of Christianity forever. It built a bridge from Jews to Gentiles, from insiders to outsiders, and sent the community of Jesus on a journey that would take it beyond the kind of religious and cultural barriers that all people erect. The message of Jesus was not for the Jews alone but for all people of all time. But as we will see, this was a hard lesson and not everyone was eager to learn it.

⁴⁴Peter wasn't planning to stop at this point, but he could go no further because the Holy Spirit suddenly interrupted and came upon all the people who were listening. ⁴⁵⁻⁴⁶They began speaking in foreign languages (just as the Jewish disciples did on the Day of Pentecost), and their hearts overflowed in joyful praises to God. Peter's friends from Joppa—all of them Jewish, all circumcised—were stunned to see that the gift of the Holy Spirit was poured out even on outsiders.

Peter: ⁴⁷Can anyone give any good reason not to ceremonially wash* these people as fellow disciples? After all, it's obvious they have received the Holy Spirit just as we did on the Day of Pentecost.

⁴⁸So he had them washed ceremonially* in the name of Jesus, the Liberating King. The new disciples asked him to stay for several more days.

11 ¹⁻²By the time Peter and his friends from Joppa returned to Jerusalem, news about outsiders accepting God's message had already spread to the Lord's emissaries* and believers there. *Some of* the circumcised believers didn't welcome Peter with joy, but with criticism.

Circumcised Believers: ³*Why did you violate divine law by* associating with outsiders and sitting at the table with them for a meal? *This is an outrage!*

⁴Peter patiently told them what had happened, laying out in detail the whole story.

Peter: ⁵I was in Joppa, I was praying, and I fell into a trance. In my vision, something like a huge sheet descended from the sky as if it were being lowered by its four corners. It landed right in front of me. ⁶It was full of all kinds of four-footed creatures *that we would call unclean*— I could identify mammals, snakes, lizards, and birds. ⁷Then I heard a voice say, "Get up, Peter! Kill these creatures and eat them!" ⁸Of course, I replied, "No way, Lord! Not a single bite of forbidden, non-kosher food has ever touched my lips." ⁹But then the voice spoke from heaven a second time: "If God makes something clean, you must not call it dirty or forbidden." ¹⁰This whole drama was repeated three times, and then it was all pulled back up into the sky.

¹¹At that very second, three men arrived at the house where I was staying. They had come to me from Caesarea. ¹²The Holy Spirit told me I should go with them, that I shouldn't make any distinction *between them as Gentiles and us as Jews*. These six brothers *from Joppa* came with me, and, yes, we entered the man's home, *even though he was an outsider*.

¹³The outsider told us the story of how he had seen a heavenly messenger standing in his house who said, "Send to Joppa and bring back Simon, also called Peter, ¹⁴and he will give you a message

---

* 10:47 Literally, immerse, in a rite of initiation and purification
* 10:48 Literally, immersed, in a rite of initiation and purification
* 11:1-2 Literally, apostles

that will rescue both you and your household." 15Then I began to speak, and as I did, the Holy Spirit fell upon them—it was exactly as it had been with us at the beginning. 16Then I remembered what Jesus had said to us: "John ritually cleansed* with water, but you will be cleansed with the Holy Spirit."* 17So, if God gave them the same gift we were given when we believed in the Lord Jesus, the Liberating King, who was I to stand in God's way?

18There was no argument, only silence.

Circumcised Believers: Well then, we must conclude that God has given to the outsiders the opportunity to rethink their lives, turn to God,* and gain a new life.

And so they stopped criticizing and started praising God.
19*Remember the persecution that began after Stephen's execution?* The believers who were scattered *from Judea* because of the persecution following Stephen's stoning kept moving out, reaching Phoenicia, Cyprus, and Antioch. Until this time, they had only shared their message with Jews. 20Then some men from Cyprus and Cyrene who had become believers came to Antioch, and they began sharing the message of the Lord Jesus with some Greek *converts to Judaism.* 21The Lord was at work through them, and a large number *of these Greeks* became believers and turned to the Lord Jesus.
22Word of this new development came to the church in Jerusalem, and they sent Barnabas to Antioch *to investigate.* 23He arrived and saw God's grace in action there, so he rejoiced and urged them to remain faithful to the Lord, to maintain an enduring, unshakable devotion. 24This Barnabas truly was a good man, full of the Holy Spirit, full of faith. A very large number of people were brought to the Lord.
25Barnabas soon was off again—now to Tarsus to look for Saul. 26He found Saul and brought him back to Antioch. The two of them spent an entire year there, meeting with the church, teaching huge numbers of

people. It was there, in Antioch, where the term "Christian" was first used to identify disciples of Jesus.
27During that year, some prophets came north from Jerusalem to Antioch. 28A prophet named Agabus stood in a meeting and made a prediction by the Holy Spirit: there would be an expansive, terrible famine in the whole region during the reign of Claudius. 29*In anticipation of the famine,* the disciples determined to give an amount proportionate to their financial ability and create a relief fund for all the believers in Judea. 30They sent Barnabas and Saul to carry this fund to the elders *in Jerusalem.*

12 *Back in Jerusalem, hard times came to the disciples.* King Herod violently seized some who belonged to the church with the intention of mistreating them. 2He ordered James (brother of John) to be executed by the sword, *the first emissary to be martyred.* 3This move pleased Jewish public opinion, so he decided to arrest Peter also. During the holy festival of Unleavened Bread, 4he caught Peter and imprisoned him, assigning four squads of soldiers to guard him. He planned to publicly bring him to trial after the Passover holiday.
5During Peter's imprisonment, the church prayed constantly and intensely to God for his safety. 6*Their prayers were not answered,* until the night before Peter's execution.

Picture this event: Peter is sound asleep between two soldiers, double-chained, with still more guards outside the prison door watching for external intruders. 7Suddenly the cell fills with light: it is a messenger of the Lord manifesting himself. He taps Peter on the side, awakening him.

Messenger of the Lord: Get up, quickly.

The chains fall off Peter's wrists.

* 11:16 Literally, immersed, to show repentance
* 11:16 Acts 1:5
* 11:18 Literally, repent

Messenger of the Lord: [8]Come on! Put on your belt. Put on your sandals.

Peter puts them on *and just stands there.*

Messenger of the Lord: Pull your cloak over your shoulders. *Come on!* Follow me!

[9]Peter does so, but he is completely dazed. He doesn't think this is really happening—he assumes he is dreaming or having a vision. [10]They pass the first guard. They pass the second guard. They come to the iron gate that opens to the city. The gate swings open for them on its own, and they walk into a lane. Suddenly the messenger disappears.

[11]Peter finally realized all that had really happened.

Peter: *Amazing!* The Lord has sent His messenger to rescue me from Herod and the public spectacle *of my execution* which the Jews fully expected.

[12]Peter immediately rushed over to the home of a woman named Mary. (Mary's son, John Mark, *would eventually become an important associate of the apostles*.) A large group had gathered there to pray *for Peter and his safety.* [13]He knocked at the outer gate, and a maid, Rhoda, answered. [14]She recognized Peter's voice, but she was so overcome with excitement that she left him standing on the street and ran inside to tell everyone.

Rhoda: *Our prayers were answered!* Peter is at the front gate!

Praying Believers: [15]*Rhoda,* you're crazy!

Rhoda: *No! Peter's out there! I'm sure of it!*

Praying Believers: Well, maybe it's his *guardian* angel *or something.*

[16]All this time, Peter was still out in the street, knocking on the gate. *Finally* they came and let him in. *Of course,* the disciples were stunned, *and everyone was talking at once.* [17]Peter motioned for them to quiet down and then told them the amazing story of how the Lord engineered his escape.

> *O*n the night before his execution, Peter slept like a baby. Here he was, chained in a room full of soldiers, James's blood still moist on the ground, and though he could only assume this was his one last night before his own torturous death, he was not afraid. So peacefully did he rest, in fact, that the heavenly messenger had to prod him to wake up, and even while he was walking, he questioned if he was dreaming. Meanwhile, the believers had dropped everything and gathered together to pray. Was this the thought that kept Peter at peace? That his friends and family were on their knees all day appealing to God for him? Maybe. But certainly Peter trusted that God was in control. A church that started with a few people was now over 8,000, and God was redeeming the world through these people.

Peter: Could you please get word to James, *our Lord's brother,* and the other believers *that I'm all right*?

Then he left to find a safer place to stay.

[18]*Meanwhile, the soldiers were having a good night's sleep.* But when morning came and Peter was gone, there was a huge uproar among the soldiers. [19]Herod *sent troops* to find Peter, but he was missing. Herod interrogated the guards and ordered their executions. Peter headed down toward the coast to Caesarea, and he remained there.

[20]*King Herod had other problems at this time. There was a major political upheaval to deal with.* Herod was at odds with the populace of neighboring Tyre and Sidon, so the two cities sent a large group of representatives to meet with him. They won over one of Herod's closest associates, Blastus, the director of the treasury; then they pressured Herod to drop his grudge. Cooperation was important to the two

cities because they *were all major trading partners and* depended on Herod's territory for food. ²¹*They struck a deal, and* Herod came over *to ratify it.* Dressed in all his royal finery and seated high above them on a platform, he made a speech, ²²and the people of Tyre and Sidon interrupted with cheers to flatter him.

The People: This is the voice of a god! This is no mere mortal!

²³Herod should have given glory to the true God, *but since he vainly accepted their flattery,* that very day a messenger of the Lord struck him with an illness. *It was an ugly disease,* involving putrefaction and worms eating his flesh. Eventually he died. ²⁴*Through all this upheaval,* God's message spread to new frontiers and attracted more and more people. ²⁵Meanwhile, the time Barnabas and Saul spent *in Jerusalem* came to an end, and they reported back *to Antioch,* bringing along John, who was also called Mark. *You may remember that Barnabas and Saul helped deliver the relief fund to Jerusalem.* Now the three men returned to Antioch.*

13 The church in Antioch *had grown strong,* with many prophets and teachers: Barnabas, Simeon (a dark man *from Central Africa*), Lucius (from Cyrene *in North Africa*), Manaen (a member of Herod's governing council), and Saul. ²Once they were engaged in a time of worship and fasting when the Holy Spirit spoke to them, "Commission Barnabas and Saul to a project I have called them to accomplish." ³They fasted and prayed some more, laid their hands on the two selected men, and sent them off on their new mission. ⁴Having received special commissioning by the Holy Spirit, Barnabas and Saul went to nearby Seleucia, *on the coast.* Then they caught a ship to the island of Cyprus. ⁵At the city of Salamis, *on the east side of Cyprus,* they proclaimed the message of God in Jewish synagogues, assisted by John Mark. ⁶⁻⁷They went *westward from*

town to town, finally reaching Paphos on the western shore. There the proconsul, Sergius Paulus, an intelligent man, summoned Barnabas and Saul because he wanted to hear their message. At his side was an occult spiritualist and Jewish false prophet named Bar-Jesus ⁸or Elymas (which means "magician"). Elymas argued with Barnabas and Saul, trying to keep Sergius Paulus from coming to faith. ⁹Saul, who is also known as Paul, was suddenly full of the Holy Spirit. He stared directly into Elymas's face.

Paul: ¹⁰You're a son of the devil. You're an enemy of justice, you're full of lies, and you steal opportunities from others. Why do you insist on confusing and twisting the clear, straight paths of the Lord? ¹¹Hear this, *Elymas:* the Lord's hand is against you, and you will be *as* blind *as a bat* for a period of time, *beginning right now*!

At that instant, *it was as if* a mist came over Elymas and then total darkness. He stumbled around, groping for a hand so he could be led *back home.* ¹²When Sergius Paulus saw this happen, he came to faith and was attracted to and amazed by the teaching about the Lord. ¹³Paul and his entourage *boarded a ship and* set sail from Paphos. They traveled *north* to Perga in Pamphylia. John Mark, however, abandoned the mission and returned to Jerusalem. ¹⁴Paul and Barnabas continued from Perga to Pisidian Antioch, and on the Sabbath, they entered the synagogue and sat down. ¹⁵After the regular reading *of the Hebrew Scriptures—including* passages from the Law and the Prophets—the synagogue leaders sent a message to them: "Brothers, if you would like to give us some exhortation, please do so." ¹⁶Paul rose to his feet, offered a gesture of greeting, and began his message.

Paul: Israelites and other God-fearing people, please hear me. ¹⁷The God of the

* 12:25 Acts 11:29-30

Israelites chose our ancestors and helped them become a large population while they were living in Egypt many years ago. He displayed His great power by leading them out *of that powerful nation.* ¹⁸For about 40 years, He endured their constant complaining in the wilderness. ¹⁹He opened up some land for them in Canaan by destroying the seven nations living there, and that land became their inheritance for about 450 years. ²⁰They had tribal leaders* through the time of the prophet Samuel. ²¹Then they asked for a king, and God gave them one—Saul, son of Kish, of the tribe of Benjamin— who reigned for 40 years. ²²After God moved Saul aside, He made David king in his place. God had this to say about David: "I have found David, son of Jesse, to be a man after My own heart. He's the kind of king who will rule in ways that please Me."* ²³God has selected one of David's descendants as the long-promised Liberator of Israel. I am speaking of Jesus.

²⁴*Before Jesus arrived on the scene, His cousin* John was hard at work, proclaiming to all the people of Israel a ritual cleansing* pointing to a new direction in thought and life. ²⁵John's ministry climaxed when he said, "Who do you assume me to be? I am not the One *you're looking for.* No, but One is coming after me, One whose sandal thong I am unworthy to untie."* ²⁶My brothers, fellow descendants of our common father Abraham, and others here who fear God, we are the ones to whom God has sent this message of salvation.

²⁷But you know the people of Jerusalem and their leaders did not recognize Jesus. They didn't understand the words of the prophets that are read *in the synagogues* on Sabbath after Sabbath. As a result, they fulfilled the ancient prophecies by condemning Jesus. ²⁸Even though they could find no offense punishable by death, still they asked Pilate to execute Jesus. ²⁹When they carried out everything that had been foretold by the prophets, they took His body down from the tree and laid Him in a tomb. ³⁰But

that was not the end: God raised Him from the dead, ³¹and over a period of many days, He appeared to those who had been His companions from *the beginning of their journey in* Galilee until *its end in* Jerusalem. They are now witnesses to everyone. ³²We are here to bring you the good news of God's promise to our ancestors, ³³which He has now fulfilled for our children by raising Jesus. *Consider the promises fulfilled in Jesus.* The psalmist says, "You are My Son; today I have become Your Father."*

³⁴Elsewhere God promises that Jesus will rise and never return to death and corruption again: "I will make You the holy and faithful promises I made to David."* ³⁵Similarly, another psalm says, "You will not abandon Me to experience suffering of a miserable afterlife. Nor leave Me to rot alone."* ³⁶*We all know* David died and was reduced to dust after he served God's purpose in his generation; ³⁷these words *obviously* apply *not to David but* to the One God raised from death before suffering decay. ³⁸So you must realize, my brothers, that through this *resurrected* man forgiveness of sins is assured to you. ³⁹Through Jesus, everyone who believes is set free from all sins—sins which the law of Moses could not release you from. ⁴⁰In light of all this, be careful that you do not fulfill these words of the prophet *Habakkuk*:

⁴¹Look, you scoffers!
    Be shocked to death.
  For in your days I am doing a
      work,
    a work you will never believe,
        even if someone tells you
        plainly!*

---

* 13:20 In the Hebrew Scriptures, these leaders were called "judges."
* 13:22 1 Samuel 13:14
* 13:24 Literally, immersion, an act to show repentance
* 13:25 Luke 3:16
* 13:33 Psalm 2:7
* 13:34 Isaiah 55:3
* 13:35 Psalm 16:10
* 13:41 Habakkuk 1:5

42Paul and Barnabas prepared to leave *the synagogue*, but the people wanted to hear more and urged them to return the following Sabbath. 43As the people dispersed after the meeting, many Jews and converts to Judaism followed Paul and Barnabas. *Privately* Paul and Barnabas continued teaching them and urged them to remain steadfast in the grace of God. 44The next Sabbath, it seemed the whole city had gathered to hear the message of the Lord. 45But some of the Jewish leaders were jealous when they saw these huge crowds. They began to *argue with and* contradict Paul's message, as well as slander him. 46Paul and Barnabas together responded with great confidence.

Paul and Barnabas: *OK, then.* It was only right that we should bring God's message to you *Jewish people* first. But now, since you are rejecting our message and identifying yourselves as unworthy of eternal life, we are turning to the outsiders. 47The Lord has commanded us to do this. *Remember His words:*

I have appointed you a light to the nations beyond Israel,
so you can bring redemption to every corner of the earth.*

48*These words created two strong reactions.* The outsiders were thrilled and praised God's message, and all those who had been appointed for eternal life became believers. 49*Through them* the Lord's message spread through the whole region *of Cyprus.* 50But the Jewish leaders united the aristocratic religious women and the city's leading men in opposition to Paul and Barnabas, and soon they were persecuted and driven out of Cyprus. 51They simply shook the dust off their feet in protest and moved on to Iconium. 52The disciples *weren't intimidated at all; rather,* they were full of joy and the Holy Spirit.

14 The results in Iconium *were similar.* Paul and Barnabas began in the Jewish synagogue, bringing a great number of ethnic Jews and Greek converts to faith in Jesus. 2But the other Jews who wouldn't believe agitated the outsiders and poisoned their minds against the brothers. 3Paul and Barnabas stayed in Iconium for a long time, speaking with great confidence for the Lord. He confirmed the message of His grace by granting them the power to do signs and wonders. 4But *over time* the people were divided; some siding with the *unbelieving* Jews and some siding with the apostles. 5Finally the Jews and outsiders who opposed them joined forces and enlisted the political leaders in their plan to beat and stone Paul and Barnabas. 6They learned of the plan and escaped to Lystra and Derbe in Lycaonia, and the surrounding countryside, 7where they continued proclaiming the good news.

8In Lystra they met a man who had been crippled since birth; his feet were completely useless. 9He listened to Paul speak, and Paul could see in this man's face that he had faith to be healed.

Paul (shouting): 10Stand up on your own two feet, man!

The man jumped up and walked! 11When the crowds saw this, they started shouting in Lycaonian.

Crowd: The gods have come down to us! They've come in human form!

12They decided that Barnabas was Zeus and Paul was Hermes (since he was the main speaker). 13*Before they knew it,* the priest of Zeus, whose temple was prominent in that city, came to the city gates with oxen and garlands of flowers so the Lycaonians could offer sacrifices in worship *to Paul and Barnabas!* 14When they heard of this, Paul and Barnabas were beside themselves with frustration—they ripped their tunics *as an expression of disapproval* and rushed out into the crowd.

Paul and Barnabas (shouting): 15Friends! No! No! Don't do this! We're just humans like

* 13:47 Isaiah 49:6

all of you! *We're not here to be worshiped! We're here to bring you good news— good news that you should turn from these worthless forms of worship and instead serve the living God, the God who made the heaven and the earth and the sea and all that they contain.* ¹⁶Through all previous generations, God has allowed all the nations to follow their own customs and religions, ¹⁷but even then God revealed Himself by doing good to you—giving you rain for your crops and fruitful harvests season after season, filling your stomachs with food and your hearts with joy.

¹⁸In spite of these words, they were barely able to keep the crowds from making sacrifices to them.

> *W*e struggle to keep the focus on the one true God. When God uses men to bless the world, many mistakenly exalt those men to the place of God. This inevitably leads to pain and disappointment. Paul and Barnabas did the right thing by shouting as loudly as possible, "We are only men!" It is time for many leaders and celebrities to follow their example, root out the religious hero worship, claim our humanity, and start sharing our own struggles—sin, depression, despair—to remind people we are all alike.

¹⁹Then *unbelieving* Jews came from Antioch and Iconium and *incited the crowds against the Lord's emissaries*. The crowds turned on Paul, stoned him, dragged him out of the city, and left him there, thinking he was dead. ²⁰As the disciples gathered around him, he suddenly rose to his feet and returned to the city. The next day he and Barnabas left for Derbe. ²¹After they proclaimed the good news there and taught many disciples, they returned to *some of the cities they had recently visited*—Lystra, Iconium, and

Antioch *in Pisidia*. ²²In each place, they brought strength to the disciples, encouraging them to remain true to the faith.

Paul and Barnabas: We must go through many persecutions as we enter the kingdom of God.

²³In each church, they would appoint leaders, pray and fast together, and entrust them to the Lord in whom they had come to believe.

²⁴They then passed through Pisidia and came to Pamphylia. ²⁵They preached their message in Perga and then went to the port of Attalia. ²⁶There they set sail for Antioch, where they were first entrusted to the grace of God for the mission they had now completed. ²⁷They called the church together when they arrived and reported all God had done with *and through* them, how God had welcomed outsiders through the doorway of faith. ²⁸They stayed with the disciples *in Antioch* for quite a while.

15 *Their peace was disturbed, however,* when certain Judeans came with this teaching: "Unless you are circumcised according to Mosaic custom, you cannot be saved." ²Paul and Barnabas argued against this teaching and debated with the Judeans vehemently, so the church selected several people—including Paul and Barnabas—to travel to Jerusalem to dialogue about this issue with the apostles and elders there. ³The church sent them on their way. They passed through Phoenicia and Samaria, stopping to report to the groups of believers there that outsiders were now being converted. This brought great joy to them all. ⁴Upon arrival in Jerusalem, the church, the apostles, and the elders welcomed them warmly, and they reported all they had seen God do. ⁵But there were some believers present who belonged to the sect of the Pharisees. They stood up and asserted,

Pharisees: *No, this is not acceptable.* These people must be circumcised, and we must require them to keep the whole Mosaic law.

⁶The apostles and elders met privately to discuss how this issue should be resolved. ⁷There was a lot of debate, and finally Peter stood up.

Peter: My brothers, you all know that in the early days *of our movement* God decided that I should be the one through whom the first outsiders would hear the good news and become believers. ⁸God knows the human heart, and He showed approval of their hearts by giving them the Holy Spirit just as He did for us. ⁹In cleansing their hearts by faith, God has made no distinction between them and us. ¹⁰So it makes no sense to me that some of you are testing God by burdening His disciples with a load that neither our forefathers nor we have been able to carry. ¹¹No, we all believe that we will be liberated through the grace of the Lord Jesus—they also will be rescued in the same way.

¹²There was silence among them while Barnabas and Paul reported all the miraculous signs and wonders God had done through them among outsiders. ¹³When they finished, James spoke.

James: My brothers, hear me. ¹⁴Simon *Peter* reminded us how God first included outsiders in His favor, taking people from among them for His name. ¹⁵This resonates with the words of the prophets:

¹⁶"After this, I will return
        and rebuild the house of David,
            which has fallen into ruins.
        From its wreckage I will rebuild it;
¹⁷ So all the nations may seek the
            Eternal One—
        including every person among
            the outsiders who have been
            called by My name."*
    This is the word of the Lord,
        ¹⁸who has been revealing
            these things since ancient
            times.*

¹⁹So here is my counsel: we should not burden these outsiders who are turning to God. ²⁰We should instead write a letter, instructing them to abstain from four things: first, things associated with idol worship; second, sexual immorality; third, food killed by strangling; and fourth, blood. ²¹My reason for these four exceptions is that in every city there are Jewish communities where, for generations, the laws of Moses have been proclaimed, and on every Sabbath, Moses is read in synagogues everywhere.

²²This seemed like a good idea to the apostles, the elders, and the entire church. They commissioned men from among them and sent them to Antioch with Paul and Barnabas. They sent two prominent men among the believers, Judas (also known as Barsabbas) and Silas, ²³to deliver this letter:

The brotherhood, including the apostles and elders in Jerusalem, send greetings to the outsider believers in Antioch, Syria, and Cilicia. ²⁴We have heard that certain people from among us—without authorization from us—have said things that, in turn, upset you and unsettle your minds. ²⁵We have decided unanimously to choose and send two representatives, along with our beloved Barnabas and Paul, ²⁶who, *as you know,* have risked their lives for our Lord Jesus, the Liberating King. ²⁷These representatives, Judas and Silas, will confirm verbally what you will read in this letter. ²⁸It has seemed good to the Holy Spirit and to us to keep you free from all burdens except these four: ²⁹abstain from anything sacrificed to idols, from blood, from food killed by strangling, and from sexual immorality. Avoid these things, and you will be just fine. Farewell.

* 15:16-17 Amos 9:11-12
* 15:17-18 Isaiah 45:21

³⁰So the men were sent to Antioch. When they arrived, they gathered the community together and read the letter. ³¹The community rejoiced at the resolution to the controversy. ³²Judas and Silas, being prophets themselves, offered lengthy encouragements to strengthen the believers. ³³After some time there, *their mission was complete so* the leaders in Antioch released Judas and Silas to return *to Jerusalem* with a blessing of peace. [³⁴But after some thought Silas decided to remain behind.]* ³⁵Paul and Barnabas stayed in Antioch, where they teamed with many others to teach and preach the message of the Lord.

³⁶Some days later, Paul proposed another journey to Barnabas.

Paul: Let's return and visit the believers in each city where we preached the Lord's message last time to see how they're doing.

³⁷Barnabas agreed and wanted to bring John Mark along, ³⁸but Paul felt that was a mistake since John Mark had abandoned them in Pamphylia and hadn't finished the previous mission. ³⁹Their difference of opinion was so heated that they decided not to work together anymore. Barnabas took John Mark and sailed to Cyprus, ⁴⁰while Paul chose Silas *as his companion.* The believers *in Antioch* commissioned him for this work, entrusting him to the grace of the Lord. ⁴¹They traveled through Syria and Cilicia to strengthen the churches there.

16 ¹⁻³When Paul reached Derbe and Lystra, he invited a disciple named Timothy to join him *and Silas.* Timothy had a good reputation among the believers in Lystra and Iconium, *but there was a problem*: although Timothy's mother was a believing Jew, his father was Greek, *which meant Timothy was uncircumcised.* Because the Jewish people of those cities knew he was the son of a Greek man, Paul felt it would be best for Timothy to be circumcised before proceeding.

⁴Leaving there, *now accompanied by Timothy*, they delivered to the churches in each town the decisions and instructions given by the apostles and elders in Jerusalem. ⁵The churches were strengthened in the faith by their visit and kept growing in numbers on a daily basis.

⁶They sensed the Holy Spirit telling them not to preach their message in Asia at this time, so they traveled through Phrygia and Galatia. ⁷They came near Mysia and planned to go into Bithynia, but again, they felt restrained from doing so by the Spirit of Jesus. ⁸So they bypassed Mysia and went down to Troas. ⁹That night Paul had a vision in which a Macedonian man was pleading with him.

Macedonian Man: Come over to Macedonia! Come help us!

¹⁰This vision convinced us all—*I should add that I, Luke, had joined Paul, Silas, and Timothy by this time*—that God was calling us to bring the good news to that region.

¹¹We set sail from the port city of Troas, first stopping in Samothrace, then the next day in Neapolis, ¹²finally arriving in Philippi, a Roman colony and one of Macedonia's leading cities. We stayed in Philippi for several days. ¹³On the Sabbath day, we went outside the city walls to the nearby river, assuming that *some Jewish* people might be gathering for prayer. We found a group of women there, so we sat down and spoke to them. ¹⁴One of them, Lydia, was *a business woman* originally from Thyatira. She made a living *buying and* selling fine purple fabric. She was a true worshiper of God and listened to Paul *with special interest.* The Lord opened her heart to take in the message with enthusiasm. ¹⁵She and her whole household were ceremonially washed.*

* 15:34 The earliest manuscripts omit verse 34.
* 16:15 Literally, immersed, in a rite of initiation and purification

Lydia: If you believe I'm truly faithful to the Lord, please, you must come and stay at my home.

We couldn't turn down her invitation.

¹⁶One day, as we were going to the place set aside for prayer, we encountered a slave girl. She made a lot of money for her owners as a fortune-teller, assisted by some sort of occult spirit. ¹⁷She began following us.

Slave Girl (shouting): These men are slaves like me, but slaves of the Most High God! They will proclaim to you the way of liberation!

¹⁸The next day as we passed by, she did the same thing—and again on the following days. One day Paul was really annoyed, so he turned and spoke to the spirit that was enslaving her.

Paul: I order you in the name of Jesus, the Liberating King: Come out of her!

It came right out. ¹⁹But when her owners realized she would be worthless now as a fortune-teller, they grabbed Paul and Silas, dragged them into the open market area, and presented them to the authorities.

Slave Owners: ²⁰These men are troublemakers, disturbing the peace of our great city. They are from some Jewish sect, ²¹and they promote foreign customs that violate our Roman standards of conduct.

²²The crowd joined in with insults and insinuations, prompting the city officials to strip them naked *in the public square* so they could be beaten with rods. ²³They were flogged mercilessly and then were thrown into a prison cell. The jailer was ordered to keep them under the strictest supervision. ²⁴The jailer complied, first restraining them in ankle chains, then locking them in the most secure cell in the center of the jail.

²⁵*Picture this:* It's midnight. *In the darkness of their cell,* Paul and Silas—*after sur-* viving the severe beating—aren't moaning and groaning; they're praying and singing hymns to God. The prisoners *in adjoining cells are wide awake,* listening to them pray and sing. ²⁶Suddenly the ground begins to shake, and the prison foundations begin to crack. You can hear the sound of jangling chains and the squeak of cell doors opening. Every prisoner realizes that his chains have come unfastened. ²⁷The jailer wakes up and runs into the jail. His heart sinks as he sees the doors have all swung open. He is sure his prisoners have escaped, *and he knows this will mean death for him.* So he *decides to do the deed himself and* pulls out his sword to commit suicide. ²⁸At that moment, Paul *sees what is happening and* shouts out at the top of his lungs,

Paul: *Wait, man!* Don't harm yourself! We're all here! *None of us has escaped.*

²⁹The jailer sends his assistants to get some torches and rushes into the cell of Paul and Silas. He falls on his knees before them, trembling. ³⁰Then he brings them outside.

Jailer: Gentlemen, please tell me, what must I do to be liberated?
Paul and Silas: ³¹Just believe—believe in the ultimate King, Jesus, and not only will you be rescued, but your whole household will as well.

³²⁻³⁴The jailer brings them to his home, and they have a long conversation with the man and his family. Paul and Silas explain the message of Jesus to them all. The man washes their wounds and *feeds them,* then they ceremonially wash* the man and his family. The night ends with Paul and Silas in the jailer's home, sharing a meal together, the whole family rejoicing that they have come to faith in God.

³⁵At dawn the city officials send the police *to the jailer's home* with a command: "Let those men go free."

---

* 16:32-34 Literally, immerse, in a rite of initiation and purification

Jailer: ³⁶The city officials have ordered me to release you, so you may go now, in peace.

Paul (*loud enough that the police can hear*): ³⁷Just a minute. This is unjust. We've been *stripped naked*, beaten in public, and thrown into jail, all without a trial of any kind. Now they want to secretly release us as if nothing happened? No way: we're Roman citizens—*we shouldn't be treated like this*! If the city officials want to release us, then they can come and tell us to our faces.

³⁸The police report back to the city officials, and when they come to the part about Paul and Silas being Roman citizens, the officials turn pale with fear. ³⁹They rush to the jail in person and apologize. They personally escort Paul and Silas from their cell and politely ask them to leave the city. ⁴⁰Paul and Silas oblige—after stopping at Lydia's home to gather with the brothers and sisters there and give them parting words of encouragement.

*P*aul and Silas planned to keep a low profile because it was clear that preaching the gospel openly was not going to advance the cause of the Liberating King. But in the course of their travels, Paul got annoyed. He was tired of the recurring mantra of this evil spirit living in a slave girl. So he performed his first miracle in the area by casting out this evil spirit, which set off a totally unexpected chain of events bringing them into the city court to be beaten before the crowds. This would seem to be the start of a very bad day. I can only imagine Silas saying, "Paul, what were you doing? Is your aggravation with this wandering girl worth all this trouble?" But they neither fought nor despaired; instead, they sang, prayed to God, and loved their captors. Paul and Silas demonstrated that we are not easily distracted or depressed as long as serving God is our priority.

17 After *leaving Philippi and* passing through Amphipolis and Apollonia, Paul and Silas came to Thessalonica. There was a Jewish synagogue there. ²⁻³As he had done in other cities, Paul attended the synagogue and presented arguments, based on the Hebrew Scriptures, that the Liberating King had to suffer and rise from the dead.

Paul: Who is this suffering and rising Liberator I am proclaiming to you? He is Jesus.

He came back the next two Sabbaths—repeating the same pattern. ⁴Some of the *ethnically Jewish* people *from the synagogue* were persuaded and joined Paul and Silas. Even more devout Greeks *who had affiliated with Judaism* came to believe—along with quite a few of the city's leading women. ⁵⁻⁶*Seeing this movement growing,* the unconvinced Jewish people became protective and angry. They found some ruffians hanging out in the marketplaces and convinced them to help start a riot. Soon a mob formed, *and the whole city was seething with tension.* The mob was *going street by street,* looking for Paul and Silas—who were nowhere to be found. Frustrated, when the mob came to the house of a man named Jason, *now known as a believer,* they grabbed him and some other believers they found there and dragged them to the city officials.

Mob: These people—they're *political agitators* turning the world upside down! *They're stirring up rebellion everywhere;* they've come here to our fine city, ⁷and this man, Jason, has given them sanctuary *and made his house a base for their operations. We want to expose their real intent:* they are trying to overturn Caesar's sensible decrees. They're saying that Jesus is king, *not Caesar!*

⁸Of course, this disturbed the crowd at large and the city officials especially, ⁹so they demanded bail from Jason and the others before releasing them.

¹⁰The believers waited until dark and then sent Paul and Silas off to Berea. When they arrived, they *repeated their usual pattern by* going to the synagogue *to proclaim Jesus from the Hebrew Scriptures.* ¹¹The Jewish people here were more receptive than they had been in Thessalonica. They warmly and enthusiastically welcomed the message and then, day by day, would check for themselves to see if what they heard *from Paul and Silas* was truly in harmony with the Hebrew Scriptures. ¹²Many of them were convinced, and the new believers included—*as in Thessalonica*—quite a few of the city's leading Greek women and important men also. ¹³Reports got back to Thessalonica that Paul and Silas were now spreading God's message in Berea; the Jewish people who had incited the riot in Thessalonica quickly came to Berea to do the same once again. ¹⁴⁻¹⁵The believers sent Paul away. A small group escorted him, first to the coast, and then all the way to Athens. Silas and Timothy, however, remained in Berea. Later they received instructions from Paul to join him in Athens as soon as possible.

¹⁶So Paul found himself alone for some time in Athens. He would walk through the city, feeling deeply frustrated about the abundance of idols there. ¹⁷*As in the previous cities*, he went to the synagogue. Once again, he engaged in debate *about Jesus* with both ethnic Jews and devout *Greek-born* converts *to Judaism. But this time, he didn't limit himself to the synagogue.* He would even wander around in the marketplace, speaking with anyone he happened to meet. ¹⁸Eventually he got into a debate with some Epicurean and Stoic philosophers. Some were dismissive from the start.

Philosophers: What's this fast-talker trying to pitch?
Others: He seems to be advocating the gods of distant lands.

They said this because of what Paul had been preaching about Jesus and the resurrection.* ¹⁹⁻²¹This stirred their curiosity, because the favorite pastime of Athenians

(including foreigners who had settled there) was conversation about new and unusual ideas. So they brought him to the *rock outcropping known as the* Areopagus, *where Athens' intellectuals regularly gathered for debate*, and they invited him to speak.

Athenians: May we understand this new teaching of yours? It is intriguingly unusual. We would love to know its meaning.
Paul: ²²Athenians, *I am a new visitor to your beautiful city. As I have walked your streets, I have observed your strong and diverse religious ethos. You truly are a religious people.* ²³I have stopped again and again to examine carefully the religious statues and inscriptions that fill your city. On one such altar, I read this inscription: "TO AN UNKNOWN GOD." I am not here to tell you about a strange foreign deity, but about this One whom you already worship, though without full knowledge. ²⁴This is the God who made the universe and all it contains, the God who is *the Caesar*, the King, of all heaven and all earth. It would be illogical to assume that a God of this magnitude could possibly be contained in any man-made structure, no matter how majestic. ²⁵Nor would it be logical to think that this God would need human beings to provide Him with food and shelter— after all, He Himself would have given to humans everything they need—life, breath, *food, shelter, and so on.* ²⁶*This is the only universal God, the One who made all of us, wherever we now live, whatever our nationality or culture or religion.* This God made us in all our diversity from one original person, allowing each culture to have its own time to develop, giving each its own place to live and thrive in its distinct ways. ²⁷*His purpose in all this was* that people *of every culture and religion* would search for this ultimate God, grope for Him *in the darkness, as it*

---

* 17:18 The philosophers misunderstand Paul's message. They think he is talking about two deities: Jesus and Anastasis (the Greek word for "resurrection").

were, hoping to find Him. Yet, in truth, God is not far from any of us. [28]For *you know the saying*, "We live in God; we move in God; we exist in God." And still another said, "We are indeed God's children." [29]*Since this is true*, since we are indeed offspring of God's creative act, we shouldn't think of the Deity as our own artifact, something made by our own hands—as if this great, universal, ultimate Creator were simply a combination of elements like gold, silver, and stone. [30]No, God has patiently tolerated this kind of ignorance in the past, but now God says it is time to rethink our lives *and reject these unenlightened assumptions*. [31]He has fixed a day of accountability, when the whole world—*including every culture and religion*—will be justly evaluated by a new, higher standard: *not by a statue*, but by a living man. God selected this man and made Him credible to all by raising Him from the dead.

[32]When they heard that last phrase about resurrection from the dead, some shook their heads and scoffed, but others were even more curious.

Others: We would like you to come and speak to us again.

[33]Paul left at that point, [34]but some people followed him and came to faith, including one from Areopagus named Dionysius, a *prominent* woman named Damaris, and others.

*T*his exchange is the most potent example of cross-cultural evangelism in the Bible. Notice how Paul provokes his audience to think and invites them to pursue God, but he does not attempt to summarize the gospel in simple propositions or acronyms. He connects their culture with the truth of the gospel and the beauty of the person who is Jesus. After that, it's the job of the Holy Spirit. How can we follow this example?

18 From Athens, Paul traveled to Corinth *alone*. [2]He found a Jewish man there named Aquila, originally from Pontus. Aquila and his wife Priscilla had recently come to Corinth from Italy because Claudius had banished all Jews from Rome. Paul visited them *in their home* [3]and discovered they shared the same trade of tent making. He then became their long-term guest and joined them in their tentmaking business. [4]Each Sabbath he would engage both Jews and Greeks in debate in the synagogue in an attempt to persuade them of his message. [5]Eventually Silas and Timothy left Macedonia and joined him in Corinth. They found him fully occupied by proclaiming the message, testifying to the Jewish people that their Liberator was Jesus. [6]Eventually, though, some of them stopped listening and began insulting him. He shook the dust off his garments in protest.

Paul: OK. I've done all I can for you. You are responsible for your own destiny before God. From now on, I will bring the good news to the outsiders!

[7]He walked out of the synagogue and went next door to the home of *an outsider*, Titius Justus, who worshiped God. [8]*Paul formed a gathering of believers there that included* Crispus (the synagogue leader) and his whole household and many other Corinthians, who heard Paul, believed, and were ceremonially washed.* [9]One night Paul had a vision in which he heard the Lord's voice.

The Lord: Do not be afraid, Paul. Speak! Don't be silent! [10]I am with you and no one will lay a finger on you to harm you. I have many in this city who are already My people.

[11]*After such turmoil in previous cities*, these words encouraged Paul to extend his stay in Corinth, teaching the message of God among them for a year and six months.

*18:8 Literally, immersed, in a rite of initiation and purification

Have you ever been frustrated by arguments and bickering with your religious friends? Maybe your frustration is a sign that you are devoting your energies in the wrong places. Like Paul, your frustration could be God pushing you into new areas or new ministries. This man kept a smile on his face when he was stripped, beaten, and imprisoned, but religious bickering brought him to his wits' end. There is nothing more depressing than religious systems corrupted by arrogance and legalism. On the other hand, the greatest joys in life may be found when we passionately pursue the dangerous mission of the Liberating King.

¹²During this time, some Jews organized an attack on Paul and made formal charges against him to Gallio, the proconsul of Achaia.

Jews: ¹³This man is convincing people to worship God in ways that contradict our Hebrew Scriptures.

Paul was about to speak, but Gallio spoke first.

Gallio: ¹⁴Look, if this were some serious crime, I would accept your complaint as a legitimate legal case, ¹⁵but this is just more of your typical Jewish squabbling about trivialities in your sacred literature. I have no interest in getting dragged into this kind of thing.

¹⁶So he *threw out their case and* drove them away from his bench. ¹⁷They *were furious and* seized Sosthenes, the synagogue official; then they beat him in front of the tribunal. Gallio just ignored them.

¹⁸At the end of 18 months, Paul said good-bye to the believers in Corinth. He wanted to travel *to the east and south* to Syria by ship, so, accompanied by Priscilla and Aquila, he went to the nearby port city of Cenchrea, where he fulfilled a vow he had made by cutting his hair. ¹⁹The three of them sailed east to Ephesus where Paul would leave Priscilla and Aquila. Paul again went to the synagogue where he dialogued with the Jews. ²⁰They were receptive and invited him to stay longer. But he *politely* declined.

Paul: ²¹⁻²²If God wills, I'll return at some point.

He caught a ship bound *south and east* for Caesarea by the sea. There he went up for a brief visit with the believers in the church at Jerusalem; then he headed north to Antioch. ²³He spent considerable time there and then left again, visiting city after city throughout Galatia and Phrygia, strengthening the disciples in each place.

²⁴Meanwhile, back in Ephesus, a Jew named Apollos *made contact with the community of believers.* He had been raised in Alexandria, *Egypt, a place where Jewish intellectuals were seeking to integrate Greek philosophy with their faith.* Apollos was eloquent and well educated in the Hebrew Scriptures. ²⁵He was partially instructed in the way of the Lord, and he added to his native eloquence a burning enthusiasm to teach about Jesus. He taught accurately what he knew, *but he had only understood part of the good news*, specifically the ritual cleansing* preached by John, *the forerunner of Jesus.* ²⁶So, when Priscilla and Aquila heard him speak boldly in the synagogue, *they discerned both his gift and his lack of full understanding.* They took him aside and in private explained the way of God to him more accurately and fully. ²⁷He wanted to head west into Achaia, *where Paul had recently been*, to preach there. The believers encouraged him to do so and sent a letter instructing the *Greek* disciples to welcome him. Upon his arrival, he was of great help to all in Achaia who had, by the grace of God, become believers. ²⁸This gifted speaker publicly demonstrated, based on the Hebrew Scriptures, that the promised Liberating King is Jesus. Then, when the Jews there raised counterarguments, he refuted them with great power.

* 18:25 Literally, immersion, an act to show repentance

19 [1,7]While Apollos was in Corinth, Paul's overland journey brought him back to Ephesus. He encountered a group of about a dozen disciples there.*

Paul: [2]Did you receive the Holy Spirit when you became believers?

John's Disciples: We've never heard about the Holy Spirit.

Paul: [3]Well then, what kind of ceremonial washing* did you receive?

John's Disciples: We received the ritual cleansing* that John taught.

Paul: [4]John taught the truth—that people should be ritually cleansed* with renewed thinking and turn toward God. But he also taught that the people should believe in the One whose way he was preparing, that is, Jesus.

[5]As soon as they heard this, they were ceremonially washed,* this time in the name of our Lord Jesus. [6]When Paul laid his hands on them, the Holy Spirit came upon them *in the same way the original disciples experienced at Pentecost*: they spoke in tongues and prophesied.

*B*oth Apollos and this small band of John's disciples heard an incomplete gospel. Our calling is not only to bring the gospel to those who have never heard, but also to expand the truth to those who understand only partial truth. If we see people as they truly are—on a journey to know God— we realize that no one has "arrived." Everyone has something more to learn because we see the truth so dimly.

[8]For three months, Paul continued his standard practice: he went *week by week* to the synagogue, speaking with great confidence, arguing with great persuasiveness, proclaiming the kingdom of God. [9-10]*Once again*, some members of the synagogue refused to believe and insulted the Way* publicly before the whole synagogue community. Paul withdrew and took those with

him who had become disciples. For the next two years, he used the public lecture hall of Tyrannus, presenting the Word of the Lord every day, debating with all who would come. As a result, everyone in the region, whether Jews or Greeks, heard the message. [11]Meanwhile, God did amazing miracles through Paul. [12]People would take a handkerchief or article of clothing that had touched Paul's skin and bring it to their sick *friends or relatives*, and the patients would be cured of their diseases or released from the evil spirits that oppressed them.

[13-14]Some itinerant Jewish exorcists *noticed Paul's success in this regard, so they* tried to use the name of Jesus, the King, in an exorcism they were performing.

Imagine this: There are seven of them, all sons of a Jewish chief priest named Sceva, *gathered around a demonized man in a house.*

One of the Jewish Exorcists: I command you to depart, by the Jesus proclaimed by Paul!

Evil Spirit: [15]Jesus I know. Paul I know. But who are you?

[16]Then the man leaps up, attacks them all, rips off their clothing, and beats them so badly that they run out of the house stark naked and covered in bruises.

[17]Word of this strange event spread throughout Ephesus among both Jews and Greeks. Everyone was shocked and realized that the name of Jesus was indeed powerful and praiseworthy. [18]As a result, a number of people involved *in various occult practices* came to faith. They confessed their secret practices and

* 19:1,7 Verses 1 and 7 have been combined to help the reader understand the continuity of the passage.
* 19:3 Literally, immersion, a rite of initiation and purification
* 19:3 Literally, immersion, an act to show repentance
* 19:4 Literally, immersed, to show repentance
* 19:5 Literally, immersed, in a rite of initiation and purification
* 19:9-10 The Christian movement (9:2)

rituals. [19]Some of them had considerable libraries about their magic arts; they piled up their books and burned them publicly. Someone estimated the value of the books to be 50,000 silver coins. [20]Again, word spread, and the message of the Lord overcame resistance and spread powerfully.

[21]Eventually Paul felt he should move on again. The Holy Spirit confirmed that he should first travel through Macedonia and Achaia and then return to Jerusalem.

Paul: I must eventually see Rome.

[22]So he sent Timothy and Erastus, two of his helpers, ahead to Macedonia while he stayed a while longer in Asia. [23]It was during this time that a major incident occurred involving the Way. [24]*This time Jews had not caused the disturbance, but outsiders, and in particular*, an idol maker named Demetrius. He had a profitable business, for himself and for others, making silver shrines for Artemis (*also known as Diana by the Romans), one of the deities worshiped in Ephesus.*

[25]*Picture this:* Demetrius calls a meeting of all the artisans who are similarly employed in idol making. *Everyone in the idol industry comes together.*

Demetrius: Men, we are all colleagues in this fine line of work. We're making a good living doing what we're doing. But we'd better wake up, or we're all going to go broke. [26]You've heard about this fellow Paul. Here in Ephesus, he's already convinced a large number of people to give up using idols. He tells them that our products are worthless. He's been doing this same kind of thing almost everywhere in Asia. [27]It's bad enough that he is slandering our fine and honorable profession, *but do you see where this will lead?* If his lies catch on, the temple of Artemis itself will be called a fraud. The great goddess of our region, the majestic deity who is revered here in Asia and around the world, will be disgraced.

[28]The crowd goes wild with rage. They start chanting.

Crowd: Great is Artemis of the Ephesians! *Great is Artemis of the Ephesians!*

[29]Soon the whole city is filled with confusion, and a mob forms. They find Paul's Macedonian travel companions, Gaius and Aristarchus, and drag them to the theater. [30]Paul wants to go confront the crowd *and protect his friends*, but the disciples hold him back. [31]Even some provincial officials of Asia who are friendly to Paul send him an urgent message, warning him to stay away from the theater.

[32]Enraged voices are shouting *on top of each other*, some saying one thing, some saying something else. The crowd is completely out of control. Most of the people don't even know what caused the commotion in the first place. [33]Some of the Jewish people push a man named Alexander to the front of the crowd, hoping he can calm the disturbance. He raises his hands to silence the crowd and gets a few sentences out; [34]but then the crowd realizes he's a Jew, and once again they start chanting.

Crowd: Great is Artemis of the Ephesians!

For two solid hours they keep the chant going. [35]Finally the town clerk manages to calm the crowd.

Town Clerk: My fellow citizens of Ephesus, everyone in the world knows that our great city is the caretaker of the temple of Artemis! Everyone knows that we are the home of the great statue that fell from heaven! [36]Our status as the economic center of the idolmaking industry is not in danger, so please, calm down. Don't do anything rash. [37]The men whom you have seized aren't temple robbers, nor have they blasphemed our great goddess. [38]If Demetrius and the artisans who share his important trade have a legal complaint, don't bring it here to the theater; take it to the courts—they're open today. [39]If you need to charge someone with a crime or launch an inquiry, take the matter to the regional judges. ⁴⁰We need to do this according to regulations, or we'll all be charged with rioting. This kind of behavior can't be justified.

⁴¹So he succeeds in dispersing the crowd.

The message of Jesus not only has the power to annihilate economic supremacy, but it can also turn the world upside down in the process. So when the kingdom of God comes, it is a good time to fine-tune your business plan, because you will not profit from dishonesty, manipulation, or selfishness. In the kingdom of God, a worker is always paid a wage worthy of his work: anyone who works will have enough to eat, and no one will be left out of the profitable bounty of God. May the Kingdom come.

20 As soon as the uproar ended, Paul gathered the disciples together, encouraged them once more, said farewell, and left *on foot*. He decided to pass through Macedonia, ²encouraging believers wherever he found them, and came to Greece. ³He spent three months there, and then planned to set sail once again for Syria. But he learned that a group of Jewish opponents was plotting to kill him, so he decided to travel through Macedonia.

⁴⁻⁵*There was a large group of us traveling with him at this time, and we decided it was best, in light of the plot, to split up and then reunite in the city of Troas.* This group included Paul, a Berean named Sopater (son of Pyrrhus), two Thessalonians named Aristarchus and Secundus, a Derbean named Gaius, two Asians named Tychicus and Trophimus, and Timothy. ⁶Some of us waited until the Days of Unleavened Bread were over; then we went to Philippi where we boarded a ship for Troas. The other group left immediately *on foot, passing through Macedonia.*

When my group landed in Troas five days later, Paul's group had already arrived. We stayed in Troas another week.

⁷⁻⁸The Sunday night before our Monday departure, we gathered to celebrate the breaking of bread. *Many wondrous events happened as Paul traveled, ministering among the churches. One evening a most unusual event occurred.*

Imagine you are celebrating with us:
We are in an upstairs room, with *the gentle light and shadows cast by* several lamps. Paul is carrying on an extended dialogue with the believers, taking advantage of every moment since we plan to leave at first light. The conversation stretches on until midnight. ⁹A young fellow named Eutychus, *seeking some fresh air*, moves to an open window. Paul keeps on talking. Eutychus perches in the open window itself. *Paul keeps talking.* Eutychus drifts off to sleep. *Paul continues talking* until Eutychus, now overcome by deep sleep, drops out of the window and falls three stories to the ground, where he is found dead. ¹⁰Paul joins us downstairs, bends over, and takes Eutychus in his arms.

Paul: It's OK. He's alive again.

¹¹Then Paul goes back upstairs, celebrates the breaking of bread, and—*just as you might guess*—keeps on conversing until first light. Then he leaves. ¹²(I should add that Eutychus had been taken home *long before*, his friends more than a little relieved that the boy was alive!)

This may be one of the strangest stories ever told. Paul is talking about faith while one young man dozes off and falls out the window. Many a pastor has secretly prayed that slumbering congregants would fall out of their chairs. It might have been funny had he not died; instead, it was a scene of great horror. That is, until God used Paul to turn horror into celebration with a death-defying miracle. But the people were so enamored with Paul's teaching about the Liberating King that they returned to their conversations, which continued until sunrise.

13Again Paul wanted us to split up. He wanted to go by land by himself while we went by ship to Assos. 14There he came on board with us, and we sailed on to Mitylene. 15From there we sailed near Chios, passing by it the next day, docking briefly at Samos the day after that, then arriving at Miletus the following day. 16This route kept us safely out of Ephesus and didn't require Paul to spend any time at all in Asia, since he wanted to arrive in Jerusalem quickly—before Pentecost, he hoped.

17In Miletus he sent word to the church in Ephesus, asking the elders to come down to meet with him. 18When they arrived, he said,

Paul: We will have many memories of our time together in Ephesus, *but of all the memories, most of all I want you to remember my way of life.* From the first day I arrived in Asia, 19I served the Lord with humility and tears, patiently enduring the many trials that came my way through the plots of my Jewish opponents. 20I did everything I could to help you; I held nothing back. I taught you publicly, and I taught you in your homes. 21I told everyone the same message—Jews and Greeks alike—that we must repent toward God and have faith in Jesus, our Liberating King. 22Now I feel that the Holy Spirit has taken me captive. I am being led to Jerusalem. My future is uncertain, 23but I know—the Holy Spirit has told me—that everywhere I go from now on, I will find imprisonment and persecution waiting for me. 24*But that's OK. That's no tragedy for me because* I don't cling to my life for my own sake. The only value I place on my life is that I may finish my race, that I may fulfill the ministry that Jesus, our King, has given me, that I may gladly tell

the good news of God's grace. 25I now realize that this is our last good-bye. *You have been like family* in all my travels to proclaim the kingdom of God, but after today none of you will see my face again. 26So I want to make this clear: I am not responsible for your destiny from this point on 27because I have not held back from telling you the purpose of God in all its dimensions.

28*Here are my instructions:* diligently guard yourselves, and diligently guard the whole flock over which the Holy Spirit has given you oversight. Shepherd the church of God, this precious church which He made His own through the blood of His own Son. 29I know that after I've gone, dangerous wolves will sneak in among you, savaging the flock. 30Some of you here today will begin twisting the truth, enticing disciples to go your way, to follow you. 31You must be on guard, and you must remember *my way of life among you.* For three years, I have kept on, persistently warning everyone, day and night, with tears.

32So now I put you in God's hands. I entrust you to the message of God's grace, a message that has the power to build you up and to give you rich heritage among all who are set apart for God's holy purposes. 33*Remember my example:* I never once coveted a single coin of silver or gold. I never looked twice at someone's fine clothing. 34No, you know this: I worked with my own two hands *making tents,* and I paid my own expenses and my companions' expenses as well. 35This is my last gift to you, this example of a way of life: a life of hard work, a life of helping the weak, a life that echoes every day those words of Jesus, our King, who said, "It is more blessed to give than to receive."

36*Once again, imagine this scene:*
As Paul finishes speaking, he kneels down, and we all join him, kneeling. He prays, and we all join him, praying. 37There's the sound of weeping, and then more weeping, and then more still. One by

one, we embrace Paul and kiss him, [38]our sadness multiplied because of his words about this being their last good-bye. They walk with us to the ship, *and we set sail.*

The last words of Paul to his Ephesian disciples are emotional, inspiring, but unbelievably arrogant. Who would place himself on a pedestal and encourage everyone to be more like him? It sounds like a cult of personality, but it is not. Paul understands that the gospel must be incarnate; it is more than a set of ideas, so someone must demonstrate how to walk the path of faith. He calls them to watch him carefully and emulate his behavior: watch how I treat people, how I eat, what I say, the way that I give—and do likewise. If only we possessed the same boldness to say, "do as I do," then the world would be a better place, and we would live with an understanding that we do not just speak the gospel; we are the gospel.

21 Cos was our next stop, and the next day, Rhodes, and the next, Patara. [2]We found another ship in Patara that would take us *south and east* toward Phoenicia. [3]We saw Cyprus to our left and sailed on to Syria, landing at Tyre where the ship had cargo to unload. [4]We found the disciples there and stayed with them for seven days. The Spirit moved them to tell Paul not to go on to Jerusalem, [5]but the day came for our departure, and the whole community of disciples, including wives and children, escorted us outside the city. We knelt down together on the beach, prayed together, said farewell, and then parted company— [6]the disciples returning to their homes, we sailing on. [7]From Tyre we docked at Ptolemais where we met with the believers and spent a day with them. [8]Then we moved on to Caesarea. In Caesarea we stayed with Philip the evangelist, one of the seven.* [9]His four virgin daughters lived with him, each having the gift of prophecy. [10]While we were with

them, another gifted prophet named Agabus came *north* from Judea. [11]He took Paul's belt and used it to bind his own feet and hands.

Agabus: This is a message from the Holy Spirit: *unbelieving* Jews in Jerusalem will in this way bind the owner of this belt and will hand him over to the outsiders.

[12]Now we all joined in imploring Paul—we, *his companions, and Philip and his daughters,* everyone present—begging him not to go one step closer to the city. [13]*Some of us were even crying.*

Paul: Please, you're breaking my heart with your tears! *I know exactly what I'm doing.* I'm fully prepared to be bound, and more—to die for the name of Jesus, the King.

[14]We realized our persuasion was fruitless, so we stopped pleading with him and simply said, "The Lord's will be done."

Paul was a man of great mystery. This persecutor-turned-preacher seemed more like a character from pages of fiction than the instigator of the spread of Christianity. He became what he had once despised and willingly suffered on behalf of his new Savior. Paul was accused of many things, but he was no fool—although he was a fool for the Liberator. He fully understood what was waiting for him in Jerusalem: persecution, suffering, and ultimately death. His friends begged him not to return to this holy city, but Paul was called to live in the footsteps of the One who was crucified—He was destined to suffer yet called for no drugs. His suffering served a greater purpose, and Paul never lost sight of this spiritual reality. You see, Paul was living in the kingdom of God.

* 21:8 Acts 6:1-6; 8:4-40

> The masses hope for a gospel that makes them happy, healthy, and wealthy. Jesus said the way of life is a hard road, with only a few on it. Ironically this hard road will end in life. The easy, broad street—which may be paved with good intentions—will always lead to death and destruction. Which road are you on?

¹⁵So we knew what we were getting into as we prepared to ascend the foothills toward Jerusalem. ¹⁶Some of the disciples from Caesarea accompanied us and led us to the home of Mnason, a Cypriot and one of the first disciples, with whom we stayed. ¹⁷We continued on to Jerusalem and were welcomed warmly by the brothers there. ¹⁸The next day, we went together to visit James, and all the elders were there with him. ¹⁹Paul greeted them and then reported account after account of what God had done through him among the outsiders. ²⁰When they heard his story, they praised God.

James and the Elders: Brother, *we have a problem.* You can see that we have thousands of Jewish believers here, and all of them are zealous law keepers. ²¹They've heard all kinds of rumors about you— that you teach all the Jews living among the outside nations to forget about Moses entirely, that you tell believers not to circumcise their sons, that you teach them to abandon all our customs. ²²We need to deal with this situation, since word will spread that you're here in the city. ²³So here's what we would like you to do. We have four men here who are fulfilling a vow. ²⁴Join them. Go through the rituals of purification with them. Pay for their heads to be shaved *according to our ritual.* That will show that the rumors are false and that you are still observing and upholding the law. ²⁵For the outside believers, we've already written in a letter our judgment on their situation: they should not eat food that has been sacrificed to idols, they should not eat meat with blood in it or meat from

animals killed by strangulation, and they should abstain from all sexual misconduct.

²⁶Paul complied with their request. The very next day, he publicly joined the four men, completed the initial purification rites, entered the temple with them, and began the *seven-day* ritual purification process, after which a sacrifice would be made for each of them.

²⁷The seven days of purification were almost completed when some Jews from Asia recognized Paul in the temple. They grabbed him.

Asian Jews (*shouting*): ²⁸Help! Fellow Israelites! This man is an enemy of our people, *our religion,* our law, and this temple! He travels around the world subverting our holiest customs! He is at this moment desecrating this holy temple by bringing outsiders into this sacred place.

²⁹*In this accusation, they were confused—* they had seen Paul elsewhere in the city with Trophimus the Ephesian, and they assumed that one of his current companions was Trophimus. ³⁰*It was too late to clarify, though, because* word spread and soon a huge crowd rushed to the temple. They held Paul and dragged him from the temple and shut the doors behind them. ³¹*They beat Paul,* and it was clear they intended to kill him. By this time, word of the uproar reached the commandant of the Roman guard assigned to Jerusalem.

³²He led a group of soldiers and officers to the scene. When the mob looked up and saw the soldiers running toward them, they stopped beating Paul. ³³The commandant took him into custody and ordered him to be bound with two chains. He conducted a preliminary interrogation— asking Paul's name, what he had done. ³⁴Members of the crowd were shouting over each other and the tribune couldn't hear a thing, so he ordered Paul to be taken back to the barracks. ³⁵When they came to the steps leading down from the temple, the crowd was seething with such

violence *toward Paul* that the soldiers had to pick him up and carry him. ³⁶Then the crowd followed.

Crowd: Away with him! *Away with him!*

³⁷They were just leaving the temple area when Paul asked the commandant,

Paul: May I say something to you?
Commandant: Do you speak Greek? ³⁸We thought you were that Egyptian who recently stirred a rebellion and led 4,000 assassins out into the desert. *But if you speak Greek, then obviously you're not the person we supposed.*
Paul: ³⁹No, I'm a Jew, originally from Tarsus in Cilicia. I'm a citizen from an important city. Please, I beg you, let me speak to the people.

⁴⁰The commandant agreed, and Paul stood there on the steps, motioning for the people to be silent. The crowd settled down, and Paul spoke in their native tongue, Aramaic.

22 Paul: Brothers and fathers, please let me defend myself against these charges.

²When they heard him speaking Aramaic, a hush came over the crowd.

Paul: ³I am a Jew, born in Tarsus in Cilicia. I was raised here in Jerusalem and was tutored in the great school of Gamaliel. My education trained me in the strict interpretation of the law of our ancestors, and I grew zealous for God, just as all of you are today. ⁴I encountered a movement known as the Way, *and I considered it a threat to our religion,* so I persecuted it violently. I put both men and women in chains, had them imprisoned, and would have killed them— ⁵as the high priest and the entire council of elders will tell you. I received documentation from them to go to Damascus and work with the brothers there to arrest followers of the Way and bring them back to Jerusalem in chains so they could be properly punished. ⁶I was on my way to Damascus. It was about noon. Suddenly, a powerful light shone around me, ⁷and I fell to the ground. A voice spoke: "Saul, Saul, why do you persecute Me?" ⁸I answered, "Who are You, Lord?" The voice replied, "I am Jesus of Nazareth, the One you persecute."

⁹My companions saw the light, but they didn't hear the voice. ¹⁰I asked, "What do You want me to do, Lord?" The Lord replied, "Get up and go to Damascus; you will be given your instructions there." ¹¹Since the intense light had blinded me, my companions led me by the hand into Damascus. ¹²I was visited there by a devout man named Ananias, a law-keeping Jew who was well spoken of by all the Jews living in Damascus. ¹³He said, "Brother Saul, regain your sight!" I could immediately see again, beginning with Ananias standing before me. ¹⁴Then he said, "You have been chosen by the God of our ancestors to know His will, to see the Righteous One, and to hear the voice of God. ¹⁵You will tell the story of what you have seen and heard to the whole world. ¹⁶So now, don't delay. Get up, be ceremonially cleansed,* and have your sins washed away, as you call on His name *in prayer.*"

¹⁷I returned to Jerusalem, and I was praying here in the temple one day. I slipped into a trance ¹⁸and had a vision in which Jesus said to me, "Hurry! Get out of Jerusalem fast! The people here will not receive your testimony about Me." ¹⁹I replied, "But, Lord, they all know that I went from synagogue to synagogue imprisoning and beating everyone who believed in You. ²⁰They know *what I was like and* how I stood in approval of the execution of Stephen, Your witness, when he was stoned. I even held the coats of those who actually stoned him." ²¹Jesus replied, "Go, for I am going to send you to distant lands to teach the outsiders."

---

* 22:16 Literally, immersed, in a rite of initiation and purification

²²They were listening quietly up until he mentioned *the outsiders*.

Crowd *(shouting)*: Away with him! Such a man can't be allowed to remain here. Kill him! He must die!

²³*Chaos broke out again*. People were shouting, slamming their coats down on the ground, and throwing fistfuls of dust up in the air. ²⁴The commandant ordered the soldiers to bring Paul to the barracks and flog him until he confessed to whatever he had done to stir up this outrage.

²⁵Back at the barracks, as they tied him up with leather thongs, Paul spoke to a nearby officer.

Paul: Is this legal—for you to flog a Roman citizen without a trial?

²⁶The officer went and spoke to the commandant.

Officer: What can you do about this? Did you know this fellow is a Roman citizen?
Commandant *(rushing to Paul's side)*: ²⁷What's this? Are you really a Roman citizen?
Paul: Yes.
Commandant: ²⁸I paid a small fortune for my citizenship.
Paul: I was born a citizen.

²⁹Hearing this, those who were about to start the flogging pulled back, and the commandant was concerned because he had arrested and bound a citizen *without cause*. ³⁰He still needed to conduct an investigation to uncover the Jews' accusations against Paul. So the next day he removed the ties on Paul and called a meeting with the chief priests and council of elders. He brought Paul in and had him stand before the group.

*T*hese Jewish leaders are prepared to fight and squabble with Paul about the law. But, in his wisdom, Paul disarms them with his story. He is one of them, and on his journey to defend Judaism against these Christian heretics, he encountered the living God. How can anyone dispute his experience? He was trained by trustworthy Jews and lived his life according to their strict interpretation of the law. When Paul invites us into his experience with the supernatural, it makes debating the finer points of the law seem ridiculous. It would be like antagonizing Moses while he reiterated God's message heard through the burning bush. But prejudice is apparently stronger than any divine message. Paul has them hanging on to every word from his mouth, until he speaks of the outsiders. The crowd immediately rises from their silence into a furious rage. The message is clear—if your revelation extends beyond our people, we will hear nothing of it. How could all of these students of the Hebrew Scriptures have been so ignorant about God's intentions to liberate all people? The prophets had declared God's plan to offer grace to Jews and non-Jews, but no one in this crowd considered that good news.

23 Paul stared at the council and spoke:

Paul: Brothers, I have always lived my life to this very day with a clear conscience before God.

²Ananias the high priest signaled those standing near Paul to hit him on the mouth.

Paul: ³You hypocrite! God will slap you! How dare you sit in judgment and claim to represent the law, while you violate the law by ordering me to be struck *for no reason*?
Bystanders: The nerve of you insulting the high priest of God!
Paul: ⁵I'm sorry, my brothers. I didn't realize this was the high priest. The law

warns us to not curse the ruler of the people.*

⁶Paul noticed that some members of the council were Sadducees and some were Pharisees, so he quickly spoke to the council.

Paul: Brothers, I am a Pharisee, born to a Pharisee. I am on trial because I have hope that the dead are raised!

⁷That got the two parties arguing with one another, ⁸because the Sadducees say there is no such thing as resurrection, heavenly messengers, or spirits, and the Pharisees believe in all three.
⁹Soon these leaders were shouting, and some of the scholars from the party of the Pharisees rose to their feet.

Pharisees: There is nothing wrong with this man. Maybe he really has encountered a spirit or a heavenly messenger.

¹⁰The two parties were about to start throwing punches, and the commandant was afraid Paul would be torn to pieces, so he sent in his soldiers to intervene. They took Paul back into custody and returned him to their barracks. ¹¹That night the Lord came near and spoke to him.

*P*aul is brilliant. If you are accused by a group of religious intellectuals, the smartest thing to do is to get them fighting with one another. Paul understood the axiom, "the enemy of my enemy is my friend." So if I pick a fight with the Sadducees, the rest of the room will defend me. The things we are against often define us, so we are easily manipulated in this way. Consider some of the conservative political pundits who have never espoused any inclination toward Christianity. They gain millions of Christian followers by opposing the political enemies of conservative Christians. Paul embraced a similar strategy here—if I can get these guys to fight, they will forget why we are actually here. In many ways, the culture wars have served the same purpose. In the middle of the battle, the church is realizing we were not placed on earth to fight about morality and culture. We are here to bring the kingdom of God to earth. His kingdom will not come by means of legislation, but by the working of the Holy Spirit within the church.

The Lord: Keep up your courage, Paul! You have successfully told your story about Me in Jerusalem, and soon you will do the same in Rome.

¹²⁻¹³That morning a group of more than 40 Jewish opponents conspired to kill Paul. They bound themselves by an oath that they wouldn't eat or drink until he was dead. ¹⁴They told the chief priests and elders about their plan.

Jewish Opponents: We've made an oath not to eat or drink until this man is dead. ¹⁵So you and the council must ask the commandant to bring Paul to meet with you. Tell him that you want to further investigate Paul's case. We'll get rid of the troublemaker on his way here.

¹⁶Now Paul had a nephew who heard about the planned ambush; he managed to gain entry into the barracks and alerted Paul. ¹⁷Paul called one of the officers.

Paul: Take this young man to the commandant. He has news the commandant needs to hear.

¹⁸The officer took him to the commandant.

Officer: The prisoner named Paul asked me to bring this man to you. He has some kind of information.

¹⁹The commandant led him away so they could speak in private.

* 23:5 Exodus 22:28

Commandant: What do you want to tell me?
Young Man: ²⁰The Jewish council is going to ask you to bring Paul down to the council tomorrow under the pretext that there will be a thorough examination. ²¹But don't agree to do it, because 40 assassins have bound themselves to an oath not to eat or drink until they've killed Paul. Their plan is in motion, and they're simply waiting for you to play your part.

²²The commandant sent the young man home with these instructions: "Don't tell a soul that you've spoken with me." ²³Then he called for two officers.

Commandant: At nine o'clock tonight, you will leave for Caesarea with 200 soldiers, 70 horsemen, and 200 spearmen. ²⁴Have a mount for Paul to ride and conduct him safely to Felix the governor.

²⁵He wrote the following letter:

²⁶*Commandant* Claudius Lysias greets his excellency, Felix, Governor. ²⁷The accompanying prisoner was seized by Jews who were about to kill him. I learned he was a Roman citizen and intervened with the guard here to protect him. ²⁸I arranged for a hearing before their council ²⁹and learned that he was accused for reasons relating to their religious law, but that he has done nothing deserving imprisonment or execution. ³⁰I was informed that a group was planning to assassinate him, so I sent him to you immediately. I will require his accusers to present their complaint before you.

³¹So the soldiers followed their orders and safely conducted Paul as far as Antipatris that night. ³²⁻³³The next day, the horsemen conducted him on to Caesarea as the foot soldiers returned to the barracks. The horsemen delivered the letter and the prisoner to Felix who read the letter. ³⁴The only question Felix asked concerned the province of Paul's birth. When he learned Paul was from Cilicia, ³⁵he said,

Felix: As soon as your accusers arrive I will hear your case.

He placed Paul under guard within Herod's headquarters.

24 The high priest Ananias came north *to Caesarea* five days later, accompanied by some elders and an attorney named Tertullus. They explained their case to Felix *without Paul present*. ²When Paul was brought in, Tertullus launched into an accusation.

Tertullus: Most Excellent Felix, through your esteemed leadership we have enjoyed a long and happy peace. Your foresight in governance has brought many reforms for the people I represent. ³We always and everywhere welcome every thought of you with high and deep gratitude. ⁴But, knowing how busy you are and how limited your time must be, I beg you to hear us briefly present our case to you with the legendary graciousness for which you are known everywhere.
    ⁵Here are the facts: this man is a disease to the body politic. He agitates trouble in Jewish communities throughout our empire as a ringleader of the *heretical* sect known as the Nazarenes. ⁶He even tried to desecrate the temple, so we seized him. [Our aim was to try him by the Jewish law. ⁷But Commandant Lysias interfered and removed this man from our control. ⁸Because of his meddling, you are now forced to hear those making the accusation.]* You will find, through your own examination, that everything we say of Paul is true.

⁹The Jewish opponents present added their vigorous testimony in support of the lawyer's opening statement. ¹⁰The governor *didn't say anything, but he* motioned for Paul to speak.

* 24:6-8 Some early manuscripts omit this portion.

Paul: I am happy now to make my defense to you, sir, knowing that you have been a judge over this nation for many years. [11]Just 12 days ago, I went up to Jerusalem to worship, as you can easily verify. [12]I wasn't arguing with anyone in the temple. I wasn't stirring up a crowd in any of the synagogues. I wasn't disturbing the peace of the city in any way. They did not find me doing these things in Jerusalem, [13]nor can they prove that I have done any of the things of which they have accused me. [14]But I can make this confession: I believe everything established by the Law and written in the Prophets, and I worship the God of our ancestors according to the Way, which they call a *heretical* sect.

[15]*Here is my crime:* I have a hope in God that there will be a resurrection of both the just and unjust, which my opponents also share. [16]Because of this hope, I always do my best to live with a clear conscience toward God and all people. [17]I have been away for several years, so recently I brought gifts for the poor of my nation and offered sacrifices. [18]When they found me, I was not disturbing anyone, nor was I gathering a crowd. No, I was quietly completing the rite of purification. Some Jews from Asia *are the ones who started the disturbance—* [19]and if they have an accusation, they should be here to make it. [20]If these men here have some crime they have found me guilty of when I stood before their council, they should present it. [21]Perhaps my crime is that I spoke this one sentence in my testimony before them: "I am on trial here today because I have hope that the dead are raised."

[22]Felix was quite knowledgeable about the Way. He adjourned the preliminary hearing.

Felix: When Lysias the commandant comes *to Caesarea,* I will decide your case.

[23]He then ordered the officer to keep Paul in custody, but to permit him some freedom and to allow any of his friends to take care of his needs.

[24]A few days later, Felix sent for Paul and gave him an opportunity to speak about faith in Jesus as Liberating King. Felix was accompanied by his wife Drusilla, who was Jewish. [25]As Paul spoke of justice, self-control, and the coming judgment, Felix became fearful.

Felix: That's enough for now. When I have time, I will send for you again.

[26]They had a number of conversations of this sort, *but Felix's motives were not as sincere as they might seem.* He actually was hoping that, by having frequent contact, Paul might offer him a bribe. [27]As a favor to the Jews, he did nothing to resolve the case and left Paul in prison for two years. Then Felix completed his assignment as governor, and Porcius Festus succeeded him.

*T*here were rumors that a large sum of money was at Paul's disposal. We know that money was the relief offering for the church in Jerusalem. But Paul did not choose to buy his freedom. Despite the corruption of the government, Paul understood that ultimately his justice was in the hands of God. In the near future, he would appear before the government of Rome, and that encounter would likely lead to his death.

25 Three days after arriving in the province, Festus traveled south from Caesarea to Jerusalem. [2-3]The chief priests and Jewish leaders still had a plan to kill Paul and gave a report to Festus about their unresolved grievances against Paul. They suggested that as a favor to them, Festus should move Paul to Jerusalem. Of course, this was part of the plan to set an ambush for Paul and kill him en route. [4]Festus *instead offered to reopen the case.* He would be going back to Caesarea soon.

Festus: [5]So let your leaders accompany me and bring your accusations against the man.

⁶Eight or ten days later, Festus returned to Caesarea, and the next day took his seat in court. He ordered Paul to be brought before him. ⁷The Jewish opponents from Jerusalem immediately surrounded Paul and from all directions bombarded him with all sorts of serious charges, none of which could be proven.

Paul *(quietly and simply)*: ⁸In no way have I committed any offense against Jewish law, against the Jewish temple and all it represents, or against the emperor.

⁹Here Festus saw an opportunity to do just the favor Paul's Jewish opponents had requested.

Festus: Would you like to have your trial in Jerusalem? I'd be willing to try your case there.
Paul: ¹⁰⁻¹¹*Sir, it's not that I'm afraid to die.* If I had committed a capital offense, I would accept my punishment. But I'm sure it's clear to you that I have done no wrong to the Jews. Since their charges against me are completely empty, it would be wrong to turn me over to them. *No, I do not wish to go to Jerusalem.* I am appealing to the court of the emperor in Rome.

¹²Festus conferred privately with his council and returned with this decision:

Festus: You have appealed to the emperor, so to the emperor you will go.

¹³Several days later, the provincial king Agrippa arrived in Caesarea with *his wife* Bernice to welcome the new governor. ¹⁴Their visit lasted several days, which gave Festus the chance to describe Paul's case to the king.

Festus: Felix left me some unfinished business involving a prisoner *named Paul.* ¹⁵When I was in Jerusalem, I got an earful about him from the chief priests and Jewish elders. They wanted me simply to decide against him, ¹⁶but I informed them that we Romans don't work that way. We don't condemn a person accused of a crime unless the accusers present their case in person so the accused has ample opportunity to defend himself against the charge. ¹⁷I arranged for them to come here for a proper hearing. In fact, the first day after I returned *to Caesarea,* I took my seat in court and heard his case without delay. ¹⁸Contrary to my expectations, the accusers brought no substantial charges against him at all. ¹⁹Instead, they were bickering about their own religious beliefs related to a fellow named Jesus, who had died, but whom Paul claimed was raised to life again. ²⁰I had no idea how to handle a religious squabble pretending to be a legal case, so I suggested Paul be taken to Jerusalem so he could be tried on Jewish turf, so to speak. ²¹But Paul refused, and instead he appealed to be kept in custody so the case could be referred to his Imperial Majesty. So I have held him until we can arrange to send him to the emperor.
Agrippa: ²²This sounds interesting. I'd like to hear this fellow in person.
Festus: You will, then. We'll bring him in tomorrow.

²³The next day, King Agrippa and Bernice arrived at the great hall with great formality, accompanied by the military commanders and the city's leading men. Festus ordered Paul to be brought before them.

Festus: ²⁴King Agrippa and all our honored guests, here is the man who has been charged with wrongdoing by the Jewish community—both in Jerusalem and here. They yelled for his execution, ²⁵but I found him guilty of no capital offense. Then he appealed to our Imperial Majesty, so I have agreed that he will be sent *to Rome.* ²⁶⁻²⁷*Here is where I need your help.* I can't send a man to our emperor without a letter logically detailing the charges against him, but I have no idea what to write. So, King Agrippa, and all of you honored guests, I'm requesting your help in determining what to write in my letter to the emperor.

26 Agrippa *(to Paul)*: Go ahead. You may speak for yourself.

Paul *(extending his hand)*: ²I am indeed fortunate to be standing before you, King Agrippa, to humbly defend myself against accusations from my Jewish opponents. ³You are extraordinarily familiar with Jewish customs and controversies, so I beg your patience as I begin. ⁴My way of life is well known to the whole Jewish community, how I have lived in the Jewish community abroad and in Jerusalem. ⁵If they are willing to speak, they themselves will tell you something they have long known— that I was a member of the strictest sect of our religion and lived *for many years* as a Pharisee. ⁶But now I am on trial here *for this simple reason:* I have hope. I have hope rooted in a promise God made to our ancestors. ⁷All our twelve tribes have hope in this promise—they express their hope as they worship day and night. How strange it is, then, Your Excellency, that I am accused by the Jews of having hope! ⁸Why would any of you think it is absurd to have hope that God raises the dead? ⁹As you know, *we're talking specifically* about Jesus of Nazareth. For a long time, I was convinced that I should work against that name. ¹⁰I opposed it in Jerusalem. I received authorization from the chief priests to lock many of His followers in prison. When they were threatened with execution, I voted against them. ¹¹I would find them in synagogues across Jerusalem and try to force them to blaspheme. My fury drove me to pursue them to foreign cities as well.

¹²On one occasion, I was traveling to Damascus, authorized and commissioned by the chief priests *to find and imprison more of His followers.* ¹³It was about midday, Your Excellency, when I saw a light from heaven—brighter than the noonday sun—shining around my companions and me. ¹⁴We all fell to the ground *in fear*, and I then heard a voice. The words were in Aramaic: "Saul, Saul, why are you persecuting Me? When you kick against the cattle prods, you're only hurting yourself." ¹⁵I asked, "Lord, who are You?" and the Lord answered, "I am Jesus, the One you are persecuting. ¹⁶Get up now and stand upright on your feet. I have appeared to you for a reason. I am appointing you to serve Me. You are to tell My story and how you have now seen Me, and you are to continue to tell the story in the future. ¹⁷I will rescue you from your Jewish opponents and from the outsiders—for it is to the outsiders I am sending you. ¹⁸It will be your mission to open their eyes so that they may turn from darkness to light and from the kingdom of Satan to the kingdom of God. This is so that they may receive forgiveness of all their sins and have a place among those who are set apart for a holy purpose through having faith in Me."

¹⁹King Agrippa, I did not disobey this vision from heaven. ²⁰I began in Damascus, then continued in Jerusalem, then throughout the Judean countryside, then among the outsiders—telling everyone they must turn from their past and toward God, and they must align their deeds and way of life with this new direction. ²¹So then, this is my crime. This is why my Jewish opponents seized me that day in the temple and tried to kill me. ²²God has helped me right up to this very moment, so I can stand here telling my story to both the humble and the powerful alike. I only say what the prophets and Moses said would happen— ²³that God's Liberating King must suffer, and then, by being the first to rise from the dead, He would proclaim light to both Jews and outsiders.

Festus *(interrupting)*: ²⁴You've gone crazy, Paul! You've read one book too many and have gone insane!

Paul: ²⁵No, most excellent Festus, I am not insane. I am telling the sane and sober truth. ²⁶The king understands what I'm talking about, which is why I could speak so freely to him. None of these things have been covered up and hidden away in a corner, so I'm sure none of these things have escaped his notice. [27]King Agrippa, do you believe the prophets? I know you must believe.

Agrippa: [28]Paul, have you so quickly moved on from defending yourself to trying to persuade me to become a Christian?

Paul: [29]Whether I have done so quickly or not, I pray to God that not only you but also everyone who is listening to me today might become what I am—minus these chains.

[30]The king stood to leave at this point, along with Festus, Bernice, and all those who had been seated; [31]and as they left, everyone was saying the same thing: "This man isn't doing anything deserving death—he shouldn't even be in prison."

Agrippa (to Festus): [32]This man could have been released completely if he had not appealed to the emperor.

27 The date was set for us to depart for Rome, and Paul and some other prisoners were transferred to the custody of a Roman officer named Julius, a member of the Augustan Division. [2]*I, Luke, was permitted to join Paul for his journey to Rome*, along with Aristarchus, a Macedonian brother from Thessalonica. We boarded a ship from Adramyttium that was stopping in ports along the coast of Asia. [3]We stopped the next day at Sidon, and Julius kindly allowed Paul to visit friends and be taken care of by them. [4]We sailed from there north of Cyprus because the winds were unfavorable. [5]We passed Cilicia and Pamphylia *on our right* and then came to Myra in Lycia. [6]There Julius found a ship from Alexandria heading directly to Italy, to which we transferred. [7]The winds were still contrary, so we made slow progress for a number of days and with difficulty passed Cnidus and sailed south toward Crete and past Cape Salmone *on its eastern end*. [8]Sailing conditions were adverse

to say the least. Finally we came to a place called Fair Havens, near the city of Lasea *on the south coast of Crete*. [9]We had lost a lot of time already—it was *late in the year for sailing*—following the Day of Atonement, and conditions had deteriorated from adverse to dangerous. Paul tried to warn those in charge.

Paul: [10]Sirs, if we proceed, I can see that our voyage will be dangerous and will involve heavy loss, not only of cargo, but of the ship itself; not only of the ship, but also of our lives.

[11]But the officer ignored Paul and instead trusted the ship's pilot and owner who felt they could proceed.

[12]*We had two choices.* We could anchor in the harbor at Fair Havens and spend the winter, or we could proceed *west along the coastline*, hoping to reach Phoenix and wait there for calmer spring weather. *Fair Havens* was not a good option, though, being vulnerable to winter storms, so most of us agreed we should try to reach Phoenix, whose harbor was more protected. [13]One day a moderate south wind began to blow, which made an attempt possible. We weighed anchor and sailed *west*, staying near shore. [14]*Then things got scary.* A violent northeaster, the Euraquilo, blew down across Crete. [15]We were caught. We couldn't turn and sail into this fierce wind, so we had no choice but to let it drive us. [16]We briefly found a bit of shelter from the wind near the island of Clauda. We had been having trouble securing the ship's lifeboat, [17]but we were able there to hoist it up and send down cables to brace the hull, *which was in danger of breaking apart under the strain of the storm. But the wind was relentless and* soon we were again being driven *southwest, at the mercy of the storm*. We feared it would drive us all the way to the Syrtis Banks, *down near the North African coast*, so we threw out the sea anchor to slow us down. [18]All through the night, the storm pounded us violently. The next day, the crew threw the ship's cargo overboard, [19]and the day after that,

they discarded any of the ship's equipment they could do without. [20]Days passed without relief from the furious winds, without a single break in the clouds to see sun or stars, even for a moment. Despair set in, as if all hope of rescue had been cast overboard as well. [21]On top of all of this, the crew had been unable to eat anything *because of the turmoil. Paul saw the crew had reached a critical moment.* He gathered them.

Paul: Men, if you had listened to my warning, we would still be safe in Crete and we would have avoided this damage and loss. [22]*I was correct in my warning,* so I urge you to believe me now: none of you will die. We will lose the ship, but we will not lose one life. So keep up your courage, men! [23]The God I belong to, the God I worship, sent a heavenly messenger to me this night. [24]He said, "Do not be afraid, Paul. *I'm not finished with you yet.* You are going to stand before the emperor! You can be certain that God has granted safety to you and all your companions." [25]So listen, men: *you must not give up hope!* Keep up your courage! I have faith in God that things will turn out exactly as I was told last night. [26]*Here's what I foresee:* we will run aground on some island.

[27-28]*Imagine what happened:* It's the 14th night *of our nightmare voyage;* we're being driven by the storm somewhere in the Adriatic Sea. It's about midnight, and the sailors are taking soundings, fearing we might run aground. "Twenty fathoms," somebody calls out in the darkness, then a little later, "Fifteen fathoms." *Suddenly you can feel a moment of hope among the crew—*we're nearing land! [29]But hope quickly gives way to a new fear. At any moment in this darkness, they realize, we could be smashed onto unseen rocks. So they drop four anchors from the stern and pray for first light.

[30]Then some of the crew decide to make a run for it on their own. They say they need to let out more anchors from the bow, and this will require lowering the ship's lifeboat. *They actually plan to abandon us; we realize what's going on.* [31]Paul quickly speaks to the officer and soldiers.

Paul: Unless these men stay on board, you won't survive.

[32]So the soldiers intervene, cut away the lifeboat, and let it drift away. [33,37]*We wait.* Just before dawn, Paul again gathers everyone on the ship—all 276 of us. He urges everyone to eat *and encourages us not to lose hope.**

Paul: *Listen, men,* we've all been under incredible stress for 14 days. You haven't eaten anything during this whole time. [34]I urge you to take some food now because it will help you survive what we're about to face. And I want to assure you—not one of you will lose a single hair from your head. *We're all going to make it—all 276 of us!*

[35]Then Paul takes a loaf of bread and gives thanks to God in front of all of them. He breaks it, takes a piece, and begins to eat. [36]A fresh surge of courage seems to fill their hearts as they also begin to eat. [38]After satisfying their hunger, the crew lightens the ship by throwing the remaining wheat overboard. [39]Day finally breaks. They survey the coastline and don't recognize it, but they do notice a bay with a beach—the best place to try to run ashore. [40]So they cut the anchor ropes, untie the steering oars, hoist the foresail to the wind, and make for the beach. [41]But *then there's a horrible sound, and* we realize we've struck a reef; the bow is jammed solid, and the waves are smashing the stern to pieces. [42]The soldiers start talking about killing the prisoners so they won't swim away and escape, [43]but the officer wants to save Paul so he stops them. He tells those who can swim to jump overboard and swim to the shore, [44]and those who can't, he tells to hold on to planks and other

---

* 27:33,37 Verses 33 and 37 have been combined to help the reader understand the continuity of the passage.

pieces of the ship when it breaks apart. *Some hours later*, we reassemble on the beach, each one safe and sound.

28 We quickly learned that we were on the island of Malta. ²The Maltese people found us and were extraordinarily kind to us. They kindled a bonfire and welcomed us around it, *which we greatly appreciated* because it was raining and cold. ³Paul was gathering firewood and helping build the fire. A viper had been hiding in some of the wood, and as it tried to escape the heat, it bit Paul on the hand. It sank its fangs in and wouldn't let go. ⁴The natives saw it dangling from his hand.

Natives: This man must be a murderer. He escaped the sea, but now justice has caught up with him.

⁵Paul simply shook the snake off into the fire and suffered no harm. ⁶The natives knew what to expect—rapid swelling followed by death—but when they waited a long time and saw that Paul suffered no ill effects of the bite, they changed their minds and concluded that he was a god.

⁷The leading man of the island, Publius, owned large amounts of land near this beach. Publius received us and hosted us for three days. ⁸Publius's father was sick, bedridden with fever and dysentery. Paul visited the invalid and prayed for him, placing his hands on Publius's father. The man was cured. ⁹Soon people from all over the island who had diseases came, and they were cured as well.

¹⁰⁻¹¹We stayed on Malta for the next three months and were treated with great honor. *When spring arrived,* we prepared to continue our journey on a ship that had wintered there—an Alexandrian vessel with the Twin Brothers as its figurehead. The Maltese people showed us a final kindness as we departed: they came with all the provisions we needed for our journey and put them on board.

¹²We *set sail from Malta and* stopped first at Syracuse. After three days, ¹³we weighed anchor and came to Rhegium. We waited there a day, and then a south wind sprang up and sped us to Puteoli. ¹⁴We found some believers there, and they invited us to stay with them for seven days. Then we reached Rome. ¹⁵The believers from Rome heard we were coming, so they traveled out to meet us at the Forum of Appius and Three Taverns. Paul thanked God and felt encouraged to see them. ¹⁶Once inside the city, Paul lived under house arrest by himself, with only one soldier to guard him.

¹⁷Three days after his arrival, he called together the local Jewish leaders.

Paul: Brothers, although I committed no wrong against our Jewish people or our ancestral customs, I was arrested in Jerusalem and handed over to the Romans. ¹⁸The Romans examined me and wanted to set me free because I had committed no capital offense. ¹⁹But my Jewish opponents objected, so I had to appeal to the emperor—even though I had no charges against me and had filed no charges against my nation. ²⁰I wanted to gather you together and explain all this to you. I want you to understand that it is because of Israel's hope that I am bound with this chain.

Jewish Leaders: ²¹We haven't received letters from Judea about you, and no visiting brother has reported anything or said anything negative about you. ²²So we are interested in hearing your viewpoint on the sect *you represent.* The only thing we know about it is that people everywhere speak against it.

²³They scheduled a day to meet again, and a large number came to his lodging. From morning until evening, he explained his message to them—giving his account of the kingdom of God, trying to convince them about Jesus from the Law of Moses and the Prophets' writings. ²⁴Some were convinced, but others refused to believe.

Paul (*adding as they left in disagreement*): ²⁵The Holy Spirit rightly spoke to your ancestors through the prophet Isaiah,

²⁶Go to this people and say:
"You certainly do hear, but you will
    never understand;
  you certainly do see, but you
    will never have insight.
²⁷Make their hearts hard,
    their ears deaf, and their eyes
      blind.
  Otherwise, they would look and
    see,
    listen and hear,
    understand and repent,
    and be healed."*

²⁸So let it be known to you that God's
liberation, *God's healing*, has been sent to
the outsiders, and they will listen.

[²⁹Then the local Jewish leaders left Paul
to discuss all he had told them.]*

³⁰For two full years, he lived there in
Rome, paying all his own expenses, receiving all who came to him. ³¹With great
confidence and with no hindrance, he
proclaimed the kingdom of God and taught
about *the ultimate authority*—Jesus, the
promised Liberating King.

*L*uke's account of the early
    church ends on a flat note: one
of the story's heroes, Paul, is under
house arrest in Rome awaiting trial. If
we wish to know what happens next,
we have to turn to other sources.
Although we don't know the details of
his captivity, we do learn that Paul was
martyred in Rome, a victim of Nero's
paranoia and cruelty.

We don't know why Luke left the
story when he did. Some think he
planned a third volume. Others speculate that he wrote this before Paul's
demise—he too was waiting to find out
what would happen. It is a possibility,
given the uncertainties of life, that our
author could not resolve the story
because of imprisonment, illness, or
his own death. What seems most likely
is that Luke finished what he started.
He was determined to trace "the Way"
as it moved geographically and culturally from Jerusalem (at the edge of the
empire) to Rome (the celebrated center of the world). And he did just that.

As it moved geographically, "the
Way," as Jesus' followers preferred to
call it, had to cross cultural, linguistic,
and religious boundaries. At each and
every point, Luke assures, the Spirit
was there demonstrating God's blessing on and approval for the apostles
who walked in the footsteps of Jesus
and in fulfillment of prophecies.
Clearly what happened in those early
decades was driven by the Spirit-wind
of heaven. No human could have done
alone what the Jewish followers of
Jesus did when they left Jerusalem to
become the church, comprised of people from every tribe, every ethnicity,
every language. Still, Luke is quick to
remind us that God's purposes were
realized through the faithful obedience
of disciples like Peter, Stephen, Philip,
and Paul.

Luke's account may have ended,
but the story about the acts of God
through the church continues into our
day. We are the characters in the current volume of salvation history.
Through our faithful obedience,
empowered by the Spirit-wind of
heaven, the plot is developing in our
day until our stories are compiled into
the wider story of God's new creation.

* 28:26-27 Isaiah 6:9-10
* 28:29 Some early manuscripts omit verse 29.

Romans

Letter to the church in Rome
From Paul, the apostle to the Gentiles

Rome was the center of the known world; it was the cradle of civilization, commerce, culture—and home to a military machine under the command of Caesar, the most powerful man in the world. The most influential city on the planet was on the frontier of the Jesus movement, a place where God was bringing together Jews and non-Jews into one community to serve the Liberating King. A group of believers was gathering, and a church of great importance was forming from ragamuffin believers who had been touched by the power of the gospel. But they do not appear to have had the leadership of the Lord's emissaries—those who had walked with and had been hand-picked by Jesus. This church would become the seedbed for the spread of the gospel across the known world, so Paul recognized the importance of articulating the whole gospel to this body of believers and preparing them for their missional calling in the world.

This letter from Paul, the emissary of Jesus, breaks all the previous molds. He is writing to many people he does not know, is instructing a church he did not plant, and is challenging them to embrace their role in bringing the gospel to the people of Italy and Spain, despite the fact that he has not been able to model the work of missions and church planting in Rome as he had in other places. What would Paul have to say to believers he had never met? How would he proclaim the gospel in a letter? In planting other churches, Paul surely told how the risen Jesus appeared to him. Paul must have preached to them for untold hours (he was known for being quite verbose) about sin, redemption, justification, the cross, adoption, grace, love, life in the Spirit, and the power of the Liberating King to redeem all things.

This letter set the church in Rome on a firm foundation and ultimately became one of the most important pieces of literature ever written. It has influenced some of the greatest minds and agents of change the world has known: Augustine, Luther, Wesley, Martin Luther King Jr., and Desmond Tutu, just to name a few. It was one of the primary inspirations for the Protestant Reformation in the 16th century. But most importantly, this letter written to Christians in an ancient city penetrates our hearts and minds today with a beautiful and persuasive view of the power of the gospel!

1 Paul, a servant of Jesus, the Liberating King, called by God to be His emissary* and appointed to tell the good news ²of the things promised long ago by God, spoken by prophets, and recorded in the Holy Scriptures. ³All of this good news is about His Son: who was (from a human perspective) born of David's royal line ⁴*and ultimately* designated to be the *true* Son of God with power upon His resurrection from death by the Spirit of holiness. I am speaking of Jesus, the Liberating King, our Lord.

> *T*he prophets express God's mind and will in the world. Sometimes their messages are a word-on-target to the people and powers of their day; at other times, they see and speak about the future. Their words not only predict the future—they speak the word of the Lord, which creates reality and shapes the future.
>
> Paul describes the gospel of Jesus, the Liberating King, by bringing in the good news on two levels: On a human level, the good news is about God's Son, David's descendant, entering into our world to begin the task of restoring the world from the damage sin and death have left behind. But the resurrection of Jesus from the dead takes Jesus' sonship beyond the human level to a spiritual level. Now He is the Son-of-God-in-Power, the One we call Lord and Master.

⁵*And here's what He's done:* He has graced us and sanctioned us as His emissaries* whose mission is to spread the *one true and* obedient faith to all people in the name of Jesus. ⁶This includes you: you have been called by Jesus, the Liberating King.

⁷To all those who are God's beloved saints in Rome:

May grace and peace from God our Father and the Lord Jesus, the Liberating King, surround you.

⁸First, I thank my God through the Liberator, Jesus, for all of you because *we are joined by faith as family, and* your faith is spreading across the world. *Because of your influence, many are becoming aware of our Savior.* ⁹⁻¹⁰For *I call* God as my witness—whom I worship in my spirit and serve in making known the gospel—He alone knows how often I mention you in my prayers. I find myself constantly praying for you and hoping it's in God's will for me to be with you soon. ¹¹I desperately want to see you so that I can share some gift of the Spirit to strengthen you. ¹²Plus I know that when we come together *something beautiful will happen as* we are encouraged by each other's faith.

¹³If, my brothers and sisters, you did not already know, my plans were set to meet you *in Rome*, but time and circumstances have forced every trip to be canceled until now. I have deeply desired to see some good fruit among you just as I have seen with so many non-Jewish believers. ¹⁴*You see,* I am in *tremendous* debt to those of various nationalities, from non-Jews to barbarians, from the wisest of the wise to the idle wanderer. ¹⁵So you can imagine how eager I am to join you and to teach the good news in *the mighty and diverse city of* Rome.

¹⁶For I am not *the least bit* embarrassed about the gospel. *I won't shy away from it,* because it is God's power to save every person who believes: first the Jew, and then the non-Jew. ¹⁷You see, in the good news, God's restorative justice is revealed. *And as we will see,* it begins with and ends in faith. As the Scripture declares: "By faith the just will obtain life."*

> *A*ccording to Paul, in and by itself, the gospel is power—God's power. The simple message of Jesus brings healing and rescue to all people. It starts with God's people, the Jews, but does not end until all people hear and respond to its call.

* 1:1 Literally, apostle
* 1:5 Literally, apostles
* 1:17 Habakkuk 2:4

The gospel reveals how right and faithful God has been all along. It begins with God's faithfulness to His creation and His covenant people. God acted, finally and decisively, in the cross of Jesus. For Paul the cross, more than any other event, displays Jesus' faithfulness to God the Father. As the Gospels tell us, in the garden of Gethsemane, Jesus entrusted Himself completely to God's will. As a result, this good news brings faith and hope to those who hear and respond to its elegant message. Because God is faithful, He acts in a most extraordinary way. Somehow in the scandal of the cross, He offers His own Son in order to redeem the fallen world.

[18]For the wrath of God is breaking through from heaven, opposing all *manifestations of* ungodliness and wickedness by the people who do wrong to keep God's truth in check—*they cloak their sin in lies and deceit.* [19]These people are not ignorant about what can be known of God, because He has shown it to them *with great clarity.* [20]From the beginning, creation in its magnificence enlightens us to His nature. Creation itself makes His undying power and divine identity clear, even though they are invisible, and voids the excuses *and ignorant claims* of these people [21]because, despite the fact that they knew the one true God, they have failed to show the *love,* honor, and appreciation due to the One who created them! Instead, their lives are consumed by vain thoughts that poison their foolish hearts. [22]They claim to be wise, but they have been exposed as fools, *frauds, and con-artists—* [23]only a fool would trade the splendor and beauty of the immortal God to worship images of the common man or woman, bird or reptile, or *the next* beast *that tromps along.* [24]So God gave them just what their lustful hearts desired. *As a result,* they violated their bodies and invited shame into their lives. [25]*How?* By choosing a foolish lie over God's truth. They gave their lives and devotion to the creature rather than to the Creator Himself, who is blessed forever and ever. Amen. [26-27]This is why God released them to their own vile pursuits, *and this is what happened*: they chose sexual counterfeits—women had sexual relations with other women and men committed unnatural, shameful acts because they burned with lust for other men. This sin was rife, and they suffered painful consequences.

[28]Since they had no mind to recognize God, He turned them loose to follow the unseemly designs of their depraved minds and to do things that should not be done. [29]Their days are filled with all sorts of godless living, wicked schemes, greed, hatred, endless desire for more, murder, violence, deceit, and spitefulness. And, *as if that were not enough,* they are gossiping, [30]slanderous, God-hating, rude, egotistical, smug people who are always coming up with even more dreadful ways to treat one another. They don't listen to their parents; [31]they lack understanding *and character.* They are simple-minded, covenant-breaking, heartless, and unmerciful; *they are not to be trusted.* [32]Despite the fact that they are fully aware that God's law says this way of life deserves death, they fail to stop. And *worse*—they applaud others on this destructive path.

*P*aul sounds a sober warning. God's wrath is here; it is not some far-off future event. Paul says that God's wrath is already at work in the world in what is effectively God's "hands-off" policy. God, he says, steps aside and gives us over to idolatry, sexual sins, and depraved minds. Human sin and depravity are both its cause and effect. You see, we are not only punished for our sins, but we are punished by our sins. If God's salvation consists essentially of His presence with us, then His wrath consists of His absence or separation from us. The bad news is this: God's wrath is real. Without the good news of Jesus, the Liberating King, no hope exists.

2 So you can see there are no excuses for any of us. If your eyes shift their focus from yourselves to others—to judge *how they are doing*—you have already condemned yourselves! *You don't realize that* you are pointing your fingers at others for the exact things you do as well. ²The judgment of God will justly fall upon hypocrites who practice such things. ³*Here's what is happening*: you attack and criticize others and then turn around to commit the same offenses yourselves! Do you think you will somehow dodge God's judgment? ⁴Do you take the kindness of God for granted? Do you see His patience and tolerance as signs that He is a pushover *when it comes to sin*? How could you not know that His kindness is guiding our hearts to turn away from *distractions and habitual* sin to walk a new path?*

⁵But because your heart is obstinate and shameless, you're storing up wrath that will count against you. On the day of His choosing, God's wrath and judgment will be unleashed to make things right. ⁶As it goes, every man will receive what his actions in life have cultivated. ⁷Whoever has labored diligently and patiently to do what is right—seeking glory, honor, and immortality—God will grant him *endless joy in* life eternal. ⁸But selfish individuals who *make trouble,* resist the truth, or sell out to wickedness *will meet a very different fate—they* will find fury and indignation *as the fruit of living in the wrong.* ⁹Suffering and pain await everyone whose life is marked by evil living (first for the Jew, and next for the non-Jew). ¹⁰But if you do what is right, you will receive glory, admiration, and peace (again, first for the Jew, then for the non-Jew).

¹¹God has no favorites. ¹²If one lives life without knowledge of the law—*the teachings of the Torah*—he will sin and die apart from the law. If someone else lives life under the law, his sin will be judged by what the law teaches. ¹³*Here's my point*: just because a person hears the law *read or recited* does not mean he is right before the one true God; it is following the law that makes one right, *not just hearing it.* ¹⁴⁻¹⁵For instance, some outsiders who are not required to follow the law often live quite naturally by its teachings. Even though the law wasn't given to them, in themselves they have the law. *Here's the thing*: their lives demonstrate that God has inscribed the law's teachings on their hearts. *On judgment day,* their consciences will testify for them, and their thoughts will both accuse and defend them. ¹⁶This good news given to me declares that this *affirmation and accusation* will take place on that day when God, through Jesus, the Liberating King, will judge every person's life secrets.

¹⁷Listen, if you claim to be a Jew, count on the law, and boast in your relationship with God; ¹⁸if you know His will and can determine what is essential (because you have been instructed in the law); and ¹⁹if you stand convinced that you are *chosen to be* a guide to the blind, a light to those who live in darkness, ²⁰a teacher of foolish wanderers and children, and have in the law what is essentially the form of knowledge and truth— ²¹then tell me—why don't you practice what you preach? If you are going to sermonize against stealing, then stop stealing. ²²If you are going to teach others not to commit adultery, then be completely faithful to your spouse. If you hate idolatry, then stop robbing the temples! ²³If you pride yourself in having God's law, then stop dishonoring God by failing to keep its teaching. ²⁴Here's what it says: "Because of you, God's reputation is slandered by those outside the covenant."*

²⁵You see, your circumcision is of value only if you keep the law's teachings. But if you break the rules, you are no different than those without the mark. ²⁶So if an uncircumcised man abides by God's just precepts, doesn't that make his standing before God the same as one who is circumcised? ²⁷The man who is naturally uncircumcised, but still keeps the law, will stand in judgment over the lawbreaker who is circumcised and yet has God's written law. ²⁸*Although you wouldn't know it by looking at him, he is indeed a Jew.* A mark that is evident doesn't necessarily make one a

* 2:4 Literally, repentance
* 2:24 Isaiah 52:5; Ezekiel 36:22

Jew, and circumcision that is evident only in the flesh is not true. ²⁹But the true Jew is Jewish on the inside—*in secret places no one but God can see*—and true circumcision involves the heart; it comes from the Spirit, not from some written code. The praise *and reputation* of that kind of Jew comes from God, not from man.

> *W*hen God's people—or people who claim to be God's people—are hypocrites, then God is the one who gets the bad name. How often do we say one thing and do another? How often have we set a standard for others only to break it ourselves? The saying is true: we practice every day what we believe; all the rest is religious talk. There is a lot of religious talk out there, a lot of smugness and self-satisfaction. But every day people readily violate their consciences and the Lord's reasonable teachings. For faith to matter, it has to get under your skin.

3 So then, do the Jews have an advantage *over the other nations*? Does circumcision do anything for you? ²The answer is yes, in every way. To begin with, God spoke to and through the Jewish people. *They have a record of His words.* ³But what if some have been unfaithful? Does the fact that they abandoned their faith zero-out God's faithfulness? ⁴Absolutely not! If every person *on the planet* were a liar *and thief*, God would still be true. It stands written:

> Whenever You speak, You are in the right.
> When You come to judge, You will prevail.*

⁵If our perpetual injustice and corruption exist merely to accentuate the purity of God's justice, what can we say? Is God unjust for unleashing His fury against us? (I am speaking from our limited human perspective.) ⁶Again, absolutely not! If this were so, how could God stand as Judge

over the world? ⁷But if my lies serve only to point out God's truth and bring Him glory, then why will I be judged for my sin? ⁸There are slanderous charges out there that we are saying things like, "Let's be as wicked as possible so that something good will come from it." Those malicious gossips will get what they deserve.

⁹So what then? Are we Jews better off? Not at all. We have made it clear that people everywhere, Jews and non-Jews, are living under the power of sin. ¹⁰Here's what Scripture says:

> No one is righteous—not even one.
> ¹¹There is no one who understands *the truth*;
> no one is seeking after the *one, true* God.
> ¹²All have turned away; together they've become worthless.
> No one does good, not even one.*
> ¹³What comes out of their mouths is as foul as a rotting corpse;
> their words stink of flattery.*
> Viper venom hides beneath their lips;*
> ¹⁴ their mouths are full of curses, lies, and oppression.*
> ¹⁵Their feet race to *violence and bloodshed*;
> ¹⁶ destruction and trouble line the roads of their lives,
> ¹⁷And they've never taken the road to peace.*
> ¹⁸ You will never see the fear of God in their eyes.*

> *S*in is more than just wrong choices, bad decisions, and willful acts of disobedience that violate God's Word and are contrary to His will. Oh, don't misunderstand; it is that

* 3:4 Psalm 51:4
* 3:10-12 Psalms 14:1-3; 53:1-3
* 3:13 Psalm 5:9
* 3:13 Psalm 140:3
* 3:14 Psalm 10:7
* 3:15-17 Isaiah 59:7-8
* 3:18 Psalm 36:1

and much more. You see, Paul knew sin as missing the mark or deliberately stepping over the line, but he also knew sin was a power at work in him and every child of Adam. As strange as it may sound, sin seems to have a will of its own, and often sin's power was more than Paul could handle. Like an addiction, sin takes hold of us and causes us to act in ways we never wanted. For Paul the cross of Jesus deals finally and definitively with the dual reality of sin. Not only are we forgiven of our sins—our willful acts of disobedience—but we are also liberated from the power of sin.

¹⁹We want to be clear that whatever the law says, it says to everyone who is under its authority. Its purpose is to muzzle every mouth, *to silence idle talk,* and to bring the whole world under the standard of God's justice. ²⁰Therefore, doing what the law prescribes will not make anyone right in the eyes of God—*that's not its purpose*—but the law is capable of exposing the true nature of our sin.

²¹But now *for the good news*: God's restorative justice has entered the world, independent of the law. Both the law and the prophets told us this day would come. ²²This redeeming justice comes through the faithfulness of Jesus,* the Liberating King, who makes salvation a reality for all who believe—without the slightest partiality. ²³You see, all have sinned, and all their futile attempts to reach God in His glory fail. ²⁴Yet they are now saved and set right by His free gift of grace through the redemption available only in Jesus, the Liberating King. ²⁵When God set Him up to be the sacrifice—the seat of mercy where sins are atoned through faith—His blood became the demonstration of God's own restorative justice. All of this confirms His faithfulness *to the promise* and His unique position to expunge the record of sin over the course of human history. ²⁶This expression of God's restorative justice displays in the present that He is just and righteous and that He makes right

those who trust and commit themselves to Jesus.

*I*n the incarnation and sacrificial death of Jesus, God is at work to extend salvation to those who fall under sin's addiction. They are liberated from its power, cleansed of its stain. By "God's restorative justice," Paul means first the justice that belongs to God and reflects His character. God is just, fair, or in a word, righteous. But character is dynamic, not static. This means that God's justice must express itself in some way. So it is in the nature of God's justice that He acts to restore and repair a world that is not the way it should be. Above all, it is God's saving actions through Jesus that constitute the gift of God's restorative justice.

²⁷So is there any place left for boasting? No. It's been shut out completely. *And how?* By what sort of law? The law of works perhaps? No! By the law of faith. ²⁸We hold to the teaching that people are justified, *that is, made right with God* through faith, which has nothing to do with the deeds the law prescribes. ²⁹Is God only the God of the Jews? *If He created all things, then doesn't that make Him* the God of all people? Jews and non-Jews, *insiders and outsiders alike*? Yes, He is also the God of all the outsiders. ³⁰So since God is one, *there is one way for Jews and outsiders,* circumcised and uncircumcised, to be right with Him. That is the way of faith. ³¹So are we trying to abolish the law because of faith? Absolutely not! In fact, we *now are free to* establish the law.

4 In light of all of this, what should we say about our ancestor Abraham? ²If Abraham was made right by performing certain works, then he would surely have something to brag about. Right? Not before *the Creator* God, ³because as the

* 3:22 Often translated "faith in Jesus"

Scriptures say, "Abraham believed God *and trusted in His promises,* so God counted it to his favor as righteousness."* ⁴Now, when you work a job, does your paycheck come to you as a gift *or as compensation for your work*? It is *most certainly* not a gift—you are only paid what you have earned. ⁵So for the person who does not work, but instead trusts in the One who makes the ungodly right, his faith is counted for him as righteousness.

⁶*Remember the psalm where* David speaks about the benefits that come to the person that God credits with righteousness apart from works? He said,

⁷Blessed are those whose wrongs
 have been forgiven
and whose sins have been covered.
⁸Blessed is the person whose sin the
 Lord will not take into account.*

⁹So is this blessing spoken only for the circumcised or for all uncircumcised people too? We remind *you what the Scripture has to say*: faith was credited to Abraham as righteousness.*

¹⁰So when was the credit awarded *to Abraham*? Was it before or after his circumcision? Well, it certainly wasn't after—it was before he was circumcised. ¹¹*Eventually* he was given circumcision as a sign of his right standing, indicating that he was credited on the basis of the faith he possessed before he was circumcised. It happened this way so that Abraham might become the spiritual father of all those who are not circumcised but are made right through their faith. ¹²In the same way, *God destined him to be* the spiritual father of all those who are circumcised as more than an outward sign, but who walk in our father Abraham's faithful footsteps—a faith he possessed while he was still uncircumcised.

¹³The promise given to Abraham and his children, that one day they would inherit the world, did not come because he followed the rules of the law. It came as a result of his right standing *before God, a standing he* obtained through faith. ¹⁴If this inheritance that we are promised is based on keeping the law, then faith is a useless commodity and the promise is canceled. ¹⁵For the law brings God's wrath *against sin*. But where law doesn't draw the line, there can be no crime.

¹⁶This is the reason that faith is the single source of the promise—so that grace would be offered to all Abraham's children, those whose lives are defined by the law and those who follow the path of faith charted by Abraham, our common father. ¹⁷As it is recorded *in the Scriptures,* "I have appointed you the father of many nations."* In the presence of the God who creates out of nothing and holds the power to bring to life what is dead, Abraham believed *and so became our father.*

¹⁸Against the odds, Abraham's hope grew into full-fledged faith that he would turn out to be the father of many nations, just as God had promised when He said, "That's how *many* your descendants will be."* ¹⁹His faith did not fail, although he was well aware that his impotent body, after nearly 100 years, was as good as dead and that Sarah's womb, too, was dead. ²⁰In spite of all this, his faith in God's promise did not falter. In fact, his faith grew as he gave glory to God ²¹because he was supremely confident that God could deliver on His promise. ²²This is why, *you see, God saw* his faith *and* counted him as righteous; *this is how he became* right with God.

²³The story of how faith was credited to Abraham was not recorded for him and him alone, ²⁴but written for all of us who would one day be credited for having faith in God, the One who raised Jesus our Lord from the realm of the dead. ²⁵He was delivered over to death for our trespasses and raised so that we might be made right *with God.*

* 4:3 Genesis 15:6
* 4:7-8 Psalm 32:1-2
* 4:9 Genesis 15:6
* 4:17 Genesis 17:5
* 4:18 Genesis 15:5

In God's plan to restore a fallen and disfigured world, Abraham became the father of all of us, the agent of blessing to every family on earth. Jesus completes what God the Father started centuries before when He established Abraham's covenant family. Those who put faith in Jesus and call Him "Lord" become part of Abraham's faith family. Because God is gracious, loving, and merciful, this family of men and women from every corner of the earth is not only declared "right," but ultimately is made right as well. It happens through God's actions—not our efforts—in the death, burial, and resurrection of Jesus who was crucified for our misdeeds and raised to repair what has been wrong all along. So the promises of God made nearly 4,000 years ago are being realized in men and women who hear the call of faith and answer "yes" to it.

5 Since we have been *acquitted and made right* through faith, we are able to experience *true and lasting* peace with God through our Lord Jesus, the Liberating King. [2]Jesus leads us into a place of *radical* grace where we are able to celebrate the hope of experiencing God's glory. [3]And that's not all. We also celebrate in seasons of suffering because we know that when we suffer we develop endurance, [4]which shapes our characters. When our characters are refined, we learn what it means to hope *and anticipate God's goodness*. [5]And hope will never fail to satisfy our deepest need because the Holy Spirit that was given to us has flooded our hearts with God's love.

[6]When the time was right, our Liberating King died for all of us who were far from God, powerless, and weak. [7]Now it is rare to find someone willing to die for an upright person, although it's possible that someone may give up his life for one who is truly good. [8]But *think about this:* while we were wasting our lives in sin, God revealed His powerful love to us *in a tangi-* ble display—the Liberating King died for us. [9]As a result, the blood of Jesus has made us right with God now, *and at the final judgment,* we will be rescued by Him from God's wrath. [10]If we were in the heat of combat with God when His Son came to reconcile us by laying down His life, then how much more will we be saved by Jesus' *resurrection* life? [11]In fact, we stand now reconciled *and at peace* with God. That's why we celebrate in God through our Lord Jesus, the Liberating King.

[12]Consider this: sin entered our world through one man, *Adam;* and through sin, death followed *in hot pursuit.* Death spread rapidly to infect all people on the earth as they engaged in sin.

God's gift of grace and salvation is so amazing. Paul struggled to find the words to describe it. He looked everywhere around him to find a metaphor, an image, a word to put into language one aspect of this awesome gift. One of those is "reconciliation." There is hardly anything more beautiful than to see two people who have been enemies or estranged or separated coming back together. When Paul reflected on what God had done through Jesus, our Liberating King, he thought about reconciliation. Before we receive God's blessing through His Son, we are enemies of God, sinners of the worst sort. But God makes the first move to restore us to a right relationship with Him.

[13]Before God gave the law, sin existed, *but there was no way to account for it.* Outside the law, how could anyone be charged and found guilty of sin? [14]Still, death plagued all humanity from Adam to Moses, even those whose sin was of a different sort than Adam's. *You see, in God's plan,* Adam was a prototype of the One who comes *to usher in a new day.* [15]But the free gift of grace bears no resemblance to Adam's crime *that brings a death sentence to all of humanity;*

in fact, it is quite the opposite. For if the one man's sin brings death to so many, how much more does the gift of God's *radical* grace extend to humanity since the One—Jesus, the Liberating King—offered His generous gift. ¹⁶His free gift is nothing like the scourge of the first man's sin. The judgment that fell because of one false step brought condemnation, but the free gift following countless offenses results in a favorable verdict—not guilty. ¹⁷If one man's sin brought a reign of death—*that's Adam's legacy*—how much more will those who receive grace in abundance and the free gift of redeeming justice reign in life by means of one other man—Jesus, the Liberating King.

¹⁸So here is the result: as one man's sin brought about condemnation *and punishment* for all people, so one man's act of faithfulness makes all of us right with God and brings us to new life. ¹⁹Just as through one man's *defiant* disobedience every one of us were made sinners, so through the *willing* obedience of the one man many of us will be made right.

²⁰When the law came into the picture, sin grew and grew; but where sin has spread, grace is there to cut it down and defeat it. *No matter how much sin crept in, there was always more grace.* ²¹In the same way that sin has reigned in the sphere of death, now grace reigns through God's restorative justice, *eclipsing death and leading to eternal life* through Jesus, the Liberating King, our Lord.

*W*e arrived here, children of a common ancestor, Adam. As such, we have inherited his traits, physically and spiritually. Although our sin may be of a different sort than his, we sin no less than Adam. The proof of that is death. Adam opened the way for sin and death to pursue us and run rampant across the earth. But from the beginning, God had a plan to reverse the curse. At just the right moment in human history, Jesus arrives, a son of Adam and the Son of God. Through His faithful obedience to His Father, He

challenges the twin powers of sin and death and defeats them. The spell is broken. Sin no longer reigns unchecked. Death no longer has the last word.

6 How should we respond to all of this? Is it good to persist in a life of sin so that grace multiplies even more? ²Absolutely not! How can we die to a life where sin ruled over us and then invite sin back into our lives? ³Did someone forget to tell you that when we were initiated into Jesus, the Liberating King, through ceremonial washing,* we entered into His death? ⁴Therefore, we were buried with Him through this ritual* into death. So when God the Father, in all His glory, resurrected our Liberating King, we were also called out of the grave to walk *confidently* into a new life. ⁵*To put it another way:* if we have been united with Him to share in a death like His, don't you understand that we will also share in His resurrection? ⁶We know this: whatever we used to be with our old sinful ways has been nailed to His cross. So our entire record of sin has been canceled, and we no longer have to bow down to sin's power. ⁷A dead man, you see, cannot be bound by sin. ⁸But if we have died with our Liberating King, we believe that we shall also live together with Him. ⁹So we stand firm in the conviction that death holds no power over our Liberator, because He was resurrected from the dead never to face death again. ¹⁰When He died, He died to whatever power sin had, once and for all, and now He lives completely to God. ¹¹So here is how to picture yourself now that you have been initiated into Jesus, the Liberating King: you are dead to sin's power and influence, but you are alive to God's rule.

¹²Don't invite *that insufferable tyrant of* sin back into your mortal body so you won't become obedient to its *destructive*

* 6:3 Literally, immersion, in a rite of initiation and purification
* 6:4 Literally, immersion, a rite of initiation and purification

desires. [13]Don't offer your bodily members to sin's service as tools of wickedness; instead, offer your body to God as those who are alive from the dead. Offer every part of your body to God as a tool for justice *and goodness in this world,* [14]because sin is no longer your tyrant and because you are under grace and not the law.

> *N*ow that sin and death no longer define us, what does? In a word, "grace." Grace is God's favor given freely to us through His Son, Jesus, who came to liberate us from sin's power. If we were at one time servants of sin, now we are subjects of grace. When we are ceremonially washed, we enter into a new reality created by the death and resurrection of Jesus.

[15]So what do we do now? Throw ourselves into a life of sin because we are cloaked in grace and don't have to answer to the law? Absolutely not! [16]Doesn't it make sense that if you sign yourself over as a slave, you will have to obey your master? The question *before you is: who will be your master?* Will it be sin—which will lead to certain death—or obedience—which will lead to a right *and reconciled* life? [17]Thank God that your slavery to sin has ended and that *in your new freedom* you pledged your heartfelt obedience *and devotion* to that teaching which was passed on to you. [18]*The beauty of your new situation is this:* now that you are free from sin, you are free to serve *a different master, God's redeeming* justice.

[19]Forgive me for using casual language to compensate for your natural weakness of human understanding. *I want to be perfectly clear.* In the same way you gave your bodily members away as slaves to corrupt and lawless living and found yourselves deeper in your unruly lives, now devote your members as slaves to right *and reconciled* lives so you will find yourselves deeper in holy living. [20]In the days when you lived as slaves to sin, you had no obligation to do the right thing. *In that regard, you were free.* [21]But what do you have to

show from your former lives besides the shame of skeletons in your closet? The outcome of that life is death, *guaranteed.* [22]But now that you have been emancipated from the death grip of sin and are God's slave, you have *a different sort of life,* a growing holiness. The outcome of that life is eternal life. [23]The payoff for a life of sin is death, but God is offering us a free gift—a payoff of eternal life through our Lord Jesus, the Liberating King.

> *G*race is no license to sin. As creatures, we are made to serve our Creator. In the absence of truth, we will serve somebody or something. It's an essential part of our nature. Our only choice is this: whom will we serve? At one time, we all served sin and grew weak under its deadly power over us. Now, through God's grace, we have become servants of obedience that sets us right with God, each other, and ourselves. We must daily decide whose servant we are and offer Him our hands, our feet, our hearts, our eyes.

7 My brothers and sisters who are well versed in the law, don't you realize that a person is subject to the law only as long as he is alive? [2]So, for example, a wife is obligated by the law to her husband until his death; if the husband dies, she is freed from the parts of the law that relate to her marriage. [3]If she is sleeping with other men while her husband is alive, she is rightly labeled an adulteress. But if her husband dies, she is free from the law and can marry another man. In such a case, she is not an adulteress.

[4]My brothers and sisters, in the same way, you have died when it comes to the law because of *your connection with* the body of our Liberating King. His death—*and your death with Him*—frees you to belong to the One who was raised from the dead so we can bear fruit for God. [5]As we were living in the flesh, the law *could not solve the problem of sin; it* only awakened

our lust for more and cultivated the fruit of death in our bodily members. [6]But now that we have died to those chains that imprisoned us, we have been released from the law to serve in a new Spirit-empowered life, not the old written code.

[7]So what is the story? Is the law itself sin? Absolutely not! *It is the exact opposite.* I would never have known what sin is if it were not for the law. *For example,* I would not have known that desiring something that belongs to my neighbor is sin if the law had not said, "Do not covet."* [8]Sin took advantage of the commandments to create a constant stream of greed and desire within me; *I began to want everything.* You see, apart from the law, sin lies dormant. [9]I was alive before I knew the law, but the commandments came *and changed everything*: sin came to life, and I died. [10]This commandment was supposed to bring me life; but in my experience, it brought death. [11]Sin took advantage of the commandment, tricked me, and exploited it in order to kill me. [12]So *hear me out:* the law is holy. The commandments are holy, right, and good.

[13]So did the good *commandment* bring me death? Absolutely not! It was sin that killed me, *not the law.* It's the nature of sin to produce death through what is good and exploit the commandments to multiply sin even more. [14]This is what we know: the law comes from the spiritual realm. *My problem is that* I am of the fallen human realm, owned by sin, *which tries to keep me in its service.*

> *G*od gave Israel the law as part of His covenant promises. The law did a great deal for His people; mainly it set them apart from all other people and gave Israel a blueprint for God's will. God's law perfectly brought sin to the surface and exposed it. The law could not free us from the power of sin and its evil twin, death.

[15]*Listen,* I can't explain my actions. Here's why: I am not able to do the things I want; and at the same time, I do the things I despise. [16]If I am doing the things I have already decided not to do, I am agreeing with the law regarding what is good. [17]But now I am no longer the one acting—*I've lost control*—sin has taken up residence in me *and is wreaking havoc.* [18]I know that in me, that is, in my fallen human nature, there is nothing good. I can will myself to do something good, but that does not help me to carry it out. [19]I can determine that I am going to do good, but I don't do it; instead, I end up living out the evil that I decided not to do. [20]If I end up doing the exact thing I pledged not to do, I am no longer doing it because sin has taken up residence in me. [21]Here's what I've discovered about the law: regardless of my desire to do the right thing, *it is clear that* evil is never far away.

[22]In my mind, I am in happy agreement with God's law; [23]but the rest of my body does not concur. My bodily members are at war with my mind (which agrees with the law), and I have become a prisoner in this war to the rule of sin that reigns supreme in my body. [24]I am absolutely miserable! Is there anyone who can cut me free from this corpse *that is tied to my back? It is slowly killing me.* [25]I am so thankful to God for the blessings of our Lord Jesus, the Liberating King! On one hand, I devotedly serve God's law in my mind; but on the other hand, in my flesh, I serve the principle of sin.

> *P*aul describes the torture from his struggle against the power of sin, and he draws a picture that would help the believers in Rome more fully grasp the struggle. The Romans were known for the ways they would slowly and painfully execute criminals or enemies of the state. A slow death on a Roman cross was one of their forms of execution, but another was executing a murderer by tying the dead body of the victim to the murderer's own flesh. As the victim decayed, the murderer would die a slow and gruesome death.

* 7:7 Exodus 20:17; Deuteronomy 5:21

Paul's struggle with sin is so significant that he chooses this grotesque analogy to explain himself to the believers in Rome.

We, like addicts, are not in control and end up falling back into painful habits again and again. Sin is at work in our flesh, fragmenting us and fracturing our world into small, broken pieces. The Liberating King is the only answer.

thanks to what Jesus has done for us. By sending His Son in "the likeness of sinful flesh," God judged sin finally and completely. The sins of the world were concentrated and condemned in the flesh of Jesus as He hung on the cross. So now there is no condemnation remaining for those who've entered into the life, death, and resurrection of Jesus.

8 Therefore, now no condemnation awaits those who are living in Jesus, the Liberating King, [avoiding sin and embracing the Spirit,]* ²because when you live in Him *a new law takes effect.* The law of the Spirit of life breathes into you and rescues you from the law of sin and death. ³God did something the law could never do. *You see, human flesh took its toll on God's law. In and of itself, the law is not weak; but* the flesh weakens it. So to condemn the sin that was ruling in the flesh, God sent His own Son, bearing the likeness of sinful flesh, as a sin offering. ⁴Now we are able to live up to the justice demanded by the law. But that ability has not come from living by our fallen human nature; it has come because we walk according to the movement of the Spirit in our lives.

⁵If you live your life animated by the flesh—*namely, your fallen, corrupt nature*—then your mind is focused on the matters of the flesh. But if you live your life animated by the Spirit—*namely, God's indwelling presence*—then your focus is on the work of the Spirit. ⁶A mind focused on the flesh is doomed to death, but a mind focused on the Spirit will find full life and complete peace. ⁷You see, a mind focused on the flesh is declaring war against God; it defies the authority of God's law and is incapable of following His path. ⁸*So it is clear that* God takes no pleasure in those who live oriented to the flesh.

The power of sin and death has been eclipsed by the power of the Spirit. The Spirit breathes life into our mortal, sin-infested bodies—

⁹But you do not live in the flesh. You live in the Spirit, assuming, of course, that the Spirit of God lives inside of you. *The truth is that* anyone who does not have the Spirit of the Liberator living within does not belong to God. ¹⁰If the Liberating King lives in you, then *God's restorative* justice is breathing life into your spirits despite the fact that sin brings death to your bodies. ¹¹If the Spirit of the One who resurrected Jesus from the dead lives inside of you, then *you can be sure that* He will cast *the light of* life into your mortal bodies through the life-giving power of the Spirit residing in you.

¹²So, my brothers and sisters, you owe the flesh nothing! You do not need to live according to its ways, *so abandon its oppressive regime.* ¹³For if your life is just about satisfying the impulses of your sinful nature, then prepare to die. But if you have invited the Spirit to destroy these selfish desires, you will experience life. ¹⁴If the Spirit of God is leading you, then *take comfort in knowing* you are His children. ¹⁵You see, you have not received a spirit that returns you to slavery, so you have nothing to fear. The spirit you have welcomes you into God's own family. You have been adopted, *and God is truly your Father.* That's why we call out to Him, "Abba! Father!" *as we would address a loving daddy.* ¹⁶*Through that prayer,* God's Spirit confirms in our spirits that we are His own children. ¹⁷If we are God's children, that means we are His heirs along with the Liberator, set to inherit everything that is His. If we will share His sufferings, *we*

* 8:1 The earliest manuscripts omit this portion.

know that we will ultimately share in His glory.

> s Paul ponders the story of redemption, he finds in the family unit a beautiful image of what salvation means. Those who enter into God's salvation are adopted into God's family. Before we receive the gift of God's grace, we are homeless orphans searching for some place to belong. But now all that has changed. The Father reaches out through His Son to all those orphaned by sin and death and brings us into His family. We are adopted into His forever family and fully enfranchised as His heirs.

18Now I'm sure of this: the pain and suffering we endure now is not even worth comparing to the glory that is coming and will be revealed in us. 19For all of creation is waiting, yearning for the time when the children of God will be revealed. 20You see, all of creation has collapsed into emptiness, not by its own choosing, but by God's. Still He placed within it a *deep and abiding* hope 21that creation would one day be liberated from its slavery to corruption and experience the glorious freedom of the children of God. 22Everything created by God, *including every bird, every beast, and every plant,* is moaning in unison with birthing pains up until now. 23*And there is more;* it's not just creation—all of us are moaning together too. Though we have already tasted the firstfruits of the Spirit, we are longing for the total redemption of our bodies that comes when our adoption as children *of God* is complete— 24for we have been saved in this hope *and for this future.* Do we hope for something we hold in our hands? No, we hope for things we have never seen. 25If we hope for things we have never seen, then we hope with true perseverance and eager anticipation.

26A similar thing happens *when we pray.* We are weak and do not know how to pray, so the Spirit steps in and articulates prayers for us with groaning too profound for words. 27*Don't you know that* He who pursues and explores the human heart *intimately* knows the Spirit's mind because He pleads to God for His saints to align their lives with the will of God? 28We are confident that God is able to orchestrate everything to create something good *and beautiful* when we love Him and accept His invitation to live according to His plan. 29-30*From the distant past,* His eternal love reached into the future, and He chose those who would be conformed to the image of His Son. *God not only knew which part they would play, but He chose them* especially to be united with His Son, the firstborn of a new family of believers, all brothers and sisters. All His chosen ones have been called to a different destiny to experience what it means to be justified and glorified together.

31So what should we say about all of this? If God is on our side, *then tell me:* whom should we fear? 32If He did not spare His own Son, but handed Him over on our account, then *don't you think that* He will graciously give us all things with Him? 33Can anyone be so bold as to level a charge against God's chosen? *Especially since* God's *"not guilty"* verdict is already declared. 34Who has the authority to condemn? Jesus, the Liberating King, who died, but *more importantly, conquered death when He* was raised to sit at the right hand of God where He pleads on our behalf. 35So who can separate us? What can disconnect us from the Liberating King's love? Can troubles, hardships, persecution, hunger, poverty, danger, or even death? *The answer is, absolutely nothing.* 36The psalm says,

> On Your behalf, our lives are endangered constantly;
> we are like sheep awaiting slaughter.*

37But no matter what comes, we will always taste victory through Him who loved us. 38For I have every confidence that nothing—not death, life, heavenly messengers, *dark* spirits, the present, the future,

* 8:36 Psalm 44:22

spiritual powers, [39]height, depth, nor any created thing—can disconnect us from the love of God that came to us in Jesus, our Lord and Liberating King.

In all of Paul's letters, there is no more triumphant note than in this declaration. He has reached the climax of what it means to live empowered by God's Spirit. We are champions, one and all. We will taste victory and sweet success made possible by His love and gifts to us. We may fear the harsh judgment of the majority. We may bristle under the scowls of others. We may even be unsettled by thoughts of death, persecution, and dark spiritual powers. But Paul celebrates the absolute assurance that no one and nothing can come between us and the love of God.

9 Now let me speak the truth *as plainly as I know it* in the Liberating King. I am not lying when I say that my conscience and the Holy Spirit are witnesses [2]to my state of constant grief. [3]*It may sound extreme,* but I wish that I were lost, cursed, and totally separated from the Liberator, if it would change *the eternal destination of* my brothers and sisters, my flesh *and countrymen. All of them are family to me; we are bound by blood.* [4]They are, *after all,* Israelites who have been placed into God's family; the glory, the covenants, the *gift of the* law, the temple-service, and God's promises are their rightful heritage. [5]The patriarchs are theirs too; and from their bloodline comes the Liberating King, who reigns supreme over all things, God blessed forever. Amen.

The tone of the letter changes abruptly. One minute Paul is celebrating the victorious power of the Liberating King's love; the next he is grieving because most of his people are not pressing their way into the Kingdom. But like his Master, Paul is willing to lay down his life for them, if that would only make a difference. But he can't, and it won't.

[6]Clearly it is not that God's word has failed. The truth is that not everyone descended from Israel is truly Israel. [7]Just because people can claim Abraham as their father does not make them his true children. But *in the Scriptures, it says,* "Through Isaac your *covenant* children will be named."* [8]The proper interpretation is this: Abraham's children by natural descent are not *necessarily* God's covenant people; what matters is that His children receive and live the promise. [9]For this is the word God promised: "In due time, I will come, and Sarah will give birth to a son."* [10]But the story didn't stop there. Remember when Rebekah conceived her twin boys by our father Isaac? [11-12]The twins were in Rebekah's womb when God said to her, "The older will serve the younger."* *This was not based on merit or actions;* the twins had not done anything to please or displease God. This was God's call on each son and His desired purposes. [13]Just as the Scriptures say, "I loved Jacob, but I hated Esau."*

[14]So how do we talk about that? Are God's dealings unjust? Absolutely not! [15]Because He said to Moses, "I will show mercy to whomever I choose to show mercy, and I will demonstrate compassion on whomever I choose to have compassion."* [16]The point is that God's mercy has nothing to do with our will or the things we pursue. It is completely up to God. [17]The Scriptures even speak to the Pharaoh himself: "I have given you a position of power so that I might show My *greater* power through you and so that My name might be declared throughout every land upon the earth."* [18]So when and where God decides to show mercy is completely up to Him. Likewise, when He chooses to harden one's heart, how can we argue?

* 9:7 Genesis 21:12
* 9:9 Genesis 18:10,14
* 9:11-12 Genesis 25:23
* 9:13 Malachi 1:2-3
* 9:15 Exodus 33:19
* 9:17 Exodus 9:16

¹⁹I can hear one of you asking, "Then how can He blame us *if He is the one in complete control*? How can we do anything He has not chosen for us?" ²⁰*Here's my answer:* Who are you, a human, to argue with God? If God takes the time to shape us from the dust, is it right to point a finger at Him and say, "Why have You made me this way?" ²¹Doesn't the sculptor have the right to shape the clay in any way he chooses? Can't he make one lump into a vase *of elegant design*, and another into a common jug, *even as lowly as a spittoon*? *Absolutely.* ²²Even though God desires to demonstrate His anger and to reveal His power, He has shown tremendous restraint toward those vessels of wrath that are doomed to be cracked and shattered. ²³And why is that? To make the wealth of His glory known to vessels of mercy that are prepared for great beauty. ²⁴*The vessels of glory* include all of us. God has invited Jews and non-Jews, *insiders and outsiders*; it makes no difference. ²⁵The prophet Hosea says:

> I will give a new name to those who
>   are not My people; I'll call them
>   "My people,"
> and to the one who has not been
>   loved, I'll rename her "beloved."*
> ²⁶And it shall turn out that in the very
>   place where it was said to them,
>   "You are not My people,"
> they will be called "children of the
>   living God."*

²⁷And *this is what* Isaiah cries out when he speaks of Israel, "Even though the number of the children of Israel had once been like the sand of the sea, only a remnant of My people will be rescued and remain. ²⁸For the Lord will waste no time in carrying out every detail of His sentence upon the earth."* ²⁹It is as Isaiah predicts:

> Except for the fraction of us who hang
>   on by the grace of the Eternal
>   One who commands armies,
> we'd be *destroyed and deserted* like
>   Sodom
> and Gomorrah, *utterly done in.**

For Paul, the astonishing truth of the gospel has to do with what God is now doing with the non-Jews. Apparently God's plan all along was to make those who are not His people into His people. All those who never experienced God's love are now experiencing it as they enter into the life of the Spirit through faith. But what does this mean for Israel? Israel, too, is included in the people of God; but again, this does not mean all of Israel. Pedigree is not what counts; faith is. As it was in the days of the prophets, so it is again. Divine judgment is falling on disobedience, but a remnant of faithful Jews—a fraction of the whole—is being saved.

³⁰So what does all of this mean? Did the non-Jews stumble into a right standing with God without chasing after it? Yes, they found it through faith. ³¹And has Israel, who has pursued the law to express their covenant relationship, failed to keep the law? Yes again. ³²And why is that? Because Israel did not follow the path of faith. They thought that whatever they needed *to be right with God* could be accomplished by doing the works of the law; they tripped over the stumbling stone. ³³As the Scriptures say,

> Look *what I am going to do* in Zion.
> I'll put in place a stone that blocks
>   and trips *those who do wrong*,
> a source of security and peace for
>   those who trust in it.*

10 My brothers and sisters, I pray constantly to God for the salvation of my people; it is the deep desire of my heart. ²What I can say about them is that they are enthusiastic about God, but

* 9:25 Hosea 2:23
* 9:26 Hosea 1:10
* 9:27-28 Isaiah 10:22-23
* 9:29 Isaiah 1:9
* 9:33 Isaiah 8:14; 28:16

that won't lead them to Him because their zeal is not based on true knowledge. [3]In their ignorance about how God is working to make things right, they have been trying to establish their own right standing with God *through the law.* But they are not operating under God's saving, restorative justice. [4]You see, God's purpose for the law reaches its climax when the Liberator arrives; now all who believe in Him can have their lives made right with God.

> *G*od's plan to restore the world disfigured by sin and death reaches its climax with the arrival of the Liberating King. When the King enters, all the prophecies, all the hopes, all the longings find in Him their true fulfillment. There may have been earlier fulfillments; but these are only partial fulfillments, signposts along the way to God's true goal. The goal has been the restoration of people to a holy God. With Jesus, we find the only perfect man with right standing before God. He comes to blaze a path defined by God's justice, not by our own sense of right and wrong. All men, women, and children who commit their lives to Him will be made right with God and will begin new lives defined by faith and God's new covenant.

[5]Moses *made this clear long ago when he* wrote about *what it takes to have* a right relationship with God based on the law: "the person devoted to the law's commands will live by them."* [6]But a right relationship based on faith sounds like this: "Do not say to yourselves, 'Who will go up into heaven?'"* (that is, to bring down the Liberating King), [7]"or, 'Who will go down into the abyss?'"* (that is, to bring the Liberating King up from the dead). [8]But what does it actually say? "The word is near you, in your mouth and in your heart"* (that is, the good news we have been called to preach to you). [9]So if you believe deep in your heart that God raised Jesus from the pit of death and if

you voice your allegiance by confessing the truth that "Jesus is Lord," then you will be saved! [10]Belief begins in the heart and leads to *a life that's* right with God; confession departs from our lips and brings *eternal* salvation. [11]Because what Isaiah said *was true*: "The one who trusts in Him will not be disgraced."* [12]Remember that the Lord draws no distinction between Jew and non-Jew—He is Lord over all things, and He pours out His treasures on all who invoke His name [13]because *as Scripture says,* "Whoever will call on the name of the Lord will be saved."*

> *F*aith is not a work. It is not something we do. Faith is a response to what God has done already on our behalf. Faith is a natural reflex, the response of a spirit restless in a fragmented, out-of-joint world. When we hear this faith-filled word proclaimed, faith arises.

[14]How can people invoke His name when they do not believe? How can they believe in Him when they have not heard? How can they hear if there is no voice proclaiming Him? [15]How can some give voice to the truth if they are not sent *by God*? As *Isaiah* said, "Ah, how beautiful the feet of those who declare the good news *of victory, of peace and liberation*."* [16]But some will hear the good news and refuse to submit to the truth they hear. Isaiah *the prophet also* said, "Lord, who would ever believe it? Who would possibly accept what we've been told?"* [17]So faith originates in hearing, as we listen to the voice that proclaims the Liberating King.

[18]One would think they had never heard, but they have heard, *for God's voice has been speaking all along*:

* 10:5 Leviticus 18:5
* 10:6 Deuteronomy 30:12
* 10:7 Deuteronomy 30:13
* 10:8 Deuteronomy 30:14
* 10:11 Isaiah 28:16
* 10:13 Joel 2:32
* 10:15 Isaiah 52:7
* 10:16 Isaiah 53:1

Yet from here to the ends of the
earth, their voices have gone
out;
the whole world can hear what
they say.*

¹⁹Did Israel hear and not understand all of
this? *Well,* Moses was the first to say,

I will make you jealous with a
people who are not a nation.
With senseless people I will anger
you.*

²⁰Isaiah the fearless prophet says it this
way:

I was found by people who did not
seek Me;
I showed My face to those who
never asked for Me.*

²¹And as to *the fate of* Israel:

All along I opened My hands
to a rebellious people, who
constantly work against Me.*

11 Now I ask you, has God rejected
His people? *Put another way: does
our God discard His own like yesterday's rubbish?* Absolutely not! *I'm living
proof that God is faithful.* I am an Israelite,
Abraham's my father, and Benjamin's my
tribe. ²God has not, *and will not,* abandon
His covenant people. He always knew they
belonged to Him. Don't you remember the
story of what happens when Elijah pleads
with God to deal with Israel? The Scrip-
ture tells us *his protest:* ³"Lord, they have
murdered Your prophets, they have demol-
ished Your altars, and I alone am left *faithful to You*; now they are seeking to kill
me."* ⁴How does God answer his pleas for
help? The divine Voice says, "I have held
back 7,000 men who are faithful to Me;
none have bowed their knee to worship the
Baal."* ⁵The same thing is happening now.
God has preserved a remnant, elected by
grace. ⁶Grace *is central in God's action here,
and it* has nothing to do with deeds pre-

scribed by the law. If it did, grace would
not be grace, would it?

*I*n every generation, God made
sure a few survived the onslaught
of judgment. The prophets called these
the "remnant." Paul sees himself living
in a crisis moment as fewer and fewer
Jews pledge obedience to the Liberating King. But the King's emissary
finds comfort in realizing how God's
faithfulness is playing out in his day. If
you ever think that you alone are
faithful to God, that somehow God has
forgotten His covenant promises, think
again. He always has a remnant.

⁷Now what does all this mean? Israel has
chased an end it has never reached. Yet
those chosen by God *through grace* have
reached it while all others were made hard
as stones. ⁸The Scriptures continue to say *it
best*:

God made them sleepy, *like they are
heavily drugged,*
eyes that are blindfolded, and ears
that are deaf,
Down to this very day.*

⁹David says *it this way,*

Let their *dinner* table be turned into
a snare and a trap,
an obstacle *to peace* and payback
for their hostility.
¹⁰Let their *bright* eyes become cloudy,
darkened so they cannot see,
and bend their *proud* backs
through it all.*

* 10:18 Psalm 19:4
* 10:19 Deuteronomy 32:21
* 10:20 Isaiah 65:1
* 10:21 Isaiah 65:2
* 11:3 1 Kings 19:10,14
* 11:4 1 Kings 19:18. Baal is the name for a Canaanite
god.
* 11:8 Deuteronomy 29:4; Isaiah 29:10
* 11:9-10 Psalm 69:22-23

[11]So I ask: did the Jewish people stumble and fall *off the deep end*? Absolutely not! *They are not lost forever;* but through their misconduct, the door has been opened for salvation to extend even to the outsiders. *This has been part of God's plan all along, and* so is the jealousy that comes when they realize *the outsiders have been welcomed into God's new covenant.* [12]So if their misconduct leads ultimately to God's riches coming to the world and if their failure turns into the blessing *of salvation* to all people, then how much greater will be the riches and blessing when they are included fully?

[13]But I have this to say to all of you who are not ethnic Jews: I am God's emissary* to you, and I honor this call by focusing on what God is doing *with and through you.* [14]I do this so that somehow my own blood brothers and sisters will be made jealous; and that, *I trust,* will bring some to salvation. [15]If the fact that they are currently set aside resolves the hostility between God and the rest of the world, what will their acceptance bring if not life from the dead? [16]If the first and best of the dough you offer is sacred, the entire loaf will be as well. If the root *of the tree* is sacred, the branches will be also.

[17]Imagine some branches are cut off *of the cultivated olive tree* and other branches of a wild olive (which represents all of you *outsiders*) are grafted in their place. You are nourished by the root of the *cultivated* olive tree. [18]It doesn't give you license to become proud and self-righteous about the fact that you've been grafted in. If you do boast, remember that the branches do not sustain the root—it is the system of roots that *nourishes and* supports you.

[19]I can almost hear some of you saying: "Branches had to be pruned to make room for me." [20]Yes, they were. They were removed because they did not believe; and you will stay attached, be strong, *and be productive* only through faith. So don't think too highly of yourselves; instead, stand in awe *of God's mercy.* [21]Besides *we know that* God did not spare the natural branches, so there is no reason to think He will spare you. [22]Witness the simultaneous balance of the kindness and severity of our God. Severity is directed at the fallen *branches withering without faith.* Yet kindness is directed at you *when God performs the delicate procedure of grafting you to the tree.* So live in the kindness of God or else prepare to be cut off yourselves. [23]If those *branches that have been cut from the tree* do not stay in unbelief, then God will carefully graft them back *onto the tree* because He has the power to do that. [24]So if it is possible for you to be taken from a wild olive tree and become part of a cultivated olive tree, imagine how much easier it would be to reconnect branches that originally grew on that olive tree.

*T*he cultivated olive tree provides Paul with a beautiful image of how believing Jews and non-Jews were organically connected in the plan of God. Life flows from the earth to the branches—some natural, some grafted in—through the rootstock. Paul wants to make sure the grafted branches know they have not arrived on their own; their spiritual life and vitality flow from the root, Israel. God is the Farmer who has tenderly grafted them into the sturdy stock on the basis of faith. So pride and arrogance are completely out of place for those grafted branches. They will bear fruit only as they remain connected by faith to the stock.

[25]My brothers and sisters, I do not want you to be in the dark about this mystery—*I am going to let you in on the plan* so that you will not become conceited *over what's really happening here.* A part of Israel has been hardened *to the good news* until the full number of those outside the Jewish family have entered in. [26]This is the way that all of Israel will be saved. As it was written, *so it also stands*:

> The Deliverer will come from Zion;
>   He will drive away wickedness
>   from Jacob.

---

* 11:13 Literally, apostle

27And this is My covenant promise to them,
> *on the day* when I take away their sins.*

28*It may seem strange.* When it comes to *the work of* the gospel, the fact that they oppose it is actually for your benefit. But when you factor in God's *eternal* election, they are truly loved because they descended from faithful forefathers. 29You see, when God gives a *grace*-gift and issues a call *to a people*, He does not change His mind and take it back. 30There was a time when you *outsiders* were disobedient to God *and at odds with His purpose*, but now you have experienced mercy as a result of their disobedience. 31In the same way, their disobedience now—*which some consider to be obedience*—will make a way for them to receive mercy due to the mercy shown you. 32For God has assigned all of us together, *Jews and non-Jews, insiders and outsiders*, to disobedience so He can show His mercy to all.

> *P*aul says that God's mysterious plan for the ages is being revealed as the number of non-Jewish outsiders swells in the churches and as a part of Israel is hardened, at least for a time. But let's not forget that hardening is not God's unilateral action. Whatever hardening takes place happens first on our side before God reluctantly agrees. That part of Israel now hardened has already rejected God's Liberating King. Yet when the full complement of non-Jewish outsiders enters God's kingdom, "all Israel will be saved." But clearly "all Israel" can't mean every last Jew, because Paul has already shown that not every son or daughter of Abraham is an heir to the promise.

33*We cannot wrap our minds around* God's wisdom and knowledge! Its depths can never be measured! We cannot understand His judgments or explain the mysterious ways that He works!

34For "who can fathom the mind of the Lord?
> Or who can claim to be His advisor?"*
35Or "who can give to God in advance so that God must pay him back?"*

36For all that exists originates in Him, comes through Him, and is moving toward Him; so give Him the glory forever. Amen.

12 Brothers and sisters, in light of *all I have shared with you about* God's mercies, I urge you to offer your bodies as a living and holy sacrifice *to God*, a sacred offering that brings Him pleasure; this is your reasonable, essential worship. 2Do not allow this world to mold you in its own image. Instead, be transformed *from the inside out* by renewing your mind. As a result, you will be able to discern what God wills and whatever God finds good, pleasing, and complete.

> *P*aul urges those who read and hear his letter to respond to the good news by offering their bodies, our bodies—eyes, ears, mouths, hands, feet—to God as a living sacrifice, an odd phrase. Paul knows well enough that sacrifices end in death, not life. But the sacrifice of Jesus changes everything. His resurrection steals life from death and makes it possible for those who trust in Him to become a sacrifice and yet live. But how do we live? We do not live as before, wrapping ourselves in the world and its bankrupt values. We live in constant renewal and transformation of our minds.

3Because of the grace allotted to me, I can *respectfully* tell you not to think of yourselves as being more important than you

---

* 11:26-27 Isaiah 27:9; 59:20-21; Jeremiah 31:33-34
* 11:34 Isaiah 40:13
* 11:35 Job 41:11

are; devote your mind to sound judgment since God has assigned to each of us a measure of faith. [4]For in the same way that one body has so many different parts, each with different functions, [5]we, too—the many—are different parts that form one body in the Liberating King. Each one of us is joined with one another, *and we become together what we could not be alone.* [6]Since our gifts vary depending on the grace poured out on each of us, *it is important that* we exercise the gifts *we have been given.* If prophecy is your gift, then speak as a prophet according to your proportion of faith. [7]If service is your gift, then serve well. If teaching is your gift, then teach well. [8]If you have been given a voice of encouragement, then use it *often.* If giving is your gift, then be generous. If leading, then be eager to get started. If sharing God's mercy, then be cheerful in sharing it.

[9]Love others *well, and* don't hide behind a mask; love authentically. Despise evil; pursue what is good *as if your life depends on it.* [10]Live in true devotion to one another, loving each other as sisters and brothers. Be first to honor others *by putting them first.* [11]Do not slack in your faithfulness and hard work. Let your spirit be on fire, bubbling up and boiling over, as you serve the Lord. [12]*Do not forget to* rejoice, for hope is always just around the corner. Hold up through the hard times that are coming, and devote yourselves to prayer. [13]Share what you have with the saints, so they lack nothing; take every opportunity to open your *life and* home to others, *even if they are outside your faith family.*

[14]If people mistreat or malign you, bless them. Always speak blessings, not curses. [15]If some have cause to celebrate, join in the celebration. And if others are weeping, join in that as well. [16]Work toward unity, and build consensus with one another. Avoid thinking you are better than others or wiser than the rest; instead, embrace common people *and undignified tasks.* [17]Do not retaliate with evil, regardless of the evil brought against you. Try to do what is good *and right and honorable* as agreed upon by all people. [18]If it is within your

power, make peace with all people. [19]*Again,* my loved ones, do not seek revenge; instead, allow God's wrath *to make sure justice is served. Turn it over to Him.* For the Scriptures say, "Revenge is Mine. I will settle all scores."* [20]But *consider this bit of wisdom:* "If your enemy is hungry, give him something to eat. If he is thirsty, give him something to drink, because if you treat him kindly, it will be like heaping hot coals on top of his head."* [21]Never let evil get the best of you; instead, overpower evil with the good.

13 It is important that all of us submit to the authorities who have charge over us because God establishes all authority *in heaven and on the earth.* [2]Therefore, a person who rebels against authority rebels against the order He established, and people like that can expect to face certain judgment. [3]You see, if you do the right thing, you have nothing to be worried about from the rulers; but if you do what you know is wrong, the rulers will make sure you pay a price. Would you not rather live with a clear conscience than always have to be looking over your shoulder? Then keep doing what you know to be good and right, and they will publicly honor you.

[4]*Look at it this way:* The ruler is a minister of God called to serve and benefit you. But he is also a minister of God executing wrath upon those who practice evil. If you do what is wrong, then you'd better be afraid because he wields the power of the sword and doesn't make empty threats.

At the time Paul writes this letter, Christians are a tiny minority within Judaism, a minor religion in the largest empire the world had ever seen. Minorities are often the subjects of rumors, suspicions, and innuendos. Because that is true, Christians don't need to add to the problem by developing a reputation as

* 12:19 Deuteronomy 32:35
* 12:20 Proverbs 25:21-22

lawbreakers and rebels. So Kingdom citizens are not to dodge taxes or cheat on fees imposed by legitimate governing authorities, local or otherwise. They are to show the proper respect for officials in power. Our presence and values may challenge the philosophical foundation of society, but we must confront people lawfully. Ultimately those who follow the truth of the gospel under the banner of the Liberator may find themselves at odds with the powers that be. Jesus, we remember, was crucified on a Roman cross. Paul, too, died a martyr's death in Rome during Nero's reign. So Paul's counsel here is not a blanket approval of any and every government that may arise in a broken world.

⁵So submission is not optional; it's imperative. But don't just submit for the sake of avoiding punishment; submit *and abide by the laws* because your conscience leads you to do the right thing. ⁶Pay your taxes for the same reason, because rulers are agents of God, giving their full attention to take care of these things. ⁷Pay all of them what you owe. If you owe taxes, then pay. If you owe fees, then pay. In the same way, pay honor and respect to those who demand it.

⁸Don't owe anyone anything, with the exception of love to one another—*that is a debt which never ends*—because the person who loves others has fulfilled the law. ⁹The commands *given to you in the Scriptures,* "Do not have sex with anyone but your spouse, do not murder, do not take what is not yours, do not envy your neighbor,"* and any other command *you have heard* are summarized in God's instruction: "Love your neighbor as yourself."* ¹⁰Does love hurt anyone? Absolutely not. In fact, love achieves everything the law requires.

*B*elievers are to not have any obligation of any kind. Borrowed money and favors granted always come with strings attached. How many lives and families have been ruined by debts and deals made in haste! There

is only one obligation Paul allows, and that is love. When we share God's care and compassion with others, we fulfill His law whether we realize it or not. Fundamentally, God's law has always been about love.

¹¹And *now consider* this. You know well the times *you are living in.* It is time to wake up *and see what is right before your eyes*: for salvation is nearer to us now than when we first believed. ¹²The darkness of night is dissolving as dawn's light draws near, so walk out on your old dark life and put on the armor of light. ¹³May we all act as good and respectable people, living today the same way as we will in the day *of His coming*. Do not fall into patterns of dark living: wild partying, drunkenness, sexual depravity, decadent gratification, quarreling, and jealousy. ¹⁴Instead, wrap yourselves in the Lord Jesus, the Liberating King, and do not fuel your sinful imagination by indulging *your self-seeking desire* for the pleasures of the flesh.

14 It's high time that you welcome all people weak in the faith without debating and disputing their opinions.

²*Here's the issue:* One person believes that nothing's off the menu; *he'll eat any food put before him with no concern whether or not it has been associated with a pagan ceremony.* But here's another believer—*we'll call him* the weaker—who eats only vegetables *because the meat is tainted through contact with an idol.* ³If you are an eater of all things, do not be condescending to your vegetarian brother or sister. In turn, those who abstain *from certain foods on religious principles* should not judge your brothers and sisters who eat meat—if God has accepted them, *you have no reason to reject them.* ⁴How could you think for a moment that you have the right to judge another person's slave? We all answer to our own Master, and we will either stand or fall in His presence. *The*

* 13:9 Exodus 20:13-15,17; Deuteronomy 5:17-19,21
* 13:9 Leviticus 19:18

good news is that both eaters and noneaters will stand because the Master is able to make it so.

[5]There may be a believer who regards one day as more sacred than any other, while another views every day as sacred as the next. *In these matters,* all must reach their own conclusions *and satisfy their own minds.* [6]If someone observes a day *as holy,* he observes it in honor of the Lord. If another eats *a particular diet,* he eats in honor of the Lord since he begins by giving thanks! If yet another abstains *from that same food,* he abstains out of respect for the Lord and begins his meal by thanking God too. [7]*The truth is that* none of us lives for ourselves, and none dies for ourselves. [8]For if we live, we live for the Lord. If we die, we die for the Lord. So in both life and death, we belong to the Lord. [9]The Liberating King died and returned to life to make this a reality: through His death and resurrection, He became Lord of the living and the dead.

[10]So how is it that you continue to judge your brother? How is it possible for you to look down on a sister? We will all stand before the judgment seat of the living God. [11]For it is written,

"As I live, *so I promise,*" says the
  Lord, "every knee will bow
  down at the sound of My name.
Every tongue will claim Me as
  their God."*

[12]So every one of us, *regardless of our eating habits,* should expect to give an account for our own lives, *not the lives of our brother or sister,* to God.

[13]In light of this, we must resolve never to judge others and never to place an obstacle or impediment in their path that could cause them to trip and fall. [14]Personally I have been completely convinced that in Jesus, our Lord, no object in and of itself is unclean, but if my fellow believers are convinced that something is unclean, then it is unclean to them. [15]If the food you eat harms your brother, then you have failed to love him. Do not let what you eat tear down your brother; after all, the Liberating King laid down His life for him. [16]Do not allow people to slander something you find to be good [17]because the kingdom of God is not about eating and drinking. *When God reigns, the order of the day is* redeeming justice, true peace, and joy made possible by the Holy Spirit. [18]You see, those who serve the Liberating King in this way will be welcomed into the whole acceptance of God and valued by all men. [19]Join us, and pursue a life that creates peace and builds up our brothers and sisters. [20]Do not sacrifice God's work for the sake of certain foods. *It is true that* all things are clean, but it's wrong to eat if you know that eating something will cause offense. [21]It is right for you to abstain from certain meats and wine (or anything else for that matter) if it prevents your brother from falling *in his faith.* [22]Hold on to what you believe *about these issues,* but keep them between you and God. A happy man does not judge himself by the lifestyle he endorses. [23]But a man who decides for himself what to eat is condemned because he is not living by his faith. Any action not consistent with faith is sin.

*P*aul says he is free to eat, but he is not free to injure another in what he eats. Personal freedom must always give way to corporate responsibility. To put it another way, the gospel of love demands that we surrender individual liberties for the sake of our brother or sister. We see this demonstrated powerfully in the example of Jesus who gave up His life and freedom for the sake of the world. When we live by this ethic, we will create a community marked by warmth and hospitality. Food, drink, and holidays may well be personal options within the Kingdom. But justice, peace, and joy are communal essentials for life in the Kingdom.

15 *So now what?* We who are strong are not just to satisfy our own desires. We are called to carry the

* 14:11 Isaiah 45:23

weaknesses of those who are not strong. [2]Each of us must strive to please our neighbors, pursuing their welfare so they will become strong. [3]The Liberating King Himself *is our model for this kind of living.* He did not pursue His own likes and avoid His dislikes. And as the Scriptures declared, "When they insult You, they insult me."* [4]You see, everything written in the days of old was recorded to give us instructions *for living.* We find encouragement through the Scriptures and a call to perseverance that will produce hopeful living. [5]I pray that our God, who calls you and gives you perseverance and encouragement, will join all of you together to share one mind according to Jesus, the Liberating King. [6]In this unity, you will all share one voice as you glorify *the one true* God, the Father of our Lord Jesus, the Liberator.

[7]So accept one another in the same way the Liberator has accepted you so that God will get the praise He is due. [8]For, as I am *fond of* saying, the Liberating King has become a servant of the circumcision in order to demonstrate God's truth. Effectively this confirms the promises He made to our ancestors [9]and causes the non-Jewish nations to glorify God for His mercy, as the Scriptures say,

For this I will praise You across the
    planet
and sing praises to Your name.*

[10]Again the Scriptures say,

Nations, celebrate with His *covenant*
    people.*

[11]And again,

Praise the Eternal One, all nations.
    Raise your voices, all people; let
        your praises flow to God.*

[12]Again Isaiah says,

Then, the *royal* line of Jesse will
    emerge—
*out of God's eternal promise to
    David.*

He rises to rule all the peoples of the
    world
who come to Him *for guidance and
    direction*
And leave with deep hope *besides.**

[13]I pray that God, the source of all hope, will infuse your lives with an abundance of joy and peace in the midst of your faith so that your hope will overflow through the power of the Holy Spirit.

[14]My brothers and sisters, I am ultimately confident that you are full of goodness, knowledge, and the ability to *help and* instruct one another. [15]I have written to you with unflinching honesty on many topics because I do not want you to ever lose sight of the *tremendous* grace God has given me. [16]*His grace makes me who* I am, a minister of our Liberator, Jesus, called to serve the nations. The good news of God is the focus of my priestly work. In effect, the nations have become an offering to God, totally acceptable, indeed made holy by the work of the Holy Spirit. [17]So in Jesus, the Liberating King, I have reason to celebrate the things I do for God. [18]I don't want to be presumptuous, so I will restrict myself to what the Liberator has accomplished through my words and actions, which has culminated in the obedience of the nations. [19]*My words and actions have been rooted* in Spirit-empowered signs and miracles. *The upshot is this:* I have been able to preach the good news of the Liberating King *in city after city* from Jerusalem all the way *around the Mediterranean* to Illyricum. [20]I have dreamed of preaching the gospel in places where no one has ever heard of Him so that I do not build on a foundation laid by anyone else. [21]But as the Scriptures say,

They will see Him even though
    they've never been told about
        Him;

* 15:3 Psalm 69:9
* 15:9 Psalm 18:49
* 15:10 Deuteronomy 32:43
* 15:11 Psalm 117:1
* 15:12 Isaiah 11:10

they will understand even though they never heard of Him.*

²²Because of many issues, I have not been able to visit you *in the city of Rome.* ²³But *my time to serve those here is coming to an end,* there's no room left for me in this region, and I have longed to come to you for many years. So I plan to visit you ²⁴on my journey to Spain. I am hoping that I will not only see you face-to-face, but that you will assist me in the journey *west* after I have enjoyed our time together. ²⁵But right now I must make the journey to Jerusalem to serve the saints there. ²⁶Those in Macedonia and Achaia decided it was a good idea to share their funds to help the poor among the saints in Jerusalem. ²⁷*I must tell you that* they were thrilled to be able to help. *They realize that* they are indebted to the believers in Jerusalem. If the nations share in the Jews' spiritual goods, then it's only right that they minister back to them in material goods. ²⁸When this work is complete and the funds we've collected are delivered, I will make my way to Spain through your *grand* city *of Rome and enjoy some of your hospitality.* ²⁹I'm sure that when I come to you I will come as a blessing and as one fully blessed by the Liberating King.

³⁰My brothers and sisters, I urgently plead with you by the name of our Lord Jesus, the Liberating King, and by the love of the Spirit to join together with me in your prayers to God for my success *in these next endeavors.* ³¹Pray that I will be rescued from those who deny *and persecute* the faith in Judea and that my service in Jerusalem will meet the approval of all the saints there. ³²If that happens, then my journey to you will be filled with joy; and, if God wills, I can be *rested and* refreshed in your presence. ³³*I pray* the God of all peace will be with you all. Amen.

*B*efore Paul treks west to Rome, he must complete an important mission he started years earlier. He must carry to Jerusalem an offering for the poor collected from the outsider churches. Paul, the emissary, hopes, not only that the offering will alleviate the human need and suffering brought on by years of famine, but that it will also build a bridge between his mainly non-Jewish churches and the mother church in Jerusalem. Paul's enemies trump up charges against him that ultimately land him in jail. So Paul makes it to Rome, but not as he planned. Several years later, after a lengthy incarceration in Caesarea and a perilous journey at sea, he is led into Rome as a prisoner of the empire.

16 I commend to you our *beloved* sister Phoebe; she serves the church in Cenchrea as a *faithful* deacon. ²*It is important* that you welcome her in the Lord in a manner befitting your saintly status. *Join her in the work she has been given,* and assist her in any way she needs you. She has spent her energy and resources helping others, and *I am blessed to have her* as my benefactor as well.

³*Give my best to Prisca and Aquila; they are not only my colleagues in my profession of tent making, but more importantly* they are my fellow servants of Jesus, the Liberating King. ⁴They put their lives on the line to keep me safe. Not only do I owe them my thanks, so do all the churches of the non-Jews. ⁵Send my regards to the church that meets in their house.

Send greetings to Epaenetus. I love him dearly *and celebrate the fact that his journey to faith in the Liberating King is historic because* he was the first to believe in all of Asia.

⁶Salute Mary for me; *she is a woman* who has worked hard for all of you.

⁷Give my regards to Andronicus and Junias, who are part of my own family and served time in prison with me. They are well known among the emissaries* and have been in the Liberator longer than I.

⁸Give my best to Ampliatus whom I love in the Lord, ⁹and greet Urbanus (our

* 15:21 Isaiah 52:15
* 16:7 Literally, apostles

fellow-worker in service to the Liberating King) and my beloved Stachys.

¹⁰Send greetings to Apelles, a tried and true *believer* in the Liberating King, and to the entire family of Aristobulus.

¹¹*Do not forget to* greet Herodion, another of my relatives, and everyone in the family of Narcissus who belong to the Lord.

¹²Greet Tryphaena and Tryphosa, *faithful* laborers in the Lord's name, and our beloved Persis, who also has accomplished a great deal in the Lord.

¹³Give my best to Rufus, clearly one of the Lord's chosen, and also his mother. She's like a mother to me.

¹⁴My regards also go to Asyncritus, Phlegon, Hermes, Patrobas, Hermas, and all the brothers and sisters who are along with them.

¹⁵Greet Philologus and Julia, Nereus and his sister, and *let me not forget* Olympas and all the saints who journey with them.

¹⁶Be sure to welcome each other with a holy kiss. All of the churches of our Liberating King *under my care* send their greetings to all of you.

¹⁷I am pleading with all of you, brothers and sisters, to keep up your guard against anyone who is causing conflicts and enticing others with teachings contrary to what you have already learned. *If there are people like that in your churches,* stay away from them. ¹⁸These kinds of people are not slaves to our Lord, the Liberating King; they have devoted their lives to satisfying their own appetites. With smooth talking and a *well-rehearsed* blessing, they lead a lot of unsuspecting people down the wrong path. ¹⁹The stories about the way you are living in obedience to God have traveled to all *the churches.* So celebrate *your faithfulness to God* that is being displayed in your lives—*but I want to warn you that it is so very easy to get offtrack.* Seek wisdom about the good life, and remain innocent when it comes to evil. ²⁰*If you do this,* the God of peace will crush Satan under your feet soon. May the grace of our Lord Jesus be ever present with you.

²¹Timothy, my coworker *in the spreading of the gospel,* also sends his greeting to all of you. As do my kinsmen, Lucius, Jason, and Sosipater.

²²I, Tertius, Paul's secretary, greet you in *the name of* the Lord. ²³Gaius, my host here as well as patron for the whole church, sends his* best to all of you. Erastus, the city administrator, sends his greetings along with brother Quartus. [²⁴May the grace of our Lord Jesus, the Liberating King, touch you all. Amen.]*

²⁵So to the One who is able to strengthen you to live consistently with my good news and the preaching of Jesus, the Liberating King, with the revelation of the ancient mystery that has been kept secret since the earliest days, ²⁶this mystery is revealed through the prophetic voices passed down in the Scriptures, as they have been commanded by the Eternal God. *In this time,* this mystery is being made known to the nations so that all may be led to faith-filled obedience.

²⁷To the one *true and* wise God we offer glory for all times through Jesus, the Liberating King. Amen.

* 16:23 Some early manuscripts read "their."
* 16:24 Some early manuscripts omit this verse.

1 Corinthians

Letter to the church in Corinth
From Paul, the apostle to the Gentiles

Jesus invested His life in 12 unlikely characters, a ragtag group of common Jews, and used them as the foundation of His church. Then He miraculously revealed Himself to Saul (also known as Paul), who had devoted his life to the destruction of Jewish Christians. Not only was Paul an unlikely emissary, but he also planted churches in unlikely places. Corinth was the last place one would imagine starting one of the first churches. This small strip of land in Achaia (southern Greece) served as a seaport on two seas and was home to sailors and merchants. It was known primarily as a place of sin, decadence, and corruption. If you were looking for prostitutes, orgies, pagan festivals, or abundant alcohol, then Corinth was your place. However, if you were looking for a faithful church, then this would seem an impossible location—but not with God.

Paul stayed in Corinth for almost two years. In that time, he led many people to faith in Jesus. Some of these people were transients who boarded ships and carried the good news of the Liberating King to distant shores, but others stayed in Corinth as members of this early Christian community. Once Paul left to plant churches elsewhere, the situation in Corinth began to deteriorate. This first generation of believers struggled with what it meant to live the gospel faithfully in this challenging and immoral city. When Paul heard reports that the church was deeply divided and immorality was rampant, he had no trouble believing it. He addressed those issues in the first part of this letter (chapters 1–6). But Paul also received a letter from the church posing to him a number of questions about celibacy, food offered to idols, spiritual gifts, and the resurrection. He dealt with their questions in the last part of his letter (chapters 7–15).

Although we refer to this letter as 1 Corinthians, it is clear Paul writes them an earlier letter (now lost?), which apparently some misunderstood (see 1 Corinthians 5:9). So 1 Corinthians is at least Paul's second letter to this church. But the situation becomes more complex, as we see in 2 Corinthians, when Paul speaks of another tearful letter written between 1 and 2 Corinthians. In all, we know of four letters Paul writes to this community, but there may have been more! Of all the churches Paul establishes, the Corinthian church is the most troubled so it receives more visits, more letters, and more instruction than any other. Paul's letters to the Corinthians exhibit his deep, pastoral concern for these urban believers who live in a truly secular city. His teachings continue to speak today to our own troubled times.

1 Paul, called out by God's will to be an emissary* for Jesus, the Liberating King, along with brother Sosthenes, ²to God's church gathering in the city of Corinth. As people who are united with Jesus, our Liberator, you have been set apart for service. You are all called into community to live as saints with all who invoke the name of our Lord Jesus, the Liberating King.

³I pray that God our Father and the Lord and Liberator, Jesus, will shower you with grace and peace.

⁴I am continuously thanking my God for you when I think about the grace God has offered you in Jesus, the Savior. ⁵*In this grace,* God is enriching every aspect of your lives by gifting you with the right words to say and everything you need to know. ⁶In this way, your life story confirms the life story of the Liberating King, ⁷so you are not ill-equipped or slighted on any necessary gifts as you patiently anticipate the day when our Liberator, the Lord Jesus, is revealed. ⁸Until that final day, He will preserve you, and on that day, He will consider you faultless. ⁹*Count on this:* God is faithful and in His faithfulness called you out into an intimate relationship with His Son, our Lord Jesus, the Liberating King.

¹⁰My brothers and sisters, I urge you by the name of our Lord and Savior, Jesus, to come together in agreement. Do not allow anything *or anyone* to create division among you. Instead, be restored, completely fastened together with one mind and shared judgment. ¹¹I have heard *troubling* reports from Chloe's people that you, my siblings, are consumed by fighting *and petty disagreements.* ¹²What I have heard is that each of you is taking sides, saying, "I am with Paul," or "I am with Apollos," or "I am with Cephas," or "I am with the Liberator." ¹³Has the Liberating King been split up *into many small pieces*? Do you think Paul was crucified for you? Were you ceremonially washed* into the name of Paul? *Absolutely not!*

P aul knows that if the work of the gospel of the Liberating King

degenerates into a cult of personality it will hardly resemble true Christianity. If the focus is on Paul, Cephas, Apollos, or any famous religious leader, then we would be distracted from the person and central message of Jesus. Any cult of personality is intoxicating, and it is often easier to claim to follow a person we can see and touch. But Christianity is founded upon the belief that Jesus is the head of the church and that all of the rest of us serve His will as a part of the royal priesthood.

¹⁴Now I am thankful that I washed* only Crispus and Gaius, ¹⁵so none of you can *falsely* declare you were washed in my name. ¹⁶*Now wait, as I think about it,* I also ceremonially washed* the household of Stephanas; if there are others in your community whom I washed, I cannot recall at this moment. ¹⁷The mission given to me by the Liberating King is not about ceremonial washing, but about preaching good news. The point is not *to impress others by* spinning an eloquent, intellectual argument; that *type of rhetorical showboating* would only nullify the cross of the Liberator.

¹⁸For people who are stumbling toward ruin, the message of the cross is nothing but a tall tale for fools by a fool. But for those of us who are already experiencing the reality of being rescued *and made right*, it is nothing short of God's power. ¹⁹This is why the Scripture says:

> I will put an end to the wisdom of
>   the *so-called* wise,
>   and I will invalidate the insight of
>   your *so-called* experts.*

²⁰*So now,* where is the philosopher? Where is the scholar? Where is the skilled

---

* 1:1 Literally, apostle
* 1:13 Literally, immersed, in a rite of initiation and purification
* 1:14 Literally, immersed, in a rite of initiation and purification
* 1:16 Literally, immersed, in a rite of initiation and purification
* 1:19 Isaiah 29:14

debater, the best of your time? *Step up, if you dare.* Hasn't God made fools out of *those who count on* the wisdom of this *rebellious, broken* world? ²¹For in God's *deep* wisdom, *He made it so that* the world could not even begin to comprehend Him through its own style of wisdom; in fact, God took immense pleasure in rescuing people of faith through the foolishness of the message we preach. ²²It seems the Jews are always asking for signs and the Greeks are always on the prowl for wisdom. ²³*But we tell a different story.* We proclaim a crucified Liberating King. For Jews this is scandalous, for outsiders* this is moronic, ²⁴but for those of us living out God's call—regardless of our Jewish or Greek heritage—we know our Savior embodies God's *dynamic* power and God's *deep* wisdom. ²⁵*You can count on this:* God's foolishness will always be wiser than mere human wisdom, and God's weakness will always be stronger than mere human strength.

²⁶Look carefully at your call, brothers and sisters. By human standards, not many of you are deemed to be wise. Not many are considered powerful. Not many of you come from royalty, right? ²⁷But *celebrate this:* God selected the world's foolish to bring shame upon *those who think they are* wise; likewise, He selected the world's weak to bring disgrace upon *those who think they are* strong. ²⁸God selected the common and the castoff, whatever lacks status, so He could invalidate the claims of those who think those things are significant. ²⁹So it makes no sense for any person to boast in God's presence. ³⁰Instead, credit God with your new situation: you are united with Jesus, the Liberating King. He is God's wisdom for us and more. He is our righteousness and holiness and redemption. ³¹As the Scripture says: "If someone wants to boast, he should boast in the Lord."*

2 My brothers and sisters, I did not pose *as an expert with all the answers.* I did not pretend to explain the mystery of God with eloquent speech and *human* wis-

dom. ²I claimed to know nothing *with certainty* other than *the reality that* Jesus is the Liberating King who was crucified on our behalf. ³I was moved to utter despair during my time with you. I would find myself trembling in *dread and* fear. ⁴The sermons I preached were not delivered with *the kind of* persuasive elegance *some have come to expect,* but they were effective because I relied on God's Spirit to demonstrate God's power. ⁵If this were not so, your faith would be based on human wisdom and not the power of God.

*C*hristianity is not merely a set of ideas and propositions. One could agree with all the truths in the Bible and still miss the power of God. Paul knows that the brothers and sisters in Corinth might attempt to reduce Christianity to a new philosophy based on human understandings, but the power of God cannot be fully grasped by our eight-pound brains. So we must approach God humbly as creations, not as those aspiring to fully explain the Creator of the universe.

⁶However, in the presence of mature believers, we do impart *true* wisdom—not the *phony* wisdom typical of this *rebellious* age or of the *hostile* powers who rule this age. *Despite what you may think,* these ruling spirits are losing their grip on this world. ⁷But we do impart God's mysterious and hidden wisdom. Before the ages began, God graciously decided to use His wisdom for our glory. ⁸This wisdom has not been grasped by the ruling powers of this age; if they had understood, they would not have crucified the Lord of Glory. ⁹But as the Scriptures say,

No eye has ever seen and no ear has
ever heard
and it has never occurred to the
human heart

* 1:23 Literally, Gentiles
* 1:31 Jeremiah 9:23-24

All the things God prepared for
those who love Him.*

¹⁰God has shown us these *profound and
startling* realities through His Spirit. The
Spirit searches all things, even the deep
mysteries of God. ¹¹Who can see into a
man's heart and know his thoughts? Only
the spirit that dwells within the man. In
the same way, the thoughts of God are
known only by His Spirit. ¹²*You must know
that* we have not received the spirit of this
rebellious and broken world but the Spirit
that comes from God, so that we may experience and comprehend the gifts that come
from God. ¹³We do not speak of these *gifts
of God* in words shaped by human wisdom;
we speak in words crafted by the Spirit
because our collective judgment on spiritual matters is accessible to those who
have the Spirit. ¹⁴But a person who denies
spiritual realities will not accept the things
that come through the Spirit of God; they
all sound like foolishness to him. He is
incapable of grasping them because they
are *disseminated,* discerned, *and valued* by
the Spirit. ¹⁵A person who walks by the
Spirit examines everything, *sizing it up
and seeking out truth.* But no one is able to
examine or size up that *kind of* spiritual
person, ¹⁶for *the Scripture asks,* "Does
anyone know the mind of the Lord well
enough to become His advisor?"* But we
do possess the mind of the Liberating
King.

3 My brothers and sisters, *I don't mean
this to sound condescending, but I must
speak truthfully to you.* I cannot
address you as people who walk by the
Spirit; I have to speak to you as people who
tend to think in merely human terms, as
spiritual infants in our Liberating King. ²I
nursed you with milk, *as a mother would
feed her baby,* because you were not, and
still are not, developed enough to digest
complex spiritual food. ³*And here's why:*
you are still living in the flesh, *not in the
Spirit. How do I know?* Are you fighting
with one another? Are you *comparing
yourselves to others and* becoming con-

sumed with jealousy? Then it sounds like
you are living in the flesh, no different
from the rest *who live by the standards of
this rebellious and broken world.* ⁴If one of
you is saying, "I am with Paul," and the
other says, "I am with Apollos," aren't you
like everybody else? ⁵So who is Apollos
really? Or Paul for that matter? *We are only*
servants, agents who led you to faith, and
the Lord commissioned each of us to do a
particular job.

> When it comes to something as
> important as our spiritual lives,
> Paul knows that he must speak hon-
> estly and that we must not get our
> feelings hurt and fail to listen. We
> may easily ignore the plain truth he is
> speaking and live as very immature
> believers. How would we know? Take
> Paul's test: Do you get in fights with
> others? (No excuses about how you
> have good reason or a defense about
> how you were right—just answer the
> question honestly.) Do you compare
> yourself to others? Are you jealous of
> others?
> If you answered "yes" to any of the
> above, then you are battling immatu-
> rity. So listen carefully to Paul's wis-
> dom about how to move forward.

⁶My job was to plant *the seed,* and Apollos
was called to water it. Any growth comes
from God, ⁷so the ones who water and
plant have nothing *to brag about.* God, who
causes the growth, is the only One who
matters. ⁸The one who plants is no greater
than the one who waters; both will be
rewarded based on their work. ⁹We are
gardeners and field workers laboring with
God. You are *the vineyard,* the garden, the
house where God dwells. ¹⁰Like a *skilled
architect and* master builder, I laid a foundation based upon God's grace given to me.
Now others will come along to build on the
foundation. Each *serves in a different way*

* 2:9 Isaiah 64:4
* 2:16 Isaiah 40:13

and is to build upon it with great care. [11]There is, in fact, only one foundation, and no one can lay any foundation other than Jesus, the Liberating King. [12]As others build on the foundation (whether with gold, silver, gemstones, wood, hay, or straw), [13]the quality of each person's work will be revealed in time as it is tested by fire. [14]If a man's work stands *the test of fire*, he will be rewarded. [15]If a man's work is consumed by the fire, his reward will be lost but he will be spared, rescued from the fire. [16]Don't you understand that together you form a temple to *the living* God and His Spirit lives among you? [17]If someone comes along to *corrupt, vandalize, and* destroy the temple of God, *you can be sure that* God will see to it that he meets destruction because the temple of God is sacred. You, *together,* are His temple.

[18]Don't let anyone deceive himself. If any one of you thinks he is wise in matters pertaining to this world, *he is going to be really disappointed.* In fact, one must be deemed a fool *by worldly standards* in order to become truly wise [19]because the wisdom of this *rebellious and broken* world looks like foolishness when put next to God. So it stands in Scripture, "He catches the wise in their deceitful plotting."* [20]And the Scriptures add, "The Lord knows the *highest* thoughts of the wise, and they are worthless."* [21]So there is no reason for anyone to boast in human leaders. You already have it all. [22]So whether it is Paul, Apollos, Cephas, the world, life or death, the present or the future—it all belongs to you. [23]*But remember you are not the ultimate owner of anything.* You belong to the Liberating King, and the Liberating King belongs to God.

4 *Do not consider our position one of power and prestige.* Think of us as servants of the Liberating King, caretakers of the mysteries of God. [2]Because we are in this particular role, it is especially important that we are people of fidelity and integrity. [3]It makes little difference to me how you or any human court passes judgment on me—*maybe I*

am your hero one day and your enemy the next;* I must resist the temptation to compare myself *to the ever-changing human standard.* [4-5]Although I am not aware of any flaw that might exclude me *from this divine service,* that's not the reason I stand acquitted—*the only supreme judge,* our Lord, will examine me in the proper time. [5]So resist the temptation to act as judges before all the evidence is in. *It is impossible for us to see all the facts as God does.* When the Lord comes, He will draw our buried motives, thoughts, and deeds (*even things we don't know or admit to ourselves*) out of the dark shadows of our hearts into His light. When this happens, the voice of God will speak to each of us the *only* praise *that will ever matter.*

[6]Right now, brothers and sisters, the best thing I can do for you is to apply these principles to the situation with Apollos and me. Maybe we can show you the meaning of the saying: "not beyond the things written." If you learn that, perhaps none of you will swell with pride because you fall into the seductive trap of pitting one against the other. [7]Is there any reason to consider yourselves better than others? What do you have that you didn't receive? If you received it as a gift, why do you boast like it is something you achieved on your own?

[8]*Now let's see if I have it straight.* You *suppose that you* already have all you need. You already are rich *and prosperous.* And without us you've already begun to reign like kings. To be honest, I wish you did reign so that we could reign with you. [9]*Based on this—assuming that what you say is true*—it seems to me that God has put His emissaries* at the end of the line, like convicts in their final walk to certain death. We have become a spectacle to the rest of the world—to all people and heaven's messengers. [10]We are nothing but fools for the cause of the Liberating King while you are wise in Him. *Am I right?* We are feeble *and tired* while you are mighty

* 3:19 Job 5:13
* 3:20 Psalm 94:11
* 4:9 Literally, apostles

and full of life. You are well respected by others while we're treated as contemptuous creatures *by pretty much everyone everywhere.* [11]Up to this very minute, we are famished, we are thirsty, and our clothes are shabby, *practically rotted to pieces.* We are homeless, *hapless wanderers.* [12]But still we labor, working with our hands *to meet our needs because, despite all of this,* when a fist is raised against us, we respond with a blessing; when we face *violence and* persecution, we stay on mission; and [13]when others choose *taunts and* slander against us, we speak words of encouragement and reconciliation. We're treated as the scum of the earth—*and I am not talking in the past tense;* I mean today! We're the scraps of society, *nothing more than the foulest human rubbish.*

---

*P*aul is explaining and exemplifying attributes of a mature believer in a way that may be easily contrasted with the patterns of immaturity. He is seeking love and truth more than popularity. In fact, he disregards popularity completely so that he might fully embrace love and truth. Can you imagine what a powerful force you could be in the world if you embraced this kind of maturity?

---

[14]I am not telling you all this so that you'll *feel guilty or* be ashamed of how you have acted. I am only trying to warn you, just as a father would warn his children. [15]You may have 10,000 instructors in the *faith of the* Liberating King, but you have only one father. In Jesus, the Liberator, I have become your father through *my efforts in spreading* the good news. [16]So as your father in the faith, *I want to encourage you to live as I have lived.* Imitate my life. [17]This is one of the reasons I sent Timothy to be with you. He is my dearly loved and faithful child in the Lord. His mission is to remind you of the way I experience life in our Liberating King. In all the churches everywhere I go, I teach the same lessons the same way, *and I live out those lessons.*

[18]But the reality is, some of you *have put yourselves on pedestals and* live like you are high above the rest—it's as if you assumed I would not return *to confront your misguided pride.* [19]But I am coming. Lord willing, I will be with you soon. Then I will know what power is backing those arrogant folks and their words. [20]The kingdom of God is not a realm of grandiose talk; it is a realm of power. [21]So tell me what you want. Should I visit you, rod in hand *ready to discipline a crew of self-important persons,* or should I *embrace you,* love you, and gently teach you *as we celebrate the blessings of God together*?

5 *Because of my deep love for you, I must express my concern about* the report brought to me regarding the *lewd and immoral behavior exhibited in your community.* This scandal has come to my attention because this kind of thing is unheard of even among the outsiders around us: I understand a man is having sexual relations with his father's wife. [2]You have turned into an arrogant lot who refuse to *see the tragedy right in front of your eyes and* mourn for it. If you would face these hard realities, the one living in this sin would be removed from the community.

[3]*I want my counsel regarding this man to be crystal clear for all of you;* despite the fact that I am not physically present with you, I am there in spirit and already have spoken judgment against the man who has engaged in this conduct. [4]When you gather in the name of the Lord Jesus and I am present with you in spirit with the infinite power of the Lord Jesus, [5]I direct you to release this man over to Satan so his rebellious nature will be destroyed and his spirit might be rescued in the day of the Lord Jesus.

[6]Your proud boasting *in this matter* is terrible. *Don't you understand that the tiniest infraction can bring about an unwelcome chain of events?* That just a little yeast causes all the dough to rise? [7]Get rid of all the old yeast; then you'll become new dough, just as you are already a people without *sin's* leavening influence. You see,

the Liberating King is our Passover lamb; He has been sacrificed for us. [8]So let the real feast begin. Get rid of all the old yeast, the yeast of hatred and evil. *Throw it out* so we can feast on the unleavened bread of sincerity and truth.

*S*in is sin. In a way, no sin is greater than another, but some sin has more grievous consequences. Sexual sin is always painful, but incest is a sexual sin that decimates families and communities, and it leaves people isolated and angry. The danger for believers who understand that sin is a reality is that they may lose sight of redemption and become complacent in their brokenness. In Corinth the believers had become so complacent that they were ignoring the sins of someone in their community who was actively committing incest with his father's wife. Ignoring the sins of others is not a loving thing to do; it actually makes their lives worse. Real love will always humbly confront the patterns in the lives of those whom we love and will lead them toward redemption and wholeness.

[9]In the letter I wrote to you *previously, I made it clear* that you are not to band together with those who have embraced immoral lives. [10]Don't misunderstand; *I'm not telling you to hole up and hunker down from the rest of the world. That's impossible.* The world is filled with immoral people consumed by their desire for more; they steal *from one another without hesitation* and will worship man-made idols *with no shame at all.* If you attempted to avoid these people, you would have to leave the world itself. [11]What I was saying is that you should not associate with someone who calls himself a brother or sister but lives *contrary to all we stand for:* committing immoral sexual acts, consumed with desire for more, worshiping tangible lifeless things, using profanity, drinking into oblivion, a crook. Do not even sit at the table with a person like this. [12]*Now do you*

understand what I am saying? Why would I ever attempt to judge those outside *the church?* Aren't we *called* to judge those within *the church?* [13]God judges the outsiders. *Your job is this:* "Expel the wicked from your own community."*

*6*Here's another troubling issue. If you have a grievance against another *follower of the Liberating King,* do you have the audacity to bring that brother or sister into the civil courts rather than submitting yourselves to the authority of God's people? [2]Don't you know that His people are destined to judge the world? If you have the authority to judge the world, can't you handle these small matters *and render a better judgment than the civil courts?* [3]Further, don't you know that we are destined to judge the heavenly messengers? *So if we are to exercise authority in the heavenly realms,* can't we take care of the conflicts that arise in this life? [4]To put it another way, if you are asking the courts to adjudicate your mundane conflicts, aren't you placing your problems under the authority of judges who have no standing within the church? [5]My words should embarrass you. Is it possible that you have no one among you with the wisdom to mediate between two siblings? [6]So one brother sues another brother *in public and drags the dispute* before outsiders who have no allegiance to the Liberating King?

[7]The truth is that these *public* lawsuits cause all of you to lose and lose big. Wouldn't it be better to be ripped off or defrauded? [8]In fact, you are guilty of ripping off and defrauding your own brothers and sisters, *not the other way around.*

[9-10]Do you need reminding that the unjust have no share in the blessings of the kingdom of God? Do not be misled. A lot of people stand to inherit nothing of God's coming kingdom, including those whose lives are defined by sexual immorality, idolatry, adultery, sexual deviancy, theft, greed, drunkenness, slander, and swindling. *People who continue on like this have*

* 5:13 Deuteronomy 17:7

no chance of inheriting the kingdom. ¹¹Some of you used to live in these ways, but *you are different* now; you have been washed clean, set apart, restored, *and set on the right path* in the name of the Lord Jesus, the Liberating King, by the Spirit of our living God.

*I*n the same way that some seek to reduce Christianity to a philosophy or a set of ideas, others seek to reduce it to a set of rules for living. If true faith was only about eating certain foods, abstaining from others, and avoiding certain practices, then we would need willpower more than the Spirit of God. But following stringent rules is not that easy. Actually, living by willpower is hard—some might say impossible. Paul was preaching about an alternative to a life governed by rules and restrictions, and that's a life of faith that embraces grace for yourself and others. Listen closely and you will see a beautiful life that surpasses a life of rule keeping.

¹²*I can hear some of you saying,* "For me, all things are permitted." But *face the facts:* all things are not beneficial. *So you say,* "For me, all things are permitted." *Here's my response:* I will not allow anything to control me. ¹³*Another chimes in:* "Food is for the stomach, and the stomach is for food." *I suppose so, but a day will come when* God will dispense with both food and the stomach. The body is not meant for sexual immorality but for the Lord; the Lord *is over all, and He* cares about your body. ¹⁴God has raised the Lord *Jesus from death,* but He won't stop there. His dynamic power will raise us up *from the grips of death* as well. ¹⁵Don't you realize that your bodies are members of the Liberating King? So should I take the members of the Liberating King and unite them to a prostitute? This *illicit union* should never take place! ¹⁶Don't you understand that when your body is joined with a prostitute you have become one body? For as it says, "The two come together as one flesh."* ¹⁷But

when you are joined with the Lord, you become one spirit with Him. ¹⁸Run from immoral behavior. All other sins are disconnected from the body, but sexual immorality is a sin against your own body. ¹⁹Don't you know that your body is the temple of the Holy Spirit who comes from God and dwells inside of you? You do not own yourself. *You and your body belong to God, so use your body for the work of God, not for selfish pursuits.* ²⁰Remember that *salvation is a costly proposition and that* you have been purchased at a great price, so use your body to bring glory to God!

7 Now to the topics you raised *in your last letter. Some have said,* "It is better for a man to abstain from having sex with his wife." ²Well, *I disagree.* Because of our tendency to embrace immoralities, each man should feel free to join together in sexual intimacy with his own wife, and each woman should join with her own husband. ³*Husbands and wives have reciprocal duties.* Each husband has the responsibility to meet his wife's *sexual* desires, and each wife should do the same for her husband. ⁴In marriage *a change takes place when two people are joined as one, so* neither the husband nor the wife should act as if his or her body is private property— your bodies now belong to one another, *and together they are whole.* ⁵So do not withhold *sex* from one another, unless both of you have agreed to devote a certain period of time to prayer. When the agreed time is over, come together again so that Satan will not tempt you when you are short on self-control. ⁶I am trying to encourage you and give you some wise counsel, so don't take this advice as a command. *It won't serve you to turn my advice into rules.* ⁷I wish that all of you could live as I do, *unmarried.* But the truth is all people are different, each gifted by God in various and dissimilar ways.

⁸To those who are unmarried or widowed, here's my advice: it is a good thing to stay *single* as I do. ⁹*But that is not an*

* 6:16 Genesis 2:24

absolute requirement. If they do not have self-control, they should go ahead and get married. It is much better to marry than to be obsessed by sexual urges.

[10]To those who are married, here's my command (*to be clear,* this isn't merely my opinion; it comes from the teaching of the Lord Jesus): it is not right for a wife to leave her husband. [11]If she does, she must either remain single or reconcile with her husband, *but she should not marry someone else.* Likewise, the husband should not divorce his wife.

> *P*aul's teaching to the Corinthians about marriage sounds like one declaring the opposite message of the Creator God in Genesis 2, where God declares that it is not good to be alone. There He sculpts the most beautiful creature in all of creation from the rib of the man: woman, who was molded to fit the man. And God blesses marriage as a good and beautiful thing.
>
> So is Paul contradicting the declaration of the Creator God when he suggests that it might be better for some people to choose an unmarried life? Absolutely not! Marriage is a sacred union, but it is possible that many will be able to serve God more fully if they do not have the limitations that come with marriage and family. Paul shares his advice humbly based on his own experience. The tension between the beauty of marriage and the freedom from marital obligations is one we should all explore. As we come to our own conclusions, we must also carry them humbly, remembering that one is not better than the other.

[12-13]To everyone else, here's my counsel (this is not a direct command from the Lord; *it is my opinion*): if a brother has a wife who does not believe in the Liberating King, he is to stay with her as long as she is willing to live with him. The same is true for any sister; you should not leave your husband even if he has no alle-giance to the Liberating King. [14]Here's the reason: An unbelieving husband is conse-crated *by that union—touched by the grace of God* through his believing wife—and *the same is true* when the husband is a man of faith and he's wed to an unbelieving wife. His wife is consecrated through their union. If this weren't so, your children wouldn't be pure; *but as it is when faith enters in,* God sets apart these children *to be used uniquely for His purposes.* [15]If the unbelieving spouse decides the marriage is over, then let him or her go; the believing partner is freed *from the marital vows* because God has called you to peace. [16]Remember that *anything is possible, so* the life you lead *and the love you show under this strain* may be what finally liber-ates your partner.

[17]So here is my instruction to all the churches: Each must live with the gifts the Lord *Jesus* grants you and with the call God offers you. [18]When you heard the voice of the Liberating King, *what were your circumstances?* Were you living as a circumcised *Jew*? If so, don't try to undo your circumcision. Were you living as an uncircumcised *outsider*? If so, you don't need to become a Jew. [19]You see, whether you are circumcised or not—these outward signs aren't the issue—the way you live out the commands of God is what really mat-ters. [20]It is important for all people to live *out faith* in the circumstances they know.

> *T*he call to faith is not a call to abandon your life, family, neigh-borhood, and culture. We must play with the hand God deals us, not look for a new deck. He works through faith to redeem broken lives and wasted years, not to provide a change of scenery. Even in the worst circum-stances, faith can change you from the inside.

[21]Did you hear God's voice while you were a slave? Don't be concerned. (But if the opportunity comes to gain your freedom, then take it.) [22]For the slave who hears the Lord's call is set free to belong to the Lord.

In the same way, the so-called free person is called to become a slave of the Liberating King. ²³A high price has been paid for your freedom, so don't *devalue God's investment by* becoming a slave to people. ²⁴My brothers and sisters, each of you should remain in whatever external circumstances you were in when God called you.

²⁵Now when it comes to unmarried young women, I do not have a command from our Lord. The best I can do is to give you my advice as a trustworthy brother who knows the Lord's mercy well. ²⁶Because of the challenging times we live in, I think the best plan is to stay as you are. ²⁷If you are married, don't divorce. If you are single, there is no need to get married. ²⁸But if you decide to get married, this is not a sin; there is nothing wrong with a young woman taking a husband, *but know that marriage is not easy* and those who marry will face hard times. I am only trying to protect you. ²⁹But *hear what* I say, brothers and sisters: the time is short *and growing shorter.* So for the time remaining, even if you have wives, live *with the undivided focus* of those who do not have them. ³⁰Those who cry should live as those who have no tears. Those who rejoice should live as those who have no pleasure. Those who buy things should live as those who do not possess anything. ³¹If you make use of this *rebellious and broken* world, live as if you have no use for it—because the form of this world is fading away.

³²My primary desire is for you to be free from the worries *that plague humanity.* A single man can focus on the things of the Lord and how to please the Lord, ³³but a married man has to worry about the details of the here and now and how to please his wife. ³⁴A married man will always have divided loyalties, *but a single man can live with the singular purpose of pleasing God. The same is true for* a young unmarried woman. She concerns herself only with the work of the Lord and how to dedicate herself entirely, body and spirit, *to her Lord.* On the other hand, a married woman has vast responsibilities for her family and a desire to please her husband. ³⁵I am not trying to give you more rules and regulations. I only want to give you advice that is fitting and helpful. I want to help you live lives of faithful devotion to the Lord without any distraction.

³⁶*But I have this advice for every single man:* If anyone thinks he is behaving badly toward his fiancée, if his desires prove to be too much for him, and if he feels they ought to marry, then he should do what he wants; it is not wrong *to marry her.* It is better that we let men *and women in this situation do as they wish and* get married. *We should celebrate their union together.* ³⁷If a man has no compulsion and chooses not to marry his fiancée, but commits himself to live *a celibate life for the sake of following God* and has the strength to live out his conviction, then he is doing a good thing. ³⁸So those who marry do a good thing, *and they will share in a holy blessing;* those who do not marry do an even better thing *because they are part of an even greater blessing in the service of God.*

³⁹A wife should stay by her husband's side all of his life. But if he dies, she is free to marry any man she wishes as long as it is in the Lord. ⁴⁰*You can likely guess that* in my opinion this woman would be better off to remain single, and I think that I have *this insight from* God's Spirit.

8 As to the concern of eating food dedicated to idols: we know that all of us have knowledge, *but knowledge can be risky.* Knowledge promotes *overconfidence and worse* arrogance, but *charity of the heart* (love, that is) looks to build up *others.* ²Just because a person presumes to have some bit of knowledge, that person doesn't necessarily have the right kind of knowledge. ³But if someone loves God, *it is certain that* God has already known that one.

⁴So to address your concerns about eating food offered to idols, let me start with what we know. An idol is essentially nothing, as there is no other God but the One. ⁵And even if *the majority believes* there are many so-called gods in heaven and on earth (certainly many *worship* such "gods"

and "lords"), *this is not our view.* [6]For us, there is one God, the Father who is the ultimate source of all things and the goal of our lives. And there is one Lord—Jesus, the Liberating King; through Him all things *were created,* and by Him we are *redeemed.*

[7]But this knowledge is not in everyone. Up until now, some have been so familiar with idols *and what goes on in the temples* that when they eat meat that has been offered first to some idol, their weak consciences are polluted. *This is the issue.* [8]*Again, here's what we know:* what we eat will not bring us closer to God—we gain nothing in feasting and lose nothing by fasting. [9]Now let me warn you: don't let your newfound liberty cause those who don't know this to fall face-first. [10]Let's say a person (*someone who knows of the Liberating King*) sees you (*who also know Him*) eating in the temple of an idol, and because the person with a weaker conscience is still unsure of things, he becomes confident, follows your lead, and eats idol food. [11]Now, because of your knowledge *on display in your conduct,* the weaker brother or sister—for whom the Liberator died—is destroyed! Ruined! [12]What's more, *by living according to your knowledge,* you have sinned against these brothers and sisters and wounded their weak consciences—and because you sinned against them, you have sinned against our Liberating King.

[13]So if any type of food is an issue that causes my brothers and sisters to fall away *from God,* then God forbid I should ever eat it again so that I would never be *the crack, the rise, or the rock on the road* that causes them to stumble.

*M*eat left over from the sacrifices was sold daily in the market. About the only option available to a host was to buy the meat for the meal from the market that sat in the shadow of a local temple. Like Paul he knows that idols are nothing really because there is only one God. But another brother thinks he is engaging in a heinous act by supporting a pagan temple and eating food that comes from a pagan sacrifice. So what is a good host to do? Well, it is not a matter of knowledge: Who's right? Who's wrong? It's a matter of love. Paul says that he has the right to eat the meat, but that he gladly gives up that right for the sake of the other. For the Lord's emissary, personal freedom was always subject to one's loving responsibility to the other.

Listen to Paul's wise counsel, and imagine how to incorporate it into places where we experience the tension that results from the tremendous freedom we find in Jesus. How might we celebrate our freedom without hurting those whose heartfelt convictions bring them to different conclusions?

9 Am I not truly free? Am I not an emissary* *of the King*? Have I not personally encountered Jesus our Lord? Are you not my work, *my mission* in the Lord? [2]Even if others don't recognize that I am His emissary,* at least you do because you are the seal, *the living proof* that the Lord commissioned me to be His representative.

[3]Let me speak in my own defense against those *keeping themselves* busy picking me apart. [4]Have we lost the right to eat and drink? [5]Have we lost the right to bring along our wives, our sisters in the Liberating King? Other emissaries travel with their wives, and so do the brothers of our Lord, not to mention Cephas. [6]Is it just Barnabas and I who have lost the right to earn a living? [7]Is a soldier in combat required to pay his own salary? Who would plant a vineyard and not enjoy one grape from it? Who would care for *and nurture* a flock but never taste the fresh milk?

[8]*Listen, these are not just my own ramblings.* These ideas aren't based on merely human notions; the law says these same things. [9]In Moses' law, it is written: "Do

* 9:1 Literally, apostle
* 9:2 Literally, apostle

not muzzle the ox while it is treading out your grain."* Is God's concern here limited to oxen, [10]or does He speak here ultimately for our benefit? These things were written for us, so as the plowman plows and the worker gathers, they can labor with the hopeful expectation that they, too, will share in the good harvest. [11]*The same principle applies here:* Is it too much to ask that we would be compensated materially for planting *life- and world-changing* spiritual realities? [12]If you have rightfully supported others, shouldn't we deserve your support even more?

But we have never insisted on this right; instead, we would rather put up with anything than to put some obstacle in the way that prevents *even one person from experiencing* the good news of the Liberating King. [13]Perhaps it has escaped your notice that leaders and priests of the temple make their living off the temple and that those who tend the altar eat their dinners from part of the sacrifices. [14]So *it shouldn't be a stretch that* the Lord has arranged for preachers of the gospel to make a living by *those who have embraced and been liberated by* the gospel.

*P*aul worked hard. He traveled the known world starting new churches and wrote letters trying to care for other churches. Simultaneously, he was working to provide for his basic needs by making tents and selling them to fund his living and travels. Would Paul's time have been better spent training young pastors or preaching to a group of church leaders rather than making tents? By giving the churches a free service, was he doing a disservice to those who would serve these churches in the future and have families to care for?

[15]*Despite what I've said here,* I have never staked a claim for such things, and I have no intention to start now; that's not why I'm writing. I would rather die than have anyone *(including me)* invalidate my right to boast. [16]You see, if I preach the good news, it's nothing to brag about. *This urgency,* this necessity has been laid on me. In fact, if I were to stop sharing this good news, I'd be in big trouble. [17]*You see, my story is different. I didn't volunteer for this.* Had I volunteered to preach the gospel, then I would deserve a wage, a reward, *or something.* But I didn't choose this. God chose me and entrusted me with this mission. [18]*You're looking for the catch. I know you're wondering,* "What reward is he talking about?" My reward, *besides being with you and knowing you,* is sharing the gospel with you free and clear. That means I don't insist on all my rights for support in the gospel; [19]that also means that I am free of obligations to all people. And, even though no one *(except the Liberating King)* owns me, I have become a slave *by my own free will* to everyone *in hopes* that I would gather more *believers.* [20]*There's almost nothing I wouldn't do for the gospel.* When around Jews, I emphasize my Jewishness in order to win them over. When around those who live *strictly* under the law, I live by its regulations—even though I have a different perspective on the law now—in order to win them over. [21]*In the same way,* I've made a life outside the law to gather those who live outside the law (although I personally abide by and live under the Liberator's law). [22]I've been *broken, lost, depressed, oppressed, and* weak that I might *find favor and* gain the weak. I'm *flexible, adaptable, and* able to do and be whatever is needed for all kinds of people so that *in the end* I can use every means at my disposal to offer them salvation. [23]I do it all for the gospel *and for the hope* that I may participate with everyone who is blessed by the proclamation of the good news.

[24]We all know that when there's a race, all the runners bolt for the finish line, but only one will take the prize. When you run, run for the prize! [25]Athletes in training *are very strict with themselves,* exercising self-control *over desires,* and for what? For a wreath that soon withers *or is crushed or simply forgotten.* That is not our race. We run for the crown that we will wear for

* 9:9 Deuteronomy 25:4

eternity. ²⁶So I don't run aimlessly. *I don't let my eyes drift off the finish line.* When I box, I don't throw punches in the air. ²⁷I discipline my body and make it my slave so that after *all this,* after I have brought the gospel to others, I will still be qualified *to win the prize.*

10 I wouldn't want you to be ignorant *of our history,* brothers and sisters. Our ancestors were once *safeguarded* under a *miraculous* cloud *in the wilderness* and brought *safely* through the sea. ²*Enveloped in water* by cloud and by sea, they were, *you might say,* ritually cleansed* into Moses. ³*Together they were sustained supernaturally:* they all ate the same spiritual food, *manna,* ⁴and they all drank the same spiritual water, flowing from a spiritual rock that was always with them, for the rock was the Liberating King. ⁵Despite all of this, they were punished in the wilderness because God was unhappy with most of them.

⁶*Do you think such things couldn't happen to us?* Look at what happened to them as an example; *it's right there in the Scriptures* so that we won't make the same mistakes and hunger after evil as they did. *So here's my advice:* ⁷Don't *degrade yourselves by* worshiping anything less than the living God as some of them did. *Remember* it is written, "The people sat down to eat and drink and then rose up in *dance and* play."* ⁸We must be careful not to engage in sexual sins as some of them did. In one day, 23,000 died *because of sin.** ⁹None of us must test *the limits of* the Liberator's patience. Some of the Israelites did, and serpents *bit them and* killed them. ¹⁰You need to stop your groaning and whining. *Remember the story.* Some of them complained, and the messenger of death came for them and destroyed them. ¹¹All these things happened for a reason: to sound a warning. They were written down and passed down to us to teach us. *They were meant especially for us because the beginning of* the end is happening in our time. ¹²So let even the most confident believers *remember their examples and* be very careful not to fall *as some of them did.*

One of the strengths of the Jewish people has been their sense of corporate identity; it has come from belonging to a unique, suffering people who are deeply loved by God. The tendency for the new, non-Jewish believers might be to create a new identity because they lack the sense of belonging that comes with belonging to a family with a shared grandfather. A new day was dawning, a day that meant all could come to God regardless of ethnicity, locale, or social class. Believers in Corinth were not part of a new movement; they were a fresh expression of the historic movement of God.

We need to hear this truth today as much as the church in Corinth did. The world has changed drastically since the time of Abraham, David, John the Prophet, and even Martin Luther. In the midst of radical economic and technological change, some within the church have begun to embrace an idea that lifts up new or contemporary practices as being somehow superior to ancient and historic practices. Paul is denouncing this idea and calling all of us to see ourselves as a part of the local, global, and historic church.

¹³Any temptation you face will be nothing new. But God is faithful, and He will not let you be tempted beyond what you can handle. But He always provides a way of escape so that you will be able to endure *and keep moving forward.* ¹⁴So then, my beloved friends, run from idolatry *in any form.* ¹⁵As wise as I know you are, understand clearly what I am saying and determine the right course of action. ¹⁶When we give thanks *and share* the cup of blessing, are we not sharing in the blood of the Liberating King? When we *give thanks and* break bread, are we not sharing in His body? ¹⁷Because there is one bread, we,

* 10:2 Literally, immersed
* 10:7 Exodus 32:6
* 10:8 Numbers 25:9

though many, are also one body since we all share one bread. [18]Look no further than Israel *and the temple practices, and you'll see what I mean.* Isn't it true that those who eat sacrificial foods are communing at the altar, sharing its benefits? [19]So what does all this mean? I'm not suggesting that idol food itself has any special qualities or that an idol itself possesses any special powers, [20]but I am saying that the outsiders' sacrifices are actually offered to demons, not to God. *So if you feast upon this food, you are feasting with demons—* I don't want you involved with demons! [21]You can't hold the *holy* cup of the Lord *in one hand* and the cup of demons *in the other.* You can't share in the Lord's table while picking off the altar of demons. [22]Are we trying to provoke the Lord *Jesus? Do we think it's a good idea* to stir up His jealousy? Do we have *ridiculous delusions about matching or even* surpassing His power?

[23]*There's a slogan often quoted on matters like this:* "All things are permitted." *Yes,* but not all things are beneficial. "All things are permitted," *they say. Yes,* but not all things build up *and strengthen others in the body.* [24]We should stop looking out for our own interests and instead focus on the people living and breathing around us. [25]Feel free to eat any meat sold in the market without your conscience raising questions about scruples [26]because "the earth and all that's upon it belong to the Lord."* [27]So if some unbelievers invite you to dinner and you want to go, feel free to eat whatever they offer you without raising questions about conscience. [28-29]But if someone says, "This is meat from the temple altar, *a sacrifice to god so-and-so,*" then do not eat it. Not so much because of your own conscience [because the earth and everything on it belongs to the Lord],* but out of consideration for the conscience of the other fellow who told you about it. So *you ask,* "Why should I give up my freedom to accommodate the scruples of another?" [30]or, "If I am eating with gratitude to God, why am I insulted for eating food that I have properly given thanks for?" *These are good questions.*

[31]*Here's my answer: God's glory.* Whatever you do—whether you eat or drink *or not*—do it all to the glory of God! [32]Do not offend Jews or Greeks or any part of the church of God *for that matter.* [33]*Consider my example:* I strive to please all people in all my actions and words—but don't think I am in this for myself—their rescued souls are the only profit.

11 So imitate me, *watch my ways, follow my example,* just as I, too, *always seek to* imitate the Liberating King.

[2]I must say how pleased I am *to hear that* you remember me in everything and continue to hold on to the traditions I have passed on to you. [3]But *it is important* that you understand this *about headship*: the Liberating King is the head of every man, the husband is the head of his wife, and God is the head of our Liberator. [4]*Knowing this,* any man wearing a covering over his head while praying or prophesying *in your gathering* disgraces his head, *the Liberator.* [5-6]On the other hand, any woman—*I mean, of course, a married woman*—not wearing a veil over her head while praying or prophesying disgraces her head, *her husband.* It wouldn't be much different than if she walked into worship with her head shaved. For if a woman isn't going to be properly veiled, she ought to *go ahead and* cut off her hair, but if it brings shame to the woman *and her husband* to have all her hair cut off or her head shaved clean, then by all means let her wear a veil.

[7]*Here's the distinction:* man is created in God's image and for His glory, so he should not cover his head. But a wife is the glory of her husband. *She ought to be covered.* [8]Man, *you remember,* was not fashioned from the body of a woman. But woman, *though she was sculpted by the hands of God,* was fashioned from *the bones and flesh of* man.* [9]Furthermore, *don't forget that* man was not created for

---

* 10:26 Psalm 24:1
* 10:28-29 Some manuscripts omit this portion.
* 11:8 Genesis 2:21-25

woman; woman was created for man *to be his helper in everything.* [10]This means that a wife should wear *a veil* on her head as a sign she is under authority, especially when gathering in the company of heavenly messengers. [11]Regardless *of how it all began,* husbands and wives should recognize they are not independent. *Man's existence would cease without woman, as woman's would without man,* [12]for just as woman was pulled from *the side of* man, man is pulled from *the womb of* woman. *In a similar way,* all things *and all people* share the same ultimate source, God.

[13]Judge for yourselves: *when you gather to worship,* is it appropriate for a woman to pray to God without covering her head? [14]*Consider the ways of nature:* doesn't nature itself teach you that a man who wears his hair long invites *shame and* dishonor to cover him? [15]But *doesn't nature also teach* that when a woman has long hair, it is her glory? It *radiates her beauty and* acts as a natural veil. [16]If you feel like debating more on this, *just know that* we, along with all other churches of God, have adopted the same custom.

[17]On this next matter, I wish I could applaud you, but I can't because your gatherings have *become counterproductive,* making things worse *for the community* rather than better. [18]Let me start *with this:* I am hearing that your gatherings are polarizing the community, and to be honest, this doesn't surprise me. [19]I've accepted the fact that factions are *sometimes useful and even* necessary so that those who are authentic *and those who are counterfeit* may be recognized. [20]*This distinction is obvious* when you come together *because* it is not the Lord's Supper you are eating *at all.* [21]When it's time to eat, some hastily dig right in; *but look—some have more than others:* over there someone is hungry, and over here someone is drunk! [22]What is going on? *If a self-centered meal is what you want,* can't you eat and drink at home? Do you have so little respect for God's people *and this community?* Is it in you to shame the poor *at the Lord's table?* I don't even know what to say to you! Are you looking for my approval? You won't find it. *Back to the basics.*

[23]I passed on to you the tradition the Lord gave to me: On the same night the Lord Jesus was betrayed, He took the bread *in His hands,* [24]and after giving thanks *to God,* He broke it and said, "This is My body, *broken* for you. Keep doing this so that you *and all who come after* will have a vivid reminder of Me." [25]After they had finished dinner, He took the cup and in the same way said, "This cup is the new covenant, *executed* in My blood. Keep doing this, and whenever you drink it, you *and all who come after* will have a vivid reminder of Me." [26]Every time you taste *the sweetness of* this bread, and every time you place the cup *to your mouths* and drink, you are declaring the Lord's death, *which is the ultimate expression of His faithfulness and love.* Until He comes again, *keep this memorial.*

[27]*As you can see, coming to the Lord's table is a sacred privilege.* So if someone takes of this bread and drinks from the Lord's cup improperly—*as you are doing*—he is guilty of *violating* the body and blood of our Lord. [28]Examine yourselves first. Then you can properly approach *the table* to eat the bread and drink from the cup [29]because otherwise, if you eat and drink without properly discerning the significance of the Lord's body, then you eat and drink *a mouthful of* judgment upon yourself. [30]Because of this violation, many in your community are now sick and weak; some have even died. [31]But if we took care to judge ourselves, then we wouldn't have to worry about being judged *by another.* [32]*In fact,* the Lord's hand of judgment is correcting us so that we don't suffer the same fate as the rest of the *rebellious* world: condemnation.

[33]From now on, brothers and sisters, *this is what I want you to do:* when you come together to eat *at the Lord's table,* wait for each other. If someone is hungry *and can't wait,* he should go home and eat. In that way, your gatherings won't result in *God's* judgment. The rest of the instructions I have *for you* will have to wait until I come.

12 Now let me turn to *some issues about* spiritual gifts, brothers and sisters. There's much you need to learn.

²Remember *the way you used to live* when you were pagans *apart from God*? You were engrossed—enchanted with voiceless idols, led astray *by mere images carved by human hands. Although they couldn't move, they somehow moved you.* ³With that in mind, I want you to understand that no one saying "Jesus is cursed" is operating under God's Spirit, and no one saying "Jesus is Lord" can do so without the Holy Spirit's inspiration.

⁴Now there are many kinds of *grace*-gifts, but they are all from the same Spirit. ⁵There are many different ways to serve, but *they're all directed by* the same Lord. ⁶There are many amazing working-gifts in the church, but it is the same God who energizes them all in all *who have the gifts.*

⁷Each believer has received a gift that manifests the Spirit's *power and presence.* That gift is given for the good of the whole community. ⁸The Spirit gives one person a word of wisdom, but to the next person the same Spirit gives a word of knowledge. ⁹Another will receive *the gift of* faith by the same Spirit, and still another gifts of healing—all from the one Spirit. ¹⁰One person is enabled *by the Spirit* to perform miracles, another to prophesy, while another is enabled to distinguish *those prophetic* spirits. The next one speaks in various kinds of unknown languages, while another is able to interpret those languages. ¹¹One Spirit works all these things in each of them individually as He sees fit.

¹²Just as a body is one whole made up of many different parts, and all the different parts comprise the one body, so it is with our Liberating King. ¹³We were all ceremonially washed* together into one body by one Spirit. *No matter our heritage*—Jew or Greek, insider or outsider—*no matter our status*—oppressed or free—we were all given the one Spirit to drink. ¹⁴*Here's why:* the body is not made of one large part but of many *different parts.* ¹⁵Would it seem right for the foot to cry, "I am not a hand, so I couldn't be part of this body"? Even if it did, it wouldn't be any less joined to the body. ¹⁶And what about an ear? If an ear started to whine, "I am not an eye; I shouldn't be attached to this body," in all its pouting, it is still part of the body. ¹⁷Imagine the entire body as an eye. How would a giant eye have the sense to hear? And if the entire body were an ear, how would it have the sense to smell? ¹⁸*This is where God comes in.* God has meticulously put this body together; He placed each part in the exact place to perform the exact function He wanted. ¹⁹If all members were a single part, where would the body be? ²⁰So now, many members *function* within the one body. ²¹The eye cannot wail at the hand, "I have no need for you," nor could the head bellow at the feet, "I won't go one more step with you." ²²It's actually the opposite. The members who seem to have the weaker functions are necessary to keep the body moving; ²³the body parts that seem less important we treat as some of the most valuable, and those unfit, untamed, unpresentable members we treat with an even greater modesty. ²⁴That's something the more presentable members don't need. But God designed the body in such a way that greater significance is given to the *seemingly* insignificant part. ²⁵That way there should be no division in the body; instead, all the parts mutually depend on and care for one another. ²⁶If one part is suffering, then all the members suffer alongside it. If one member is honored, then all the members celebrate alongside it. ²⁷You are the body of our Liberating King; each and every one of you is a *vital* member. ²⁸God has appointed *gifts* in the assembly: first emissaries,* second prophets, third teachers, then miracle workers, healers, helpers, administrators, and then those who speak with various unknown languages.* ²⁹Are all members gifted as emissaries? Are all gifted with prophetic utterance? Are all teachers? Do all work miracles? ³⁰Or are all gifted in healing arts? Do all speak or

---

* 12:13 Literally, immersed, in a rite of initiation and purification
* 12:28 Literally, apostles
* 12:28 Literally, tongues

interpret unknown languages? *The answer to each of these questions, of course, is no.* ³¹Pursue the greater gifts, and let me tell you of a more excellent way—*love.*

13 What if I speak in the *most elegant* languages of people or in the *exotic* languages of the heavenly messengers, but I live without love? Well then, anything I say is like the clanging of brass or a crashing cymbal. ²What if I have the gift of prophecy, am blessed with knowledge and insight to all the mysteries, or what if my faith is strong enough to scoop a mountain *from its bedrock,* yet I live without love? If so, I am nothing. ³I could give all that I have to feed the poor, I could surrender my body to be burned *as a martyr,* [that I may brag,]* but if I do not live in love, I gain nothing *by my selfless acts.*

> *P*aul boils it all down for the believers in Corinth. Religious people often spend their time practicing rituals, projecting dogma, and going through a routine that might look like Christianity on the outside but that lacks the essential ingredient that brings all of it together—love! It is a loving God who birthed creation and pursued a broken people in the most spectacular way. That same love must guide us, lest we become meaningless noise.

⁴Love is patient; love is kind. Love isn't envious, doesn't boast, *brag, or strut about.* There's no arrogance in love; ⁵it's never rude, crude, or indecent—it's not self-absorbed. Love isn't easily upset. Love doesn't tally wrongs ⁶or celebrate injustice, but truth—*yes, truth*—is love's delight! ⁷Love puts up with anything and everything that comes along; it trusts, hopes, and endures no matter what. ⁸Love will never become obsolete. Now as for the prophetic gifts, they will not last; unknown languages will become silent, and the gift of knowledge will no longer be needed. ⁹Gifts of knowledge and prophecy are partial at best, *at least for now,* ¹⁰but when the

perfection *and fullness of God's kingdom* arrive, all the parts will end. ¹¹When I was a child, I spoke, thought, and reasoned in childlike ways *as we all do.* But when I became a man, I left my childish ways behind. ¹²For now, we can only see a dim and blurry picture of things, as when we stare into polished metal. I realize that everything I know is only part of the big picture. But one day *when the Liberating King arrives,* we will see clearly, face-to-face. In that day, I will fully know just as I have been wholly known *by God.* ¹³But now faith, hope, and love remain; these three *virtues must characterize our lives.* The greatest of these is love.

14 So *in everything* strive to love. Passionately seek the gifts of the Spirit, especially the gift of prophecy. ²*You see,* a person speaking in an *unknown* language is not addressing the church because he is really addressing God—those who overhear don't understand because he is speaking in the Spirit the depths of the mysteries *of the Liberating King.* ³But a person who has the gift of prophecy teaches in a way that builds up the community, draws them near, and comforts them. ⁴Those who speak in an unknown language only strengthen themselves, but those who prophesy strengthen the community. ⁵While I'd like for you all to be able to speak *by the Spirit* in unknown languages, my preference would be for you all to prophesy *by the Spirit.* Those who speak prophetically *are God's mouthpiece and* are far more useful to the church than those who speak in exotic languages—unless there is another who interprets so that the community may be strengthened.

⁶If I come to you, brothers and sisters, talking in unknown languages, what good would that be for any of you? *What service to the community would that provide?* You receive no benefit unless I speak to you some word of revelation, knowledge, prophecy, or instruction *in your own lan-*

---

* 13:3 Most early manuscripts omit this portion.

guage. ⁷Look, if inanimate objects, *musical instruments* like a pipe or harp, don't make a clear, distinct sound, how would you know whether you're listening to someone blow a pipe or strum a harp? ⁸If the bugle blares more like a clank, who would know to prepare for battle? ⁹It's the same with you. Unless you speak a message in a language everyone understands, they won't know what you're talking about. You'll be talking into the wind. ¹⁰This world is full of languages, each and every one of them having meaning, ¹¹but if I don't understand the meaning of some sound, then I become like a foreigner to the person speaking and the person speaking will be like a foreigner to me. ¹²It's the same with you; in your passion for spiritual gifts, seek to strengthen the community of believers *and you will all be better off.*

¹³So anyone who speaks in an unknown language should pray for the ability to interpret ¹⁴because if I pray in such a language, although my spirit prays, my mind isn't productive. ¹⁵What do I do then? I pray. I pray with my spirit but also with my mind engaged; I sing with my spirit but also with my mind engaged. ¹⁶If you speak a word of blessing in the spirit only, then how will an uninformed person who can't understand your prayer say "Amen" when you are done giving thanks? ¹⁷Even though you give thanks *to God* well, the unknowing person doesn't benefit. ¹⁸I thank God that I speak in unknown languages more than the rest of you, ¹⁹but when the church gathers, I would rather speak five words with my mind so I can be understood and train others than utter 10,000 exotic words.

²⁰Brothers and sisters, don't think like children. Be innocent of malice but mature in understanding. ²¹In the law, it states:

"I will send My message to this
people
with strange languages and
foreign lips.
And even when that happens,
they will not listen to Me,"

says the Lord.* ²²So speaking in unknown languages is not a sign to the believing but *a miracle* to the unbelieving; prophecy, though, is not a sign to the unbelieving but for the believing. ²³*Imagine what would happen* if the entire church gathered together speaking in different languages, *one foreign to the next.* Then people who have never heard of such a thing or unbelieving people walk up on all that's going on. Would they not think each and every one of you were raving lunatics? ²⁴But let's say an outsider or unbeliever walks in on a different scene: all are speaking for God with great power and insight *in a language they know. What then?* Well, the outsider would come under the conviction *of his own sins* and be called to accountability by the words of all *the prophets.* ²⁵The very secrets of his heart would be revealed, *and right there—mystified—*he would fall on his face in worship to God, proclaiming *all the while* that God most certainly dwells among you.

²⁶What should you do then, brothers and sisters? When you come together, *each person has a vital role because each has gifts.* One person might have a song, another a teaching, still another a revelation *from God.* One person might speak in an unknown language, another will offer the interpretation, but all of this should be done to strengthen *the life and faith of the community.* ²⁷But if any do speak in an exotic language, limit it to two or three people at the most, and have them speak one at a time, while another interprets for the rest. ²⁸If there is not an interpreter present, then the one should stay silent during the gathering, speaking only to himself and God. ²⁹Have two to three prophets speak, and let others *with discerning gifts* evaluate the messages they hear. ³⁰Now if *in the course of things* a message comes to another who is seated, then the first one speaking should be silent *until this new message can be spoken.* ³¹To *avoid confusion and* create a space where all can learn and be encouraged, let only one prophet speak at a time *without interruption.* ³²*You see,* the prophetic spirits are under the control of the prophets

* 14:21 Isaiah 28:11-12

33because God is the author of order, not confusion. This is how it is in all gatherings of the saints. 34Wives should be respectfully silent at the gatherings, as they are not allowed to speak, and they should yield *themselves to those in authority* just as it is written in the law. 35When they want to learn anything *in particular,* they should ask their husbands when they get home. It creates a shameful situation for them to speak at church. 36Do you think the word of God came to the world by you? Or that it came only to you?

37Let any person who thinks he is a prophet or a spiritual person affirm that these things I write to you are the commands of the Lord. 38Whoever chooses to be ignorant of this will be treated as ignorant. 39So, my dear brothers and sisters, passionately desire to prophesy, but don't ban the gift of speaking in unknown languages. 40Just maintain the proper order in all things.

15 Let me remind you, brothers and sisters, of the good news that I preached to you *when we first met.* *It's the essential message* that you have taken to heart, the central story you now base your life on, 2and through this gospel, you are liberated—unless, of course, your faith has come to nothing. 3-4For I passed down to you the crux of it all which I had also received *from others,* that the Liberating King died for our sins and was buried and raised from the dead on the third day. All this happened to fulfill the Scriptures; *it was the perfect climax to God's covenant story.* 5Afterward He appeared alive to Cephas* *(you may know him as Simon Peter),* then to the rest of the twelve. 6*If that were not amazing enough,* on one occasion, He appeared to more than 500 believers at one time. Many of those brothers and sisters are still around *to tell the story,* though some have fallen asleep* in Jesus. 7Soon He appeared to James, *His brother and the leader of the Jerusalem church,* and then to all the rest of the emissaries* *He Himself commissioned.* 8Last of all, He appeared to me;* I was like a child snatched from his mother's womb. 9You see, I am the least of all His emissaries, not fit to be called His emissary because I hunted down and persecuted God's church. 10Today I am who I am because of God's grace, and *I have made sure that* the grace He offered me has not been wasted. I have worked harder, *longer, and smarter* than all the rest, but *I realize* it is not me— it is God's grace with me *that has made the difference.* 11In the end, *it doesn't matter* whether it was I or the other witnesses *who brought you the message.* What matters is that we keep preaching and that you have faith in this message.

12Now if we have told you about the Liberating King (how He has risen from the dead *and appeared to us fully alive),* then how can you *stand there and* say there is no such thing as resurrection from death? 13*Friends,* if there is no resurrection of the dead, then even the Liberator hasn't been raised; 14if that is so, then all our preaching has been for nothing and your faith *in the message* is worthless. 15And what's worse, all of us *who have been preaching the gospel* are now guilty of misrepresenting God because we have been spreading the news that He raised the Liberating King from the dead (which must be a lie if what you are saying about the dead not being raised is the truth). 16*Please listen.* If *you* say, "the dead are not raised," then *what you are telling me is that* the Liberating King has not been raised. *Friends,* 17if the Liberator has not been raised *from the dead,* then your faith is worth less *than yesterday's garbage,* you are all doomed in your sins, 18and all the *dearly* departed who trusted in His liberation are left decaying *in the ground.* 19If what we have hoped for in the Liberator doesn't take us beyond this life, then we are world-class fools, deserving everyone's pity.

---

* 15:5 Luke 24:34
* 15:6 Literally, died
* 15:7 Literally, apostles
* 15:7 Acts 1:3-4
* 15:8 Acts 9:3-6

²⁰But the Liberating King was raised from death's slumber and is the firstfruits of those who have fallen asleep *in death*. ²¹For since death entered *this world* by a man, it took another man to make the resurrection of the dead *our new* reality. ²²*Look at it this way*: through Adam all of us die, but through the Liberating King all of us can live again. ²³But this is how it will happen: the Liberator's *awakening* is the firstfruits. It will be followed by the resurrection of all those who belong to Him at His coming, and ²⁴then the end will come. After He has *conquered His enemies and* shut down every rule and authority vying for power, He will hand over the Kingdom to God, the Father *of all that is*. ²⁵And He must reign as King until He has put all His enemies under His feet. ²⁶The last hostile power to be destroyed is death itself. ²⁷*All this will happen to fulfill the Scripture that says*, "You placed everything on earth beneath His feet."* (Although it says "everything," it is clear that this does not also pertain to God, *who created everything* and made it all subject to Him.) ²⁸Then, when all creation has taken its rightful place beneath God's sovereign reign, the Son will follow, subject to the Father who exalted Him over all created things; then God will be God over all.

> esurrection is central to the gospel of the Liberating King. In Jesus, God personified His redeeming work in this world. He created us from dust, and upon death He will resurrect us to be with Him. Our God is a God who brings things back from the dead. Out of wars, He brings peace. Out of bankruptcy, He brings prosperity. Out of famine, He brings a great bounty. If you seek to follow the Liberator, will you embrace death so that you might know true life?

²⁹*You have probably heard that* some people are undergoing ritual cleansings* for the dead. Why are they doing that? If the dead are not going to be raised, then why are people being ritually cleansed* for

them? ³⁰Why are we putting our lives on the line all the time *if there's no resurrection*? ³¹I die every day! I swear that it's true! That's something you take pride in, brothers and sisters, as I do in our Lord Jesus, the Liberating King. ³²But if I have fought against the wild beasts in Ephesus for some human cause, then what good has that done me? If the dead are not raised, then there's nothing more to do than—*as the saying goes*—eat and drink, for tomorrow we die.*

³³But don't be so naïve—*there's another saying you know well*—Bad company corrupts good habits. ³⁴Come to your senses, live justly, and stop sinning. *It's true that* some have no knowledge of God. I am saying this to shame you *into better habits*.

³⁵Now I know what some of you are thinking: "Just how are the dead going to be raised? What kind of bodies will they have when they come *back to life*?" ³⁶*Don't be a* fool! The seed you plant doesn't produce life unless it dies. *Right?* ³⁷The seed doesn't have *the same look*, the same body, *if you will*, of what it will have once it starts to grow. It starts out a single, naked seed—whether wheat or some other grain, *it doesn't matter*— ³⁸and God gives to that seed a body just as He has desired. For each of the different kinds of seeds God prepares a unique body. ³⁹*Or look at it this way*: not all flesh is the same. *Right?* There is *skin* flesh on humans, *furry* flesh on animals, *feathery* flesh on birds, and *scaly* flesh on fish. ⁴⁰*Likewise* there are bodies made for the heavens and bodies made for the earth. The heavenly bodies have a different kind of glory *or luminescence* compared to bodies below. ⁴¹*Even among the heavenly bodies, there is a different level of brilliance*: the sun shines differently than the moon, the moon differently than the stars, and the stars themselves differ in their brightness.

⁴²It's like this with the resurrection of those who have died. The body planted in

---

* 15:27 Psalm 8:6
* 15:29 Literally, immersions, to show repentance
* 15:29 Literally, immersed, to show repentance
* 15:32 Isaiah 22:13

the earth decays. But the body raised from the earth cannot decay. ⁴³The body is planted in disgrace and weakness. But the body is raised in splendor and power. ⁴⁴The body planted *in the earth* was animated by the physical, material realm. But the body raised *from the earth* will be animated by the spiritual. Since there is a physical, material body, there will also be a spiritual body. ⁴⁵That's why it was written, "The first man Adam became a living soul"*; the last Adam has become a life-giving spirit. ⁴⁶*Everything has an order.* The body is not animated first by the spiritual but the physical; then the spiritual *becomes its life-giving source.* ⁴⁷The first man, *Adam,* came from the earth and was made from dust; the second man, *our Liberating King,* has come from heaven. ⁴⁸The earth man shares his earth nature with all those made of earth; likewise the heavenly man shares His heavenly nature with all those made of heaven. ⁴⁹Just as we have carried the image of the earth man in our bodies, we will* also carry the image of the heavenly man *in our new bodies at the resurrection.*

⁵⁰Now listen to this: brothers and sisters, this present body is not able to inherit the kingdom of God any more than decay can inherit that which lasts forever. ⁵¹Stay close because I am going to tell you a mystery—something you may have trouble understanding: we will not all fall asleep with death, but we will all be transformed. ⁵²*It will all happen so fast,* in a blink, a mere flutter of the eye. The last trumpet will call, and the dead will be raised from their graves with a body that does not, cannot decay. All of us will be changed! ⁵³We'll step out of our mortal clothes and slide into immortal bodies, *replacing everything that is subject to death with eternal life.* ⁵⁴And, when we are all redressed with bodies that do not, cannot decay, when we put immortality over our mortal frames, then it will be as *Scripture* says:

> *Life everlasting* has victoriously
>   swallowed death.*

⁵⁵Hey, Death! What happened to your
    big win?

Hey, Death! What happened to
    your sting?*

⁵⁶Sin came *into this world,* and death's sting *followed.* Then sin took aim at the law and gained power *over those who follow the law.* ⁵⁷Thank God, then, for Jesus, the Liberating King, who brought us victory *over the grave.*

⁵⁸My dear brothers and sisters, stay firmly planted—be unshakable—do many good works in the name of God, and know that all your labor is not for nothing when it is for God.

16 Now I call you, just as I did the churches gathering in Galatia, to collect funds to support God's people *in Jerusalem.* ²On *Sunday,* the first day of the week, *I want* each of you to set aside an amount, as God has blessed you, so the funds will be collected by the time I come. ³When I get there, I will send those you recommend by your own letters to carry your *generous and gracious* donation to Jerusalem. ⁴If you think it seems appropriate for me to travel with them, then we'll go together.

⁵*Get ready.* I will come your way after traveling through Macedonia. For I'm just passing through Macedonia ⁶and will probably stay with you through the winter so that you may provide for my next journey (wherever that may be). ⁷I want to reconnect with you, not just pass through; if the Lord is willing, I hope to stay awhile. ⁸But until Pentecost, I plan to stay in Ephesus ⁹because, not only has *God* opened a significant door here for me to serve, but also there is a lot of opposition against me.

*C*hurches love to throw around words like "independent" and "autonomous." But one would be hard-pressed to find any of these ideas in

* 15:45 Genesis 2:7
* 15:49 Other manuscripts read "so let us."
* 15:54 Isaiah 25:8
* 15:55 Hosea 13:14

the Scriptures. Instead, Paul seems to be modeling submission and interdependence. We must always consider others and shape our actions to bless them. But he does not stop there—it is clear that we are responsible to care for one another in physical and monetary ways. What might Paul say to the church today, given the drastic disparity between the wealthy churches of the West and the brothers and sisters in the rest of the world who lack food, water, or shelter?

[10]If Timothy comes, see that he is comfortable and untroubled; his work is the Lord's, as is mine. [11]No one should treat him badly. Send him on to meet me in peace because the brothers and sisters here and I are looking for him. [12]You shouldn't expect to see our brother Apollos, although I tried to persuade him to come to you with the rest of the brothers and sisters, because now is not the best time for him to come. When it's his time, he will come.

[13]*Listen,* stay alert, stand tall in the faith, be courageous, and be strong. [14]Let love prevail in your life, words, and actions.

[15]*Finally,* brothers and sisters, I call on you *to follow your leaders.* People like those in the house of Stephanas—you know they were among the first believers in Achaia, and they have devoted their lives to serving God's people— [16]*I urge you* to submit to the authority of such leaders, to every coworker, and to those who *offer their backs and shoulders for the* work. [17]I celebrate the arrival of Stephanas, Fortunatus, and Achaicus, as they have supplied me with what you could not. [18]They have been a breath of fresh air for me as I know they are for you, so respect and honor those like them.

[19]The churches in Asia salute you. Aquila and Prisca send a heartfelt greeting in the Lord along with those who gather at their house. [20]The entire family in faith here sends their greetings. *Be sure you* greet one another by a holy kiss.

[21]This *closing* greeting is written by my own hand—Paul's: [22]May those who have no love for the Lord be cursed. Maranatha, *"Our Lord, come!"* [23]May the grace of the Lord Jesus be with you. [24]My love to you all in *the name of* the Liberating King, Jesus. [Amen.]*

* 16:24 Some manuscripts omit this word.

2 Corinthians

Letter to the church in Corinth
From Paul, the apostle to the Gentiles

After Paul wrote 1 Corinthians, he heard from Timothy that the situation between him and the church he loved was deteriorating. Apparently in Paul's absence, a number of false teachers had instructed the church and claimed that Paul was not a true emissary of the Liberating King. They criticized his message and his methods; they charged that he was inferior to the real emissaries. So Paul made a hasty trip across the Aegean from Ephesus—where he was working—in hopes of repairing the rift between them. But the visit backfired. Instead of making things better, it made things worse. He returned to Ephesus from the "agonizing visit," as he later characterized it, and wrote a letter "covered with tears." This time Paul dispatched Titus with the letter. Perhaps he could intervene before a permanent break resulted.

When Titus caught up with Paul in Macedonia, he had good news and bad news. The good news was that a majority of believers in Corinth were back with Paul. The tearful letter—now lost—and Titus's vigilant efforts apparently worked. The bad news was that there was a minority of believers and influential leaders who were still unconvinced. So Paul wrote the letter we now call 2 Corinthians to congratulate the majority and to confront the minority, urging both to stay with the true gospel of the Liberating King and His emissary and to pave the way for a peaceful, positive visit.

More than any letter Paul writes, 2 Corinthians offers insight into his work as the Liberator's emissary. As he responds to the accusations of his opponents, he articulates clearly his understanding of the gospel and his call as one divinely commissioned to carry the good news to both Jews and outsiders. It's clear he is embarrassed by the way he has to defend himself at times; still he refuses to sit idly by as his work and church are in jeopardy. At the heart of the letter is an appeal for the Corinthians to join in the collection for the Jerusalem church. The initiative has a dual purpose. First, Paul hopes to provide substantial relief to the poor in Judea after a lengthy period of famine and hard times. Second, he wants to build a bridge from the churches he is establishing in Asia and Greece to the "mother church" in Jerusalem. Paul understands well the heart of his Lord, and he does everything he possibly can to promote peace and unity among all the churches.

1 Paul, an emissary* of Jesus, the Liberating King, *pressed into service* by the will of God, and our brother Timothy to God's church that gathers in Corinth and all the saints in the region of Achaia.

²May grace and peace from God our Father and the Lord Jesus, our Liberator, surround you.

³All praise goes to God, Father of our Lord Jesus, the Liberating King. He is the Father of compassion, the God of all comfort. ⁴He consoles us as we endure the pain and hardship of life so that we may draw from His comfort and share it with others in their own struggles. ⁵For even as His suffering continues to flood over us, through our Liberator we experience the wealth of His comfort just the same. ⁶If we are afflicted *with such trouble and pain*, then know it is so that you might ultimately experience comfort and salvation. If we experience comfort, it is to encourage you so that you can hold up while you endure the same sufferings we all share. ⁷Remember that our hope for you stands firm, *unshaken and unshakable*. That's because we know that as you share in our sufferings, so you will also share in our comfort.

⁸My brothers and sisters, we have to tell you that when we were in Asia the troubles we faced were nearly more than we could handle. The burdens we bore nearly crushed us. Our strength dwindled to nothing. For a while, we weren't sure we would make it through the whole ordeal. ⁹We thought we would have to serve out our death sentences right then and there. As a result, we realized that we could no longer rely on ourselves and that we must trust solely in God, who possesses the power to raise the dead. ¹⁰*Miraculously* God Himself delivered us from the cold hands of death. We again place our hope in Him alone, and we know He will deliver us. ¹¹Join us in this work. Lend us a hand through prayer so that many will give thanks for the gift that comes to us when God answers the prayers of so many.

*S*ome believe that prosperity and comfort are the markers of a faithful Christian; in order to believe that, you have to ignore completely the life and writings of Paul, the emissary. It is only when you suffer that you can meet God as your comforter. In these letters, and often in our own lives, it is when we seem to have come to the end of our rope that we see and experience the fullness of God in entirely new ways. This is not to say that any of us should or would seek out the kind of suffering Paul experienced; we do not long to be imprisoned, beaten, shipwrecked, or hunted by authorities. But when our dark days come, we should be ready to learn, grow, and experience the fullness of God in the midst of our troubles.

¹²We are proud of the fact that we have lived before the world and especially before you with clear consciences, living holy lives mixed with genuine sincerity before God. We have not relied on any human wisdom but on the grace *and favor* of God. ¹³We are not writing to you in anything *resembling codes or riddles*; we only write those lessons you are ready to read and understand. I hope you will *study them, value them, and* truly understand them until the end. ¹⁴You have already begun to grasp what we mean in part, but on the day when our Lord Jesus returns, we will be as proud of you as you are of us.

¹⁵⁻¹⁶In *this spirit of* trust and confidence, I was intending to come your way first *on my current journey*. So that you might have a double dose of this grace and assurance, my plan was to visit you on my way to Macedonia and return to you again on the journey back so that you could assist me on the trip to Judea. ¹⁷*And now, because I didn't make it back to Corinth as planned, I understand some are criticizing me. Was I just being indecisive? Were my plans made*

* 1:1 Literally, apostle

in the flesh *rather than by God's Spirit*? How can I say "yes" and "no" in the same breath? [18]Because our God is always faithful *to His promises*, our word to you was not both "yes" and "no"—*"Yes, I'll come," and then, "No, I've changed my mind."* [19]For the Son of God—Jesus, the Liberating King, who we (Silvanus, Timothy, and I) have preached to you—was not both "yes" and then "no." With Him the answer is always "yes." [20]In Jesus, *our Liberator,* we hear a resounding "yes" to all of God's many promises. This is the reason we say "Amen" to and through Jesus when giving glory to God. [21]*Remember that* God has established our relationship with you in the Liberating King, and He has anointed *and commissioned* us *for this special mission.* [22]He has marked us with His seal and placed His Spirit in our hearts as a guarantee, a down payment *of the things to come.*

[23]*If I were in court today,* I'd call God as a witness to my soul. *Here's the truth:* I decided not to come back to Corinth in order to spare you *further pain and sorrow.* [24]It's not that we want to coerce you in any matter of faith; we are coworkers called to increase your joy because you have stood firm in faith.

*I*n many ways, the church in Corinth is the example of what not to do: these guys were exhausting to Paul and to one another with their negativity and criticism. Nothing destroys the beauty of Christian community more aggressively than these kinds of patterns. How can you infuse your community with grace rather than negativity?

2 I finally determined that I would not come to you again for yet another agonizing visit. [2]If my visits create such *pain and* sorrow for you, who can cheer me up except for those I've caused such grief? [3]This is exactly what I was writing to you about earlier so that when we are face-to-face I will not have to wallow in sadness in the presence of friends who should bring me the utmost joy. For I felt sure that my delight would also become your delight.

[4]My last letter to you was covered with tears, composed with great difficulty, and *frankly,* a broken heart. It wasn't my intention to depress you *or cause you pain;* rather, I had hoped you would see it for what it was—a demonstration of the overwhelming love I have for all of you.

[5]But if anyone has caused harm, he has not so much harmed me as he has—and I don't think I'm exaggerating here—harmed all of you. [6]*In my view,* the majority of you have punished him well enough. [7]So instead of continuing to ostracize him, I encourage you to offer him *the grace of* forgiveness and the comfort *of your acceptance.* Otherwise, *if he finds no welcome back to the community,* I'm afraid he will be overwhelmed with extreme sorrow and lose all hope. [8]So I urge you to demonstrate your love for him once again. [9]I wrote these things to you with a clear purpose in mind: to test whether you are willing to live and abide by all *my counsel.* [10]If you forgive anyone, I forgive that one as well. Have no doubt, anything that I have forgiven—when I do forgive—is done ultimately for you in the presence of the Liberating King. [11]*It's my duty* to make sure that Satan does not win even a small victory over us, for we don't want to be naïve *and then fall prey* to his schemes.

[12]When I arrived at Troas, bringing the good news of the Liberating King, the Lord opened a door there for me. [13]Yet my spirit was restless because I could not find my brother Titus. Eventually I told them goodbye and set out for Macedonia.

[14]Yet I am so thankful to God, who always marches us to victory under the banner of our Liberator, and through us He spreads the beautiful fragrance of His knowledge to every corner of the earth. [15]*In a turbulent world* where people are either dying or being rescued, we are the sweet smell of the Liberating King to God *our Father.* [16]To those who are dying, they smell the stench of death in us. And to those being rescued, we are the unmistakable scent of life. Who is worthy of this calling? [17]For we are nothing like the others who sell the word of God like a commodity. *Do not be mistaken;* our words

come from God with the utmost sincerity, always spoken through the Liberating King in the presence of God.

3 Are we back to page one? Do we need to gather some recommendations *to prove our validity* to you? Or do we need to take your letter of commendation to others *to gain credibility*? [2]You are our letter, every word burned onto our* hearts to be read by everyone. [3]You are the living letter of the Liberating King, nurtured by us and inscribed, not with ink, but with the Spirit of the living God—*a letter too passionate* to be chiseled onto stone tablets, but *emblazoned* upon the human heart.

[4]This is the kind of confidence we have in and through the Liberating King toward our God. [5]*Don't be mistaken;* in and of ourselves we know we have little to offer, but any competence *or value* we have comes from God. [6]Now God has equipped us to be capable servants of the new covenant, not by authority of the written law which only brings death, but by the Spirit who brings life.

pparently Paul is responding to repeated questions from the church in Corinth requiring him to justify his actions and explain himself. But instead of responding to each separately, Paul suggests a new course of action: let my record be based on the fruit in your lives. How do we stand up to the same test? If our lives were judged based on the fruit of the seeds we have planted and nurtured in the lives of others, would we be proud or mortified?

[7]Now *consider this:* if the ministry of death, which was chiseled in stone, came with so much glory that the Israelites could not bear to look at Moses' face even as that glory was fading, [8]imagine the kind of greater glory that will accompany the ministry of the Spirit. [9]If glory ushered in the ministry that offers condemnation, how much more glory will attend the ministry

that promises to restore and set the world right? [10]In fact, what seemed to have great glory will appear entirely inglorious in the light of the greater glory *of the new covenant.* [11]If something that fades away possesses glory, how much more intense is the glory of what remains?

[12]In light of this hope that we have, we act with great confidence and speak *with great courage.* [13]We do not act like Moses who covered his face with a veil so the children of Israel would not stare as the glory *of God* faded *from his face.* [14]Their minds became as hard *as stones*; for up to this day when they read the old covenant, the same veil continues *to hide that glory*; this veil is lifted only through the Liberating King. [15]Even today a veil covers their hearts when the words of Moses *found in the first five books of Scripture* are read, [16]but in the moment when one turns toward the Lord, the veil is removed. [17]*By* "the Lord" *what I mean* is the Spirit, and *in any heart* where the Spirit of the Lord is present, there is liberty. [18]Now all of us, with our faces unveiled, are transfixed by the glory of the Lord, gazing—like we'd gaze into a mirror—*at His splendor,* and so we are being transformed, *metamorphosed,* into His same image from one radiance of glory to another, just as the Spirit of the Lord accomplishes it.

4 Since we are *joined together* in this ministry as a result of the mercy *shown to all of us* by God, we do not become discouraged. [2]Instead, we have renounced all the things that hide in shame; we refuse to live deceptively or use trickery, and we do not pollute God's Word *with any other agenda.* Instead, we aim to plainly tell the truth appealing to the conscience of every person under God's watchful eye. [3]Now if our gospel remains veiled, it is only veiled from those who are *lost and* dying, [4]because the *evil god of this age* has blinded the minds of unbelievers. As a result the light of the gospel, the radiant glory of the Liberating King—who is

* 3:2 Other manuscripts read "your hearts."

the very image of God—cannot shine down on them. [5]We do not preach about ourselves. The subject of all our sermons is Jesus, the Liberator. He is Lord *and Master* of all. For Jesus' sake we are here to serve you. [6]The God who spoke *light into existence,* saying, "Let light shine from the darkness,"* is the very One who sets our hearts ablaze to shed light on the knowledge of God's glory *revealed* in the face of Jesus, the Liberating King.

[7]But this beautiful treasure is contained in us—*cracked* pots made of earth and clay—so that the transcendent character of this power will be clearly seen as coming from God and not from us. [8]We are dented and dinged on all sides from our afflictions, but we are not crushed by them. *We are greeted with pain at every turn, but we are not trampled and defeated.* We are bewildered at times, but we do not give in to despair. [9]We are persecuted, but we have not been abandoned. We have been knocked down, but we are not destroyed. [10]We always carry around in our bodies the reality of the brutal death *and suffering* of Jesus. As a result, His *resurrection* life *rises and* reveals its wondrous power in our bodies as well. [11]For while we live, we are constantly handed over to death on account of Jesus so that His life may be revealed even in our mortal bodies of flesh. [12]So death is constantly at work in us, but life is working in you.

[13]We share the same spirit of faith as the one who wrote *the psalm,* "I believed; therefore I spoke."* We also believe, and that belief leads us to acknowledge [14]that the same God who resurrected the Lord Jesus will raise us with Jesus and will usher us all together into His presence. [15]All of this is happening for your good. As grace is spread to the multitudes, there is a growing sound of thanks being uttered by those relishing in the glory of God.

[16]So we have no reason to despair. Despite the fact that our outer humanity is falling apart and decaying, our inner humanity is breathing in new life every day. [17]You see, the short-lived pains of this life are creating for us an eternal glory that does not compare to anything we know here. [18]So we do not set our sights on the things we can see *with our eyes.* All of that is fleeting; *it will eventually fade away.* Instead, we focus on the things we cannot see, which live on and on.

5 *Let me try to explain what I'm talking about in a way that makes the most sense to me as a tentmaker.* We know that if our earthly house—a mere tent *that can easily be taken down*—is destroyed, we will then live in an eternal home in the heavens, a building crafted by divine—not human—hands. [2]Now in this tent of a house, we continue to groan *and ache* with a deep desire to be sheltered in our permanent home [3]because then we will be truly clothed *and comfortable,* protected by a covering for our *current* nakedness. [4]The fact is that in this tent we anxiously moan, *fearing the naked truth of our reality.* What we crave above all is to be clothed so that what is *temporary and* mortal can be wrapped completely in life. [5]The One who has worked *and tailored* us for this is God Himself, who has gifted His Spirit to us as a pledge *toward our permanent home.*

[6]In light of this, we live with a daring passion and know that our time spent in this body is also time we are not present with the Lord. [7]The path we walk is charted by faith, not by what we see with our eyes. [8]There is no doubt that we live with a daring passion, but in the end we prefer to be gone from this body so that we can be at home with the Lord. [9]Ultimately it does not matter whether we are here or gone; our purpose stays fixed, and that is to please Him. [10]*In time* we will all stand in judgment before the throne of the Liberating King to receive what is just for our conduct (whether it be good or bad) while we lived in this temporary body.

[11]So because we stand in awe of the *one true* Lord, we make it our aim to convince all people *of the truth of the gospel;* God sees who we really are, and I hope *in some*

* 4:6 Genesis 1:3
* 4:13 Psalm 116:10

way that you'll look deeply into your consciences to see us as well. [12]*But we hope you understand that* we are not trying to prove ourselves to you *or pull together a résumé that will impress you.* We are simply hoping that you will find a sense of joy in connecting with us. And when you are approached by others (who may value appearances more than the heart) *seeking questions about us,* you will be able to offer an answer for them. [13]If we *seem out of control and* act like fanatics, it is for God. But if we act in a coherent and reasonable way, it is for you. [14]You see, the controlling force in our lives is the love of the Liberating King. And our confession is this: One died for all; therefore, all have died. [15]The reason He died for us is so that we will all live, not for ourselves, but for Him who died and rose from the dead. [16]*Because of all that God has done,* we now have a new perspective. We used to show regard for people based on worldly standards and interests. No longer. We used to think of the Liberating King the same way. No longer. [17]Therefore, if anyone is united with the Liberator, that person is a new creation. The old life is gone—and see— a new life has begun! [18]All of this is *a gift* from *our Creator* God, who has *pursued us and* brought us into a restored *and healthy* relationship with Him through the Liberator. And He has given us *the same mission,* the ministry of reconciliation, *to bring others back to Him.* [19]*It is central to our good news that* God was in the Liberating King making things right between Himself and the world. This means He does not hold their sins against them. But it also means He charges us to proclaim the message that heals and restores our broken relationships *with God and each other.*

[20]So we are now representatives of the Liberating King; God has given us a charge to carry through our lives—urging all people on behalf of the Liberator to become reconciled to *the Creator* God. [21]He orchestrated this so that He who had never experienced sin would become sin for us so that *through the Liberating King* we might embody the very righteousness of God.

6 As for those of us working as His emissaries,* we beg you not to take the grace of God lightly. [2]For God says *through Isaiah,*

> When the time was right, I listened to you,
> and that day you were delivered, I was your help.*

Look, now the time is right! See, your day of deliverance is here! [3]*We are careful in what we teach* so that our words won't be a stumbling block and so that no one will discredit our ministry. [4]But as God's servants, we commend ourselves in every situation: with great endurance, through anguish and hardship, cornered *by the enemy—* [5]in beatings, imprisonments, uproars, toil, sleeplessness, and starvation— [6]in purity and understanding; patience and kindness; in the Holy Spirit and sincerest love; [7]with the voice of truth and power of God; armed on the right and armed on the left with righteousness *from God;* [8]whether respected or loathed, praised or criticized as frauds, and yet true; [9]as unknown *to this world,* yet well known *to God;* as dying, and yet we live; as punished, and yet not executed; [10]as sorrowful, yet we continually rejoice; as *the poorest of* the poor, yet bringing richness to all; as possessing nothing, yet holding *the key to* all things.

[11]Corinthians, we have been completely open to you. *We've exposed the truth,* holding nothing back while our hearts open wide *to take you in.* [12]We have revealed our affection toward you—though *it's obvious* you have a hard time showing your affection toward us. [13]If I could offer some fatherly advice: open yourselves up as children; share your hearts with us as we have done for you.

[14]Don't develop partnerships with those who are not followers of the Liberating King. For what real connection can exist between righteousness and rebellion? How can light participate in darkness? [15]What harmony can exist between the Liberating King and Satan?* Do the faithful and the

---

* 6:1 Literally, apostles
* 6:2 Isaiah 49:8
* 6:15 Literally, Belial

unfaithful have anything in common?
¹⁶Can the temple of God find common
ground with idols? Don't you see that we
house the temple of the living God within
us? *Remember when* He said:

"I will make My home with them and
 walk among them.
 I will be their God,
 and they will be My people."*
¹⁷"So then turn away from them,
 turn away and leave *without
 looking back*,"* says the Lord.
"Stay away from anything unclean,
 anything impure,
 and I will welcome you."*
¹⁸"And I will be for you as a father,
 and you will be for Me as sons and
 daughters,"*
Says the Lord Almighty!

One of the most important "partnerships" in life is found in marriage. There are other kinds of union,
but the union of husband and wife
transcends any other. God created
sexual intimacy as a unique gift to
marriage. Its purpose goes beyond
pleasure and procreation. As a man
and a woman join their bodies together, the Spirit does a unique work
of binding these two individuals as one
person. But the involvement of the
Spirit is not possible when a believer is
intimate with a nonbeliever. They are
not filled with the same Spirit and
cannot experience the fullness that
God intended. Paul's instructions are
practical, simple, and clear.

7 Because we have these promises,
dearly loved ones, out of respect for
God we should scour the filth from
our flesh and spirit and move toward perfect *beauty and* holiness.

²Take us into your hearts; *love us as we
love you. You have nothing to fear.* We have
hurt no one, ruined no one, swindled no
one. ³I am not writing these things to condemn you, as I said before. Our hearts

embrace you, so we stand beside you
whether facing life or death. ⁴I am completely confident and incredibly proud of
you. Even in all this turbulence I am at
peace—I am overflowing with joy.

⁵When we came into Macedonia, we
were completely worn out. Under attack
from every angle—nagging opposition on
the outside, *our own nagging* fears from the
inside. ⁶But God, who comforts the downcast, brought us comfort when Titus
arrived *from Corinth*. ⁷We were relieved,
not just to see him, but because he told us
how he was encouraged to learn about
your longing, your grieving, and your continued enthusiasm for me. So these were
all more reasons for me to rejoice!

Jesus said you are blessed when
you mourn (Matthew 5:4). The
very thought sounds ridiculous to
some, but from Paul's perspective, God
uses our weakness and is present in
our pain. This truth is revolutionary.
In the midst of mourning, we lose our
pretense and self-consciousness.
There we meet God and one another
in honest ways that open the doors to
redemption when we are willing.

⁸*To be honest, I've been conflicted.* I knew
you would be upset with my last letter, but
I do not regret sending it. If there were
times I did have second thoughts, it was
because I could see that the letter did hurt
you, even if only for a while. ⁹Now I am
glad—not because it caused you grief but
because you were moved to make a permanent change* that can happen only with
the realization that your actions have gone
against God—I'm glad to know you suffered no long-term loss because of what
we did. ¹⁰Now *this type of deep sorrow*,
godly sorrow, is not so much about regret,
but it is about producing a change of mind

* 6:16 Leviticus 26:12; Ezekiel 37:27
* 6:17 Isaiah 52:11
* 6:17 Ezekiel 20:34,41
* 6:18 2 Samuel 7:14
* 7:9 Literally, repentance

and behavior* that ultimately leads to salvation. But *the other type of sorrow,* worldly sorrow, *often is fleeting and* only brings death. [11]*Look at what is happening among you!* Notice how authentic and diligent you have become because this godly sorrow has been at work *in your community. But there's more:* your desire to clear your name, your *righteous* anger, your respect, your longing, your zeal, your *concern for* justice. All these demonstrate how you have been made clean. *There's no part of you untouched by God's work.* [12]So when I wrote my *last difficult* letter, it was not to comfort the victim or confront the perpetrator—it was to stir up your sincere devotion for us under God's watchful eye. [13]In the midst of all that has happened, *though it has been difficult,* we are comforted *and encouraged.* When we saw the *relief and* joy on Titus's face, we celebrated even more because his spirit had been totally refreshed by you. [14]Now if I have bragged *in the past* about you to Titus, I have nothing to be ashamed of. Just as we've spoken the whole truth to you, I'm glad to know that our *modest* boasts to Titus *about you* have proven true as well. [15]His love for you overflows even more as he recalls your obedience and how you *respectfully and somewhat nervously,* with fear and trembling, took him in. [16]I have great joy *now* because I have great confidence in you.

8 Now, brothers and sisters, let me tell you about the *amazing* gift of God's grace that's happening throughout the churches in Macedonia. [2]Even in the face of severe anguish *and hard times,* their elation and poverty have overflowed into a wealth of generosity. [3]I watched as they willingly gave what they could afford and then went beyond to give even more. [4]They came to us *on their own,* begging to take part in this work *of grace* to support the *poor* saints *in Judea.* [5]*We were so overwhelmed*—none of us expected their reaction—that they truly turned their lives over to the Lord and then gave themselves to support us in our work as we answer the call of God. [6]That's why we asked Titus to finish what he started among you regarding this gracious work of charity. [7]Just as you are rich in everything—in faith and speech, in knowledge and all sincerity, and in the love we have shown among you*—now I ask you to invest richly in this gracious work too. [8]I am not going to command you, but I am going to offer you the chance to prove your love genuine in the same way others have done. [9]You know the grace *that has come to us* through our Lord Jesus, the Liberating King. He set aside His infinite riches and was born into the lowest circumstance so that you may gain great riches through His humble poverty. [10-11]Listen, it's been a year *since we called your attention to this opportunity to demonstrate God's grace,* so here's my advice: pull together your resources and finish what you started.

God chose a people for Himself—a people that make up a body, bound together in a covenant. The forces of this world seek to divide and isolate, but God seeks to unite and reconcile. We must all learn to serve one another and hold our self-interest in abeyance to find a greater good in community.

The believers in Corinth were struggling to find unity and harmony in their local church. Some were living selfishly by eating all the food at the feast of communion or finding an issue that created division among their brothers and sisters. For Paul it was not enough that they learn to live well with one another, although that was important. They must know that they were part of a larger body—they belonged to the churches in Jerusalem, Ephesus, Philippi, and the new frontier of Christianity. We are also part of a global church. What would happen if the church began to live this simple truth and generously share all that we have with all of our brothers and sisters across the globe?

* 7:10 Literally, repentance
* 8:7 Other manuscripts read "you have shown us."

Remember how excited you were at first; it's time to complete this task in the same spirit. [12]Now if there is a willingness to help, give within your means. That's perfectly acceptable. No one expects you to go without or borrow to give. [13-14]The objective is not to go under so others will have some relief; the objective is to use this opportunity today to supply their needs out of your abundance. *One day it may be the other way around,* and they will need to supply your needs from what they have. That's equality. [15]As it is written, "The one who gathered plenty didn't have more than he needed; the one who gathered little didn't have less."*

[16]I praise God who lovingly burdened Titus's heart for you just as He did mine. [17]You see, when we approached him about you, he eagerly stepped up, not only because of our request, but because of his own desire to help. [18]We're also sending with him a brother who is well known among the gatherings of believers because of how well he proclaims the good news. [19]And there's more *you should know*: he has been handpicked by the churches to accompany us as we carry on this work of grace. *All this is being done* for the glory of the Lord and to show our own good will. [20]We're being careful so that no one can claim that we are mishandling the funds we've collected. [21]For we are taking every precaution to remain aboveboard—not only in the Lord's eyes, but in the eyes of the people too. [22]So we are also sending another brother who's proven himself time and again. He's certainly *trustworthy and enthusiastic for the gospel, and after hearing about all you are doing,* he's even more excited because he has confidence in you. [23]If anyone asks about Titus, he's my partner and coworker in this ministry to you. If there's any question about who the other brothers and sisters are, they are emissaries* of the churches, traveling to bring glory to the Liberating King. [24]So welcome them before the community in love; show the churches *they represent* that I have not exaggerated about your charity and kindness.

9 There's nothing further I could add about your efforts for God's people *in Judea.* [2]I know you are ready. I bragged on you throughout Macedonia, telling them how the people in Achaia have been prepared since last year, and your passion has been contagious. [3]Still I thought it would be best to send these brothers and sisters ahead to help you finish the final details so all my bragging wouldn't be for nothing. [4]If some of the Macedonians decide to travel with me, all of us would be more than embarrassed if we arrived and you weren't ready to give after the way we've been going on about you. [5]So to help you get your previously promised gift ready, it made sense to me to ask the brothers and sisters to go on ahead so you will have *all the time you need to* put it together as planned and so it doesn't look *thrown together or* coerced.

[6]But I will say this *to encourage your generosity*: the one who plants little harvests little, and the one who plants plenty harvests plenty. [7]Giving grows out of the heart—otherwise, you've reluctantly grumbled "yes" because you felt you had to or because you couldn't say "no," *but this isn't the way God wants it.* For *we know that* "God loves a cheerful giver."* [8]God is ready to overwhelm you with more blessings than you could ever imagine so that you'll always be taken care of in every way and you'll have more than enough to share. [9]Remember what is written *about the one who trusts in the Lord*:

> He scattered abroad; He gave *freely*
>   to the poor;
>   His righteousness endures
>   throughout the ages.*

[10]The same One who has put seed into the hands of the sower and brought bread to fill our stomachs will provide and multiply the resources you invest and produce an abundant harvest from your righteous

* 8:15 Exodus 16:18
* 8:23 Literally, apostles
* 9:7 Proverbs 22:8 (Septuagint)
* 9:9 Psalm 112:9

actions. ¹¹You will be made rich in everything so that your generosity *will spill over in every direction. Through us* your generosity is at work inspiring praise and thanksgiving to God. ¹²For this mission will do more than bring food and water to fellow believers in need—it will overflow in a cascade of *praises and* thanksgivings for our God. ¹³When this mission *reaches Jerusalem and* meets with the approval *of God's people there*, they will give glory to God because your confession of the gospel of the Liberating King led to obedient action and your generous sharing with them and with all exhibited your sincere concern. ¹⁴Because of the extraordinary grace of God at work in you, they will pray for you and long for you. ¹⁵Praise God for this *incredible, unbelievable,* indescribable gift!

10 I, Paul, appeal to you in the same gentle and loving spirit of the Liberator—*yes,* I who am humble when I'm face-to-face with you but audacious to you *in these letters* when I'm away *(I know what they say).* ²If it were up to me, I'd rather not have to be so bold when I'm with you, especially with the kind of forceful confidence I can work up when I confront those who have accused us of walking in a worldly way. ³For though we walk in the world, we do not fight according to this world's rules of warfare. ⁴The weapons of the war we're fighting are not of this world but are powered by God and effective at tearing down the strongholds *erected against His truth.* ⁵We are demolishing arguments and ideas, every high-and-mighty philosophy that pits itself against the knowledge of *the one true* God. We are taking prisoners of every thought, *every emotion,* and subduing them into obedience to our Liberator. ⁶As soon as you choose obedience, we stand ready to punish every act of disobedience.

⁷Look at what is going on right in front of you. If anyone is convinced that he belongs to the Liberating King, then he should think again; even if he belongs to Him, so do we. ⁸I'm not embarrassed, even

if it seems to others I have gone overboard in speaking about the power the Lord has given us to edify and encourage you and not to destroy anyone who strays. ⁹I don't want it to seem as if I'm simply trying to scare you with my letters; *they are not hollow.* ¹⁰For some people are saying, "Paul's letters sound authoritative and strong, but in person he just doesn't measure up—even his speeches don't deliver." ¹¹They need to understand this: whatever we say through our letters when we are away, that is exactly what we will do when we are looking you in the eye.

¹²For we would never dare to compare ourselves with people who have based their worth on self-commendation. They check themselves against and compare themselves with one another. *It just shows that* they don't have any sense! ¹³So we will carefully limit our boasting to the extent only of what God has done in and through us, a reach that extends as far as you. ¹⁴For it wasn't as if we were overreaching *into someone else's territory* by reaching out to you; *I mean, weren't we there in the beginning?* Weren't we the first ones to bring you the good news of the Liberating King? ¹⁵We carefully put limits on our boasting and avoid taking credit for what others do. But we do hope to see your faith grow so that we can watch our mission really expand all the way to the limits *God has set for us.* ¹⁶*The plan includes* taking the good news to people and lands beyond you. We've no interest in or intention of staking claim to other people's accomplishments in their arenas. *As the Scripture says,* ¹⁷"The one who boasts must boast in the Lord."* ¹⁸Now *let's be clear,* it's not the one who commends himself who is approved; it's the one the Lord commends.

11 Please endure a little foolishness on my part; you have come so far with me already. ²*To be completely honest,* I am extremely jealous for you, but it's the same kind of jealousy God has for you. You see, *like an attentive father,* I have pledged

* 10:17 Jeremiah 9:24

your hand in marriage and promised to present you as a pure virgin to *the man who would be your husband,* the Liberating King. [3]But now I'm afraid that as that serpent tricked Eve with his wiles, so your *hearts and* minds will be tricked and you will stray from the single-minded love and pure devotion to Him. [4]So then, if someone comes along and presents you with a Jesus different from the one we told you about, or if you receive a spirit different from the one gifted *through our Lord Jesus,* or even if you hear a gospel different from the one you heard *through us,* you're ready to go with it.

[5]I consider myself in league with the *so-called* great emissaries; I lack nothing. [6]Even if I'm not the greatest speaker, I make up for it by what I know *of God* and have proved it time and again to you. [7]Was it a sin to humble myself *and serve* you so that you might be lifted up? *Did I wrong you somehow* by instructing you in the good news of God without charge? [8]*In a sense,* I robbed other churches by accepting their support just so I could serve you. [9]If any need arose while I was with you, I didn't trouble anyone. When the brothers and sisters arrived from Macedonia, they covered all my needs so that I didn't become a burden to any of you, and I plan on keeping it that way. [10]*For I tell you,* as the truth of the Liberating King lives in me, I will continue to boast about this all throughout Achaia. [11]Why am I doing this? It's not because I don't love you—God knows I do— [12-13]but I will continue doing what I am doing to cut off any opportunity—*clearly* some are looking for one—for these false emissaries, these *low-down,* untrustworthy preachers, these posers who act as emissaries of the Liberator to claim that they work under the same terms that we do. [14]No wonder *they are so good at it.* Satan* himself poses as a messenger of heavenly light, [15]so why should we expect less from his servants— *plodding over the earth,* pretending to be ministers of righteousness—but in the end, they'll get what's coming to them.

[16]So as I said before, please don't mark me a fool, but if you must, then please accept me even as that and give me a little more room to boast. [17]What I am saying now is not in character with our Lord but is the bragging of a self-assured fool. [18]Just as other fools brag according to their worldly accomplishments, so I, too, will have to boast— [19]meanwhile, you—so wise, so tolerant—gladly bear this *kind of* foolishness. [20]How easily you tolerate becoming another's slave, having them consume you, letting them rob you *blind,* or allowing them to edge their way past you or slap you in the face. [21]Embarrassingly I admit that next to them we must look very weak!

But in whatever way they dare to boast—*remember,* I'm speaking *in character* as a fool—I dare to boast *even more!* [22]Are they Hebrews, *God's chosen*? So am I. Are they true Israelites? So am I. Are they descendants of Abraham? So am I. [23]Are they servants to the Liberating King? I am even more so! (I can't believe how foolish I sound.) I have worked harder *for God's kingdom,* taken more beatings, been dragged in and out of prisons, and have been eye-to-eye with death. [24]Five times I have withstood thirty-nine lashes from Jewish authorities, [25]three times I was battered with rods, once I was almost stoned to death, three times I was shipwrecked, and I spent one day and night adrift on the sea. [26]I have been on many journeys *and faced the most extreme circumstances*: perilous rivers, violent thieves, and threats by my own people and by the Gentile outsiders alike. I have faced dangers in the city, in the wilderness, and at sea; and danger from spies among our brothers and sisters. [27]I have survived toil and hardships, sleepless nights, hunger and thirst without a crumb in sight, bare to the cold. [28]As if these external trials weren't enough, there is the daily stress I feel and anxiety I carry for all the churches *under my care.* [29]Who is weak without my empathy? Who is hurt and offended without my burning anger?

[30]*So as you can see,* if I have to boast, I will, but only in my own weaknesses. [31]The God and Father of our Lord Jesus, He who is worthy of eternal blessing, can confirm that I am telling you the truth. [32]Once, in Damascus, the governor under King Aretas

---

* 11:14 Literally, "the Satan"

had his people in the city looking for me in order to arrest me. ³³But I crouched in a basket and was lowered out of a window in the city wall, and I narrowly escaped his tight grip.

---

*S*incerity is a difficult thing to judge. The commitment that people have to a cause can only be determined over time. One test might be: do they persevere through hardships and challenges? In this regard, Paul is without equal. If the cause of the Liberating King were a fleeting interest or a halfhearted pursuit, then he would have given up after his first beating. But Paul's compassion for those who did not know the beauty of the gospel of the Liberating King was stubborn and unyielding. This former persecutor turned emissary always had his critics. But who could call him insincere?

12 Boasting like this is necessary, but it's *unbecoming and probably unavailing. Since you won't hear me any other way,* let me tell you about visions and revelations I received of the Lord.

²Fourteen years ago, there was this man I knew—a believer in the Liberator who was caught up to the third heaven. (Whether this was an in- or out-of-body experience I don't know; only God knows.) ³⁻⁴This man was caught up into paradise (*let me say it again,* whether this was an in- or out-of-body experience I don't know; only God knows), and he heard inexpressible words—words a mortal man is forbidden to utter. ⁵I could brag about such a man, but as for me, I have nothing to brag about outside my own shortcomings. ⁶So if I want to boast, I won't do so as a fool because I will be speaking the truth. But I will stop there, since I don't want to be credited with anything except exactly what people see and hear from me. ⁷To *keep me grounded and* stop me from becoming too high and mighty due to the extraordinary character of these revelations, I was given a thorn in the flesh—a nagging nuisance of Satan,* a messenger to plague me! ⁸I

begged the Lord three times to liberate me *from its anguish,* ⁹and *finally* He said to me, "My grace is enough to cover and sustain you. My power is made perfect in weakness." *So ask me about my thorn,* inquire about my weaknesses, and I will gladly go on and on—*I would rather stake my claim in these* and have the power of the Liberator at home within me. ¹⁰I am at peace *and even take pleasure* in any weaknesses, insults, hardships, persecutions, and afflictions for the sake of our Liberating King because when I am at my weakest, He makes me strong.

---

*P*aul is speaking of himself here in an odd, third-person way. He writes cryptically for a purpose: to direct us away from the fact that, at least for the moment, he is boasting of something other than weakness. In heavenly journeys, Paul has seen amazing sights and heard amazing sounds— sights and sounds no human can or should ever speak of.

But God adds something to keep Paul from being carried away by such ecstasies: He gives His emissary "a thorn in the flesh." We don't know what Paul means by this. Perhaps it is a chronic physical or emotional illness he suffers. Perhaps it is the steady stream of opponents who follow Paul wherever he goes. In God's wisdom, Paul doesn't say because we'd likely fixate on whatever problem he has in unhealthy ways. That's what we humans do. Still Paul believes that God sent this unwelcome messenger, so he pleads with God three times to remove it. Why just three times? Why doesn't he bombard heaven daily with his pleas? Well, it's likely because he knows that Jesus prayed three times in the garden for the cup of suffering to be removed. Ultimately Jesus surrendered to the will of the Father, and Paul does too: "Grace is enough, Paul. Grace is enough."

---

* 12:7 Literally, "the Satan"

11I have become a fool, but you drove me to it. Why didn't you stick up for me? I may not be much, but you could have shown me the same respect as you did the other *so-called* great emissaries.* I am not inferior to them in the least. 12Miracles, wonders, and signs were all performed right before your eyes, proving I am who I say, a true emissary *of the Liberating King.* 13With the exception of not asking you to shoulder the burden of my care, I have treated you no different from any other churches. Forgive me for wronging you *by not charging for my services!*

14Now listen, for the third time, I am ready to travel to you, and *once again* I will not burden you because there's nothing of yours that I want: the only thing I want is you. You see, it's not right for children to have to save up for their parents because it's the parents' job to care for their children. 15I would happily spend until I had nothing left if it was for you. But just because I love you more, should you love me less? 16Because even though you didn't have to lift a finger for me, *lies abound that* I deceived you by some clever act. 17Did I cheat you somehow through one of the coworkers I sent your way? *If any of them defrauded you, I'd like to see it.* 18I was the one who insisted Titus come to you with the brother I sent along. Did Titus take advantage of you in some way? *Wouldn't you agree that we are alike in our ways?* Didn't we work in the same spirit and follow the same direction?

19I hope you don't think that all this time we've been defending ourselves to you. We come as the voice of the Liberator; God will judge whether all our work has been useful in building you up, beloved. 20*And quite honestly*, I am afraid that when I come, we may both be disappointed with what we find; in my fear, *my thoughts go from bad to worse—into a drama* of friction, rivalry, fevered tempers and fists, selfishness, slander, defamation, pride, and complete chaos. 21I am worried that when I come to visit that my God will humble me *somehow* before you, that I

will have to grieve over all those who have sinned before and then refused to turn away* from their addictions to impure practices, immoral sex, and reckless perversions.

13 This is my third trip to your city and community. *As the Scripture says,* "Every charge must be confirmed by two or three witnesses."* 2As I said before on my second visit, I say now again while absent. Consider this an advance warning, *if you wish,* to those of you still caught up in your old sins and to all the rest as well: when I come the next time, I will not spare anyone *who is out of order.* 3You asked to see evidence that *the power of* the Liberating King is at work in me. *Well, you will see it* because He won't be weak in dealing with you. Instead, He will do great things in you. 4Now it's true that He was crucified in weakness, but *it's also true that* He lives by God's power. For we *who belong to Him* are weak in Him, but we will live with Him by God's power for you.

5Examine yourselves. Check your faith! Are you really in the faith? Do you still not know that Jesus, the Liberating King, is in you?—unless, of course, you have failed the test. 6Surely you will realize we have not failed the test, 7but we pray to God that you will stay away from evil. *What's important is* not whether we appear to have passed the test, but that you do what is right *and act honorably,* even if it appears that we have failed. 8For there's nothing we can do to oppose the truth; all we can do is align ourselves with it. 9You see, we celebrate when we are weak but you are strong. Our prayer is *simple*: that you may be *whole and* complete. 10*How I hope I* am saving you by writing this to you in advance; this letter will spare me from using the Lord's authority to come down

---

* 12:11 Literally, apostles
* 12:21 Literally, repent
* 13:1 Deuteronomy 19:15

on you when I arrive. His intention in giving me this authority is to build you up, not tear you down.

¹¹Finally, brothers and sisters, keep rejoicing and repair whatever is broken. Encourage each other, think as one, and live at peace; and God, *the Author* of love and peace, will remain with you. ¹²Greet each other with a holy kiss, *as brothers and sisters*. ¹³All the saints *here with me* send you their greeting.

¹⁴May the grace of the Lord Jesus—the Liberating King, the love of God, and the fellowship of the Holy Spirit remain with you all. [Amen.]*

* 13:14 The earliest manuscripts omit this word.

Galatians

Instruction to those who live in Galatia
From Paul, the apostle to the Gentiles

In the decades following Jesus' death and resurrection, the churches were locked in an extremely difficult dispute that had far-reaching consequences. The earliest followers of Jesus were mostly Jews who recognized Him as the Liberator for Israel. Some of them taught that all believers—both Jews and non-Jews—had to observe Jewish law in order to enter into the benefits and community created through God's actions in the Liberator. These people were called "Judaizers" because they insisted that non-Jews live like Jews. Paul writes Galatians to counter this threat to Christian liberty. The tone of this letter is harsh because Paul believed the very truth of the gospel and his ministry were in jeopardy. Since circumcision was the act that initiated non-Jews into Jewish faith, it became a symbol for the whole controversy. In this brief book, Paul lays the groundwork for what became the orthodox understanding of salvation; namely, that Jews and non-Jews alike enter into a positive relationship with God by grace through faith, not through observing the law.

Paul begins the letter by insisting that his call as an emissary came directly from the Liberating King, not any human institution. Apparently some were criticizing him, not only for his deficient gospel, but also for his lacking credentials. So Paul responds by recounting his own story of how he persecuted the church until he experienced a revelation of Jesus, our Savior. He sees his call largely in prophetic terms and begins his ministry without any kind of human blessing or instruction. When Paul does present his understanding of the good news years later to the Jerusalem leaders, they affirm his message and confirm his call as the emissary to the Gentiles. But this does not put an end to the controversy. As this letter shows, it was played out again and again in the churches.

Paul argues his case from both the experience of the Galatians and the Hebrew Scriptures. The Galatians had received the Spirit, not because they kept the law, but because they received the gospel in faith. Likewise in Scripture he discovered that faith had always been the way Abraham and his spiritual children related to God and entered into His promises. Therefore those who put faith in Jesus as Lord and Savior become the true sons and daughters of Abraham.

1 Paul, an emissary* commissioned directly by Jesus, the Liberating King, and God the Father (who raised Him from the dead)—not *(as some claim)* an agent of men or any person— [2]and all the brothers and sisters with me to you, the churches of Galatia.

[3]May the grace and peace of God the Father and the Lord Jesus, our Liberator, live in you; [4]*He is the very Savior* who rescues us from this present, *perverse* age dominated by evil by giving His life according to our Father's will to deal with our sins. [5]May God's glorious name forever receive honor. Amen.

> *F*rom the opening address, it is clear that Paul is angry with what is going on among the churches in Galatia. He feels compelled to defend himself from opponents who are attacking his call as the Liberator's emissary. Paul counters the attack by distancing himself from any human institution: he was not called by any church or committee. God the Father and the Lord Jesus commissioned Paul directly to be the emissary to the nations.

[6]*Frankly* I am stunned. I cannot believe that you have abandoned God so quickly—even after He called you through the grace of the Liberating King—and have fallen for a different gospel. [7]Actually there is only one true gospel, and you—because of divisive prodding by others—are accepting a distorted version of the Liberator's promise, which is not the gospel at all! *People are deceiving you with some cut-up imitation of the true gospel, and you have bought into it. Their words are nothing but twisted lies.* [8]No matter the source of the false gospel, even if it is preached by us or a heavenly messenger, *ignore it.* May those *who add to or subtract from the gospel of Jesus* be *eternally* cursed! [9]Listen again *because I am going to make it crystal clear*: if anyone preaches to you a gospel other than what you have accepted, may he find

himself cursed! *Take this message for what it is: a truthful warning.*

[10]*I am not writing to win you over.* Do you think I care about the approval of men or about the approval of God? Do you think I am on a mission to please people? If I am still *spinning my wheels* trying to please men, then there is no way I can be a servant of the Liberating King.

[11]Know this, dear brothers and sisters: the good news I brought to you isn't *the latest in fiction or* the product of some creative mind. [12]It is not a legend I learned or one that has been passed down from person to person, *ear to ear.* I was gifted with this message as Jesus, the Liberator, revealed Himself *miraculously to me.* [13]Surely you are familiar with my personal history, with my dedication to the teachings and traditions of Judaism. I persecuted *those who belonged to this emerging movement that I now recognize as* the church of God—in fact, I meant to destroy it. *In my blindness, I believed it was a dangerous sect.* [14]I excelled in the teachings of Judaism far above other Jewish leaders *(in fact, I was advanced for my age)*, and I was zealous to practice the ways of our ancestors. [15]But God—who set me apart even before birth and who called me by His grace—chose, to His great delight, [16]to reveal His Son in me so I could tell His story among the outsider nations. I didn't confer with anyone right away, [17]nor did I go to those who were already emissaries* of the Liberating King in Jerusalem. I went straight to Arabia and later returned to Damascus.

[18]After *living this adventurous mission for* three years, I made my way to Jerusalem and spent 15 days with Cephas, *whom you know as Peter.* [19]But I didn't see any emissary* other than James, our Lord's brother. [20](You can be certain that what I am offering you *is an authentic account.* Before God, it's the whole truth—I wouldn't lie.) [21]Later I journeyed to Syria

* 1:1 Literally, apostle
* 1:17 Literally, apostles
* 1:19 Literally, apostle

and Cilicia, ²²and *since I had spent so little time in* Judea among the churches of our Liberator, no one there could pick me out of a crowd. ²³But stories of my call and mission preceded me: "The very man who wanted to kill us all is now preaching the faith he once labored to destroy." ²⁴And so they praised God for the miracle He did in my life.

---

*O*ne of the great stories in the Bible is the transformation of Saul, the Pharisee, from a persecutor of the church to the greatest missionary history has ever witnessed. Seldom does Paul relate that story in his letters. He doesn't need to because he usually does that in person when he is planting a church. But on this occasion, as he defends his call and gospel, he retells a bit of his personal history to underscore the complete metamorphosis that has taken place in his life. In his former life, Paul admits—quite painfully, no doubt—that he had tried to destroy this movement. Borrowing language from the prophets, Paul narrates how God unveiled to him the truth about Jesus, the Liberating King. At just the right moment, even while Paul was an active enemy, God revealed His Son to Paul and called him to be heaven's emissary to the nations. Paul immediately stopped his campaign against the church, which was just beginning to emerge from its Jewish roots and spread to the Gentile nations.

---

2 ¹⁻²As a result of a revelation, I returned to Jerusalem 14 years later, and *this time* Barnabas and Titus accompanied me. *When I arrived,* I shared the *exact* gospel that I preach to the outsiders. I first shared God's truth privately with those who were people of influence and leadership because I thought *if they did not embrace the freedom of my good news, then* any work *I had done for the Liberator here* and any in the past would be spoiled.

³*Listen carefully.* None of the Jerusalem leaders insisted that Titus be circumcised, although *it was plain that* he is Greek. ⁴Some people who were pretending to be our brothers and sisters were brought in to spy on the freedom we enjoy in Jesus, the Liberating King—*their agenda was clear:* they wanted to enslave us. ⁵But we didn't give in to them. We didn't entertain their thoughts for a minute! We resisted them so the true gospel—*and not some counterfeit*—would continue to be available to you.

⁶It makes no difference to me (or to God for that matter) if people have power or influence. God doesn't choose favorites *among His children.* Even the so-called pillars *of the church* didn't contribute anything new to my understanding *of the good news.* ⁷But it quickly became obvious to them *what God was doing*: He had entrusted me to carry the good news to the uncircumcised, just as Peter was called to preach to those who were circumcised. ⁸God was at work in the ministry of Peter, as emissary* to the Jews, and was also *moving and* working with me in my ministry to the outsider nations.

⁹When James, Cephas *(whom you know as Peter)*, and John—three men purported to be pillars *among the Jewish believers*—saw that God's favor was upon me *to fulfill this calling,* they welcomed and endorsed* both Barnabas and me. *They agreed that our ministries would work as two hands,* theirs *advancing the mission of God* among the Jews and ours toward the outsider nations, *all with the same message of redemption.* ¹⁰*In parting,* they requested we always remember to care for the poor *among us,* which was something I was eager to do *and knew in my heart was exactly what the Liberator would want.*

¹¹But when Cephas came to Antioch, *there was a problem.* I got in his face and exposed him *in front of everyone.* He was clearly wrong. ¹²*Here's what was going on:* before certain people from James arrived, Cephas used to share meals with the

---

* 2:8 Literally, apostle
* 2:9 Literally, gave the right hand of fellowship

Gentile outsiders. And then, after they showed up, Cephas suddenly became aloof and distanced himself from the outsiders because he was afraid of those believers who thought circumcision was necessary *for all Gentile believers before they could interact with Jewish believers.* [13]*I couldn't believe what happened next.* The rest of the Jewish believers followed his lead, including Barnabas! Their hypocritical behavior was so obvious— [14]their actions were not at all consistent with everything the good news *of our Lord* represents. So I approached Cephas and told him in plain sight of everyone: "If you, a Jew, have lived like the Gentile outsiders and not like the Jews, then how can you turn around and urge the outsiders to start living like Jews?" [15]We are natural-born Jews, not "sinners" from the godless nations. [16]But we know that no one is made right *with God* by meeting the demands of the law. It is only through the faithfulness of Jesus,* the Liberator, *that salvation is even possible.* This is why we put faith in Jesus as our Savior: so we will be put right with God. It's His faithfulness, not works prescribed by the law, that puts us in right standing with God because no one will be acquitted and declared "right" for doing what the law demands. [17]Even though we are seeking a right relationship *with God* through the Liberating King, *the fact is* we have been found out. We are "sinners." But does that mean our Liberator is the one responsible? Absolutely not! [18]If I reconstruct something I have worked so hard to destroy, then I prove myself a sinner.

So why all this personal history? Paul thinks it is useful. You see, the people preaching the false gospel in Galatia claim to be operating under the authority of some of the followers of Jesus from Jerusalem, the mother church. Paul doesn't have their pedigree and, according to them, doesn't deserve the rank he claims as the emissary to the nations. They say that not only is Paul deficient, but his

gospel is, too, because it doesn't bring outsiders to follow the law. So Paul goes toe-to-toe with them, defending not only his call but also his gospel. The good news he preaches comes directly from the risen Jesus.

[19]The law has provided the means to end my dependence on it *for righteousness. Now I have found the freedom* to truly live for God. [20]I have been crucified with the Liberating King—I am no longer alive—but the Liberator is living in me, and whatever life I have left in this failing body I live by the faithfulness of God's Son, the One who loves me and gave His body *on the cross* for me. [21]*I say all that to make this point:* I can't dismiss God's grace, *and I won't.* If being right *with God* depends on how we measure up to the law, then the Liberating King's sacrifice *on the cross* was the most tragic waste in all of history!

3 Galatians, don't act like fools! Has someone cast a spell over you? Did you miss the crucifixion of Jesus, the Liberator, that was reenacted right in front of your eyes? [2]Tell me this, did the Holy Spirit come upon you because you lived according to the law? Or was it because you heard *His message of grace* through faith? [3]Are you so foolish? Do you think you can perfect something God's Spirit started with any human effort? [4]Have you suffered so greatly for nothing—if it was indeed for nothing? [5]You have experienced the Spirit He gave you *in powerful ways.* Miracle after miracle has occurred *right before your eyes* in this community, so tell me: did all this happen because you have kept certain provisions of God's law, or was it because you heard *the gospel* and accepted it by faith?

Paul stays on offense, accusing the Galatian believers of abandoning the true gospel for a counterfeit

* 2:16 Some translations say "faith in Jesus."

version that is not good news at all. He's amazed at how quickly the situation has deteriorated. The tone of the letter is now set. Paul is angry. The gospel he has worked so hard to proclaim is in jeopardy, and he won't let it go without a fight. Some things, you see, are worth fighting for.

⁶*You remember Abraham.* Scripture tells us, "Abraham believed God *and trusted in His promises,* so God counted it to his favor as righteousness."* ⁷Know this: people who trust in God are the true sons and daughters of Abraham. ⁸For it was foretold to us in the Scriptures that God would set the Gentile nations right by faith when He told Abraham, "I will bless all nations through you."* ⁹So *this is not breaking news; God made it plain to us from the beginning that* those who have faith *in Him* are blessed along with Abraham, our faithful ancestor.

¹⁰*Listen,* whoever seeks *to be righteous* by following *certain* works of the law actually falls under the law's curse. I'm giving it to you straight from Scripture *because it is as true now as when it was written:* "Cursed is everyone who doesn't live by and do all that is written in the law."* ¹¹Now it is absolutely clear that no one is made right with God through the law because *the prophet Habakkuk told us,* "By faith the just will obtain life."* ¹²The law is not *the same thing as life* formed by faith. In fact, *you are warned against this when God says,* "The one who observes My laws will live by them."* *I am trying to tell you that* ¹³the Liberating King has redeemed us from the curse of the law by becoming a curse for us. It was stated *in the Scriptures,* "Everyone who hangs on a tree is cursed by God."* ¹⁴*This is what God had in mind all along:* the blessing He gave to Abraham might extend to all nations through Jesus, the Liberator, and we are the beneficiaries of this promise of the Spirit that comes *only* through faith.

¹⁵My dear brothers and sisters, here's a real-life example I can give you: *A father sits down to decide how to distribute his properties in his last will and testament.*

When all the property is accounted for, the document is signed, witnessed, and notarized, and afterward, no one can make changes to it. ¹⁶*In a similar way, God's* promises established *a binding agreement* with Abraham and his offspring. *In the Scriptures,* it is carefully stated, "And to your descendant" (meaning one), not "And to your descendants"* (meaning many). Therefore, *in these covenant promises, God was* not *referring* to every son and daughter *born into Abraham's family* but to the One *to come—Jesus,* the Liberating King. ¹⁷What this all means is that the law, recorded some 430 years after the promise, does not invalidate the promise He made to Abraham. *God's promise is still in effect.* ¹⁸You see, if the law became the sole basis for the inheritance, then it would put God in the position of breaking a covenant. Because He had promised it to Abraham, *He had every intention of following through with it.*

*T*hroughout this argument, there is one critical question that remains: why would God give us the law if it would not bring us into a right standing with Him? Couldn't God have found a better way of doing this? The truth is that people are naturally selfish and ignore God unless life becomes too difficult to bear; we needed the law for us to recognize what was to come. The law kept sin in check until the time was right for the saving justice that comes through faith in Jesus. The law served as a tutor or a schoolmaster, revealing our great need for salvation and pointing us toward the promised Liberator, Jesus.

* 3:6 Genesis 15:6
* 3:8 Genesis 12:3; 18:18; 22:18; 26:4; 28:14
* 3:10 Deuteronomy 27:26
* 3:11 Habakkuk 2:4
* 3:12 Leviticus 18:5
* 3:13 Deuteronomy 21:23
* 3:16 Genesis 12:7; 13:15; 24:7

[19]*Now you're asking yourselves, "So why did God give us the law?"* God commanded His heavenly messengers to deliver it into the hand of a mediator for this reason: to help us rein in our sins until the Offspring, about whom the promise was made *in the first place,* would come. [20]A mediator represents more than one, but God is *only* one. [21]*"So,"* you ask, *"does the law contradict God's promise?"* Absolutely not! Never was there written a law that could lead to *resurrection and* life; if there had been, then surely we could have experienced saving righteousness through keeping the law. *But we haven't.* [22]Scripture has subjected the whole world to sin's power so that the faithful obedience of Jesus, the Liberator, might extend God's promises to everyone who has faith. [23]Before faith came on the scene, the law did its best to keep us in line, restraining us until the faith that was to come was fully revealed. [24]So then, the law was like a tutor, assigned to *train us and* point us to the Liberating King, so that we will be acquitted *of all wrong* and made right by faith. [25]But now that *true* faith has come, we have no need for a tutor. *We now stand unbound.* [26]It is your faith in the Liberator Jesus that makes all of you children of God [27]because all of you who have been initiated into the Liberating King through ceremonial washing* have put Him on. [28]It makes no difference whether you are a Jew or a Greek, a slave or a freeman, a man or a woman, because in Jesus, the Liberator, you are all one. [29]Since you belong to Him *and are now subject to His power,* then you are the descendant of Abraham and the heir *of God's glory* according to the promise.

4 Listen. I am going to explain *how this all works:* When a minor inherits an estate *from his parents,* although he is the owner of everything, he is the same as a slave. [2]Until the day set by his father, the minor is subject to the authorities or guardians *whom his father put in charge.* [3]It is like that with us; there was a time when we were like children held under the elemental powers of this world. [4]When the right time arrived, God sent His Son into this world (born of a woman, subject to the law) [5]to free those who, *just like Him,* were subject to the law. Ultimately He wanted us all to be adopted as sons and daughters. [6]Because you are now part of God's family, He sent the Spirit of His Son into our hearts, *and the Spirit* calls out, "Abba, Father." [7]You no longer have to live as a slave because you are a child *of God.* And since you are His child, God guarantees an inheritance *is waiting* for you.

[8]During the time before you knew God, you were slaves to powers that are not gods at all. [9]But now, when you are just beginning to know *the one true* God—actually, *He was showing how completely* He knows you—how can you turn back to weak and worthless *idols made by men—icons of these* spiritual powers? Haven't you endured enough bondage to these powerless idols? [10]You are observing particular days, months, *festival* seasons, and years; [11]you have me worried that I may have wasted my time laboring among you.

[12]Brothers and sisters, I have become one of you. Now *it's your turn*—become as I am. You have never wronged me. [13]Do you remember the first time I preached the good news to you? I was sick, and [14]I know my illness was a hardship to you, but you never drew back from me or scorned me. You cared for me as if I were a heavenly messenger of God, possibly as well as if I were Jesus, the Liberator, Himself! *Don't you remember?* [15]What has happened to your *joy and* blessing? I tell you, *the place was so thick with love that* if it were possible, you would have plucked out your eyes and handed them to me. [16]And now, do I stand as your enemy because I tried to bless you with the truth? [17]*I'll tell you what these false brothers and sisters are counting on:* your flattery. They are ravenous for it. They are not acting *honorably or* in your best interests. They want to keep you away *from the good news we proclaim* so they can have you all to themselves. [18]Listen, there's

---

* 3:27 Literally, immersion, in a rite of initiation and purification

nothing wrong with zeal when you're zealous for *God's* good purpose. And what's more, you don't have to wait for me to be with you to seek the good. [19]My dear children, I feel the pains of birth upon me again, and I will continue in labor for you until the Liberating King is formed completely in you. [20]I wish I were there. *Maybe it's not as bad as I think—I cannot help but think* this letter is really harsh, yet I am really perplexed by you.

[21]*Now it's your turn to* instruct me. All of you who want to live by the rules of the law, are you really listening to and heeding what the law teaches? *Listen to this:* [22]it's recorded *in the Scripture* that Abraham was the father of two sons. One son was born to a slave woman, *Hagar,* and the other son was born to a free woman, *Abraham's wife, Sarah.* [23]The slave woman's son was born through only natural means, but the free woman's son was born through a promise *from God. Stay with me, because this applies to what is going on with you.* [24]I'm using an allegory. *Here's the picture:* these two women stand for two covenants. The first *represents the covenant God made* on Mount Sinai—this is Hagar, who gives birth to children of slavery. [25]Hagar is Mount Sinai in Arabia, and she stands for the Jerusalem *we know* now. She has lived in slavery along with her children. [26]But there is a Jerusalem *we know* above. She is free, and she is our mother. [27]*Isaiah* wrote:

> Be glad, you who feel sterile and
> never gave birth!
> Raise a joyful shout, childless
> woman, who never went into
> labor!
> For the barren woman produces
> many children,
> more than the one who has a
> husband.*

[28]So you *see now,* brothers and sisters, you are children of the promise like Isaac. *Stay focused on the significance of this story; it is basically the same issue we are dealing with.* [29]The *slave's* son, born through only what flesh could conceive, *resented and* perse-cuted the one born *into the freedom* of the Spirit. *The slave's son picked at Isaac,* just as you are being picked at now. [30]So what does the Scripture say? "Throw out the slave and her son, for the slave's son will never have a share of the inheritance coming to the son of the free woman."* [31]So, brothers and sisters, we are not children of the slave woman, but *sons and daughters* of the free.

5 So stand strong for our freedom! The Liberating King freed us so we wouldn't spend one more day under the yoke of slavery; *don't let anyone get you turned around and trapped under the law.*

[2]Listen because I, Paul, am going to make this message very clear *so it cannot be misunderstood:* if you undergo the rite of circumcision, then all that the Liberating King accomplished will be lost on you. [3]And understand this: if you choose to be circumcised, then you will oblige yourself to do every single rule of the law *for the rest of your life.* [4]You, *and anyone else* who seeks to be on the right side of God through the law, have effectively been cut off from the Liberator, *circumcised from grace,* and cast off from the favor of God—*the favor that could have set you free.* [5]We, on the other hand, *continue to live* through the Spirit's power and wait confidently in the hope that things will be put right through faith. [6]Here's the thing: in Jesus, the Liberator, whether you are circumcised or not makes no difference. What makes a difference is faith energized by love.

[7]Who has impeded your progress and kept you from obeying the truth? You were off to such a good start. [8]*I know for certain* the pressure isn't coming from God. He keeps calling you *to the truth.* [9]*You know what they say,* "Just a little yeast causes all the dough to rise," *so even the slightest detour from the truth will take you to a destination you do not desire.* [10]*Despite this,* I'm confident because the Lord *reassures me that* you will *truly hear and* take my

* 4:27 Isaiah 54:1
* 4:30 Genesis 21:10

message to heart. Besides, *I also know that these troublemakers, whoever they are,* will answer to God and be judged accordingly. [11]As for me, brothers and sisters, if I continue to preach circumcision—*as these agitators claim*—then why do I still face persecution? *If I were to preach a compromised version of the good news,* then the scandal of the cross would come to an end. [12]I really wish that these people who weigh you down with corrupt counsel would mutilate themselves!

[13]Brothers and sisters, God has called you to freedom! *Hear the call,* and do not *spoil this gift by* using your liberty to engage in what your flesh desires; instead, use it to serve each other *as the Liberator taught* through love. [14]For the whole law comes down to this one instruction: "Love your neighbor as yourself,"* so [15]why all this vicious gnawing on each other? If you are not careful, you will find you've eaten each other alive!

[16]Here's my instruction: walk in the Spirit, and let the Spirit bring order to your life. If you do, you will never give in to your selfish and sinful cravings. [17]For everything the flesh desires goes against the Spirit, and everything the Spirit desires goes against the flesh. There is a constant battle raging between them that prevents you from doing *the good* you want to do. [18]But when you are led by the Spirit, you are no longer a subject under the law.

[19]It's clear that our flesh entices us into practicing some of its most heinous acts: participating in corrupt sexual relationships, impurity, unbridled lust, [20]idolatry, witchcraft, hatred, arguing, jealousy, anger, selfishness, contentiousness, division, [21]envy *of others' good fortune,* drunkenness, drunken revelry, and other shameful vices *that plague humankind.* I told you this clearly before, and I only tell you again *so there is no room for confusion:* those who give in to these ways will not inherit the kingdom of God.

*P*aul has finished with his correction of the Galatians. Now he is preaching about the call of God to

freedom. We are done with the demands of the law; now we are free to live in the Spirit and to be truly right with God. As free people, the Spirit gives us the characteristics of the Liberator. We can freely love in joy and peace. We can have patience along with kindness and faithfulness that can only come from the Father. We can reflect the goodness of God while being gentle in operating with self-control. For the follower of the Liberator, who is in the Spirit, these characteristics or fruits are a gift from God. As we grow in the faith, we find that we belong to God, and we can walk daily in the Spirit.

[22]The Holy Spirit produces a different kind of fruit: *unconditional* love, joy, peace, patience, kindheartedness, goodness, faithfulness, [23]gentleness, and self-control. You won't find any law opposed to fruit like this. [24]Those of us who belong to Jesus, the Liberator, have crucified our old lives and put to death the flesh and all the lusts and desires that plague us.

[25]*Now* since we have chosen to walk with the Spirit, let's keep each step in perfect sync with God's Spirit. [26]This will happen when we set aside our self-interests *and work together to create true community* instead of a culture consumed by provocation, *pride,* and envy.

[6]My spiritual brothers and sisters, if one *of our faithful* has fallen into a trap and is snared by sin, *don't stand idle and watch his demise.* Gently restore him, being careful not to step into your own snare. [2]Shoulder each other's burdens, and then you will live as the law of the Liberator taught us. [3]Don't *take this opportunity to* think you are better than those who slip because you aren't; then you *become the fool and* deceive even yourself. [4]Examine your own works so that if you are proud, it will be because of your own

* 5:14 Leviticus 19:18; Matthew 7:12; 22:39-40

accomplishments and not someone else's. [5]Each person has his or her own burden to bear *and story to write.*

[6]Remember to share what you have with your mentor in the Word, *for it is right to make sure your teacher's needs are met.*

[7]Make no mistake: God can't be mocked. *What you give, you get.* What you sow, you harvest. [8]Those who sow seeds into their flesh will be pulling thorns from their skin! *The flesh knows only destruction.* But those who sow seeds into the Spirit shall harvest everlasting life from the Spirit. [9]May we never tire of doing what is good and right before our Lord because in His season we shall bring in a great harvest if we can just persist. *This is a truth upon which we can build our lives,* [10]so seize any opportunity *the Lord gives you* to do good things *and be a blessing* to everyone, especially those within our faithful family.

[11]Look at how giant these letters are now that I am writing with my own hand! [12]The troublemakers who are putting pressure on you to be circumcised are trying to impress the flesh. They want to avoid the persecution that always comes from preaching the cross of the Liberating King. [13]But even those who receive circumcision can't keep the law—*although they think they can*—and they hope to influence which way you go with your own skin so they can have bragging rights over your flesh.

[14]May I never put anything above the cross of our Lord Jesus, our Liberator. Through Him, the world has been crucified to me and I to this world. [15]Let me be clear: circumcision *won't save you—* uncircumcision won't either *for that matter*—for both amount to nothing. God's new creation *is what counts, and it* counts for everything. [16]May peace and mercy come to all of you who live by this rule and to the Israel of God.

[17]In the future, don't let anyone cause trouble for me because I bear in my body the marks that wounded Jesus.

[18]May the grace of our Lord Jesus, the Liberating King, infuse your life *with His Spirit*, brothers and sisters. Amen.

Ephesians

Letter to the church in Ephesus
From Paul, the apostle to the Gentiles

During Paul's time, Ephesus was one of the great cities of the world. It was a wealthy commercial seaport on the Cayster River, not far from the Aegean Sea in what is western Turkey today. The Ephesians were a proud people; their city was home of the ancient temple of Diana (a goddess known to the Greeks as Artemis), one of the Seven Wonders of the World. The city was immersed in the magical arts, a kind of religion that promised people protection from fate, demons, curses, and incantations. This is why Paul's letter is filled with power language and promises that the Liberating King has defeated them through His death and resurrection.

According to Luke, Paul spent nearly three years in Ephesus planting and nurturing a church there, so it seems a bit odd that the letter itself is so generic. Unlike most of Paul's other letters, Ephesians lacks a personal touch, a personal message to specific members of the church at Ephesus. There's good evidence to suggest that Paul intended this letter to be circulated among a number of churches in Asia, but eventually it came to rest in and was identified with the city of Ephesus. It seems clear from the themes and content that Ephesians is not a letter for any particular church; it's a letter for every church in every age.

Writing from his prison cell, possibly in Rome, Paul pictured all liberated believers occupying a new spiritual location he calls "the heavenly realms." In this place, they enjoy all the spiritual blessings God has prearranged for them, but they also wait for the next act in the drama of redemption. They have already been raised to live in this new reality, but the world is still not yet what it will be when the Liberating King comes again. Even now Jesus is positioned at God's right hand, reigning over the spiritual powers the Ephesians fear most, so Paul assures them that as they belong to the Liberator and take up the full armor of God, they have nothing to fear.

1 Paul, an emissary* of Jesus, the Liberating King, *directly commissioned as His representative* by the will of God, to the saints [in Ephesus]* faithful in Jesus, the Liberator.

²May God the Father and the Lord Jesus, the Liberating King, surround you with grace and peace.

³Blessed be God, the Father of our Lord Jesus, the Liberator, who grants us every spiritual blessing in these heavenly realms *where we live* through the Liberator—*not because of anything we have done, but because of what He has done for us.* ⁴God chose us to be in a relationship with Him even before He laid out plans for this world; He wanted us to live holy lives characterized by love, *free from sin,* and blameless before Him. ⁵He destined us to be adopted as His children through *the covenant* Jesus, the Liberating King, *inaugurated in His sacrificial act.* This was His pleasure and His will *for us.* ⁶Ultimately God is the one worthy of praise for showing us His grace; *He is merciful and marvelous,* freely giving us these gifts in His Beloved. ⁷*Visualize this:* His blood *freely flowing down the cross,* setting us free! We are forgiven for our sinful ways by the richness of His grace, ⁸which He has poured all over us. With all wisdom and insight, ⁹He has enlightened us to the great mystery *at the center* of His will. With immense pleasure, He laid out His intentions *in the Liberator,* ¹⁰a plan that will climax when the time is right *as He returns to create order and unity*—both in heaven and on earth—when all things are brought together *under His royal rule.* In Him ¹¹we stand to inherit even more. As His heirs, we are predestined *to play a key role* in His *unfolding* purpose that is energizing everything to conform to His will. ¹²As a result, we, the first to place our hope in the Liberating King, will live in a way to bring Him glory and praise. ¹³Because you, too, have heard the word of truth—the good news of your salvation—and because you believed *in the One who is truth,* your lives are marked with His seal. This is *none other than* the Holy Spirit who was promised ¹⁴as the guarantee toward the inheritance we are to receive when He liberates and rescues all who belong to Him. To God be all praise and glory!

*T*his letter begins with praise and thanksgiving offered to God. Paul celebrates all the spiritual "blessings" available to us through the gospel. These benefits come to all believers "in Christ," the Liberating King. This means that He is the one through whom God has acted to rescue the world. But more than that, He is the Lord to whom we belong and the spiritual place where all believers are presently located. In God's purpose, heaven has come down to where we live so that we now occupy this wonderful realm where salvation is at work, where God's truth and beauty are a reality, and where we wait as the rest of His plan is worked out.

¹⁵This is why, when I heard of the faith in the Lord Jesus that is present in your community and of your great love for all God's people, ¹⁶I haven't stopped thanking Him for you. I am continually speaking to Him on your behalf in my prayers. *Here's what I say:*

God of our Lord Jesus, the Liberating King, Father of Glory: *I call out to You on behalf of Your people.* Give them a mind ready to receive wisdom and revelation so they will truly know You. ¹⁸Open the eyes of their hearts, *and let the light of Your truth flood in. Show them what You have promised them.* Shine Your light on the hope You are calling them to embrace. Reveal to them the glorious riches You are preparing as their inheritance. ¹⁹Let them see the full extent of Your power that is at work in those of us who believe, and may it be done according to Your might and power.

* 1:1 Literally, apostle
* 1:1 Some early manuscripts omit this portion.

Friends, it is this same might and *resurrection* power that [20]He used to raise our Liberating King from the dead and to position Him at His right hand in heaven. *There is nothing over Him.* [21]He's above all rule, authority, power, and dominion; over every name invoked, *over every title bestowed* in this age and the next. [22]God has placed all things beneath His feet and anointed Him as the head over all things for His church. [23]This church is His body, the fullness of the One who fills all in all.

*O*ften in his letters, Paul lets us overhear his prayers for his churches. He is constantly talking with God about those he considers his spiritual children. He prays that God will grant them wisdom, knowledge, and great power. This is the same power that was at work when God raised Jesus from the dead and seated Him in heaven. Ultimately Paul knows all powers have been subjected to Jesus, the God-man, and He is destined to be head over all creation. In the resurrection of Jesus, the ultimate redemption of the cosmos has begun, and the church is the first act of God's glorious drama.

2 As for you, *don't you remember how you used to just exist? Corpses,* dead *in life,* buried by transgressions, [2]wandering the course of this *perverse* world. *You were the offspring* of the prince of the power of air—*oh, how he owned you,* just as he still controls those living in disobedience. *I'm not talking about the outsiders alone;* [3]we were all guilty of falling headlong for the persuasive passions of this world, and we all have had our fill of indulging the flesh and mind, *obeying impulses to follow perverse thoughts conceived of dark powers.* As a result, our natural inclinations led us to be children of wrath, and we, like the rest of humankind, *were due to receive the full weight of God's fury.*

[4]But God, with the *unfathomable* richness of His love and mercy focused on us,

[5]united us with the Liberator and infused our lifeless souls with life—even though we were buried under mountains of sin—and saved us by His grace. *Then do you know what He did?* [6]He raised us up with Him and seated us in the heavenly realms with *our beloved* Jesus, the Liberating King. [7]*He did this for a reason:* so that for all eternity we will stand as a living testimony to the incredible riches of His grace and kindness that He freely gives to us by uniting us with Jesus, the Liberator. [8-9]For it's by God's grace that you have been saved. You receive it through faith. It was not *our plan or* our effort. It is God's gift, *pure and simple.* You didn't earn it, *not one of us did,* so don't go around bragging *that you must have done something amazing.* [10]For we are the product of His hand, *heaven's poetry etched on lives,* created in Jesus, the Liberator, to accomplish the good works God arranged long ago.

*T*he relationship between faith and works is often misunderstood. Some think that salvation is God's reward for a life of good deeds. If that's true, then it can't possibly be a gift. If it were a reward, then heaven would be a place where people might compare notes on what they did to make it through the gates. But Paul is confident in the truth of the gospel. The truth is that salvation is God's gift through Jesus, the Liberating King. Grace and faith make salvation real in us. When we are transformed by grace, then we become His new creation and we begin to live out the good works He has planned for us. Works, then, aren't the cause of salvation; they are its result. To put it another way, works aren't the means of salvation; they are its presence.

[11]So never forget how you used to be. Those of you born as outsiders *to Israel* were *outcasts,* branded "the uncircumcised" by those who bore the sign of the covenant in their flesh, a sign made with human hands. [12]You had absolutely no connection to the

Liberating King; you were strangers, separated from God's people. You were aliens to the covenant they had with God; you were hopelessly stranded without God in a *fractured* world. [13]But now, because of Jesus, the Liberator, *and His sacrifice, all of that has changed.* God gathered you who were so far away and brought you near to Him in the royal blood of our Liberating King.

[14]He is the embodiment of our peace, *sent once and for all* to take down the great barrier of hatred and hostility that has divided us so that we can be one. *Here's what He did:* [15]He offered His body *on the sacrificial altar* to bring an end to the law's ordinances and dictations *that separated Jews from the outside nations. His desire was* to create in His body one new humanity from the two *opposing groups,* thus creating peace. [16]*Effectively* the cross becomes God's means to kill off the hostility *once and for all* so that He is able to reconcile them both to God in this one new body.

[17]The Great Preacher of peace *and love* came for you, and *His voice* found those of you who were near and those who were far away. [18]By Him both have access to the Father in one Spirit. [19]And so you are no longer called outcasts and wanderers but citizens with God's people, *members of God's holy family,* and residents of His household. [20]You are being built on a *solid* foundation: *the message* of the prophets and *the voices* of God's chosen emissaries* with Jesus, the Liberator Himself, the *precious* cornerstone. [21]The building is joined together *stone by stone—all of us chosen and sealed* in Him, rising up to become a holy temple in the Lord. [22]In Him you are being built together, creating a *sacred* dwelling place *among you* where God can live in the Spirit.

> or Paul there are two kinds of people: Jews and Gentiles, or to put it another way, insiders and outsiders. The Prince of Peace is establishing peace where division and hostility once ruled unchallenged. In the Jerusalem temple, a stone wall separated Jewish from non-Jewish

worshipers. According to Paul, the cross is God's instrument to dismantle the wall, end the segregation, and make the two into one. You see, the one true God wants one people of God. That has been His plan all along.

In our day, walls continue to exist, erected strategically to separate people by race, religion, class, culture, and sex. Those who erect these walls, protect them, and maintain them will find that they are enemies of the gospel.

3 All this is exactly why I, Paul, am a prisoner of Jesus, the Liberating King, His representative to the outsider nations. [2]You have heard, haven't you, how God appointed me to bring you His message of grace? [3]And how the mystery was made known to me in a revelation? I wrote about it earlier in brief. [4]When you read what I have written, you will be better able to understand *the depth of* my insight into the mystery of the Liberating King, [5]a mystery that has never before been shown to past generations. Only now are *these secrets* being revealed to God's chosen emissaries* and prophets through the *Holy* Spirit. [6]Specifically, *the mystery* is this: by trusting in the good news, the Gentile outsiders are becoming *fully enfranchised* members of the same body, heirs alongside *Israel,* and beneficiaries of the promise *that has been fulfilled* through Jesus, the Liberator.

[7]I became a servant *and preacher* of this gospel by the gift of God's grace as He exercised His *amazing* power over me. [8]I cannot think of anyone more unworthy to this cause than I, the least of the least of the saints. *But here I am,* a grace-made man, privileged to be *an echo of His voice and* a preacher to all the nations of the riches of the Liberating King, riches that no one ever imagined. [9]*I am privileged* to enlighten all *of Adam's descendants* to the mystery concealed from previous ages by God, the Creator of all. [10]*Here's His*

* 2:20 Literally, apostles
* 3:5 Literally, apostles

objective: through the church, He intends now to make known His infinite and boundless wisdom to all rulers and authorities in heavenly realms. [11]This has been His plan from the beginning, one that He has now accomplished through the Liberating King, Jesus our Lord. [12]His faithfulness* *to God* has made it possible for us to have the courage we need and the ability to approach the Father confidently. [13]So I ask you not to become discouraged because *I am jailed for speaking out* on your behalf. *In fact,* my suffering is something that brings you glory.

[14]It is for this reason that I bow my knees before the Father, [15]after whom all families in heaven above and on earth below receive their names, *and pray*:

[16]*Father,* out of Your *honorable and glorious riches*, strengthen Your people. Fill their souls with the power of Your Spirit [17]so that through faith the Liberating King will reside in their hearts. May love be *the rich soil* where their lives take root. May it be the bedrock where their lives are founded *so that together* [18-19]with all of Your people they will have the power to understand that the love of the Liberator is infinitely long, wide, high, and deep, surpassing everything anyone previously experienced. God, may Your fullness flood through their entire beings.

[20]Now to the God who can do so many *awe-inspiring things, immeasurable things,* things greater than we ever could ask or imagine through the power at work in us, [21]to Him be all glory in the church and in Jesus, the Liberating King, from this generation to the next, forever and ever. Amen.

4 As a prisoner of the Lord, I urge you: *Walk as Jesus walked.* Live a life that is worthy of the calling He has *graciously* extended to you. [2]Be humble. Be gentle. Be patient. Tolerate one another in *an atmosphere thick with* love. [3]Make every effort to preserve the unity the Spirit has already created, with peace binding you together.

> Now that Paul has described the new world as God would have it, he urges believers to live out their calling with humility, patience, and love. These are the ways of the Liberating King. Paul encourages them to do whatever it takes to hold onto the unity that binds people together in peace. He does not ask them to create that unity; this has already been accomplished through the work of our Liberator and His Spirit. Rather, he calls believers to guard that unity—a more modest but no less significant task. As we will see, that unity is founded on God's oneness and work in the world.

[4]There is one body and one Spirit, just as you were all called to pursue one hope. [5]There is one Lord *Jesus*, one *living* faith, one ceremonial washing,* and [6]one God, the Father over all who is above all, through all, and in all. [7]*This God* has given to each of us grace in full measure according to the Liberator's gift [8]as *the Scripture* says,

> When He ascended to the heights,
>   He put captivity in chains,
> And *in His triumph* He gave gifts to
>   the people.*

[9](Well, when it says "He ascended," then that must mean that He had descended earlier to the lower levels, that is, to the earth. [10]The One who descended is the same One *who rose from the dead* to ascend far above all the heavens so that He could fill all things.)
[11]It was the *risen* One who handed

---

* 3:12 Some translations read "faith in Him."
* 4:5 Literally, immersion, in a rite of initiation and purification
* 4:8 Psalm 68:18

down *to us such gifted leaders*—some emissaries,* some prophets, some evangelists, as well as some pastor-teachers— [12]so that God's people would be *thoroughly* equipped to minister and build up the body of the Liberating King. [13]*These ministries will continue* until we are unified in faith and filled with the knowledge of the Son of God, until we stand mature *in His teachings* and fully formed in the likeness of our Liberator. [14]Then we will no longer be like children, tossed around here and there upon ocean waves, picked up by every gust of religious teaching spoken by liars or swindlers or deceivers. [15]Instead, by truth spoken in love, we are to grow in every way into Him—Jesus, the Liberating King, the head. [16]He joins and holds together the whole body with its ligaments providing the support needed so each part works to its proper design to form a healthy, *growing, and mature* body that builds itself up in love.

[17]Therefore, as a witness of the Lord, I insist on this: that you no longer walk in the outsiders' ways—with minds devoted to worthless pursuits. [18]They are blind to *true* understanding. They are strangers and aliens to the kind of life God has for them because they live in ignorance *and immorality* and because their hearts are *cold,* hard stones. [19]And now, since they've lost all *natural* feelings, they have given themselves over to sensual, greedy, and reckless living. They stop at nothing to satisfy their impure appetites.

[20]But this is not *the path of* the Liberating King, which you have learned. [21]If you have heard Jesus and have been taught by Him according to the truth that is in Him, [22]then you know to take off your former way of life, your *crumpled* old self— *that dark blot of a soul* corrupted by deceitful desire and lust— [23]*to take a fresh breath* and to let God renew your attitude and spirit. [24]Then *you are ready to* put on your new self, modeled after the very likeness of God: truthful, righteous, and holy.

[25]So put away your lies and speak the truth to one another because we are all part of one another. [26]When you are angry, don't let it carry you into sin.* Don't let the sun set with anger in your heart or [27]give the devil room to work. [28]If you have been stealing, stop. Thieves must go to work *like everyone else* and work honestly with their hands so that they can share with anyone who has a need. [29]Don't let even one rotten word seep out of your mouths. Instead, offer only fresh words that build others up when they need it most. That way your good words will communicate grace to those who hear them. [30]It's time to stop bringing grief to God's Holy Spirit; you have been sealed with the Spirit, marked as His own for the day of liberation. [31]Banish bitterness, rage and anger, shouting and slander, and any and all malicious thoughts—*these are poison.* [32]Instead, be kind and compassionate. *Graciously* forgive one another just as God has forgiven you through the Liberating King.

*T*he truth of the good news must be manifest in how we live. We may come to God as sinners, but He doesn't leave us there. He wants to transform us through the power of the Spirit. Certain habits, attitudes, and practices must be laid aside, like old, worn-out clothes. But, like nature, souls abhor a vacuum. We must replace the old ways we once knew with the new ways of the Liberating King. His life, revealed to us in the Gospels, becomes the script for us to imitate. To live as He lived. To forgive as He forgave. To love as He loved.

5 So imitate God. *Follow Him* like adored children, [2]and live in love as the Liberator loved you—so much that He gave Himself as a fragrant sacrifice, pleasing God.

[3]*Listen,* don't let any kind of immorality be breathed among you. Any demoralizing behavior (*perverse sexual acts, uncleanliness,* greediness, *and the like*) are inappropriate topics of conversation for those set apart as God's people. [4]Don't swear or

---

* 4:11 Literally, apostles
* 4:26 Psalm 4:4

spurt nonsense. Don't make harsh jokes *or clown around.* Make proper use of your words, and offer them thankfully in praise. ⁵This is what we know for certain: no one who engages in loose sex, impure actions, and greed—which is just a form of idolatry—has any inheritance in the kingdom of God and His Liberating King.

⁶Don't be fooled by people whose sentences are compounded with *useless words, empty words—it just shows they are empty souls.* For, in His wrath, God will judge all the children of disobedience for these kinds *of sins.* ⁷So don't *be persuaded into their ignorance, and don't* cast your lot with them ⁸because, although you were once the personification of darkness, you are now light in the Lord. So act like children of the light. ⁹For the fruit of the light is all that is good, right, and true. ¹⁰Make it your aim to learn what pleases our Lord. ¹¹Don't get involved with the fruitless works of darkness; instead, expose them *to the light of God.* ¹²You see, it's a disgrace to speak of their secrets (so don't even talk about what they do when no one is looking). ¹³⁻¹⁴When the light shines, it exposes *even the dark and shadowy* things and turns them into *pure reflections of* light. This is why they sing:

Awake, you sleeper!
  Rise from your grave,
And the Liberating King will shine
    on you.

¹⁵So be careful how you live; *be mindful of your steps.* Don't run around like idiots *as the rest of the world does.* Instead, walk as the wise! ¹⁶Make the most of every *living and breathing* moment because these are evil times. ¹⁷So understand *and be confident in* God's will, and don't live thoughtlessly. ¹⁸Don't drink wine excessively. The drunken path *is a reckless path. It* leads nowhere. Instead, let God fill you with the Holy Spirit. ¹⁹*When you are filled with the Spirit, you are empowered to* speak to each other in *the soulful words of* pious songs, hymns, and spiritual songs; to sing and make music with your hearts attuned to God; ²⁰and to give thanks to God the Father every day through the name of the Lord Jesus, the Liberating King, for all He has done.

> *W*isdom is a rare commodity. Paul urges believers, then and now, to walk wisely. It involves living well every day you are given. Time itself seems to be co-opted by dark forces. But when believers understand God's will, avoid drunkenness, and allow God to fill them with His Spirit, they are able to walk wisely and live well. The Spirit-filled life is not just for fanatics; it is the normal Christian life, and it affects everything, including how we live in community and how we treat others at home.

²¹*And the Spirit makes it possible to humbly* submit to one another out of respect for the Liberator. *So give yourselves away. After all, He was the first to give.* ²²Wives, *it should be no different* with your husbands. Submit to them as you do to the Lord, ²³for God has given husbands a *sacred* duty to lead as the Liberator leads the church and serves as the head. (The church is His body; He is her Savior.) ²⁴So wives should submit to their husbands, *respectfully,* in all things, just as the church yields to the Liberating King.

²⁵⁻²⁶Husbands, you must love your wives so *deeply, purely, and sacrificially that we can understand it only when we* compare it to the love the Liberating King has for *His bride,* the church. *We know* He gave Himself up completely to make her His own, washing her clean of all her impurity with water and *the powerful presence of* His word. ²⁷*He has given Himself* so that He can present the church as His radiant bride, unstained, unwrinkled, and unblemished—*completely free from all impurity*—holy and innocent before Him. ²⁸So husbands should care for their wives *as if their lives depended on it,* the same way they care for their own bodies. As you love her, you ultimately are loving *part of* yourself (*remember, you are one flesh*). ²⁹No one really hates his own body; he takes care to

feed and love it, just as the Liberating King takes care of His church, [30]because we are *living* members of His body. [31]"And this is the reason a man leaves his father and his mother and is united with his wife; the two *who once lived as "me's"* come together as *"we,"* one flesh *and blood."** [32]There is a great mystery *reflected* in this *Scripture,* and I say that it has to do with *the marriage of* the Liberating King and the church. [33]Nevertheless, each husband is to love *and protect* his own wife as if she were his very heart, and each wife is to respect her own husband.

6 *Now to you,* children, obey your parents in the Lord because this is right *in God's eyes.* [2]This is the first commandment onto which He added a promise: "Honor your father and your mother, and [3]if you do, you will live long and well in this land."*

[4]And, fathers, do not drive your children mad, but nurture them in the discipline and teaching *that comes* from the Lord.

[5]Slaves, respect and fear your earthly masters. Obey and serve them with the same sincerity of heart as you serve the Liberating King. [6]Don't put on a show just because they are looking (as if you were a people-pleaser); but as a slave of the Liberator, do the will of God from your heart. [7]Serve them in good faith as if you were serving the Lord, not men, [8]because all good deeds are gifted back from the Lord, and they are yours whether you are a slave or not.

[9]Masters, hear this: act in kind to your slaves. Stop *terrorizing and* threatening them. Don't forget that you have a Master in heaven who does not take sides or pick favorites.

[10]Finally, *brothers and sisters,* draw your strength and might from God. [11]Put on the full armor of God to protect yourselves from the devil and his evil schemes. [12]We're not waging war against enemies of flesh and blood alone. No, this fight is against tyrants, against authorities, against *supernatural* powers *and demon-princes*

that slither in the darkness of this world, and against wicked *spiritual armies* that lurk about in heavenly places.

[13]And this is why you need *to be head-to-toe in* the full armor of God: so you can resist during these evil days and be fully prepared to hold your ground. [14]Yes, stand—truth banded around your waist, righteousness as your chest plate, [15]and feet protected in preparation to proclaim the good news of peace. [16]Don't forget to raise the shield of faith above all else, so you will be able to extinguish flaming spears hurled at you from the wicked one. [17]Take also the helmet of salvation and the sword of the Spirit, which is the word of God.

P aul knows that the real battles and dangers we face are not against flesh and blood. The enemies we see are real enough, but they are animated by spiritual forces of darkness that stay strategically hidden from view. These "powers" often reveal themselves in institutional evils—genocide, terror, tyranny, and oppression—but the weapons needed to combat them are not earthly weapons at all. What is needed, Paul advises, is to stand firm in God's power and to suit up in the full armor of God. Although the devil and his demon armies are destined for destruction, they are serious threats now and must be resisted and beaten back. For Paul, the best offensive weapons we have are the word of God and prayer.

[18]Pray always. Pray in the Spirit. Pray about everything in every way you know how! And keeping all this in mind, pray on behalf of God's people. Keep on praying feverishly, and be on the lookout *until evil has been stayed.* [19]And please pray for me. Pray that truth will be with me before I even open my mouth. *Ask the Spirit to*

* 5:31 Genesis 2:24
* 6:2-3 Exodus 20:12; Deuteronomy 5:16

guide me while I boldly defend the mystery that is the good news— [20]for which I am an ambassador in chains—so pray that I can bravely pronounce the truth, as I should do.

[21]I am sending to you Tychicus, my dear brother and faithful minister in the Lord. He will tell you everything that has been going on here with me [22]so you will know how I am and what I am doing. He's coming with news that will hopefully comfort your hearts. [23]Brothers and sisters, *let me leave you with a blessing:*

May peace and love with faith be yours from God the Father and our Liberating King, Jesus. [24]May His grace surround all who love our Lord Jesus, the Liberator, with a never-ending love.

Philippians

Letter to the church in Philippi
From Paul, the apostle to the Gentiles

This little letter has had a big impact on the church in Paul's day and ours. At the heart of it is Paul's consistent plea that the Philippians "rejoice in the Lord." For Paul, joy is not a good feeling based on favorable happenings; it is a decision, a deliberate choice to celebrate God's work through the Liberating King in any and every circumstance. Ironically Paul writes this letter from a prison probably in Rome or Caesarea; we don't know for certain. What is certain is that, despite his chains, Paul is content where he is, in part, because he sees the gospel progressing. As a servant and prisoner of the Lord Jesus, that thrills and satisfies him.

Paul writes this letter to thank the Philippians for a gift he had just received and to announce some travel plans, assuming he'd be freed from prison. For years he had enjoyed a warm and intimate friendship with the believers of this little Roman colony, the first church in Europe. From the moment he preached the message of the Liberating King in Philippi, the church there had supported and encouraged Paul in ways no other church had. Now they have renewed their concern for him with another act of generosity. No wonder the emissary feels closer to them than to any other church he founded!

One of the most beautiful moments in this letter is a hymn to the Liberator in 2:6-11. Whether Paul composes this hymn himself or quotes it from another source, no one knows. Nevertheless this hymn recounts a beautiful story of love and humility as the Liberating King descends into our world to serve humanity and face the horrors of the cross; then He is exalted by God, given a unique name, and declared "Lord" by all creatures to the glory of God. Paul makes Jesus the lordly example of humility and urges others to follow Him and adopt His attitude. As disciples of the Liberating King, Paul, Timothy, and Epaphroditus demonstrate that same spirit of service as they pour themselves out for the gospel and for the Philippians.

1 Paul and Timothy, slaves of the Liberating King, Jesus, greet you, *our friends* in Philippi—those set apart by Jesus, the Liberator—*and we greet the* elders and deacons *who serve* with you. ²Grace and peace be with you from God our Father and the Lord Jesus, the Liberator.

³Whenever you cross my mind, I thank my God for you *and for the gift of knowing you.* ⁴My spirit is lightened with joy whenever I pray for you (and I do constantly) ⁵because you have partnered with me to spread the gospel since the first day *I preached to you.*

⁶I am confident that the Creator, who has begun such a great work among you, will *not stop in mid-design but will* keep perfecting you until the day Jesus, the Liberating King, *returns to redeem the world.* ⁷It is only right that I should feel such admiration for you all—you hold me close to your hearts. And, since we are partners in *this great work of* grace, you have never failed to stand with me as I have defended and stood firm for the gospel—even from this prison cell. ⁸Before God I want you to know how much I long to see you and love you with the affection of the Liberating King, Jesus.

⁹Here's what I pray for you:

Father, may their love grow more and more in wisdom and insight— ¹⁰so they will be able to *examine and* determine the best *from everything else.* And on the day of the Liberating King, *the day of His judgment,* let them stand pure and blameless, ¹¹filled with the fruit of *authentic* righteousness that ripens through Jesus, the Liberator.

All this I pray, with a view to God's ultimate praise and glory.

¹²*I have good news,* brothers and sisters, and I want to share it. *Believe it or not,* my imprisonment has actually helped spread the good news *to new places and populations.* ¹³Word has spread through the ranks of the imperial guard and to everyone else *around me* that I am in prison because of my faith in the Liberating King. *Many have come and listened to me tell the story of His life, death, and resurrection.* ¹⁴My imprisonment has instilled courage in most of our brothers and sisters, so they *are trusting God more and* have been even more daring as they speak the good news without fear.

¹⁵⁻¹⁷*I am well aware that* some people out there are preaching the message of the Liberating King because of jealousies and rivalries. Their motives aren't pure. They're driven by selfish ambitions and personal agendas, hoping somehow to add to my pain here in prison. *And I also know* there are others who are preaching the Liberating King from true goodness, motivated by love. *They wish me the best because* they know I'm here in prison in defense of the gospel. *My focus, as they know, is this mission God has placed before me.*

¹⁸So what *do we do* then? *Listen. What matters is* that in every way, *regardless of the motives*—whether pure or shady—the great story of the Liberating King *and God's grace is spreading. This is what I care about,* and it's a cause for joy. I will continue to rejoice ¹⁹because I know that through your *encouragement and* prayers and through the help of the Spirit of Jesus, the Liberator, I will soon be released from this dark place. ²⁰I don't expect that dishonor and shame will plague me in any way, but I do hope that I will continue to be able to speak freely and courageously *about Jesus,* and that now and forever the Liberating King will be glorified and placed above all else through this body of mine—whether I live or die. ²¹For my life is about the Liberator *and Him alone.* And my death, *when that comes,* will mean great gain for me. ²²So, if it's His will that I go on serving here, my work will be fruitful *for the gospel.* I honestly wouldn't know how or what to choose (*and I'm glad it's not up to me*); ²³I would be hard-pressed to decide. I lean toward leaving this world to be with the Liberating King because I can only think that would be much better. *But as I said, my life is no longer about me.* ²⁴To stay in this body of flesh—*even with all its pains and weaknesses*—would best serve your needs. ²⁵Now that I think of it, I am

sure of this: I would prefer to remain to share in the progress and joy of your growing belief. 26When I return to you, we will celebrate Jesus, our Liberator, even more *and we will share in the joy of faith that is a result of my return to you.*

27*So here is what I want you to do:* conduct yourselves as *true and* worthy citizens of our Liberator's gospel, so that whether I make it or don't make it to see you, I will *at least* hear that you continue to stand, united in one spirit, single-minded *in purpose* as you struggle together for the faith in the gospel. 28Don't be paralyzed in any way by what your opponents are doing. Your steadfast faith in the face of opposition is a sign that they are doomed and that you have been graced with God's salvation. 29And now, you have been given the privilege of not only believing in *Jesus,* the Liberating King, but *being chosen* to suffer for Him as well. 30You have seen me suffer for Him. *Since I've been away,* you've heard of the other agonizing conflicts I've had to face. Now you know firsthand the pains of this battle.

2 If you find any comfort from being in the Liberator, if His love brings you some encouragement, if you experience true companionship with the Spirit, if His tenderness and mercy fill your heart, *then, brothers and sisters,* 2*here is one thing that would* complete my joy—come together as one in mind and spirit and purpose, sharing in the same love. 3Don't let selfishness and prideful agendas take over. Embrace true humility, and lift your heads to extend love to others. *We will get nowhere if our motives spring from selfish ambition or from indifference to the plight of those around us.* 4Get beyond yourselves and protecting your own interests; *be sincere,* and secure your neighbors' interests first.

5*In other words,* adopt the mind-set of Jesus, your Liberating King. *Live with His attitude in your hearts. Remember:*

6Though He was in the form of God,
   He chose not to cling to equality
      with God.

7But poured Himself out *to fill a
      vessel brand-new;*
   a servant in form
      and a man indeed.
   The very likeness of humanity,
8He humbled Himself,
      obedient to death—
   a merciless death on the cross!
9So God raised Him up to the highest
      place
   and gave Him the name above all.
10So when His name is called,
      every knee will bow,*
   in heaven, on earth, and below.
11And every tongue will confess*
   "Jesus, the Liberating King, is Lord,"
      to the glory of God our Father!

I magine the kind of church Paul describes: a community where every person considers the needs of others first and does nothing from selfishness; a group that pulls together rather than pulls apart, and a body that knows its purpose and lets nothing interfere with it. It would be the kind of extended spiritual family where others would want to belong. Outsiders would line up to become part of this sacred assembly and to make it their home because they see the welcome, feel the encouragement, and know they are truly loved. So Paul urges the Philippians to strive for this radical unity and fulfill his joy by having the mind of the Liberating King. That mind is expressed beautifully as Paul retells the story of how Jesus humbled Himself, became a servant, and suffered the death of the cross. Jesus becomes the lordly example of humility and service, leading to the kind of unity Paul imagines.

12So now, my beloved, obey as you have always done, not only when I am with you,

* 2:10 Isaiah 45:23
* 2:11 Isaiah 45:23

but even more so when I can't be. Continue to work out your salvation, with great fear and trembling, [13]because God is energizing you so that you would desire and do what always pleases Him.

[14]Do all things without complaining or bickering with each other, [15]so you will be found innocent and blameless; *you are God's children called to live without a single stain on your reputations among this perverted and crooked generation. Don't let the darkness lead you astray. Instead, friends,* shine like stars across the land, *reflections of the Liberator's love.* [16]Cling to the word of life so that on the day of judgment when the Liberating King returns I may have reason to rejoice, because it will be plain that I didn't turn from His mission nor did I work in vain. [17]Even if my lifeblood is to be poured out like wine as a sacrifice of your faith, I have great reason to celebrate with all of you. [18]And for the same reason, you can be glad and celebrate with me.

[19]I hope in the Lord Jesus to send Timothy your way. He will visit soon *so that he may report to me how you are doing.* To hear all that is going on with you will truly encourage my heart. [20]There is no one like Timothy. *He's a special blessing in my life.* What sets him apart from others is his deep concern for you *and your spiritual journey. This is rare, my friends,* [21]for most people only care about themselves, not about what is *dear to the heart* of our Liberating King, Jesus. [22]You know Timothy is genuine *in the Lord's ways; he has proven this time and again.* He has been a faithful partner to me in *this work of* the gospel, as much as my own flesh and blood would have been. [23]I expect to send him soon, and I will as soon as I see how things turn out here. [24]I trust in the Lord that it won't be very long before I can come *and be with you in person, and we can renew the friendship that we have always enjoyed.*

[25]But for now, I think it is best to send Epaphroditus home to you. *Know that you did well by sending this man to me; he has become* my dear brother in the Lord. We have worked well together and fought great battles together, and he was an encouraging minister to me in my time of need. [26]He could not wait to see you all; *he has missed you dearly.* He was concerned for you when he found out you knew how sick he really was. [27]In fact, he nearly died. But once again, God *was exceedingly kind and* covered him with His mercy. And I, too, by His mercy, have been spared sorrow on top of sorrow. *To lose him would have caused me more grief than I can express. But instead, there is cause to celebrate.*

[28]I am so excited to be sending him back to you! I can picture the joy on your faces when he arrives; I can feel my worries falling away. *The Lord will be glorified by your praise and joy. I am relieved to know he will be there soon!* [29]Welcome him joyfully in the Lord. Esteem all spiritual leaders like Epaphroditus *who risk their lives for the gospel,* [30]and honor the commitment of your brother Epaphroditus to the work of our Liberating King, for he placed his life in grave danger to come to me when you could not.

3 It is time that I wrap up these thoughts to you, my brothers and sisters. Rejoice in the Lord! (I don't mind writing these things over and over to you, as I know it keeps you safe.)

[2]Watch out for the dogs—wicked workers who *run in packs* looking for someone to maul with their false circumcision.

*C*ircumcision had become a flash point for the early church. Some taught that non-Jews had to become Jews to follow Jesus completely, including circumcision, dietary regulations, keeping weekly and annual holy days, and other Jewish practices. Since the time of Abraham, circumcision had been the mark of the covenant with Abraham's spiritual children. Things were changing: outsiders, non-Jews, were entering into the new covenant.

Do they enter by faith alone, or is it faith plus following God's law for Israel? Paul's answer is clear: it is faith alone that makes Jews and outsiders right with God. So he cautions the Philippians to watch out for those who would chastise them into a false circumcision. Real followers of Jesus know that salvation doesn't come from the blade of a knife but from the cross of the Liberating King.

3We are the true circumcision—those who worship God in Spirit and make our boast in Jesus, the Liberating King—so we do not rely on *what we have accomplished in* the flesh.

4If any try to throw around their pedigrees to you, remember my résumé—which is more impressive than theirs. *Listen, I used to be in the elite among them:* 5I was circumcised on the eighth day—*as the law prescribes*—born of the nation of Israel, descended from the tribe of Benjamin. I am a Hebrew born of Hebrews; I have observed the law according to *the strict piety of* the Pharisees, *separate from those embracing a less rigorous kind of Judaism.* 6Zealous? Yes. I ruthlessly *pursued and* persecuted the church. And when it comes to the righteousness required by the law, my record is spotless.

7But whatever I used to count as my greatest accomplishments, I've written them off as a loss because of the Liberator. 8And more so, I now realize that all I gained *and thought was important* was nothing but yesterday's garbage compared to knowing my Lord Jesus, the Liberating King. Because for Him I have thrown everything aside—*it's nothing but a pile of waste*—so that I may gain Him *and make room for what He has planned for me.* 9*When it counts,* I want to be found belonging to Him, not clinging to my own righteousness based on law, but actively relying on the faithfulness of our Liberator. *This is true* righteousness, supplied by God, acquired by faith. 10I want to know Him *inside and out.* I want to experience the power of His resurrection. *I want to find myself deeper in the path of the Liberating King,* joined in His suffering, shaped by His death, 11so that I may arrive *safely* at the resurrection from the dead.

12I'm not there yet, nor have I become perfect, but I am charging on to gain anything *and everything* the Liberator, Jesus, has in store for me—*and nothing will stand in my way* because He has grabbed me *and won't let me go.* 13Brothers and sisters, *as I said,* I know I have not arrived, but there's one thing I am doing: I'm leaving my old life behind, putting everything on the line for this mission. 14I am sprinting toward the only goal that counts: *to cross the line,* to win the prize, and to hear God's call *to resurrection life found exclusively* in Jesus, the Liberator. 15All of us who are mature ought to think the same way about these matters. If you have a different attitude, then God will reveal this to you as well. 16For now, let's hold on to what we have been shown *and keep in step with these teachings.*

17Imitate me, brothers and sisters, and look around to those already following the example we have set. 18I have warned you before (and now say again through my tears) that we have many enemies—people who reject the cross of our King and Liberator. 19They are ruled by their bellies, their glory comes by shame, and their minds are fixed on the things of this world. They are doomed. 20But we are citizens of heaven, *exiles on earth* waiting eagerly for our Liberator, the Lord Jesus the King, to come and 21transform these humble, *earthly* bodies into the form of His glorious body by the same power that brings all things under His control.

4 For this reason, brothers and sisters, my joy and crown whom I dearly love, I cannot wait to see you again. Continue to stand firm in the Lord, *and follow my instructions in this letter,* beloved. 2Euodia and Syntyche, I urge you to *put aside your differences,* agree, and work together in the Lord. 3Yes, *Syzygus,** loyal friend, I enlist you to please help these women. They, along with brother Clement and many others, have worked by my side

* 4:3 Literally, companion

to spread the good news of the gospel. They have their names recorded in the book of life.

⁴*Most of all, friends,* always rejoice in the Lord! I never tire of saying it: Rejoice! ⁵Keep your gentle nature so that all people will know *what it looks like to walk in His footsteps.* The Lord is ever present with us. ⁶Don't be anxious about things; instead, pray. Pray about everything. *He longs to hear your requests,* so talk to God about your need and be thankful for what has come. ⁷And know that the peace of God (*a peace* that is beyond any and all of our *human* understanding) will stand watch over your hearts and minds in Jesus, the Liberating King.

⁸Finally, brothers and sisters, fill your minds with *beauty and* truth. Meditate on whatever is honorable, whatever is right, whatever is pure, whatever is lovely, whatever is good, whatever is virtuous and praiseworthy. ⁹Keep to the script: whatever you learned and received and heard and saw in me—do it—and the God of peace will walk with you.

¹⁰I could hardly contain my joy in the Lord when I realized you have started to show your care for me once again. Since you have not had the opportunity to show how much you cared until now, *I want you to know how it touched me.* ¹¹I am not saying this because I am in need. I have learned to be content in whatever circumstances, *whether meager or bountiful, where I find myself.* ¹²I know how to survive in tight situations, and I know how to enjoy having plenty. In fact, I have learned how to face any circumstances: fed or hungry, with or without. ¹³I can be content in any and every situation through the One who is my power and strength. ¹⁴Nevertheless, it was admirable of you to participate in my affliction.

*T*rue contentment is a beautiful thing. It is the result of a heart committed to the risen Lord and guarded by His peace. Think of all the sins, pain, and brokenness that come from coveting. Adultery, murder, stealing, and lying can all be traced directly to a prior condition when hearts and minds are frustrated and discontent.

Notice that Paul says he learned contentment, because it doesn't come naturally. The normal, natural state is discontent and quiet desperation. It takes a powerful, spiritual presence to transform anxiety into joyous satisfaction. Ironically, it may have been the shackles more than his freedom that schooled Paul in the art of contentment. Despite the chains, Paul discovered this beautiful state of inner peace through the power of the Liberating King residing in him.

¹⁵You remember, Philippians, at the beginning of my gospel journey after I left Macedonia, no church offered me the financial assistance I needed to do the Lord's work, except you alone. ¹⁶Even when I took the message to Thessalonica, you sent provisions to me. Twice even! ¹⁷Not that I am looking for a gift—I am just looking toward your reward that comes from your gift. ¹⁸With what Epaphroditus delivered to me from your generous pockets, I have even been blessed in excess. I am fully satisfied. I know God is pleased with your dedication and accepts this gift as a fragrant offering, a holy sacrifice, on His behalf. ¹⁹*Know this:* my God will also fill every need you have according to His glorious riches in the Liberating King, Jesus. ²⁰So may our God and Father be glorified forever and ever. Amen.

²¹Greet every saint there in the Liberator, Jesus, for my brothers and sisters and I send our greetings to you. ²²All of the saints, especially those serving in Caesar's household, also send salutations to you. *Though we are not together, we are one in our King.* ²³May you all continue *the journey* with your spirits strengthened by the grace of the Lord Jesus, the Liberating King. [Amen.]*

---

* 4:23 Some manuscripts omit this word.

Colossians

Letter to the church in Colossae
From Paul, the apostle to the Gentiles

Paul wrote this letter about 25 years after his call to be an emissary for the Liberating King. The headstrong Paul who had planted churches and pioneered the gospel had now become an elder states- man for the growing movement. His reputation was so great that he could send a letter to a church he had neither planted nor even visited and expect to be received as a voice that must be heard.

When Paul wrote this letter, he was in prison. The people in Colossae would have known where, so there was no need to put it in the letter. But that important detail escapes us today. It is often said that he wrote it from prison in Rome, although Ephesus or Caesarea cannot be ruled out. The fact is that the Lord's emissary often found himself in prison because his message clashed with the local political, economic, and religious powers. But even as a prisoner, Paul was able to find a secretary or urge a coworker to help him craft and dispatch a letter.

Colossae was an important city located about 100 miles east of Ephesus. There were many religious options in Colossae, Jewish and pagan, and apparently some in Colossae thought that Jesus should simply be added into the mix. But for Paul, Jesus is no "add-on." As the Creator and Sustainer, as the head of the church, Jesus deserves their full and undivided attention. According to Paul, Jesus came to liberate not only individuals but all of creation from the powers of darkness.

Paul prays that God will encourage the believers in Colossae to live with a spiritual perspective and that their lives will reflect the transforming power of Jesus (1:9-10). One of the best-known passages in this letter is the wonderful hymn to Christ found in 1:15-20; it cele- brates not only His role as the Creator and Sustainer of the world, but also as the Reconciler and head of the church, which is His body. He then challenges the believers in Colossae to turn from their past, as if their old selves were dead, and to keep their eyes fixed on the goal of new life hidden in Jesus (3:2-4). Paul speaks individually to wives, husbands, children, slaves, and masters and finally asks them to pray with him that "we can go on telling the mystery of the Liberating King." Paul truly sees all believers as sharing in his min- istry and his imprisonment.

1 Paul, an emissary* of Jesus, the Liberating King, *serving* at God's pleasure, *along* with our brother Timothy, ²to you, *dear* holy and faithful brothers and sisters in *the family of* the Liberator, who live in Colossae. May grace and peace from God our Father [and the Lord Jesus, the Liberating King]* envelop you.

³As always, we've been praying for you, thanking God, the Father of our Lord Jesus, the Liberating King, ⁴ever since we heard of your faith in Jesus, our Liberator, and your love for His holy ones— ⁵*a faith and love* that emerge from the hope you have heard about in the word of truth—the gospel—the very hope that awaits you in heaven. ⁶⁻⁷The same gospel that was brought to you is growing and bearing fruit all over the world, just as it has been growing among you since the day you heard and took in the truth of God's grace from our beloved fellow servant Epaphras. (He is a faithful minister of the Liberator on our* behalf.) ⁸He was the one who told us how you demonstrate your love in *the power of* the Spirit. ⁹Since the day we got this good news about you, we have not stopped praying for you. We ask:

Father, may they clearly know Your will and achieve *the height and depth of* spiritual wisdom and understanding. ¹⁰May their lives be a credit to You, Lord; and *what's more,* may they continue to delight You by doing every good work and growing in the true knowledge that comes from being close to You. ¹¹Strengthen them with Your infinite power, according to Your glorious might, so that they will have everything they need to hold on and endure hardship patiently and joyfully. ¹²Thank You, Father, as You have made us* eligible to receive our portion of the inheritance given to all those set apart by the light. ¹³You have rescued us from dark powers and brought us safely into the kingdom of Your Son, whom You love ¹⁴and in whom we are redeemed and forgiven of our sins [through His blood].*

¹⁵He is the *exact* image of the invisible God, the firstborn of creation, *the eternal.* ¹⁶It was by Him that everything was created: the heavens, the earth, all things within and upon them, all things seen and unseen, thrones and dominions, *spiritual* powers and authorities. Every detail was crafted through His design, *by His own hands,* and for His purposes. ¹⁷He has always been! *It is His hand* that holds everything together. ¹⁸He is the head of this body, the church. He is the beginning, the first of those to be reborn from the dead, so that *in every aspect, at every view,* in everything—He is first. ¹⁹God was pleased that all His fullness should *forever* dwell in the Son, ²⁰who, *as predetermined by God,* bled peace into the world by His death on the cross as God's means of reconciling the whole creation to Himself—all things in heaven and all things on earth.

> As Paul gives thanks to God—a normal thing to do in a letter—he remembers a hymn he heard in the churches. The Colossian hymn (verses 15-20), as we call it, is all about Jesus, the Liberating King. It celebrates His reign, first as the Creator and Sustainer of the cosmos and second as the head of the church and the One who reconciles every broken thing to God by what He accomplished on the cross. In this hymn, the story of redemption is a witness to God's love. Paul wants the Colossians to understand who they are, but to do that, they must first know to whom they belong.

²¹You were once at odds *with God,* wicked in your ways and evil in your minds, ²²but now the Liberating King has reconciled you in His body—in His flesh through His death—so that He can present you to God

---

* 1:1 Literally, apostle
* 1:2 Some manuscripts omit this portion.
* 1:6-7 Some manuscripts read "your."
* 1:12 Other manuscripts read "you."
* 1:14 Early manuscripts omit this portion.

holy, blameless, and *totally* free of imperfection [23]as long as you stay planted in the faith. So don't venture away from what you have heard *and taken to heart*: the *living* hope of the good news that has been announced to all creation under heaven and has captured me, Paul, as its servant.

[24]Now I rejoice in what I've suffered on your behalf, *but even more suffering is ahead for me* as I *take on and* complete what remains of the Liberator's suffering for the sake of His body, the church. [25]I am a servant appointed by God to preach the Word of God until it is known to you and all over—*what I am talking about is nothing less than* [26]the mystery *of the ages!* What was hidden for ages, generations and generations is now being revealed to His holy ones. [27]He decided to make known to them His blessing to the nations; the glorious riches of this mystery is the indwelling of the Liberating King in you! The very hope of glory.

[28]We are preaching Him—spreading the Word to all with *equal amounts of* wise warning and instruction—so that, *at the final judgment,* we will be able to present everyone *to his Creator* fully mature because of what the Liberating King has done. [29]This is why I continue to toil and struggle—because His amazing power and energy surge within me.

*G*od calls Paul to preach the Word and to embody the sufferings of our Liberating King. At the heart of the good news is a mystery hidden in ancient Scriptures but now exposed to the world through the lives of the church's holy ones. If you pay close attention, you'll see that Paul never refers to just one "holy one"; he always uses the plural. And why is that? He knows that holiness is too difficult to accomplish on your own. One has to be called and equipped by God, but one also has to be accompanied by others who've answered the call. Those who say "yes" to Jesus become the church, the company of those rescued from darkness and ultimately from death. Paul is fond of calling the church the body of our Liberating King. Our own hopes and dreams for the future are concentrated in Him. Not only do we dwell in Him, but He dwells in us.

2 This battle I am facing is huge. And, I want you to know, I do it for you, for all those at Laodicea, and for everyone else (even those who have never seen my face). [2]I'm working hard to *comfort and* encourage them so *that they would be knit together*—that many hearts would become one through His love. I do it so they will be rich in understanding and have full knowledge of God's mystery, which is the Liberator Himself— [3]in Him all the treasures of wisdom and knowledge are concealed. [4]I only tell you this to warn you about those who would try and deceive you with their arguments. They seem plausible enough, *but in the end, they are false.* [5]Even though I cannot be there in the body, my spirit is with you, and I'm happy to know of your good order and your solid commitment to the Liberating King.

[6]Now that you have welcomed Jesus, the Liberator, as Lord of your lives, continue to journey with Him *and allow Him to shape your lives.* [7]Let your roots grow down deeply in Him, and let Him build you up on a firm foundation. Be strong in the faith, just as you were taught, and always spill over with thankfulness. [8]Make sure no predator makes you his prey through some *misleading* philosophy and empty deception based on traditions fabricated by mere mortals. These are sourced in the elementary principles originating in this world and not in the Liberating King (*so don't let their talks capture you*). [9]You see, all that is God, all His fullness, resides in the body of the Liberator. [10]You, too, are being completed in Him, the One who has dominion over all rule, all authority. [11]In Him you were also circumcised, set apart by a spiritual act performed without hands. The Liberator's circumcision cut you off from the sinfulness of your flesh. *And here is where it all happened; this is where your*

salvation began: [12]you were buried with Him beneath the waters of ceremonial washing* and then were raised up with Him by faith in the *resurrection* power of God, who brought Him back from the dead. [13]And when your flesh was still uncircumcised—dead in transgression *and swathed in its sinful nature*—it was God who brought us* to life with the Liberator, forgave all our sins, and [14]eliminated the massive debt we incurred by the law that stood against us. He took it all away; He nailed it to the cross. *But that's not all.* [15]He disarmed those who once ruled over us—those who had overpowered us. *Like captives of war,* He put them on display to the world to show His victory over them *by means of the cross.*

[16]So don't let anyone stand in judgment over you and dictate what you should eat or drink, what festivals you should celebrate, or how you should observe a new moon or Sabbath days—[17]all these are only a shadow of what shall come. The reality, *the core, the import,* is found in the Liberator. [18]Don't be cheated out of the prize by others who are peddling the worship of heavenly beings and *false* humility. People like this run about telling *whoever will listen* what they claim to have seen, but in reality they testify only to an inflated mind, saturated in conceit—*not in the Spirit.* [19]They are detached from the very head that nourishes and connects the whole body with all of its nerves and ligaments, a body that grows by the kind of growth that can only come from God.

[20]Listen, if you have died with the Liberating King to the elemental spirits of the cosmos, then why are you submitting yourselves to its rules as if you still belonged to this world? [21]*You hear:* "Don't handle this! Don't taste that! Don't even touch it!" [22]But everything they are obsessed about will eventually decay with use. These rules are just human commands and teachings. [23]*Here's what they are promoting:* fabricated religion, self-humiliation, and bodily abuse. *As to what may seem like wisdom on their part, I tell you this*: no matter which way they try to

tether their bodies, they cannot harness their desires.

*P*aul knew the people in Colossae were facing many religious and philosophical options, none of which were neutral. Notice Paul didn't say "Just add Jesus to what you already believe" or "Factor Jesus into your philosophy" or "Include Jesus in this or that ritual." The claim that "Jesus is Lord" does not allow that. If Jesus is Creator, Sustainer, and Redeemer of all creation, then all other teachings must give way. All people must bow before Him and only Him.

3 So *it comes down to this*: since you have been raised with the Liberating King, set your mind on heaven above. The Liberator is there, seated at God's right hand. [2]Stay focused on what's above, not on earthly things, [3]because your *old* life is dead and gone. Your *new* life is now hidden, enmeshed with the Liberator who is in God. [4]On that day when the Liberating King—who is our* very life—is revealed, you will be revealed with Him in glory! [5]So kill your earthly impulses: loose sex, impure actions, unbridled sensuality, wicked thoughts, and greed (which is *essentially* idolatry). [6]It's because of these that God's wrath is coming [upon the sons and daughters of disobedience],* *so avoid them at all costs.* [7]These are the same things you once pursued, and together you spawned a life of evil. [8]But now make sure you shed such things: anger, rage, spite, slander, and abusive language. [9]And don't go on lying to each other since you have sloughed away your old skin along with its evil practices [10]for a fresh new you, which is continually renewed in knowledge according to the image of the One who created you. [11]In this re-creation there is no distinction between Greek and Jew,

* 2:12 Literally, immersion, a rite of initiation and purification
* 2:13 Some manuscripts read "you."
* 3:4 Some manuscripts read "your."
* 3:6 Some early manuscripts omit this portion.

circumcised and uncircumcised, barbarian and conqueror,* or slave and free, because the Liberator is the whole and He dwells in us all.

¹²Since you are all set apart by God, made holy and dearly loved, clothe yourselves with *a holy way of life*: compassion, kindness, humility, gentleness, and patience. ¹³Put up with one another. *Stay together—no matter what!* Forgive. Pardon any offenses against one another, as the Lord has pardoned you, because you should act in kind. ¹⁴But above all these, put on love! Love is the perfect tie to bind these together. ¹⁵Let your hearts fall under the rule of the Liberator's peace (the peace you were called to as one body), and be thankful.

¹⁶Let the word of the Liberating King richly inhabit your lives. With all wisdom teach, *counsel,* and instruct one another. Sing the psalms, *compose* hymns and songs inspired by the Spirit, and keep on singing—*sing to God* from hearts *full and spilling over* with thankfulness. ¹⁷Surely, no matter what you are doing (speaking, *writing,* or working), do it all in the name of Jesus our Master, sending thanks through Him to God our Father.

For Paul it wasn't enough just to believe the right things. Right belief always produces right living. The gift of salvation demands that we put into practice the character of our King. Just as we take off and throw away old, worn-out clothes, we must strip off certain attitudes and actions. They are the remainders of our old selves. Since our lives have been swallowed up in His wider, glorious life, then things like sexual immorality, greed, anger, lying, and the rest must find no place in us. But it is not enough to strip off the old; we must put on the new. And that new creation looks suspiciously like the life of Jesus: compassion, gentleness, humility, putting up with each other, forgiving each other, and above all, loving each other. These are the ways of the Liberator. So they must be our ways too.

¹⁸Wives: be submitted to your husbands as is appropriate in the Lord. ¹⁹Husbands: love your wives, and don't treat them harshly *or respond with bitterness toward them.*

²⁰Children: obey your parents in every way. The Lord is well pleased by it. ²¹Fathers: don't infuriate your children, so their hearts won't *harbor resentment and* become discouraged. ²²Slaves: obey your earthly masters in all things. Don't just act as if you are earnest in your service only when they are watching; *don't be one of those who lives to be seen by others.* Serve with a sincere heart (*even when others aren't watching*), fearing the Lord *who is always watching*! ²³So no matter what your task is, work hard. *Always do your best* as the Lord's servant, not as man's, ²⁴because you know your reward is the Lord's inheritance. You serve the Lord, the Liberating King, and ²⁵anyone who does wrong will be paid his due because He doesn't play favorites.

4 And to you masters: treat your slaves fairly and do what is right, knowing that you, too, have a Master in heaven.

Families and family life have changed since Paul's day. Today, sociologists talk about modern families as "nuclear": two parents with fewer than two children. In Colossae, as elsewhere in Paul's world, the family consisted of a husband, a wife, lots of children, servants, friends, and other family members. So when Paul addresses the family, he does not envision our modern version of it. He addresses the main family members: wives, husbands, children, fathers, and then slaves. The family reflects the order God desires in the church. Each member is to be responsible to the whole, and love and respect are to serve as the guiding principles within family relationships. Paul and Peter

* 3:11 Literally, Scythian

both use the term "submission" within family and church relationships. While we may not identify with that language in our society, the biblical description is of order and support.

2Pray, *and keep praying.* Be alert and thankful when you pray. 3And while you are at it, add us to your prayers. Pray that God would open doors *and windows and minds and eyes and hearts* for the word so we can go on telling the mystery of the Liberating King, for this is exactly why I am currently imprisoned. 4Pray that I will proclaim this message clearly, *fearlessly,* as I should.

5Be wise when you engage with those outside *the faith community;* make the most of every moment *and every encounter.* 6When you speak the word, speak it gracefully (as if seasoned with salt), so you will know how to rightly respond to everyone.

7-9I am sending this letter by Tychicus and Onesimus, both dear brothers. Tychicus has been a faithful minister and fellow servant in the Lord. He will update you on me and my* situation here, and he will no doubt be an encouragement to you. Onesimus is one of you, and he, too, has been faithful. You will get the whole story from them.

10My cellmate Aristarchus sends his love, as does Mark, Barnabas's cousin. (You've been sent instructions about him, so if he comes to you, welcome him.) 11Jesus, also called Justus, also sends greetings. These are the only workers in God's kingdom here who are of the circumcision, and they are a great comfort to me.

12Epaphras, another one of your hometown fellows and a servant of Jesus, the Liberating King, sends his regards and wants you to know how passionately and sincerely he speaks to the Lord about you. He prays *for your spiritual journey,* that you will continue to mature and stand tall in the kind of confidence that comes from knowing God's will. 13I can testify to his zeal for you and those in Laodicea and Hierapolis.

14Luke, the beloved doctor, says hello, and so does Demas. 15Send my well wishes to the brothers and sisters of Laodicea, especially Nympha and the church that meets in her house. 16After this letter has been read among you, see that it is also read to the church of Laodicea, and make sure you get and read aloud the letter I am sending to them. 17Tell Archippus, "Take care that you complete the service you received in the Lord."

18I, Paul, am signing this letter in my own hand. Remember that I am chained. Grace be with you all.

* 4:7-9 Some manuscripts read "so he may know about your."

＿1 Thessalonians

Letter to the church in Thessalonica
From Paul, the apostle to the Gentiles

Not long after Paul first went to Europe, he arrived in Thessalonica. After only three weeks of ministering in the local synagogue, the Jews rebelled and started a riot. In their indictment of Paul and his coworkers before the local judge, they said, "These people—they're *political agitators* turning the world upside down!"* Paul had spent just a few short weeks with the believers in Thessalonica, but he was greatly blessed by them.

In this warm, fatherly letter, he recalls their true faith, tireless love, and enduring spirit. They truly touched his heart. One can sense the instant affection between these new believers and their spiritual parent. He describes himself as a nursing mother caring for her children and as a father soothing his own children. After encouraging them to continue to grow in the faith and telling how word of their response to the good news has spread throughout the regions of Macedonia and Achaia, Paul pleads with them to avoid sexual defilement because their bodies are the dwelling place of the Holy Spirit and should be kept in holiness and purity. He reminds them of the riches that belong to them, warning them of Satan's activities. He then writes of Timothy's report about their faith. Timothy had been left behind when Paul was forced to move out of the area; later Paul's spirit was buoyed when Timothy spoke of their growth in the faith in the midst of a period of stressful days for Paul.

At this stage in the development of the young church, they were not as greatly hindered by false teachers as were the churches in Asia Minor. But there were some who came from Judea sowing seeds of unrest. Still Paul reminds them of his message of grace to the Gentiles. He then turns to one particular doctrinal issue about those believers who have died and of their standing before God on the coming day of the Lord. Paul tells them that all believers should have confidence whether they die before the return of the Liberating King or they are present at the time of His return. All have obtained salvation and should not fear that they will miss out on the joy of the King's return. He concludes by emphasizing the importance of encouraging and caring for one another while guarding the truth.

* **Note** Acts 17:5-6

1 Paul, Silvanus, and Timothy to the church gathering in Thessalonica, *those living* in God the Father and in the Lord Jesus, the Liberating King.

May grace and peace be yours [from God our Father and the Lord Jesus, our Liberator].*

²We always thank God for all of you in our prayers. ³Your actions on behalf of the *true* faith, your *tireless* toil of love, and your unfailing, unwavering, unending hope in the Master *of us all*—Jesus, the Liberating King—before God our Father, have put you consistently at the forefront of our thoughts. ⁴O brothers and sisters loved by God, we know He has chosen you. ⁵*And here is why: what you experienced in* the good news we brought you was more than words *channeling down your ears*; it came to you as a *life*-empowering, Spirit-infused message that offers complete *hope and* assurance! *We lived transparently before you so that* you would know what sort of people we *truly* are. *We did it* for your sake, ⁶*and apparently it worked.* You have modeled your lives after ours just as we are modeling ours after the Lord. You took *to heart* the word *we taught* with joy inspired by the Holy Spirit, even in the face of trouble. ⁷As a result, you have turned into a model *of faith* yourselves for all the believers in Macedonia and Achaia. ⁸In fact, not only has the message of our Lord thundered from your gathering into Macedonia and Achaia, but everywhere *we go,* your faith in God is talked about so we don't even have to say a thing! ⁹You see, they go on and on telling us *the story of* how you welcomed us *when we were introduced to you;* how you turned toward God and realigned your life to serve the one true living God—leaving your idols *to crumble in the dust*— ¹⁰and how you now await *the return of* His Son from heaven, whom He raised from the dead—namely, Jesus—our rescuer from the wrath to come.

I t's not by chance but by the Spirit that these first-generation church planters would find themselves living their mission to harmonize humankind under God's gentle reign in this most disagreeable city (although it seems there's no place Paul can go without instigating a stripping, a beating, or an imprisoning). Likewise, it is neither by chance (although Paul is known for fueling some pretty powerful conversational flames), nor any human power that would draw people out of their comfy old habits into a radical new way of living. But the miracle really starts to take shape when they find that by trading in their old ways of living, believers took to heart the message of Jesus, and their unshakable faith was shaking up conversations everywhere.

Kingdom work begins at the surrender of life, by giving yourself away and expecting nothing in return. Real change will be ushered in by the loving touch of the Spirit, moving out from people living transparently faithful lives even in the middle of commotion.

2 Brothers and sisters, you yourselves know that our coming to you was not a waste of time. *We accomplished what we set out to do.* ²You remember how we had just suffered through brutal and insulting attacks in Philippi, but because of God, we boldly *stepped into the open to* tell you His good news, even though it would likely mean more conflict for us. ³For we haven't approached you—*or anyone else for that matter*—with some error or impure motives or deceitful agenda, ⁴but as we have been approved by God and entrusted with the good news, that's how we are telling the world. We aren't trying to please everybody, but God, the only One who can truly examine our motives. ⁵As you know, we didn't sandwich the truth between cunning compliments; *we told it straight,* and before the eye of God, we never conspired to make a single cent *off of you.* ⁶We didn't come seeking respect from people—not from you or anyone else— although we could have leveraged our position as emissaries* of the Liberating

* 1:1 Some early manuscripts omit this portion.
* 2:6 Literally, apostles

King. [7]Instead, we proved to be gentle among you, like a nursing mother caring for her own children. [8]We were so taken by you that we not only eagerly shared with you God's good news, but we also shared with you our own lives. That's how much you've come to mean to us.

[9]Don't you remember, my brothers and sisters, how hard we worked and struggled? We worked day and night so that we wouldn't be a burden to any of you and so that we could *continue to* proclaim to you the good news of God. [10]Both you and God can confirm how well we treated the believers: we were always holy, just, and blameless. [11-12]As you know, we comforted and consoled each of you as a father soothes his own children, encouraging you to live lives worthy of God—of the One calling you into His own kingdom and into His glory.

[13]So we have good reason to give thanks to God without pausing. For you have taken into yourselves the word of God we brought to you and received it as a message from God—not just something whipped up by someone like you or us—and that word is at work in you who believe. [14]And, brothers and sisters, you even became imitators of the churches of God in Jesus, the Liberator, that gather in Judea because you were willing to suffer at the hands of your own countrymen as they suffered from the *unbelieving* Judeans. [15]*These are the same people* who killed the Lord Jesus, as well as the prophets, and *continued attacking until they* drove all of us out. They don't just offend God; they are *clearly* hostile to the rest of the people [16]because they are trying to silence our life-saving message to the nations, and as a result, their sins are always filling up *and overflowing*. But in the end, they will face God's wrath.

[17]Brothers and sisters, we are like orphans, separated from you for a short time (in presence, yes, but not in heart), and we desperately desire to see your faces *again*. [18]However, as much as we wanted to come to you—I, Paul, assure you we tried again and again—Satan thwarted our plans. [19]For what is our *true* hope, our *true* joy, our victor's crown in all this? It is nothing if it isn't you standing before our Lord Jesus, the Liberating King, at His arrival. [20]You are our glory! You are our joy!

3 But after all our attempts *to come to you* were frustrated, we decided it was best for Silvanus and me to stay behind in Athens by ourselves [2]and to send Timothy (our dear brother [and servant of God],* our partner in the good news of the Liberating King) to strengthen, *comfort,* and encourage you in your faith [3]so that you won't be shaken by the sufferings *and wither under this stress* that we know lies ahead. [4]*Certainly you remember that* when we were with you, we warned you of the suffering we would have to endure; now, as you well know, it has happened. [5]This is why I couldn't stand it anymore and sent *Timothy* to report on *the state of* your faith: because I was worried the tempter had tested you and, if so, all of our hard work would have come to nothing.

[6]*You can imagine my relief and joy* when Timothy returned to us with such good news about you, about your faith and love *for us,* about how you have such good memories of us and long to see us as much as we long to see you. [7]Hearing this *about your faith,* brothers and sisters, brought comfort to us in our *stress-filled* days of trouble and suffering. [8]For if you are set firmly in the Lord, then we can truly live. [9]What thanks would ever be enough to offer God about you for all the jubilant celebration we'll feel before our God because of you? [10]We remain vigilant in our prayers, night and day praying to *once again* see your faces and to help complete whatever may be lacking in your faith.

*I*t is obvious Paul loved Jesus, and His Spirit reinforced Paul in every way. How else would he be able to walk away from beating after beating or endure trials of the heart and mind? He must have constantly been praying for backup, for those he could and couldn't reach, for those he was with,

* 3:2 Some manuscripts omit this portion.

and for those he had to leave behind. Paul loved Jesus, and so he could not help but embrace the world as passionately as he did.

11May God Himself, our Father, along with our Lord Jesus, [the Liberating King,]* navigate our way to you. 12May the Lord flood you with an *unending, undying* love for one another and for all humanity, like our love for you 13so that your hearts will be reinforced *with His strength*, held blameless and holy before God, our Father, when our Lord Jesus, [the Liberator,]* appears along with all His holy ones. [Amen.]*

4 So finally, brothers and sisters, in the *name of our* Lord Jesus, we ask you, we beg you to remember what we have taught you: live a life that is pleasing to God as you are already doing. Yes, we urge you to keep living and thriving in that life! 2For you know the instructions we gave you; instructions that came through the Lord Jesus. 3Now this is God's will *for you*: set yourselves apart and live holy lives; avoid *polluting yourselves with* sexual defilement. 4Learn how to take charge over your own body, maintaining purity and honor. 5Don't let the swells of lustful passion run your life as they do the outsiders who don't know God. 6Don't violate or take advantage of a fellow believer in such matters. *After all, they are family.* As we told you before and warned you: the Lord will settle the score with anyone who does these things. 7Here's why: God did not call us to live impure, *adulterous, scandalous* lives, but to seek holiness *and purity*. 8If you ignore this message, then you're not only rejecting us but you're rejecting God, the One who has given His Holy Spirit to *live in* you.

9Now there's no need for us to send you instructions on caring for your faith family because God Himself has already taught you how to love outside yourselves. 10And it's evident *you learned that lesson well* by the way you love all the people of Macedonia. Brothers and sisters, we urge you to love even more 11and make it your goal to lead a peaceful life, mind your own business, and keep your hands busy in your work, as we have instructed you. 12That way you will live peacefully with those on the outside, and all your needs will be met without depending on others.

What a beautiful, dramatic transformation! What we're reading is a progression from spoon-feeding people better moral choices to trusting them to live by love according to the conviction of the Spirit, their guide to becoming active participants in the kingdom of God. Paul is acknowledging that there is a power at work that is much greater than his pen. In fact, the same Spirit that inspires Paul's words in these letters is teaching the believers in Thessalonica to live as true believers and teaches us still today.

13Brothers and sisters, we want you to be fully informed about those who have fallen asleep in death so that you will not be overwhelmed with grief like those who live outside of the *true* hope. 14Here's what we believe: since Jesus died and rose again, in the same way, God will bring with Jesus all who have died through Him. 15For we can say all this to you *confidently* because it is the word of the Lord: we who are still alive and left behind when the Lord comes will not precede those who have fallen asleep in death. 16*On that day*, with a command *that thunders into the world*, with a voice of a chief heavenly messenger, and with a blast of God's trumpet, the Lord Himself will descend from heaven; and all those who died in the Liberator will rise *from the dead* first. 17Then we who are alive and left behind will be snatched up together with them into the clouds to meet the Lord in the air. This is how we, *the resurrected and the living*, will be with Him forever. 18So comfort one another *with this hope*, and encourage one another with these words.

* 3:11 The earliest manuscripts omit this portion.
* 3:13 The earliest manuscripts omit this portion.
* 3:13 Most manuscripts omit this word.

Many people fear death; perhaps it's the idea of the unknown that stirs the imagination. Whatever the reason, Paul uses the gentle image of the faithful being asleep as a new perspective on the finality of death. One minute you close your eyes to this world; the next you are celebrating with the Liberating King. Those sleeping will not even miss a moment; it will all happen in the blink of an eye.

5 Now, brothers and sisters, you don't need further instruction *from us or anyone else for that matter* regarding how the seasons and times *will play out.* ²That's because you know *the truth* well enough. The day of the Lord will *race onto the scene and* surprise us like a thief in the night. ³People will be going about their business chanting, "All is well! All is at peace!" and in the next moment, *ruin and destruction* will suddenly seize them as labor pains grip a woman about to give birth; for them there will be no escape. ⁴My brothers and sisters, *it will be different for you.* You do not dwell in the darkness, so that day will not surprise you like a thief. ⁵For you are all children of light. You are sons and daughters of the day. We are not *created* of night, nor are we *owned by* darkness. ⁶So then let's not *give in to sleep or wander around in a stupor* as some do, but let's stay awake and in control. ⁷You see, sleepers sleep through the night, and drunkards drink the night away; ⁸but since we belong to the day, we should stay sober *and in control,* covered with a breastplate of faith and love and a helmet of the hope of salvation. ⁹For God has not destined us, *His chosen,* to face His wrath but to be the heirs of salvation through our Lord Jesus, the Liberating King, ¹⁰who died for us. So regardless of whether we are awake or asleep, we will live together with Him. ¹¹So support one another. Keep building each other up as you have been doing.

¹²Brothers and sisters, we ask you to show appreciation to those who are working hard among you and those who are your leaders as they guide and instruct you in the Lord—*they are priceless.* ¹³When you think about them, let it be with great love in your heart because of all the work they have done. Let peace live *and reign* among you.

¹⁴Brothers and sisters, we strongly advise you to scold the rebels *who devote their lives to wreaking havoc,* to encourage the downcast, to help the *sick and* weak, and to be patient with all of them. ¹⁵Make sure no one returns evil for evil, but always pursue what is good as it affects one another *in the church* but also all people. ¹⁶Celebrate always, ¹⁷pray constantly, and ¹⁸give thanks *to God* no matter what circumstances you find yourself in. (This is God's will for all of you in Jesus, the Liberator.) ¹⁹Don't suppress the Spirit. ²⁰Don't downplay prophecies. ²¹Take a close look at everything, *test it,* then cling to what is good. ²²Put away every form of evil.

²³So now, may the God of peace *make you His own* completely *and* set you apart from the rest. May your spirit, soul, and body be preserved, kept intact and wholly free from any sort of blame at the coming of our Lord Jesus, the Liberating King. ²⁴For the God who calls you is faithful, and He can *be trusted to* make it so.

²⁵Brothers and sisters, *we ask you to* pray for us. ²⁶Greet one another *warmly* with a holy kiss. ²⁷Here is my charge to you before the Lord: have this letter read to all our brothers and sisters [in the faith].*

²⁸May the grace of our Lord Jesus, the Liberating King, be with *all of* you.

Paul calls believers to use the healing power of a hug to comfort those who are hurting or feeling alone. He was not only speaking to the church in Thessalonica; he was addressing all those who long to be a part of a loving and warm community. If you are an integral part of a church that embraces each other and warmly greets one another, rather than merely tolerating one another, then you will find the hardest days to be easier, and even at your loneliest, you will never be alone.

---

* 5:27 Omitted in some early manuscripts

2 Thessalonians

Letter to the church in Thessalonica
From Paul, the apostle to the Gentiles

Compared to the gentle, pastoral tone in Paul's first letter to the Thessalonians, in this letter, he seems anxious over what is going on in this robust capital of Macedonia. First, the intensity of persecution against the gatherings of believers is clearly on the rise in and around Thessalonica. But we cannot know exactly who is bringing the pressure on this young community of faith or why they are doing it. What we do know is that it is increasingly dangerous to be a follower of Jesus in this area. Paul assures these new believers that relief is coming when the Lord returns. God's justice will be satisfied when He punishes those who brought such misery on His people.

Second, apparently someone has forged a letter in Paul's name. In that letter, Paul is said to have written that the day of the Lord has already arrived. He is quick to point out that the letter is not from him and to assure the Thessalonians that the day has not arrived. In fact, it won't come, he says, until restraints are removed and "the rebellious one" is unleashed to start a "great rebellion." But as awful as this sounds, Paul again assures them that almost as soon as it begins, the rebellion will be over when the Lord Jesus returns to annihilate the enemy and his minions.

Third, for reasons not altogether clear, a number of people in the community have quit their jobs and are no longer working. As a result, they have become a nuisance and a burden on the rest. Paul confronts them: "Anyone not willing to work shouldn't get to eat!" As he often does, Paul points to his own example. Although as a traveling missionary he had the right to live off of the hospitality of others, he didn't exercise that right and, instead, went to work daily to take care of his own needs. So he urges the lazy Thessalonians to follow his example. With all these issues going on in the church, no wonder Paul is a bit nervous.

The themes that dominate both 1 and 2 Thessalonians have much to do with matters of last or ultimate things: death, the afterlife, the second coming, judgment, and eternity. Paul addresses these subjects not long after he had planted the church. They were clearly salient issues facing the church in Thessalonica, and they continue to fascinate us today. Still Paul doesn't answer every question we might have about what will happen next as the story of redemption unfolds.

1 Paul, Silvanus, and Timothy, to the church of the Thessalonians *that gathers* in God our Father and in the Liberating King, our Lord Jesus. [2]May grace and peace from God our Father and from the Lord Jesus, our Liberator, be with you.

[3]Brothers and sisters, we cannot help but to thank God for you, which is only appropriate because your faith is growing and expanding and because the love *demonstrated by* each and every one of you is overflowing for one another. [4]So, *of course,* we've proudly bragged about you *within circles of God's people* at other churches *near and far* because, even in *the grip of* much persecution and affliction, you've stood firm in your faith and have persevered. [5]Your sufferings prove that God's judgment is right! The result: your sufferings have made you worthy—worthy of the kingdom of God, which is the very reason why you are suffering *in the first place*! [6]It is only right that God would repay with trouble those who have troubled you [7]and give relief to all of you still bandaging your wounds, as well as to all the rest of us. On that day—when *the clouds draw back displaying* His powerful heavenly messengers, Jesus the Lord will appear from heaven [8]in a fiery blaze dealing out perfect justice to anyone who doesn't know God and anyone who disobeys the good news of our Lord Jesus. [9]*And what's to become of them?* They'll pay for what they've done; their punishment will be eternal destruction. *And what's worse?* They'll be banished from the Lord's presence and glorious power. [10]On that day when He comes, all the saints *in heaven and on earth* will celebrate the glory *of His power* and all who believe will *stand and* be amazed—*this includes you* because you believed us when we testified *on His behalf.* [11]All this is why we are constantly praying for you, so God will make you worthy of the *great* calling *you have received from Him* and will give you the power to accomplish every good intention and work of faith. [12]Then the *great* name of Jesus our Lord will be glorified through your lives, and you will be glorified in Him according to the grace of our God and the Lord Jesus, the Liberating King.

On that day—though men and women have spent lifetimes scanning the skies for the chance that "perhaps today" is the day of salvation—on that day, the confessed lovers of God and the Liberating King will glow with all the wonder of children at Christmas.

There are clear premonitions in the Bible about what we can expect on that day; but can anyone, with our rudimentary human knowledge, know what to expect from God? Jesus confessed that even He did not know the day or the hour when these final moments of history will play out, so how can we truly know? Likely this fear of the unknown is what took root and began to spread like weeds within the Thessalonians' community. And, where fear takes root, faith withers, and people who once focused toward the bright hope of the Son have turned away.

2 Since, brothers and sisters, we are on the topic of the coming of our Lord Jesus, the Liberating King, and how we will all gather together to meet Him, we ask [2]that you don't let your minds get quickly rattled or become anxious because of someone else's so-called "spiritual revelation" or because someone gave you a message or claimed to know of a letter allegedly from us reporting that the day of the Liberating King has already come! [3]Don't be deceived by anyone! *Don't be fooled in any way!* That day, *that amazing day,* won't come until after the *great* rebellion and the unveiling of the rebellious one*—*he who has absolutely no regard for God's law. As the spawn of death,* he delights in destruction. [4]He sets himself up as the *great* adversary *of God* and vies for

* 2:3 Other manuscripts read "man of sin."

a place above all other so-called gods or objects of worship. *If it were possible*, he would even take a seat—*yes, exalt himself*—in the temple of *the one true* God, declaring that he himself is God! [5]Don't you remember me telling you all this the last time we were together? [6]You know what restrains him now *and what will hold him* until the exact time when he will be revealed. [7]For the mystery of sin is already working *its way through the world*; He who holds him back now *will continue to suppress him only until He* is pulled out of the way. [8]It is then that this rebellious one will be *finally* unleashed. But the Lord will slay him with the breath of His mouth, and with the splendor of His coming, He will bring him to his *predetermined* end. [9]Still the rebellious one arrives with all sorts of power, performing signs and fake miracles sanctioned by Satan; [10]he employs every manner of wicked deception to wile away those who are destined for *eternal* death because they reject the love of the truth that leads to salvation. *And do you know what happens next?* [11]Because of this, God sends a deceptive influence over them so they will wander from the truth and believe the lie. [12]As a result, God will judge all of those who did not entrust themselves to the truth *when it faced them* but instead reveled in wickedness.

[13]*But this is not you,* dearly beloved brothers and sisters of the Lord. We cannot help but thank God for you at all times, because from the beginning He handpicked you for salvation through the Spirit's sanctifying work and your belief in the truth. [14]He called you to this when we shared our good news with you. Now you can take part in the glory of our Lord, the Liberating King, Jesus. [15]So, brothers and sisters, *all you need to do now is* stand firm and hold tight to the line of teachings we have passed on to you, whether in person or in a letter. [16-17]Now may our Lord Jesus, the Liberating King, and God our Father, who has loved us, comforted us eternally, and given us a good hope by His grace, bring comfort to your hearts and strengthen *your wills to accomplish* every good work and word.

*P*aul brings the situation to life for them: on one side, the rebellious one opposes God by corrupting God's world, telling lies, and instigating fear; but on the other side, there's Jesus, who came from above and rained mercy over the world with His blood. He stands ready to return to face these enemies. Paul is trying to explain this epic battle with eternal consequences to his friends who have been led astray by false revelations.

3 Brothers and sisters, having shared all this, let me ask you to pray for us. Pray that this message of the Lord will spread quickly and receive the praise and respect *it deserves* from others as it has with you. [2]Pray also that we would all be rescued from *the snares of* harmful, wicked people—after all, not all people are believing. [3]Still, the Lord is true to His promises; He will hold you up and guard you against the evil one. [4]We do not doubt the Lord's intentions for you; we are confident that you are carrying out, and will continue to carry out, the commands we are sending your way. [5]May the Lord guide your hearts into God's *pure* love and keep you headed straight into the strong and sure grip of our *patient* Liberator.

[6]*For the sake of the church,* brothers and sisters, we insist in the name of our Liberating King, the Lord Jesus, that you withdraw from any brother or sister who is out of order and unwilling to work, who is straying from the line of teaching we passed on to all of you. [7]You know how essential it is to imitate us *in the way we live life.* We were never undisciplined [8]nor did we take charity from anyone *while we were with you.* Instead, *you saw* how we worked very hard day and night so we wouldn't be a burden to even one person in the community. [9]We had the right *to depend on your help and hospitality, as you know,* but we wanted to give you a model you could follow, *to lay a path of footprints for you to walk in.* [10]This is exactly why, while with you, we commanded you:

"Anyone not willing to work shouldn't get to eat!" [11]You see, we are hearing that some folks in the community are out of step *with our teaching*; they are idle, not working, but really busy doing nothing—*and yet still expect to be fed*! [12]If this is you or someone else in the community, we insist and urge you in the Lord Jesus, the Liberating King, that you go to work quietly, *earn your keep, put food on your own table,* and supply your own necessities. [13]And to the rest of you, brothers and sisters, never grow tired of doing good.

[14]If someone disregards the instructions of this letter, make a note of who it is and don't have anything to do with that person so that this one may be shamed. [15]Don't consider someone like this an enemy *(he is an enemy only to himself)* but warn him as *if you were redirecting* your own brother.

> *S*ome people in the community are no longer working and have become a burden on everyone else.

Paul tells them to go back to work and stop depending on others for their needs. As he often does, Paul appeals to his own example. Work, properly understood, is not a burden; it is a blessing. God has made us to work; it's in our DNA. It's part of being made in God's image. In fact, we are at our best and happiest when we are using our energy and God-given talents to create, fashion, and make. Those who refuse to work—for whatever reasons—will find they are unfulfilled and a burden to those around them.

[16]And now, *dear friends,* may the Lord of peace Himself grace you with peace always and in everything. May the Lord be present with all of you.

[17]This *final* greeting is by me, Paul, *written* by my own hand. This is my signature, *letting you know that* this is a *genuine* letter from me, and so I write to you:

[18]May the grace of our Lord Jesus, the Liberating King, be with all of you.

1 Timothy

Personal letter to Timothy
From Paul, the apostle to the Gentiles

In the first three decades after Jesus launched the Christian movement, no one was more influential than Paul, the former Jewish zealot. Many of the early churches were begun through his ministry or were strengthened by the "teaching of the apostles" by Paul or his associates. Because misunderstandings and false teachings were enormous problems in those early years of the church, Paul traveled throughout the eastern Mediterranean basin bringing authoritative teaching, church order, and a strong apologetic to control heresy and divisive elements. Paul mentored a select group of apprentices as they traveled together. Those dedicated coworkers included Barnabas, Silas, Luke, John Mark, and Apollos. Although many others are also mentioned in his letters, possibly those closest to him were two young men he called his sons: Timothy and Titus.

Several of Paul's letters have survived, most of which are addressed to groups of believers at various locations. Four of his letters are addressed to individuals: Philemon, 1 and 2 Timothy, and Titus. While each letter is uniquely personal, it's clear that Paul intends that these letters be read in the churches.

In this first letter to Timothy, there is conversational warmth that is not found in the church letters Paul wrote. When Paul moved into Macedonia, he had Timothy remain behind in Ephesus for the purpose of confronting false teaching and bringing order to this influential church through qualified elders and deacons. Timothy is encouraged, despite his young age, to handle difficult problems with authority and maturity. He is told to confront elders, to silence overbearing women, and to avoid activities that will call into question his position and standing in the church. In some ways, Timothy is being thrown into the fire; but he is gifted, called, and well equipped. He will make mistakes; but God is with him, and his spiritual father, Paul, shows great confidence in his young son.

It has become traditional to refer to 1 Timothy, 2 Timothy, and Titus as the Pastoral Epistles because they share a number of common features and themes Paul considered useful to those who lead churches.

1 Paul, an emissary* of Jesus, the Liberating King, commissioned by order of God our Savior and Jesus, the Liberator, our *living and certain* hope, ²to you, Timothy, my true son in the faith.

May the grace, mercy, and peace *that come only* from God the Father and our Lord Jesus, the Liberating King, *mark your life and the lives of everyone touched by your words and deeds.*

³As I said that day I left for Macedonia, stay in Ephesus and instruct the *unruly* people *in the church, once and for all,* to stop teaching a different doctrine. ⁴*Tell them* to turn away from fables and endless genealogies. These activities just cause more arguments and confusion *which end up stalling God's work.* Instead, they should concern themselves with *welcoming in and bringing about* the reign of God, which is all about faith. ⁵Our teaching *about this journey* is intended to bring us to *a single destination—a place where self-giving* love *reigns* from a pure heart, a clean conscience, and a genuine faith. ⁶*Yes,* some have walked away from these traits and have fallen into *a life of endless* blabber and nonsense— ⁷they wish to become scholars of the law, but they don't know what they are talking about, and they make these *grand* pronouncements *but clearly don't understand what they just said.*

⁸You and I know the law is good (if used in the right way), and ⁹we also know the law was not designed for law-abiding people but for lawbreakers and criminals, the ungodly and sin-filled, the unholy and worldly, the father killers and mother killers, the murderers, ¹⁰the sexually immoral and homosexuals, slave dealers, liars, perjurers, and anyone else who acts against the sound doctrine ¹¹laid out in the glorious, *holy, and pure* good news of the blessed God that has been entrusted to me.

¹²I thank our Lord Jesus, the Liberating King, who empowers me, because He saw me as faithful and appointed me to this ministry. ¹³Despite the fact that at one time I was slandering the things of God, persecuting and attacking *His people,* He was still merciful to me because I acted in ignorance apart from faith. ¹⁴But He poured His grace over me, *and I was flooded* in an abundance of the grace and faith and love that can only be found in Jesus, the Liberator.

¹⁵Here's a statement worthy of trust: the Liberator Jesus came into the world to save sinners, and I am the worst of them all. ¹⁶But it is for this reason I was given mercy: by displaying His perfect patience in me, the very worst of all sinners, the Liberator Jesus could show that patience to all who would believe in Him and gain eternal life. ¹⁷May the King eternal, immortal, and invisible, the one and only God, now be honored and glorified forever and ever. Amen.

It is fair to say that Paul never got over the fact that he violently persecuted the church. Even though his rampage against the first followers of Jesus had ended over 20 years earlier, he still grieved because of what he had done. But when Paul was older, he was moved to celebration and praise because God's mercy is always greater than sin. The Lord Jesus called Paul in the midst of his campaign against Him so that he became a public display of our Liberating King's patient love. So, if we think somehow we are too far from God's mercy, then we should think again.

---

¹⁸Timothy, my dear child, I am placing before you a charge *for the mission ahead.* It is in total agreement with the prophecies once spoken over you. *Here it is: with God's message* stirring and directing you, fight the good fight, ¹⁹armed with faith and a good conscience. Some have tried to silence their consciences, wrecking their *lives and ruining their* faith. ²⁰Hymenaeus and Alexander are among these; I have had to hand them over to Satan so they might learn not to speak against God.

---

* 1:1 Literally, apostle

2 So, first and foremost, I urge *God's people to pray*. They should make their requests, petitions, and thanksgivings on behalf of all humanity. ²*Teach them* to pray for kings, or anyone in high places *for that matter* so that we can lead quiet, peaceful lives—reverent, godly, *and holy*—³all of which is good and acceptable before the eyes of God, our Savior ⁴who desires for everyone to be saved and know the truth. ⁵Because

> There is one God
>   and one Mediator between God
>   and us—
> The man Jesus, the Liberator,
> 6 who gave His life as a ransom for all
>   *so that we might have freedom.*

The testimony was given *to me* at just the right time. ⁷This is exactly what I was appointed *to do—tell everyone His story—*as a herald, an emissary,* a teacher of the outsiders in faith and truth. (*Listen, I promise* it's all true. I'm not lying.)

⁸*So here's what you tell them;* here's what I want to see. Men, pray wherever you are. Reach your holy hands *to heaven—*without rage or conflict—*completely open.* ⁹Women, the same goes for you: dress properly, modestly, and appropriately. Don't get carried away in grooming your hair or *seek beauty in* glittering gold, pearls, or expensive clothes. ¹⁰Instead, as is fitting, let good works *decorate your true beauty and* show that you are a woman who claims reverence for God. ¹¹*It's best if* a woman learns quietly and orderly in complete submission.

¹²*Now, Timothy,* it's not my habit to allow women to teach in a way that wrenches authority from a man. *As I said, it's best if* a woman learns quietly and orderly. ¹³*This is* because Adam was formed first *by God*, then Eve. ¹⁴Plus, it wasn't Adam who was tricked; it was she—the woman was the one who was fooled and disobeyed *God's command first.* ¹⁵Still, God, in His faithfulness, will deliver her through childbearing as long as she* remains in faith and love and holiness with self-restraint.

Even in Paul's day, many people were more concerned about their outward appearance than they were about their inner beauty. But with cosmetic surgery and designer labels, we've taken "looks" to a whole new level. Women, in particular, feel the need to lose weight, look beautiful, and carry the right accessories. Paul wants women to pursue the right kind of beauty, the beauty of an inner life fashioned after godliness. In Paul's day, that meant proper respect for their husbands, a willingness to learn the truth, and—unlike Eve—avoiding the enticing claims of the false teachers. It meant, too—more often than not—that they would bear children. But childbirth was a particularly precarious event in the life of a woman; in that day, many women died trying to deliver their babies. While Paul was not promising lack of pain or assurance of safety in childbirth, he was speaking of God's faithfulness and spiritual rewards to those women who lived in faith, love, and holiness, supporting the family and the church in which God placed them.

3 *Here's another* statement you may trust: if anyone is seeking a position as overseer *in the church*, he desires an honorable and important work. ²*Here are the qualifications to look for in* an overseer: a spotless reputation, the husband of one wife, sober-minded, sensible, respectable, welcoming to strangers (*allowing them into his home*), and gifted to teach. ³Disqualify any drunk or violent man. Look for a gentle man; no belligerent fellow can follow this calling. And he should be free from money-lust. ⁴He should exert good control over his own household, and his children should obey and honor him. ⁵(If someone can't manage his own household, then how can he take care of God's family?) ⁶He mustn't be someone recently converted;

* 2:7 Literally, apostle
* 2:15 Literally, they

otherwise, he may become arrogant and fall into the devil's condemnation. [7]He should also be respected *for his character and known as an honorable person* by people outside *of the church* so as to avoid the *trips,* traps, *and pitfalls* of the devil.

[8]The same standards apply to deacons: they should be dignified. Double-talking *hypocrites,* heavy drinkers, and those greedy for ill-gotten gain *should* not *be considered.* [9]They should be people who hold tight to the great mystery of faith with a clear conscience. [10]Put these deacon-candidates to the test first, and if they come through without stumbling, then send them out to serve.

[11]Again the same applies to women *in key positions*; they should also be dignified, not *backstabbing* gossips but self-controlled and faithful to the core.

[12]Now deacons should live faithfully as the husband of one wife and be in control of their households, including their children. [13]Those deacons who serve well will achieve a good standing for themselves *in the community* and have great confidence to walk in the faith that is in Jesus, the Liberating King.

*I*f the church lacks qualified, positive leaders, then it will not succeed in its mission. Paul never provided a job description for "overseers" and "deacons." What he did offer was a list of character traits or qualifications that challenge even the most outstanding disciple. Essentially they were servant-leaders of the church. They gave themselves to the church's well-being by teaching the truth, living a life in imitation of Jesus, and defending the church from false teaching. Paul knew first-hand how important it was to discover, train, and empower capable leaders. Everywhere he went, he invested a lot of himself in coworkers like Timothy. Now it was Timothy's turn to train the next generation.

[14]I am writing all this to you, hoping I can come to you before too long, [15]but in case I am delayed, you will know how one ought to behave as a member of God's family—the assembly of the living God, the pillar and foundation that support the truth—[16]and I think you will agree that the mystery of godliness is great:

> He* was revealed in the flesh,
>   proven right in the Spirit;
> He was seen by the heavenly
>   messengers,
>   preached to outsider nations.
> He was believed in the world,
>   taken up *to the heavens* in glory.

[4] But even so, the Spirit very clearly tells us that in the last times some will abandon the *true* faith because of their devotion to spirits *sent to* deceive *and sabotage,* and *mistakenly they will end up* following the doctrine of demons. [2]*They will be carried away* through the hypocrisy of liars whose consciences have been branded with a red-hot iron, [3]saying, "Don't marry. Don't eat *such-and-such* foods." But God created all these to be received with gratitude by people who hold fast to the faith and really comprehend the truth. [4]For everything God made is good. *That means* nothing should be rejected as long as it's received with a grateful heart, [5]for by God's word and prayer, it is made holy.

*P*aul has addressed moral character. Now he turns to doctrine built on solid truth. The church in Ephesus had both Jewish legalism and pagan immorality in its midst. As members of the church were repeating untruth, various divisions were arising. Some people were believing strange doctrines and passing rumors among themselves. Timothy was expected, as a young man, to step forward and confront these deceptive teachings. Clarifying what is true and exposing what is false is the beginning of healing and right thinking.

* 3:16 Some manuscripts read "God."

⁶Place these *truths* before the brothers and sisters; *let them hear with their own ears so they will truly listen. If you do,* you will be a good servant of Jesus, the Liberator, raised and fed on words of true belief, trained in the good instruction you have so clearly followed. ⁷Reject worldly fables. Refuse old wives' tales. Instead, train yourself toward godliness. ⁸Although training your body has certain payoffs, godliness benefits all things—holding promise for life here and now and promise for the life that is coming. ⁹This statement is worthy of trust and our full acceptance. ¹⁰This is what we work so hard for! This is why we are constantly struggling, because we have an assured hope fixed upon a living God who is the Savior of all humankind—especially all of us who believe.

¹¹So go out and insist on these things. Teach them. ¹²Don't let anyone belittle you because you are young. Instead, show the faithful, *young and old,* an example of how to live: set the standard for how to talk, act, love, and be faithful and pure. ¹³Until I get there, make sure to devote yourself to the public reading of Scripture, to exhortation, and to teaching. ¹⁴Don't neglect the gift that was given to you through the prophecy spoken when the company of the elders laid their hands on you. ¹⁵Cultivate *all* these practices; live by them so that all will see *how* you are advancing *and growing.* ¹⁶Take care of yourself, concentrate on your teaching, and stick with these things. If you do, then you will be effective in bringing salvation to yourself and all who hear you.

Timothy's young age made him an easy target for those who preferred a seasoned leader. But youth, in and of itself, does not disqualify someone from leading (nor is it an automatic qualification). So Paul instructed Timothy not to let his youth and inexperience cause distraction. Instead, he can meet this objection with loving speech, faithful conduct, pure action, and living publicly and transparently as an example for all. According to Paul, this would make it possible for Timothy to lead the church in the public reading of Scripture, encouragement, and teaching.

5 Respect an elderly man. Don't speak to him sharply; appeal to him as you would a father. Treat younger men as brothers, ²elderly women as mothers, and younger women as sisters in all purity.

³Honor widows, *but be discerning about* which ones are truly widows. ⁴If any widow has children or grandchildren, then go to the descendants first and teach them that it is their spiritual responsibility to care for their own family, to repay their parents *and grandparents* because this is what pleases God. ⁵*Here's how you know* if she is a true widow: she is all alone with her hope fixed in God, crying her pleas, prayers, and appeals to God day and night. ⁶But the woman who is living for pleasure is dead as she stands. ⁷You should command these things to everyone to keep them free of blame. ⁸And listen, if someone is not providing for his own relatives and especially his own household, then he is denying the faith and is worse off than an unbeliever.

⁹Now only these should be put on the widow registry: a woman who is at least 60 years old, was a faithful wife to one husband, ¹⁰is well thought of for her good works, has raised children, was hospitable, has washed the feet of the saints, has tended to the sick and suffering, and has devoted herself to do good wherever possible. ¹¹Don't add younger women *to the widow roll* because when their desires for pleasure overtake them, they get careless in their devotion to the Liberating King. Their constant thoughts become, "I want to get married," ¹²and such thoughts disqualify them because they have tossed aside their first commitment *to the Liberator.* ¹³Plus, they get into the habit of being idle—*have you seen them? Watch for them*—not only are they idle, *but they are busy being useless!* They *band together and* roam from house to house, gossiping and

meddling into other people's business; they talk about all sorts of things that should never be spoken of. [14]That's why I think it's best to have the younger widows remarry, have children, and take care of their households so that the enemy gains no opportunity to come with accusations. [15](Unfortunately some have already lined up behind Satan!) [16]Tell any woman of faith: if you have a widow in your family, help her so the church is unencumbered and is free to extend aid to the widows who are truly in need of its help.

[17]Elders who are leading well *should be admired and valued*. Double up on the honor shown them; *care for them well*—especially those *constantly and consistently* teaching the word and preaching. [18]For the Scripture agrees, "Don't muzzle the ox while it is treading out *your* grain,"* and, "The worker deserves his wages."*

[19]Listen, when or if a charge comes against an elder, don't even acknowledge the accusation unless there are two or more witnesses. [20]*Bring any believers* who persist in sinning before the community and publicly scold them so that all the rest will know to fear *sin and its consequences. This is a serious situation.* [21]I challenge you—in front of God, Jesus, the Liberating King, and His select heavenly messengers—to keep these instructions. *Don't back down, never decide a matter beforehand,* and don't do anything out of favoritism.

[22]Don't be too quick to lay hands *upon anyone* or share in the sins of others—stay clean.

[23]*I am worried about your health, Timothy.* Don't just drink water; drink a little wine. It is good for your stomach and will help with your frequent ailments.

[24]Some people's sins are clearly on display *before the world.* They lead the way to the *final* judgment—*the guilty are sentenced practically before they get there to testify! But it's not so easy* with other people because their sins trail behind *and don't catch up to them until later.* [25]The same is true regarding good works; some are there for all to see. Other people's works can be inconspicuous, but *at the final judgment,* they cannot remain hidden.

6 Tell all who labor under the yoke of slavery to treat their masters with honor *and respect, whether or not their masters deserve it.* This will keep God's name and doctrine from being smeared. [2]If their masters are believers, then they should not be insolent toward them just because they are your brothers and sisters. Actually they should be even more determined to serve them because the gains from their good works benefit those who are faithful and loved.

Timothy, teach these *instructions,* and appeal *to those under your ministry to live by them.* [3]If others are teaching otherwise and bringing unhealthy conversations to the community, if they are not sticking to the sound words in the teaching of the Liberating King, our Lord Jesus, if they are not teaching godly principles— [4]then they are swollen with conceit, *filled with self-importance,* and without any proper understanding. *My bet is that* they probably have a gross infatuation with controversy and will endlessly debate over meanings of words. That kind of talk leads to envy, discord, slander, and evil mistrust, [5]and these people constantly bicker because they are depraved in their minds and bereft of the truth. They think somehow that godliness is the way to get ahead. [6]This is ironic because godliness, along with contentment, does put us ahead *but not in the ways some imagine.* [7]You see we came into this world with nothing, and nothing is going with us on the way out! [8]So as long as we are clothed and fed, we should be happy. [9]But those who chase riches are constantly falling into temptation and snares. They are regularly caught by their own stupid and harmful desires, dragged down and pulled under into ruin and destruction. [10]For the love of money—*and what it can buy*—is the root of all sorts of evil. Some already have wandered away from the true faith because they craved what it had to offer, *but when reaching for the prize,* they found their *hands and* hearts pierced with many sorrows.

* 5:18 Deuteronomy 25:4
* 5:18 Compare Luke 10:7

[11]*Timothy, don't let this happen to you—* run away from these things! You are a man of God. Your quest is for justice, godliness, faithfulness, love, perseverance, and gentleness.

> *P*aul shows his confidence in
> Timothy and his great love for
> the young man when he asks him to
> shepherd this divided congregation
> through one problem after another.
> This was truly a heavy load for such a
> young leader even if he was "a man of
> God." He is commanded to "fight the
> good fight" and to hold on to his "good
> confession." With each new genera-
> tion, some individuals are called to
> stand and lead. Paul points to a time
> when the Liberating King will show up
> to set this world straight. In our time,
> we are also called to stand and fight,
> to speak truth into faulty thinking, and
> to stand with others who will follow
> Jesus at any cost.

[12]Fight the good fight of the faith! Cling to the eternal life you were called to when you confessed the good confession before witnesses. [13]Before God, the life-giving Creator of all things, and Jesus, the Liberator, who made the good confession to Pontius Pilate, I urge you: [14]keep His commandment. Have a spotless, indisputable record until the Lord Jesus, our Liberating King, appears *to set this world straight.* [15]In His own perfect time, He will come—blessed is the only Sovereign, the King of kings, and the Lord of lords. [16]He alone possesses immortality; He makes His home in matchless, blinding, brilliant light that no one can approach— no mortal has ever even seen Him, and no human can. So let it be that all honor and eternal power are His. Amen.

[17]Here's what you say to those wealthy in regard to this age: "Don't become high and mighty or place all your hope on a gamble for riches; instead, fix your hope on God, the One who richly provides everything for our enjoyment." [18]*And don't stop there, Timothy.* Tell them to use their wealth for good things; be rich in good works! If they are willing to give generously and share everything, [19]then they will send ahead a great treasure for themselves and build their futures on a solid foundation. As a result, they will surely take hold of eternal life.

[20]O Timothy, protect what was entrusted to you! Walk away from all the godless, empty voices *out there,* and turn aside from objections and arguments that arise from false knowledge. [21](By professing such knowledge, some are missing the mark when it comes to *true* faith.)

May God's grace be with you.

2 Timothy

Personal letter to Timothy
From Paul, the apostle to the Gentiles

This is probably the last letter Paul ever wrote. His tone is different
in this letter as he writes from his prison in Rome, not long before
dying a martyr's death. Gone is his typical optimism that he will soon
be released; now he is all but certain that he has come to the end of
his life. Yet, while there is an air of acceptance of what is to come,
there is also a triumphant tone to this last of the letters from Paul to
individuals. You see, Paul will face whatever may come with a clean
conscience and a clear sense that he has fulfilled the work God had
for him to do. He has run the race of faith and run it well. He will
cross the finish line a winner ready to receive the welcome, the acco-
lades, and the crown from his King, Jesus, the Liberator. But Paul
knows he is not in this race alone. What awaits him is the same victorious destiny that awaits all who love God and long for His kingdom.
For Paul, no one longs more and loves greater than Timothy.

In writing what may have been his last letter to his younger colleague in Ephesus, Paul effectively deputizes him to carry on proclaiming the gospel. As Paul passes from this world to the next, he
wants to be certain that the good news is in good hands. With
Timothy he knows that is the case. Paul encourages Timothy to
become a leader and teacher who stands above the pettiness that
threatens to tear the church apart. But before the martyr's blade sev-
ers Paul's head from his body, Paul wants to see Timothy one last
time. So Paul asks Timothy to come to Rome before winter sets in to
bring a cloak to keep Paul warm in his prison cell and to collect some
books and papers for him.

In this letter, we overhear Paul reminding Timothy of his rich
spiritual heritage and the need to center his attention on the truth
that Paul himself taught. False teachers surround the church, upsetting many and harming the whole community. Jewish legalists are
trying to divide the believers; Gentile pagans are introducing
immorality into the church fellowships; Rome is seeking to destroy
their leaders. Timothy is Paul's last and best hope to counter their
negative influences. To protect the church, the young leader must
avoid their deceptions, follow Paul's example, and be ready to pass
the faith along to the next generation of faithful witnesses.

1 Paul, an emissary* of Jesus, the Liberating King, *commissioned* by God's will according to the promise of life *found only* in Jesus, the Liberator, ²to *you,* my dear child Timothy.

May grace, mercy, and peace from God our Father and the Lord Jesus, our Liberating King, be yours.

³⁻⁴*Timothy,* you are constantly in my prayers. Day and night I remember you before God and give thanks to Him whom I serve with a clean conscience, as did my ancestors. I really want to see you, especially when I remember how you cried *the last time we were together.* Yes, I know it would make me joyful *to see you again.* ⁵What strikes me most is how *natural and* sincere your faith is. I am convinced that the same faith that dwelt in your grandmother, Lois, and your mother, Eunice, abides in you as well. ⁶This is why I *write to* remind you to stir up the gift of God that *was conveyed* to you when I laid my hands upon you. *Even if the embers have cooled, fan them again and keep them ablaze.* ⁷You see, God did not give us a cowardly spirit but a powerful, loving, and disciplined spirit. ⁸So don't be embarrassed to testify about our Lord or for me, His prisoner. Join us in suffering for the good news by the *strength and* power of God. ⁹God has *already* saved us and called us to this holy calling—not because of any good works we may have done, but because of His own intention and because eons and eons ago *(before time itself existed),* He gave us this grace in Jesus, the Liberating King. ¹⁰And now, *the time has come!* That grace has been revealed when our Savior, Jesus, the Liberator, appeared, and *through His resurrection,* He has wiped out death and brought to light life and immortality by way of this good news. ¹¹I was appointed a preacher, emissary, and teacher of this message. ¹²This is exactly why I am suffering. But I am not ashamed because I know Him and I have put my trust in Him. And I am fully certain that He has the ability to protect what I have placed in His care until that day.

¹³Remember the words that you heard from me. Retain them as the model for *healthy and* sound teaching in the faith and love that are *available* in Jesus, the Liberating King. ¹⁴*As for* the precious thing entrusted to you, protect it with the help of the Holy Spirit who dwells within us.

*P*aul singles out several individuals in this letter, some for praise, others for harsh criticism. Timothy is an example of one who stayed true to Jesus and His emissary, the imprisoned Paul. Later Paul mentions Hymenaeus and Philetus as victims of a cancer within the church who have turned from the truth. Demas, too, is drawn into the attractions of the world, while Alexander the coppersmith opposes their message. With so many who have abandoned and opposed Paul, it's refreshing to hear of Onesiphorus, who—against all odds—has stayed true to Paul and often visited him in prison to keep up his spirits. Clearly the message is that many may fall away, but a few will continue to be strong for the Lord.

¹⁵You may know *by now* that all those in Asia have turned their backs on me, including Phygelus and Hermogenes. ¹⁶⁻¹⁷But Onesiphorus was not ashamed of my chains. So when he arrived in Rome, he searched for me and found me. May the Lord show mercy to his house because he has often *stopped by to* refresh my *weary* soul. ¹⁸And may the Lord shower him with divine mercy on the last day. You are well aware of all he did to serve me in Ephesus.

2 But as for you, my child, be empowered by the grace that is in Jesus, the Liberating King. ²Whatever you heard me teach before an audience of witnesses, I want you to pass along to trustworthy people who have the ability to teach others too. ³As a good soldier of Jesus, the Liberating King, *be ready to* suffer with me. ⁴*Remember that* soldiers on active duty

---

* 1:1 Literally, apostle

don't get wrapped up in civilian matters because they want to satisfy those who recruited them. ⁵*Look at it another way:* if someone competes as an athlete, he won't *win the race and* be crowned with the wreath if he breaks the rules. ⁶And the farmer who exhausts himself *in the field* should be the first to taste his harvest. ⁷Think about what I am telling you, *spend time with my words,* and let the Lord give you clarity on all of it.

---

*P*aul has spent his entire life passing the faith along, not only by teaching but by example. He mentored no one more privately and successfully than Timothy. Now, as time marches on, he charges Timothy to pass the faith along to the next generation. Finding and training men and women who will be loyal to God and His emissary is priority one.

---

⁸Remember Jesus, the Liberating King, raised from the dead, descended from David's *royal* line. This is *the crux of* my good news! ⁹This is why I suffer and why I am *bound and* chained like a lawbreaker. But God's word is not in chains! ¹⁰That's why I endure everything for the sake of God's chosen: so that they might experience salvation with lasting, eternal glory through Jesus, the Liberating King. ¹¹Here's a statement you can trust:

If we died with Him,
  we will live with Him.
¹²If we remain *with Him,*
  we will reign alongside Him.
If we deny Him,
  we will be denied by Him.
¹³If we are unfaithful,
  He remains faithful,
For He is not able to deny Himself.

¹⁴Remind others about these things *that I'm telling you.* Warn them before God to stop their useless bickering over words. *After all, splitting hairs* does no good; it only ruins those *forced to* listen *to their meritless arguments.* ¹⁵Timothy, do every-thing you can to present yourself to God as *a man who is fully* genuine, a worker unashamed *of your mission,* a guide capable of leading others *along the correct path defined* by the word of truth. ¹⁶Stay away from ungodly babbling because it will only lead deeper into a godless lifestyle. ¹⁷Once these empty voices start to speak, *Timothy,* they infect and spread, and soon the body is consumed with its cancer.* Hymenaeus and Philetus fell victim to it, and ¹⁸they walked away from the truth by claiming that the day of resurrection has already arrived. They are clearly disrupting the faith of some *who are not well grounded.* ¹⁹Regardless *of what they do or say,* God's foundation is strong and firmly in place, etched with this seal: "The Lord knows the ones who belong to Him,"* and, "Everyone who invokes the name of the Lord ought to stop doing what they know to be wrong."

²⁰*Look,* in the mansions *of the rich and powerful* you will find everything from silver and gold serving bowls to wooden containers and clay jars; some are used for special occasions—*where honor is important*—others are used for more mundane tasks. ²¹So *tell them,* if they will clean up their lives and purify themselves from dishonorable teachings *that lead people astray,* then they can become honorable vessels, consecrated and useful to the Master, made ready for every good work *He has in store.*

²²*Timothy,* run away from youthful desires. Instead, *direct your passion to* chasing after righteousness, faithfulness, love, and peace, along with those who call upon the Lord with pure hearts. ²³Excuse yourself from any *conversation that turns into a* foolish and uninformed debate because you know they only provoke fights. ²⁴As the Lord's slave, you shouldn't *exhaust yourself in* bickering; instead, be gentle—no matter who you are dealing with—*ready and* able to teach, tolerant without resentment, ²⁵gently instructing those who stand up against you. Besides,

---

* 2:17 Literally, gangrene
* 2:19 Numbers 16:5

the time may come when God grants them a change of heart* so that they can arrive at the full knowledge of truth. ²⁶And if they come to their senses, they can escape the devil's snare and walk freed from his captivity and evil bidding.

3 And know this: in the last days, times will be hard. ²You see, the world will be filled with narcissistic, money-grubbing, pretentious, arrogant, and abusive people. They will rebel against their parents, be ungrateful, unholy, ³uncaring, coldhearted, accusing, without restraint, savage, and haters of anything good. ⁴*Expect them to be* treacherous, reckless, swollen with self-importance, and given to love pleasure more than they love God. ⁵Even though they may look or act like godly people, they're not. They deny His power. *I tell you:* Stay away from the likes of these. ⁶They're *snakes* slithering into the houses of vulnerable women, women gaudy with sin, to seduce them. *These reptiles can* capture them because these women are weak and easily swayed by their desires. ⁷They seem always to be learning, but they never seem to gain the full measure of the truth. ⁸And, just like Jannes and Jambres rose up against Moses,* these *ungodly* people defy the truth. Their minds are corrupt, and their faith is *absolutely* worthless. ⁹But they won't get too far because their stupidity will be noticed by everyone, just as it was with Jannes and Jambres.

P aul challenges Timothy to be prepared. Hard times are coming. Things will go from bad to worse, he warns, because pretentious, hostile, hateful, and betraying people are out there. He tells Timothy to stay away from them and to continue to look to Paul's example, enduring in love and recalling how Paul himself has followed Jesus. For if the Liberating King was persecuted, then what should we expect for ourselves? In the midst of this warning, Paul encourages Timothy.

¹⁰*You have been a good student.* You have closely observed how I have lived. You've followed my instructions, my habits, my purpose, my faith, my patience. You've watched how I love and have seen how I endure. *You have been with me* ¹¹through persecutions and sufferings—remember what they did to me in Antioch? in Iconium and Lystra? I endured all of it, and the Lord rescued me from it all! ¹²*The plain truth for all of us who walk this road is that* anyone wishing to live a godly life in Jesus, the Liberator, will be *hunted down and* persecuted. ¹³But as for the wicked and the imposters, they will keep leading and following each other further and further away from the truth. ¹⁴So surely you ought to stick to what you know is certain. All you have learned comes from people you know and trust ¹⁵because since childhood you have known the holy Scriptures, which enable you to be wise *and lead* to salvation through faith in Jesus, the Liberating King. ¹⁶All of Scripture is God-breathed; *in its* inspired *voice, we hear* useful teaching, rebuke, correction, *instruction, and* training for a life that is right ¹⁷so that God's people may be up to the task ahead and have all they need to accomplish every good work.

4 *And now* I bring you this charge before God and Jesus, the Liberating King, the one *destined* to judge the living and the dead, and by His *glorious* appearance and His kingdom: ²*go out and* preach the word! Go out whether it's an opportune time or not! Reprove, warn, and encourage, *but do so* with all the patience and instruction *needed to fulfill your calling* ³because a time will come when some will no longer tolerate sound teaching. Instead, they will live by their own desires; they'll scratch their itching ears by surrounding themselves with teachers who *approve of their lifestyles and* tell them what they want to hear. ⁴They will turn away from the real truth *you have to offer* because

* 2:25 Literally, repentance
* 3:8 Exodus 7:11,22

they prefer the sound of *fables and* myths. [5]But you *must stay focused and* be alert at all times. Tolerate suffering. Accomplish the *good* work of an evangelist, and complete the ministry to which you have been called.

> *T*he message to Timothy is simple: stay focused and fulfill your calling. Paul tells Timothy that he has all that he needs to accomplish the task for which God has prepared him. Over the centuries, this message has been passed down from one generation to the next. As we overhear Paul's encouragement to young Timothy, we can sense that it is our time to stay focused . . . suffer hardships . . . be confident . . . do the work. The church has always moved ahead based upon the faithfulness of a few dedicated saints.

[6]For I am already being poured out, *and the last drops* of this drink offering *are all that remain*; it's almost time for me to leave *and cross the threshold to the next world.* [7]I have fought the good fight, I have *stayed on course and* finished the race, and *through it all,* I have kept believing. [8]I look forward to what's in store for me: a crown of righteousness that the Lord—the always right *and just* judge—will give me that day (but it is not only for me, but for all those who love *and long for* His appearing).

[9]Come to me, *Timothy,* as soon as you can. [10]You see, Demas has fallen for this world, abandoned me, and headed off to Thessalonica. Crescens took off for Galatia. Titus has gone to Dalmatia. [11]Luke is the only one left. Bring Mark with you because he is useful in this work and will help look after me. [12]I sent Tychicus to Ephesus. [13]On your way here, pick up the cloak I left with Carpus in Troas and bring the scrolls—especially the parchments.

[14]*Keep your eye out for* Alexander the coppersmith! He came against me with all sorts of evil—may the Lord pay him back accordingly— [15]so watch your back because he has gone overboard to oppose our message.

[16]*When it was time* for my first defense, no one showed up to support me. Everyone abandoned me (may it not be held against them), [17]except the Lord. He stood by me, strengthened me, and backed the truth I proclaimed with power so it may be heard by all the non-Jews. He rescued me, pried open the lion's jaw, *and snatched me from its teeth.* [18]And *I know* the Lord will continue to rescue me from every *trip, trap, snare, and pitfall of* evil and carry me safely to His heavenly kingdom. May He be glorified throughout eternity. Amen.

[19]Give my regards to Prisca, Aquila, and everyone over at Onesiphorus's house. [20]Erastus stayed in Corinth, and I left Trophimus in Miletus because he was sick. [21]Try your best to come before winter blows in. Eubulus says hello and so do Pudens, Linus, Claudia, and all the brothers and sisters. [22]May the Lord *Jesus, the Liberating King,* be with your spirit, and may His grace be with you. [Amen.]*

* 4:22 The earliest manuscripts omit this word.

Titus

Personal letter to Titus
From Paul, the apostle to the Gentiles

Titus was a young coworker with Paul, a part of the emissary's mission team as he planted churches in Asia Minor and Greece. Because of his affection for and trust in Titus, whom Paul described as his "dear son birthed through our shared faith," Paul often delegated to Titus sensitive and difficult situations. One such situation was in Crete, an island in the Mediterranean with a reputation for dishonesty and thievery that was a haven for pirates. We can infer from this letter that the church on Crete was in its infancy and needed to be taught the basics about church government and foundational doctrine. The primary message of this letter is that good works come from sound doctrine, the shared faith of believers, and the resulting character that reflects a life lived serving God. In spite of the serious nature of the subject matter and the Cretans' situation, Paul managed to convey his teachings on leadership, sound teaching, and church order in a warm, conversational style.

Titus is the only book in Scripture where Jesus is specifically addressed as "our amazing God and Savior, Jesus, the Liberating King." Three times God is identified as the source of salvation, and three times Jesus is referred to as the instrument of salvation. It is one of the few places where the role that each Person in the Trinity has in salvation is isolated: "God our Savior . . . came to save us . . . made us completely new through the Holy Spirit . . . through Jesus, the Liberating King."

Paul makes it abundantly clear that we are each in need of redemption, but we cannot achieve it by anything that we do on our own. Rather, it is the work that only God can do that brings us salvation. Then Paul comes back and commands Titus to remind believers to "be constant in doing the right things." The last imperative in the book is for all believers to learn to "do what is good."

Paul trusted Titus to appoint elders, to sort out unfinished business, and to set a good example for everyone; the future of the church on Crete rested on Titus's shoulders. In this personal look into the work of a young church planter, we find courage, wisdom, and a zeal for serving God. We see what Jesus was looking for when He called a few to follow Him. Here in Titus we find what a truly devoted follower of Jesus looks like.

1 Paul, servant of God and emissary* of Jesus, the Liberating King, on behalf of the faith *that is accepted* by God's chosen people and the knowledge of the *undeniable* truth that leads to godliness.

*P*aul is ready to defend "the undeniable truth that leads to godliness." This truth is pure and honorable, coming from God. In contrast, Paul perceives the constant threat of false teaching that produces chaos, overturns entire families, and is filled with myths and instructions taught by those outside the faith. This counter-truth is filled with lusts and passions that tear down others, and it results in petty debates over family trees with fights and disagreements over the law. The line is clearly drawn between these two truths. Paul leaves no room to sit on the fence; there is no partial truth—the future of the church is at stake.

²*We rest in this hope we've been given*—the hope that we will live forever with our God—*the hope that* He proclaimed *ages and ages* ago (even before time began). And our God *is no liar; He* is not even capable of uttering lies. ³*So we can be sure that* it is in His exact right time that He released His word *into the world—it is now exploding with absolute clarity and life-saving knowledge* through the preaching that God our Savior has commanded into my care.

⁴To you, Titus, my dear son birthed through our shared faith: may grace and peace rest upon you from God the Father and the Liberating King, Jesus our Savior.

⁵I left you on Crete so you could sort out the chaos and the unfinished business and appoint elders *over communities* in each and every city according to my earlier orders. ⁶*Here's what you should look for in an elder:* he should be above suspicion; *if he is married, he should* be the husband of one wife, raise children who believe, and be a person who can't be accused of rough and raucous living. ⁷It is necessary that any overseer *you appoint* be blameless, as he is entrusted with God's mission. *Look for*

someone who isn't pompous or quick to anger, who is not a drunkard, violent, or chasing after seedy gain *or worldly fame.* ⁸*Find a person* who lovingly opens his home to others, who honors goodness, who is thoughtful, fair, devout, self-controlled, and ⁹who clings to the faithful word that was taught because he must be able, not only to encourage people with sound teaching, but also to challenge those who are against it.

¹⁰You see antagonists everywhere; they are rebellious, loose-lipped, and deceitful (especially those who are from the circumcised lot). ¹¹*Their talk must be quashed—* their mouths sealed up because impure teaching is *flying out of their lips and* overturning entire families for the sake of their own squalid gain. ¹²*I'll tell you,* even their own prophet was heard saying, "Chronic liars, foul beasts, and lazy gluttons—that's who you'll meet in Crete." ¹³And he's right! This is why we have to scold them, sometimes severely, so they will be sound in the faith ¹⁴and be able to ignore Jewish myths as well as any commandments given by those who turn away from the truth.

¹⁵*Listen:* to those who are pure, all things are pure. But to those who are tainted, *stained,* and unbelieving, nothing is pure because their minds and their consciences are polluted. ¹⁶They claim, "I know God," but their actions are a slap to His face. They are wretched, disobedient, and useless to any worthwhile cause.

2 As to you, *Titus:* talk to them; give them a good, healthy diet of solid teaching *so they will know the right way to live.*

²*Here's what I want you to* teach the older men: enjoy everything in moderation, respect yourselves *and others*, be sensible, and dedicate yourselves to *living an unbroken* faith demonstrated by your love and perseverance.

³*And here's what I want you to* teach the older women: Be respectful. Steer clear of gossip or drinking too much so that you

* 1:1 Literally, apostle

can teach what is good ⁴to young women. *Be a positive example,* showing them what it is to love their husbands and children, and teach them to ⁵control themselves *in every way* and to be pure. *Train them* to manage the household, to be kind, and to be submissive to their husbands, all of which honor the word of God.

⁶Encourage the young men in the same way: *in every situation,* they should learn to control themselves.

⁷⁻⁸*Titus, you have to* set a good example for everyone. Go out of your way to do what is right, speak the truth with the weight and authority that come from an honest and pure life. No one can argue with that. Then your enemies will cower in shame because they have nothing bad to say against us.

⁹Advise all the servants: Work hard for your masters, and be loyal to them. Strive to please. Don't be rude or sarcastic. ¹⁰Don't steal or embezzle *your masters' property.* Show them you are trustworthy, and all the credit will go to the teaching of God our Savior.

¹¹*We have cause to celebrate* because the grace of God has appeared, offering *the gift of* salvation to all people. ¹²*Grace arrives* with its own instruction: run away from anything that leads us away from God; abandon the lusts and passions of this world; live life now in this age *with awareness* and self-control, doing the right thing and keeping yourselves holy. ¹³*Watch for His return*; expect the blessed hope *we all are to share* when our amazing God and Savior, Jesus, the Liberating King, appears again. ¹⁴He gave His body for our sake and will not only break us free from *the chains of* wickedness, but He will also prepare a community uncorrupted by the world that He would call His own—people who are passionate about doing the right thing.

*A*t times Paul can be unrelenting. As he challenged Timothy in the two letters he addressed to him, Paul also challenges Titus to live the truth he teaches. People are drawn toward God, not through bold argu-ments, but by passionate godliness. We must be passionate about doing the right thing. Our actions tell the story. Our lives are living parables, shouting the mystery of godliness. Paul tells Titus to be bold, to teach with authority, and to not let anyone belittle him. We get a clear picture of a strong, courageous, giant of a man. Titus was sent to the people of Crete—a people short on virtue and long on vice—to fashion a church of loving disciples.

¹⁵*So, Titus,* tell them all these things. Encourage and teach them with all authority—and rebuke them with the same. *You are a man called to serve, so* don't let anyone belittle you.

3 And remind them of this: respect the rulers and the courts. Obey them. Be ready to do what is good and honorable. ²Don't tear down another person with your words. Instead, keep the peace, and be considerate. Be truly humble toward everyone ³because there was a time when we, too, were foolish, rebellious, and deceived—we were slaves to sensual cravings and pleasures, and we spent our lives being spiteful, envious, hated by many, and hating one another. ⁴But then *something happened:* God our Savior and His overpowering love and kindness for humankind entered our world; ⁵He came to save us. It's not that *we earned it* by doing good works or righteous deeds; He came because He is merciful. *Here's what He did:* He brought us *out of our old ways of living* to a new beginning through the washing of regeneration, and He made us completely new through the Holy Spirit, ⁶who was poured out in abundance through Jesus, the Liberating King, our Savior. ⁷*All of this happened* so that through His grace we would be accepted *into God's covenant family* and appointed to be His heirs, full of the hope that comes from *knowing you have* eternal life. ⁸This is a faithful statement *of what we believe.*

Concerning this, I want you to put it out there boldly so that those who believe in

God will be constant in doing the right things, which will benefit all of us. ⁹*Listen,* don't get trapped in brainless debates; avoid competition over family trees *or pedigrees*; stay away from fights and disagreements over the law. They are a waste of your time. ¹⁰If a person is causing divisions *in the community*, warn him once, and if necessary, warn him twice. After that, avoid him completely ¹¹because by then you are sure that you are dealing with a corrupt, sinful person *who has a distorted sense of what's important.* He is determined to condemn himself.

*I*t's easier to ignore a problem than to address it. We do it all the time. But the more we ignore it, the more the problem grows. Paul's advice: deal with it. Go straight at it. Don't beat around the bush. So if someone in the community is causing divisions, Paul prescribes a course of action. Church discipline may sound like something "they" used to do in the days of scarlet letters and the stocks, but if we ignore division, it won't go away. For the church to be strong and God to be honored, the church is to be one.

¹²I am sending either Artemas or Tychicus to you. When one of them arrives, try your best to make your way to me at Nicopolis (I plan to spend the winter there). ¹³Do what you can to get Zenas (the lawyer) and Apollos on their way; make sure they have everything they need. ¹⁴Our people must learn to get involved when a need arises, particularly when the need is urgent. Teach them to do what is good so they won't become unproductive *members of the community.*

¹⁵Everyone with me sends his greetings. Greet all our friends in the faith. May grace be with all of you. [Amen.]*

* 3:15 Some manuscripts omit this word.

Philemon

Personal letter to Philemon of Colossae
From Paul, the apostle to the Gentiles

There's a story behind every letter Paul wrote, and this is an especially vivid one: While Paul was in prison, he wrote to his friend Philemon, a Christian leader in Colossae, about this man's slave Onesimus. Philemon was apparently a well-to-do follower of Jesus, having a house large enough for a church to gather there. He had a good reputation as a man of faith and love. Somewhere he met Paul, and they became good friends and coworkers in Kingdom causes. Onesimus was Philemon's slave who encountered Paul in prison—tradition tells us that Onesimus was a runaway slave who happened to meet Paul when he was under house arrest—and became a believer. For a time, the Lord's imprisoned emissary found Onesimus to be a useful assistant, but eventually he sent Onesimus back to Philemon with an appeal rather than a command: Paul asked Philemon to receive Onesimus back as more than a slave—as a beloved brother.

Surprisingly, Paul addressed this letter to Philemon and the entire church that gathered in his home. What seems at first to be a private letter was meant for public reading. Perhaps Paul hoped to bring a bit of social pressure on Philemon, or perhaps Paul wanted to address the issue of slave treatment to all Christian slave owners. It is clear that Paul used the story of the runaway slave to discuss the larger issues of forgiveness and equality. In the kingdom of God, all relationships must exhibit forgiveness and acceptance of each other, and everyone is an equal participant in salvation, regardless of his or her station in life. The history of humankind is stained by the guilt and pain of slavery. May the words of Paul the emissary echo into our own culture so that we treat all human beings as our brothers and sisters in Jesus, the Liberating King.

¹Paul, a prisoner of Jesus, the Liberating King, *our Savior,* with our brother Timothy to you, beloved Philemon, our fellow worker, and ²to Apphia our sister, to Archippus our fellow soldier, and to the church that gathers in your house. ³May grace and peace from God our Father and the Lord Jesus, the Liberator, surround you.

⁴I am constantly thanking God for you in my prayers ⁵because I keep hearing about your love and faith toward our Lord Jesus and all those set apart for His purposes. *Here's what I've been praying on your behalf:*

> ⁶*Thank You, Father, for Philemon.* I pray that as he goes and tells his story of faith, *he would tell everyone so that* they will know for certain all the good that comes to those who put their trust in the Liberating King.

⁷My brother, because you are out there encouraging and reviving the hearts of fellow saints with such love, this brings great joy and comfort to me.

⁸Although I am bold enough in our Liberator to insist you do the right thing, ⁹instead I choose to appeal to you on account of love. I do this for my own sake since I, Paul, am an old man and am held prisoner because of *my service to* Jesus, the Liberator. ¹⁰I make this request on behalf of my child, Onesimus,* whom I brought to faith during my time in prison. ¹¹Before, he was useless to you, but now he is useful to both you and me. ¹²Listen, I am sending my heart back to you as I send him to stand before you, *although truly* ¹³I wished to keep him at my side to take your place as my helper while I am bound for the good news. ¹⁴But I didn't want to make this decision without *asking for* your permission. This way, any goodwill on your part wouldn't be *seen as* forced, but as your *true and* free desire.

¹⁵Maybe this is the reason why he was supposed to be away from you for this time: so that now you will have him back forever— ¹⁶no longer as a slave, but as more than a slave—as a dear brother. Yes, he is dear to me, but I suspect he will come to mean even more to you, both in the flesh *as a servant* and in the Lord *as a brother.*

> *P*aul knew the truth about the gospel. The good news of Jesus is a powerful social force, capable of making rich and poor, slave and free into beloved brothers. While we erect barriers and put up walls to keep "those people" out—whoever they may be—the cross of Jesus successfully dismantles those walls brick by brick.

¹⁷So if you look upon me as your partner *in this mission,* then I ask you to open your heart to him as you would welcome me. ¹⁸And if he has wronged you or owes you anything, charge it to me. ¹⁹*Look,* I'll put it here in my own handwriting: I, Paul, promise to repay you everything. (Should I remind you that you owe me your life?) ²⁰Indeed, brother, I want you to do me this favor out of obedience to our Lord. It will refresh my heart in the Liberating King. ²¹This letter comes, written with the confidence that you will not only do what I ask, but will also go beyond all I have asked.

²²One more thing: you should get a room ready for me as I hope to be released to you soon in answer to your prayers. ²³Epaphras (my fellow prisoner in Jesus, the Liberating King) greets you, ²⁴as well as my fellow workers Mark, Aristarchus, Demas, and Luke.

²⁵May the grace of the Lord Jesus, the Liberating King, be with your spirit. [Amen.]*

* Verse 10 Literally, useful one
* Verse 25 Some early manuscripts omit this word.

Hebrews

Instruction to Jewish believers
From a leader in the early church

This letter is addressed to Christian believers of Jewish descent in the last half of the first century A.D. Possibly the original audience lived in Rome, since it was written by an unknown leader residing in Italy. For years it was thought that Paul wrote it, but the letter lacks his typical letter-writing features. Still, the themes of the letter, its style, and the reference to Timothy (13:23) suggest that Hebrews comes from somewhere within Paul's circle of friends and coworkers. Because of its tone and structure, some have wondered whether this magnificent letter may have originally been a sermon that was written down and later circulated as a letter. As Origen said, only God knows who wrote it.

The Jewish Christians had faced severe persecution, so severe that some were ready to abandon the faith. The frequent warnings that punctuate the letter indicate that the danger of drifting away was real and imminent. So the author pulls out every argument he can think of to persuade them not to drift away from the Liberating King. Throughout the letter, he compares the person and work of Jesus to the institutions of the Jewish faith. It may well be that those who were in danger of walking away from faith in Him were going back to their Jewish roots. While it is clear that the writer has appreciation for the Hebrew prophets, the mediation of heavenly messengers, Moses, Joshua, the priesthood, and the temple, he argues that in every way the new covenant brought by Jesus is better than, more than, greater than the old covenant.

Throughout the letter, he appeals to Scripture itself to demonstrate how Jesus fulfills the Old Testament promises. At the heart of the letter, he presents Jesus as the Great High Priest, offering Himself as the perfect sacrifice once and for all. Although Jesus' death as a sacrifice is discussed in other New Testament writings, it is central in Hebrews. Further, according to our author, all the earlier promises of God are concentrated in His person and work, particularly in His work on the cross. Jeremiah prophesies that God will one day establish a new covenant, creating a permanent relationship with people of faith and erasing completely the guilt of their sins. Unlike the earlier promises, God's work in reconciling the world through the Liberating King is not a temporary measure because Jesus is the final, full, definitive revelation of God.

1 Long ago, at different times and in different ways, God's voice came to our ancestors through the *Hebrew* prophets. ²But in these last days, it has come to us through His Son, the One who has been given dominion over all things and through whom all worlds were made.

³This is the One who—imprinted with God's image, shimmering with His glory—sustains all that exists through the power of His word. He was seated at the right hand of the *royal* God once He Himself had made the offering that purified all our sins. ⁴This Son of God is elevated as far above the heavenly messengers as His holy name is elevated above theirs.

*M*ost of our images of angels are influenced by art and pop culture—and are far removed from the Bible. The word "angel" literally means "messenger," and it can refer to either a human being or a heavenly being. The Hebrews author is writing about heavenly messengers.

In the Bible, heavenly messengers have several functions—executors of God's judgment, guardians of God's people, heralds of God's plans. They appear at critical moments to chosen people who play important roles in God's salvation, arriving to announce the birth and resurrection of Jesus and to transmit God's law to Moses. They are no more than messengers, created beings, who serve the will of God and His Son. Recognizing their place, they bow before the Son in loving adoration.

⁵For no heavenly messengers have ever heard God address them with these words *of the Psalms*:

You are My Son.
Today I have become Your Father.*

Or *heard Him promise*,

I will be to You a Father,
and You will be My Son.*

⁶Now, when the Son, the firstborn *of God*, was brought into the world, God said,

Let all My heavenly messengers
worship Him.*

⁷Concerning the heavenly messengers, God said,

I make My angels like the winds,
and My servants like a flame.*

⁸But to the Son He said,

God, Your throne is eternal;
You will rule Your kingdom with
the scepter of justice.
⁹You have loved what is right
and hated what is evil;
That is why God, Your God, has
anointed You
with the oil of gladness and lifted
You above Your companions.*

¹⁰And *God continues*,

In the beginning, You, Lord, laid the
foundation of the earth
and set the skies above us with
Your own hands.
¹¹*But while* they will someday pass
away,
You remain *forever*;
when they wear out like old
clothes,
¹²You will roll them up
and change them into something
new.
But You will never change;
Your years will never come to an
end.*

¹³Did God ever say to any of the heavenly messengers,

---

* 1:5 Psalm 2:7
* 1:5 2 Samuel 7:14
* 1:6 Deuteronomy 32:43 (LXX and DSS only)
* 1:7 Psalm 104:4
* 1:8-9 Psalm 45:6-7
* 1:10-12 Psalm 102:25-27

Sit here, at My right hand, *in the seat
of honor;*
and I'll put all Your enemies under
Your feet?*

¹⁴*No, of course not.* The heavenly messengers are only spirits and servants, sent out
to minister to those who will certainly
inherit salvation.

2 That is why we ought to pay even
closer attention to the voice that has
been speaking so that we will never
drift away from it. ²For if the words *of
instruction and inspiration* brought by
heaven's messengers were valid, and *if we
live in a universe where* sin and disobedience receive their just rewards, ³then how
will we escape *destruction* if we ignore this
great salvation? We heard it first from our
Lord Jesus, then from those who passed on
His teaching. ⁴God also testifies to this
truth by signs and wonders and miracles
and the gifts of the Holy Spirit lighting on
those He chooses.

*T*his letter is punctuated with
passages that sound an alarm:
danger, both imminent and eternal, is
at hand. The real danger is the gentle
erosion of rock-solid commitments.
How often it happens! A person
makes a decision to follow the Liberator. He practically explodes with joy.
Then life happens and the invisible
forces that shape culture—in our
world, the idols of consumerism, rela-
tivism, and materialism—begin their
exacting work to shape us into an
image that no longer reflects our
Savior. Over and over again, the writer
warns us to be careful. Don't neglect
this great salvation. Make sure the
anchor holds.

⁵Now clearly God didn't set up the heavenly messengers *to bring the final word or
to rule over the world that is coming.* ⁶I
have read something somewhere:

I can't help but wonder why You
care about mortals
or choose to love the son of man.
⁷⁻⁸Though he was born below the
heavenly messengers,
You honored the son of man like
royalty,
crowning him with glory and
honor,
Raising him above all earthly things,
placing everything under his feet.*

*H*ere is God's Son: Creator—
Sustainer—Great High Priest.
What made Jesus perfect for the task
was something that could only happen
on earth. He had to enter our fallen
world, take on our feeble flesh, and
suffer a violent death at the hands of
an angry mob. Suffering is what ultimately made Jesus right for what we
needed. What happened next was
nothing short of brilliant!

When God placed everything under the
Son of Man, He didn't leave out anything.
Maybe we don't see all that happening yet;
⁹but what we do see is Jesus, born a little
lower than the heavenly messengers, who
is now crowned with glory and honor
because He *willingly* suffered and died.
And He did that so that through God's
grace, He might taste death on behalf of
everyone.
¹⁰It only makes sense that God, by
whom and for whom everything exists,
would choose to bring many of us to His
side by using suffering to perfect Jesus, *the
founder of our faith,* the pioneer of our salvation. ¹¹*As I will show you,* it's important
that the One who brings us to God and
those who are brought to God become one,
since we are all from one Father. This is
why Jesus was not ashamed to call us
His family, ¹²saying, *in the words of the
psalmist,*

* 1:13 Psalm 110:1
* 2:6-8 Psalm 8:4-6

I will speak Your Name to My
brothers and sisters
when I praise You in the midst of
the community.*

[13]And, *in the words of Isaiah,*

I will wait for the Eternal One.*

And, again,

Look, here I am with the children
God has given Me.*

[14]Since we, the children, are all creatures
of flesh and blood, Jesus took on flesh and
blood, so that by dying He could destroy
the one who held power over death—the
devil— [15]and destroy the fear of death that
has always held people captive.

[16]So notice—His concern here is not for
the welfare of the heavenly messengers,
but for the children of Abraham. [17]He had
to become as human as His sisters and
brothers *so that when the time came,* He
could become a merciful and faithful high
priest of God called to reconcile a sinful
people. [18]Since He has also been tested by
suffering, He can help us when we are
tested.

3 So all of you who are holy partners in
a heavenly calling, let's turn our attention to Jesus, the Emissary *of God* and
High Priest, who brought us the faith we
profess, [2]and compare Him to Moses, *who
also brought words from God.* Both of them
were faithful to their missions, to the One
who called them. [3]But we value Jesus more
than Moses, in the same way that we value
a builder more than the house he builds.
[4]Every house is built by someone, but the
builder of all things is God. [5]Moses *brought
healing and redemption to his people* as a
faithful servant in God's house, and he was
a witness to the things that would be spoken later. [6]But *Jesus,* the Liberating King,
was faithful as a Son of that house. (We
become that house, if we're able to hold on
to the confident hope we have *in God* until
the end.)

For the first-century Jewish-
Christian audience, Moses was
the rescuer of Hebrew slaves out of
bondage in Egypt—the receiver of
God's law and the covenant. He shepherds the children of Israel safely
through the desert for 40 years and
leads them to the brink of the promised land. He was indeed a remarkable
man. Yet what Jesus accomplished for
us is on a totally different level. Moses
was indeed faithful to God and accomplished a great deal as God's servant.
Jesus, too, was faithful to God, but He
accomplished what Moses could not
because He's God's very own Son.

[7]Listen now, to the voice of the Holy Spirit.
The psalmist wrote,

Today, if you listen to His voice,
[8]Don't harden your hearts the way
they did
in the bitter uprising *at Meribah*
[9]Where your ancestors tested Me
though they had seen My
marvelous power.
[10]For the 40 years *they traveled on
to the land that I had promised
them,*
That generation *broke My heart.*
Grieving and angry, I said, "Their
hearts are unfaithful;
they don't know what I want from
them."
[11]That is why I swore in anger
they would never enter *salvation's*
rest.*

[12]Brothers and sisters, pay close attention
so you won't develop an evil and unbelieving heart that causes you to abandon the
living God. [13]Encourage each other every
day—for as long as we can still say
"today"—so none of you let the deceitful-

* 2:12 Psalm 22:22
* 2:13 Isaiah 8:17
* 2:13 Isaiah 8:18
* 3:7-11 Psalm 95:7-11

ness of sin harden your hearts. [14]*There's no need for it.* For we have become partners with the Liberating King—if we can just hold on to our confidence, *gained when we became faithful,* until the end.

[15]Look at the lines *from the psalm* again:

> Today, if you listen to His voice,
> Don't harden your hearts the way
>   they did
>   in the bitter uprising *at Meribah.*

[16]Now who, *exactly, was God talking to then?*—who heard and rebelled? Wasn't it all of those whom Moses led out of Egypt? [17]And who made God angry for an entire generation? Wasn't it those who sinned *against Him,* those whose bodies are still buried in the wilderness, *the site of that uprising?* [18]It was those disobedient ones who God swore would never enter into salvation's rest. [19]And we can see that they couldn't enter because they did not believe.

4 That's why, as long as that promise of entering God's rest remains open to us, we should be careful that none of us seem to fall short ourselves. [2]Those people in the wilderness heard *God's* good news, just as we have heard it, but the message they heard didn't do them any good since it wasn't combined with belief. [3]We who believe are entering into salvation's rest, as He said,

> That is why I swore in anger
>   they would never enter *salvation's*
>   rest,*

even though God's works were finished from the very creation of the world. [4](For didn't God say that on the seventh day *of creation* He rested from all His works?* [5]And doesn't God say in the psalm that they would never enter into *salvation's* rest?*)

*T*here is much discussion of "rest" in what we are calling the First Testament. God rests on the seventh day after creation. In the Ten Commandments, God commands His people to remember the Sabbath, to keep it holy and rest. The God who released them from oppressive work commands them to remember the Sabbath day, keep it holy, and do no work. But think about what this means. By letting go of daily work, they declared their absolute dependence on God to meet their needs. In our hustle-and-bustle world, we, too, should remember that we do not live by the work of our hands, but by the bread and Word that God supplies.

But as wonderful as this rest is, a greater rest is yet to come when we will be released from all suffering, and when we will inherit the earth and all its beauty. Jesus, the Liberating King, embodies this greater rest that still awaits the people of God, a people fashioned through obedience and faith. If some fail to enter that rest, it is not because God has not called. It is because we fail to answer the call.

[6]So *if God prepared a place of rest, and* those who were given the good news didn't enter because they chose disobedience *over faith,* then it remains open for us to enter. [7]Once again, God has fixed a day, and that day is "today," as David said so much later when he wrote *in the psalm* quoted earlier:

> Today, if you listen to His voice,
> Don't harden your hearts.*

[8]Now if Joshua had been able to lead those who followed him into God's rest, would God then have spoken this way? [9]There still remains a place of rest, a true Sabbath, for the people of God [10]because those who enter into salvation's rest lay down their labors in the same way that God entered into a Sabbath rest from His.

* 4:3 Psalm 95:11
* 4:4 Genesis 2:2
* 4:5 Psalm 95:11
* 4:7 Psalm 95:7-8

[11]So let us move forward to enter this rest, so that none of us fall into the kind of faithless disobedience that prevented them from entering. [12]The word of God, *you see*, is alive and moving; sharper than a double-edged sword; piercing the divide between soul and spirit, joints and marrow; able to judge the thoughts and will of the heart. [13]No creature can hide from God: God sees all. Everyone and everything is exposed, opened for His inspection, and He's the One we will have to explain ourselves to.

> *T*he word of God is powerful. By God's word, everything finds a rhythm, a place, an order. God's word fills, empowers, enlivens, and redeems us. But its powers of creation and redemption are only one edge of God's double-edged sword. The word cuts both ways. The same word that creates and redeems also divides and destroys. It pierces and exposes us. It lays us bare.

[14]Since we have a great High Priest, Jesus, the Son of God who has passed through the heavens *from death into new life with God,* let us hold tightly to our faith. [15]For Jesus is not some high priest who has no sympathy for our weaknesses *and flaws.* He has already been tested in every way that we are tested; but He emerged victorious, without failing God. [16]So let us step boldly to the throne of grace, where we can find mercy and grace to help when we need it most.

5 *Remember what I said earlier about the role of the high priest,* even the ones chosen by human beings? The job of every high priest is reconciliation: approaching God on behalf of others and offering Him gifts and sacrifices to repair the damage caused by our sins *against God and each other.* [2]The high priest should have compassion for those who are ignorant of the faith and those who fall out of the faith because he also has wrestled with human weakness, [3]and so the priest must

offer sacrifices both for his sins and for those of the people. [4]*The office of high priest and* the honor that goes along with it isn't one that someone just takes. One must be set aside, called by God, just as God called Aaron, *the brother of Moses.*

[5]In the same way, the Liberating King didn't call Himself but was appointed to His priestly office by God, who said to Him,

You are My Son.
   Today I have become Your Father,*

[6]and who also says elsewhere,

You are a priest forever—
   in the *honored* order of
      Melchizedek.*

> *W*hen Hebrews refers to Jesus as the Great High Priest, it is because He accomplishes something beautiful and unique by becoming the sacrifice that atones for sins once and for all. But the fact that Jesus is our High Priest and the ultimate sacrifice doesn't set aside our need—or God's call—that we be priests for each other. You see, the same Bible that assigns Jesus so lofty a role as Great High Priest, seated with God upon the throne of heaven, also says, "own up to your sins to one another and pray for one another. In the end, you may be healed." These are not mutually exclusive ideas.
>
> Whenever you share a cup of cold water in Jesus' name, you're a priest. You're communicating the grace of God in the gift of cool, clean water. Whenever you pray for another person, you're a priest. You're carrying the concerns and needs of another to heaven. Whenever you share the good news of God's love with someone, you're working as a priest. You are a

* 5:5 Psalm 2:7
* 5:6 Psalm 110:4

conduit for the best news anyone could ever hear.

But if we are honest, there are times that we need a priest too, right? If we are to be like Him, we must be a priest and allow someone else to be a priest for us. There are problems and pains so deep and sins so intractable that we need a person of flesh and blood. When we say, "Pray for me," we're saying, "I need a priest." We need someone to join us in carrying our concerns to God.

[7]When Jesus was *on the earth, a creature of* flesh *and blood,* He offered up prayers and pleas, groans and tears to the One who could save Him from death. He was heard because He approached God with reverence. [8]Although He was a Son, Jesus learned obedience through the things He suffered [9]and was perfected *through that suffering* so that He could become the way of eternal salvation for all those who hear and follow Him [10]and could be—as God called Him to be—a High Priest in the order of Melchizedek.

[11]I have a lot more to say about this, but it may be hard for you to follow since you've become dull in your understanding. [12]By this time, you ought to be teachers yourselves, yet I feel like you want me to reteach you the most basic things that God wants you to know. It's almost like you're *a baby again, coddled at your mother's breast,* nursing, not ready for solid food. [13]No one who lives on milk alone can know the ins and outs of what it means to be righteous *and pursue justice;* that's because he is only a baby. [14]But solid food is for those who have come of age, for those who have learned through practice to distinguish good from evil.

6 So let's push on toward a more perfect understanding and move beyond just the basic teachings of the Liberating King. There's no reason to rehash the fundamentals: repenting from *what you loved in* your old dead lives, believing in God *as our Creator and Redeemer,* [2]teaching about

the importance of ceremonial washings, *setting aside those called to service through* the *ritual* laying on of hands, the coming resurrection of those who have died, and God's final judgment *of all people for all time.* [3]No, we will move on toward perfection, if God wills it.

*I*t's clear that Jesus wanted us to grow and mature in our faith. Those who don't move beyond the basics—tasting the gifts and powers of the new creation, partaking in the Spirit and the word of God—and then fall away bring shame to the Liberating King and produce nothing but briars and brambles. There is no stagnant life in the Kingdom. Either you grow and produce a blessing or you languish and descend into a curse. Be warned.

[4-6]It is impossible to restore the changed heart of the one who has fallen from faith—who has already been enlightened, has tasted the gift of new life from God, has shared in the power of the Holy Spirit, and has known the goodness of God's revelation and the powers of the coming age. If such a person falls away, it's as though that one were crucifying the Son of God all over again and holding Him up to ridicule. [7]*You see,* God blesses the ground that drinks of the rain and then produces a bountiful crop for those who cultivate it. [8]But land that produces nothing but thorns and brambles? That land is worthless and in danger of being cursed, burned to the bare earth.

[9]But *listen,* my friends—we don't mean to completely discourage you with such talk. We are convinced that you are made for better things, the things of salvation, [10]because God is not unjust *or unfair.* He won't overlook the work you have done or the love you have carried to each other in His name while doing His work, as you are still doing. [11]We want you all to continue working until the end so that you'll realize the certainty that comes with hope [12]and not grow lazy. We want you to walk in the footsteps of the faithful *who came before*

you, from whom you can learn to be steadfast in pursuing the promises *of God.*

[13]Remember when God made His promise to Abraham? He had to swear by Himself, there being no one greater: [14]"Surely I will bless you and multiply your descendants."* [15]And after Abraham had endured with patience, he obtained the promise he had hoped for. [16]When swearing an oath to confirm what they are saying, humans swear by someone greater than themselves and so bring their arguments to an end. [17]In the same way, when God wanted to confirm His promise as true and unchangeable, He swore an oath to the heirs of that promise. [18]So God has given us two unchanging things: *His promise and His oath.* These prove that it is impossible for God to lie. As a result, we who come to God for refuge might be encouraged to seize that hope that is set before us. [19]That hope is real and true, an anchor to steady our *restless* souls, a hope that leads us back behind the curtain *to where God is (as the high priests did in the days when reconciliation flowed from sacrifices in the temple)* [20]and back into the place where Jesus, who went ahead on our behalf, has entered since He has become a High Priest forever in the order of Melchizedek.

7 *In the Book of Genesis, we read about when* Melchizedek, the king of Salem and priest of the Most High God, met Abraham as he returned from defeating King *Chedorlaomer* and his allies. Melchizedek blessed our ancestor, and [2]Abraham gave him a tenth of everything captured in the battle.*

Let's look more closely at Melchizedek. First, his name means "king of righteousness"; and *his title,* king of Salem, means "king of peace." [3]The Scriptures don't name his mother or father or descendants, and they don't record his birth or his death. We could say he's like the Son of God: eternal, a priest forever.

*M*elchizedek is perhaps the most mysterious figure in Scripture. He appears for the first time in Genesis 14:17-20 as Abraham returns from battle against Chedorlaomer and his allies. The name "Melchizedek" shows up again in Psalm 110, a song of David that is widely used to celebrate the coronation of the Davidic kings in Jerusalem. When God installs His king upon the throne of Jerusalem, He promises to vanquish his enemies and establish him as an eternal priest according to the honored order of Melchizedek.

But who was Melchizedek? In the Book of Hebrews, Jesus is often referred to as "a priest forever according to the order of Melchizedek." Psalm 110 was never far away as the writer unpacked this theme. Melchizedek is taken as a type of Jesus, and the few details we know about him are mined and sculpted into a beautiful image of how Jesus' priesthood belongs to an ancient, perhaps heavenly, order of priests that contrasts the temple priests in Jerusalem.

Some have wondered whether Melchizedek is actually the Liberating King, a manifestation of God's Son in the early, raw days of God's dealings with Abraham and his people. After all, the name "Melchizedek" means "king of righteousness," and his role as king of Salem makes him the "king of peace (*shalom*)." But this letter doesn't demand this association. It demands only that we see what prophets and sages had seen already. This mysterious Melchizedek, king of righteousness and peace, was a precursor to the Prince of Peace. In his brief appearance in Genesis and in Psalms, he opened a window into the mystery of God and His plan to redeem the world. With Melchizedek, we see an eternal priest who represents a higher order of kings and priests that includes Jesus who comes to rule the world with justice and to exercise perfectly an eternal priesthood.

* 6:14 Genesis 22:17
* 7:2 Genesis 14:17-20

[4]And just imagine how great this man was, that even our *great and honorable* patriarch Abraham gave him a tenth of the spoils. [5]Compare him to the priests *who serve in our temple,* the descendants of Levi, who were given a commandment in the law *of Moses to collect one-tenth of the income of the tribes of Israel.* The priests took that tithe from their own people, even though they were also descended from Abraham. [6]But this man, *Melchizedek,* who did not belong to that Levite ancestry, collected a tenth part of Abraham's income; and although Abraham had received the promises, it was Melchizedek who blessed Abraham. [7]Now I don't have to tell you that it is the lesser one who receives a blessing from the greater, *so Melchizedek must be considered superior even to the patriarch from whom we descend.* [8]*In the case of the priests descended from Levi,* they are mortal men who receive a tithe *of one-tenth;* but the Scriptures record no death of *Melchizedek,* the one who received Abraham's tithe. [9]I guess you could even say that Levi, who receives our tithes, originally paid tithes through Abraham [10]because he was still unborn and only a part of his ancestor when Abraham met Melchizedek.

[11]If a perfect method *of reconciling with God*—a perfect priesthood—had been found in the sons of Levi (a priesthood that communicated God's law to the people), then why *would the Scriptures* speak of another priest, a priest according to the order of Melchizedek, instead of, say, from the order of Aaron? What would be the need for it? *It would reflect a new way of relating to God* [12]because when there is a change in the priesthood there must be a corresponding change in the law as well. [13]We're talking about someone who comes from another tribe, from which no member has ever served at God's altar. [14]It's clear that *Jesus,* our Lord, descended from the tribe of Judah, but Moses never spoke about priests from that tribe. [15]Doesn't it seem obvious? *Jesus is* a priest who resembles Melchizedek *in so many ways;* [16] He is someone who has become a priest, not because of some requirement about human lineage, but because of the power of a life without end. [17]*Remember, the psalmist says,*

> You are a priest forever—
> in the *honored* order of
> Melchizedek.*

[18]Because the earlier commandment was weak and did not reconcile us to God effectively, it was set aside— [19]after all, the law could not make anyone or anything perfect. God has now introduced a new and better hope, through which we may draw near to Him, [20]and confirmed it by swearing to it. [21]The *Levite order of* priests took office without an oath, but this man *Jesus* became a priest through God's oath:

> The Eternal One has sworn an oath
> and cannot change His mind:
> You are a priest forever.*

[22]So we can see that Jesus has become the guarantee of a *new and* better covenant. [23]Further, the prior priesthood *of the sons of Levi* has included many priests because death cut short their service, [24]but Jesus holds His priesthood permanently because He lives His resurrected life forever. [25]From such a vantage, He is able to save those who approach God through Him for all time because He will forever live to be their advocate *in the presence of God.*

[26]It is only fitting that we should have a High Priest who is devoted to God, blameless, pure, *compassionate toward but* separate from sinners, and exalted by God to the highest place of honor. [27]Unlike other high priests, He does not first need to make atonement every day for His own sins, and only then for His people's, because He already made atonement, reconciling us with God once and forever when He offered Himself as a sacrifice. [28]The law made imperfect men high priests; but after that law was given, God swore an oath that made His perfected Son a high priest for all time.

* 7:17 Psalm 110:4
* 7:21 Psalm 110:4

8 So let me sum up what we've covered so far, *for there is much we have said*: we have a High Priest, *a perfect Priest* who sits *in the place of honor* in the highest heavens, at the right hand of the throne of the Majestic One, [2]a Minister within the *heavenly* sanctuary set up by the Lord, not by human hands.

[3]*As I have said*, it is the role of every high priest to offer gifts and sacrifices *to God*, so clearly this Priest of ours must have something to offer as well. [4]If He were on earth, then He would not be a priest at all because there are already priests who can offer gifts according to the law *of Moses, and they offer worship daily in a sanctuary set up according to the laws of God given to Moses—* [5]a sanctuary that is only a copy and shadow of the heavenly sanctuary. *We know this because* God admonished Moses as he set up the tent for the Lord's sanctuary: "Be sure that you make everything according to the pattern I showed you on the mountain."* [6]But now Jesus has taken on a new and improved priestly ministry; and in that respect, He has been made the Mediator of a better covenant established on better promises. [7]Remember, if the first covenant had been able to reconcile everyone to God, there would be no reason for a second covenant.

---

*J*eremiah was known as the prophet of the new covenant. Hundreds of years before the birth of the Liberating King, Jeremiah heard the voice of God and saw what God had planned: a new day. A new law inscribed in the mind, written on the heart. A new and abiding knowledge of God. A new covenant where mercy runs deep and sins are forgiven and forgotten.

---

[8]God found fault with the priests when He said *through the prophet Jeremiah*:

"Look! The time is coming," the
   Eternal Lord says,
   "when I will bring about a new
covenant with the people of
   Israel and Judah.
[9]It will not be like the covenant I
   made with their ancestors
   when I took them by the hand
   and led them out of *slavery in* the
      land of Egypt.
They did not remain faithful to that
   covenant,
   so," the Eternal One says, "I turned
      away from them.
[10]But when those days are over," the
   Eternal One says, "I will make
   this *kind of* covenant with the
      people of Israel:
I will put My laws on their minds
   and write them upon their hearts.
I will be their God,
   and they will be My people.
[11]*In those days*, they won't need to
   teach each other *My ways*
   or to say to each other, 'Know the
      Eternal.'
In those days, all will know Me,
   from the least to the greatest.
[12]I will be merciful when they fail,
   and I will erase their sins *and
      wicked acts* out of My memory
   as though they had never existed."*

[13]With the words "a new covenant," God made the first covenant old, and what is old and no longer effective will soon fade away completely.

9 Think about that first covenant for a moment. Even that covenant had *rules and* regulations about how to worship and *how to set up* an earthly sanctuary *for God*. [2]*In the Book of Exodus*,* we read how the first tent was set aside for worship—we call it the holy place—how inside it they placed an oil lamp, a table, and the bread that was consecrated *to God*. [3]Behind a second *dividing* curtain, there was another tent which is called the most holy of holy places. [4]In there they placed the golden

* 8:5 Exodus 25:40
* 8:8-12 Jeremiah 31:31-34
* 9:2 Exodus 25–26

incense altar and the golden ark of the covenant. Inside the ark were the golden urn that contained manna (*the miraculous food God gave our ancestors in the desert*), Aaron's rod that budded,* and the tablets of the covenant *that Moses brought down from the mountain.* ⁵Above the ark were the *golden images of* heavenly beings* of glory who shadowed the mercy seat.

I cannot go into any greater detail about this now; *I don't have the time and space.* ⁶*Here's my point:* When all is prepared as it is supposed to be, the priests go back and forth daily into the first tent to carry out the duties described in the law. ⁷But once a year, the high priest goes alone into that second tent, the holy of holies, with blood to offer for himself and the unwitting errors of the people. ⁸As long as that first tent is standing, the Holy Spirit shows us, the way into the most holy of holy places has not yet been revealed to us. ⁹That first tent symbolizes the present time, when gifts and sacrifices can be offered; but it can't change the *heart and* conscience of the worshiper. ¹⁰These gifts and sacrifices deal only with regulations for the body—food and drink and various kinds of *ritual* cleansings necessary until the time comes to make things truly right.

¹¹When the Liberating King arrived as High Priest of the good that comes to us, *He entered* through a greater and more perfect sanctuary that was not part of the earthly creation or made by human hands. ¹²He entered once for all time into the most holy of holy places—entering, not with the blood of goats or calves *or some other prescribed animal*, but offering His own blood and thus obtaining redemption for us for all time. ¹³*Think about it:* if the blood of bulls or of goats, or the sprinkling of ashes from a heifer, restores the defiled to bodily cleanliness *and wholeness*, ¹⁴then how much more powerful is the blood of the Liberating King, who through the eternal Spirit offered Himself *as a* spotless *sacrifice* to God, purifying your conscience from the dead things *of the world* to the service of the living God?

¹⁵This is why Jesus is the mediator of the new covenant: through His death, He

delivered us from the sins that we had built up under the first covenant, and His death has made it possible for all who are called to receive God's promised inheritance. ¹⁶For whenever there is a testament—a will—the death of the one who made it must be confirmed ¹⁷because a will takes effect only at the death of its maker; it has no validity as long as the maker is still alive. ¹⁸Even the first *testament—the first covenant*—required blood to be put into action. ¹⁹When Moses had given all the laws of God to the people, he took the blood of calves and of goats, water, hyssop, and scarlet wool, and he sprinkled the scroll and all the people, ²⁰telling them, "This is the blood of the covenant that God has commanded for us."* ²¹In the same way, he also sprinkled blood upon the sanctuary and upon the vessels used in worship. ²²Under the law, it's almost the case that everything is purified in connection with blood; without the shedding of blood, sin cannot be forgiven.

*H*ere we are reminded that what is most real, what is most true, is the unseen reality. Take the temple in Jerusalem, the holiest place on earth. It seemed real enough, with its massive stone construction, constant flurry of rituals, and daily offerings. But the writer tells us that it was merely a copy or shadow of another place, the heavenly temple. Whatever took place in this shadowy temple could not change the realities of alienation from God, sin, and death.

Every year on a most special day, the Day of Atonement, the high priest would don his priestly garb and enter the most holy of holy places in the temple. His task was profound, his duty dangerous: he must appear before God carrying the sins of his people. All the sins of Israel were

* 9:4 Numbers 17:1-13
* 9:5 Greek *cheroubin*, a class of angels
* 9:20 Exodus 24:8

concentrated in him as he carried the blood of the sacrifice into the divine presence. But there was another day, a Day of Atonement unlike any other, when Jesus, the Liberating King, concentrated in Himself the sins of the world, hanging on a cross not far from the temple's holiest chamber. Indeed, for a time, He became sin.* But unlike the high priest in the earthly copy of the temple, the crucified and risen Jesus entered the true temple of heaven and was ushered into the divine presence. He who had embodied the sins of the world carried His own blood into the holy presence. At that moment, everything changed.

23Since what was given in the old covenant was the earthly sketch of the heavenly reality, this was sufficient to cleanse the earthly sanctuary; but in heaven, a more perfect sacrifice was needed. 24The Liberating King did not enter into handcrafted sacred spaces—imperfect copies of heavenly originals—but into heaven itself, where He stands in the presence of God on our behalf. 25There He does not offer Himself over and over as a sacrifice (as the high priest on earth does when he enters the most holy of holy places each year with blood other than his own) 26because that would require His repeated suffering since the beginning of the world. No, He has appeared once now, at the end of the age, to put away sin forever by offering Himself as a sacrifice.

27Just as mortals are appointed to die once and then to experience a judgment, 28so the Liberating King was offered once in death to bear the sins of many and will appear a second time, not to deal again with sin, but to rescue those who eagerly await His return.

10 We have seen how the law is simply a shadow of the good things to come. Since it is not the perfect form of these ultimate realities, the offering year after year of these imperfect sacrifices cannot bring perfection to those who

come forward to worship. 2If they had served this purpose, wouldn't the repetition of these sacrifices have become unnecessary? If they had worked—and cleansed the worshipers—then one sacrifice would have taken away their consciousness of sin. 3But these sacrifices actually remind us that we sin again and again, year after year. 4In the end, the blood of bulls and of goats is powerless to take away sins. 5So when Jesus came into the world, He said,

Sacrifices and offerings were not
what You wanted,
but instead a body that You
prepared for Me.
6Burnt offerings and sin offerings
were not what pleased You.
7Then I said, "See, I have come to do
Your will, God,
as it is inscribed of Me in the scroll
of the book."*

8Now when it says that God doesn't want and He takes no real pleasure in sacrifices, burnt offerings, and sin offerings (even though the law calls for them), 9and follows this with "See, I have come to do Your will,"* He effectively takes away the first—animal sacrifice—in order to establish the second, more perfect sacrifice. 10By God's will, we are made holy through the offering of the body of Jesus, the Liberating King, once and for all time.

11In the first covenant, every day every priest stands at his post serving, offering over and over those same sacrifices that can never take away sin. 12But after the Liberator stepped up to offer His single sacrifice for sins for all time, He sat down in the position of honor at the right hand of God. 13Since then, He has been waiting for the day when He rests His feet on His enemies' backs,* as the psalm says. 14With one perfect offering, Jesus has perfected forever those who are being made holy,

* Note 2 Corinthians 5:16
* 10:5-7 Psalm 40:6-8
* 10:9 Psalm 40:7
* 10:13 Psalm 110:1

¹⁵as the Holy Spirit keeps testifying to us *through the prophet Jeremiah.* After he says:

¹⁶"But when those days are over," says
　　the Eternal One, "I will make
　　this *kind of* covenant with the
　　people *of Israel:*
I will put My laws in their hearts
　　and write them upon their
　　minds."*

Then He adds,

¹⁷I will erase their sins and wicked
　　acts out of My memory
　　as though they had never existed.

¹⁸When there is forgiveness such as this, there is no longer any need to make an offering for sin.

¹⁹So, my friends, Jesus by His blood gives us courage to enter the most holy of holy places. ²⁰He has created for us a new and living way through the curtain, that is, through His flesh. ²¹Since we have a great High Priest who presides over the house of God, ²²let us draw near with true hearts full of faith, with hearts rinsed clean of any evil conscience, and with bodies cleansed with pure water.

---

*T*he word translated "church" in English Bibles means literally "assembly of the called"; it implies that we have said "yes" to God's call in our lives. We assemble because we are "the called," called into being by God Himself. Some people, for reasons only they know, choose to live their Christian faith in isolation. When they do, they cut themselves off from the gifts, encouragement, and vitality of others. And perhaps, just as tragically, they deprive the church of the grace and life God has invested in them.

---

²³Let us hold strong to the confession of our hope, never wavering, since the One who promised it to us is faithful. ²⁴Let us consider how to inspire each other to greater love and to righteous deeds, ²⁵not forgetting to gather as a community, as some have forgotten, but encouraging each other, especially as the day *of His return* approaches.

²⁶Now if we willfully persist in sin after receiving such knowledge of the truth, then there is no sacrifice left for those sins— ²⁷only the fearful prospect of judgment and a fierce fire that will consume God's adversaries. ²⁸*Remember that* those who depart from the law of Moses are put to death without mercy based on the testimony of two or three witnesses.* ²⁹Just think how much more severe the punishment will be for those who have turned their backs on the Son of God, trampled on the blood of the covenant by which He made them holy, and outraged the Spirit of grace *with their contempt.* ³⁰For we know the God who said, "Vengeance belongs to Me—I will repay,"* also said, "The Eternal One will judge His people."* ³¹It is truly a frightening thing to be on the wrong side of the living God.

³²Instead, think back to the days after you were first enlightened *and understood who Jesus was:* when you endured all sorts of suffering *in the name of the Lord,* ³³when people held you up for public scorn and ridicule, or when they abused your partners and companions in the faith. ³⁴Remember how you had compassion for those in prison and how you cheerfully accepted the seizure of your possessions, knowing that you have a far greater and more enduring possession. ³⁵Remember this, and do not abandon your confidence, which will lead to rich rewards. ³⁶Simply endure, for when you have done as God requires of you, you will receive the promise. ³⁷*As the prophet Habakkuk said,*

In a little while, *only a little longer,*
　　the One who is coming will come
　　　　without delay.

---

* 10:16 Jeremiah 31:33
* 10:17 Jeremiah 31:34
* 10:28 Deuteronomy 17:6
* 10:30 Deuteronomy 32:35
* 10:30 Deuteronomy 32:36

[38]But My righteous one must live by
faith,
    for if he gives up his commitment,
My soul will have no pleasure in
    him.*

[39]*My friends*, we are not those who give
up hope and so are lost; but we are of the
company who live by faith and so are
saved.

11 Faith is the assurance of things you
have hoped for, the absolute conviction that there are realities you've
never seen. [2]It was by faith that our forebears were approved. [3]Through faith we
understand that the universe was created
by the word of God; everything we now see
was fashioned from that which is invisible.

> Stories of faith and faithfulness
> make up most of the First
> Testament. The writer of Hebrews
> recalls some of the most memorable
> examples of how people of faith lived
> their lives. But what is faith? Faith is
> more than belief; it is trust, assurance,
> and firm conviction. Ironically most of
> those who lived by faith never fully
> realized the promises God had made.
> Like us they journeyed as strangers
> and exiles, longing for another country.
> We should remember their patient
> faith when we face prolonged hard-
> ships and allow the trials we face to
> strengthen our faith rather than
> destroy it.

[4]By faith Abel presented to God a sacrifice
more acceptable than *his brother* Cain's. *By
faith* Abel learned he was righteous, as God
Himself testified by approving his offering.
And by faith he still speaks, although his
voice was silenced by death.

[5]By faith Enoch was carried up *into
heaven* so that he did not see death; no
one could find him because God had taken
him. Before he was taken up, it was said
of him that he had pleased God. [6]Without
faith no one can please God because the
one coming to God must believe He exists,
and He rewards those who come seeking.

[7]By faith Noah respected God's warning
regarding *the flood—the likes of* which no
one had ever seen—and built an ark that
saved his family. In this he condemned the
world and inherited the righteousness that
comes by faith.

[8]By faith Abraham heard God's call to
travel to a place he would one day receive
as an inheritance; and he obeyed, not
knowing where God's call would take him.
[9]By faith he journeyed to the land of the
promise as a foreigner; he lived in tents, as
did Isaac and Jacob, his fellow heirs to the
promise [10]because Abraham looked ahead
to a city with foundations, a city laid out
and built by God.

[11]By faith *Abraham's wife* Sarah became
fertile long after menopause because she
believed God would be faithful to His promise. [12]So from this man, who was almost at
death's door, God brought forth descendants,
as many as the stars in the sky and as impossible to count as the sands of the shore.

[13]All these I have mentioned died in
faith without receiving the full promises,
although they saw the fulfillment as
though from a distance. These people
accepted and confessed that they were
strangers and foreigners on this earth
[14]because people who speak like this make
it plain that they are still seeking a homeland. [15]If this was only a bit of nostalgia for
a time and place they left behind, then certainly they might have turned around and
returned. [16]But such saints as these look
forward to a far better place, a heavenly
country. So God is not ashamed to be
called their God because He has prepared
a *heavenly* city for them.

[17]By faith Abraham, when he endured
God's testing, offered *his beloved son* Isaac *as
a sacrifice.* The one who had received God's
promise was willing to offer his only son;
[18]God had told him, "It is through Isaac that
your descendants will bear your name,"*
[19]and he concluded that God was capable

* 10:37-38 Habakkuk 2:3-4
* 11:18 Genesis 21:12

of raising him from the dead, which, figuratively, is indeed what happened.

²⁰By faith Isaac spoke blessings upon his sons, Jacob and Esau, concerning things yet to come.

²¹By faith Jacob, when he was dying, blessed the sons of *his son* Joseph, bowing in worship as he leaned upon his staff.*

²²By faith Joseph, at his life's end, predicted that the children of Israel would make an exodus from Egypt; and he gave instructions that his bones *be buried in the land they would someday reach.*

²³By faith Moses' parents hid him for three months after he was born because they saw that he was handsome; and they did not fear Pharaoh's directive *that all male Hebrew children were to be slain.*

²⁴By faith Moses, when he was grown, refused to be identified solely as the son of Pharaoh's daughter ²⁵and chose instead to share the sufferings of the people of God, not just living in sin and ease for a time. ²⁶He considered the abuse *that he and the people of God had* suffered in anticipation of the Liberator more valuable than all the riches of Egypt because he looked ahead to the coming reward.

²⁷By faith Moses left Egypt, unafraid of Pharaoh's wrath and moving forward as though he could see the invisible God. ²⁸Through faith, he instituted the Passover and the sprinkling of blood *on the doorposts among the Hebrews* so that the destroyer of the firstborn would pass over their homes without harming them. ²⁹By faith the people crossed through the Red Sea as if they were walking on dry land, although the pursuing Egyptian *soldiers* were drowned when they tried to follow.

³⁰By faith the walls of Jericho toppled after the people had circled them for seven days. ³¹By faith the prostitute Rahab welcomed the *Hebrew* spies *into her home* so that she did not perish with the unbelievers.

³²I could speak more *of faith*; I could talk until time itself ran out. If I continued, I could speak *of the examples* of Gideon, Barak, Samson, and Jephthah, of David and Samuel and all the prophets. ³³*I could give accounts of* people alive with faith who conquered kingdoms, brought justice,

obtained promises, and closed the mouths of hungry lions. ³⁴*I could tell you how people of faith* doused raging fires, escaped the edge of the sword, made the weak strong, and—stoking great valor among the champions of God—sent opposing armies into panicked flight.

³⁵I could speak of faith bringing women their loved ones back from death and how the faithful accepted torture instead of earthly deliverance because they believed they would obtain a better *life in the* resurrection. ³⁶Others suffered mockery and whippings; they were placed in chains and in prisons. ³⁷The faithful were stoned, sawn in two,* killed by the sword, clothed only in sheepskins and goatskins; they were penniless, afflicted, and tormented. ³⁸The world was not worthy of these saints. They wandered across deserts, crossed mountains, and lived in the caves, cracks, and crevasses of the earth.

³⁹These, though commended by God for their great faith, did not receive what was promised. ⁴⁰That promise has awaited us, who receive the better thing that God has provided *in these last days,* so that with us, our forebears might finally see the promise completed.

12 So since we stand surrounded by *all those who have gone before,* an enormous cloud of witnesses, let us drop every extra weight, every sin that clings to us *and slackens our pace,* and let us run with endurance the long race set before us.

We are not alone. We may feel like we are the only ones, but we aren't. We are surrounded by a cloud of martyrs, an army of witnesses. They have run the race of faith and finished well. They have passed the baton to us. It is now our turn.

* 11:21 Genesis 47:31
* 11:37 Some early manuscripts read "sawn in two." Other early manuscripts read "tempted." Later manuscripts have both.

[2]Now stay focused on Jesus, who designed and perfected our faith. He endured the cross and ignored the shame *of that death* because He focused on the joy that was set before Him; and now He is seated beside God on the throne, *a place of honor.*

[3]Consider *the life of* the One who endured such *personal attacks and* hostility from sinners so that you will not grow weary or lose heart. [4]Among you, in your striving against sin, none has resisted *the pressure* to the point of death, as He did.

---

*G*od "disciplines" His "disciples." The words look so similar because at the heart of both is "training." Life—with all its hardships and hostilities—is God's training ground for those who belong to Him. What is He training us for? Not just to live here and now, but to have life in the age to come. He's training us to share His life and holiness. He's training us so that our lives might be instruments of peace and justice.

---

[5]Indeed, you seem to have forgotten the proverb directed to you as children:

My child, do not ignore the
     instruction that comes from the
     Lord,
  or lose heart when He steps in to
     correct you;
[6]For the Lord disciplines those He
     loves,
  and He corrects each one He takes
     as His own.*

[7]Endure hardship as God's discipline *and rejoice* that He is treating you as His children, for what child doesn't experience discipline from a parent? [8]But if you are not experiencing the correction that all true children receive, then it may be that you are not His children after all. [9]Remember, when our human parents disciplined us, we respected them. *If that was true,* shouldn't we respect and live under the correction of the Father of all spirits even more? [10]Our parents corrected us for

a time as seemed good to them, but God only corrects us to our good so that we may share in His holiness.

[11]*I'll admit it:* when punishment is happening, it never seems pleasant, only painful. Later, though, it yields the peaceful fruit called righteousness to everyone who has been trained by it. [12]So lift up your hands that are dangling and brace your weakened knees. [13]Make straight paths for your feet so that what is lame *in you* won't be put out of joint, but will heal.

[14]Pursue peace with everyone, and holiness, since no one will see God without it. [15]Watch carefully that no one falls short of God's favor, that no well of bitterness springs up to trouble you and throw many others off the path. [16]Watch that no one becomes wicked and vile like Esau, *the son of Isaac,* who for a single meal sold his invaluable birthright. [17]You know *from the stories of the patriarchs* that later, when he wished to claim his blessing, he was turned away. He could not reverse his action even though he shed bitter tears over it.

---

*T*he Bible is a brutally honest book. It contains stories of liars, murderers, and adulterers; and these are the good guys. If we read the Bible looking only for positive role models, we'll be quickly disappointed. But if we are honest with ourselves and confess our own faults, we will find in Scripture, particularly in the First Testament, that we have much in common with many broken saints of the past. But we must not stay broken. We must follow their path to transformation through repentance and faith. Repentance means a change of heart, a change of mind, and ultimately a change of how we live. God's grace comes to us and enables us to turn away from our sin and to turn back to Him.

---

[18]You have not come to the place that can be touched (*as Israel did at Mount Sinai*),

* 12:5-6 Proverbs 3:11-12

to a mountain crowned with blazing fire, darkness, gloom, and a windstorm, [19]or to the blast of a trumpet and the sound of a voice—a voice and message so harsh that the people begged not to hear another word. [20](They could not bear the command that was given: that if even a beast touches the mountain, it must be stoned. [21]The sight was so terrible that even Moses said, "I am trembling with fear.")*

[22]No, instead you have come to Mount Zion, to the city of the living God, to the heavenly Jerusalem, to heavenly messengers unnumbered, to a joyful feast, [23]to the assembly of the firstborn registered as heaven's citizens, to God the righteous Judge of all, and to the spirits of all the righteous who have been perfected. [24]You have come to Jesus, the mediator of a new covenant between God and humanity, and to His sprinkled blood, which speaks a greater word than the blood of Abel crying out from the earth.

[25]See that you don't turn away from the One who is speaking; for if the ones who heard and refused the One who spoke on earth faced punishment, then how much more will we suffer if we turn away from the One speaking from heaven— [26]the One whose voice in earlier times shook the earth now makes another promise: "Yet once more I will shake not only the earth, but also the heavens"?* [27]The phrase, "Yet once more," means that those things that can be shaken will be removed and taken away, namely, the first creation. As a result, those things that remain cannot be shaken. [28]Therefore, let us all be thankful that we are a part of an unshakable Kingdom and offer to God worship that pleases Him and reflects the awe and reverence we have toward Him [29]for He is like a fierce fire that consumes everything.*

13 Let love continue among you. Let it be the air you take in, that uncurls within you, and that extends between you. [2]Don't forget to extend your hospitality to all—even to strangers—for as you know, some have unknowingly shown kindness to heavenly messengers in this way. [3]Remember those imprisoned for their beliefs as if you were their cellmate; and care for any who suffer harsh treatment, as you are all one body.

[4]Hold marriage in high esteem, all of you, and keep the marriage bed pure because God will judge those who commit sexual sins.

[5]Keep your lives free from the love of money, and be content with what you have because He has said, "I will never leave you; I will always be by your side."* [6]Because of this promise, we may boldly say,

> The Lord is my help—
> I won't be afraid of anything.
> How can anyone harm me?*

[7]Listen to your leaders, who have spoken God's word to you. Notice the fruits of their lives and mirror their faith.

[8]Jesus, the Liberating King, is always the same: yesterday, today, and forever. [9]Do not be carried away by diverse and strange ways of believing or worshiping. It is good for the heart to be strengthened by grace, not by regulations about what you can eat (which do no good even for those who observe them). [10]We approach an altar from which those who stand before the altar in the tent have no right to eat. [11]In the past, the bodies of those animals whose blood was carried into the sanctuary by the high priest to take away sin were all burned outside the camp. [12](In the same way, Jesus suffered and bled outside the city walls of Jerusalem to sanctify the people.)

*I*f we are honest, we have to admit that coming to Christ and entering into His church ruins us—at least as far as this world is concerned. If we identify with Him in His suffering and

* 12:20-21 Exodus 19:12-13; Deuteronomy 9:19
* 12:26 Haggai 2:6,21
* 12:29 Deuteronomy 4:24
* 13:5 Deuteronomy 31:6
* 13:6 Psalm 118:6

rejection, we will become a reproachful irritation to the powers that rule this culture. If we ever felt at home in this world—if we ever sensed that we belonged—then we would wake up one day to discover that we will never be at home again until we enter the city of God. By entering through Jesus, our Liberating King, we become citizens of another city, subjects of another king. As long as we are here, we should live as resident aliens longing to go home.

[13]Let's then go out to Him and resolve to bear the insult and abuse that He endured. [14]For as long as we are here, we do not live in any permanent city, but are looking for the city that is to come.

[15]Through Jesus, then, let us keep offering to God our own sacrifice, the praise of lips that confess His name without ceasing. [16]Let's not neglect what is good and share what we have, for these sacrifices also please God.

[17]Listen to your leaders and submit to their authority *over the community,* for they are on constant watch to protect your souls and someday they must give account. Give them reason to be joyful and not to regret their duty, for that will be of no good to you.

[18-19]Pray for us, for we have no doubt that our consciences are clean and that we seek to live honestly in all things. [9]But please pray for me that I may be restored to you even more quickly.

[20]Now may the God of peace, who brought the great Shepherd of the sheep, our Lord Jesus, back from the dead through the blood of the new everlasting covenant, [21]perfect you in every good work as you work God's will. May God do in you *only* those things that are pleasing in His sight, through Jesus, the Liberating King, to whom we give glory always and forever. Amen.

[22]Please, brothers and sisters, pay attention to this word of exhortation, for I have written only a few words to you.

[23]I want to tell you that our brother Timothy has been set free; and if he arrives soon, he will come with me when I see you next.

[24]Give my greetings to your leaders and to all of God's people. Those of Italy greet you.

[25]May grace always be with you.

James

Letter to Jewish believers
From James, the brother of Jesus

Can you imagine what it would be like to grow up with Jesus as your brother? Now there's a reason for some serious sibling rivalry! Picture yourself in a devout Jewish home during the first century. The Scriptures are recited from memory, and the faith is celebrated in festivals that provide a rhythm to life. Then one day at the synagogue your brother gets up and starts preaching, healing the sick, and casting out demons. Some people in the community are calling Him a lunatic. Others think He has made a deal with the devil. How would you handle the situation? Jesus' family tried to interrupt His public displays on several occasions because they wanted to protect Him and guard the family from shame.

As an adult son, it was James's responsibility to defend the family honor. At first, James was not convinced that his brother was the Savior and Liberating King. What turned this skeptic into a passionate believer and the prominent leader of the Jerusalem church? It was after the crucifixion, when he saw the risen Jesus with his own eyes, that James's doubts disappeared. Later, at a time when the church was divided over how to incorporate Gentile believers into the formerly all-Jewish group, James stepped forward and showed great leadership. He boldly said, "So here is my counsel: we should not burden these outsiders who are turning to God."* Thus James endorsed Paul's ministry, and with his leadership the brother of Jesus enabled the spread of Christianity to the world.

In this letter, James is writing to his fellow Jewish Christians scattered throughout the world in the first century. He is concerned with preserving a connection between his Jewish heritage and the movement begun by Jesus. James does not see himself as a leader of a new religion, but as a Jew who follows the Jewish Liberator. Like Peter and Paul, James views the gospel as the fulfillment of promises in the Hebrew Scriptures. But now, through the work of Jesus, outsiders are invited to follow as well. James takes honoring the law very seriously; in this letter, he encourages all believers to simply practice what they preach.

* **Note** Acts 15:19

1 James, a servant of God and our Lord Jesus, the Liberating King, to *all the people of God,* the twelve tribes *of Israel* who are spread across the earth: I send you my warmest welcome!

²⁻⁴Don't run from tests and hardships, brothers and sisters. *As difficult as they are, you will ultimately* find joy in them; if you embrace them, your faith will blossom under pressure *and teach you true patience* as you endure. *And true patience brought on by* endurance will equip you to complete the long journey *and cross the finish line*—mature, complete, and wanting nothing. ⁵If you don't have all the wisdom needed *for this journey,* then all you have to do is ask God for it, and God, *who is never stingy when it comes to wisdom,* will grant all that you need. He gives lavishly and never scolds you for asking.

> *W*e all need wisdom for the journey of life. Wisdom, as James understands it, is the ability to live life well and make good decisions. Wisdom doesn't come from old age or hard knocks. Wisdom begins with knowing and depending absolutely on God. He supplies all the wisdom we need when we ask. But when we try to go it alone—without God and on our own—trouble is around the corner.

⁶The key is that your request be anchored by your single-minded commitment *to God.* Those who depend only on their own judgment are like *those lost on* the seas, carried away by any wave or picked up by any wind. ⁷Those *adrift on their own wisdom* shouldn't assume the Lord will *rescue them or* bring them anything. ⁸*The splinter of* divided loyalty *shatters your compass and* leaves you dizzy and confused.

⁹If you are a brother of humble means, celebrate the fact that God has raised you up. ¹⁰If you are rich *and seemingly invincible,* savor the humble reality that you are a mere mortal who will vanish like a flower withering in the field. ¹¹The sun rises with a blazing heat that *dries the earth and* causes the flower to wither and fall to the ground and its beauty to fade and die. In the same way, the rich will fall and die in the midst of their busy lives.

¹²Happy is the person who can hold up under the trials of life. *At the right time,* he'll know God's sweet approval and will be crowned with life *by God—the ultimate Victor.* As God has promised, the crown awaits all who love Him.

¹³No one who is tempted should *ever be confused and* say that God is testing him. The One who created us is free from evil and can't be tempted, so He doesn't tempt anyone. ¹⁴⁻¹⁵When a person is carried away with desire, lured by lust, and when desire becomes the focus and takes control (*even when the thing we desire may seem good*), it gives birth to sin. Sin, *left to itself,* becomes full-grown; *as it gathers strength, it chokes out life* and produces death.

¹⁶My dearly loved brothers and sisters, don't be misled. ¹⁷When you receive a good gift, a perfect gift, *an unexpected gift, do not be surprised.* It comes to us courtesy of the Father of lights. *But remember this:* He is not one to trick you or hide in the shadows. He *is consistently good and* does not change. ¹⁸*Remember, too, that* we have a special role in His plan. He calls us to life by His message of truth so that we will show the rest of His creatures *His goodness and love.*

¹⁹ Listen, open your ears, harness your desire to speak, and don't get worked up into a rage so easily, my brothers and sisters. ²⁰Human anger *is a futile exercise that* will never produce God's kind of justice *in this world.* ²¹So walk out on your corrupt liaison with smut and depraved living, and humbly welcome the word *of truth that will blossom like the seed* of salvation planted in your souls.

²²*Prove that you are real.* Put the word into action. If you think hearing is what matters most, *you're delusional*—you are going to find you have been deceived.

> *G*od the Father is the giver of all things and is looking for every opportunity to bless us. But many people have difficulty trusting and receiving

good things, even when those things come from God. The problem is that we not only have trouble trusting God's work in our lives, but we also don't always respond to God's Word. People often hear the Scriptures but don't really listen. People store truths in their brains but never put them to use. For James, the only good religion is religion lived out every day.

²³⁻²⁴*It seems like some people have amnesia.* If they fail to do what God requires, it's like they forget the word as soon as they hear it. One minute they look in the mirror, and the next they forget who they are and what they look like. *It sounds ridiculous, but it is true.* ²⁵However, it is possible to open your eyes and take in the beautiful, perfect truth found in God's law of liberty *and live by it.* If you pursue that path and actually do what God has commanded, then you will avoid *the many distractions that lead to* an amnesia of all true things and you will be blessed.

²⁶If you *put yourself on a pedestal,* thinking you have become a role model in all things religious, but you can't control your mouth, then think again. Your mouth exposes your heart, and your religion is useless. ²⁷Real, true religion from God the Father's perspective is about caring for the orphans and widows who suffer needlessly and resisting the evil influence of the world.

2 My brothers and sisters, *I know you've heard this before, but* stop playing favorites! Do not try to blend the genuine faith of our glorious Lord Jesus, the Liberating King, *with your silly pretentiousness.* ²If an affluent gentleman enters your gathering wearing the finest clothes and priceless jewelry, *don't trip over each other trying to welcome him.* And if a penniless bum crawls in with his shabby clothes *and a stench that fills the room, don't look away or pretend you didn't notice—offer him a seat up front, next to you.* ³⁻⁴If you tell the wealthy man, "Come sit by me; there's plenty of room," but tell the vagrant, "Oh,

these seats are saved. Go over there," then you'll be judging *God's children* out of evil motives, *and who are you to judge anyway?*

⁵My dear brothers and sisters, listen: God has picked the poor of this world to become *unfathomably* rich in faith and to ultimately inherit the Kingdom, which He has pledged to those who love Him. ⁶*By favoring the rich,* you have mocked the poor *in the midst of their suffering. And, correct me if I'm wrong,* but isn't it the rich who step on you while climbing the ladder of success? And isn't it the rich who *take advantage of you and* drag you into court? ⁷Aren't they the ones mocking the noble name *of our God,* the One calling us?

*W*e are often mesmerized by the rich, powerful, and beautiful people of the world. We dream of associating with them, but when we focus our attention on the fashionable people of this world, it is often at the expense of those who need it the most.

Ignoring the needy and favoring the wealthy is completely contrary to the example Jesus modeled for us while walking on earth. God often chooses those who are the poorest materially to be the richest spiritually. We should welcome everyone equally into God's kingdom, even if it means upsetting boundaries like class and race. The rule is simple: we should treat others in the same way we want to be treated. God does not play favorites, and neither should we.

⁸*Remember His call and* live by the royal law. *It's the very heart of Scripture:* Love others as you love yourself.* You'll be doing very well if you can get this down. ⁹But if you *start running around* paying attention only to those who can help you *in some way, while ignoring those who seem to need all the help,* you'll be sinning and

* 2:8 Leviticus 19:18

condemned by the *royal* law. [10]*Here's the thing: the law doesn't pick favorites either.* If you break just one law or commit only one sin, *to God* it's like breaking every law or committing every sin. [11]The same God who said, "Do not commit adultery,"* *or to put it another way, "Save your bed and your body for your spouse,"* also says, "Do not murder."* If you break either of these commands, you're a lawbreaker, *no matter how you look at it.* [12]So live your life in such a way that acknowledges that one day— *maybe one day soon*—you will be judged. But the law that judges also gives freedom, [13]although you can't expect to be shown mercy if you refuse to show mercy. *But hear this: mercy always wins against judgment! Thank God!*

[14]Brothers and sisters, it doesn't make any sense to say you have faith and act in a way that denies that faith. *Mere talk never gets you very far, and* a commitment to Jesus only in words will not save you. [15]It would be like seeing a brother or sister is without any clothes *out in the cold* and begging for food, and [16]saying, "Shalom, *friend*, you should get inside where it's warm and eat something," but doing nothing about their needs—*leaving them cold and alone on the street*. What good would your words alone do? [17]The same is true with faith. Without actions, *faith is useless. By itself*, it's *as good as* dead. [18]I know what you're thinking: "OK, you have faith. And I have actions. Now let's see your faith without works. *And I'll go one better*. I'll show you a faith that works." *Don't you realize that one without the other is useless: a glove without a hand, a hat without a head?* [19]Do you think that just believing there's one God is going to get you anywhere? All demons believe there's a God, *and to tell you the truth*, it terrifies them! *And it should terrify you too.* [20]*The fact is*, belief has to show itself through works performed in faith. If you don't recognize that, then you're an empty soul.

*S*ome passages of the Bible seem to contradict others. James is one of the most frequently cited exam-

ples. On the one hand, it appears James is saying that salvation is achieved by works; on the other, writers like Paul emphasize that salvation comes by faith alone.* How can we reconcile these seemingly conflicting accounts?

A careful look at the Scriptures demonstrates that the contradiction lies only on the surface. Essentially Paul and James are talking about different issues. Paul is in the middle of a debate with some Jewish Christians over whether Gentiles must live like Jews to enter the family of faith. He says that no one is made right with God by performing the works of the law such as circumcision, Sabbath observance, dietary rules and regulations. Instead, all people are made right by faith, thanks to God's grace. For James the situation is entirely different. The works he is talking about refer to God's people helping the poor, not whether non-Jews must live like Jews. He's concerned about a shallow, insincere, and hypocritical faith. To put it another way, it is the difference between the "root" of salvation and the "fruit" of salvation. The root of salvation is the grace of God, what grounds our faith. The fruit of salvation is our works, what flows from our faith. Even though we are saved by grace, we should still have a faith that works. In fact, Paul reminded Titus eight times in his letter to him that good works are to be a natural result of faith.

[21]Wasn't our father Abraham made right with God by laying his son Isaac on the altar? [22]The faith *in his heart* was made known in his behavior. In fact, his commitment was perfected by his obedience. [23]That's what Scripture means when it says, "Abraham entrusted himself to God, and God credited him with righteousness."*

* 2:11 Exodus 20:14
* 2:11 Exodus 20:13
* **Note** Galatians 2
* 2:23 Genesis 15:6

And living a faithful life earned Abraham the title of "God's friend." ²⁴*Just like our father in the faith,* we are made right with God through good works, not simply by what we believe or think. ²⁵Even Rahab the prostitute was made right with God by hiding the spies and aiding in their escape.* ²⁶Removing action from faith is like removing breath from a body. All you have left is a corpse.

3 My brothers and sisters, do not encourage a large number of you to become teachers because teachers will be held to a higher standard. ²We all stumble along the way. If a person never speaks hurtful words *or shouts in anger or profanity,* then he has achieved perfection. The one who can control his tongue can also control the rest of his body. ³It's like when we place a metal bit into a horse's mouth to ride it; we can control its entire body *with the slightest movement of our hand.* ⁴Have you ever seen a massive ship *sailing effortlessly across the water? Despite its immense size* and the fact that it is propelled by mighty winds, a small *tongue-shaped* rudder directs the ship in any direction the pilot chooses. ⁵It's just the same with our tongues! It's a small, *awkward* muscle, capable of marvelous undertakings.

But do you know how many forest fires begin *with a single ember* from a small campfire? ⁶The tongue is a *blazing* fire seeking to ignite an entire world of vices. The tongue is unique among all parts of the body because it is capable of corrupting the whole body. *If that were not enough,* it ignites *and consumes* the course of creation with a fuel that originates in hell itself. ⁷Humanity is capable of taming every bird and beast in existence, even reptiles and sea creatures *great and small.* ⁸But no man has ever demonstrated the ability to tame his own tongue! It is a spring of restless evil, brimming with toxic poisons. ⁹*Ironically* this same tongue can be *both an instrument* of blessing to our Lord and Father and *a weapon* that hurls curses upon others who are created in

God's own image. ¹⁰One mouth streams forth both blessings and curses. My brothers and sisters, this is not how it should be. ¹¹Does a spring gush crystal-clear freshwater and moments later spurt out bitter salt water? ¹²My brothers and sisters, *let's be reasonable.* Does a fig tree produce olives? Is there a grapevine capable of growing figs? Can salt water give way to freshwater?

¹³Who in your community is understanding and wise? Let his example, which is marked by wisdom and gentleness, blaze a trail for others. ¹⁴If your heart is one that bleeds dark streams of jealousy and selfishness, do not be so proud that you ignore your depraved state. ¹⁵The wisdom of this world should never be mistaken for heavenly wisdom; it originates below in the earthly realms, with the demons *that make uninspired souls their homes.* ¹⁶Any place where you find jealousy and selfish ambition, you will discover chaos and evil thriving under its rule. ¹⁷Heavenly wisdom centers on purity, peace, gentleness, *reason,* deference, mercy, and other good fruits untainted by hypocrisy. ¹⁸The seed that flowers into righteousness will always be planted in peace by those who embrace peace.

Worldly wisdom may promise the good life but will take you down the wrong path to chaos and destruction every time. Ultimately true wisdom comes from God. We hear it in the words of Scripture. We see it incarnate in the face of our Liberator. If we listen carefully, we can hear wisdom calling us to embrace exquisite gifts.

4 Where do you think your fighting and *endless* conflict come from? Don't you think that they originate in the *constant pursuit of* gratification that rages inside of each of you *like an uncontrolled militia? No wonder community is so hard to achieve!* ²You crave something that you do

* 2:25 Joshua 2:1-16

not possess, so you murder to get it. You desire the things you cannot earn, so you *sue others and* fight for what you want. You do not have because you have chosen not to ask. ³And when you do ask, you still do not get what you want because your motives are all wrong—because you continually focus on self-indulgence. ⁴You are adulterers, *every one of you*. Don't you know that making friends with this corrupt world order is open aggression toward God? So, anyone who aligns with this bogus world system is declaring war against the one true God. ⁵Do you think it is empty rhetoric when the Scriptures say, "the spirit that lives in us is addicted to envy and jealousy"?* ⁶*You may think that the situation is hopeless,* but God gives us more grace *when we turn away from our own interests.* That's why Scripture says:

> God opposes the proud,
>   but He pours out grace on the
>   humble.*

⁷So submit yourselves to the one true God and fight against the devil *and his schemes.* If you do, he will run away *in failure.* ⁸Come close to the one true God; *He has been pursuing you all along*—and He will draw close to you. Wash your hands; you have dirtied them in sin. Cleanse your heart, because your mind is split down the middle *by your love for God and selfish pursuits.*

> *J*ames echoes an amazing and beautiful reality that is often heard throughout the story of Scripture. Since the beginning, our loving Creator has been pursuing us, wooing us, and drawing us closer to Him. Like a loving husband, He waits for His bride. He invites us to move closer to Him so we can be fully His.

⁹Now is the time to lament, to grieve, and to cry. Dissolve your laughter into sobbing and exchange your joy for depression. ¹⁰Lay yourself *bare, facedown to the ground,* in humility before the Lord, and He will lift your head *so you can stand tall.* ¹¹My brothers and sisters, do not assault each other with criticism. If you decide your job is to accuse and judge another believer, then you are a self-appointed critic and judge of the law; if so, then you are no longer doers of the law *and subject to its rule;* you stand over it as a judge. ¹²*Know this*—there is One who stands supreme as Judge and Lawgiver. He alone is able to save and to destroy, so who are you *to step in and try* to judge another?

¹³Listen carefully, those of you *making your plans and promoting your agenda,* saying, "We are traveling to this city in the next few days. We'll stay there for one year while our business explodes and revenue is up." ¹⁴The reality is you have no idea where your life will take you tomorrow. You are like a mist that appears one moment and then vanishes another. ¹⁵It would be best to say, "If it is the Lord's will and we live long enough, we hope to do this project or pursue that dream." ¹⁶But your current speech indicates an arrogance *that does not acknowledge the One who controls the universe,* and this kind of big-talking is the epitome of evil. ¹⁷So, if you know the right way to live, and you ignore it, it is sin—*plain and simple.*

5 Hey, you rich folk, misery is on its way. *Don't get too comfortable with your wealth and extravagance;* cry and moan—*you might as well start now.* ²*You have banked your lives on accumulating things, and* now you will watch your riches rot before your eyes as the moths devour your fine clothes. ³Your stockpile of silver and gold is tarnished and corroded: and this rust will stand up in the final judgment and testify against you. It will eat your flesh like fire *and become a permanent and painful reminder that* you have hoarded your wealth, *and it will not last* through these last days. ⁴Listen; *this is for you.* You held back a just wage from the laborers who mowed your fields, and that

* 4:5 Genesis 6:5
* 4:6 Proverbs 3:34

money is crying out against you, *demanding that justice be done.* The cries of the people who harvested your crops *and made you a profit* have fallen upon the ears of the supreme Lord of heavenly armies. [5]Your life on the earth has been one of luxury, pleasure, and endless consumption; you have feasted to your hearts' content *on animals you slaughtered, but now* the day of slaughter comes *for you.* [6]You have condemned and murdered the righteous man, and he did not defend himself.

[7]For this reason, my brothers and sisters, be patient as you wait for the return of the Lord. Look! The farmer knows how to wait patiently for the land to produce *vegetables and fruits. He cannot harvest a freshly planted seed.* Instead, he waits for the early and the late showers *to nourish the soil.* [8]You need this same kind of patience, *so in the meantime,* strengthen your resolve because the Lord will be coming soon.

[9]Brothers and sisters, don't waste your breath complaining about one another. If you judge others, you will be judged yourself. Be very careful! *You will face* the one true Judge who is right outside the door. [10]The prophets who declared the word of the Lord are your role models, my brothers and sisters, for what it means to live patiently in the face of suffering. [11]Look, we bless and honor the memory of those who persevered *under hardship.* Remember Job's endurance and how the Lord orchestrated the triumph of his final circumstances as a grand display of His mercy and compassion.

[12]It is even more important, my brothers and sisters, that you remember not to make a vow by the heavens or the earth or by anything. *Keep it simple.* When you say "yes," it should always mean yes, and "no" should always mean no. *If you can keep your word,* you will avoid judgment.

[13]Are any in your community suffering? They should pray. Are any celebrating? They should sing praises *to God.* [14]Are any sick? They should call the elders of your church and ask them to pray. They will *gather around and* anoint them with oil in the name of the Lord. [15]Prayers offered in faith will restore them from sickness *and bring them to health.* The Lord will lift them up *from the floor of despair,* and if the sickness is due to sin, then God will forgive their sin. [16]So own up to your sins to one another and pray for one another. In the end, you may be healed. Your prayers are powerful when they are rooted in a righteous life. [17]*Remember* Elijah? He was a man, no different from us. He prayed with great intensity asking God to withhold the rain; God *answered his prayers and* did not allow a single drop of rain to fall for three and a half years. [18]It did not rain until Elijah prayed again *for God to open the skies,* when the rain came down and the earth produced a great crop.

*W*hy should we bother to pray if God already knows what we are going to ask for? Prayer involves so much more than making personal requests.

How, then, should we pray? First, James tells us to pray in community, not just by ourselves and for ourselves. When we pray together, life is shared and community is born. We also confess our sins, not just to God, but to each other. Through this vulnerable transparency, God knits souls together in authentic community, and we discover the true benefit of prayer.

[19]Brothers and sisters, if someone you know loses his way and rebels *against God, pursue him in love and* bring him back to the truth. [20]Know this: If you turn a sinner back from the error of his ways, then you will rescue him from the grips of death and cover *the pain and consequences of* untold sins.

1 Peter

Instruction to the church scattered
From Peter, the apostle to Jewish Christians

This letter was written by Peter, a fisherman from Galilee who
became one of the most prominent leaders of the early church.
Though his name was Simon, Jesus gave him the nickname "Peter,"
which means "rock." Jesus said Peter would be the rock or foundation the church would be built on. Although Peter knew he was a key
leader in the movement, he was humble enough to know that it was
Jesus who would always be the cornerstone, the One who holds the
church together. That's why the image of a temple, crafted from
stone, touches Peter so deeply. As "the rock," Peter urges them to
come to Jesus, the cornerstone, and join Him in building a new temple and forming a new priesthood where spiritual sacrifices are
offered to God.

Peter addressed Christians scattered throughout Asia Minor
(modern Turkey). Whether he knew these churches personally, we
cannot say. But as one of Jesus' original disciples, a member of "the
twelve," his stature and reputation were such that he could gain a
hearing as the churches gathered. He refers to them as "living as
aliens" because he knew they were having a difficult time relating to
the pagan world around them. Like strangers on a journey in a culture and land not their own, citizens of the Liberating King felt out of
step with everyone else. In times of persecution, it became common
for Christians to identify themselves as aliens and sojourners, living
as strangers even among their own people. Peter writes this letter
"from Babylon," probably a cryptic designation for Rome, the imperial capital where the fires of persecution burned the hottest.

Peter wrote this letter to encourage believers who were going
through intense persecution. According to him, followers of the
Liberating King should not be surprised by the fiery ordeals that
come their way. In fact, when they experience social ostracism,
imprisonment, torture, and even death, they are participating in the
ongoing sufferings of Jesus. So Peter calls them to entrust themselves
to God and to have courage in the face of persecution. Suffering that
lacks meaning or purpose is suffering without hope. So Peter tries
to infuse them with hope by reminding them of who they are and
urging them to imitate the One who called them.

1 Peter, an emissary* of Jesus, the Liberating King, to God's chosen people living as aliens scattered *among the unbelievers* in Pontus, Galatia, Cappadocia, Asia, and Bithynia. ²*I am sending this letter to those* who have been selected and destined by God the Father and made holy by *God* the Spirit that you may be obedient to Jesus, our Liberator, and *purified* by the sprinkling of His blood. May grace and peace beyond all reckoning be yours.

³Blessed is God, the Father of our Lord Jesus, the Liberator! Because He has raised Jesus, the Liberator, from death, through His great mercy we have been reborn into a living hope— ⁴reborn for an eternal inheritance, held in reserve in heaven, that will never fade or fail. ⁵Through faith, God's power is *standing watch,* protecting you for a salvation that you will see completely at the end of things. ⁶You should greatly rejoice *in what is waiting for you,* even if now for a little while you have to suffer various trials. ⁷*Suffering tests* your faith which is more valuable than gold (remember that gold, although it is perishable, is tested by fire) so that, if it is found genuine, you can receive praise, honor, and glory when Jesus, the Liberating King, is revealed at last.

⁸Although you haven't seen Jesus *in the past,* you *still* love Him. Although you don't yet see Him, you do believe in Him and celebrate with a joy that is glorious and beyond words. ⁹You are receiving the salvation of your souls as the result of your faith.

¹⁰The prophets who spoke of this *outpouring of* grace upon you *were filled with wonder as they* diligently searched and inquired *of the Lord* about this salvation. ¹¹To whom and to what time was the Spirit of the Liberating King who was in them referring when He told them about the suffering of the Liberator and the honor that would follow it? ¹²The Spirit revealed to them they were not serving themselves but you. And you have learned from those who told you the good news by the Spirit that was sent down from heaven. Even the heavenly messengers would like to explore this news.

¹³So *get yourselves ready,* prepare your minds to act, control yourselves, and look forward in hope as you focus on the grace that comes when Jesus, the Liberating King, *returns and* is completely revealed to you. ¹⁴Be like obedient children as you put aside the desires you used to pursue when you didn't know better. ¹⁵Since the One who called you is holy, be holy in all you do. ¹⁶For the Scripture says, "You are to be holy, for I am holy."* ¹⁷If you call on the Father who judges everyone without partiality, *strictly* according to their actions, then you should live in reverence and awe while you live out the days of your exile.

¹⁸You know that a price was paid to redeem you from following the empty ways handed on to you by your ancestors; it was not paid with things that perish (like silver and gold), ¹⁹but with the precious blood of the Liberating King, who was like a perfect and unblemished sacrificial lamb. ²⁰God determined to send Him before the world began, but He came *into the world* in these last days for your sake. ²¹Through Him, you've been brought to trust in God, who raised Him from the dead and glorified Him for the very reason that your faith and hope are in Him.

²²Now that you have *taken care to* purify your souls through your submission to the truth, you can experience real love for each other. So love each other deeply from a [pure]* heart. ²³You have been reborn—not from seed that eventually dies but from seed that is eternal—through the word of God that lives and endures forever. ²⁴For *as Isaiah said,*

All life is like the grass,
  and its glory like a flower;
The grass will wither *and die,*
  and the flower falls,
²⁵But the word of the Lord will endure
  forever.*

Interpreted: this is the word that has been preached to you.

---

* 1:1 Literally, apostle
* 1:16 Leviticus 11:44-45; 19:2; 20:7
* 1:22 Not in all manuscripts
* 1:24-25 Isaiah 40:6b-8

2 So get rid of hatefulness and deception, of insincerity and jealousy and slander. ²Be like newborn babies, crying out for spiritual milk that will help you grow into salvation ³if you have tasted *and found* the Lord to be good.

⁴Come to Him—the living stone—rejected by people, but *accepted* by God as chosen and precious. ⁵Like living stones, let yourselves be assembled into a spiritual house, a holy order of priests who offer up spiritual sacrifices that will be acceptable to God through Jesus, the Liberating King. ⁶For it says in the words *of the prophet Isaiah,*

> See here—I am laying in Zion a
>   stone,
>   a cornerstone, chosen and
>   precious;
> Whoever depends upon Him will
>   never be disgraced.*

⁷To you who believe *and depend on Him,* He is precious, but to you who don't, *remember the words of the psalmist,*

> The stone that the builders rejected
>   has been laid as the cornerstone—
>   the very stone *that holds
>   together the entire foundation,*

⁸and, *as in Isaiah,*

> A stone that blocks their way,
>   a rock that trips them.*

They stumble because they don't follow the word of God, as they were destined to do.

⁹But you are a chosen people, *set aside to be* a royal order of priests, a holy nation, God's own, so that you may proclaim the wondrous acts of the One who called you out of *inky* darkness into shimmering light. ¹⁰Once you were not a people, but now you are God's people; once you had not received mercy, but now you have received it.

¹¹Beloved, remember *you don't belong in this world.* You are resident aliens, living in exile, so resist those desires of the flesh that battle against the soul. ¹²Live honorably among the outsiders so that, even when some may be inclined to call you criminals, when they see your good works, they might give glory to God when He returns in judgment.

¹³For the Lord's sake, accept the decrees and laws of all the various human institutions, whether they come from the highest human ruler ¹⁴or agents he sends to punish those who do wrong and to reward those who do well. ¹⁵You see, it is God's will that by doing what is right *and good* you should hush the gabbing ignorance of the foolish. ¹⁶Live as those who are free and not as those who use their freedom as a pretext for evil; but live as God's servants. ¹⁷Respect everyone. Love the community of believers. Reverence God. Honor your ruler.

For many, acceptance of another's authority (or submission) refers solely to how Christian women are to behave in marriage and in the church. However, a variety of other relationships call all Christians to submit. Peter describes the submission of believers to God, citizens to rulers, slaves to masters, and younger men to older men.

Even when applied to various groups, the word "submission" still evokes concerns about sexism, racism, and dehumanization. Unfortunately many Christians have provided good reason for others to draw such conclusions. The true purpose of biblical submission is not to sanction any type of inequality but to honor the Liberating King even in the most difficult of circumstances. Offering an attitude of humility toward those who are undeserving of it mirrors the unmerited favor God graciously gives to us. When submission is modeled evenly by all believers—male and female, young and old—it is no longer enslaving, but liberating.

* 2:6 Isaiah 28:16
* 2:7 Psalm 118:22
* 2:8 Isaiah 8:14

18*If you are a* slave, submit yourself to the master who has authority over you, whether he is kind and gentle or harsh *as he deals with you.* 19For grace is clearly at work when a person accepts undeserved pain and suffering and does so because he is mindful of God. 20For what credit is there in enduring punishment you deserve? But if you do what is right and yet are punished and endure it patiently, God will be pleased with you. 21-22For you were called to this *kind of life*: *as Isaiah said,*

> He did no wrong deed,
>   and no evil word came from His
>   mouth.*

The Liberating King suffered for us and left us His example so that we could follow in His steps. 23When He was verbally abused, He didn't return the abuse; when He suffered, He didn't make threats *to cause suffering in return*; instead, He trusted that all would be put right by the One who is just when He judges. 24He took on our sins in His body *when He died* on the cross* so that we, being dead to sin, can live for righteousness. *As the Scripture says,* "Through His wounds, you were healed." 25For there was a time when you were like sheep that wandered from the fold, but now you have returned to the Shepherd and Guardian of your lives.

3 1-2In the same way, wives, you should patiently accept the authority of your husbands. This is so that even if they don't obey God's word, as they observe your pure, respectful behavior, they may be persuaded without a word by the way you live. 3*Wives, adjust your priorities:* don't focus on decorating your exterior by doing your hair or putting on fancy jewelry or wearing fashionable clothes; 4let your adornment be what's inside—*the real you,* the lasting beauty of a gracious and quiet spirit, in which God delights. 5This is how, long ago, holy women who put their hope in God made themselves beautiful: by respecting the authority of their husbands. 6Consider how Sarah, *our mother,* obeyed her husband, Abraham, and called him "lord," and you will be her daughters as long as you boldly do what is right without fear *and without anxiety.*

7In the same way, husbands, as you live with your wives, understand *the situation* women *face* as the weaker vessel. *Each of you should respect your wife* and value her as an equal heir in the gracious gift of life. Do this so that nothing will get in the way of your prayers.

8Finally, all of you, be like-minded and show sympathy, love, compassion, and humility to and for each other— 9not paying back evil with evil or insult with insult, but repaying the bad with a blessing. It was this you were called to do, so that you might inherit a blessing. 10*It is written in the psalms,*

> If you love life
>   and want to live a good, long time,
> Then be careful what you say.
>   Don't tell lies or spread gossip or
>   talk about improper things.
> 11Walk away from the evil *things in the world—just leave them behind,*
>   and do what is right,
>   and *always* seek peace and pursue
>   it.
> 12For the Lord watches over the
>   righteous,
>   and His ears are attuned to their
>   prayers.
> *He is always listening,*
> But His face is set against *His enemies;*
>   *He will punish* evildoers.*

13Why would anyone harm you if you eagerly do good? 14Even if you should suffer for doing what is right, you will receive a blessing. Don't let them frighten you. Don't be intimidated, 15-16but exalt the Liberating King as Lord in your heart. Always be ready to offer a defense, humbly and respectfully, when someone asks why

* 2:21-22 Isaiah 53:9
* 2:24 Literally, tree
* 3:10-12 Psalm 34:12-16

you live in hope. Keep your conscience clear so that those who ridicule your good conduct in the Liberator and say bad things about you will be put to shame.

*P*eter urges us always to be ready to give a reason for the hope that lives within us. We do not need to be afraid when others ask us tough questions about why we believe what we believe. We can prepare for attacks on our faith by prayerfully anticipating objections and carefully crafting responses to them in advance. It is important that when it is time to present our defense that it is done with gentleness and love, not arrogance and contempt. Giving an account for our hope is not about outsmarting the other person or making ourselves feel superior about our beliefs. It is about humbly offering our minds to God as a form of worship and as a loving act of obedience. This is one way we can glorify Jesus as King over all our lives—by exalting Him with both our emotions and our intellect.

[17]For if it is the will of God that you suffer, then it is better to suffer for doing what is right than for doing what is wrong. [18]Because the Liberating King suffered for sins once for all time—the righteous *suffering* for the unrighteous—so that He might bring us to God. Though He died in the flesh, He was made alive again through the Spirit. [19]And in the Spirit He went and preached to those spirits held captive. [20]*It was these* who long ago lived in disobedience as God waited patiently as Noah was building the ark. At that time, only a tiny band—eight people—was spared from the flood.

[21]The water *through which the ark safely passed* symbolizes now the ceremonial washing *that initiates* you into salvation. You are saved not because it cleanses your body of filth but because of your appeal to God from a good conscience, through the resurrection of Jesus, the Liberating King. [22]Now He has entered heaven and sits at the right hand of God as heavenly messengers and authorities and powers submit to His supremacy.

4 Since the Liberating King suffered in the flesh, prepare yourselves to do the same—anyone who has suffered in the flesh *for the Lord* is no longer in the grip of sin— [2]so that you may live the rest of your life on earth *controlled* not by earthly desires but by the will of God.

*T*he reality of suffering in the world causes many to question the existence of an all-powerful and all-loving God. A God of power and love is expected to be both able and willing to remove suffering from our lives. However, God allows suffering to persist, and He calls us to consider it a blessing and to rejoice in the midst of it. Contrary to how we think God ought to behave, He prioritizes His glory over our happiness. This may seem downright selfish of God. But we should ask ourselves this: if humanity's greatest purpose is to glorify God, then how could God have a lesser one? He is the majestic Creator of all things, existing in Himself and for Himself, and yet He has wounds. Just because God calls us to suffer does not mean He is immune to it. At the cross, Jesus entered into our suffering. Now we enter into His.

[3]You have already wasted enough time living like those outsiders in the society around you: losing yourselves in sex, in addictions and desires, in drinking and lawless idolatry, in *giving your time and allegiance to things that are not godly.* [4]When you don't play the same games they do, they notice that you are living by different rules. That's why they say such terrible things about you. *So what? Let them.* [5]Someday they, too, will have to give an account *of themselves* to the One who judges the living and the dead. [6](This is

why the good news had to be brought to those who are dead so that although they are judged in the flesh, they might live in the spirit in the way that pleases God.) [7]We are coming to the end of all things, so be serious and keep your wits about you in order to pray *more forcefully.* [8]Most of all, love each other steadily and unselfishly, because love makes up for many faults. [9]Show hospitality to each other without complaint. [10]Use whatever gift you've received for *the good of* one another so that you can show yourselves to be good stewards of God's grace in all its varieties. [11]If you're called upon to talk, speak as though God put the words in your mouth; if you're called upon to serve others, serve as though you had the strength of God behind you. In these ways, God may be glorified in all you do through Jesus who is the Liberating King, to whom belongs glory and power, now and forever. Amen.

[12]Dear ones, don't be surprised when you experience your trial by fire. It is not something strange and unusual, [13]but it is something you should rejoice in. In it you share the Liberator's sufferings, and you will be that much more joyful when His glory is revealed. [14]If anyone condemns you for following *Jesus as* the Liberating King, consider yourself blessed. The glorious Spirit of God rests on you. [15]But none of you should ever merit suffering like those who have murdered or stolen, meddled in the affairs of others or done evil things. [16]But if you should suffer for being a Christian, don't think of it as a disgrace, *as it would be if you had done wrong.* Praise God that you're permitted to carry this name.

[17]For the time for judgment has come, and it is beginning with the household of God. If it is starting with us, what will happen to those who have rejected God's good news? [18]*It is written in Proverbs,*

> If it is hard for the righteous ones to
> be saved,
> what will happen to the ungodly and
> the sinners?*

[19]So even if you should suffer now for doing God's will, continue doing good and trust your futures to the judgment and mercy of a faithful Creator.

5 Now for the elders *of the church.* I want to encourage you. *As you know,* I am an elder, too, like you. I have witnessed *firsthand* the sufferings of the Liberating King as well as shared in the glories which are soon to be revealed. [2]*When you* shepherd the flock God has given you, watch over them not because you have to but because you want to. For this is how God would want it not because you're being compensated somehow but because you are eager to watch over them. [3]Don't lead them as if you were a dictator, but lead your flock by example; [4]and when the Chief Shepherd appears, you will be crowned with honor that will shine brightly forever. [5]You who are younger *in the faith:* do as your elders *and leaders* ask. All of you should treat each other with humility, *for as it says in Proverbs,*

> God closes the door to the proud,
> but opens it to the humble.*

[6]So bow down under God's strong hand; then when the time comes God will lift you up. [7]Since God cares for you, let Him carry all your burdens and worries. [8]*Most importantly,* be disciplined and stay on guard. Your enemy the devil is prowling around outside like a roaring lion, just waiting *and hoping for the chance* to devour someone. [9]Resist him and be strong in your faith, knowing that your brothers and sisters throughout the world are fellow sufferers with you. [10]After you have suffered for a little while, the God of grace who has called you [to His everlasting presence]* through the Liberating King, Jesus, will restore you, support you, strengthen you, and ground you. [11]For all power belongs to God, now and forever. Amen.

* 4:18 Proverbs 11:31
* 5:5 Proverbs 3:34
* 5:10 Omitted in the earliest manuscripts

¹²Silvanus, whom I consider a trustworthy and faithful brother, is carrying this brief letter to encourage you and to testify that here is the true grace of God. Hold on to it. ¹³The church in Babylon *(our exile in Rome),* that is chosen with you, sends you its greetings. So does my son Mark.

¹⁴Greet each other with a kiss of love, and may peace come to all who follow *Jesus,* the Liberating King.

2 Peter

Instruction to the church scattered
From Peter, the apostle to Jewish Christians

Later tradition credits this letter to Peter, one of "the twelve," an eye-witness to much of Jesus' public ministry and the same disciple who, according to tradition, when sentenced to die requested to be crucified upside down because he felt unworthy to die in the same way his Lord did. Initially there were questions about this letter, so it was one of the last letters accepted as authentic and part of the New Testament canon. Peter wrote this second letter to the same churches he addressed in 1 Peter. But the address here is more generic, which suggests that he expects this letter to be read broadly to anyone who shares his faith in Jesus.

Peter begins by celebrating God's power and the true knowledge of God, which leads to salvation. For him salvation consists of escaping the corruption that characterizes this world and sharing in God's very nature. But believers must cooperate with God's work in them in order to fully live into the promises God has for those who believe. Virtue, knowledge, self-control, godliness, and love: these are the characteristics that form the life of any true believer.

At the heart of the letter is a warning against the growing influence of false teachers who have infiltrated the churches. With their greed, sensuality, arrogance, and hatred for authority, these false believers are undermining the church. Peter looks back over Jewish history and notices that God did not spare the disobedient angels and people in the past, so God's judgment on the present false teachers is sure.

Some of the false teachers were mocking the hope that Jesus would return again. But Peter assures his audience that any delay in the Liberator's return has to do with God's patience: He wishes for all to change their ways and enter the Kingdom. The day of the Lord will come, he writes, like a thief in the night, and the old world as we know it will give way to a new world as only God can make it.

There are a number of similarities between the second chapter of this letter and Jude. Both letters cite the same examples from the Scriptures to recall how God has judged disobedience in the past. Both describe the false teachers who are threatening the church in similar ways. The correspondences are such that it is unlikely they are working independently. Letters were often collaborative and not solo efforts, and it was common for writers to borrow from another when it suited their purpose.

Simon Peter, a servant and emissary*
of Jesus, the Liberator, to those who
have received the same precious faith
we share through the righteousness of our
God and Savior Jesus, the Liberating King.
²I wish you a full measure of grace and
peace *as you grow* in the knowledge of God
and of Jesus our Lord.

³His divine power has given us everything we need to experience life and to
reflect God's true nature through the
knowledge of the One who called us by His
glory and virtue. ⁴Through these things,
we have received God's great and valuable
promises, so we might escape the corruption of worldly desires and share in the
divine nature.

> The Christian faith does not
> begin with us; it begins with
> God. He took the first step to rescue
> us from this corrupt world. He has
> granted us His power, revealed to
> us true knowledge, and spoken to us
> great promises. He has done all this for
> a reason: that we might participate in
> God's own nature and reflect God's
> own life. But we are not passive
> observers to God's saving actions.
> We must receive His grace, grow in
> knowledge, and join Him in this work
> of redemption.

⁵To achieve this, you will need to add
virtue to your faith, and then knowledge to
your virtue; ⁶to knowledge, add discipline;
to discipline, add endurance; to endurance,
add godliness; ⁷to godliness, add affection
for others as sisters and brothers; and to
affection, *at last,* add love. ⁸For if you possess these traits and multiply them, then
you will never be ineffective or unproductive in your relationship with our Lord
Jesus, the Liberating King; ⁹but if you don't
have these qualities, then you will be near-
sighted and blind, forgetting that your past
sins have been washed away. ¹⁰Therefore,
brothers and sisters, work that much
harder to confirm that God has called you
and claimed you. If you do this, then you

will never fall along the way, ¹¹and you can
be sure that you will be richly welcomed
into the eternal kingdom of our Lord and
Savior Jesus, the Liberating King.

¹²That is why I will keep reminding you
of these things, even though I know that
you believe them and have made these
truths a part of your lives; ¹³as long as I
draw breath, I know it is right for me
to keep on stirring you up with these
reminders. ¹⁴I know that soon I must *die
and* lay down this *old* body that's been my
home—our Lord Jesus, the Liberating
King, has told me so. ¹⁵*But before my exodus from this life,* I want to be certain you
will be able to call these things to mind
anytime you need them even after I am
gone.

¹⁶For *I want to remind you that* when
we told you about the power and coming
of our Lord Jesus, the Liberating King, we
were relying on what our eyes had seen of
His *glorious* majesty, not on cleverly told
fables. ¹⁷You see, God the Father lavished
honor and glory upon Jesus when the
voice of the Majestic Glory echoed *from
heaven* and said, "This is My beloved Son,
and My favor rests on Him."* ¹⁸*We witnessed this*—we ourselves heard this voice
from heaven—when we were with Jesus on
that holy mountain. ¹⁹We have a fuller confirmation of the message of the prophets.
You would do well to pay close attention to
this word; it is like a light that shines for
you in the darkness of night until the day
dawns when the morning star rises in your
own hearts.

> The Christian faith does not rest
> upon cleverly devised fables or
> stories invented by creative minds; it
> begins in history. It rests upon the tes-
> timony of eyewitnesses who faithfully
> passed down what they saw and heard
> to others. Peter was not an eyewitness
> to every event in Jesus' life. But he was
> part of a small group of disciples who

* 1:1 Literally, apostle
* 1:17 Matthew 17:5; Mark 9:7; Luke 9:35

ascended a mountain in Galilee one day to see Jesus transfigured right before his eyes. This miracle confirmed Jesus' true identity and was a prelude to the greatest miracle of all—the resurrection.

[20]But notice first that no prophecy found in Scripture is a matter of the prophet's own interpretation. [21]For prophecy has never been a product of human initiative, but it comes when men *and women* are moved to speak on behalf of God by the Holy Spirit.

2 Just as false prophets rose up *in the past* among *God's* people, false teachers will rise up *in the future* among you. They will slip in with their destructive opinions, denying the very Master who bought their freedom and dooming themselves to destruction swiftly, [2]but not before they attract others by their unbridled and immoral behavior. Because of them *and their ways,* others will criticize *and condemn* the path of truth *we walk as seedy and disreputable.* [3]These *false teachers* will follow their greed and exploit you with their fabrications, but *be assured that* their judgment was pronounced long ago and their destruction does not sleep.

[4]For God did not spare the heavenly beings who sinned, but He cast them into the dark pits* of hell* to be kept until the time of judgment; [5]and He did not spare the ancient world, but He sent a flood swirling over the ungodly (although He did save Noah, God's herald for what is right, with seven other *members of his family*); [6]and God condemned the cities of Sodom and Gomorrah, reducing them to ash as a lesson of what He will do with the ungodly in the days to come [7-8](although again He did rescue Lot, a person who did what was right in God's eyes and who was distressed by the immorality *and the lawlessness* of the society around him. Day after day, the sights and sounds of their lawlessness were like daggers into that good man's soul). [9]*If all this happened in the past,* it

shows clearly the Lord knows how to rescue the godly from their trials and how to hold the wicked in punishment until the day of judgment. [10]And above all, it shows He will punish those who let the desires of their bodies rule them and who have no respect for authority. People like this are so bold and willful that they aren't even afraid of offending heavenly beings, [11]although the heavenly messengers—in spite of the fact that they have greater strength and power—make no such accusations against these people before the Lord. [12]These people who speak ill of what they do not understand are no different from animals— without sense, operating only on their instincts, born to be captured and killed— and they will be destroyed just like those animals, [13]receiving the penalty for their evil acts. They waste their days in *parties and* carousing. As they feast with you, these stains and blemishes *on your community* are feasting on their deceptions.* [14]Their eyes are always looking for their next adulterous conquests; their appetite for sin cannot be satisfied. They seduce the unwary soul, and greed is the only lesson they have learned by heart. God's curse lies upon them. [15]They have veered off the right road and gotten lost, following in the steps of Balaam, the son of Beor, *the false prophet.* Balaam loved the reward he could get by doing evil, [16]but he was rebuked for crossing the line into sin; his own speechless donkey scolded him in a human voice, *an amazing miracle* that reined in the prophet's insanity.*

[17]These *people I'm talking about* are *nothing but* dried-up springs, mists driven by fierce winds; the deepest darkness has been set aside for them. [18]They speak *in loud voices* empty and arrogant. They exploit the desires of the flesh, *take advantage of* sensual natures, to entangle people who have just escaped from those who live by deception. [19]They claim to offer them

* 2:4 Other manuscripts read "into chains of darkness."
* 2:4 Literally, Tartarus
* 2:13 Other manuscripts read "in their love feasts."
* 2:16 Numbers 22–24

freedom, but they themselves are enslaved by corruption because whatever a person gives in to soon becomes his master. [20]Those who have been pulled out of the cesspool of worldly desires through the knowledge of our Lord and Savior Jesus, the Liberating King, yet have found themselves mired in it again, are worse off than they were before. [21]They would have been better off never knowing the way of righteousness than to have known it and then abandoned the sacred commandment they had previously received *and dived back into the muck!* [22]In their case, the words from Proverbs hold true, "The dog goes back to his own vomit,"* and, *as the Greeks say,* "The sow is washed to wallow in the mud."

3 This is now, my dear friends, my second letter to you. In both of them, I *have tried to* inspire you to a sincere *and pure* way of thinking by reminding you *of what you already know.* [2]Remember the words spoken earlier by God's holy prophets and the commandment that our Lord and Savior *gave to you* through your emissaries.* [3]Above all, be sure to remember that in the last days mockers will come, following their own desires and taunting you, [4]saying, "So what happened to the promised *second* coming of Jesus? For everything keeps going just the way it has since our ancestors fell asleep *in death;* since the beginning of creation, nothing's changed."

[5]*When they make fun of you,* it's as if the scoffers are deliberately forgetting that long ago when God spoke the word, the heavens came into existence and the earth formed from water and by water— [6]the waters *that eventually arose from below and fell from above* and flooded and destroyed that world. [7]By that same word, the heavens and earth *we see* now are being reserved for *destruction by* fire, preserved until the time comes for the godless on the day of judgment.

[8]Don't imagine, dear friends, *that God's timetable is the same as ours; as the psalm says,* for with the Lord, one day is like a thousand years, and a thousand years is like one day.*

> hese believers faced persecution every day and eagerly awaited the day when the Liberating King would return and judge their enemies. But what was taking so long? Scoffers who made fun of believers used the delay to question if the Liberator was going to return at all. Peter responds by saying that God's perspective on time is not like ours. What seems long from a finite, human perspective is incredibly short from an eternal one. Peter also describes how God is not slow, but patient. God wants to allow the time needed for as many sinners as possible to turn from their sinful ways.
>
> Unlike some depictions of God as a vindictive being who enjoys inflicting punishment on people, the God we see here desires that all would be saved and not destroyed. If we had true spiritual insight, we would not be amazed by the severity of eternal judgment, but by the intensity of God's mercy.

[9]*Now* the Lord is not slow about enacting His promise—slow is how some people want to characterize it—*no, He is not slow* but patient *and merciful* to you, not wanting anyone to be destroyed, but wanting everyone to turn away from following his own path and to turn toward God's.*

[10]The day of the Lord will come *unexpectedly* like a thief in the night, and on that day, the sky will vanish with a roar, the elements will melt with intense heat, and the earth and all the works done on it will be seen as they truly are.* [11]Knowing that one day all this will come to pass, think what sort of people you ought to be— how you should be living faithful and godly

* 2:22 Proverbs 26:11
* 3:2 Literally, apostles
* 3:8 An allusion to Psalm 90:4
* 3:9 Literally, repent
* 3:10 Other manuscripts read "be burned up."

lives, [12]waiting *hopefully* for and hastening the coming of God's day when the heavens will vanish in flames and the elements melt away with intense heat. [13]*What will happen next,* and what we hope for, is what God promised: a new heaven and a new earth where justice reigns.

[14]So, my friends, while we wait for the day of the Lord, work hard to live in peace, without flaw or blemish, [15]and look at the patience of the Lord as your salvation. Our dearly loved brother Paul, according to the wisdom given him, has written about this. [16]He says *essentially* the same in all of his letters, although uneducated and unstable readers misinterpret the difficult passages, just as they always misread Scripture, to their *spiritual* ruin.

[17]So *hear my final words,* my friends. Now that I have warned you about what's ahead, keep up your guard and don't let unprincipled people pull you away from the sure ground *of the truth* with their lies and misunderstandings. [18]Instead, grow in grace and in the *true* knowledge of our Lord and Savior Jesus, the Liberating King, to whom be glory, now and until the coming of the new age. Amen.

1 John

Instructions to believers everywhere
From John, the apostle

This letter was written by John the emissary, one of Jesus' earliest
followers. Before he became a disciple, John worked as a fisherman
with his father, Zebedee, and his brother James on the Sea of Galilee.
Once he joined Jesus, John became one of Jesus' closest friends, part
of an inner circle within "the twelve" that included Peter, Andrew,
and James. But out of all the disciples, it seems that John had the
closest relationship with Jesus. He was known as "the disciple loved
by Jesus."*

John wrote this letter from Ephesus, then a bustling seaside city
whose ruins are now found in Western Turkey. Although we classify
1 John as a letter, it doesn't have all the elements of a letter written
in its day. It has no typical opening or closing. In fact, it was not written to one person or church in particular, but was sent to several different churches made up mainly of non-Jews. He wrote this letter
when he was an old man, after serving in ministry for a very long
time. He used a tender, fatherly tone toward people he viewed as his
spiritual "little children"—the new generation of Christians who had
not seen Jesus with their own eyes as John had.

John begins this letter much as he did his Gospel. In both writings, he opens by stressing the eternal nature of Jesus. He explains
how Jesus was with the Father from the beginning, before the creation of the world and before He was revealed to the world in human
flesh. John then describes God as light and encourages believers to
walk in the light by stepping away from the darkness of sin. Like
other New Testament writers, he also warns believers to beware of
false teachers who deny the true identity of the Liberating King. But
most of all, John focuses on love—how God lavishes His love on us
and how we are to do the same to one another. The love of God must
overwhelm the believer's desire for the material things of this life.
John goes so far as to say, "Don't fall in love with this *corrupt* world
or *worship* the things it can offer. Those who love its corrupt ways
don't have the Father's love living within them" (2:15).

In John's Gospel and Epistles, the notes are written in first person.
Who better to comment on Jesus' life than the one who had walked
so closely with Him?

* **Note** John 19:26; 21:7,20

1 We want to tell you about the One who was from the beginning, *the One who started everything.* We have seen Him with our own eyes, heard Him with our own ears, and touched Him with our own hands. This One is *the manifestation of* the life-giving Voice *who came down from the heavens.* ²He appeared as a human being and showed us real life, *eternal life.* We have seen it *all. And we can't keep what* we witnessed *quiet*—we have to share it with you. *We've been telling all of you what happened, inviting you to experience* eternal life through the One who was with the Father and came down to us. ³What we saw and heard we pass on to you so that you, too, will be connected with us intimately *and become family.* Our family is united by our connection with the Father and His Son Jesus, our Liberating King, ⁴and we write all this because retelling this story fulfills our* joy.

⁵What we are telling you now is the very message we heard from Him: God is *pure* light, undimmed by darkness of any kind. ⁶If we say we have an intimate connection with the Father but we continue stumbling around in darkness, then we are lying because we do not live according to truth. ⁷If we walk *step by step* in the light, where the Father is, then we are ultimately connected to each other *through the sacrifice of* Jesus, His Son. His blood purifies us from all our sins. ⁸If we go around bragging, "We have no sin," then we are fooling ourselves and are strangers to the truth. ⁹But if we own up to our sins, God shows that He is faithful and just by forgiving us of our sins and purifying us from the pollution of all the bad things we have done. ¹⁰If we say, "We have not sinned," then we depict God as a liar and *show that* we have not *responded to His life-giving voice or* let His word find its way into our hearts.

D o you ever sin? Do you even know what sin is? These may seem like silly questions, but the word "sin" has virtually disappeared from our vocabularies. Afraid of sounding judgmental and preachy, we excuse sin in our lives and in the lives of others by calling it something else or by ignoring it altogether in favor of tolerance and diversity.

We displease God by just doing the wrong things, but when we substitute rules for grace or otherwise force people to do seemingly good things, we also displease God. We don't have to murder to be sinful. Each of our sins, small and large, makes us imperfect and separates us from the perfect God. Sure, we are all born as slaves to sin, which is not our choice, but we do have a choice in whether we accept the freedom from sin offered to us by the Liberating King. If we confess our sins to God each day, He will purify our hearts and draw us closer to His.

2 *You are* my little children, so I am writing these things to help you avoid sin *and the pain and guilt that come with it.* If, however, any believer does sin, we have a *high-powered* defense lawyer *arguing on our behalf* before the Father— Jesus, the righteous Liberating King, *the redeeming force.* ²It was through His sacrificial death that our sins were atoned. But He did not stop there—He died for the sins of the whole world.

I am affectionately addressing this letter to my "little children," and I am writing to help them and you not only avoid sin, but the pain and guilt that come with it. The glamour of decadent lifestyles devoid of God is often advertised as the epitome of joy and freedom. But what are often conveniently left out of these portrayals are the agonizing consequences of such destructive lifestyles. Meaningful pleasure comes not when we are enslaved by the empty promises of the world, but when we are living in loving obedience to God.

* 1:4 Other manuscripts read "your."

³We know we have joined Him in an intimate relationship because we live out His commands. ⁴If someone claims, "I am in an intimate relationship with Him," but this big talker doesn't live out His commands, then this individual is a liar and a stranger to the truth. ⁵But if someone *responds to and* obeys His word, then God's love has truly taken root and filled him. This is how we know we are in an intimate relationship with Him: ⁶anyone who says, "I live in intimacy with Him" should walk the path Jesus walked.

⁷My loved ones, *in one sense,* I am not writing a new command for you. I am only reminding you of the old command. It's a word you already know, a word that has existed from the beginning. ⁸However, in another sense, I am writing a new command for you. The new command is the truth that He lived, and now you are living it, too, because the darkness is fading and the true light is already shining *among you.*

⁹Anyone who says, "I live in the light," but hates his brother or sister is still living in the shadows. ¹⁰Anyone who loves his brother or sister lives in the light and will not trip *because his conscience is clear*. ¹¹But anyone who hates his brother is in the darkness, stumbling around with no idea where he is going, blinded by the darkness.

> *T*he mark of a Christian is love. It sets us apart and makes us different. On the one hand, I admit, there is nothing new in this teaching. In the Hebrew Scriptures, the people of the first covenant are told to love God and neighbor. On the other hand, it is new because it was newly defined when God sent His Son to be our Liberating King. The truth is we are deeply loved by God. We receive and celebrate that love when we turn and love those members of our faith family whom God loves.

¹²I am writing to you, my children, because *I want you to know the truth about Jesus and how* your sins have been forgiven by the authority of His name.

¹³I am writing to you, fathers *and mothers*, because you have known Him *as the Creator*, as the One who started everything.

I am writing to you, young people, because *He has conquered the evil one and has given you the power to* conquer the evil one as well.

¹⁴I have written to you, my children, because you have known the Father.

I have written to you, fathers *and mothers*, because you have known Him, the Creator.

I have written to you, young people, because the voice of God remains *and is heard* among you. *Remember that* you have conquered the evil one.

¹⁵Don't fall in love with this *corrupt* world or *worship* the things it can offer. Those who love its corrupt ways don't have the Father's love living within them. ¹⁶Everything the world can offer to you—the allure of pleasure, the passion to have things, and the pompous sense of superiority—does not come from the Father. These are *the rotten fruits* of this world. ¹⁷This *corrupt* world is already wasting away, as are its selfish desires. But the person really doing God's will—*that person* will never cease to be.

¹⁸My children, this is the final hour. You have heard that the antiChrist, *the greatest enemy to the Liberator's kingdom,* is coming, but, in fact, many antiChrists* are already here. This development tells us how late it really is. ¹⁹A group has left us, but they were not part of our family. If they were truly our brothers and sisters, they would have remained *for the duration* with us. When they left, they made it *ever so* obvious that they were not part of us.

²⁰You have been given an anointing, *a special touch* from the Holy One. You know *the truth*.* ²¹I am not writing to you because you do not know the truth, but because you do know it. You know that no lie belongs to the truth. ²²The liar is the one who says, "Jesus is not really the

---

* 2:18 Literally, those who oppose the Liberating King and His kingdom
* 2:20 Other manuscripts read "all things."

Liberating King." This is the antiChrist,* the one denying both the Father and the Son. ²³Anyone who denies the Son does not know the Father. The one affirming the Son enjoys an intimate relationship with the Father as well.

²⁴Let *the gospel*, the story you have heard from the beginning of your journey, live in *and take hold of* you. If that happens *and you focus on the gospel*, then you will always remain in a relationship with the Son and the Father. ²⁵This is what He promised us: eternal life.

²⁶I also am writing to warn you about some who are attempting to deceive you. ²⁷You have an anointing. You received it from Him, and His anointing remains on you. You are not lacking any teaching. But as His anointing teaches you all *the essentials* (all the truth uncontaminated by darkness and lies), His teaching is: "Remain connected to Me."

²⁸So now, my little children, live in Him, so that whenever He is revealed, we will have confidence and not have *to hang our heads in* shame before Him when He comes. ²⁹If you know that He is just *and faithful*, then you also know that everyone who lives *faithfully* and acts justly has been born into a new life through Him.

3 Check out the kind of extravagant love the Father has lavished on us—He calls us children of God! It's true; we are His *beloved* children. And in the same way the world didn't recognize Him, the world does not recognize us either.

*H*ow can we be certain that we are doing enough to please God? When we feel like we are not good enough to love as God loves, or not good enough to be loved by God at all, we should remember that God is greater than our doubts. We must silence the sounds of condemnation so we can hear the voice of God's loving assurance and remember that He has made us part of His family.

²My loved ones, *we have been adopted into God's family, and* we are officially His children now. The full picture of our destiny is not yet clear, but we know this much: when Jesus appears, we will be like Him because we will see Him just as He is. ³All those who focus their hope on Him *and His coming* seek to purify themselves just as He is pure.

⁴Everyone who lives a life of habitual sin is living in moral anarchy. That's what sin is. ⁵You realize that He came to eradicate sins, that there is not the slightest bit of sin in Him. ⁶The ones who live in *an intimate relationship with* Him do not persist in sin, but anyone who persists in sin has not seen and does not know the real Jesus.

⁷Children, don't let anyone pull one over on you. *If you are wondering about someone, take a look at his or her life. Does he do what is right?* The one doing the right thing is just imitating Jesus, the Righteous One. ⁸The one persisting in sin belongs to the diabolical one, who has been all about sin from the beginning. That is why the Son of God came into our world: to destroy the plague of destruction inflicted *on the world* by the diabolical one.

⁹Everyone who has been born into God's family avoids sin *as a lifestyle* because the genes of God's children come from God Himself. Therefore, a child of God can't live a life of persistent sin. ¹⁰So it is not hard to figure out who are the children of God and who are the children of the diabolical one: those who lack right standing and those who don't show love for one another do not belong to God.

¹¹The central truth—*the one I continue to repeat*, the one you have heard since the beginning *of your faith*—is that we must love one another. ¹²Please do not act like Cain, who was of the evil one. He *brutally* murdered his own brother.* Why would he do something so despicable? Because his life was devoted to evil *and selfishness* and his brother chose to do what is right.

---

* 2:22 Literally, one who opposes the Liberating King
* 3:12 Genesis 4:8

¹³Brothers and sisters, don't be shocked if the *corrupt* world despises you. ¹⁴We know that we have crossed over from death to real life because we are devoted to true love for our brothers and sisters. Anyone who does not love lives among corpses.

> o you ever wonder if you are really living or if you are just silently sleeping through days, months, and years? There is one indicator of real life: true love for others.

¹⁵Everyone who hates other members of God's family is a murderer. Does a murderer possess the *beautiful* life that never ends? No. ¹⁶We know what true love looks like because of Jesus. He gave His life for us, and He calls us to give our lives for our brothers and sisters. *This is a portrait of true love.*

¹⁷If a person owns the kinds of things we need to make it in the world but refuses to share with those in need, is it even possible that God's love lives in him? *Once God's love takes hold of a person, it is impossible for him to close his heart to his brothers and sisters in God's family.* ¹⁸My little children, don't just talk about love as an idea or a theory. Make it your true way of life, and live in *the pattern of gracious love.*

¹⁹⁻²⁰There is a sure way for us to know that we belong to the truth. Even though our inner thoughts may condemn us *with storms of guilt and constant reminders of our failures,* we can know in our hearts in His presence that God Himself is greater than any accusation. He knows all things *and has chosen to offer grace instead of condemnation.* ²¹My loved ones, if our hearts cannot condemn us, we can stand with confidence before God. ²²Whatever we may ask, we receive it from Him because we follow His commands and take the path that pleases Him. ²³His command is clear: believe in the name of His Son, Jesus, our Liberating King, and love one another as He commanded. ²⁴The one who follows His teaching and walks this path lives in an intimate relationship with God. How do we know that He lives in us? By the gift of His Spirit.

4 My loved ones, *I warn you*: do not trust every spirit. Instead, examine them carefully to determine if they come from God, because the *corrupt* world is filled with *the voices of* many false prophets. ²*How do you test the spirits?* If a spirit affirms *the truth* that Jesus, the Liberating King, has come in human flesh, then that spirit is from God. ³If a spirit does not affirm *the true nature of* Jesus, then that spirit does not come from God and is, in fact, an agent of the antiChrist.* You have heard about his coming, whose spirit already is active in the world. ⁴My children, you have come from God and have conquered these spirits because the One who lives within you is greater than the one in this world. ⁵But they are of this world, and they articulate the views of the *corrupt* world, which the world understands. ⁶We come from God, and those who know God hear us. Whoever is not from God will not listen to us. This is the way we discern the difference between the spirit of truth and the spirit of deception.

> warn you, my spiritual children, do not believe everything you hear; instead, you should test the prophets to find out if their voices are really from God. So how do we test the spirits to discover who is telling the truth? The most important question is whether they acknowledge that Jesus, our Liberator, is fully God and fully human. You see, in my day, most people were so convinced that this material world was corrupt and evil that they couldn't imagine how a perfect God could wrap Himself in imperfect skin.
> Modern issues are different. Many people today accept Jesus' humanity

* 4:3 Literally, enemy of the Liberator's kingdom

but deny His divinity. He may have been a great teacher, they say, but certainly not the incarnation of the Eternal God. However, Jesus made bold claims about fulfilling prophecy, living sinlessly, and conquering death. These are not the things a great teacher would have said or done if they had not been true. It is fair to say that no other life has drawn so much scrutiny, and no other life has ever elicited such praise.

[7]My loved ones, let us devote ourselves to loving one another. Love comes straight from God, and everyone who loves is born of God and truly knows God. [8]Anyone who does not love does not know God, because God is love.

[9]Because of this, the love of God is a reality among us: God sent His only Son into the world so that we could find *true* life through Him. [10]This is *the embodiment of true* love: not that we have loved God *first*, but that He loved us and sent His *unique* Son *on a special mission* to become an atoning sacrifice for our sins. [11]So, my loved ones, if God loved us so *sacrificially*, surely we should love one another. [12]No one has ever seen God *with human eyes*. But if we love one another, God *truly* lives in us. Consequently God's love has accomplished its mission among us.

[13]How can we be sure that He *truly* lives in us and that we *truly* live in Him? *By one fact:* He has given us His Spirit. [14]We have watched *what God has done* and we stand ready to provide eyewitness testimonies to the reality that the Father sent the Son to be the Savior of the world. [15]If anyone unites with our confession that Jesus is God's own Son, then God truly lives in that person and that person lives in God. [16]We have experienced and we have entrusted our lives to the love of God in us.

God is love. Anyone who lives *faithfully* in love also lives *faithfully* in God, and God lives in him. [17]This love is fulfilled with us, so that on the day of judgment we have confidence based on our identification with Jesus in this world. [18]Love will never invoke fear. Perfect love expels fear, particularly the fear of punishment. The one who fears *punishment* has not been completed through love.

[19]We love because He has first loved us. [20]If someone claims, "I love God," but hates his brother or sister, then he is a liar. Anyone who does not love a brother or sister, whom he has seen, cannot possibly love God, whom he has never seen. [21]He gave us a *clear* command, that all who love God must also love their brothers and sisters.

*I*t's easy to say "I love God"; it's easy to love in general, hard to love in particular; easy to love in theory, hard to love in practice. But genuine love is about the One willing to enter our poverty and suffering and make us rich with life. If we belong to that God, then we will love each other regardless of how hard love is.

*5*Everyone who trusts Jesus as the long-awaited Liberating King is a child of God, and everyone who loves the Father cannot help but love the child fathered by Him. [2]Then how do we know if we truly love God's children? We love them if we love God and keep His commands. [3]You see, to love God means that we keep His commands, and His commands don't weigh us down. [4]Everything that has been fathered by God overcomes the *corrupt* world. This is the victory that has conquered the world: our faith.

[5-6]Who is the person conquering the world, but the one who truly trusts that Jesus is the Son of God? Jesus, the Liberating King, is the One who came by water and blood—not by the water only, but by the water and the blood.

*J*ust as we do not get to choose our biological brothers and sisters, we do not get to choose our spiritual brothers and sisters either. But what comes along with loving the

Father is to love all His other children—even the really annoying ones! It is easy to say we love God with our words once a week at a church service and then go off and live in isolation from others and focus on ourselves. Another way to worship God is by loving our Christian brothers and sisters during the other six days of the week as well. How we treat the people around us on a daily basis is the real test of our love for God.

The Spirit of God testifies to this truth because the Spirit is the truth. [7]So there are three testifying witnesses: [8]the Spirit, the water, and the blood. All three are in total agreement.* [9]If we accept the testimony of people, then we must realize the testimony of God is greater *than that of any person.* God certified *the truth* about His own Son. [10]Anyone who trusts the Son of God has this truthful testimony at the core of his being. Anyone who does not trust God calls God a liar because he ignores God's truthful testimony regarding His own Son. [11]The truth is: God has given us *the gift of* eternal life, and this life is in His Son. [12]If you have the Son *and know Him intimately*, you have eternal life. If you do not have the Son of God, you are not acquainted with *true* life.

[13]I am writing all of this to you who have entrusted your lives to the Son of God—so you will realize that eternal life already is yours. [14]We live in the bold confidence that God hears our voices when we ask for things that fit His plan. [15]And if we have no doubt that He hears our voices, we can be assured that He moves in response to our call.

[16]*In this regard,* if you notice a brother or sister *in faith* making moral missteps and blunders, disregarding and disobeying God *even to the point of God* removing this one *from the body* by death, then pray for that person, and God will grant him life on this journey. *But to be clear,* there is a sin that is ultimately fatal *and leads to death.* I am not talking about praying for that fatal sin, [17]but I am talking about all those wrongs and sins that plague God's family that don't lead to death.

[18]We all know that everyone fathered by God will not make sin *a way of life* because God protects His children *from the evil one,* and the evil one can't touch them. [19]Have confidence in the fact that we belong to God, but also know that the world around us is in the grips of the evil one. [20]We also can be sure of the fact that the Son of God has come and given us a mind so that we may know Him as *the embodiment of all that is* true. We live in this truth, in His Son Jesus, the Liberating King. He is the true God and eternal life.

[21]My little children, keep away from idols.

M y final bit of pastoral advice sounds an alarm against idolatry. If we look carefully at our cultures and into our own hearts, we will find we are ultimately concerned about ourselves, our entertainment, our comforts, and our wallets. None of these are objects worthy of our highest devotion, but we put more time, energy, money, and emotion into these than we do into the one true God. So heed my warning: watch out for the steady impulse to love other things more than God.

---

* 5:7-8 Late Latin manuscripts include "in heaven: the Father, the Word, and the Holy Spirit. All three are in total agreement. And there are three testifying witness on the earth."

2 John

Letter to a lady and her children
From John, the apostle

John, the emissary of the Liberating King, writes this second letter shortly after his first. But unlike his first letter, where he jumps into the heart of the matter with a direct witness about Jesus, John begins this brief letter in the customary way by stating who wrote the letter and to whom it is written. He describes himself as "the elder." This is probably an affectionate title his readers knew him by, referring both to his old age and to his authority as an eyewitness to the life of Jesus. As with his first letter, the recipients are not completely disclosed. John is writing to "a lady . . . along with her children." Since he doesn't list any of their names, it is possible that he is using the phrase to signify a church and its members. Regardless of the specific recipient, this letter addresses the concerns of all believers, not just a few individuals, just as his first letter did.

Two major themes stand out in the letter: love and truth. Even though John emphasizes love in his first letter, he proves its importance by further discussing it in this one. He describes love as measurable action—not sentimental emotion or academic theory. He says love is accomplished when we obey the teachings of Jesus, our Liberating King. Next he warns of the danger of false teachers, as he did in his first letter. False teachers who deny that Jesus is both fully God and fully human are not to be tolerated. Welcoming them in any way, especially with hospitality, promotes their deceptive plans.

John sees love and truth embodied flawlessly in the person of Jesus. He wants to encourage his readers to reflect the true love of God by knowing who Jesus is, resisting false teachers, and serving each other selflessly.

¹I, the elder, to *you*, a lady chosen *by God* along with her children. I truly love *all of* you and *am confident that* all who know the truth share in my love for you. ²The truth, which lives *faithfully* within all of us and will be with us for all eternity, is the basis *for our abounding love.* ³May grace, mercy, and peace from God the Father and Jesus, the Liberating King (God's own Son), surround you *and be with you always* in truth and love.

⁴I was so filled with joy to hear stories about your children walking in truth, in the very way the Father called us to live. ⁵So now, dear lady, I am asking you to live by the command we received in the beginning *from our Lord*, and not by some new commandment: love one another. ⁶Love is defined by our obedience to His commands. This is the same command we have known about from the very beginning. *It is not an abstract idea;* we must live it. ⁷The *corrupt* world is filled with liars and frauds who deny the reality of Jesus, the Liberator, coming *into the world* as a man. These people *advance this lie and oppose the Liberating King*—they are deceivers and antiChrists.* ⁸Ensure that you do not lose what we have worked for so that you will be fully rewarded.

⁹Any person who drifts away and fails to live in the teachings of the Liberating King does not have God. The person who lives in this teaching will have both the Father and the Son *and remain in their presence.* ¹⁰If any person comes to you with a teaching that does not align with the true message *of Jesus*, do not welcome that person into your house or greet him or her *as your true brother or sister.* ¹¹Anyone who welcomes this person (*and his teaching*) *as a true brother* has become a partner in advancing his wicked agenda.

¹²I have so much more to tell you, but I would rather meet with you personally than try to capture these sentiments by ink on paper. I hope to come and see you so that our joy will be complete.

¹³The children of your chosen sister send you warm greetings.

---

* Verse 7 Literally, those who oppose the Liberating King and His kingdom

3 John

Letter to believers in the first century
From John, the apostle

The elder John writes this third letter specifically to a dear friend of his named Gaius. John wants to commend Gaius for his outstanding Christian lifestyle, so John sends this uplifting personal word to Gaius and his community. What most impresses John about Gaius is how Gaius regularly opens up his home to house, feed, and encourage traveling ministers. At this time, many prophets, missionaries, and teachers travel from place to place to serve new congregations. Given the Christian perspective on love, it is appropriate for them to rely on the generosity of their fellow believers. While John's third letter points out the importance of refusing hospitality to false teachers, it emphasizes the importance of showing hospitality to true ones.

John contrasts the hospitable behavior of Gaius with the selfish behavior of a man named Diotrephes. Diotrephes is a controlling leader within the church who refuses to welcome ministers into his home and forces out any members of the church who are caught helping them. John urges Gaius to avoid being influenced by the bad example of Diotrephes. He explains that welcoming ministers into believers' homes is about more than just hospitality—it is about reflecting the goodness of God.

John closes his letter by praising another man named Demetrius. John assures Gaius that unlike Diotrephes, Demetrius is a man of truth who may be trusted. Just like John's two previous letters, this letter focuses on living the truth found in Jesus by serving others in love. We don't have to travel full-time to spread the message of Jesus. Being generous with our time, money, and energy from our very own homes is a powerful way to serve God and fellow believers.

¹*I, the elder, to Gaius, who is much loved by all and loved* in truth by me.

²My beloved friend, I pray that things are going well for you and that your body is healthy, as your soul is prosperous. ³I was thrilled when all the brothers and sisters would tell stories of your faithfulness as you continue to walk in the truth. ⁴The greatest joy in my life is hearing how my children are walking in the truth.

⁵My friend, you demonstrate your faithfulness in all the things you do for the brothers and sisters; even when they are strangers to you, *you treat them as family.* ⁶These friends tell the entire church how you have extended your hand to them in love. You will do well to send them forward in a way that is in keeping with God. ⁷They have gone out to serve under the banner of the Name, and they do not accept gifts from those outside our faith community *so that their motives may not be questioned.* ⁸We should give people like this our full support so that we can share in this work for the truth.

⁹I wrote some things specifically to the church, but Diotrephes, who loves to be the one up front, rejects us. ¹⁰If I come, you can be sure that I will call him out and draw attention to his actions. He assails us with lies and deceit. As if that were not enough, he does not welcome the traveling missionaries *into his home.* Instead, he hinders any who do so and expels them from the church.

¹¹Dear friend, don't follow his evil ways. Instead, imitate the good *and righteous* life. The one doing what is good belongs to God, but those who pursue evil have never even laid eyes on God.

¹²Demetrius has a good reputation with everyone *we know.* The truth stands on his side, and we add our unreserved recommendation *to the long list of accounts on his behalf.* You can rest assured that our story is the truth.

¹³There is so much I would like to say to you, but I do not want to say it with ink and pen. ¹⁴I expect us to be together soon and talk about these things face-to-face.

¹⁵May you experience true peace. I send you greetings from the fellow believers here. Greet all our friends there personally.

Jude

Letter to Christians everywhere
From Jude, a Christian leader

The letter Jude is named for its author rather than for its recipients. Identifying this "Jude" is a bit of a challenge since Jude (or Judas) was a common name at the time. Because the hero of the Maccabean wars bore the name Judas, Jewish parents often named their boys Judas during this period. The author describes himself as a servant of the Liberating King and the brother of James. But which James? That, too, was a common name. Church tradition suggests that he was James, the brother of Jesus, the head of the Jerusalem church and author of the letter James. If so, this makes Jude the second New Testament letter written by a family member of Jesus. During Jesus' public ministry, Jude was not a disciple of Jesus. As with other members of his family, Jude likely became a follower of Jesus after the resurrection when the crucified and risen Jesus appeared to His followers and family.

Jude writes this letter in the last half of the first century A.D. to an audience facing critical problems related to the influx of false teachers in their church. These false teachers are not out in the world to be easily avoided; they have infiltrated the church and are making inroads into the leadership of the young and vulnerable community. He writes this letter to encourage believers to keep up the struggle for the true faith. Some things are worth fighting for, and the truth of the gospel is one of them. Jude has often seen God's grace perverted by those who want to turn freedom into a license to sin. This was a common problem, then and now. If God is loving and forgiving, and if God's grace is free, then it is easy to take His goodness for granted. Jude counters that to do so denies our central confession: Jesus is Lord and Master.

After urging his audience to fight for the true faith, Jude looks back over a number of stories from the Bible and Jewish tradition that demonstrate how God's judgment has fallen upon those who disobey Him. In the same way, vile characters have slithered into Christian congregations in various places and are dismantling the spiritual community by grumbling, faultfinding, and promoting sexual perversion. Yet Jude is hopeful that if true believers will pray in the Spirit and continue in God's love, these defectors will be judged and defeated.

A careful comparison of this letter and Peter's second letter demonstrates a lot of common ideas and themes. Clearly the audiences for both letters were facing similar troubles. The problem of false teaching in the church was not just an ancient problem. As we see it today, Jude's authoritative counsel still holds.

¹Jude, a slave of Jesus, the Liberating King, and a brother of James, to *you*, the ones whom God our Father loves and has called and whom Jesus, the Liberator, has kept. ²Kindness, peace, love—may they never stop blooming in you and from you *into all of God's creation.*

³Friends, all I think about is our communal redemption, *the story of our Father sweeping us up together in His salvation hands. But these days my heart is troubled,* and I am compelled to write to you and encourage you to continue struggling for our common faith that was entrusted to the saints once and for all. ⁴Vile men have slithered in among us. Depraved souls who stand condemned have made a mockery of the grace given to us, using it as a pretext for a life of excess, lived without any thought of God. These *poor fools* have denied Jesus, the Liberating King, our one Lord and Master.

⁵*But even you, in your knowledge, forget God's saving acts.* You have heard the stories many times, *and the Spirit has enlightened you about their meaning,* but you still need to be reminded. Remember when the One *who scooped us from the earth* saved our ancestors by scooping them from the land in Egypt? *He breathed life into our earthen lungs* and took back the life from those who did not believe.

⁶So has God kept the *rebellious* heavenly messengers bound and chained in utter darkness—*shadowy gloom*—until the time when His judgment arrives, because they failed to keep their rightful positions and abandoned their appointed realms. ⁷Sodom and Gomorrah and all their neighbors were defeated by their own sexual perversions as they pursued the strange and unnatural impulses of the flesh. Let these who *went their own way and* are experiencing the eternal heat of God's vengeance—a punishment by fire—be a warning to you. *Let it be known: God will be glorified.*

⁸*These stories are examples to help you understand the fate of* those dreamers who have *slipped in and* defiled your community, rejected those in charge, and insulted the glorious majesty of the heavenly mes-

sengers. ⁹Even their chief, Michael, when disputing with the devil over Moses' body, did not offer his own taunting judgment against him. Michael simply said, "May the Lord's rebuke fall on you."*

¹⁰The deceivers among you despise what they do not understand; they live without reason like animals, reacting only with primal instincts, and their ways are corrupting them. ¹¹Woe to these *deceivers! They are doomed!* They have followed in the footsteps of *their father* Cain, sold their souls for profit into Balaam's deceit, and suffered the devastation of Korah's rebellion.

¹²These men are cold stones on the warm hearth of your love feasts as they glut themselves without fear, thinking only of their own benefit. They are waterless clouds, carried away by the wind; autumn's lonely and barren trees, twice dead, uprooted; ¹³violent waves of the sea *breaking over the bow*, foaming with shame; *lost and* wandering stars destined to live forever in gloomy darkness. *They are hopeless and without a home.*

¹⁴During the seventh generation after Adam, the prophet Enoch said, "Look! The Lord came, and with Him tens of thousands of His holy messengers ¹⁵to judge wicked men and convict the impious and ungodly for all they have said and all the hard things they have done against the Holy One." ¹⁶These men are complainers who look long and hard to find the faults of other men. They are led by their own lustful desires *like fools down the path of destruction*. They are arrogant liars who want only to get ahead of others, *and they will say whatever they must to reach that sick goal.*

¹⁷But you, friends, remember the words of the emissaries* of the Lord Jesus, our Liberating King: ¹⁸"At the end of time, some will ridicule *the faithful* and follow their lusts *to the grave*." ¹⁹These are the men among you—those who divide friends, those concerned ultimately with this

---

* Verse 9 Compare Zechariah 3:1-10.
* Verse 17 Literally, apostles

world, those without the Spirit. [20]You, however, should stand firm *in God's love* like builders constructing a life within the holy faith, praying the Spirit's prayer, [21]and staying with the love of your Creator. Wait eagerly for the kindness of our Lord Jesus, the Liberating King, which will deliver you to eternal life.

[22]Keep being kind to those who waver *in this faith*. [23]Pursue those who are singed by the flames *of God's wrath* and bring them safely *to Him*. Show mercy to others with fear, despising every garment soiled by the *weakness of human* flesh.

[24]Now to the One who can keep you upright and plant you firmly in His presence—clean, unmarked, and joyful in the light of His glory— [25]to the *one and* only God, our Savior, through Jesus, the Liberating King, our Lord, be glory and greatness and might and authority; just as it has been since before He created time, may it continue now and into eternity. Amen.

Revelation

Letter to the seven churches
From John, the apostle

On the Island of Patmos in the Aegean Sea, a prophet named John writes to congregations of faithful, but frightened, Christians in Asia Minor. Under the dim light of an oil lamp, John paints a picture of the vision he was given of the world that is and that is to come. This book of letters and visions is to be sent to the hardy churches that have stood strong through persecutions, heresies, and many temptations. However, knocking at the door are Satan and his forces. They are encroaching on the domain of God's kingdom.

Satan's minions, led by the beast and the false prophet, are ready to battle the armies of heaven. This war that begins in the celestial realm will spill over to the world below. While the nations of earth rally around the banner of the evil one, heavenly messengers prepare for a battle that has all of creation at stake.

Still, as John knows, the Lamb-King has already vanquished evil in the world. John's ink-stained hands write of the One who is renewing all of creation and establishing an everlasting order. God has Rome and all the powers that rule the earth on a short leash. Soon the nations of the earth will see the All Powerful, the One who has given His life for the many. This is the future as it has been unveiled to John.

John writes of what he sees and hears in his vision. Sometimes he hears one thing but turns to see something altogether different. Sometimes he sees multiple images of the same event as if he views it from different perspectives. These visions are dynamic; they far exceed the imagery we experience in our contemporary world and are far superior to what can be produced on film or through television. John's apocalyptic images challenge the imagination. The imagery in Revelation involves numbers, word pictures, and symbols that held religious and political significance for the churches in Asia Minor. Many of the images come from the Hebrew prophetic literature of Isaiah, Ezekiel, and Daniel. John's audience did not need a guide to interpret the "ciphers"; each image already held relevance for them. However, those of us living in a twenty-first-century context must "decipher" these images to see what they meant for John's world and what they mean for us today.

1 Prologue: This is the revelation of Jesus, the Liberating King: *an account of visions and a heavenly journey.* God granted this to Him so He would show His followers the realities that *are already breaking into the world and* soon will be fulfilled. Through His heavenly messenger, He revealed to His servant John *signs and insight into these mysteries.* ²John, *in turn,* gave witness to the word of God and to the *glorious* truth revealed about Jesus, the Liberator, *the Chosen Ruler,* by *carefully* describing everything he saw.

³Blessings come to those who read *and proclaim* these words aloud; blessings come to those who listen closely and put the prophetic words recorded here into practice. The finale is approaching.

⁴*I, John,* to the seven churches in Asia:

May you experience God's favor *and rest* in the peace that comes from the One who is, the One who was, and the One who is coming; from the seven Spirits, *the Perfect Spirit,* constantly before God's throne; ⁵and from Jesus, the Liberating King, the Witness who is *true and* faithful, the first to emerge from death's cold womb, the *chosen* Ruler over all the kings *and rulers* of the earth.

To the One who loves us and liberated us from *the grip of* our evil deeds through His very own blood ⁶and who established us to be *His* kingdom and priests for God, His Father. May glory and power be His throughout all the ages. Amen.

⁷Look! He is coming with the clouds,
    in glory.
He will capture every eye;
Even those who pierced Him
    through *will not be able to avert
    their eyes.*
All the nations of the earth will be
    pierced with grief when He
    appears.

Yes, may all this be *done according to His plan.* Amen.

Lord God: ⁸I am the Alpha and the Omega, [the very beginning and the very end,]* the One who is, the One who was, and the One who is coming: the All Powerful.

⁹I, John, your brother who shares with you *this journey* in persecution and the *establishment of the* Kingdom and endurance in Jesus, was on the island called Patmos because *of the ministry* of the word of God and my testimony about Jesus. ¹⁰I was in the Spirit on the Lord's Day *(the first day of the week),* and I heard a voice behind me. It sounded like the blast of a trumpet.

A Voice: ¹¹[I am the Alpha and the Omega, the very beginning and the very end.]* Make a book of what you see, write it down, and send it to the seven churches [which are in Asia]*: Ephesus, Smyrna, Pergamum, Thyatira, Sardis, Philadelphia, and Laodicea.

¹²When I turned around to see what sort of voice this was that was addressing me, I saw seven golden lampstands. ¹³And among the lampstands, I saw One like the Son of Man *right in front of me* dressed in a long robe. Across His chest was draped a golden sash. ¹⁴His head and hair were pure white, white as wool and white as snow; His eyes blazed like a fiery flame; ¹⁵His feet gleamed like brightly polished bronze, purified *to perfection* in a furnace; His voice *filled the air and* sounded like a roaring waterfall. ¹⁶He held seven stars in His right hand, from His mouth darted a sharp double-edged sword, and His face shone a brilliant light, like the blinding sun.

¹⁷When I saw Him, I fell at His feet. It was as though I were dead. But He *reached down and* placed His right hand on me.

The One: This is not the time for fear; I am the First and the Last, ¹⁸and *I am* the living One. I entered the realm of the dead; but see, I am alive now and for all the

* 1:8 Most manuscripts omit this portion.
* 1:11 Early manuscripts omit this portion.
* 1:11 Most manuscripts omit this portion.

ages—even ages to come. [Amen.]* I possess the keys *to open the prison* of death and hades.

¹⁹Now write down all you have seen—all that is and all that will be. ²⁰Regarding the mystery of the seven stars you saw in My right hand and of the seven golden lampstands—*let Me tell you so you will know:* the seven stars are the messengers who preside over the seven churches, and the seven lampstands are the seven churches *themselves*.

> he initial vision in this book of visions is of "the Son of Man." John and his audience know that this cryptic title, taken from the Book of Daniel, was Jesus' favorite way of talking about Himself. Here John tells us how the Son of Man appears to him in bright, shining glory. He uses the language of Scripture to try to describe the indescribable: what he saw, heard, and experienced that fateful Lord's Day. This bright, shining Son of Man walks and moves among the lampstands.
>
> As the story unfolds, we're told that the lampstands signify the churches. During harsh times of persecution, the faithful often wonder where their Master is. Is He even aware of what they are experiencing? John's vision confirms what the gospel already teaches: Jesus is present with them even in their suffering, moving among those who dare to bear the light. Lampstands, of course, are not the light. They only carry the light. The true Light that has come into the world is none other than Jesus, the Son of Man.

2 The One: Write *down My words and send them* to the messenger of the church in Ephesus, "These are the words of the One who holds the seven stars in His right hand, the One who walks *and moves* among the golden lampstands:

²"I know your deeds, your *tireless* labor, and your patient endurance. I know you do not tolerate those who do evil. Furthermore, you have *diligently* tested those who claim to be emissaries,* and *you have found that they* are not *true witnesses.* You have *correctly* found them to be false. ³*I know* you are patiently enduring and holding firm on behalf of My name. You have not become faint.

⁴"However, I have this against you: you have abandoned your first love—*your love for Me and your love for others.* ⁵Do you remember what it was like before you fell? *It's time to* rethink and change your ways;* go back to how you first acted *when your love was fresh and new.* However, if you do not return,* I will come quickly* and *personally* remove your lampstand from its place. ⁶But you do have this to your credit: you despise the deeds of the Nicolaitans *and how they concede to evil.* I also hate what they do.

⁷"Let the person who is able to hear, listen to *and follow* what the Spirit proclaims to all the churches. I will allow the one who conquers *through faithfulness even unto death* to eat from the tree of life found in God's *lush* paradise."

⁸Write *down My words and send them* to the messenger of the church in Smyrna, "These are the words of the First and the Last, the One who was dead and returned to life:

⁹"I know [your deeds and]* the difficult ordeal you are enduring and your poverty, although you are actually rich. I am aware of the offensive accusations preached by those who call themselves 'Jews.' But these people are not the Jews *they pretend to be;* they are actually the congregation of Satan. ¹⁰In the face of suffering, do not fear. *Suffering is inevitable.* Watch; the devil will throw

---

* 1:18 The earliest manuscripts omit "Amen."
* 2:2 Literally, apostles
* 2:5 Literally, repent
* 2:5 Literally, repent
* 2:5 Some manuscripts omit "quickly."
* 2:9 The earliest manuscripts omit this portion.

some of you into prison shortly so that you might be tested, and you will endure great affliction for 10 days. Be faithful throughout your life, until the day you die, and I will give you the *victor's* wreath of life.

[11]"Let the person who is able to hear, listen to *and follow* what the Spirit proclaims to all the churches. The one who conquers *through faithfulness even unto death* will escape the second death."

[12]Write *down My words and send them* to the messenger of the church in Pergamum, "These are the words of the One with the sharp double-edged sword:

[13]"I know [your deeds and]* where you live. It is where Satan, *the adversary,* has established his throne. *In the face of his presence,* you have stayed true to My name, and you did not deny your trust in Me even in the *eventful* days of My faithful witness, Antipas. He was killed among you *in that place* where Satan dwells.

[14]"However, I have a few matters against you: some *who live* among you hold to the teaching of Balaam, who instructed Balak to set up a stumbling block before the people of Israel.* *As a result,* some among you are eating food prepared for idol worship and committing immoral sexual acts. [15]You have others who are holding firm to the teaching of the Nicolaitans. [16]Therefore, change your ways and turn to Me.* If you do not, I will quickly come to where you live and will battle them with the sword of My mouth.

[17]"Let the person who is able to hear, listen to *and follow* what the Spirit proclaims to all the churches. To the one who conquers *through faithfulness even unto death*, I will feed you with hidden manna and give you a white stone. Upon this stone, a new name is engraved. No one knows this name except for its recipient."

[18]Write *down My words and send them* to the messenger of the church in Thyatira, "These are the words of the Son of God, the One whose eyes blaze like flames of fire and whose feet gleam like brightly polished bronze:

[19]"I know your deeds, your love, faithfulness, service, and endurance. Your labors greatly increase *in quality* as you travel along this journey.

[20]"However, I have this against you: you have tolerated that woman Jezebel, who is a self-anointed prophetess and who misleads My followers to commit immoral sexual acts and to eat food prepared for idol worship. [21]I have provided her enough time to turn away* *from her indecency,* but she refuses to turn from these immoral acts. [22]Watch; I will throw her back into her sickbed with those who committed adultery with her, and I will make *them a bed of* great affliction if they do not abandon her indiscretions and turn* *to follow Me.* [23]I will *punish her by* striking her children dead. Through this all the churches will know I am the One who *relentlessly* explores the mind and heart, and I will deal to each of you as you deserve according to your acts.

[24]"I say to the rest of you in Thyatira, those who have not held to the teachings *of Jezebel* and who remain ignorant of *the real meaning of what is called* the deep things of Satan, I will not burden you with anything more. [25]Just keep on task and keep the faith until I return.

[26]"And as for those who conquer *through faithfulness even unto death* and continue to labor with Me until the *close of the* final curtain,

I will give them authority over the
 nations.
[27]And they will rule the nations with
 an iron scepter,
  as fragile clay jars are shattered
  to pieces.*

As I received this authority from My Father, [28]I will bestow the morning star to the victor.

---

* 2:13 The earliest manuscripts omit this portion.
* 2:14 Numbers 22–24
* 2:16 Literally, repent
* 2:21 Literally, repent
* 2:22 Literally, repent
* 2:26-27 Psalm 2:8-9

29"Let the person who is able to hear, listen to *and follow* what the Spirit proclaims to *all* the churches."

For centuries many Jews had been scattered throughout the known world, exiled to the lands east of the Jordan River from the promised land by powerful invading nations. After Jerusalem fell in A.D. 70, even more Jews left Judea, this time crossing the Mediterranean looking for some place far from Roman cruelty. That's why, as John writes these letters to churches in Asia Minor, he recalls some of the most infamous characters from Israel's past: Balaam, Balak, and Jezebel. You see, the ordeals facing John's churches are not all that different from those Israel faced hundreds of years before, and many of the same struggles plague churches in the West to this day. The names may change, but the problems confronting God's faithful do not.

3 The One: Write *down My words and send them* to the messenger of the church in Sardis,

"These are the words of the One who has the seven Spirits of God, *the Perfect Spirit,* and the One who holds the seven stars:

"I know the things you do—you've claimed a reputation of life, but you are actually dead. 2Wake up *from your death-sleep,* and strengthen what remains *of the life you have been given* that is in danger of death. I have judged your deeds as far from complete in the sight of My God. 3Therefore, remember what you have received and heard; *it's time to* keep these instructions and turn back from your ways.* If you do not wake up *from this sleep, I will come in judgment.* I will creep up on you like a thief—you will have no way of knowing when I will come. 4But there are a few in Sardis who don't have the stain *of evil works* on their clothes. They will walk alongside Me in

white, *spotless garments* because they have been proven worthy.

5"The one who conquers *through faithfulness even unto death* will be clothed in white garments, and I will *certainly* not erase that person's name from the book of life. I will acknowledge this person's name before My Father and before His heavenly messengers.

6"Let the person who is able to hear, listen to *and follow* what the Spirit proclaims to all the churches."

7Write *down My words and send them* to the messenger of the church in Philadelphia,

"These are the words of the holy
   One, the true One,
and the One who possesses the
   key of David,
which opens *the possibilities* so
   that no one can shut them.
The One who closes *all
   options* so that no one can
   open:

8"I know your deeds. See, I have placed before you an open door, which no one can shut. *I have done this* because you have limited strength, yet you have obeyed My word and have not denied My name. 9Watch, and I will make those of the congregation of Satan—those who call themselves 'Jews' but are not because they lie—come before you penitent, falling at your feet. Then they will know how much I have loved you. 10Because you have obeyed My instructions to endure and be patient, I will protect you from the time of trial which will come upon the whole earth and put everyone in it to the test. 11I will soon return. Hold tight to what you have so that no one can take away your *victor's* wreath.

12"As for the one who conquers *through faithfulness even unto death,* I will plant that person as a pillar in the temple of My God, and that person will never have to leave *the presence of God. Moreover,* I will inscribe this person with

* 3:3 Literally, repent

the name of My God and the name of the city of My God, New Jerusalem—which descends out of heaven from My God—and My own new name.

¹³"Let the person who is able to hear, listen to *and follow* what the Spirit proclaims to all the churches."

¹⁴Write *down My words and send them* to the messenger of the church in Laodicea, "These are the words of the Amen, the Faithful and True Witness, the Beginning of God's creation:

¹⁵"I know your works. You are neither cold *with apathy* nor hot *with passion*. It would be better if you were one or the other. *But you are neither.* ¹⁶So because you are lukewarm, neither cold nor hot, I will vomit you out of My mouth. ¹⁷You claim: 'I am rich, I have accumulated riches, and I need nothing.' But you do not realize that you are miserable, pathetic, poor, blind, and naked. ¹⁸So here is what I suggest you do: buy *true gold* from Me (gold refined by fire so that you can be *truly* rich), white garments (to cover you so that you can keep the shame of your nakedness from showing), and eye ointment (to treat your eyes so that you may see clearly).

¹⁹"Those I love I also correct and discipline. Therefore, be shamelessly committed *to Me* and turn back.* ²⁰Now pay attention; I am standing at the door and knocking. *Don't you hear?* If anyone hears My voice and opens the door, then I will come in to *visit with* you and to share a meal at your table, and you will be with Me.

²¹"The one who conquers *through faithfulness even unto death* I will place next to Me on My throne, just as I Myself conquered and took a place *of honor* with My Father on His throne.

²²"Let the person who is able to hear, listen to *and follow* what the Spirit proclaims to all the churches."

4 After I wrote down these messages, I saw a door standing open in heaven and heard again the first voice that sounded like a trumpet.

A Voice: Come up here, and I will show you what must happen after this.

> *J*ohn's next vision begins sometime later when he sees an open door in heaven. The same voice that called to him earlier to see the Son of Man moving through the lampstands now beckons him to come into heaven and enter through the door. What happens next would have been impossible for John to imagine.

²Immediately I was *caught up* in the Spirit, and I saw a throne that stood in heaven and One seated on the throne. ³The One enthroned gleamed like jasper and carnelian, and a rainbow encircled the throne with an emerald glow. ⁴Encircling that *great* throne were twenty-four *smaller* thrones with twenty-four elders clothed in white robes with wreaths fashioned of gold on their heads. ⁵Out of the *great* throne came flashes of lightning, sounds of voices, and peals of thunder. In front of the great throne, seven torches were ablaze, which are the seven Spirits of God. ⁶Also in front of the throne was a glassy sea of shimmering crystal.

In the midst of the throne and encircling the throne were four living creatures, covered all over with eyes, front to back. ⁷The first living creature was like a lion, the second creature was like an ox, the third creature had a face like the face of a human, and the fourth creature was like an eagle in full flight. ⁸These four living creatures, each of which had six wings and was covered with eyes—eyes on the outside and on the inside—did not cease chanting. All day and night *they were singing.*

Four Living Creatures:
Holy, holy, holy
Is the Lord God who is the All
Powerful,
who was, and who is, and who is
coming.

* 3:19 Literally, repent

[9]And when the living creatures declared glory and honor and thanksgiving to the One seated on the throne, the One who lives throughout all the ages, [10]the twenty-four elders fell prostrate before the One seated on the throne, worshiped the One who lives throughout all the ages, cast their *golden* wreaths before the throne, and chanted *to Him.*

24 Elders:

> [11]Worthy are You, O Lord; worthy
> are You, O God,
> to receive glory and honor and
> power.
> You *alone* created all things,
> and through Your will *and by
> Your design,* they exist and
> were created.

*T*hroughout this book of letters and visions, numbers play an important role. Numbers and their multiples are signs of great mysterious realities. We've already seen how the Son of Man moved among seven lampstands and held seven stars in His right hand. The number "seven" represents perfection and completeness. Another important number is the number "twelve" because it represents the people of God. The children of Israel consisted of twelve tribes, and Jesus called "the twelve" to follow Him and embody the new covenant. The number "twelve" and multiples of "twelve" recur throughout the book to signify the people of God, so here the twenty-four elders (12 + 12) signify the people of God, both the old and new covenants.

*5*And then I saw a scroll in the right hand of the One seated upon the throne, a scroll written both on the inside and on the outside. It had been sealed with seven seals. [2]Then a mighty heavenly messenger proclaimed with a loud voice,

Mighty Messenger: Who is worthy to break the seals and open the scroll?

[3]No creature *of creation* in all heaven, on all the earth, or even under the earth could open the scroll or look into its *mysteries.* [4]Then I began to *mourn and* weep bitterly because no creature *of creation* was found who was worthy to open the scroll or to look into its *mysteries.* [5]Then one of the elders consoled me.

One of the 24 Elders: Stop weeping. Look there—the Lion of the tribe of Judah, the Root of David. He has conquered and is able to break its seven seals and open the scroll.

[6]I looked, and between the throne and the four living creatures and the *twenty-four* elders stood a Lamb who appeared to have been slaughtered. The Lamb had seven horns and seven eyes (the eyes are the seven Spirits of God sent out over all the earth).

*J*ohn hears that the Lion of the tribe of Judah, the Root of David, has arrived and will open the seals to reveal the scroll's mysteries. But when he turns to see the Lion, he sees a Lamb instead. Not everything is as it appears. The Lamb stands, even though He has been slaughtered as a sacrifice, because He has been resurrected from the dead. And now in his vision, John sees things as they truly are: the Lamb-King has seven horns and seven eyes, signifying the perfect power and perfect sight He possesses to rule the world.

[7]The Lamb came and took the scroll from the right hand of the One seated upon the throne. [8]And when He took it, the four living creatures and twenty-four elders fell prostrate before the Lamb. *They worshiped Him, and* each one held a harp and golden bowls filled with incense (the prayers of God's holy people). [9]Then they sang a new song.

Four Living Creatures and 24 Elders:

> You are worthy to receive the
> scroll,
> to break its seals,

Because You were slain. With Your
  blood, You redeemed for God
people from every tribe and
  language, people from every
  race and nation.
¹⁰You have made them a kingdom;
  You have appointed them
  priests to serve our God,
and they* will rule upon the
  earth.

¹¹When I looked *again,* I heard the voices
of heavenly messengers (numbering
myriads of myriads and thousands of
thousands). They surrounded the throne,
the living creatures, and the elders.

Thousands of Messengers *(with a great voice)*:
  ¹²Worthy is the Lamb who was slain.
  Worthy is the Lamb to receive
    authority and wealth and
    wisdom and greatness
  And honor and glory and praise.

¹³Then I heard every creature in heaven
and on earth and beneath the earth and in
the sea and all things in them echoing *the
messengers.*

Every Creature:
  To the One who sits on the throne
    and to the Lamb
  Be blessing and honor and glory
    and power
  Throughout the ages.

¹⁴And the four living creatures kept on
repeating:

Four Living Creatures: Amen. *Amen.*

And the elders fell down and worshiped
[Him who lives forever].*

6 Then I saw the Lamb break the first of
the seven seals, and I heard one of the
four living creatures call out with a
thundering voice.

First Living Creature: Come!

²Then I looked, and what a sight! There was
a white horse carrying a rider with a bow.
He wore a wreath and came riding like a
conqueror, intent on complete victory.
  ³The Lamb broke the second seal, and
the second living creature called out.

Second Living Creature: Come!

⁴Then another horse, fiery red, sped forth.
Its rider was granted the power to steal
peace from the earth and received a large
sword so that people would slaughter each
other.
  ⁵The Lamb broke the third seal, and the
third living creature called out.

Third Living Creature: Come!

Then I looked, and behold, there was a
black horse! Its rider held in his hand a balance scale. ⁶And I heard a voice emanating
from the middle of the four living creatures.

A Voice: A quart* of wheat for a whole day's
wage,* three quarts of barley for a whole
day's wage, but do not harm the olive oil
and the wine!

⁷And when the Lamb broke the fourth seal,
the fourth living creature called out.

Fourth Living Creature: Come!

⁸I looked, and behold, there was a pale
green horse! Its rider's name was Death,
and Hades accompanied him. Together
they were granted authority over one-
fourth of the earth to kill with weapons,
with famine, with disease, and with wild
animals that roamed the earth.

*T*he breaking of the seals
  releases the four riders and a
series of disasters and plagues. Even

* 5:10 Other manuscripts read "we."
* 5:14 Some manuscripts omit this portion.
* 6:6 Literally, choinix, a Roman unit of measure
* 6:6 Greek denarius

though what follows appears to be extreme violence unleashed against the earth and its inhabitants, there is a limitation to what follows. Death and Hades have the authority to kill, but their authority extends only to one-fourth of the earth. The slaughtered souls cry out for vengeance, but they will have to wait a little longer until more martyrs are killed for their testimony.

⁹When the Lamb broke the fifth seal, I saw under the *heavenly* altar the souls of those murdered for holding fast to the word of God and their testimony. ¹⁰They cried out in a great, *singular* voice.

Murder Victims: How much longer, O Lord, the holy One, the true One, until You pronounce judgment on the inhabitants of the earth? Until You avenge our blood?

¹¹Then they were each given a white robe and told to rest for a little while longer—soon their number would be complete. In a little while, more of their fellow servants, brothers, *and sisters* would be murdered as they had been.

¹²When the Lamb broke the sixth seal, a great earthquake shook the earth and the sun *grew dark and* became black (like mourning sackcloth) and the full moon became red like blood. ¹³The stars of heaven fell to earth as a fig tree drops its fruit during a *winter* storm. ¹⁴The sky snapped back as a scroll when it is rolled up. Every mountain was shaken off its foundation, and every island melted into the sea. ¹⁵The rulers of the earth, the important and the great, the generals, the wealthy and the powerful, the slave and the free person, hid themselves in the caves and among the mountains' rocks. ¹⁶They pleaded with loud *suicidal* requests to the rocks and mountains.

People of the Earth: Fall on us. Hide us from the *fierce* presence of the One who sits on the throne, from the wrath of the

Lamb. ¹⁷The great day of their* wrath has come. Who can withstand it?

7 After this *vision*, I saw four heavenly messengers standing at the four corners of the earth. They were holding back the four winds so that the earth would not be *overcome by violent, rushing* winds blowing over the land or over the sea or blowing down any tree. ²Then I saw a *fifth* messenger, coming up with the sun as it was rising *in the east*, carrying the seal of the living God. He called with a *great and* loud voice to the four messengers who had authority to harm the earth and its seas.

Fifth Messenger: ³Do not harm the land or the sea or the trees until we seal the servants of our God *with a mark of ownership* on their foreheads.

⁴⁻⁸Then I heard that 144,000 would receive the seal, 12,000 from every tribe of Israel: Judah, Reuben, Gad, Asher, Naphtali, Manasseh, Simeon, Levi, Issachar, Zebulun, Joseph, and Benjamin. ⁹After *I heard about* these *who would be sealed*, I looked and saw a huge crowd of people, which no one could *even begin to* count, representing every nation and tribe, people and language, standing before the throne and before the Lamb, wearing white robes and waving palm branches. ¹⁰They cried out with one loud voice.

Crowd: Salvation comes only from our God, who sits upon the throne, and from the Lamb.

John hears that 144,000 people out of Israel are destined to be sealed, but then he turns to see an innumerable multitude from every people group in the world. What he sees reveals the truth of what he

---

* 6:17 Other manuscripts read "His."

hears: the number "144,000" is not an exact count of who will be saved but is a symbolic number (12 x 12 x 1000). Remember, "twelve" is a number that signifies all the people of God, from both the Old and New Testaments. In reality, between the sixth and seventh seal, there is an interlude, an opportunity for people from every nation to enter into the people of God, to receive God's mark, and to take their places among the redeemed.

[11]All the heavenly messengers stood up, encircling the throne and the elders and the four living creatures, and they fell prostrate before the throne and worshiped God.

Heavenly Messengers, Elders, and Living Creatures:
> [12]Amen! Praise and glory and wisdom
> And thanksgiving and honor
> And power and might
> Be to our God on and on
> throughout all the ages.
> Amen.

One of the Elders (to me): [13]Who are these people clothed in white robes, and where have they come from?
John: [14]Sir, surely you know *the answer to your own questions.*
One of the Elders: These are coming from the *time of* great suffering and affliction. They have washed their robes in the blood of the Lamb, cleansing them *pure* white.

> [15]Responding *out of a heart filled with praise,* they congregate before the throne of God
> and constantly worship Him day and night in His temple.
> The One seated on the throne will *always* live among them.
> [16]They will never be hungry or thirsty again.
> The sun or blazing heat will never scorch them *as it did in the past,*

> [17]Because the Lamb *who stands* at the center of the throne is their shepherd *and they are His sheep,*
> and He will lead them to the water of life.
> And God will dry every tear from their eyes.

8 When the Lamb cracked open the seventh *and final* seal, *a great* silence filled all heaven *penetrating everything* for about half an hour. *Nothing was heard— only silence.* [2]Then I saw seven heavenly messengers, the ones who stand before God, receive seven trumpets.

[3]An *eighth* messenger came and stood before the altar carrying a golden censer. He received a large portion of incense to complement the prayers of all the saints on the golden altar *that sits* in front of the throne. [4]From the hand of the *eighth* messenger, the smoke of the incense mixed with the prayers of God's people and billowed up before God. [5]The messenger filled the censer with fiery *coals* from the altar and cast it upon the earth, causing *a great commotion of* thunder, rumblings, flashes of lightning, and an earthquake.

[6]The seven heavenly messengers raised the seven trumpets and prepared to sound them.

[7]The first messenger sounded *his trumpet,* and a blast of hail and fire mixed with blood was cast down to the earth. *As a result,* one-third of the land was set ablaze, one-third of the trees were burned, and all the green grass was scorched.

[8]The second messenger sounded *his trumpet,* and something like a great mountain, *with bright flames of* burning fire, was cast into the sea. *As a result,* one-third of the sea turned into blood, [9]one-third of the living sea creatures died, and one-third of the ships were obliterated.

[10-11]The third messenger sounded *his trumpet,* and a great star called Wormwood dropped out of heaven, flaming like a torch as it fell on one-third of the rivers and the springs. *As a result,* one-third of the waters turned *bitter like the herb* wormwood so

that many people died from the *poisonous bitter waters.*

[12]The fourth messenger sounded *his trumpet,* and one-third of the sun, one-third of the moon, and one-third of the stars were darkened. *As a result,* one-third of their light *flickered and* failed. For one-third of the day, *the sun* did not shine and likewise, for one-third of the night, *the moon and stars* did not give their light.

[13]Then I saw an eagle flying through midheaven, and I heard it cry with a loud voice.

Eagle: Woe, woe, woe—*horror, disaster, and calamity*—to the earthdwellers! The rest of the trumpet blasts from the last three messengers are about to sound.

*W*hen the heavenly messengers blast their trumpets, another cycle of disasters begin. In this round, each calamity affects one-third of the earth, its inhabitants, and its cosmic partners—the sun, moon, and stars. Time is now flying by as the level of the disasters grows.

9 Then the fifth messenger sounded *his trumpet.* I saw a star that had dropped out of heaven to earth. He received the key *that unlocks the shaft leading* to the abyss, *the pit that falls away to nothingness,* and [2]he opened *the shaft to* the abyss. *Huge columns of* smoke rose from the depths of the cavern—*a black, ugly* smoke as if from a great furnace so that the sun was darkened and the air was thickened by the *blanket of* smoke from the shaft. [3]From the smoke, locusts appeared *and swarmed* upon the earth. They were given power, like the power of scorpions on the earth. [4-5]However, they were instructed not to damage any grasses, plants, or trees that grow from the earth. Instead, they were given power for five months to torture, but not to kill, the people without the seal of God upon their foreheads. The torment they inflicted was like the sting of a scorpion when it strikes. [6]During those days, people will seek any

way possible to kill themselves, but death will not befriend them. They will long to die *and end their miseries,* but death will elude them.

[7]The locusts looked like horses *clad in armor,* ready for battle. They wore golden wreaths on their heads, and their faces appeared human [8]with hair as *long as* women's hair, but they had teeth as *sharp as* lions' teeth. [9]They had armor that appeared to be iron-plated, and when their wings flapped, they sounded like an army of horse-drawn chariots rushing into battle. [10]They have tails like scorpions with stingers, and the power invested in them to inflict torture on people for five months lies in their tails. [11]They were ruled by the messenger of the abyss, whose Hebrew name is Abaddon, and whose Greek name is Apollyon, *both meaning "the Destroyer."*

[12]The first disaster has occurred; there are two more disasters to come.

[13]Then the sixth messenger sounded *his trumpet,* and I heard a voice from the four corners of the golden altar that is before God, [14]commanding the sixth messenger with the trumpet.

A Voice: Set loose the four messengers who are bound *in chains* at the great river Euphrates.

[15]Then the four messengers, who had been held *in chains* until the hour and the day and the month and the year when they would kill one-third of humanity, were released.

[16]I heard that 200 million soldiers rode in the cavalry. [17]This is how these horses and their riders appeared in my vision: the riders wore breastplates of fiery red, smoky blue,* and sulfur yellow. The heads of the horses seemed to be like the heads of lions; they breathed fire and smoke and sulfur from their mouths, [18]killing one-third of humanity with the three plagues coming out of their mouths. [19]The *lethal* power of these horses was not only in their mouths but also in their tails because their

---

* 9:17 Literally, jacinth (a semiprecious blue stone)

tails, which resembled snakes, had heads that inflicted injury.

²⁰The rest of humanity, those not killed by these plagues, did not rethink their course and turn away* from the devices of their own making. *Despite all these calamities,* they continued worshiping demons and idols crafted in gold, silver, bronze, stone, and wood. *They bowed down to images* which cannot see or hear or walk. ²¹They failed to turn away* from their murders, their sorceries, their sexual immoralities, and their thefts.

10 Then I saw another extremely powerful messenger descending out of heaven. He wore a cloud wrapped around him, and a rainbow was covering his head. His face *shone* like the sun, and his legs *blazed* like columns of fire. ²In his hand, he held a little scroll that had been unrolled. He placed his right foot on the sea and his left foot on dry land; ³then he shouted with a voice that sounded like a roaring lion. When he cried out, the seven thunders answered with their own rumbling voices. ⁴As I was about to record the thunders' answer, a voice from heaven stopped me.

A Voice: Seal up all the seven thunders have spoken; do not write it down!

⁵Then the messenger, whom I saw standing on the sea and on the dry land, raised his right hand into heaven ⁶and swore *an oath* to the Eternal One—who always lives, who created heaven, earth, the sea, and all that is in them.

Heavenly Messenger: Time has run out. ⁷Whenever the days arrive and the seventh messenger sounds his trumpet, the mystery of God will be accomplished just as He announced to His servants, the prophets.

⁸Again, the voice I heard from heaven addressed me.

A Voice: Go. Take the *little* scroll that is unrolled in the hand of the messenger

standing both on the sea and on the dry land.

⁹I then went to the messenger and asked him to give me the little scroll.

Heavenly Messenger: Take it, and eat it. Although in your mouth it will be sweet to the taste, sweet as honey, it will become bitter when it reaches your stomach.

¹⁰I took the little scroll from the hand of the messenger and ate it. In my mouth, it was sweet like honey, but my stomach became bitter after I swallowed it.

Heavenly Messengers (*repeating*): ¹¹Once again, you are to prophesy about many peoples, nations, languages, and kings.

> *T*he scroll John eats is taken from the hand of the powerful messenger who announces the fulfillment of all the prophecies. Just as it did for the Old Testament prophet Ezekiel (2:8–3:4), the scroll represents the message John is required to proclaim, but first he must take it in and it must become a part of him. Initially it tastes sweet, but as it settles deep within him, it becomes bitter. God's message is always bittersweet. It is sweet joy for those who turn to God, but bitter sadness for those who do not accept the gospel.

11 Then I received a measuring rod. It resembled a staff, and I was commanded *to take some measurements of the temple in Jerusalem.*

A Voice: Get up, and measure the temple of God, the altar, and those who worship in it. ²However, do not measure the court outside of the temple. Separate that area

---

* 9:20 Literally, repent
* 9:21 Literally, repent

out because it has been handed over to the nations. They will trample over the holy city for 42 months. ³I will authorize my two witnesses to prophesy for 1,260 days dressed in sackcloth, *the clothes that mourners wear.*

⁴These *two witnesses* are the two olive trees and two lampstands standing in front of the Lord of the earth. ⁵If anyone wishes to harm the witnesses, fire spews out of the witnesses' mouths and consumes their foes *in flames.* Anyone who wishes to harm them is *destined* to die this way. ⁶They have the authority to shut up the sky so that no rain may fall during the time of their prophecies. They also have authority to turn the waters into blood and to strike the earth with any plague whenever they desire.

> *T*he two witnesses bear a striking resemblance to the faithful prophets of Israel and the faithful martyrs of the churches. Together they stand speaking God's message as the nations rant and rave and trample the holy city. As we saw earlier, the lampstands signify the churches. They are not the light, but they welcome the light and present it to the world. The olive tree, even today, is a symbol of Israel. Olive trees supply the oil for the lamps so that they may burn bright in the darkness. For a season, the two witnesses enjoy God's protection, but a time is coming when they will fall victim to the nations and then lie silent.

⁷On the day they finish their testimony, the beast from the abyss will declare war on them and win victory by killing them. ⁸Their dead bodies will lie in the street of the great city, which, spiritually speaking, is called Sodom and Egypt, where their Lord was crucified. ⁹For three and a half days, representatives of the peoples and ethnicities, languages and nations stare down at their lifeless bodies and refuse

them a proper burial. ¹⁰Because these two prophets tormented the earthdwellers *by speaking God's message*, the people will rejoice over their dead bodies and celebrate their deaths by exchanging gifts with one another.

¹¹At the end of the three and a half days, the spirit of life that comes from God entered their corpses, *resurrected them,* and they stood *again* on their feet. Those who looked on were terrified by what they saw. ¹²Then they heard a great voice from heaven.

A Voice: Come up here!

Their enemies watched *the spectacle* as the witnesses ascended into heaven in a cloud. ¹³In that same hour, a great earthquake shook *the earth* causing one-tenth of the city to crumble *into dust,* and 7,000 people were killed in the earthquake. Then the rest *who were left alive,* quaking in fear, *turned and* glorified the God of heaven. ¹⁴The second disaster has passed; watch as the third disaster comes quickly.

¹⁵The seventh messenger sounded *his trumpet,* and great voices in heaven confessed:

Voices from Heaven:
> The kingdom of the world has
> given way to the kingdom of
> our Lord
> and of His Liberating King.
> He will reign throughout the ages.

> *W*hen the seventh messenger blows his trumpet, the kingdom of this world comes to an end. Life as we know it is never the same. With the blast of this trumpet, the rule and reign of God and His Liberating King has arrived in full to eclipse the rogue kings who rebelled against the Creator and mocked His good name. God's kingdom entered our world in the incarnation, death, and resurrection of Jesus. It slipped in almost unnoticed beneath the noses of the powers

that be. It grows silently as a seed in the earth until it fills the cosmos. In our day, Christians live between the times: we live as aliens and strangers rescued from this present darkness, but we also live as citizens who long for the Kingdom that is to come. Until then we are to seek His kingdom and help carve out the territories for the Liberating King.

¹⁶Then the twenty-four elders, who sit before God on their thrones, fell prostrate and worshiped God.

24 Elders:

¹⁷We give You thanks, Lord God, the
All Powerful,
who is and who was.
For You have wielded Your great
power
and have begun Your reign.
¹⁸The nations have raged *against*
You,
but Your wrath has *finally* come.
It is now time to judge *all of* the
dead,
To give a just reward to Your
servants, the prophets,
and to the saints and all who
honor Your name,
both the small and the great,
And to destroy those who cause
destruction to the earth.

¹⁹Then God's temple in heaven was opened up, and the ark of His covenant could be seen within His temple. Lightning flashed *all around*. Noises and thunder rumbled. The earth trembled. Heavy hailstones fell *from the sky*.

12 *As I looked,* a great sign appeared in heaven: a woman *came into view* clothed in *the radiance of* the sun, *standing* with the moon under her feet, and she was crowned with a wreath of twelve stars on her head. ²She was *painfully* pregnant and was crying out in the agony of labor. ³Then a second sign appeared in heaven, *ominous, foreboding*: a great red dragon, with seven crowned heads and ten horns. ⁴The dragon's tail brushed one-third of the stars from the sky and hurled them down to the earth. The dragon crouched in front of the laboring woman, waiting to devour her child the moment it was born.

⁵She gave birth to a male child, who is *destined* to rule the nations with an iron scepter. *Before the dragon could bite and devour her son,* the child was whisked away and brought to God and His throne. ⁶The woman fled into the wilderness, where God had prepared a place *of refuge and safety* where she could find sustenance for 1,260 days.

The sign that appears in the vision is of a celestial woman who gives birth to a son. While it's possible that this could refer to Mary, the mother of Jesus, it is also possible this is a symbol of God's chosen people. The faithful remnant of Israel is the womb that carried the Liberating King and delivered Him to the world. While the great red dragon did his best to destroy and devour Him, God had another plan. Since then, the dragon and his minions have done their best to harangue and persecute the woman's children. But again he does not have the final word.

⁷A battle broke out in heaven. Michael, along with his heavenly messengers, clashed against the dragon. The dragon and his messengers returned the fight, ⁸but they did not prevail and were defeated. *As a result,* there was no place left for them in heaven. ⁹So the great dragon, that ancient serpent who is called the devil and Satan, the deceiver of the whole world, was cast down to the earth along with his messengers. ¹⁰Then I heard a great voice in heaven.

A Voice:

Now the salvation and the power
and the kingdom of our God

and the authority of His
Liberating King have come.
For the accuser of our brothers
and sisters,
who relentlessly accuses them
day and night before our
God, has been cast down *and
silenced.*
[11]By the blood of the Lamb
and the word of their witnesses,
they have become victorious
over him,
For they did not hold on to their
lives, even under threat of
death.
[12]Therefore, rejoice, all you heavens;
celebrate, all you who live in
them.
But disaster will befall the earth
and the sea,
for the devil has come down to
your spheres,
And he is incredibly angry
because he knows his time is
nearly over.

[13]*Down below the scene was very different.*
When the dragon realized he had been cast
down to the earth, he pursued the mother
of the male infant. [14]In order to escape
the serpent, she was given the two wings
of the great eagle to fly *deeper* into the
wilderness to her own special place where
she would find sustenance for a time, and
times, and half a time. [15]Then from his
mouth the serpent spewed water like a
raging river that chased after the woman,
trying to sweep her away in the flood. [16]But
the earth came to her rescue. It opened its
gaping mouth and swallowed the river
that spewed from the dragon's mouth.
[17]*As a result*, the dragon was enraged at the
woman and went away to make war on the
rest of her children—those who keep the
commandments of God and hold fast to the
testimony of Jesus, His Liberating King.

[18]And the dragon* stood *waiting* on the
sand of the seashore, *for another horror
was about to arise.*

13 I saw a beast with ten horns and
seven heads rising out of the
blackness of the sea. On its horns

hung ten crowns, and on its heads were
inscribed blasphemous names. [2]This beast
was like a leopard, its feet were like the
claws of a bear, and its mouth was like the
jaws of a lion. The dragon bestowed it
with his power and his throne and his
great authority. [3]One of the beast's heads
appeared to have suffered a fatal blow,
but its mortal wound had *somehow* been
healed. Amazed *at the miracle and its
power*, all the earth followed the beast.
[4]People worshiped the dragon because he
had given his authority to the beast, [4]and
they worshiped the beast *because of its
power.*

Earth: Who can match the beast? Who can
fight against it?

*T*he beast emerges from the
murky waters resembling the
dragon, but it has other features,
too, that resemble the four beasts
as described in Daniel 7. Daniel, in
his visions, learns that the beasts
represent the empires that terrorized
Israel and the rest of the world: the
Babylonians, Persians, Medes, and
Greeks. This beast in John's vision may
well be none other than the Roman
Empire with its own beastly authority,
the Caesar, who demanded worship.
"Caesar is Lord," they dared to claim.
But John knew better. In every generation, powerful people and institutions
arise—political predators that demand
loyalty at least, sometimes even worship.

[5]And the beast was given a mouth that bel-
lowed arrogant boasts and uttered great
blasphemies, and it was permitted to do
what it willed for 42 months. [6]Its mouth
opened with a stream of insults against
God, blaspheming His name, cursing His
dwelling and those who live in heaven.
[7]Also it received permission to declare war
against the saints and conquer them. Not a

* 12:18 Some late manuscripts read "I."

single nation, people, language, or ethnicity could escape its dominion. ⁸The inhabitants of the earth will worship it, *that is,* all those whose names have not been recorded before the foundation of the world in the book of life of the Lamb who was slaughtered.

⁹Let the person who is able to hear, listen *carefully*:

¹⁰If someone is destined for captivity,
    a captive he will be.
If someone is destined [to die]* by
        the sword,
    by the sword he will die.

The endurance and faithfulness of the saints will be *tested* here.

¹¹As I watched, I saw a second beast, *this one* rising up from the earth. It had two horns like a lamb, but it was speaking with the voice of a dragon.

> *T*he second beast, which later becomes "the false prophet," has horns like the lamb, but its true nature is revealed in its dragonlike voice. Many pretenders and posers exist in the spiritual world. This new beast would have us believe it represents the true God, the only King worthy of worship. But it's a deceiver, a counterfeit of the true King; it steals devotion away from the one true God, producing signs to dazzle the inhabitants of the earth.

¹²This earth-beast exercises all of the authority given to it by the first beast, and it forces the earth and all its inhabitants to *bow down and* worship the first beast, whose mortal wound had been healed. ¹³And the earth-beast performs fantastic miracles. *Like Elijah on Mount Carmel,* it even causes fire to blaze down from heaven to earth for all to see. ¹⁴Since it is allowed to perform these miracles in the presence of the first beast, the earth-beast deceives the inhabitants of the earth, commanding them to make an image of the first beast that had survived the mortal

wound inflicted by the sword. ¹⁵And the earth-beast was granted permission to breathe into the image *and to animate it* so that it could even speak. It decreed that those who refuse to worship the image of the *first* beast must be killed, ¹⁶and the earth-beast mandates that all humans must carry a mark on their right hands or foreheads: both great and small, both rich and poor, both free and slave. ¹⁷Those who do not carry this mark, that is, *those who do not have* the name of the *first* beast or the number representing its name *inscribed on them,* are not allowed to sell *their wares* or buy *in the market.*

¹⁸Here is *divine* wisdom: let anyone who understands *these mysteries* figure out the number of the beast because it is the number of a person. Its number is 666.*

> *T*he number "666" is the number associated with the beast and its followers. The beast demands worship and requires that all people carry its mark prominently as a witness to their loyalty. Those who do not follow the beast face severe social ostracism, deprived of their livelihoods and cut off from their basic needs.
>
> The number "666" stands in contrast to the perfection of the Lamb and the Spirit. The allure of the imperfect is but a cheap substitute for what is real and complete. Because we're told this number is "the number of a person," people have tried to pin down the identity of this person throughout history. In John's day, the name and title "Nero Caesar" was a likely candidate for the beast because Nero persecuted and executed believers, demanding obedience and even worship. For centuries the name "Nero" was synonymous with anyone who opposed the church. Every era seems to have its Neros, those beastly characters who occupy seats of power and yet use their power to

* 13:10 Other manuscripts read "to kill."
* 13:18 Some manuscripts read 616.

oppress God's people. The speculation continues as to this person's identity, but what has not changed is the message of hope in the midst of extreme persecution; that is the beauty proclaimed in this vision given to John.

14 *The scene changed.* I looked and saw the Lamb standing on top of Mount Zion, and with Him were the 144,000 who had His name and His Father's name inscribed on their foreheads. 2And I heard a voice from heaven roaring like a waterfall and clapping like thunder. The voice I heard was like a symphony of harpists playing their instruments. 3*As I watched,* they began to sing a new song before the throne, the four living creatures, and the *twenty-four* elders. The only ones with the ability to learn this song were the 144,000 who had been rescued from the earth, 4virgins who had not given themselves to sexual relations. They follow the Lamb wherever He goes. They have been purchased from among humanity as the firstfruits, *set apart* for God and the Lamb. 5In their mouths, no lie was found; no blemish marred them.

6I saw another messenger flying through midheaven. He carried an eternal gospel, bringing good news to all the citizens of the earth—every ethnicity, nation, language, and people.

Heavenly Messenger (*with a loud voice*):
7Fear God. Give Him glory, for the time of judgment has arrived. Worship the One who fashioned heaven and earth and created the seas and the springs.

8Another messenger, a second, came along.

Second Messenger: Fallen, fallen is Babylon, the great city! She has intoxicated all the nations with the wine of the wrath of her sexual perversion.

9Another messenger, a third, followed.

Third Messenger (*with a loud voice*): Those who worship the beast and its image,

and all who receive its mark on their foreheads or on their hands, 10will *be forced to* drink the wine of God's wrath, poured out undiluted into the cup of God's anger. And they will face the torment of fire and *the agony of* sulfurous flames before the holy messengers and the Lamb. 11The smoke of their torment will rise throughout the ages for eternity. Day and night will come and go without pause or cessation. There will be no end to the torture experienced by those who worship the beast and its image and by those who receive the mark of its name.

12Here is the patient endurance of the saints, those who keep the commandments of God and remain faithful to Jesus. 13Then I heard a voice call out from heaven.

A Voice: Record this: "Blessed are the dead who have died in the Lord from now until the end."
Spirit: Yes, they will rest from their labors because their deeds remain with them.

14Then I saw a white cloud, and seated on the cloud was one like the Son of Man, a golden wreath atop His head and a sharp sickle in His hand. 15Another messenger proceeded from the temple and called with a loud voice to the One who sat on the cloud.

Heavenly Messenger: Take Your sickle and reap *the harvest,* because the harvest of the earth is full and ripe and because the time to harvest has come.

16Then the One seated on the cloud swung His sickle over the earth, and the earth gave up its harvest.

17Just then another messenger proceeded out of the heavenly temple. He also had a sharp sickle. 18Then another messenger (the one with authority over fire) came out from the altar, and he called with a loud voice to the one who had the sharp sickle.

Messenger of Fire: Take your sharp sickle and gather together the clusters *of grapes* from the vines of the earth, for the grapes are ripe *and ready for harvest.*

¹⁹So the heavenly messenger swung his sickle over the earth, gathered the fruit of the vine from the earth, and threw it into the great winepress, which is the wrath of God. ²⁰And the winepress was trampled outside of the city, and blood flowed from the winepress. *The blood ran deep.* It reached as high as the bridle on a horse and ran for the distance of about 185 miles.*

15 Then I saw another sign in heaven, great and amazing: seven messengers with seven plagues—plagues that marked the end. With these the wrath of God reached its end.

²And then I saw something like a sea made of glass mixed with fire *flashing through it.* Those who had been victorious over the beast, its image, and the number of its name were standing on the sea of glass, holding the harps of God in their hands. ³*As they stand and play their harps,* they sing the song of Moses, the servant of God, and the song of the Lamb.

Victors:
> Great and amazing are Your works,
> Lord God, the All Powerful.
> Right and true are Your ways,
> King of all nations.
> ⁴Who will not fear You, Lord?
> Who will not glorify Your
> name?
> Because You alone are holy,
> all the nations will come
> and worship before You,
> For Your righteous judgments have
> been revealed.

⁵After I had taken all this in, I looked *again,* and the inner part of the tabernacle of witness opened in heaven. ⁶Out of the temple came seven messengers, clothed in pure linen, bright *and shining,* their chests clad in a golden sash, carrying seven plagues. ⁷Then one of the four living creatures *stepped over to* give to the seven mes-

sengers seven golden bowls brimming with the wrath of God who lives throughout the ages. ⁸The temple was full of the smoke *billowing* from the *magnificent* glory of God and from His power, and no one could enter the temple until the seven plagues of the seven messengers accomplished their *God-ordained* end.

16 Then I heard a great voice coming from the temple ordering the seven heavenly messengers.

A Voice: Go and pour out the seven bowls of the wrath of God upon the earth.

²So the first messenger poured out his bowl onto the earth. *When he did,* a foul-smelling, painful sore broke out on each person who bore the mark of the beast and who worshiped its image.

³The second messenger poured out his bowl into the sea. *When he did,* the waters became like the blood *that spills* from a dead body, and every living creature in the sea died.

⁴The third messenger poured out his bowl into the rivers and springs of *fresh* water. *When he did,* they, too, became blood. ⁵And I heard the messenger over the waters speak.

Messenger over the Waters:
> You are just, O holy One who is
> and who was,
> for You have judged these
> things *rightly.*
> ⁶Because people shed the blood of
> the saints and prophets,
> You have given them blood to
> quench their thirst.
> They are deserving of these
> punishments.

*T*he judgment of God is always true and just. Violent men and women were thirsty for the blood of

* 14:20 Literally, 1,600 stadia

God's people, so God gave them blood to drink. Sometimes judgment means receiving what you desire.

[7]And I heard *a voice from* the altar agree.

A Voice:

Yes, Lord God, the All Powerful,
true and right are Your
judgments!

[8]The fourth messenger poured out his bowl on the sun. *When he did,* the sun was permitted to blister people with its fire. [9]The incredible heat *of the sun* burned their skin, but instead of rethinking their actions* and glorifying God, they cursed God's name because He had the power to carry out these plagues.
[10]The fifth messenger poured out his bowl on the throne of the beast. *When he did,* its kingdom was blanketed in darkness. People chewed on their tongues out of *the depth of* their agony. [11]Still they refused to change their wicked ways,* so they cursed the God of heaven because of their painful afflictions and *ulcerous* sores.
[12]The sixth messenger poured out his bowl on the great river Euphrates. *When he did,* the river dried up and became a road so that the kings from the east *and their armies* could make their way. [13]What I saw next *troubled me deeply*: three foul spirits like frogs appeared, belched from the mouth of the dragon, the mouth of the beast, and the mouth of the earth-beast. [14]These frogs are demonic spirits. *As they go into the world,* they perform miracles persuading the kings of the world to gather for the *last* battle on the great day of God, the All Powerful.

*T*he dragon, beast, and false prophet are an unholy trinity who send out demonic spirits. The demonic spirits include frogs that remind the reader of the mighty plague used against Egypt. This is a spawning of slimy creatures of the night. These spirits roam about the world, persuad-

ing the kings of the earth to assemble together to do battle. Their words are to exert influence on the rulers rather than on the common people. Words hold sway in the world of politics. They are a source for either good or evil.

A Voice: [15]See, I am coming like a thief! Blessed is the person who watches and waits, dressed and ready to go, so as not to wander about naked, exposed to disgrace.

[16]And the kings gathered at the place called Har-Magedon in Hebrew.

*H*ar-Magedon—which is sometimes transliterated "Armageddon"—is the battleground where the armies of the earth, led by the forces of evil, will assemble to mount their final attack against God. This place is often associated with the plain of Megiddo in northern Israel because the fertile land there has often been turned into fields of blood during gruesome battles. In a place like this, for one last time, evil will raise its ugly head against good.

[17]*Finally,* the seventh messenger poured out his bowl into the air. *When he did,* a great voice came out of the temple, from the throne.

A Voice: It is accomplished!

[18]*At the sound of the voice,* there were flashes of lightning, sounds *of voices,* rumblings of thunder, and tremors of an earthquake. In all of human history, there had never been an earthquake of this magnitude. [19]The great city was torn into three parts, and the cities of all the nations fell. God remembered the great city, Babylon, and made her drink the cup of His fury

* 16:9 Literally, repenting
* 16:11 Literally, repent

and wrath. ²⁰Every island sank *into the ocean*, and no mountains were left to be discovered. ²¹And great hailstones, each weighing nearly 100 pounds,* fell from the sky onto the people until they cursed God because the plague of hail was so severe.

17 And then one of the seven messengers entrusted with the seven bowls came over to me.

Guide: Come, and I will show you the *true nature and righteous* judgment of the great whore who is sitting on the many waters. ²She has seduced all the kings of the earth into committing lewd, sexual acts, and *most* earthdwellers have become intoxicated with the wine of her harlotry.

³*Immediately* I was in the Spirit, and the guide picked me up and carried me off. In the middle of a *vast* desert, I saw a woman sitting on a scarlet-colored beast covered with blasphemous names. The beast had seven heads and ten horns *like the beast I had seen earlier rising out of the sea.* ⁴The woman was dressed in purple and scarlet fabrics; she shimmered with gold and jewels and pearls. *I looked closer and saw that* her hand held a golden cup brimming with abominations, *bubbling over* with the impurities of her sexual exploits. ⁵On her forehead was inscribed a name, a mystery: "Babylon the great, the mother of whores and the abominations that defile the earth." ⁶I looked and saw that the woman was drunk because she had gorged herself on the blood of the saints and the blood of those people who refused to deny Jesus *even to save their own lives.* When I saw her, I was filled with wonder.

Guide: ⁷Why are you so amazed? I will reveal to you the mystery of this woman and of the beast with seven heads and ten horns that carries her. ⁸The beast you saw was, and is not, and is about to come up out of the abyss and go away into *eternal* destruction. And the earthdwellers, whose names have not been

inscribed in the book of life from the foundation of the world, will be astonished when they see the beast because it was and is not and is to come.

⁹Here is the mind possessing wisdom: The seven heads signify the seven mountains where the woman is seated. They also stand for seven kings. ¹⁰Five have fallen, one is alive, and the last has not yet come *to reign.* But when he does come, he will be allowed to reign only a short time. ¹¹Regarding the beast that was and is not, it is *actually* an eighth *ruler* that springs from the seven and goes away into *eternal* destruction. ¹²The ten horns you saw stand for ten kings who have not yet ascended to power, but they will be invested with royal authority for a single hour *and will reign* together with the beast. ¹³These come together for one purpose *and one purpose alone*: to yield their power and authority to the beast. ¹⁴Together they will make war on the Lamb, and the Lamb will be victorious over them because He is the Lord over all lords and the King over all kings, and those who stand with Him are called, elect, and faithful.

(continuing to speak to me) ¹⁵The waters you saw, where the whore is seated, represent the peoples and multitudes, ethnicities and languages. ¹⁶The beast and the ten horns you saw will despise the whore; they will make her a wasteland and strip her naked. They will gorge themselves on her flesh and incinerate her with fire. ¹⁷For God has placed in their hearts to do what He has purposed, *that is,* to become one in mind and to surrender their kingdoms over to the beast until the words of God accomplish their end. ¹⁸And the woman you saw—she is the great city that rules over the kings of the earth.

*B*ecause Babylon was the city responsible for the destruction of Jerusalem's first temple in 586 B.C.,

* 16:21 Literally, the weight of a talent

John uses this ominous symbol to describe the Babylon of his day—Rome, the city that sat on seven hills. In A.D. 70, the Roman armies marched against Jerusalem, destroyed the second temple, and scattered the Jewish people.

The whore, who is identified as Babylon, was a symbol to readers in John's day of Rome and its allure. Its beauty and power were legendary, but beneath the surface lies the truth of its nature. People who ally themselves with Rome and all that it represents are partners with ruin. In the years since John's Revelation was first written, the whore has been seen as many different world forces. What Rome represents in John's day has been replicated by many different world powers and their material attractions.

18 Next I saw another messenger descending from heaven. *I knew he possessed great authority because his glory illuminated the earth with a warm light that chased away all the shadows.*

Heavenly Messenger (*with a powerful voice*):
> ²Fallen, fallen, is Babylon the great
> city!
> It has become a habitat for
> demons,
> A haunt for every kind of foul
> spirit,
> a prison for every sort of
> unclean bird, and
> a den for every foul and hateful
> beast.
> ³For all the nations have drunk
> *deeply*
> from the wine of the wrath of
> her immorality,
> And the kings of the earth have
> *disgraced themselves by*
> engaging in *gross* sexual acts
> with her,
> and the merchants of the earth
> have grown fat and rich,
> profiting off the power
> *purchased with* her luxury.

⁴Then I heard another voice from heaven urge:

A Voice:
> My people, get away from her—*fast.*
> Make sure you do not get
> caught up in her sins.
> *Put some distance between you* so
> that you do not share in her
> plagues,
> ⁵For her sins *are higher than the
> highest mountain.* They reach
> far into the heavens,
> and God has not forgotten even
> one of her missteps.
> ⁶Deal out to her what she has dealt
> out *to others,*
> and repay her double according
> to her deeds.
> In the cup where she mixed her
> drink, mix her a double.
> ⁷Whatever glory she demanded and
> whatever luxury she lived,
> give back to her the same
> measure in torment and
> sorrow.
> *Secretly* she says in her heart:
> "I rule as queen;
> I am not like a widow;
> I will never experience grief."
> ⁸Because of this *arrogance,* in a
> single day, plagues will
> overwhelm her.
> *Her portion will be* death and
> sorrow and famine,
> And she will be incinerated with
> fire,
> for mighty is the Lord God who
> exacts judgment on her.

⁹And the kings of the earth, who committed lewd, sexual acts and lived lavishly off of her, will weep and wail over their loss when they see the smoke from her burning *body rise into the sky. They will not go to her.* ¹⁰They will stand at a distance, fearing they, too, might fall victim to her torment. They will moan:

> Woe to you, our great city!
> Babylon, the *most* powerful city
> *in the world.*

In a single hour, your day of
    judgment has come.

¹¹And the merchants *and the magnates*
of the earth weep and mourn over her
demise because no one is buying their
goods any longer. ¹²*Warehouses full* of
gold, silver, jewels, and pearls; fine fab-
rics, purple, silk, and scarlet *cloth*; fragrant woods, items made of ivory, and
items finely crafted out of expensive
wood; bronze, iron, and marble; ¹³cinna-
mon, spices, incense, myrrh, and frankincense; wine, olive oil, rich flour, and
wheat; cattle, sheep, horses, chariots, and
human cargo, *trafficking in the* souls of
humanity.

¹⁴Everything your heart desired
    has gone away;
All the glitz and glitter
    are lost to you forever;
    you'll never have them again!

¹⁵The sellers of these goods, who
made a fine profit from her, will stand
at a distance. *Like the kings,* they will
fear her punishment *might fall on them
too.* They will weep and mourn *their
loss.*

¹⁶Woe to you, our great city,
    dressed in finest linens, in
        purple and scarlet *fabrics,*
    dazzling in gold and jewels and
        pearls.
¹⁷In a single hour, all this wealth is
    gone.

And all the sea captains, all those
who sail the seas, sailors, and those who
make a living by the sea, stood at a distance. ¹⁸*Strong men* were reduced to
tears as they gazed on the smoke that
rose from her ruins: "Was there ever any
city like her?" they asked. ¹⁹They threw
dust in the air covering their heads.
They wept *bitterly* and mourned *their
loss.*

Woe to you, our great city;
    all who had ships at sea
    became rich off your wealth!
In a single hour, you have been
    utterly ruined.

²⁰Rejoice over her *torment,* O heaven.
Join in the celebration, you saints, emissaries,* and prophets, because God has
judged in your favor and against her.

²¹Then a mighty messenger picked up a
huge stone—it looked like a great millstone—and he cast it into the sea.

Mighty Messenger:
    Watch and see. This is how
        Babylon, the great city,
        will be thrown down; violently
        will she go down,
        and they will search for her in
            vain.
    ²²Never again will the sound of
        music grace your streets.
    The melodies and harmonies of the
        harpists and musicians and
        flutists and trumpeters
        will never be heard again.
    And never again will an artisan of
        any craft
        be found *in your markets,*
    And never again will the grinding
        of the millstone
        provide rhythm to your city,
    ²³And never again will the light of a
        lamp
        bring warm light *to your houses,*
    And never again will the voice of
        the bridegroom and bride
        bring joy *to your festivities.*
    For the merchants were the
        magnates of the earth,
        and all the nations fell prey to
            your sorceries.
    ²⁴And in her *streets* the blood of the
        prophets and the saints
        and of all who have been
            slaughtered upon the earth,
            ran freely.

* 18:20 Literally, apostles

19 *The scene changed.* After this, I heard the great sound of a multitude *echoing* in heaven.

Multitude:
> Praise the Lord!
> Salvation and glory and power
>> *truly* belong to our God,
> ² for true and just are His
>> judgments.
> He has judged the great whore
>> who polluted the *entire* earth
>> with her sexual immorality,
> And He has vindicated the blood
>> of His servants, which she
>> shed.

³Again praise *spilled from heaven*:

Multitude:
> Praise the Lord!
> The smoke rises up from her *ruins*
>> forever and ever.

⁴And the twenty-four elders and four living creatures fell on their faces and worshiped God who reigns on the throne.

Four Living Creatures and 24 Elders:
> Amen, Praise the Lord!

A Voice from the Throne:
> ⁵Give praise to our God,
>> all of you, God's servants,
> All who reverence Him,
>> small and great.

⁶And I heard what seemed to be an immense crowd speaking with one voice— it was like the sound of a roaring waterfall, like the sound of clashing thunder.

Multitude *(in unison)*:
> Praise the Lord!
> For the Lord our God,
>> the All Powerful, reigns
>> *supreme.*
> ⁷Now is the time for joy and
>> happiness.
>> *He deserves* all the glory we can
>> give Him.
> *For the wedding feast has begun;*
>> the marriage of the Lamb to

His bride has commenced,
and His bride has prepared
herself *for this glorious day.*

> *T*he church that suffered and remained pure is now prepared for a time of glorious celebration. As Israel has been the bride of God, now the church, the bride of the Liberating King, will be intimately united with the Lamb. God and His people are about to become one. The marriage feast has been arranged at great expense, and the festivities are about to take place. But before the wedding, some things need to be put in order.

⁸She had been given the finest linens
>> to wear,
>> linens bright and pure,

woven from the righteous deeds of the saints.

Guide: ⁹Write this down: "Blessed are those who are invited to the marriage feast of the Lamb." What I am telling you are the true words of God.

¹⁰At that, I fell down at his feet to worship him, *but he refused my praise.*

Guide: Stop it. Don't you see? I am a servant like you and your brothers and sisters, all who hold fast to the testimony of Jesus. Address your worship to God, *not to me!* For the testimony about Jesus is *essentially* the prophetic spirit.

¹¹*In what seemed to be no time at all,* I looked up and saw that heaven had opened. Suddenly, a white horse appeared. Its rider is called Faithful and True, and with righteousness He exercises judgment and wages war. ¹²His eyes burn like a flaming fire, and on His head are many crowns. His name was written *before the creation of the world,* and no one knew it except He Himself. ¹³He is dressed in a robe dipped in blood, *stained red by the blood of the murdered saints, and* the name He was known

by is The Word of God. [14]And the armies of heaven, outfitted in fine linen, white and pure, were following behind Him on white steeds. [15]From His mouth darts a sharp sword with which to strike down the nations. He will rule over them with a scepter made of iron. He will trample the winepress of the fury of the wrath of God, the All Powerful. [16]And there on His robe and on His thigh was written His name: King of kings and Lord of lords.

[17]Then I *looked up and* saw a messenger standing in the sun, and with a loud voice, he called to all the birds that fly through midheaven:

Heavenly Messenger: Come. Gather for the great feast God is preparing *for you* [18]where you will feast on the flesh of kings, the flesh of captains, the flesh of the *rich and* powerful, the flesh of horses and their riders—all flesh—both free and slave, both small and great.

[19]*I looked down,* and I saw the beast *I had seen earlier* and the kings of the earth with their armies gathered together to wage war against the One riding the white horse and His *heavenly* army. [20]The beast was soon captured along with the false prophet, *the earth-beast I had seen earlier* who performed signs to deceive those who had agreed to receive the mark of the beast and those who worshiped its *detestable* image. Both of them were thrown alive into the lake of fire that burns with sulfur. [21]And all who remained met death at the blade of the sword that proceeded from the mouth of the One riding on the *white* horse. All the birds feasted fully on their flesh.

*I*n one of the final, decisive battles, the rider on the white horse leads the armies of heaven against the armies led against Him by the beast and the false prophet. His enemies are easily defeated, and the beast and the false prophet are thrown into the lake of fire. When the battle is over, the rider known as the King of kings and Lord of lords turns His attention to the dragon.

20 Then I saw a messenger coming from heaven. In his hand was a key to the abyss and a great chain *that had been forged in heaven.* [2]He seized the dragon, that ancient serpent who is the devil and Satan, and bound him for 1,000 years *with the great chain.* [3]The messenger cast him into the *bottomless* abyss and locked it and sealed him in it so that he could not go about deceiving the nations until the 1,000 years had come to completion. Afterward he must be released for a short time.

[4]Then I saw some thrones, and those seated in judgment were given the right to judge. Standing there were the souls of those who were beheaded because of their testimony of Jesus and the word of God. They had refused to worship the beast or its *detestable* image and had not received the mark upon their foreheads or upon their hands. They had come back to life and reigned with the Liberating King for 1,000 years. [5]Now as for the rest of the dead, they were not given life until the 1,000 years were completed. This is the first resurrection.

[6]Blessed and holy are the ones who take part in the first resurrection. Over these, the second death has no power; they will serve as priests of God and of the Liberator, and they will reign with Him for 1,000 years.

[7]When the 1,000 years are completed, Satan will be released from his prison. [8]And he will crawl out *of the bottomless abyss* in order to deceive the nations located at the four corners of the earth, Gog and Magog *as Ezekiel described them,* in order to rally them together for *one final* battle. They are in number as the grains of sand on the shore. [9]They marched in *unholy array* over the expanse of the earth and surrounded the camp of the saints and the beloved city. *As they laid siege to the city,* fire rained down from heaven and incinerated them. [10]And the devil who had deceived them was cast into the lake of fire and sulfur, where the beast and the false prophet had already been thrown, and the *unholy* trio will be tortured day and night throughout the ages.

Since the beginning, Satan, the dragon, has brought trouble on all the sons and daughters of Adam. Now John sees the truth of his destiny. Ultimately the one who brings such pain and sorrow upon the world will be bound and thrown into the lake of fire. Lest we think evil is somehow easily defeated, however, John watches as he mounts one last, futile attack against God's people and His beloved. Never again will he raise his ugly head against those who remain faithful to the One who sits on the throne and to the Lamb.

[11]*The scene changed.* I saw a great white throne and One was seated upon it. The earth and heaven receded from His presence; there was no place for them. [12]And I saw the dead, great and small, standing *motionless* in front of the throne. Some books were opened. Then another book was opened; it was called the book of life. And the dead were judged according to what had been recorded in the *first* books; *these were the records* of everything they had done. [13]And the sea surrendered its dead. Death and Hades gave up their dead as well. And all were judged according to their works. [14]Then Death and Hades were cast into the lake of fire. This is the second death, the lake of fire. [15]And everyone whose name could not be found *among the names* written in the book of life was thrown into the lake of fire.

21 I looked again *and could hardly believe my eyes.* Everything above me was new. Everything below me was new. *Everything around me was new* because the heaven and earth that had been had passed away, and the sea was gone, completely. [2]And I saw the holy city, the new Jerusalem, descending out of heaven from God, prepared like a bride *on her wedding day,* adorned for her husband *and for His eyes only.* [3]And I heard a great voice, coming from the throne.

A Voice:

> See, the home of God is with *His* people.
> He will live among them;
> They will be His people,
> And God Himself will be with them.
> [4]*The prophecies are fulfilled:*
> He will wipe away every tear from their eyes.*
> Death will be no more;
> Mourning no more, crying no more, pain no more,
> For the first things have gone away.

[5]And the One who sat on the throne announced *to His creation,*

The One: See, I am making all things new. (turning to me) Write *what you hear and see,* for these words are faithful and true. [6]It is done! I am the Alpha and the Omega, the beginning and the end. I will see to it that the thirsty drink freely from the fountain of the water of life. [7]To the victors will go this inheritance: I will be their God, and they will be My children. [8]*It will not be so* for the cowards, the faithless, the sacrilegious, the murderers, the sexually immoral, the sorcerers, the idolaters, and all those who deal in deception. They will inherit *an eternity in* the lake that burns with fire and sulfur, which is the second death.

John sees an amazing sight. It is something no one had ever seen nor would ever see again until that day. Scene by blessed scene passes before the prophet. Finally he is transported to the end of history only to discover it is no end at all; it is a new beginning. The prophecies—every last one of them—are coming true. God's plan will be accomplished on earth as it is in heaven when the new Jerusalem comes down and He lives among His people. All things will become new.

* 21:4 Isaiah 25:8

⁹And then one of the seven messengers in charge of the seven bowls filled with the seven last plagues came over to me.

Heavenly Messenger: Come *with me, and* I will show you the bride, the wife of the Lamb.

¹⁰He took me away in the Spirit and set me on top of a great, high mountain. *As I waited for what I thought was a bride,* he showed me the holy city, Jerusalem, descending out of heaven from God. ¹¹It gleamed *and shined* with the glory of God; its radiance was like the most precious of jewels, like jasper, and it was as clear as crystal. ¹²It was surrounded with a wall, great and high. There were twelve gates. Assigned to each gate was a messenger, twelve in all. And on the gates were inscribed the names of the twelve tribes of Israel's sons. ¹³*There was a beauty and symmetry to its perfection.* On the east *wall were* three gates. On the north *wall were* three gates. On the south *wall were* three gates. On the west *wall were* three gates. ¹⁴And the city wall sat *perfectly* on twelve foundation stones, and on them were *inscribed* the names of the twelve emissaries* of the Lamb.

¹⁵My guide held a golden measuring rod. With it he measured the city and the gates and the walls. ¹⁶And the city is laid out with four corners in a *perfect* square, the length the same as its width. He measured the city with his measuring rod, and *the result was that* its length and width and height are equal: 1,444 miles,* *a perfect cube.* ¹⁷And my guide measured the wall; it was nearly 72 yards* *high,* in human measurements, which was the instrument the guide was using. ¹⁸The wall was made of jasper, while the city itself was made of pure gold, yet it was as clear as glass. ¹⁹The foundation stones of the wall of the city were decorated with every kind of jewel: the first was jasper, the second sapphire, the third agate, the fourth emerald, ²⁰the fifth onyx, the sixth carnelian, the seventh chrysolite, the eighth beryl, the ninth topaz, the tenth chrysoprase, the eleventh jacinth, the twelfth amethyst. ²¹The twelve gates were twelve pearls, each gate *expertly* crafted from a single *beautiful* pearl. And the city street was pure gold, yet it was as transparent as glass.

²²And in the city, I found no temple because the Lord God, the All Powerful, and the Lamb are the temple. ²³And in the city, there is no need for the sun to light *the day* or moon *the night* because the resplendent glory of the Lord provides the city with *warm, beautiful* light and the Lamb illumines every corner *of the new Jerusalem.* ²⁴And *all peoples of* all the nations will walk by its *unfailing* light, and the rulers of the earth will stream into the city bringing with them the symbols of their grandeur and power. ²⁵During the day, its gates will not be closed; the darkness of night will never settle in. ²⁶The glory and grandeur of the nations will be *on display there,* carried to the holy city by people *from every corner of the world.* ²⁷Nothing that defiles or is defiled can enter into its *glorious gates.* Those who practice sacrilege or deception will never walk its streets. Only those whose names are written in the Lamb's book of life *can enter.*

*J*ohn had never seen a city without a temple. In fact, every city John had ever entered had many temples dedicated to many gods—all, of course, except Jerusalem. But now in his vision, he saw a different kind of city, the holy city, the new Jerusalem. As he looked around its streets of gold and magnificent buildings, he saw no temple reaching into the sky. No temple will be needed in this city because God and the Lamb will live with them, constantly in view. Their throne will sit prominently in the city. Their light will forever illumine its streets and citizens.

* 21:14 Literally, apostles
* 21:16 Literally, 12,000 stadia
* 21:17 Literally, 144 cubits

22 My heavenly guide brought me to the river of *pure* living waters, *shimmering as* brilliantly as crystal. It flowed out from the throne of God and of the Lamb, ²flowing down the middle and dividing the street of the holy city. On each bank of the river stood the tree of life, *firmly planted*, bearing twelve kinds of fruit and producing its sweet crop every month *throughout the year*. And the *soothing* leaves that grew on the tree *of life* provided precious healing for the nations.

> *F*ed by a crystal clear river is the tree of life. In the beginning, Adam and Eve were prevented from eating from the tree because they were expelled from the garden of Eden. Divine creatures and a flaming sword then stood guard at the entrance to the garden.* Now the tree of life returns into our story, a single tree situated on both sides of the river. No one is denied access to its luscious fruit and healing leaves.

³No one or nothing will labor under any curse any longer. And the throne of God and of the Lamb will sit *prominently* in the city. God's servants will *continually* serve *and worship* Him. ⁴They will be able to look upon His face, and His name will be written on their foreheads. ⁵Darkness will never again fall *on this city*. They will not require the light of a lamp or of the sun because the Lord God will be their illumination. *By His light*, they will reign throughout the ages.

Guide (*speaking to me*): ⁶These words are faithful and true.

And the Lord, the God who inspired the prophets, has sent His heavenly messenger to show to His servants what must soon take place.

The Liberating King: ⁷Look now, I am coming soon! The one who remains true to the prophetic words contained in this book will truly be blessed.

⁸I, John, am the one who heard and witnessed these visions. And when I heard and witnessed them, I fell prostrate at the feet of the heavenly guide who showed them to me. ⁹But he refused.

Guide: You must not do that! I am a servant with you, with your brothers and sisters the prophets, and with those who keep the words contained in this book. Worship God instead!
   (continuing) ¹⁰Do not seal up the prophetic words contained in this book *for another day*, for the finale is near. ¹¹Let the one given to evil continue down evil's path and the one addicted to filth continue to be its servant. But let the one who is righteous journey along the righteous road, and let the holy continue in holy ways.

The Liberating King: ¹²See, I am coming soon, and I will bring My reward with Me. I will pay back every person according to the deeds he has done. ¹³I am the Alpha and Omega, the First One and the Last One, the beginning and the end.

¹⁴Blessed are those who wash their garments. *In the end,* they have rightful access to the tree of life and will enter the city through its gates. ¹⁵The dogs, the sorcerers, those who commit immoral acts, the murderers, the idolaters, and all who love and practice deception must remain outside *the gates for all eternity.*

Jesus: ¹⁶I, Jesus, have sent My messenger to *show you and guide* you so that you in turn would share this testimony with the churches. I am the Root and the Descendant of David, the Bright Morning Star.

The Spirit and the Bride: ¹⁷Come.

And let everyone who hears these words say, "Come."

* **Note** Genesis 3:24

And let those who thirst come.
All who desire *to drink*, let them
    drink *deeply* from the water of
    life, as a gift.

18Beware, everyone who hears the prophetic words of this book. *Know this for certain:* if anyone adds to these words, God will add to that person the plagues described in this book. 19And if anyone subtracts from the prophetic words of this book, God will remove that person's access to the tree of life and to the holy city which are described in this book.

20The One who testifies to these realities makes this promise:

The Liberating King: Yes. I am coming soon.

To which we say: "Amen. Come, Lord Jesus."
    21May the grace of the Lord Jesus [the Liberating King]* be with all [the saints].* Amen.

* 22:21 Some manuscripts omit this portion.
* 22:21 The earliest manuscripts omit this portion.

Index to Biblical References

Index

Index

Index